# Praise for *Microsoft Content Management Server 2002*

"This is one of those rare books that you will read to learn about the product and keep re-reading to find those tidbits that you missed before. Need to know how to setup CMS? *Microsoft Content Management Server 2002: A Complete Guide* will tell you. Need to know how the information is being processed before the user views it? *Microsoft Content Management Server 2002: A Complete Guide* will tell you. A great book no matter what your experience level is with Content Management Server."

—*Gary Bushey, SharePoint Portal Server MVP*

"A concise and accurate guide to Microsoft's enterprise development tool for content-centric applications. An invaluable resource for any developer who wants to get the best out of Microsoft Content Management Server."

—*Ed Robinson, Lead Program Manager, Microsoft Corporation*

"Content management is a complex, multifaceted application area, and Microsoft's CMS Server is a complex product. This book sets out everything you could possibly need or want to know about CMS. The title could easily be *The CMS Resource Kit* since it will be an essential addition to the library of any IT professional or developer working on content management and Microsoft's CMS."

—*Thomas Lee, Chief Technologist, QA*

# Microsoft Content Management Server 2002

# Microsoft Content Management Server 2002

## A Complete Guide

*Bill English*
*Olga Londer*
*Shawn Shell*
*Todd Bleeker*
*Stephen Cawood*

✦✦Addison-Wesley

Boston • San Francisco • New York • Toronto • Montreal
London • Munich • Paris • Madrid
Capetown • Sydney • Tokyo • Singapore • Mexico City

Many of the designations used by manufacturers and sellers to distinguish their products are claimed as trademarks. Where those designations appear in this book, and Addison-Wesley was aware of a trademark claim, the designations have been printed with initial capital letters or in all capitals.

The authors and publisher have taken care in the preparation of this book, but make no expressed or implied warranty of any kind and assume no responsibility for errors or omissions. No liability is assumed for incidental or consequential damages in connection with or arising out of the use of the information or programs contained herein.

The publisher offers discounts on this book when ordered in quantity for bulk purchases and special sales. For more information, please contact:

U.S. Corporate and Government Sales
(800) 382-3419
corpsales@pearsontechgroup.com

For sales outside of the U.S., please contact:

International Sales
(317) 581-3793
international@pearsontechgroup.com

Visit Addison-Wesley on the Web: www.awprofessional.com

*Library of Congress Cataloging-in-Publication Data*

Microsoft Content management server 2002 : a complete guide /
Bill English . . . [et al.].
      p.    cm.
Includes bibliographical references and index.
ISBN 0-321-19444-6 (pbk. : alk. paper)
1. Microsoft Content Management Server (Electronic resource) 2. Web
sites—Design—Computer programs. 3. Web sites—Management—Computer
programs. 4. Database management. I. English, Bill, 1961–
TK5105.8885.M52M4497 2004
005.2'76—dc22

                                  2003019169

Pearson Education, Inc.
Rights and Contracts Department
75 Arlington Street, Suite 300
Boston, MA 02116
Fax: (617) 848-7047

ISBN 0-321-19444-6
Text printed on recycled paper
1 2 3 4 5 6 7 8 9 10—CRS—0706050403
First printing, October 2003

*To Kathy, David, and Anna—I love you three
more than I could ever fully express.
—W.F.E.*

*To Gregory, Michael, and Dina
—O.M.L.*

*To Lauren, my alpha and omega.
—S.A.S.*

*To my Lord Jesus Christ and my lovely wife,
Kathryn Alicia Bleeker. In memory of our firstborn son,
Landen Jamison Bleeker, and to all
of our precious living children: Landis Jarin Bleeker,
Lake Justus Bleeker, Lissa Jeneé Bleeker,
Logan Joshua Bleeker, Lawson Jens Bleeker,
and Lexa Joelle Bleeker
—T.C.B.*

*To my parents.
Thanks for all the support.
—S.G.C.*

# Contents

# Preface

*Microsoft Content Management Server 2002* is intended to be an outstanding reference on this emerging product. This book takes an in-depth look at CMS 2002 and outlines all areas of this product: from architecture to content authoring and publishing. In addition, we have chapters that detail how to create a site framework, administer a site, secure the site, and deploy the site in a production environment. There are several chapters on the Publishing API and how to extend CMS in your environment.

While most of this book is written for the developer in your organization, there are key chapters that will assist your infrastructure team in installing and monitoring a CMS 2002 production server.

In the first part of the book, we cover introductory information and the fundamentals of CMS 2002. This part has a short introduction to CMS 2002, discusses how to install CMS 2002, and then outlines the architecture for CMS 2002 in Chapter 3. Chapter 4 gives a sample outline on how to plan for a CMS 2002 implementation.

The second part of the book covers content authoring and publishing activities. We start this part by discussing the Web Author; then we move on to discussing publishing workflow in CMS 2002 and the Authoring Connector. This part is chock-full of examples and instructions on how to complete these tasks.

The third part of the book focuses on creating the site framework. We'll show you how to create a new CMS site and how to structure the channel, template galleries, and resource galleries hierarchies in your site. We also have inserted an excellent chapter on how to develop for CMS using Visual Studio .NET, with special attention paid to how a CMS project is different from a generic project. This part also includes several chapters that focus on templates, including a chapter on template-based page processing, one on creating templates, and other chapters that discuss planning, creating, and debugging CMS templates. Finally, we'll discuss working with placeholders in Visual Studio .NET, creating dynamic navigation elements, and connected postings.

The fourth part of this book focuses on site administration and security. Hence, we discuss how to work with containers, how to set up user security, how to use the Server Configuration Application, and how to secure access to your CMS site.

In Part V, we focus on site deployment issues, such as using the Site Deployment Manager and discussing various site deployment scenarios.

Part VI is for the folks who love the nitty-gritty and the details of CMS 2002. In this part, we cover PAPI, obtaining contexts, traversing channels, managing postings, manipulating postings, and finding CMS assets.

In Part VII, we discuss how to extend the functionality of CMS 2002. We cover topics like developing custom controls, customizing the Web Author console in Visual Studio .NET, extending the publishing workflow, publishing dynamic data in CMS, and building a Web service for CMS.

Part VIII is for those who administer a CMS 2002 server but don't code in the CMS environment. In this part, we cover capacity planning and performance monitoring issues, to help you run your servers more smoothly and efficiently. We also provide tips on troubleshooting.

Part IX has migration information for those of you who need to migrate from CMS 2001 to CMS 2002.

Complete source code for the examples in this book is available for download at www.awprofessional.com/titles/0321194446.

No technical book has ever been written that can answer all the questions for every reader who picks it up. But this book will be able to answer most of your questions and show you how to install, manage, troubleshoot, extend, configure, and develop for CMS 2002.

Also, when it comes to purchasing a book, most readers evaluate the strength of a book, in part, based on who the authors are. Rarely has such a strong author team been assembled to write a book on a specific product. One of our authors works on the CMS team for Microsoft. Three other authors are very experienced developers, including one who is responsible for a nationwide CMS rollout on the CMS 2002 platform. By adding to that the direct support and enthusiasm of the CMS team at Microsoft, and three technical editors, we believe this book will be the benchmark work on CMS 2002.

We trust that you will find this book to be an excellent reference as you work toward a full CMS deployment in your organization.

# Acknowledgments

There are five names on the front of this book, but there are many more people who are responsible for creating the book you are now holding. There were several people, who, behind the scenes, made this book possible. First, we'd like to thank Sondra Scott, Senior Acquisitions Editor for Addison-Wesley Professional. She went well beyond the call of duty to ensure that all the contracts were worked out to meet everyone's needs while keeping this book on track and on focus. Sondra, without you, this book would not have materialized.

We also would like to thank Debby English, copy editor, and Kathy Glidden, project manager, who went through a rather rough manuscript with a fine-toothed comb and made the sentences flow well and caught a number of minor errors, all while keeping us on schedule. Both of you did a great job and we are indebted to you.

We would also like to thank those that helped ensure this manuscript is as free of technical errors as possible: Gary Bushey (SharePoint MVP, Microsoft Corporation), Scott Brown (Microsoft UK Corporation), and Thomas Lee (QA, London). Thank you all for your work and dedication to this book and for giving us additional insight into how to make this book better!

**Bill English:** It is not often that such an outstanding group of authors come together to produce a great work, but this is what is happened. As I was reading through the chapters, I was struck over and over again with the quality of writing from the authors on this team and found myself repeatedly impressed with their effort, attention to detail, and the professionalism that they demonstrated. It is rare to be in such great company, and so to Olga, Steve, Todd, and Shawn: You guys are great! Thank you for working on this project and for adding significant value to the original vision and concept for this book. You all have been great to work with and I hope we can do more together in the future.

On a personal note, I'd like to thank Neil Salkind at StudioB for supporting this project and for helping with the contractual issues. As usual, Neil, you did your outstanding work and I appreciate your efforts. I also want to thank Kathy, my wife, who continues to support and love me when I'm writing books. As usual, you're a great person to whom to be married.

Finally, I'd like to thank Jesus Christ, who gave me the opportunity to write this book and without whom I would be lost forever.

**Olga Londer:** My very personal thanks go to the author team—Bill, Shawn, Steve, and Todd. I have thoroughly enjoyed working with all of you, and I sincerely hope we will have opportunities to work together in the future.

I would also like to thank all at AQ for supporting me throughout the writing of this book. Without the kind help and support of all my colleagues at QA this book would have never been written. Special thanks go to Justin Turner and Thomas Lee for their endless encouragement, understanding, and help.

I'm grateful to Henry Winkler and David Frearson of Microsoft CMS team for reviewing my chapters and suggesting valuable additions and alterations. It was Henry who provided an identity matrix for Chapter 19, "Managing User Access"—thank you!

Last, but not least, I would like to thank my husband, who stoically coped with my nearly constant work in the evenings and over the weekends, always maintained his good humor, and never complained.

**Shawn Shell:** I'd like to start by thanking the other authors. Bill, Steve, Olga, and Todd—you were all fantastic to work with and I enjoyed our partnership. I don't believe I could have worked with a better group.

I would also like to thank folks in the following organizations:

At Dell, first and foremost, I would like to thank Sue Hanley. You have been nothing but encouraging, constructively critical, and someone who is always willing to listen (when you're not checking e-mail ☺); I couldn't have picked a better manager or mentor. I would like to thank Neil Isford, whose support of this project helped make my participation possible. I would like to thank Paul Kolinsky, who initially hired me and made my time at Dell possible. In addition, I would like to thank all of my friends across DPS. You guys are a great group of people to work with and I'm lucky to have had the opportunity to be a part of such a fantastic team.

At Microsoft, I would like to thank all of my friends, spread across various groups. Specifically (listed in no particular order): Anne Weiler, Mike Van Snellenberg, Jean Pierre Poissant, Steve Cawood (of course), Ben Heng, Pat Miller, Jan Shanahan, Arpan Shah, Jim Lorenz, Ro Dhanda, Laura Nance, and Ivan Smigoc. I've known some of you since the NCompass days, others only since the acquisition. I appreciate your help, professionalism, and the occasional tasty tidbit of knowledge (and pre-release code . . . hint hint . . .).

Outside of Microsoft and Dell, I would like to thank the following people. . . . Although no longer at Microsoft, I would like to thank Paul Loughlin. Without you, I probably would never have gotten to know NCompass or Resolution. Thanks, man! I would also like to thank Brian Fildes and John Crane. You both served as guiding figures early in my career and you taught me a great many things; I feel my successes are, in part, due to your tutelage.

On a personal note, I would like to thank my wife, who has been a constant source of support, encouragement, and understanding. While she wasn't thrilled about my very late nights in the office, her love and support never wavered. I would also like to thank my parents for providing me with a solid foundation to achieve whatever I set my mind to.

Note: For those of you who haven't figured out where BOTS Consulting got its name . . . **B**ill**O**lga**T**odd**S**teve**S**hawn (two S's at the end would have been a few too many consonants).

**Todd Bleeker:** A resounding "thank you" to my outstanding co-authors, the talented people at Addison-Wesley Professional, StudioB, IPCS Consulting, and Microsoft. I also appreciate the strong support I received from my wife and kids (see my dedication); my mom and dad, Millie and Gary Bleeker; my inlaws, Marcy and Ron Olson; and my entire extended family. Finally, I'm grateful for the extended technical discussion my younger brother, Troy, and I had over ice cream one Sunday afternoon. BZ (bravo zulu) and Godspeed to all y'all.

**Steve Cawood:** This book could not have been written without the help of the Microsoft Content Management Server product group. I would like to thank the whole team. In addition to this, I would like to specifically thank the following people for their help: Jan Shanahan, David Frearson, Pat Miller, Charles Morris, Kristian van der Hoek, Christa Peters, John Keinanen, Stefan Goßner, Henry Winkler, Mike Taghizadeh, Chris White, Luke Nyswonger, Mark Poernbacher, Arpan Shah, Tarun Banga, Glen Buhlmann, Sigrid Elenga, and Rasool Rayani.

I would also like to thank Christa for her tireless encouragement and support.

# About the Authors

An author, trainer, and consultant specializing in knowledge management and collaboration technologies, **Bill English** (MCSE, MCT, CTT+, MVP, GSEC) is the owner of Networknowledge (www.networknowledge. com), a consulting and training business dedicated to planning, architecting, and securing information for companies of all sizes. He has authored/coauthored eight books, including the *The Administrator's Guide*  *to SharePoint Portal Server 2001.* Bill has been given the prestigious Most Valuable Professional (MVP) award from Microsoft for his work on the SharePoint Portal Server platform. Bill is also the owner of a very popular Web site dedicated to SharePoint Portal Server (www. sharepointknowledge.com). Bill lives in Nowthen, Minnesota, with his wife and two children.

**Olga Londer,** MCSE/MCT, is a principal technologist at QA, the UK's biggest independent IT training company. Olga has been involved with Web development, infrastructure, and authoring since 1992, and has seen and worked with all leading products in this area. In 1993, Olga wrote the first Internet training course in the UK. She has authored most of QA's courses on Web development, design, and support,  including "Building an Effective Website," "Intranet Technologies and Services," "E-commerce Masterclass," and many others. As a consultant, Olga has been a technical lead for numerous projects for blue-chip clients. Her current responsibilities include teaching, consulting, and technical leadership for the Internet/e-commerce curriculum at QA. Olga holds an M.S. in applied math and computer science, and has over 15 years of experience in IT consulting and training.

**Shawn Shell** is an industry-recognized expert in the area of content management and on Microsoft's Content Management Server. He leads Dell Professional Services' Content Management practice, a nationally focused competency practice that leverages the group's expertise in content management solutions to help clients achieve business objectives. Shawn has been with Dell for more than three years, following an 11-year career at Warner-Lambert Company. Shawn joined Warner-Lambert Company (now Pfizer) in 1989 as a help desk analyst. Throughout his career, he held various positions within divisional and corporate information technology groups, from running the Legal Division's help desk to managing a divisional data center and participating in a cross-divisional team to develop Warner-Lambert's standard desktop. In 1999, Shawn became the Manager of Internet/Intranet Technologies, responsible for Warner-Lambert.com, the global intranet, and various product-specific sites like Trident.COM. In addition to his time at Warner-Lambert Company, Shawn has been a part-time lecturer at Rutgers University's Department of Computer Science and an instructor at the Rutgers Internet Institute.

With over a decade of Microsoft-centric software development in his wake, **Todd C. Bleeker**, Ph.D., is regarded as an innovative, resourceful, and competitive IT executive with an intense desire to excel. Early in his career, Todd built shrewd customer service solutions for P&G, pioneered new technologies to revolutionize the transportation logistics systems for Fingerhut, shaped the disease management tools for UHG (United Healthcare), and drove the human capital procurement vision to an internationalized, commercial-grade, global solution for Itiliti (now PeopleClick). Currently the CTO for International Project Consulting Services, Inc. (http://ipcs.net), Todd manages offshore software development operations in New Delhi, India, while actively participating in various roles on stateside and Canadian projects. For instance, Todd recently architected the software that Air Canada uses to track its roughly $30 million of annual in-flight cash sales. From a content management perspective, Todd helped the State of Minnesota webify and manage over 40,000 pages of systems documentation; implemented on behalf of Microsoft Consulting Services an MCMS solution for Bank of Montreal, AnytimeLoan.com, and Bancsoft; and presented on Web

Services and MCMS at TechEd 2003. In his spare time, Todd loves to soak up whatever technology Microsoft is churning out and spend countless hours in Minnesota with his wife, Kathryn, and six "high energy" children: Landis, Lake, Lissa, Logan, Lawson, and Lexa.

**Stephen Cawood** is a Microsoft employee and has been working with Microsoft Content Management Server for over four years. Stephen joined the MCMS product team as a Web developer and has recently transitioned to the role of program manager. He is currently focused on MCMS security. Over the last few years, Stephen has spoken at the University of Washington Graduate Studies Department and at  conferences such as the MCMS Technical Airlift and Microsoft TechEd.

# CMS Fundamentals

# CHAPTER 1

# Introduction to Content Management Server

Microsoft Content Management Server (CMS) is the future of building Web sites. CMS represents a dramatic departure from conventional methods of building and conceptualizing Web sites. CMS offers significant improvement in how Web sites are built and maintained, in terms of both economies of scale and time savings.

Moreover, CMS offers a compelling story that you will learn about as you read this book. There are strong reasons to implement CMS in your environment—especially if you manage a large number of Web servers with content that often changes. These reasons include scalability, flexibility, and extensibility of your Web site.

Hence, in this chapter, we will outline the features of CMS and offer reasons for implementing CMS in your environment. CMS is an exciting product, so let's get going!

## The CMS Story: Why You'll Want to Implement CMS in Your Environment

When Web sites were being initially developed and published on the Internet, the designers of these sites were driven primarily by the need for the sites to be attractive and to hold the viewers' interest. They were right, of course, but we soon learned that sites had to be more than attractive. They also needed to be easy to navigate and offer timely, accurate information that was relevant to the site visitor.

This was difficult to achieve because information was static on Web sites. In fact, many sites were little more than glorified company brochures. The information presented in these sites was the same for every visitor, making personalization of the site impossible. Hence, we

**3**

were faced with trying to build sites that contained information that would be relevant to a wide audience and yet meet the needs of multiple, distinct audiences.

In addition, updating static information was expensive because of the coding efforts of creating each page. And common workflows that were used to update existing data in these sites were cumbersome and not able to quickly react to changing conditions.

The upshot of all these factors was that the promise of the Internet becoming the delivery vector for commerce did not meet expectations. What we learned was that if we were going to use Web applications and the Internet for commerce in any serious manner, these problems we've outlined here needed to be addressed and solved from both a development and an infrastructure viewpoint. What was needed was a new way to conceptualize and deliver content on Web sites.

What CMS represents is a new way of conceptualizing Web sites. Instead of being primarily concerned about the design of the Web site, we are now most concerned about the *content* of the Web site. In other words, by using CMS, we can develop and deliver content-driven Web sites instead of design-driven sites. This is a fundamental shift in how we think about Web sites.

Content-driven Web sites address the challenge of frequent changes to the site content by separating the design of the site from the content of the site. This approach enables the design and the content to be created and managed separately. More to the point, your Web designers and graphics people can concentrate on what they do best: developing great site designs from both a navigational and a visual perspective. On the other hand, your business people can concentrate on what they do best: developing great content for your customers and other interested parties. There is no need for your business users to learn about the site design, and the reverse is true too: Your site developers have no need to learn about the business content that will appear on your site.

The advantages to this separation are multiple:

- Workflow is simplified because business users can create, approve, and manage content without needing to understand one whit of site design.
- Site designs can be customized for every type of content.
- Content can be changed quickly to meet changing business needs and goals.
- Workflows can be customized for different parts of the site, avoiding a one-size-fits-all workflow.

Obviously, content-driven Web sites are more difficult to secure than design-driven Web sites. With a traditional Web site, you had to concern yourself with who had access to the site over the Internet and from within your own organization. With a content-driven Web site, you'll need to be concerned about giving different levels of permissions to those within your organization who will have different roles in developing and delivering content on your Web site. Rights can be granted or denied to users based on the role that user has for the site. Content-driven Web sites will require more administrative effort, but this effort is more than offset by the efficiencies gained through the use of CMS.

## Features of Content Management Server

CMS offers a rich set of features that form a compelling reason to purchase this product. These fall into two broad categories: design features and content features.

The design features of CMS include the ability to create templates that define the layout of the pages for your Web site. These templates will contain placeholders for content that is created by your business users.

The content features of CMS include the use of two tools to which we'll refer from time to time in this book: the Web Author tool and the Authoring Connector tool. These tools allow business users to create and manage content efficiently and effectively. Using the Web Author tool, users can:

- Create, modify, and delete pages
- Copy and move pages
- Create connected pages that share source content with other pages but display that information in different ways
- Submit pages for review and approval

The Authoring Connector can be used to submit a Microsoft Word document to the Web site and associate that document with a particular task that has been created in the Web site. When the author selects a task, the task itself will perform the required functions, abstracting the author from the workflow required to correctly publish the document to the Web site. Hence, it becomes as simple as using Word to create the document and then submitting the document under a chosen task to ensure the document is approved and published as desired.

Other features of CMS include the ability to schedule content publication for a future point in time. Pages can be expired or set to remain on the site indefinitely. Moreover, before content is actually published, authors will have the opportunity to review exactly how that information will appear on the Web page, giving the author the ability to ensure that the information is both technically and visually correct.

CMS is integrated in Visual Studio .NET (VS.NET). The integrated development environment allows you to create and maintain CMS templates in VS. In addition, full support for template debugging is included in the VS debugger. Finally, template files can be managed and secured using Visual Source Safe or third-party source control tools. This allows your developers to maintain template integrity in a multideveloper environment. In addition, CMS also allows for third-party integration by using the .NET framework, Web services, and support for Extensible Markup Language (XML).

CMS also allows for a rapid deployment of a large Web site. In addition, CMS offers flexibility in quickly changing data across a large deployment to meet changing needs and demands. And because content can be kept up-to-date, visitors will find the site more informative and useful, leading to an increased positive end-user experience.

At a detailed level, Table 1–1 offers an overview of the new features that can be found in CMS 2002.

In short, CMS offers three overall features that form the foundation for an excellent e-commerce site:

- A comprehensive system for Web site content management
- A dynamic, up-to-date content delivery system
- Rapid, efficient time-to-market for e-commerce sites

In addition to these features, you'll find that CMS stores content as objects, enabling reuse of content throughout your site. Because of the template-driven nature of presenting content, you'll also be able to target which content appears based on audience membership, device, and/or individual account information.

You'll install CMS on top of Internet Information Services (IIS) 6.0 or later. For developers, you'll install CMS on top of Visual Studio .NET.

CMS dynamically generates Web pages from content objects and templates. But there are other components that ship with CMS 2002 that increase productivity for business and technical users. These components

**Table 1–1**  New Features in CMS 2002

| New Feature | Explanation |
| --- | --- |
| .NET-based Publishing API | The CMS 2002 Publishing API is .NET based, meaning that CMS 2002 objects can be called from any Common Language Runtime (CLR). |
| Improved authentication model | Authentication can be customized and can use either the ASP.NET authentication model or accounts in Active Directory. |
| Improved caching and performance | Caching can be implemented via rule-based commands on each page. |
| Improved event model | CMS provides event classes that make it easier to extend the CMS workflow model. |
| Improved multilingual support | You can use the .NET features to add multiple cultures to your initial deployment. After the templates are created, you won't need to worry about them. |
| Web services support | You can use XML Web services that provide or consume Web services for your CMS site. |
| XML support | The new XML placeholders support XML content, XML Schema Definitions (XSD), and Extensible Stylesheet Transformations (XSLT). |
| Integration with Visual Studio .NET | Placeholders are implemented as ASP.NET controls, code can be stored in files so that source control tools are used in large deployments, and debugging is easier too. |
| Simplified publishing process | Site managers can publish information more easily directly from Word into the Web site. |
| Separation of authoring and site management tasks | Authoring of content is left to the business user, while site management tasks are left to administrators and/or developers. |

speed up site development, simplify integration and interoperability, and provide rapid deployment. These components are:

- **Web Author:** This tool enables authors and editors to create, edit, and publish Web content. A site can be updated quickly because multiple users can work on different parts of the Web site at the same time. The Web Author is a browser-based tool that requires no additional client software.
- **Authoring Connector:** This tool enables content creators to author and edit documents in Microsoft Word XP and to submit them for approval and publication to a CMS Web site.
- **Site Manager:** This tool enables CMS administrators to create a site structure, including channels, templates, and resource galleries, and to assign rights and roles to content creators, developers, and users.
- **Site Deployment Manager:** This tool enables CMS administrators to update the Web site using an export and import package transfer method. Site Deployment Manager is invoked through the Site Manager. Developers can also schedule deployment of content using ASP scripts.
- **Database Configuration Application (DCA):** This tool selects and populates a SQL database, specifies the virtual Web site, and selects a system account and initial administrator for a new installation. Once installation is complete, the Database Configuration Application is used to configure the database on an ongoing basis.
- **Server Configuration Application (SCA):** This tool is used to view and change the configuration values for the CMS 2002 Server.
- **Publishing Application Programming Interface (API):** This API enables developers to build highly customized, dynamic Web sites that integrate easily with other applications.

There are a number of possible deployment scenarios. Each scenario will depend on the site requirements, the size of your organization, and the resources available at the time the site is deployed.

CMS is highly flexible and can be used in any number of situations to enhance Web site design, deployment, and timeliness.

In this book, we'll discuss each feature of CMS and illustrate how to use the tools and the product to deploy sites more quickly and more efficiently than ever has been possible.

## Summary

CMS 2002 is Microsoft's most advanced Web site building and deployment tool. It achieves economies of scale by reusing code and templates and improves efficiency by allowing content workers to directly publish their work to the Web site. CMS 2002 can reduce costs and improve customer relations while allowing you to build an outstanding Web site that is rich in features, design, and up-to-date content.

In the next chapter, we'll discuss how to install CMS 2002.

# CHAPTER 2

# Installing Microsoft Content Management Server

Installing Microsoft Content Management Server (CMS) is a pretty straightforward process. In this chapter, you'll find information on how to install CMS, elements that should be considered before you install CMS, and some troubleshooting issues too. Because this book is primarily a developer-oriented book, we'll not dive into all the nooks and crannies of a CMS installation. However, if you need introductory information on how to install CMS, then this chapter is for you.

## Elements to Consider before a CMS Installation

The minimum hardware and software requirements vary, depending on the type of server you're planning to install. For instance, if you are planning to install CMS for your developers, then the following laundry list applies:

- Windows 2000 Professional, Server, or Advanced Server with Service Pack 2 or later
- Internet Explorer 6.0 or later
- Internet Information Services (IIS) 5.0 with these components: Common Files, IIS services snap-in, and the World Wide Web Server
- IIS Security Hotfix MS02-018
- SQL Server with Service Pack 2 or later
- .NET Framework with Service Pack 2 or later

- Visual Studio .NET
- Internet Explorer WebControls 1.0 or later

It is also recommended that you have installed the Data Access Components 2.7 RTM Refresh, and the Windows High Security Template and the CMS template for the IIS Lockdown Tool.

For a production environment, you should ensure that your server meets these minimum hardware requirements:

- Pentium III processor or higher
- 1GB of RAM or more
- 2GB of free disk space or more
- CD-ROM drive
- Working network card
- 800x600 monitor resolution
- Mouse or pointing device

For a production server, you should also ensure that you have this minimum software ready for the installation:

- Windows 2000 Server or Advanced Server with Service Pack 2 or later
- Internet Explorer 6.0 or later
- IIS 5.0 with these components: Common Files, IIS services snap-in, and the World Wide Web Server
- IIS Security Hotfix MS02-018
- SQL Server 2000 Client Utilities with Service Pack 2 or later
- .NET Framework with Service Pack 2 or later
- Internet Explorer WebControls 1.0

For a Site Manager box, you'll only need Windows 2000 Professional with Service Pack 2 or later.

If you are running Windows 2003, you'll need to install CMS and then Service Pack 1 for CMS. With SP1 for CMS, you'll find that Windows 2003 domains are supported. There are some known issues surrounding a CMS/SP1 installation on Windows Server 2003.

First, the CMS console may not run properly if your Internet Explorer zone is set to High Security. This setting will interfere with the downloading of the JavaScript file that supports the Switch to Edit Site link. To work around this problem, either lower your security setting or add the CMS site to your trusted sites in Internet Explorer.

Second, if you stop the AESecurityService and then attempt to access your CMS console, the console will not appear and the AESecurity Service will not automatically restart. You'll need to start this service manually, and then the console should appear just fine.

Third, Visual Studio.NET presents some problems when it is installed on Windows 2003 Server because of the way it stores .tmp files; IIS 6.0 blocks all file types that are not explicitly mapped, and the .tmp file type is not explicitly mapped by default. The workaround for this problem is to either use Visual Studio .NET 2003 when working with Windows 2003 or map the .tmp file extension as a text/plain file type in the MIME type box in IIS.

Generally speaking, the process of installing CMS contains four steps: creating the Windows user accounts, creating the database, installing the CMS components, and configuring the database.

## Creating the Necessary Windows User Accounts

CMS uses a system account to access resources on the network and to work with the Active Directory (AD) directory service. For example, the system account will need permissions to browse the AD in order to enumerate objects in the director. In addition, the account (essentially) performs impersonation for all users connecting to the Web site so that the administrator isn't forced to list each user account on each resource for permissions to access the resource.

The system account will need read/write permissions on the SQL database. In addition, ensure that this account is not the same as the local administrator account and that it is not the IIS anonymous account.

In reality, you'll need to create two accounts, not one. The first will be the CMS system account. The other will be the CMS administrator account. The system account will be used to read and write data to the database. The administrator account will need to be the first administrator to access the CMS Web application. This account can use Site Manager to add other users as needed.

After you have created the necessary accounts in the local server's account database, you'll want to install the required software. The only software that we'll illustrate here is the CMS installation.

One thing to note about the CMS setup routine is that it is context sensitive in the sense that it will evaluate the environment into which CMS is being installed and notify you with a pop-up box of any configuration problems. This type of self-checking of the server before running setup saves us from ourselves. Setup will not allow us to set up CMS in a poorly or wrongly configured environment. Hence, if you get a screen saying that you need a certain piece of software installed while you're running setup, then pay attention! You'll need to resolve that issue before setup will be able to continue past that point in the setup routine.

## Running the CMS Setup Program

To install CMS, place the CMS CD-ROM in your CD-ROM drive and allow autoplay to start the process. On the initial splash screen, select Install Components. On the next screen, select Install MCMS Components. Setup will then run through a series of internal checks while it displays a Preparing to Install screen to ensure your server meets the requirements for a CMS installation. If your server passes the tests, you'll be presented with the Welcome to the Installation for Microsoft Content Management Server screen. At this point, you'll want to click Next to continue.

The ensuing screen will ask you to read and agree to the licensing agreement. After agreeing to the licensing agreement, you'll click Next and be presented with the Custom Setup screen (Figure 2–1). Notice

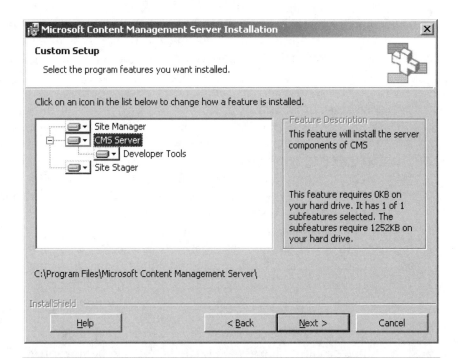

**Figure 2–1** Custom Setup screen in the CMS setup routine

that your screen may appear different from ours in this illustration if you
have installed Visual Studio .NET on your server.

After you have made your selections on the Custom Setup screen,
click Next and enter the product key code on the Customer Information
screen. Then click Next to bring up the Disk Cache Folder screen (Figure 2–2). The size selected here will default to 2GB (2,048MB). The
minimum is 50MB and the maximum is 7,429MB. After making your
selection, click Next.

---

**NOTE:** At this juncture, you'll only need to install the developer tools if
you are installing CMS on a server that already has Visual Studio .NET
installed.

---

The next screen will ask you to start the installation and will let you
choose whether you want to launch the Database Configuration Application (DCA) after setup has completed. The DCA allows you to make
configuration changes and modifications to your SQL databases. We'll
discuss the DCA in more detail under the Creating the Database section
in this chapter.

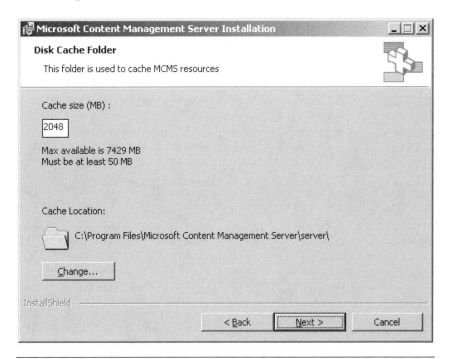

**Figure 2–2** Disk Cache Folder configuration screen

After you click Next, the installation will start. You'll see a status bar indicating setup's progress. When setup ends, you'll be presented with a Finish screen if you didn't choose to start the DCA automatically or the DCA welcome screen if you did choose to start the DCA automatically.

If you encounter installation problems, you can look at the CMSInstall log file, located (by default) in the program files\Microsoft Content Management Server\LogFiles directory. It will open with Notepad or any other text editor, and you can read the error messages in the log file and then troubleshoot as necessary.

## Creating the Database

After you have installed the required software, if you selected to have the DCA run, then the DCA will start automatically. There is an opening splash screen to this application, which you can just click through to the next screen. This screen will ask you if you want to operate in ASP.NET mode or mixed mode (Figure 2–3). The difference here is that ASP.NET mode will restrict CMS to hosting read-only sites in

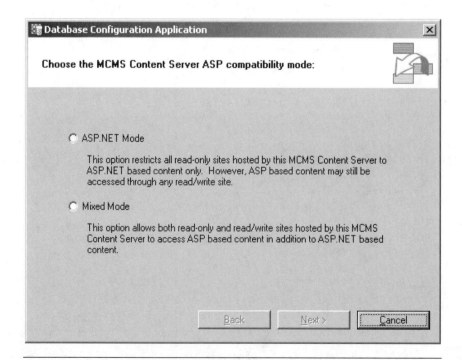

**Figure 2–3** Selecting the CMS mode

ASP.NET as opposed to earlier versions of Active Server Pages (ASP). In mixed mode, read-only sites can be hosted in either version of ASP code.

Once you've made your selection, you can click Next. The following screen will ask you which existing Web sites on your server should host the CMS server installation. In our running example here, we'll select the Default Web site (Figure 2–4). You can also choose whether the site will be read-only or read/write.

The next screen will ask you which Web site should be the SCA Web entry point. Select the Administration Web Site at this point and click Next. Note that if you select the Default Web site or any Web site that is operating over port 80, you will receive a warning message that says, essentially, don't use this site. Then click Next.

The following screen will ask you for a user name and password account that will be used for the CMS system account. Enter the correct user name and password, and then click Next.

The DCA application will then stop all IIS services and present you with the screen from which you can select the database that you'd like CMS to use. If this screen comes up with a "[none]" selection, as illustrated in Figure 2–5, click the Select Database button, and you'll receive

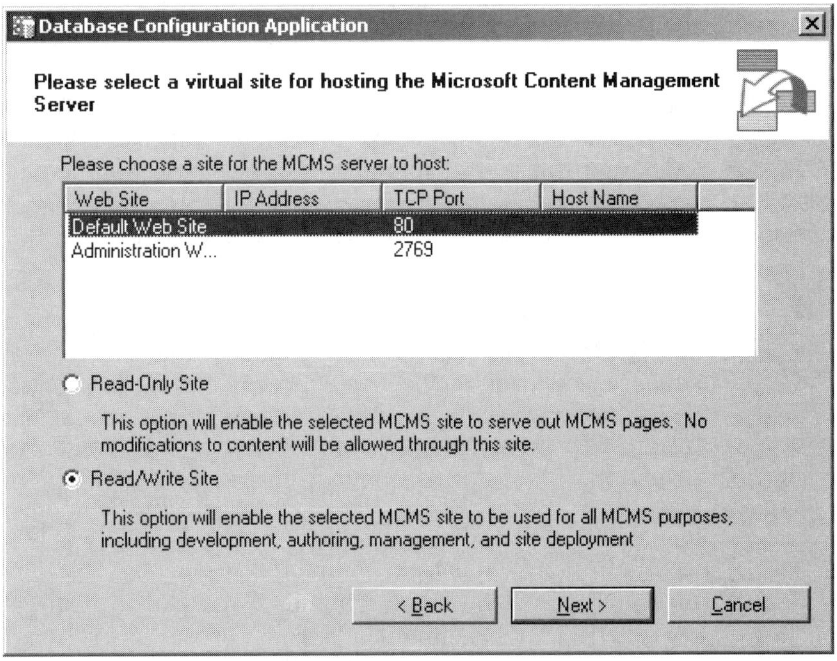

**Figure 2–4** Selecting a Web site to host the CMS server installation

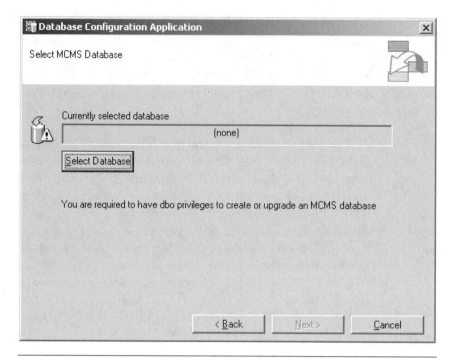

**Figure 2–5** Database selection screen

a list of all the SQL servers in your environment. From there, you can select which server and database you'd like this CMS installation to use. You'll want to use the Options button (which is dimmed in Figure 2–6 because we already selected it to illustrate the Options features) to select the exact database on that server, along with the language.

---

**NOTE:**  Best practice is to create the empty SQL database before installing CMS on your server. If you wait until this point to create the SQL database, you'll need to bounce out of the installation program, create the database, and then come back and perform these actions again.

---

If the database is empty, you'll be asked if you'd like CMS to populate the database. Click Yes on that pop-up, and the database population will begin. After the schema is built in the new database and the changes are committed, you'll be asked whether you'd like to restrict Site Stager access to the local machine. The default is to say Yes. Make your selection there and then click Next. You'll then receive a pop-up box indicating that

**Figure 2–6** Options screen that allows us to select a SQL database on a different server

SQL services need to be running on the remote SQL box. This DCA ends by defaulting to starting the SCA when you click Finish.

If you choose to start the SCA, you'll be presented with the General tab in the Server Configuration Application. This application is discussed in detail in Chapter 18. The DCA is also discussed in Chapter 8.

At this point, you'll have CMS installed and ready to build your Web site. There are some other installation issues that we'll discuss now in the following sections. These issues include installing CMS on multiple computers.

## Installing SQL and CMS on the Same Server

The SQL server can reside on the same physical box as CMS. In our preceding example, we demonstrated how to install CMS on one server and place the SQL database on a different server. The reason this illustration was selected was that we felt in most environments the SQL server and the CMS server would be two different servers.

However, this is not required. If you want to install CMS and SQL on the same server, you can. And, in fact, you can use the local SQL databases to host your CMS installation.

So, the only difference in how CMS would be installed is that on the database selection screen (refer to Figure 2–5), you would select a local database instead of a remote database. After that, the installation should proceed as normal.

## Installing Site Manager and/or Site Stager

There is not much to installing either of these packages. Essentially, you'll want to run the CMS setup routine and then make your selections during this setup routine on the Custom Setup screen (Figure 2–7). Incidentally, this is where you can select to uninstall a package as well.

## Installing the Authoring Connector

The Authoring Connector (AC) is used to allow users to publish information directly from Word. The Authoring Connector runs from within the Word application and is a wizard-based utility.

The AC is installed on the client computer, not the server. Any user with rights to contribute to the content on a CMS site can install and use

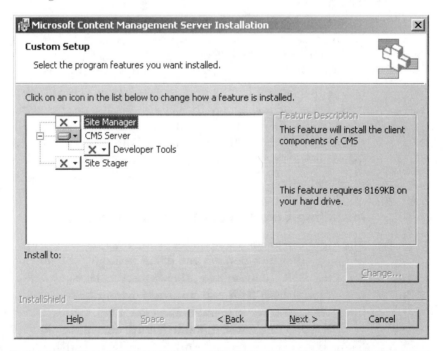

**Figure 2–7**  Selecting Site Manager on the Custom Setup screen in the CMS setup routine

the AC. There are essentially two steps involved in installing the AC on a client machine:

- Install the AC component.
- Enable the AC component in the Word application.

In order to install the AC, you must meet these prerequisites:

- The operating system must be Windows 2000 based or Windows XP based.
- You'll need to be running at least Service Pack 2 if Windows 2000 based.
- You must be running Word XP.
- You must be running Internet Explorer 5.0 or later.

To install the Authoring Connector, you'll need to first install Word 2002. Without this installed, the AC setup routine will not even begin. The first three screens in the setup wizard are the Welcoming screen, the Company Information screen, and the location screen where you can tell setup where you want the AC installed. These are generic screens that don't need to be illustrated here.

The fourth screen will ask you which CMS server you'd like to connect to. Enter the CMS server name and click Next. Then click Next again and the installation will start. The installation is short, and you'll finish the wizard by clicking Finish on the Finish Setup screen.

Enabling the AC in Word 2002 is not terribly intuitive. First, you'll need to navigate to the Tools menu and select Options. On the Security tab (Figure 2–8), you'll click the Macro Security button. This will bring up the Security dialog box. On the Trusted Sources tab, ensure that the "Trust all installed add-ins and templates" check box is selected (Figure 2–9).

This series of steps will enable the AC in Word 2002. These options should already be selected for you because of the AC installation on your client computer. However, it is a good idea to go through these steps and ensure that you have the proper configurations assigned as we just described.

What changes in Word 2002? Well, on the File menu, you'll find a Send to MCMS menu option that will allow you to send a document directly to CMS from Word 2002. This menu option is illustrated in Figure 2–10.

---

**NOTE:** You can learn how to create a page in Word 2002 and publish it to a CMS Web site by referencing Chapter 7.

---

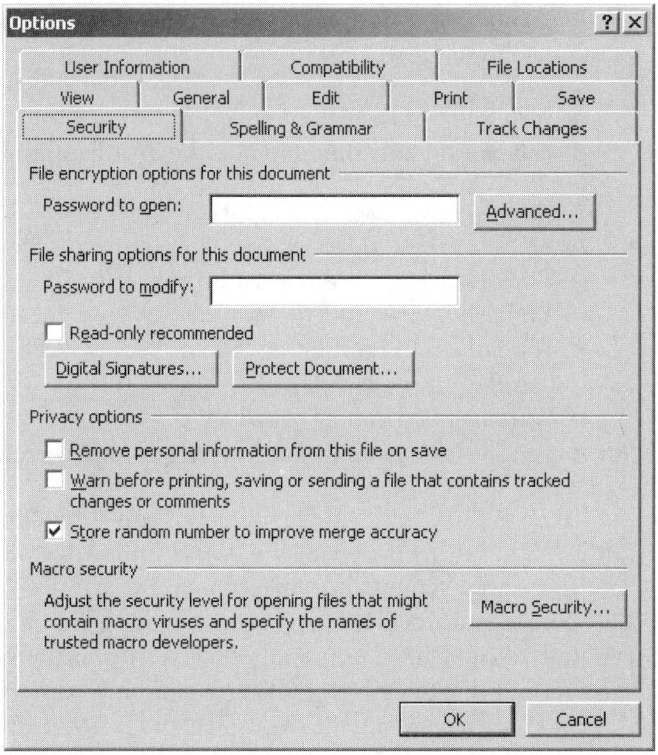

**Figure 2–8**  Security tab in the Options area of Word 2002

## Enabling Guest Rights on Your CMS Web Site

In order for guest users or subscribers to view your site, you'll need to enable this feature in CMS 2002. To do this, navigate to the Security tab in the MCMS Configuration Application (Figure 2–11).

From the Security tab, click the Configure button and then select Yes from the Allow Guests on Site drop-down menu (Figure 2–12). Enter the account that guests will be automatically logged in as, and then click OK.

## Installing the CMS Documentation Only

If you need to install the CMS documentation that ships with CMS 2002, then you'll simply need to copy the .chm files from the installation CD to your local hard drive. There is no separate installation program for installing the CMS documentation by itself. The .chm file will run on

**Figure 2–9**  Trusted Sources tab in Word 2002

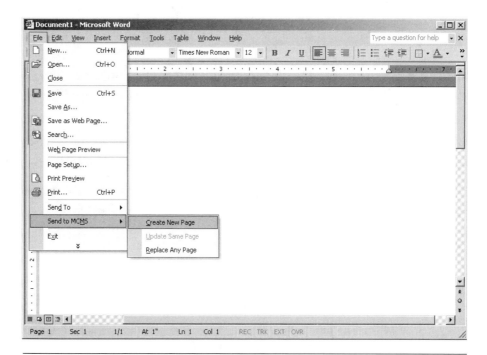

**Figure 2–10**  Send to MCMS menu option

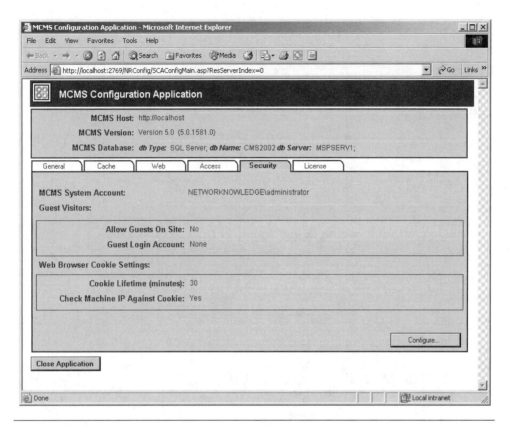

**Figure 2–11**  Security tab in the MCMS Configuration Application

its own without running any installation routine. The .chm files can be found in the documentation folder on the server CD-ROM. These documents are also available from Microsoft's Web site at http://www.microsoft. com/cmserver/default.aspx?url=/CMServer/techinfo/productdoc/.

## Uninstalling CMS

Microsoft has made uninstalling simple. If you ever need to uninstall CMS 2002, then you can use the Add/Remove Programs utility in the Control Panel. Alternatively, you can run the CMS setup program and select to run none of the features on your server. This too will uninstall CMS from your server. When you select to uninstall CMS, you will not affect the CMS database or the files on the file system.

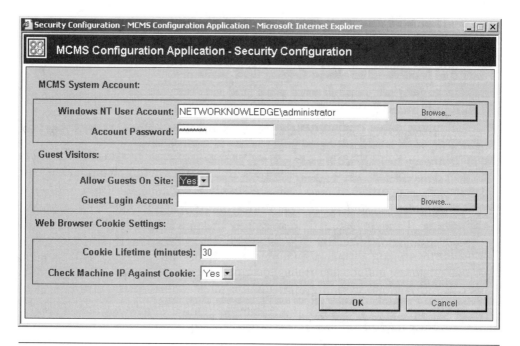

**Figure 2–12**  Enabling guest account access in the Security Configuration area

This procedure is the same for the AC and the Site Manager too.

## Upgrading from CMS 2001

Please reference Chapter 37 on how to upgrade from CMS 2001 to CMS 2002. That chapter is devoted to this function. However, there are a couple of things to note here:

- Your CMS 2001 database will be upgraded by the DCA when the CMS 2002 setup is run. Therefore, you'll want to ensure that you select to run the DCA after setup is complete.
- The DCA will upgrade the schema of the CMS 2001 database to accept the new objects in CMS 2002.
- The DCA will create a template file for each CMS 2001 template and will delete historical revisions of templates.
- DCA will create a directory called IIS-NR named Templates that mirrors the CMS 2001 template gallery hierarchy. Placeholders are also converted to use the correct placeholder definition.

- Resources that were embedded in the templates are moved to the file system. Hence, if you have any templates in CMS 2001 that will rely on embedded information, they may not work properly in CMS 2002.

### Installing CMS 2002 with SP1 on a Windows 2003 Server

To install CMS 2002 with SP1 on a Windows 2003 Server, you'll need to perform the installation as we described earlier in this chapter. However, it is important to note that *you should not launch the DCA until after you have installed SP1*. Therefore, once CMS is installed, do not select the Launch Database Configuration Application check box. Let the installation finish, then install SP1 for CMS, and then run the DCA.

Remember that Windows 2003 installs without IIS, so you'll need to install IIS 6.0 with the components ASP.NET, ASP, and server side includes *before* you install CMS or SP1.

In Windows 2003, the maximum amount of allowed data upload is configurable in IIS. However, the default number is too low for CMS resources. You'll need to raise this limit to at least 50MB. For information on how to do this, please see the SP1 documentation. XML code will need to be added to the metabase.xml file, and then services will need to be restarted.

## Summary

In this chapter, we have highlighted how to install CMS 2002. We have seen that installation is not difficult, but if there are misconfigurations on your server, setup will notice this and inform you of the problem before continuing the routine. Installing CMS server, in the larger scheme of things, is probably the least of your problems. Understanding the architecture of CMS and knowing how to plan for a CMS implementation is crucial if you are going to be successful in your implementation.

In the next chapter, we'll discuss the architecture of CMS. Then, in Chapter 4, we'll discuss the planning issues surrounding a CMS implementation. Both chapters are crucial, so it's time we go on to learning about and understanding the architecture of CMS 2002.

# CHAPTER 3

# CMS Architecture

When Microsoft Content Management Server (CMS) was envisioned, it was designed to do something that was not popular. At that time, most people felt that dynamically assembling Web pages was not a good strategy—especially on a public-facing Web site. The main reason for this was the potential performance implication. Sites that consisted of static pages did not have to spend server resources generating HTML. But this is precisely what CMS was designed to do. Today it is clear that this practice has become extremely popular. Many sites are moving toward serving up pages of dynamic content. People expect personalized sites that offer them real-time information. They expect dynamic Web sites. Technologies such as CMS make this possible.

Furthermore, the design of CMS exposes traditionally static concepts as programmable objects. For example, CMS developers can programmatically access properties of a CMS page. This enables them to build content-centric applications on top of CMS.

In this chapter, we will discuss the architecture of CMS. Although the discussion might be a bit "low level," knowing *how* a program is put together will help you take full advantage of its potential.

## The History of CMS

Content Management Server was originally developed in Canada at NCompass Labs Inc. as ActiveEnterprise. The prefix "Active" was a reference to NCompass's work in the creation of the ActiveX technology. The software was later renamed Resolution. Some components within CMS continue to use the naming conventions of "AE" and "RE".

Microsoft Corporation acquired NCompass Labs in 2001 and renamed the software Microsoft Content Management Server. Shortly after the acquisition, Microsoft released CMS 2001. CMS 2001 was essentially a point release of NCompass Resolution 4.0.

# CMS Architecture—Overview

Figure 3–1 shows a high-level representation of the CMS architecture. It is clear that there are a number of components and technologies involved. These components work together to create the functionality present in CMS. There are four basic elements involved in the CMS architecture:

- A database for storing information
- A Web server for presenting pages
- The CMS software
- Connectors to integrate functionality from other sources

It is not surprising that CMS uses SQL Server 2000 as its data store. CMS pages are presented using the Internet Information Services (IIS) Web server. In addition, CMS integrates with IIS to produce other functionality. Examples of this are described later in this chapter. The CMS server software is installed on a system running Windows 2000 Server and IIS 5.0. CMS 2002 SP1 will support Windows 2003 Server and IIS 6.0. The CMS server software also enables connectors that allow users to populate CMS template pages with content generated by other applications—for example, Microsoft SharePoint or custom Web services applications.

It is important to bear in mind that each component has an important role that is enmeshed with the roles of the other components. Some components may be used more often than others, but few could be removed altogether. In the following sections, we will take a granular look at each component. We will learn about the component's functionality, the services it performs, and how it integrates into the overall CMS picture. There is much to learn, so let's get going.

# History of a CMS Page Request

To clarify an important part of the CMS server architecture, let's trace the path of a CMS page request (Figure 3–2). First, the client requests a CMS URL. This request goes to IIS and passes through the Internet Server Application Programming Interface (ISAPI) filters loaded on the server. The CMS ISAPI filter examines the URL to see if it maps to a posting in the CMS server. If there is a matching posting, the URL is

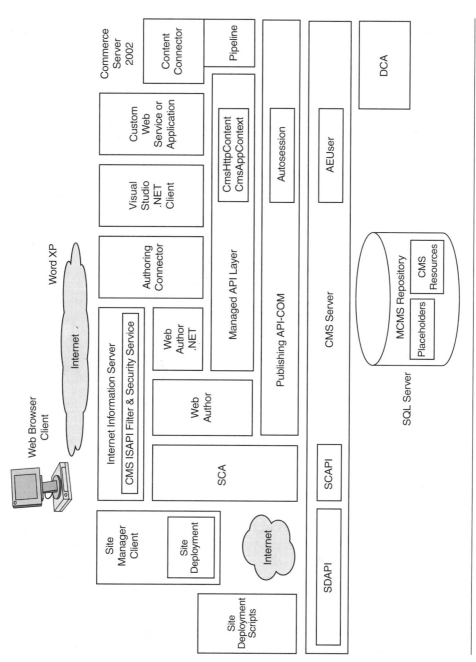

**Figure 3-1** CMS architecture

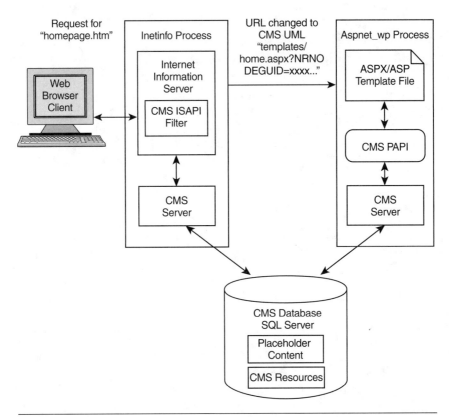

**Figure 3–2** The path of a CMS page request

modified to point to the ASPX template file for the posting. The new URL also includes a query string that specifies the posting to render. For example, the URL homepage.htm might point to a posting that uses a template file called home.aspx. The URL would be modified to be /home.aspx?NRNODEGUID="xxxxx," where "xxxxx" is the Globally Unique Identifier (GUID) of homepage.htm. This URL is returned to IIS, and it runs the specified ASPX page to render the posting. In the live site mode, CMS can translate this GUID-based URL to a more readable hierarchical URL (e.g., http://www.botsconsulting.com/home.htm).

To create the page's HTML, IIS runs the specific ASPX page template. This page may contain server controls and a code-behind page that interacts with the CMS system. If the needed information has not been requested before, the CMS server requests the required content and resources from the CMS database. If the page has been requested before, the many CMS caching strategies limit trips to the database. This dynamic page assembly process is one of the fundamental features of CMS. Each time an author edits a page and goes through the CMS workflow, the changes are saved by the CMS system. The next time the pieces are requested, the updated HTML will be served to the user. By combining the CMS caching features with ASP.NET output caching, it is possible to serve up ASP.NET pages much faster than with regular ASP pages. Considering that CMS 2001 only supported ASP, this provides a significant improvement over CMS 2001 performance.

# CMS Architecture—Component Discussion

These are the CMS components:

- CMS server
- CMS database
- Web Author
- Web Author .NET
- Authoring Connector
- Templates and placeholder server controls
- Placeholder objects
- Site Manager
- Visual Studio .NET client
- Publishing API
- Site Deployment/SDAPI
- Sample data
- Database Configuration Application (DCA)
- Server Configuration Application (SCA)
- Content Connector (provided with the Microsoft Solution for Internet Business, or MSIB)

Essentially all the parts can be categorized according to four distinct purposes:

- Managing and rendering content
- Authoring content
- Developing CMS templates
- Managing CMS servers

# Managing and Rendering Content

## Internet Information Server Layer

The IIS server is at the top level of a CMS deployment. Just as Microsoft SQL Server 2000 is fundamental to the CMS server tier, Microsoft IIS is essential to the CMS front end. CMS is not a Web server; IIS is the application that serves up the pages to a Web browser.

CMS installs two ISAPI filters: Resolution filter and Resolution HTML Packager. The first ISAPI filter recognizes when a request for a CMS page is made and rewrites the URL to point to the actual template file. The Resolution filter is the main filter responsible for detecting CMS URLs and targeting the correct template files. The REHtml Packager filter is only used for one purpose. It aids the historical revision comparison feature by packaging HTML so that it is safe for JavaScript code. The filter puts the HTML into JavaScript variables that the browser then sends to an ASP page on the CMS server. This page then checks the differences between the two pieces of HTML and uses this information for the compare historical revisions feature.

## CMS Server Layer

The CMS server layer is one of the original CMS components. When CMS was conceived, the server layer was tasked with a tremendous amount of the processing load. Before the Publishing API (PAPI), the Authoring Connector, or even the Web Author came along, the server did almost all of the work. At that time, the Site Manager was the only interface to the server layer. Both authors and administrators used the Site Manager to do their jobs. However, as CMS has evolved, the work has been distributed over a number of components. Authoring, for example, has been removed entirely from the Site Manager.

The CMS server is one of the only components that write changes directly to the CMS database. The private server object called AEServer is used for such interactions. There are some CMS features that are only exposed from within the AEServer API. For example, CMS user rights management is only available through the Site Manager; it is not exposed through the PAPI. At this time, there is no plan to expose AEServer to CMS customers. However, the CMS group at Microsoft is considering how they could expose the same functionality through the PAPI.

There are few components that interact directly with the CMS server. The Site Manager client is one of these interfaces. The Site Manager is used by CMS users to perform actions such as creating or assigning rights to resource galleries and other CMS containers. Developed before the introduction of the PAPI, the Site Manager communicates directly with the CMS server. Originally, the Site Manager was the only exposed interface to the CMS server. Partially for this reason, it is also one of the components that can be used remotely over HTTP. Two other components that interact directly with the CMS server are the SCA and the DCA. These components are described later in this chapter.

The CMS server is also responsible for managing the various CMS caches. The following sections will explain the purpose of these caches.

## CMS Server Caches

### Caching Background

Because of the architecture of CMS, caching plays a very important role. For example, .NET output caching can improve performance by 100 to 200 times. The CMS server also uses memory caches to enhance system performance. Instead of retrieving the information from the database every time the information is required, CMS temporarily stores the most frequently used data in the server memory caches.

The CMS server maintains memory caches and a disk cache for resources. Together, these caches allow the server to readily access data and files that are stored in the database. Examples of this data include CMS template metadata and placeholder content.

Here is a description of the various types of caching that CMS uses.

### .NET Output Caching

.NET output caching can cache the rendered HTML of Web pages. When a cache hit occurs, the entire rendered page can be served to the client. It is possible that no CMS template code would be invoked. This offers a large performance increase because very little needs to be done to fulfill the request. Other than some rights checking, all CMS has to do is return the cached HTML.

### Placeholder Definition Caching

This cache exists only in managed code. When a template is accessed, the particular version of the placeholder definitions contained within it is used as an index to the inflated placeholder definitions. Because the definitions are inflated using XmlSerialization, there is a performance hit when they are used. Multiplying that hit over every placeholder of every page is unacceptable. Fortunately, the placeholder definitions do not change very often. This makes them a prime candidate for caching.

### Fragment Caching

Fragment caching involves gathering chunks of HTML and storing the content for later use. In ASP, this is the only form of caching that the template designer can implement. In the case of content blocks—that are used in many pages—it still has its uses in conjunction with .NET output caching. For example, all pages may share the same navigation code, and this code may be expensive to generate. If the cache hit is low on a large number of the pages, the output cache may not have a lot of use. In this scenario, the template designer could generate the navigation code once for the entire site and cache this fragment. All subsequent page renderings would use the pregenerated navigation HTML.

### String Caching

Quite a few strings are repeated often in CMS. For example, every page has a list of placeholders. If there are 10,000 pages loaded into memory based on the same template with 10 placeholders, the 10 strings are replicated 10,000 times in memory. Thus, it makes a lot of sense to cache these strings and reuse them via shallow copying. In order to increase the effectiveness of the cache and to decrease the time spent in critical sections searching and updating the cache, each type of object that string caching is used on contains a specific string cache. For example, placeholders, node properties, and layout properties have their own string caches.

### Hierarchy Caching

There is a collection object that contains the list of child GUIDs for a given node. The collection cache keeps track of these objects, as well as a backward list that maps every node to its parent collection. This allows for quick lookups when you are moving nodes, so that you can remove a node from the old parent and add it to the new parent easily. Similar to the node cache, the collection cache is represented by an LRK Hash table that maps the GUID to a collection class. This collection class is simply a list of GUIDs of child nodes. The child nodes themselves are not present in this collection. The collection only contains references to them.

Since CMS is running in a multithread process, cache access conflicts could compromise the integrity of the server. To prevent this, a special resource synchronization mechanism called "WNT critical section" is used to prevent conflicting access among different threads. Since CMS runs within the IIS process, CMS does not manage these threads. IIS schedules different HTTP requests to be processed by different threads.

### Disk-Resident Cache

When a user uploads a file into a placeholder or adds a file to the CMS resource gallery, these files are stored within the CMS database. Examples of these resources are image files, Microsoft Word documents, and Microsoft PowerPoint presentations. These resources tend to be big (100K or more), and it may be slow to retrieve them from the database every time a user wants to access them.

The job of the disk-resident cache is to store the most often used resources on the server file system. Since local file access is much faster than reading an object file from a database, the retrieval of information is greatly improved.

This disk-resident cache also provides a temporary holding place for all URL-accessible files. In order for IIS to access the resources, these files must be stored on the local file system and referenced by an IIS virtual directory. These files are not deleted once the HTTP request is complete; they are stored on the file system so that they are ready to be downloaded by future users. This disk-resident cache is emptied every time the system starts. It is important to note that CMS templates are persistent files, so they are not cached by the disk-resident cache.

### Node Cache

Once the CMS server is running, and users are accessing the system, node objects are instantiated in the server. These objects include concepts such as the CMS channels, postings, template gallery items, and resource gallery items. These objects are then filled with information from the relational database. Some of these node objects, known as the shared objects, stay in IIS server process memory space. These shared objects retain their information so that they can possibly be reused by the next user request. Because the database does not have to be accessed every time, information retrieval is accelerated.

In order to maintain and locate these objects and their relationship with the database, a special static control object is used. This object is called the node cache. The node cache stays in memory and holds references to the most often used nodes. This increases performance because it keeps more objects in memory and minimizes the calls to the SQL server. The size of the node cache is set in the SCA (Figure 3–3).

The node cache periodically checks for changes in the database. This check happens every six seconds and on every edit request. Only nodes that have been modified are removed from the cache.

### Node Collection Cache

A node collection object is used to store the relationship between child nodes and their parent node. It contains the parent node GUID and the list of GUIDs associated with the child nodes. As with the node cache, after the node collection object is instantiated, it can be initialized from information stored in the database. These node collection objects remain in the server process memory as long as there is sufficient space. This allows them to be accessed quickly. In order to maintain and locate these node collection objects, a special static control object is used. This is called the shared node collection cache.

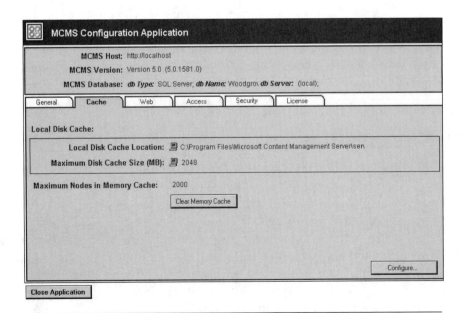

**Figure 3–3** The SCA cache configuration settings

### User Node Cache

Currently, CMS users must be either NT users or Active Directory users. In order to find information about a particular user quickly, a user node cache is created. The user node cache consists of a map between the user name and the database ID of the AEUser table in the database. The map enables a user name to be quickly translated to the proper database ID.

Before a CMS asset is read or accessed, the user's rights are verified by the CMS server. A page node contains a reference to a list of rights groups, and each rights group contains its members. Using the map, the server can quickly determine the database ID of the user and determine what rights the user has to the appropriate page node.

### High-Level Caches

There are a series of caches inside CMS that are used to speed up certain operations. High-level caches are contained entirely within the CMS system. They are not accessible via any API. The purpose of these caches is to store frequently used items that are computationally expensive. One example of this is the URL transformations that are done for the ISAPI filter. The same URL is transformed into the same new URL, so it does not need to be calculated every time. This would normally involve traversing the channel hierarchy, grabbing and inflating all the items, comparing their names, drilling down to the next level, and grabbing the appropriate template. Since the information does not normally change, we can simply store an entry in a cache that maps the friendly URL to the file system URL.

Unlike the node cache, these caches are not able to just toss out one item when a node changes in the database. The reason for this is that if you happen to rename your root CMS channel, every URL in the entire system will be different. This is the one problem with the high-level caches; they are based on an aggregation of data. On the plus side, changes to the system are generally few compared with the number of page hits.

There are also high-level caches for the rights of the guest user, placeholder content inflation, resource lookup, URL generation, and the fragment cache that can be used with ASP templates.

### The Sandbox

The sandbox is where transient uncommitted data is held and operated on. It is quite similar to the master cache in that it contains a collection cache, a series of interfaces to allow for manipulation of nodes, and a node cache. This is a smaller node cache retrieved from the master cache.

The node cache in a sandbox is owned entirely by the sandbox for the duration of the request. It cannot be accessed by any other session, which allows it to be free of thread synchronization. Whenever a node in the sandbox cache is modified, it is cloned, the original is removed, and the clone is kept to be operated on. This again makes sure that object synchronization is maintained. The collection cache in the sandbox is very similar to the node cache in that it is the same object as the master cache, but it is cloned before being operated on.

When a transaction has been committed, the sandbox passes itself to the master cache to examine and synchronize with the master cache's internal state. At this point, modified objects are moved over, collections are updated, and derived behavior (high-level cache and so on) is enacted.

## CMS Database

At the base level there is a Microsoft SQL Server 2000 database. The architecture of CMS relies heavily upon Microsoft SQL Server 2000. Without the database layer, it would not be possible to provide the key features of CMS.

The CMS server executes complex procedures against the database. These actions cannot be easily reproduced by manually manipulating the data store. For this reason, the database schema is not published, and customers are discouraged from direct interaction with the CMS database. CMS is designed such that almost all the interaction with the CMS database is handled by the CMS server layer. By using the CMS API, customers can be assured that their interface to the database has been fully tested.

The database schema consists of 40 tables. CMS data is stored in various formats within these tables. Opening the AEUser table, for example, plainly shows the users and groups that have been added to the CMS rights model (Figure 3–4).

However, finding information stored in a particular placeholder is more difficult. The reason for this is that CMS was designed to be used through the PAPI, not via direct access to the database. Placeholder data is often stored in binary large object (BLOB) format and cannot be easily found or read. Resources within placeholders are stored in the "blob" table, but placeholder data is stored in the NodePlaceholderContent

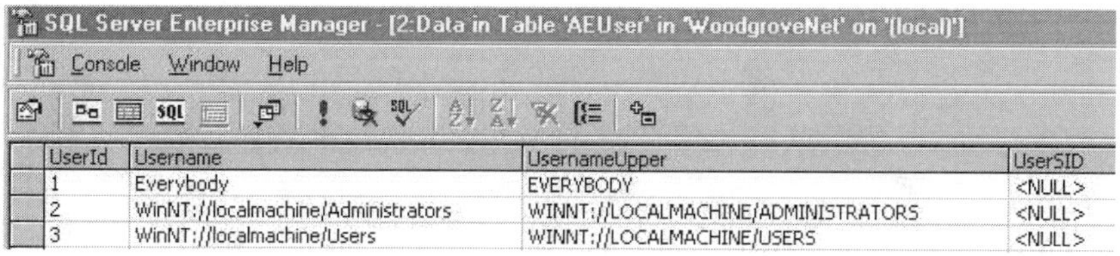

**Figure 3–4** AEUser table shown in SQL Server Enterprise Manager

table. It is difficult to find placeholder data, because CMS assembles various pieces of content from this table.

Although it is possible to create a cluster of CMS servers, CMS only supports an "active passive" SQL Server cluster. The reason for this is that the CMS 2002 database is restricted to one Microsoft SQL Server 2000 machine. In contrast to Commerce Server 2002, it is not possible to split CMS tables between different Microsoft SQL Server 2000 boxes. Also, the CMS server will recognize if tables have been added or deleted. Altering the database schema in either of these ways will render the CMS database invalid for new installs or upgrades.

When the CMS server is in read-only mode, roughly 90% of interaction with the database is through stored Structured Query Language (SQL) procedures. An example of this is a read-only CMS server caching CMS pages. When the server is writing—such as creating new CMS pages—approximately half of the database queries are ad hoc server queries and the other half are stored procedures.

As mentioned earlier, the schema for the CMS data store is not published, and direct requests to the database are not supported by Microsoft. However, many people are curious about the architecture of the data store. Here is some information that will allow you to perform read-only tasks on the CMS data store. One of the more interesting tables in the CMS database is the Node table. This table contains the core information about the CMS system.

Table 3–1 shows some examples of node types that are stored within the CMS Node table.

Using this information, you can do simple read-only queries against the CMS database. Under no circumstances should write operations be performed directly against the database. The PAPI is the appropriate interface for writing to the CMS database. Note that since the schema has not been released, these queries may not work on future releases of CMS.

**Table 3–1** CMS Node Types

| Node Type | Type of Object |
|---|---|
| 1 | Server |
| 4 | Channel |
| 16 | Page or posting |
| 64 | Resource gallery |
| 256 | Resource gallery item |
| 16384 | Template gallery |
| 65536 | Template |

These are examples of read-only SQL queries that can be run against the CMS database:

- Find the page/posting by name:
  Select * From Node Where type=16 AND name='Page Name'
- Find the page and posting GUID from the page name:
- Select posting.nodeguid posting,page.nodeguid page From Node page inner join node posting on page.nodeguid = posting.followguid and page.name='Page Name' AND page.type=16 and page.isshortcut=0
- Find the posting from the page followguid:
- Select * From Node Where followguid = '{87B29228-3CFC-426A-8DD0-7B5E33CXXXXX}'
- Find information about the posting (add your own GUID):
- Select * From Node Where nodeguid = '{0369528B-943B-40A0-8B57-C5E3578XXXXX}'

# Authoring Content

## Web Author

Many CMS users will only use the Web Author interface. In fact, many probably think that the Web Author *is* CMS. Since the CMS 2002 release, all authoring happens through this thin client interface. The Web Author is built using ASP, JavaScript, and the PAPI. A few elements, such as the toolbar and the HTML placeholder control, are

ActiveX components. The Web Author consists of a number of user interfaces and code that interacts with the PAPI. Because the Web Author is a thin client interface, it can be used remotely over HTTP. It is also possible to use HTTPS with the Web Author interface.

The Web Author default install location is C:\Program Files\Microsoft Content Management Server\Server\IIS_NR\System\WBC. The directory is called WBC because the Web Author was originally called the Web Browser Client.

Inside the WBC directory are the following folders:

- Customizable: This folder contains the Web Author files that are still supported after customer modifications. For example, the Hooks directory contains scripts that allow ASP access to some Web Author events.
- Internals: Most of the Web Author code is under this directory. For example, the user interfaces for the Web Author console are located in the WBCFuncPages directory. The legal statement (InternalsDirectoryLegal.txt) provided in these directories clearly states that these files are not meant to be modified.
- SiteInterface: This directory contains only one file, Placeholders Support.inc. The file is simply a warning that this former interface has been deprecated.

## Web Author .NET

The .NET version of the Web Author has been designed to offer the same functionality as the nonmanaged version. Therefore, the two applications are very similar. Without this similarity, people might have become frustrated by two different user experiences. The Web Author .NET interface and dialogs were developed using JavaScript and .NET server controls.

The default install location for Web Author .NET is C:\Program Files\Microsoft Content Management Server\Server\bin. Unlike the ASP version of the Web Author, the managed version is compiled. This is the way that .NET works, but for CMS customers, there are positive and negative arguments about the compiled version of Web Author. Some people argue that customers and partners are hurt by the fact that they are not able to view all of the code. However, other people feel that the compiled version of the code has advantages. Two common positive arguments are that hackers are not able to comb the code looking for weaknesses and that customers can be sure that their Web Author code has not been inadvertently altered.

On an ASP.NET CMS site, the Web Author .NET handles all the authoring duties. It is not necessary to install the ASP version of the Web Author if the site will not be using it. Web Author .NET also supports HTTPS. The architecture of the Web Author .NET is discussed in detail in Chapter 30.

## Authoring Connector

The Authoring Connector is a new interface for CMS. Introduced in CMS 2002, this feature promises to be popular with CMS authors. The Authoring Connector component enables content creation and editing directly through Microsoft Word XP. The Authoring Connector consists of a client-side component and a server-side component.

- Client side: A Word add-on featuring a user interface wizard. This wizard allows CMS authors to easily specify the location for their content to be published.
- Server side: ASPX files and ASP.NET server controls that write to CMS via their interaction with the PAPI.

The Authoring Connector client uses the Word API to convert Word documents into HTML. The HTML and any inline images are then submitted to a designated placeholder within a CMS page. After that submission, a link to the newly created Web page is stored in the properties of the Word document. This makes it easier for the author to update or replace the page at a later date. The next time the same Word document is submitted, Authoring Connector recognizes the reference to the page and allows the user to update the corresponding page.

The default location for the Authoring Connector is C:\Program Files\Microsoft Content Management Server\Authoring Connector. There are a number of subfolders installed in this client-side location. Each numbered folder corresponds to a Locate Identifier (LCID) and contains the localized version of the client-side portion of the Authoring Connector application. This allows CMS authors from all over the world to use their localized versions of Microsoft Word XP to create and edit content on CMS servers.

Although this is currently the only localized portion of CMS, other components have been designed to be localizable. For example, the Web Author, the Web Author .NET, and the Visual Studio integration have all been designed to be localizable. Based on this, various people have produced their own localized versions of the Web Author. Also, a white paper on the subject of localizing the Web Author is available from the MSDN Web site (http://msdn.microsoft.com).

## CMS Placeholders

CMS placeholders have evolved substantially over the last few years. Placeholders are the parts of a CMS Web page that contain editable content. Placeholders come in various types, with special features associated with each type.

Examples of placeholder types are:

- Image: Can only contain images
- HTML: Can contain HTML
- XML: Contains XML

Placeholders consist of three parts:

- Placeholder object: The underlying object that controls the behavior of the interface to the placeholder content. Custom placeholder objects can be created. For example, if you wanted a placeholder that contained a method such as GetPieceOfContent, you might want to create a custom placeholder.
- Placeholder definition: The description of the placeholder that is set from within Visual Studio .NET. Placeholder objects must be bound to a placeholder definition before they can be used. The placeholder definition can be thought of as controlling the behavior of a placeholder—for example, the XSD that an XML placeholder should validate against.
- Placeholder server control: The .NET server controls that CMS users actually interact with. Custom placeholder controls can be created to control the rendering of the placeholder object in different modes.

The new model for placeholder controls is to use .NET server controls. Placeholder server controls are designed to allow an ASPX template to be bound to placeholder object data. The controls also render the placeholder data in various modes. The model for custom placeholder controls allows developers to choose the controls used for modes such as presentation and authoring. Most of the logic behind these services is provided by the BasePlaceholderControl object. Custom placeholder server controls built on top of this object only need to specify the logic for data reading, data writing, and rendering.

The rendering implementation of placeholder server controls is not restricted. This leaves the logic for rendering the authoring or presentation display up to the CMS developer. Rendering is generally handled by aggregating other controls designed specifically for this purpose. These controls could be ASP.NET controls (e.g., a TextBox or Literal), or they could be more complex custom controls. The BasePlaceholderControl provides the implementation for loading data into placeholders and saving data from placeholders into the CMS database.

The placeholder server control is not responsible for committing data to the database. It is notified by the BasePlaceholderControl when it should be loading content from the bound placeholder object and when it should be saving content. Therefore, the placeholder is only used as a data storage mechanism. It appears as though the placeholder server control reads and writes the data. But within the implementation of the placeholder server control, it is the PAPI that is responsible for committing data to the CMS database.

Before the .NET layer was added, placeholders were COM objects that rendered contents from the CMS database. This interface was previously hidden by the deprecated Template Designer interface. In other words, CMS developers did not need to write any code to get their placeholders to work; the code was automatically added to the template by the Template Designer. In CMS 2002, the template files have been moved from the CMS database to the server file system. This means that the CMS server no longer manages this placeholder code. To create an ASP site with CMS 2002, CMS developers need to manage this connection in their templates. The ASP version of the placeholder controls might be removed in the next release of CMS.

When you are creating custom placeholder server controls, the logic contained within the controls is only available from within an ASPX file. If you happen to need this logic outside a server control, you may need to duplicate your effort. One example of this would be if you were using the control through a Web service. A better solution in this scenario is to put that logic into a custom placeholder and then create a server control to interact with it. In this way, the placeholder object will be available via the PAPI directly, for use in Web services or more programmatic access like code behind in templates.

# CMS Development

## Publishing API

The CMS Publishing API was introduced in NCompass Resolution 3.0. Originally, the PAPI was referred to as the Resolution Object Model (ROM). Before the introduction of the PAPI, Resolution developers used the Template Builder API (TBA). But the TBA only offered a small fraction of the functionality that the PAPI offers today. For example, the properties for pages were read-only.

Originally, the PAPI was written as a COM-compliant application. The COM interface alone offers well over 400 methods and properties. Today the PAPI is widely used by CMS developers. For example, most CMS developers use the PAPI to create their site navigation. This allows them to take advantage of the dynamic nature of a CMS site. Furthermore, the ASP Web Author component was written on top of this COM layer.

In CMS 2002, an ASP.NET managed layer is provided on top of the original PAPI. The application context allows CMS developers to develop ASP.NET WinForm applications on top of the CMS managed layer. Components that use the managed layer of the PAPI include the Authoring Connector, the CMS integration with Commerce Server 2002 (Content Connector), and the new Web Author .NET.

Examples of PAPI applications include:

- Web Author: An ASP application used for CMS page authoring through a Web browser.
- Web Author .NET: An ASP.NET application used for authoring through a Web browser.
- Authoring Connector: An ASP.NET application used for authoring with Microsoft Word XP.
- Visual Studio .NET client: An ASP.NET application used for developing CMS sites. This application uses the new CMS application context.
- Content Connector: An ASP.NET (and Visual Basic) application that allows for integration with Microsoft Commerce Server 2002. This component is provided with the Microsoft Solution for Internet Business.

### Autosession

The base object within the COM PAPI is called Autosession3. The Authenticate.inc file creates a variable called Autosession and assigns the PAPI Autosession3 object to it. All other objects, such as Posting or Channel, depend on this main object. In other words, it is necessary to create an Autosession object if you wish to use the CMS COM PAPI. You do this by referencing the Resolution.inc file within your ASP page. This file then calls Authenticate.inc, and the Autosession object is instantiated like this:

```
AutoSession = Server.CreateObject("ResolutionObjectModel.
        AutoSession3")
```

Authenticate.inc also handles the security for the CMS COM PAPI. A user cannot use the Autosession object unless they have been authenticated as a valid CMS user. A user could actually instantiate the Autosession object, but they would not be able to call any of its methods or properties until they had been authenticated as a valid CMS user.

Autosession is automatically instantiated within CMS templates, but it can also be used within any ASP pages that are on the CMS server. In previous versions of CMS, this particular point was hidden from view. The Authenticate.inc file was always readable on the file system. However, the fact that CMS automatically inserted an include statement to include Authenticate.inc was hidden from the end user's eyes.

Template files were once stored within the CMS database and edited only using the Site Manager's custom Template Designer. The Template Designer interface did not expose the method used by the templates to automatically instantiate an Autosession object. However, in CMS 2002, the template files have been moved to the file system, and anyone can plainly see how the Autosession object is instantiated.

### Managed PAPI

The new ASP.NET interface for the PAPI is a tremendous step forward for CMS developers. Using this interface, developers can program against the CMS PAPI using the Visual Studio .NET environment and numerous ASP.NET languages (including VB.NET and C#). It is this new feature that allowed the Visual Studio .NET integration to be developed. The managed layer of the CMS PAPI offers access to the PAPI through Interop assemblies. This layer was written using the C# language.

There are two interfaces within the ASP.NET layer of the PAPI:

- CmsHttpContext: The CmsHttpContext interface allows managed code to access the CMS PAPI. This interface can be used to develop .NET Web applications on top of CMS. This interface relies on the HTTP context provided within IIS.
- CmsApplicationContext: The application context is new to CMS. Although there is currently no remote interface, the application context is a fantastic step forward for CMS developers. Using the application context, CMS developers can create Windows .NET Forms applications. The application context also enables the impressive CMS VS.NET integration. This interface does not require the IIS HTTP context.

Looking forward, you can reasonably assume that future CMS components will only interact with the server though the managed PAPI layer. After all, this interface has been designed to allow developers to build applications on top of the CMS server.

## Visual Studio .NET Client

The Visual Studio .NET (VS.NET) interface is a new feature. This client application depends on the Microsoft .NET Framework and the new CMS PAPI application context. The custom Template Designer used in previous versions of CMS has been replaced by this application. Instead of using a custom template authoring environment, CMS developers can use Visual Studio .NET to code their templates. The client was developed using the CmsApplicationContext class within the managed layer of the PAPI.

Because the CMS application context provides a method to authenticate the current Windows user, CMS developers do not need to log in to this client application. They can open their CMS solution in Visual Studio .NET and automatically access CMS features such as the placeholder collections and the template galleries.

The Visual Studio .NET integration is not installed by default. The reason for this is that the component is only necessary on developer boxes. The current version of Visual Studio .NET does not support remote connections for client applications such as the CMS integration. For this reason, the CMS VS.NET integration must be installed on the CMS server. The default install location for the client is C:\Program Files\Microsoft Content Management Server\DevTools.

Once this component is installed, it allows a CMS developer to work in an extremely powerful development environment. For example, developers can use the Visual Studio integration to manage components of CMS templates that are stored within the database. One of these components is the collection of placeholders that is associated with a particular template.

A compelling feature for a CMS developer is the fact that CMS templates can be debugged in VS.NET just like any other ASP.NET pages. Not only can a developer use tools such as breakpoints in their code, they can also debug CMS pages within their specific CMS context. For example, when a CMS developer launches a debugging session, the page can be displayed exactly as a specific CMS user would see it. At any given breakpoint, the local variables will show the values that a specific CMS user would see. This level of contextual debugging has not been offered in the past.

## Sample Data

To help CMS developers get off the ground, a sample Web site is provided with CMS 2002. The WoodgroveNet site is an ASP.NET example of how to build a CMS site. The source code for the sample site is also provided on the CMS 2002 CD. Included in this code are a number of ASP.NET user controls, and server controls. Examples include the navigation control and the custom XML placeholder control. This sample code is one of the key resources for a new CMS developer.

It is important to mention that the CMS sample site should not be used directly as the starting point for a production CMS site. As written in the CMS ReadMe.html file, it is not a good idea to build an application on top of the sample objects. The reason for this is that the objects are accessed by the Site Deployment feature by their GUID. If a site is built on top of the sample objects, you could overwrite parts of the site by reinstalling the sample data.

The default install location for the CMS WoodgroveNet sample site is C:\Program Files\Microsoft Content Management Server\Sample Data. Microsoft plans to release new sample sites; you might want to check the CMS Web site for updates (http://www.microsoft.com/cmserver).

## Content Connector

The Content Connector component is used to integrate CMS with Commerce Server 2002 features. For example, developers can use the Content Connector to display Commerce Server catalog information within a CMS page. Content Connector is not included in CMS 2002. This component is included with MSIB.

Content Connector is essentially a bridge between the Commerce Server 2002 API and the CMS PAPI. It was originally written using VBScript and Visual Basic. In the new version of Content Connector, the ASP pieces have been rewritten against the managed layers of the Commerce Server 2002 API and the CMS PAPI. The Visual Basic components, such as the Personalized Content Objects pipeline, have remained the same.

# CMS Administration

## Site Manager

The Site Manager has probably changed more than any other component of CMS. Originally called the Desktop Client, it was later renamed the Site Builder. At one point, the Site Manager was the only business user interface to the CMS application. Before the PAPI, the Authoring Connector, the Web Author, or the Server Configuration Application, the Site Manager was being used by CMS customers. At that point, almost all authoring and administration was done using the Site Manager.

In CMS 2002, authoring features were removed from the Site Manager. The intent was that the Web Author (and Web Author .NET) would handle authoring, and the new Site Manager would be used purely as an administrative interface. CMS administrators and channel managers can use the Site Manger for site maintenance tasks. These tasks include administering user roles and rights, and working with CMS containers.

The Site Manager exposes four types of virtual containers: channels, resource galleries, template galleries, and user roles. Originally there were five types of containers. Pages were stored in containers called folders. At this time, a distinction was made between a "page" and a "posting." Pages contained content, and postings determined the location and schedule for publication. However, authors found this separation to be confusing, and eventually it was decided that the folders container would be hidden. Since this change, "page" and "posting" are used interchangeably.

It is interesting to point out that, under the covers, the folders and pages still exist. The server layer was not altered a great deal when this level of abstraction was removed.

These are the CMS 2002 container types:

- Channels: Contain pages (aka postings). Channels have no physical representation; they are an abstraction created by the CMS server.
- Resource Galleries: Contain CMS resources. Resources can be virtually any type of file. They are stored within the CMS database.
- Template Galleries: Contain templates. In CMS 2002, templates have been moved onto the file system. However, meta information about templates (such as the placeholder collection data), is still stored within the CMS database. This information is referred to as the template gallery item (TGI).
- User Roles: Contain user authorization and authentication information. This is one of the few CMS features not exposed through any other interface (including the PAPI).

Note that these containers have no physical representation; they are an abstraction created by the CMS server.

The properties of the Site Manager shortcut show that the application is called NRClient.exe. This is short for NCompass Resolution Client. The shortcut also shows the path to the ASP interface for the Site Manager (http://localhost/NR/System/ClientUI/login.asp). This is the login page that is shown when the Site Manager is launched.

It is possible that the Site Manager will be phased out in the next release of CMS. There are various reasons for this change. If the Site Manager features were available elsewhere, they could be easier to maintain, they could be updated for new features of CMS, and they could be built with remote interfaces.

The Site Manager has a remote interface, but this ability is provided through a custom proxy. Since there are better ways to provide remote interfaces, the custom proxy will most likely be removed. Using port 80, the Site Manager client sends and receives XML messages. The proxy was originally written in Java. However, for the CMS Service Pack 1 release, the proxy has been written using the J# managed language.

The Site Deployment feature is also partially exposed through the Site Manager. In addition to the Site Manager, it is possible to access Site Deployment through its own API. However, the only graphical user interface for Site Deployment is within the Site Manager client.

## Server Configuration Application

The Server Configuration Application exposes a Web interface for managing CMS sites. The application is written in ASP and is built on top of the CMS server's private Server Configuration API (SCAPI).

The SCA is used to write CMS settings to the system registry, assign the CMS system account file system Access Control Lists (ACLs), configure settings within the CMS database, and create the CMS structure within the IIS metabase. Some of the properties set by the SCA are local to the particular server; other settings are global across a CMS server farm. In the SCA interface, the local settings are distinguished by a small server icon. This allows a CMS administrator to easily see whether the setting will affect one machine or the entire server farm.

An example of a default install location for the SCA is http://localhost:9291/NRConfig/SCAConfigMain.asp. On Windows Server, the default install location is in the administration Web site. However, XP only supports one Web site, so the default install location is the less secure default Web site.

The SCAPI interface is installed via the ServerConfigurationAPI.dll file. The SCA and the Site Manager are the only remote administration interfaces to the CMS server. They both function over HTTP, and they handle almost all of the configuration and maintenance of the CMS server.

## Database Configuration Application

The Database Configuration Application is used to manage the connection between the CMS server and the Microsoft SQL Server 2000 database. The DCA is triggered automatically during the CMS server install, but it can also be run manually at any point. A CMS administrator would use the DCA to change the CMS database that the server is using. Once CMS is installed, it is unusual for an administrator to run the DCA. It is more common for CMS developers to use the DCA to change from one development database to another.

The DCA application is installed as the file NRDCApplication.exe. The application uses the private SCAPI interface to perform many of the same tasks as the SCA. The DCA also triggers the code necessary for migrating one version of CMS to the next version.

## Site Deployment

The CMS Site Deployment feature has evolved considerably over the last few releases. From its creation, Site Deployment used XML packages to move CMS objects from one server to another. Site Deployment Object (SDO) packages can contain various CMS objects. For example, SDO files (which were previously referred to as Resolution Object Packages or ROP files) can be used to move CMS template objects, pages, or CMS resources.

SDO files use the Windows Cabinet compression format. By changing the .sdo extension to .cab, you can open the package and view the contents. Inside the package are XML files (that describe the SDO file) and various other file types that contain the CMS data.

Previously, the Site Deployment feature was only exposed via the Site Manager. However, Site Deployment has recently been enhanced to use a component called the Site Deployment API (SDAPI). The SDAPI allows CMS developers much more flexibility than was previously possible. Using the SDAPI, a developer can write a script that will trigger Site Deployment events.

Site Deployment can also be used as part of a backup or versioning strategy. Regular SDO exports can be backed up and used to store versions of the CMS site.

# Summary

CMS has been designed to address the Webmaster bottleneck. To eliminate this problem, CMS uses a number of different components and interfaces. The components serve four basic purposes: to enable dynamic Web page rendering, to help authors publish their content, to manage the CMS server, and to enable developers to build CMS sites.

The server component is the heart of CMS. Previously, this piece was responsible for a good portion of the CMS workload. However, over the last few releases, CMS has evolved and distributed a number of functions to other components. The primary client used to be the Site Manager application. However, the Web Author applications and the Visual Studio .NET integration are now used for many features previously available only through the Site Manager.

Support for the .NET platform has brought more flexibility into the architecture of CMS. For example, the new application context provides CMS developers with new development and integration options.

CMS is a powerful platform for creating content-centric applications. As new technologies have emerged, CMS has leveraged them. At the time of writing, the next release of CMS is still being designed. However, it is logical to expect that CMS will provide more features built on top of the .NET platform.

# Planning a Content Management Server Engagement

Just because this is a planning chapter doesn't mean you can skip it, OK? It always seems that the planning chapter is one that people tend to read *last* in a book, primarily because these chapters are viewed (wrongly) as so boring as to not possibly be of any benefit. Well, nothing could be further from the truth. Although this chapter might not be as exciting as watching a sporting event or tending to your garden, this chapter is important. If there is one thing you can count on, it is this: *A poorly planned CMS deployment will lead to a poor CMS implementation.*

As with everything else in information technology, you'll need to do your due diligence in planning your Web site before implementing it. Often, a pilot program is used to help with the planning process, but you also need to understand that the pilot alone cannot create your plan: You must do this yourself.

In this chapter, we'll discuss how to plan your CMS 2002 deployment. We'll discuss four key areas:

- Envisioning the project
- Planning the project
- Developing the project
- Stabilizing the project

If you are developing a site for a customer and acting as a consultant on the project, be sure to read this chapter with an added element: You'll need to pay very close attention to document specifications. Usually, it is the customer's IT department that is responsible for setting up the environment into which the site is deployed. A poorly written specification will lead to a poorly deployed CMS site.

There's much to discuss, so let's get going!

# Envisioning the Project

If this is the first time your organization has been introduced to a product with functionality like Content Management Server (CMS), then you'll need to ensure that you've planned for the "people" side of this engagement.

Unfortunately, most IT people are ill prepared for the political and interpersonal side of implementing technology change in an organization. It is one thing to ask your users to change operating systems or upgrade to a new version of Office; it is entirely another to ask your users to *manage* their information differently than they do today.

For example, if a content creator is accustomed to creating Web information in a Word document and then sending that document through an approval process before e-mailing it to the Webmaster for posting on the Web site, then the Authoring Connector is going to lead to changes in how content is posted to the Web site. Discussion about workflow, approval, and using the features of CMS will need to occur before you can deploy CMS to your overall environment. Moreover, although some of these discussions can take place during the pilot phase, it is better for you if they occur while you're still in the design and vision stage of the project. Keeping affected parties in the loop on upcoming changes in information management will help ensure that your project is deployed smoothly and that the changes are accepted by all in your organization. Don't underestimate the amount of culture and process change that CMS may introduce. This would be a grave mistake.

Remember that if you want to bring about change in your organization, you'll need the following five elements:

■ Champion: A person at vice president level or higher who is personally vested in seeing the project succeed. This person can help convince other people high in the organization of the importance of this project's success.
■ Grassroots support: You'll need some level of support from the folks who will use this project on a day-by-day basis. A good way

to develop this is to throw a CMS party with food and beverages and then give them a demonstration on the cool features and time-saving elements of CMS.

- Project definition: Your project needs to be defined in terms of objective criteria. Stay away from defining the project with relative terms like "more," "less," and so forth. Define the project in terms that are verifiable, such as numbers and/or percentages.
- Project control: If you're going to get the blame if the project goes bad, then you should get the glory if the project goes well. If you can't control all aspects of the project, then ask for such control.
- Approved, funded budget: There is no sense in doing any of this if the money isn't available to be spent on hardware, software, support, and training. Ensure that your project plan includes monies for all four aspects of the project.

Some of your efforts should focus on getting support from every affected party in your organization or in your customer's organization. This will mean doing things such as giving demonstrations, holding meetings, and discussing the cultural and information management changes that will occur by implementing CMS.

The importance of such meetings cannot be underestimated. One of your first objectives should be to get a person high in your organization on board with the vision of the project based on the benefits and cost savings CMS will introduce to your organization. If you can't get your top-level people on board with the project's vision, then it will be difficult to find funding for the project. Hence, getting a person at the vice president level or higher on board is a key to the success of any CMS deployment.

Once you have your top-level people sold on the CMS engagement, then it's time to make the rounds to your department heads and help them understand the benefits and goals of a CMS implementation. Inherent in these discussions should be the realization of the change in business processes and information management that will occur. You will have better credibility if you recognize these changes up front and discuss this with your department heads. These folks will be more open to change if they feel that they have input into the change process.

You'll also need to discuss how CMS will change your IT and Web-based departments. There might be positions that will become obsolete because of the ability for users to directly publish content from Word to the Web site.

Also, most content will need to go through an approval process before being placed on the Web site. Your workflow models may need to change to accommodate the features of CMS. This doesn't mean that you give up your approval processes, only that the way information is passed through the approval process may change because of the Authoring Connector.

When gathering the interested parties, you should talk to each party individually and then also address them as a group. The purpose of getting them all together is so that they can see and understand the needs of other groups, which may be dissimilar from their own needs. Enabling them to understand the needs of other groups in your organization will help everyone understand why some decisions are made that, at first, might appear foolish or unwise. Understanding the context in which decisions are made is often helpful to those who usually see only a portion of the overall project plan and focus.

Be sure to have your kickoff meeting to start the project only after you have secured your champion and buy-in from your department heads. This way, nobody is taken by surprise. Moreover, the kickoff meeting can be a time to get all the interested parties together and generate some excitement and enthusiasm for the project. It is also a great time to deliver the overall project plan, go over the vision once again, and ensure that everyone is on board with the CMS engagement.

As part of the envisioning stage, you'll need to determine the goals, objectives, and business requirements of the CMS deployment at this stage. And you'll need to communicate this to each interested party in your organization.

What you want your site to do and accomplish will directly impact the objectives and business requirements of your CMS deployment. Therefore, presenting the CMS engagement in terms of how it solves a current problem or set of problems is an excellent way to describe the engagement's objectives and business requirements.

Your project proposal will be a high-level document that indicates the goals and scope of the project. Sign-off on this document is usually required before you can move to the next phase.

You'll also need to design a proof-of-concept site whereby the Web team prototypes a CMS site with templates and content. Such content can often be reused in the pilot and deployment phases.

You should plan to scope the project in such a way that you define the current "pain points" and how a CMS implementation will solve those pain points. You'll want to describe your current system and workflows and then point out specific challenges with your current system.

The need for a content management system should be a logical conclusion as you describe the ideal solutions that will solve your problem(s).

You'll also need to do some competitive analysis between various content management products and be able to articulate reasons for selecting CMS 2002 over other products.

If you are consulting, you'll need to spend time understanding your customer's current environment, their Web content, and their authoring/publishing requirements. If you don't have a good understanding of these three elements, chances are good that your CMS deployment at their site will encounter setbacks and misreads—neither of which you or your customer will enjoy very much.

Hence, from an outline perspective, here are the opening points to discuss in your CMS project plan as you scope out the CMS deployment:[1]

**I.** The envisioning phase
   **A.** Understanding business pain points
      **1.** Company background
      **2.** Current system
      **3.** Challenges with current system
      **4.** Why the need for a content management system?
      **5.** Why the choice of Microsoft Content Management Server 2002?

After you have demonstrated a thorough understanding of your pain points or your customer's pain points, you can begin to investigate other areas of a CMS deployment. The first area to look at is the requirements of the project. Be sure to include documentation that demonstrates you understand the current environment, the content that will be placed on the CMS site, and the publishing requirements for the site. Detailing the publishing requirements—such as who will be publishing, the type of content that will need to be published, and/or the place in the workflow models where publishing will occur—will help flesh out this area.

Another area to look at in this phase is identifying which supporting products are currently installed in the environment. For instance, does the customer use Exchange 2003 Server or GroupWise or SendMail? Does the customer use Visual Studio .NET? What homegrown applications has the customer built that they want to interoperate with CMS 2002? How will the Web sites be presented to the Internet? What products will be involved in the passage of packets between the Internet and your CMS server?

1. A sample document outline is included later in this chapter.

Finally, detail the budget and cost of the required CMS servers. If you will have multiple servers, be sure to explain the purpose of each physical server and why it is necessary to install. Part of your planning process will be to estimate the number, size, and cost of each CMS server. Many environments will have only one server or a few servers. Other environments will have multiple servers. Not only should your plan include budget and cost information, but it should also estimate the amount of site traffic that each server will support. Issues like these, and others, can be covered in this portion of the outline:

    **B.**  Gathering customer requirements
        **1.**  Understand the current environment
        **2.**  Analyze the customer's content
        **3.**  Investigate your customer's authoring/publishing requirements
    **C.**  Identifying supporting products for integration
        **1.**  Applications built in-house
        **2.**  Third-party applications
        **3.**  Other Microsoft products and servers
    **D.**  Determining the required number of CMS servers
        **1.**  Budget and cost
        **2.**  Site traffic
        **3.**  Hardware

The environment into which CMS will be installed is crucial to the planning process. The staging environment, source control, testing processes, and deployment solutions should all be explained. Here is a sample outline to help stir your thinking in this area:

    **E.**  Content Management Server 2002 environments
        **1.**  Managing different environments
        **2.**  Development environments
            **a)**  managing team development efforts
            **b)**  Source control
            **c)**  Build servers and the build process
        **3.**  Testing and staging environments
            **a)**  Aims of testing and staging
            **b)**  Setting up testing and staging environments
            **c)**  Testing and staging processes for Content Management Server 2002 solutions

4. Production environments
   a) Deploying solutions to the production environment
   b) Managing and maintaining the production environment

As you continue with your planning of the CMS deployment, it will behoove you to consider the skill set that each interested party will need to posses in order to get a high return on investment (ROI) of your CMS investment dollars. Don't be shy at this stage. Outline the ideal skill set for each party and then pursue doing a formal training program for them. Here is a possible outline for this portion of your planning document:

F. Team model and resources
   1. Skill set for administrators
   2. Skill set for authors/editors/moderators
   3. Skill set for infrastructure and operations staff
   4. Skill set for developers
   5. CMS team skill set document
      a) Identify team members
      b) Evaluate skill set
      c) Assign CMS tasks to individuals

As part of your client planning, you should include security and authentication requirements for your CMS site:

G. Identify security and authentication requirements
   1. Type of authentication
   2. Need for a single sign-on
   3. Need for private content

Be sure to include notes on the current network environment that details where the CMS database will reside, the location of domain controllers (or other authenticating servers), and where the CMS sites will ultimately live. Be sure to note any changes to your TCP filter that will need to be instituted as a result of your CMS deployment:

H. Identify network topology designs
   1. Location of database

    **2.**  Location of domain controller

    **3.**  DMZ setup

    **4.**  Firewall setup

# Planning the Project

Aside from the meetings, you'll need to create a plan on paper that will describe the project's vision, scope of work, and milestones. You'll also need to describe the interested parties in the project and who will perform which actions.

At this stage, you are most interested in defining all the elements of the Web site and the project work that is required to build it with CMS. Hence, you'll be looking at overall design issues, the site's functionality, CMS-related components such as templates, and how to deploy this site. End-user training should also be included in this step—especially use of the Authoring Connector.

The project plan should include information related to the project schedule, budget estimates, and any other project specifications that might exist for the project to be successful. Business users and content experts should develop a content plan that becomes a part of the overall project plan. Developers should create a development plan that becomes a part of the overall project plan.

The project plan identifies all the types of content and functionality that will be placed into the site. The content plan should also specify the sources of the content for your site.

Your development team may also need to craft a plan that explains how content in an existing site will be ported to the new CMS-based site (see Chapter 37 on how to migrate from CMS 2001 to CMS 2002). They may also need to outline how to import content from external sources, such as a newsfeed or a streaming data source.

The project vision and scope document should define the size of the project and the areas of responsibility for each party in the project. It is also essential to define what "success" means to a given project. Setting expectations at this stage will help keep the project rolling along and remove misunderstandings that would naturally arise in the absence of such definitions:

**II.** The planning phase
- **A.** Create project vision and scope
    - **1.** CMS vision/scope document
        - **a)** Project vision
        - **b)** Solution concept
        - **c)** Project scope
        - **d)** Success criteria
        - **e)** Dependencies
- **B.** Risk management
- **C.** Resource management
- **D.** CMS project plan documents
    - **1.** Envisioning document
        - **a)** Planning phase
        - **b)** Development phase
        - **c)** Deployment phase
        - **d)** Stabilizing phase
    - **2.** CMS risk document and risk matrix
        - **a)** Risk management process
        - **b)** Identify risks
        - **c)** Analyze and prioritize risks
        - **d)** Plan risks
        - **e)** Track risks
        - **f)** Control risks
        - **g)** Top risks

During the planning phase, you'll want to gather and discuss detailed information about security, authentication, site architecture, operations management, and capacity planning. Be sure to argue for a test lab with a good configuration to enable you to work offline with a production version of your CMS environment so that you can test proposed changes to your production environment in your test lab.

Some of the elements in the following portion of the outline will be difficult to quantify, such as the CPU cost per transaction or a theoretical maximum number of users. Don't spend a great deal of time on these types of details unless they play a prominent role in the customer's requirements. Here, then, are some additional outline elements that should be addressed in your planning documents:

- **E.** Planning for security and authentication
- **F.** Existing content management planning
- **G.** Planning site architecture

**H.** Operations planning
**I.** Performance planning
1. Capacity planning and usage profiling
   a) Capacity planning fundamentals
   b) Understanding transaction characteristics
   c) Understanding page requests
   d) Establishing a usage profile
   e) Example: Establishing a usage profile
2. Capacity planning and transaction cost analysis
   a) Maximum throughput per transaction
   b) CPU cost per transaction
   c) Cost per user
   d) Theoretical maximum number of users
   e) Strategy for handling peaks
   f) Consideration of other factors
   g) Result verification
3. Test plans
4. Test cases
5. Test lab requirements
6. Test lab configuration
7. Test tools
8. Availability planning
   a) Acceptable uptime
   b) Software solutions for high availability
   c) Hardware solutions for high availability

Although some of the following points might be a bit redundant to earlier outline entries in this chapter, what you need to keep in mind is that the planning portion of the deployment is much more detailed than the envisioning portion. Hence, even though you might have discussed the number and type of CMS servers in your environment, you may need to do so again from a functional and design perspective:

**J.** Planning site design
1. Network design and topology
   a) Basic network topology and servers
      (1) Web servers
      (2) Read-only MCMS servers
      (3) Authoring MCMS servers
      (4) Clustering Web servers
      (5) Database servers

    **b)**   Additional network components and servers
- **(1)** Switches and hubs
- **(2)** Firewalls and proxies
- **(3)** Network load balancing
- **(4)** Leveraging application center in network design
- **(5)** Monitoring with MOM

    **c)**   Integrating with SharePoint Portal Server
- **(1)** SharePoint Portal Server and Content Management Server 2002
- **(2)** Integration pack

## Developing the Project

Once the project has been mapped out on paper, it is time to implement the project on your CMS server. The site development phase includes a number of tasks that are unique to a CMS implementation.

There are generally two areas in which you'll need to focus your attention. The first area is having the Web team build the site, including the framework and templates. Testing the functionality of these elements is essential before handing off the site to the content people for content development. While the content team is working on supplying the site with content, the Web development team can busy themselves with other development work.

Because CMS is modular in format, your Web team can build one channel complete with templates, hand that off to the content people, and then work on other channels while the content teams are developing content for the first channel. It is not necessary for all the channels and templates to be developed before you hand the site off to the content people.

The testing and approval workflow processes can be honed and refined during this phase. Your content teams should view the development phase as a chance to ensure that their workflow processes are adjusted and refined to make their future work flow as well as possible.

At the end of this phase, you should have several elements ready to go. The first element is a working Web site that uses CMS for its content management. The second element should be documentation that contains instructions for those who will interact with the site, from both a development and a content user's perspective. A third element should be training for those who will need to learn how to use the Authoring Connector wizard to populate the site with content.

Any project can be kept on track better through the use of milestones. Milestones are used to break up an overall project into bite-sized chunks. Holding people accountable to meet milestone deadlines ensures that the project continues to move forward.

Be sure that before you release a channel and templates, you've tested each template's functionality and navigation elements. Nothing will irritate your nontechnical content developers more than a template that doesn't do what it purports to do.

In large measure, the success of any CMS deployment depends on the ease of use experienced by the content developers. This ease of use comes from a well-designed template that is easy to use. Be sure to build your templates so that they display all the relevant information without being cumbersome or difficult to use.

When you are planning the number and type of templates to host on your site, there will be a trade-off. One consideration is that the more templates you have, the tighter control you will gain for content exposure on your site. The balancing consideration is that the more templates you have, the more maintenance you will experience in keeping your site updated as new changes come down the pike.

When planning your template types, depending on the type of content you wish to display, you may need to write several versions of the template for specific browsers and devices. Be sure to address these needs as well.

Navigation elements include the links that people will use to navigate the site. Because CMS navigation is dynamically generated, when a page is added to the site, it can automatically appear in a list of links created by a script that uses the CMS API. If the script has been well planned, you will rarely need to touch it. And this is the stage at which these scripts will need to be planned.

---

**NOTE:** Always keep accurate documentation on each script that is developed for your CMS site, including scripts used to build navigation elements and scripts used to build workflow in your site.

---

When creating such a script, be sure to consider several elements. First, be sure to consider the overall site navigation design. Second, decide between text-based and image-based navigation schemes. Text-based navigation schemes can be automatically updated when a new channel is added. Image-based navigation may require a graphics designer and/or Web designer to implement the new navigation element. Third, identify any hard-coded or static navigation elements early in your navigation design. And then ensure that these static navigation elements are not lost as the overall site design continues.

Many sites will have global navigation elements, local navigation elements, and some type of breadcrumb trail that loops back up the channel structure to the current root channel, adding each step to the left-hand side of a series of links. When planning your navigation elements, you can probably use this three-tiered approach to your planning process.

There are workflow specifications that ship with CMS. You can also implement a customized workflow, and if you do, you'll need to account for several considerations. First, you'll need to see if there are any existing Windows NT or Active Directory security principles that can be directly mapped to the CMS security roles. If so, you've just saved yourself some time.

Second, you may need to have new groups created. This may involve the cooperation of your server group, so be sure to ping them early on to ensure the groups are created and are populated with the appropriate user accounts.

Third, are there any unique CMS rights that need to be created? If so, can you clearly define the purpose of these rights and the groups with which the rights will be associated? If so, you'll need to plan these out as they relate to your CMS deployment.

Any workflow paths should include how e-mail notifications will be used. How many e-mail triggers will exist in each workflow path? Will e-mail notifications be included for content that is outside a workflow path, such as expired content? You'll also need to determine how an e-mail address is derived from the user name and ensure that the same alias format is appended to each user's mailbox to ensure smooth delivery of e-mail. For example, if your users log on as *gwashington* (George Washington), but their current e-mail alias is *george.washington@<domain_name_here>*, then you'll need to ensure that your messaging administrators have added a recipient policy that creates a second e-mail address for *gwashington@<domain_name_here>*.

Here is the developing-phase portion of the outline for your overall CMS deployment documentation:

    **III.** The developing phase
        **A.** Installation

     **B.** Site design
        **1.** Managing channel hierarchies
          **a)** Determining basic site structure
          **b)** Preventing channel proliferation
          **c)** Identifying channel managers
        **2.** Managing resource gallery structure
          **a)** Grouping resources with Site Manager
          **b)** Adding resources with Resource Manager
        **3.** Managing template gallery structure
          **a)** Grouping templates
          **b)** Identifying template designers
        **4.** Workflow design
          **a)** Basic workflow
          **b)** Designing extended workflow scenarios
    **C.** Site architecture
    **D.** CMS customizations
    **E.** Template creation
    **F.** Content creation

# Stabilizing the Project

This is the final stage in the delivery of the CMS engagement. This step involves deploying the site to the production environment, system testing the site in that environment, and keeping backup copies of the project. This is also the stage at which the final Web site is launched.

At this point, your Web site should be fully installed, tested, designed, and operational. Training for end users should have been completed at this point, and training for any personnel who will now assume management of the site should have been completed as well.

## Future Releases for Your Web Site

As your site content and focus change, you will need to have your templates and navigation elements updated accordingly. Remember that you can implement additional, specific releases without reworking the entire site. Be sure to create a process of continual improvement, scheduling regular releases and updates to add functionality without undertaking an entirely new project. Timeliness can be important in many sites, so having a methodical, regular plan in place to meet the changing demands of the site will help keep your site up-to-date and focused on your core business functions. Here is a sample outline for this phase in your planning documents:

    **IV.** The stabilizing and monitoring phase
        **A.** Testing
        **B.** Site deployment

## Sample Planning Document Outline

In this section, we've pulled together all the portions of the overall outline discussed previously in this chapter, and we present it here for your consideration.

    **I.** Envisioning the project
        **A.** Understanding business pain points
            **1.** Company background
            **2.** Current system
            **3.** Challenges with current system
            **4.** Why the need for a content management system?
            **5.** Why the choice of Microsoft Content Management Server 2002?
        **B.** Gathering customer requirements
            **1.** Understand the current environment
            **2.** Analyze the customer's content
            **3.** Investigate your customer's authoring/publishing requirements
        **C.** Identifying supporting products for integration
            **1.** Applications built in-house
            **2.** Third-party applications
            **3.** Other Microsoft products and servers
        **D.** Determining the required number of CMS servers
            **1.** Budget and cost
            **2.** Site traffic
            **3.** Hardware
        **E.** Content Management Server 2002 environments
            **1.** Managing different environments

      **2.**   Development environments
          **a)**   Managing team development efforts
          **b)**   Source control
          **c)**   Build servers and the build process
      **3.**   Testing and staging environments
          **a)**   Aims of testing and staging
          **b)**   Setting up testing and staging environments
          **c)**   Testing and staging processes for Content Management Server 2002 solutions
      **4.**   Production environments
          **a)**   Deploying solutions to the production environment
          **b)**   Managing and maintaining the production environment

   **F.**   Team model and resources
      **1.**   Skill set for administrators
      **2.**   Skill set for authors/editors/moderators
      **3.**   Skill set for infrastructure and operations staff
      **4.**   Skill set for developers
      **5.**   CMS team skill set document
          **a)**   Identify team members
          **b)**   Evaluate skill set
          **c)**   Assign CMS tasks to individuals

   **G.**   Identify security and authentication requirements
      **1.**   Type of authentication
      **2.**   Need for a single sign-on
      **3.**   Need for private content

   **H.**   Identify network topology designs
      **1.**   Location of database
      **2.**   Location of domain controller
      **3.**   DMZ setup
      **4.**   Firewall setup

**II.**   The planning phase
   **A.**   Create project vision and scope
      **1.**   CMS vision/scope document
          **a)**   Project vision
          **b)**   Solution concept
          **c)**   Project scope
          **d)**   Success criteria
          **e)**   Dependencies

**B.** Risk management
**C.** Resource management
**D.** CMS project plan documents
    **1.** Envisioning document
        **a)** Planning phase
        **b)** Development phase
        **c)** Deployment phase
        **d)** Stabilizing phase
    **2.** CMS risk document and risk matrix
        **a)** Risk management process
        **b)** Identify risks
        **c)** Analyze and prioritize risks
        **d)** Plan risks
        **e)** Track risks
        **f)** Control risks
        **g)** Top risks
**E.** Planning for security and authentication
**F.** Existing content management planning
**G.** Planning site architecture
**H.** Operations planning
**I.** Performance planning
    **1.** Capacity planning and usage profiling
        **a)** Capacity planning fundamentals
        **b)** Understanding transaction characteristics
        **c)** Understanding page requests
        **d)** Establishing a usage profile
        **e)** Example: Establishing a usage profile
    **2.** Capacity planning and transaction cost analysis
        **a)** Maximum throughput per transaction
        **b)** CPU cost per transaction
        **c)** Cost per user
        **d)** Theoretical maximum number of users
        **e)** Strategy for handling peaks
        **f)** Consideration of other factors
        **g)** Result verification
    **3.** Test plans
    **4.** Test cases
    **5.** Test lab requirements
    **6.** Test lab configuration
    **7.** Test tools

       **8.** Availability planning
          **a)** Acceptable uptime
          **b)** Software solutions for high availability
          **c)** Hardware solutions for high availability
    **J.** Planning site design
       **1.** Network design and topology
          **a)** Basic network topology and servers
             **(1)** Web servers
             **(2)** Read-only MCMS servers
             **(3)** Authoring MCMS servers
             **(4)** Clustering Web servers
             **(5)** Database servers
          **b)** Additional network components and servers
             **(1)** Switches and hubs
             **(2)** Firewalls and proxies
             **(3)** Network load balancing
             **(4)** Leveraging application center in network design
             **(5)** Monitoring with MOM
          **c)** Integrating with SharePoint Portal Server
             **(1)** SharePoint Portal Server and Content Management Server 2002
             **(2)** Integration pack
**III.** The developing phase
    **A.** Installation
    **B.** Site design
       **1.** Managing channel hierarchies
          **a)** Determining basic site structure
          **b)** Preventing channel proliferation
          **c)** Identifying channel managers
       **2.** Managing resource gallery structure
          **a)** Grouping resources with Site Manager
          **b)** Adding resources with Resource Manager
       **3.** Managing template gallery structure
          **a)** Grouping templates
          **b)** Identifying template designers
       **4.** Workflow design
          **a)** Basic workflow
          **b)** Designing extended workflow scenarios
    **C.** Site architecture
    **D.** CMS customizations

       **E.** Template creation
       **F.** Content creation
   **IV.** The stabilizing and monitoring phase
       **A.** Testing
       **B.** Site deployment

## Summary

In this chapter, we introduced essential concepts for writing a planning document for a CMS engagement. We used a four-phase approach of envisioning the project, planning the project, developing the project, and stabilizing the project. We have also provided a sample outline from which you can begin to write your own CMS planning documents.

# PART II

# Content Authoring and Publishing

# CHAPTER 5

# The Web Author

## Overview

The key features of CMS are providing nontechnical users with the ability to easily create and manage content, and the automation of the Web publishing process.

Traditionally, content authors use tools such as Microsoft FrontPage or Macromedia Dreamweaver to create Web content. Then the content is forwarded to a Webmaster, who checks it and then puts it on a Web site. The Webmaster's main responsibility is the technology, not the content. It takes some time for the Webmaster to check the technical correctness of Web pages created by the business users and then to put them on the Web site, thus creating a publishing bottleneck. CMS removes this bottleneck by putting content publishing in the hands of the business users.

In the traditional model, content creators are required to understand HTML and the Web. They are usually disconnected from the published content and need to involve the Webmaster to change it. Furthermore, the technical staff is often expected to understand the content and be able to edit it.

CMS-based Web sites provide business users with an environment that enables them to create and publish their content without any prior HTML knowledge and without involving the technical staff. At the same time, Web developers and Webmasters are able to focus on the overall site design and structure, without having to create or maintain the content. In other words, the coders can worry about writing code.

CMS provides the ability to separate the site development process from the content authoring process, as shown in Figure 5–1. First, the Web designers and developers create the site framework, which includes page templates. Page templates have permanent elements that don't change from page to page—for example, a company logo or a navigation

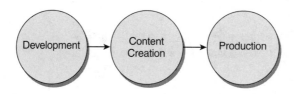

**Figure 5–1** CMS site creation

bar—as well as placeholders for content to be provided by the content creators. After the site framework has been created, the content creators populate the site with the content. For example, Figure 5–2 shows the BOTS Consulting home page; BOTS Consulting is a fictional consulting company that we will use as the sample site throughout the book. The graphic at the top of the page and the navigation bar directly underneath it come from a template; however, the content of the page is provided by the content creators.

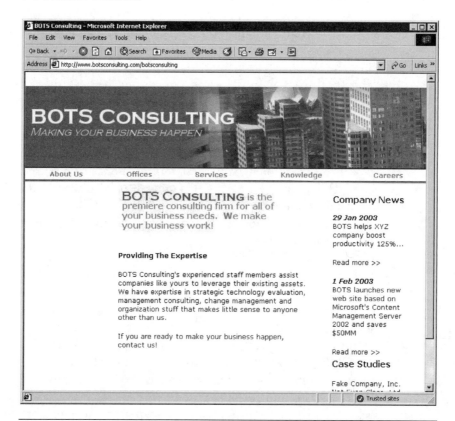

**Figure 5–2** A template-based Web page

Content creators with little or no Web development knowledge can easily add, update, and even delete content without having to contact the Webmaster. Content creators don't need any special technical skills. Rather than having to install and learn a Web development tool, they can do the authoring in CMS either using the Web browser interface or using Microsoft Word XP.

---

**NOTE:** Content authoring from Word XP is achieved by installing and using the CMS Authoring Connector component in addition to Word XP on the content authors' client computers. We will discuss the Authoring Connector in detail in Chapter 7.

---

After the content has been created or modified by the content authors, it goes through the publishing workflow, which allows content editors and moderators to approve the page for publishing. The pages are published on the live site only after they have been approved; otherwise, they are not available to the site visitors.

In the next two chapters, we will focus on the content authoring and publishing workflow in the CMS environment using the Web browser; then we will look into content authoring using Word XP with the Authoring Connector.

In this chapter, we will concentrate on creating and editing a CMS page in a Web browser.

## Browser-Based Publishing

To give business users the ability to create content using a Web browser, CMS provides a framework called the Web Author. There are two version of the Web Author in CMS 2002: ASP-based and ASP.NET-based. We are going to focus on the ASP.NET-based version.

The Web Author framework consists of client-side and server-side components. On the client side, the Web Author functionality includes a console with a link to switch between the CMS presentation and authoring modes, and a set of links to authoring actions (Figure 5–3), as well as a number of dialog boxes that provide and gather information (Table 5–1). We will be looking into these components in the next two chapters. On the server side, the Web Author functionality is implemented using ASP.NET server controls. These controls will be discussed in Chapter 30 later in the book.

**Table 5–1** Web Author Dialogs

| Dialog | What It Does |
| --- | --- |
| Create New Page | Provides an interface to create a new page |
| Save New Page | Provides an interface to enter the name and description of a new posting |
| Insert Image | Provides an interface to insert an image from the resource gallery or the local computer |
| Edit Image Properties | Provides an interface to edit the properties of an image |
| Insert Attachment | Provides an interface to insert an attachment from the resource gallery or the local computer |
| Edit Attachment Properties | Provides an interface to edit the properties of an attachment |
| Insert Table | Provides an interface to insert a table |
| Edit Hyperlink | Provides an interface to insert or edit a hyperlink |
| Select Color | Provides an interface to set the foreground and background colors |
| Page Properties | Provides an interface to change the properties of the page |
| Copy Page | Provides an interface to copy the current page into another channel |
| Move Page | Provides an interface to move the page into another channel |
| Create Connected Page | Provides an interface to create a connected page |
| Go to Connected Pages | Lists hyperlinks of all connected postings |
| Production Manager | Lists not yet published pages created by the user |
| Approval Assistant | Lists pages waiting for approval by the user |
| Resource Manager | Provides an interface to manage resources in the galleries to which the user has rights |
| Revision History | Lists revisions to the page, and provides an interface to compare two revisions of the page |
| View Revisions By Date | Provides an interface to view a revision of a page |
| Channel Properties | Provides an interface to change the properties of the channel |

| Switch To Live Site |
|---|
| **Page Status:** Published |
| **Lock Status:** *Not Locked* |
| Production Manager |
| Approval Assistant |
| Resource Manager |
| Preview |
| Create New Page |
| Create Connected Page |
| Edit |
| Delete |
| Copy |
| Move |
| Page Properties |
| Revision History |
| View Revisions by Date |
| Channel Properties |

**Figure 5–3** Full default console

**NOTE:** Dialog files are located in the folder *<installation drive>*/ Program Files/Microsoft Content Management Server/Server/ IIS_CMS/WebAuthor/Dialogs/.

The default Web Author console (Figure 5–3) is implemented using the DefaultConsole.ascx user control. This user control is added to the page templates by the template designers. The actions in the console are presented to a user depending on that user's rights in CMS; each user only sees the actions they are allowed to perform. Figure 5–3 shows the full list of options in the console; this console would be displayed to a user with administrative rights. Figure 5–4 shows the console that would be displayed to a user with authoring rights.

The console is displayed as a table with the authoring commands available. The commands are grouped together based on the general functions they perform. The console provides several options to perform various editing functions on pages, such as creating pages, editing pages, and previewing pages. Options for the publishing workflow include submitting pages, approving pages, and declining pages. There are also several options related to the content management lifecycle, such as Production Manager, Resource Manager, and Approval Assistant. Table 5–2 lists and explains each option. The options in the console display a series of the Web Author dialogs; therefore, don't be surprised that Tables 5–1 and 5–2 overlap.

**Figure 5–4**  Default console as displayed to site authors

**Table 5–2**  Web Author Console Options

| Option | What It Does |
|---|---|
| Page Status | Shows the current status of the page |
| Lock Status | Provides a Locked/Not Locked status for the current page |
| Production Manager | Lists saved pages that are in production |
| Approval Assistant | Lists pages awaiting approval |
| Resource Manager | Lists available resource galleries and resources in those galleries |
| Preview | Provides a preview of the current page |
| Create New Page | Creates a new page based on a selected template |
| Create Connected Page | Creates a page that is connected to an existing page |
| Edit | Edits a page |
| Delete | Deletes a page |
| Copy | Copies a page to another channel |
| Move | Moves a page to another channel |
| Page Properties | Displays and allows modification of the properties of the current page |
| Revision History | Displays all page versions |
| View Revisions by Date | Displays versions of a page for a specified date |
| Channel Properties | Displays properties for a channel |

**NOTE:** The look, feel, and functionality of the default console can be customized by the template designers. We will discuss how to do this in Chapter 30.

To separate the page design from the page content creation, the Web Author provides the ability to use placeholders for content authoring. A *placeholder* is a predefined area on a page template where content creators can put their content. A blueprint for the page is provided by a template; it can contain both static elements, such as images, and dynamic elements, such as navigation links. These elements cannot be changed by the content creators. A template designer defines the areas on the page template where the content will be inserted by the content creators; these areas are the placeholders. The designer may restrict the type of content that a placeholder can contain—for example, only text and no images. An example of a placeholder is shown in Figure 5–5.

The Web Author client interface is implemented using HTML forms, JavaScript, and ActiveX controls. For content creation, the supported browsers are Microsoft Internet Explorer 5.*x* and later.

**NOTE:** The HTML placeholders are implemented using two ActiveX controls: ncbmprdr.dll and NRDHtml.dll. One control provides the functionality of the toolbar and the other of the placeholder itself. These controls are downloaded to a browser on the first use in a .cab file, nrdhtml.cab. If the ActiveX controls download is restricted on the client browser, these controls can be preinstalled on the client machine by unzipping the .cab file and registering the .dlls. On the server, the .cab file is located in the folder <*installation drive*>:\Program Files\ Microsoft Content Management Server\Server\IIS_CMS\WebAuthor\ Client\PlaceholderControlSupport\.

**Figure 5–5** A placeholder

# CMS Page Modes

The Web Author provides the ability for content authors to switch between two CMS page modes, as follows:

- Presentation mode, which is displayed within the Web Author as Live mode
- Authoring mode, which is displayed within the Web Author as Edit mode

When users browse the site, the pages are displayed in presentation, or Live, mode. In presentation mode, the Web Author console is displayed to the users with predefined editing rights as a single link that provides the ability to switch to authoring, or Edit, mode. Therefore, in order to see the link and to start authoring or editing content, the content creators need to log in to the site (Figure 5–6).

In CMS, the users who browse the site are called *subscribers*. Figure 5–2 shows the BOTS Consulting home page in presentation mode as it is displayed to the subscribers. The Web Author console is not displayed; there is no link that allows a user to switch to Edit mode. Figure 5–7 shows the same page in presentation mode displayed to the user with authoring rights; you can see that there is a link that reads "Switch to Edit Site."

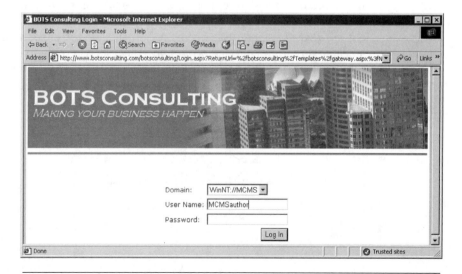

**Figure 5–6** Login dialog

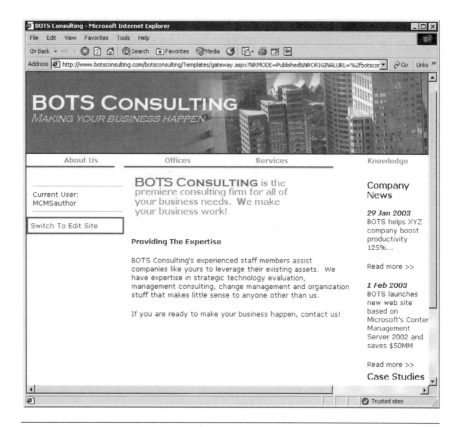

**Figure 5–7** CMS page in Live mode presented to a user with authoring rights

When a user clicks this link, the site is switched from presentation mode into authoring mode, and the Web Author console options are displayed (Figure 5–8). On the top of the console there is a link that allows the user to switch back to the live site. When the site is in Live mode, the URL of the page is presented in the hierarchical way that reflects the page's location in the site structure. In Edit mode, the URL is modified; it includes various parameters in the query string after the question mark, including the page's Globally Unique Identifier (GUID) that is assigned and maintained by CMS.

Depending on the rights of the logged-on user, the options presented in the Web Author console will be different. For example, the console in Figure 5–8 displays the options that are available to the content authors because we are logged on as a user with authoring rights (Figure 5–6).

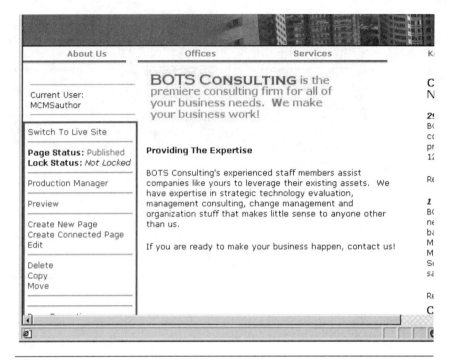

**Figure 5–8** CMS page in Edit mode

Let's click the Edit link in the console to see what we can edit in the page (Figure 5–9). We can see the placeholders on the page: The top placeholder contains the graphic representing BOTS Consulting; the Body Page Title placeholder contains the title; and there is also a bottom placeholder that provides the actual text. (The bottom placeholder needs to be scrolled to in the browser window in Figure 5–9; this placeholder is similar to the one we have already seen in Figure 5–5) The page is presented as a combination of content defined in the page template—such as the graphic on the top of the page—and the content provided within the placeholders. Since we are now in Edit mode, we can change the data within the placeholders if need be.

When we edit the page, the options in the console change to provide access to actions that may be required during or after editing (Figure 5–9). Because the console and the placeholders are displayed in the page, the page looks quite different in authoring mode. This can be confusing for the authors; therefore, there is a Preview option available. Clicking Preview causes a new window to appear, with the page shown as it would be

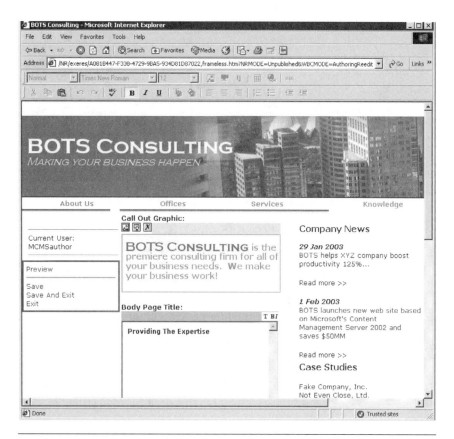

**Figure 5–9** Editing the page

displayed in Live mode to the subscribers. Other options allow us to save the page, to save the page and exit page editing, and to exit without saving the changes. We are not going to change the page, so we will click Exit on the console. An exit warning is displayed by the Web Author (Figure 5–10); we will click OK to continue, and then we will be taken to the page in authoring mode, as shown in Figure 5–8. From there, to go to presentation mode, we can click the Switch to Live Site link in the Web Author console; then the page is displayed in Live mode, as we have already seen in Figure 5–7.

**Figure 5–10**  Web Author exit warning

# Creating a New Page

The Web Author console provides a link that allows content authors to create new pages. However, before you click this link, you need to navigate to a site location where you want the page to be created. This location is referred to as a *channel*. Traditional Web sites store pages in virtual directories; CMS Web sites provide virtual storage spaces for pages that are called channels. A channel can contain pages and other subchannels. Channels are organized in a hierarchical way; the channels hierarchy defines the navigational structure of the CMS site. CMS site administrators create and maintain the channels hierarchy. For example, in our sample site the horizontal navigation bar underneath the BOTS Consulting graphic represents the site top-level channels (Figure 5–2).

**NOTE:** We will look into the channels structure and site navigation in Chapter 9.

When we want to create a new page, first of all we need to navigate to a channel where this page will be stored, and then switch to Edit mode to display the Web Author console. When you navigate to the channel, you see the page that is configured as a default for this channel. If you are creating the first page in the channel, the default CMS channel page is displayed. The default CMS channel page displays the channel within the channels hierarchy immediately surrounding the current channel: the parent channel above the current channel, and the subchannels within the current channel.

**NOTE:** The channel default page is an ASP page called cover.asp located in the folder *<installation drive>*:\Program Files\Microsoft Content Management Server\Server\IIS_NR\Shared\.

Figure 5–11 shows the CMS channel default page for the Knowledge channel in Edit mode. Depending on whether you are creating the first page in the channel or not, the console will look different. However, as we have seen in Figures 5–8 and 5–11, in both cases the Create New Page option is present; to create a new page, you need to click this link.

---

**NOTE:** Another console option for creating pages is Create Connected Page. Connected pages are pages that are based on the same template, or a set of connected templates. You can use connected pages, for example, for multilingual sites. Creating connected pages will be discussed in detail in Chapter 15.

---

Our next step is to choose a page template on which we are going to base our page. In CMS, the *template galleries* provide virtual storage spaces for templates. A template gallery can contain templates and other template galleries. Site administrators and developers organize templates into the template galleries.

After you've clicked Create New Page, the Web Author displays the Select Template Gallery dialog, as shown in Figure 5–12. Each template gallery is displayed by name; the number in parentheses at the end of each gallery name shows how many templates are available in

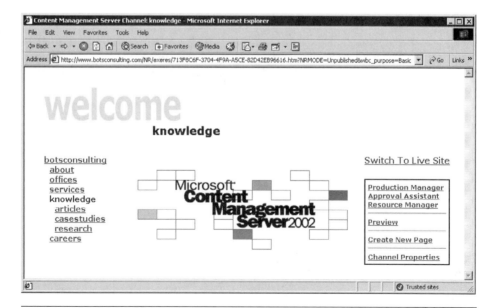

**Figure 5–11** Default page for an empty channel

## CMS Templates

In CMS 2002, templates are divided into two parts: a template file and a template metadata. The template file is an ASPX file in the file system that contains the code for the template and provides a blueprint for a page. The template metadata is a list of properties that is stored within a template gallery. It includes the location of the template file as well as additional properties and definitions that are set up by the template designers in order to fully define the functionality of a page based on this template. For example, we may need two different page templates that use the same template file but have different properties set up for a particular placeholder: Pages based on the first template allow both text and images in this placeholder, while pages based on the second template allow only text in the same placeholder.

The template metadata is stored as an item in the template gallery. This item is referred to as a template gallery item (TGI). When we select a template from a template gallery, in effect we select a TGI that contains the location of the template file as well as custom properties and placeholder definitions that are required for the page based on this template. We will discuss TGIs in detail in Chapter 10.

this gallery. The order of the list can be sorted by the template gallery name, location, or the last modified date by clicking the appropriate column heading. Template galleries in Figure 5–12 are listed by template gallery name.

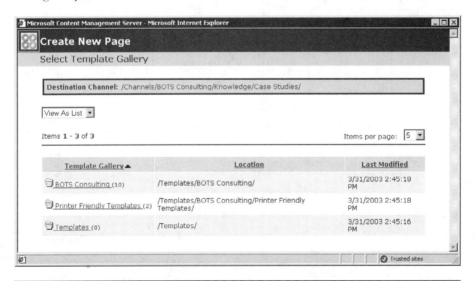

**Figure 5–12** Select Template Gallery dialog in the list view

**NOTE:** The template galleries in Figure 5–12 are displayed in the list view; they can also be displayed in a tree view, which outlines the galleries hierarchy, as shown in Figure 5–13. However, if the user does not have access rights to all template galleries on the site, the tree view may display nothing. To avoid this, make sure you view the galleries using the list view.

To select the gallery, you need to click the gallery name. In our example, we are going to select the BOTS Consulting template gallery.

After we've selected the template gallery, the Select Template dialog is displayed, as shown in Figure 5–14. The templates list can be sorted either by a template name or by the last modified date and time. You can define how many templates per screen are listed using the drop-down box in the top right of the screen; there are navigation links to navigate between the screens at the bottom of the list. The magnifying glass icon in the first column provides the ability to preview the template in a browser; the hand icon in the Select column allows us to select the template on which to base our new page. Table 5–3 shows the functionality of icons used within the Web Author interface.

**NOTE:** You don't have to add content to all page placeholders; if you leave a placeholder empty, the page will not display any data in this placeholder's location.

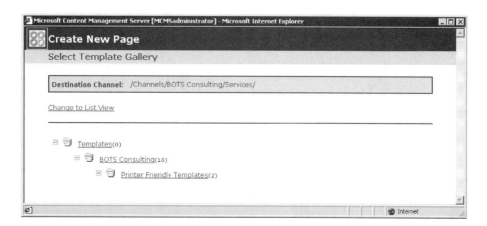

**Figure 5–13** Select Template Gallery dialog in the tree view

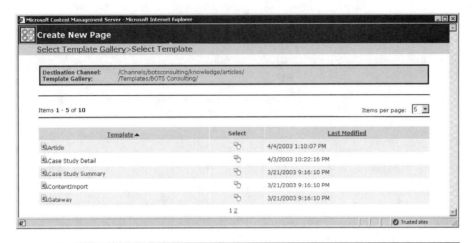

**Figure 5–14** Select Template dialog

**Table 5–3** Web Author Icons

| Icon | Functionality |
|------|---------------|
| | Preview |
| | Select template |
| | Select resource |
| | Replace resource |
| | Properties |
| | Go to page |
| | Go to connected page |
| | Calendar |

After you have selected a page template—for example, a template called Article—a new instance of this template is displayed in the browser, as shown in Figure 5–15. The next step is to add content to the page placeholders.

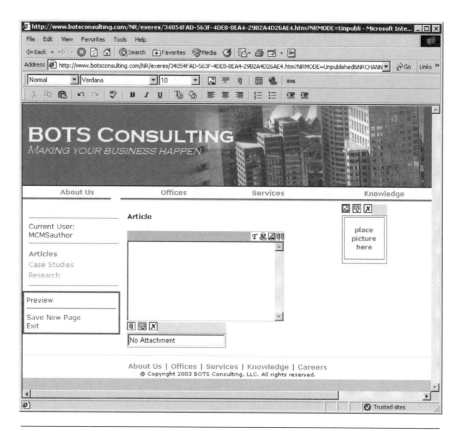

**Figure 5–15** New page with empty placeholders

# Adding Content

As we have discussed already, the template provides the placeholders for content to be entered. The type of content a placeholder may contain is defined by the placeholder's properties, which are set up by the template designers at the development stage.

**NOTE:** Information about the placeholder properties is one of the details stored in the template's TGI (you may want to refer to the CMS Templates sidebar earlier in this chapter for the definition of a TGI).

CMS provides three types of placeholders where the content authors can enter content, as follows:

- Multipurpose HTML placeholder
- Single image placeholder
- Single attachment placeholder

Template designers may create additional custom placeholders—for example, a drop-down list or a specific placeholder for XML content.

**NOTE:** We will discuss custom placeholders in detail in Chapter 29.

An example of an empty multipurpose HTML placeholder is shown in Figure 5–16. The icons displayed on the top of a placeholder indicate the content that is allowed within this placeholder; they are listed in Table 5–4. The placeholder is referred to as "multipurpose" because it

**Figure 5–16** HTML placeholder

**Table 5–4** HTML Placeholder Icons

| Icon | What It Indicates |
|------|-------------------|
| T | Allow plain text |
| B*I* | Allow bold and italics formatting |
| 𝔗 | Allow fully formatted text |
| 🖧 | Allow hyperlinks |
| 🖼 | Allow multiple images |
| 📎📎 | Allow multiple attachments |
| <> | Allow HTML styles |

may contain different content; however, technically speaking, it generates HTML; therefore, it is formally called the HTML placeholder.

Examples of content that an HTML placeholder may contain include the following:

- Text, either formatted or plain
- Text formatted with HTML styles
- Images
- Hyperlinks
- File attachments

It is worth mentioning that the content of a placeholder is validated against the placeholder properties before the page is saved; the content that is not allowed is deleted.

A single image placeholder is shown in Figure 5–17. It is currently empty; the default graphic displayed is provided for CMS to remind the page authors to insert the graphic into the placeholder. The icons on the top of the placeholder are clickable buttons. They allow us, from left to right, to add an image to the placeholder, edit image properties, and remove the image from the placeholder. When you work with the image placeholder, you can use only these buttons; the buttons on the CMS toolbar on top of the page, if present, will be disabled.

A single attachment placeholder provides the same functionality for file attachments as the single image placeholder provides for images. A file attachment is a resource that is displayed in a page as a link; it cannot be displayed inline within a browser window. The default presentation of an empty single attachment placeholder in a page template is shown in Figure 5–18. As with the image placeholder, the icons on the top of an attachment placeholder are clickable buttons. These buttons, from left to right, allow us to add an attachment, edit the attachment's properties, and remove the attachment. When you work with the attachment placeholder, you can use only these buttons; the CMS toolbar buttons will be disabled if present.

**Figure 5–17** Default single image placeholder

**Figure 5–18** Default single attachment placeholder

In the Web Author, content may be added to placeholders in a number of different ways, as follows:

- HTML placeholders:
  - Typing inside a placeholder
  - Copying and pasting text and images
  - Dragging and dropping images and file attachments from the desktop
  - Adding images and file attachments using buttons on the toolbar
- Single image and single attachment placeholders:
  - Adding single images and file attachments using buttons on the top of a placeholder

**NOTE:** Empty placeholders may contain the default elements that the designers incorporate in the template to help users when they need to add content to the placeholders. When you add your own content, you should delete these default elements.

## Adding Text and Hyperlinks

The HTML placeholder provides a simple inline authoring environment for the content creators. When you are creating or editing a page, two new toolbars appear in the browser at the top of the page (Figure 5–19). These toolbars provide the ability to edit and insert content into the placeholders on the page.

Depending on the current placeholder properties set up at the template design stage, certain buttons on these toolbars are enabled or disabled. Figure 5–19 shows the toolbars with all buttons enabled; however,

**Figure 5–19** CMS toolbars

it may not be the case for the placeholders in your templates. When you add content to the placeholder, CMS creates HTML for this content.

The toolbars provide the following options:

- The style drop-down allows us to select a style from the predefined list of styles (Figure 5–20). Each style inserts different HTML tags and provides a different look and feel; these are summarized in Table 5–5, later in this section.

**Figure 5–20** Style selection

- Font and size drop-down lists allow us to select the font and the size for the text; the appropriate <FONT> tag is inserted in HTML.
- The next section of the toolbar contains three buttons that allow us to insert images, video, and file attachments into the page; we will look into these buttons and their functionality in the next section.
- The Insert Table button allows us to insert a table in the placeholder. If you click this button, a Table dialog appears (Figure 5–21) asking you to specify the number of columns and rows, and whether you'd like the table border to be shown. After you've set up the table options and clicked OK, the table is inserted into the placeholder, as shown in Figure 5–22. The following HTML tags are inserted: <TABLE> for the overall table, <TBODY> for the table body, <TR> for table rows, and <TD> for table cells.

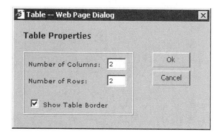

**Figure 5–21** Table dialog

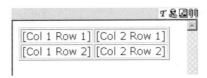

**Figure 5–22** Table within a placeholder

When the table is inserted, each cell in an empty table has default text showing its position in the table—for example, "[Col 2 Row 1]." You need to replace this text; otherwise, it will show in the page.

- The Edit Hyperlink button allows us to make part of the placeholder content a hyperlink. To create a hyperlink, select content you'd like to become a link—such as text, an image, or a combination of both—and click this button. The Edit Hyperlink dialog appears, as shown in Figure 5–23. This dialog provides the ability to either type in the URL for the link or browse to the channel or page on the CMS site you'd like to link to (Figure 5–24).

  Browsing to an internal CMS object, such as a page or channel, has the advantage that CMS will maintain a link if the object linked to is moved to another location. Internal links will use the object GUID rather than the URL. This ensures that the links are always valid, even if the original object is moved. If the link to an internal object is entered manually in the URL box using the hierarchical URL http://server/channel/page, the link will be broken when the page is moved.

  In the Edit Hyperlink dialog, you can also type in a tooltip for the link and define where you'd like the link to be opened.

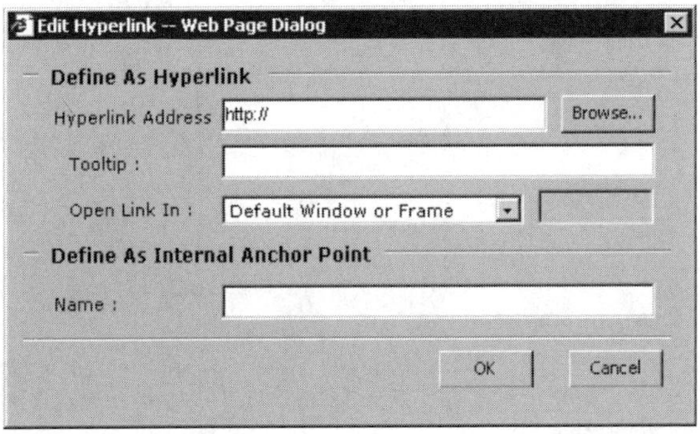

**Figure 5–23** Edit Hyperlink dialog

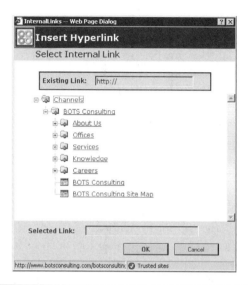

**Figure 5–24**  Insert Hyperlink dialog

Depending on what you select, the target will be shown in the box next to the Open Link In drop-down list. The choices include:

- Default window or frame.
- Same window or frame; the target is _self.
- Parent window or frame; the target is _parent.
- Full browser window; the target is _top.
- New unnamed window; the target is _blank.
- Custom named window; you need to type the name for the target window yourself.

If you'd like to create an internal anchor point so that you can link to it later on, type a name for an anchor in the Name field.

When you click OK, the link is created; the <A HREF=…> tag for the link is inserted into the HTML. The link text is displayed as underlined and highlighted in blue. If you have created an internal anchor, then the <A NAME=…> tag is inserted in the HTML, and the text is displayed as before; it is neither highlighted nor underlined.

If a linked-to CMS page is not available, then the links that are pointing to this page will automatically be converted into so-called *sleepy links*. For example, a page may be unavailable when the page content has been changed but hasn't yet been approved for publishing. In this case, CMS maintains the link, but will not display the link on the site. Sleepy links are rendered with the HREF attribute changed to ZHREF—that is, <A ZHREF=...>. The only way to remove a sleepy link is to remove the original hyperlink that points to an unavailable object.

■ The HTML button allows us to edit the HTML source code. When you click this button, the content of the current placeholder is displayed as HTML (Figure 5–25); you can type within the placeholder and edit the HTML by hand. Usually, the template designers don't enable this button on the toolbar so that nontechnical users cannot break the HTML within the placeholder.

■ The buttons on the second toolbar are similar to the buttons in Microsoft Word. Starting from the left, these buttons are Cut, Copy, and Paste; Undo and Redo (one action only); Spell Check; Bold, Italic, and Underline; Foreground and Background color; Left, Center, and Right alignment; Numbered and Bulleted lists; Decrease Indent and Increase Indent.

The Foreground and Background buttons allow us to select the foreground and background colors from the dialog shown in Figure 5–26. The Foreground color button changes the color of the

**Figure 5–25** HTML source editing

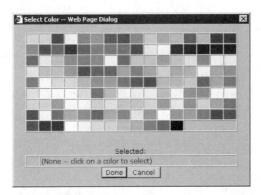

**Figure 5–26** Select Color dialog

selected text; the chosen color is inserted in HTML as a color attribute of the FONT tag—for example, <FONT color=#ff69b4>. The Background color button changes the background of the selected text; a chosen color is inserted in HTML as an inline style in the FONT tag—for example, <FONT style="BACKGROUND-COLOR: #eee8aa">.

**Table 5–5** HTML Placeholder Styles

| Style | What It Does |
|---|---|
| Normal | <P> tags are inserted into the HTML that is created for the placeholder. |
| Formatted | <PRE> tags are inserted; the text is displayed using a fixed font such as Courier. |
| Address | <ADDRESS> tags are inserted; the text is displayed in italics. |
| Headings 1–6 | <H1>–<H6> tags are inserted for different levels of headings; in IE the text is made boldface, with sizes of 24, 18, 14, 12, 10, and 8, respectively. |
| Numbered List | <OL> tags are inserted for the list, and <LI> tags are inserted for the list items; the text is displayed as a numbered list with Arabic numbers starting at 1. |
| Bulleted List | <UL> tags are inserted for the list, and <LI> tags are inserted for the list items; the text is displayed as a bulleted list with a small round black bullet. |
| Directory List | <DIR> tags are inserted for the list, and <LI> tags are inserted for the list items; the text is displayed as a bulleted list with a small round black bullet. |
| Menu List | <MENU> tags are inserted for the list, and <LI> tags are inserted for the list items; the text is displayed as a bulleted list with a small round black bullet. |
| Definition Term and Definition | <DL> tags are inserted for the list, and <DT> and <DD> tags are inserted for the list items, respectively; the definitions are indented. |
| Paragraph | <P> tags are inserted around selected text. |

## Adding Images and File Attachments

Any file that can be inserted in or attached to a page is known as a site *resource*. Examples include images, audio and video files, Adobe PDF files, and other files that are required on the CMS site. A file of any type can be a resource. Resources can be shared between multiple pages using resource galleries. A *resource gallery* provides virtual storage space for the site resources. The resource gallery can contain individual resources and other resource galleries. The resource gallery hierarchy is created and maintained by site administrators and resource managers.

**NOTE:** We will look into management of resource galleries and resources in Chapter 16.

Resource types that can be rendered inline and viewed in a browser are images and video files in the following formats:

- Image formats: GIF, JPEG, PNG, BMP
- Video formats: ASF/ASX, AVI, MPEG/MPG, MOV/QT

All other resources are rendered not inline, but as links pointing to a resource; therefore, they are called file attachments. File attachments can be of any type; a file attachment may be displayed with an icon showing the file type. How the linked file is viewed is determined by a client's browser and the applications available on the client computer. For example, Adobe PDF files require an additional viewer (Acrobat Reader) to be installed on the client machine.

**NOTE:** By default, Flash animations will display as an attachment rather than an embedded inline page element. It is possible to change this behavior programmatically using the Publishing API. For example, the content authors add the Flash animation as an attachment, but the code in the template dynamically accesses the attachment's URL and displays the content inline. Another approach is to create a custom placeholder control for Flash resources. Custom placeholders are discussed in Chapter 29.

Images and attachments can be added to placeholders from the resource galleries and from a local or network file system. The template designer may restrict this choice for a particular placeholder to resource galleries only.

Images can be added to HTML placeholders and single image placeholders. Attachments can be added to HTML placeholders and single attachment placeholders. Images and attachments are added to the multipurpose HTML placeholders using the buttons on the CMS toolbar on the top of the screen. Single image and single attachment placeholders provide clickable buttons at the top of the placeholder for adding images and attachments.

To add an image to an HTML placeholder, click the Insert Image button on the CMS toolbar; to add an image to a single image placeholder, click the Add Image button on the top of the placeholder. If the placeholder allows images from the file system and shared images from resource galleries, the dialog shown in Figure 5–27 is displayed. This dialog allows us to select images from resource galleries and local or network files. If the placeholder in the template doesn't allow the file system images, then the dialog shown in Figure 5–28 is displayed. This dialog only allows us to insert shared images from a resource gallery.

Let's insert an image from a resource gallery; we will click the Insert Shared Image link. The Web Author displays the list of resource galleries set up on the CMS site that the current user has permissions to access (Figure 5–29).

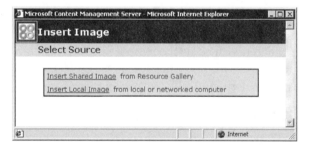

**Figure 5–27**  Insert Image Select Source dialog, with local files permitted

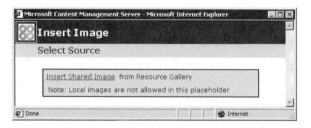

**Figure 5–28**  Insert Image Select Source dialog, with local files not permitted

**Figure 5–29**  Select Resource Gallery dialog

---

**NOTE:**  As with the template galleries, it is possible to switch to the tree view in the Select Resource Gallery dialog. However, the same warning applies: If you don't have sufficient rights to view all galleries in the tree, you may not see the resource gallery you require.

---

The interface in the Select Resource Gallery dialog is organized in the same way as the interface in the Select Template Gallery dialog that we have discussed before. You can navigate to the resource gallery that stores the resource you need, and then click its name to open the Select Image dialog, as shown in Figure 5–30.

You can preview and then select the images by clicking the appropriate icon (refer to Table 5–4 for the icons and their functionality). After you've selected the image, the Insert Image dialog is displayed by the Web Author, asking you to provide optional properties for an image (Figure 5–31). If you want an image to become a hyperlink, then you need to provide a URL for the image to link to. You can either type the URL or use the Browse button to navigate to the page or channel you would like to link to using the Insert Hyperlink dialog (Figure 5–24). The alternate text for the image you specify becomes a value of the ALT attribute of the IMG tag for the image; some browsers display this text as a mouse tip. It is a good practice of Web design to provide all images on the site with the text for alternative representation. There are multiple uses for

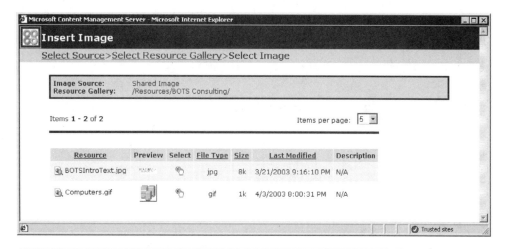

**Figure 5–30**  Select Image dialog

this text; for example, when the images are disabled in the browser, this text is displayed instead.

After you've typed the text for alternative representation, click Insert, and the image is inserted into a placeholder. Figure 5–32 shows an image inserted into the single image placeholder; Figure 5–33 shows the same image inserted into the HTML placeholder.

If you want to insert an image from local storage, you need to click the Insert Local Image link in the Select Source dialog (Figure 5–27),

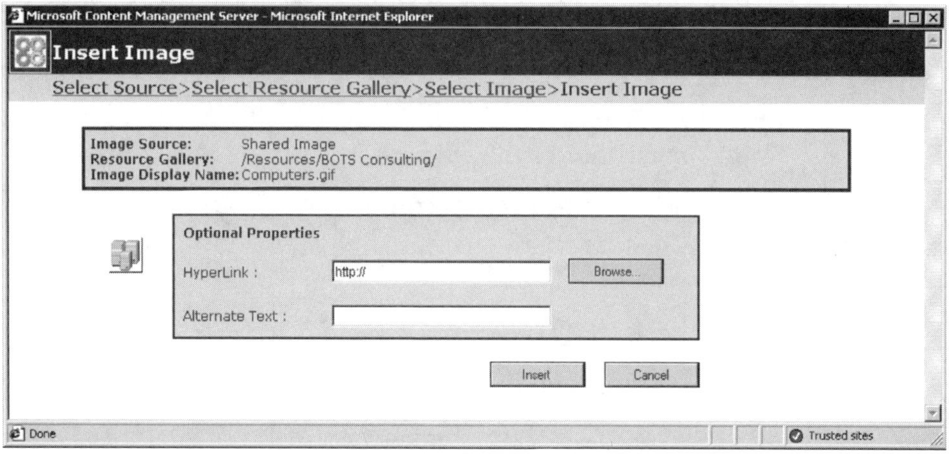

**Figure 5–31**  Insert Image dialog

**Figure 5–32** Image inserted into a single image placeholder

**Figure 5–33** Image inserted into an HTML placeholder

and the Web Author displays an Insert Image dialog for the local image source, as shown in Figure 5–34. This dialog provides the ability to browse to the required image; to preview the image; to select a file type from a list of GIF, JPEG, PNG, and BMP image types; and to type in alternate text for the image. After you've specified the necessary parameters, click Insert, and the image is inserted into a placeholder. You can also copy and paste, or drag and drop, images into an HTML placeholder, provided the local images are allowed in this particular placeholder.

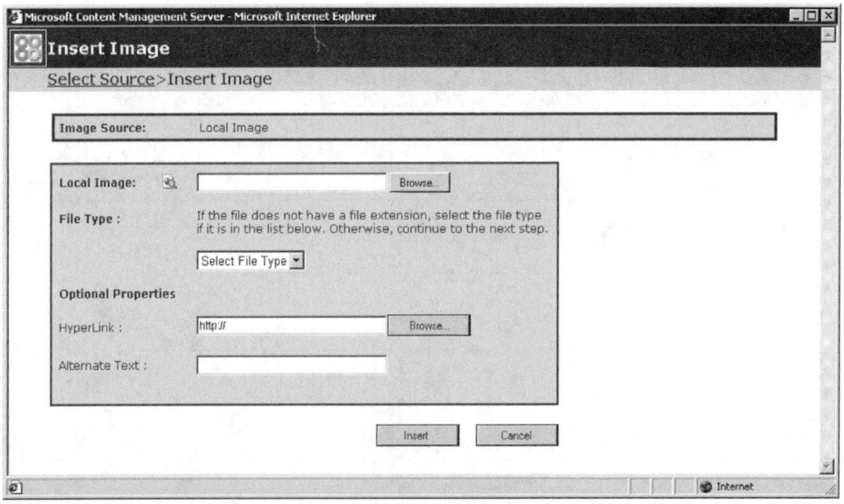

**Figure 5–34** Insert Image dialog for local image

**NOTE:** Local files aren't added to the CMS resource gallery. For example, if you want to use a file on multiple pages, it may be better to import it into a resource gallery first and then insert it into the page. In this case, there is only one copy of the resource in the CMS database that is shared between multiple pages.

Attachments are inserted in the placeholders in the same way as images. To add an attachment to an HTML placeholder, click the Insert Attachment button on the CMS toolbar; to add an attachment to a single attachment placeholder, click the Add Attachment button on the top of the placeholder. The Web Author displays the Insert Attachment Select Source dialog (Figure 5–35), which allows us to browse the resource galleries and the file system, if the latter is allowed by the placeholder's properties set up by the template designers.

After the attachment has been selected, the Web Author displays the Insert Attachment dialog box (Figure 5–36), which allows us to set the text for the link to this attachment. An example of an attachment inserted into a single attachment placeholder is shown in Figure 5–37.

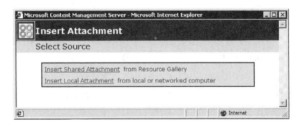

**Figure 5–35** Insert Attachment Select Source dialog

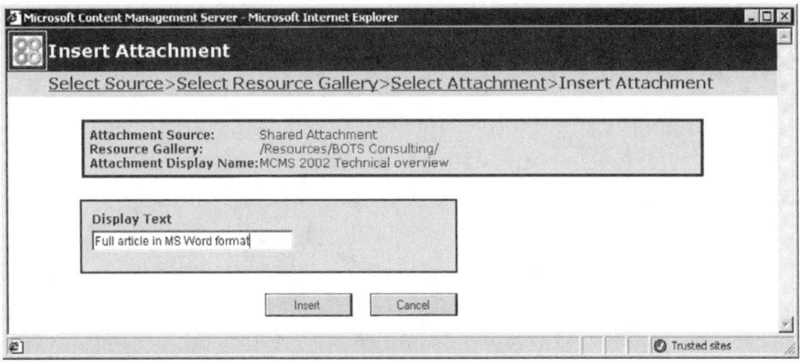

**Figure 5–36** Insert Attachment dialog

**Figure 5–37** Placeholder with inserted attachment

# Saving the Page

After you've added content to the required placeholders and previewed the page, the page has to be saved. When the page is being saved, the content of the placeholder is validated against the allowed content set up by the template designers in the placeholder properties.

> **NOTE:** As we have seen already, the HTML placeholder saves the text as HTML; the buttons on the toolbar allow only the formatting and flow tags to be inserted in the resulting HTML. All other tags are stripped out of the placeholder content before it is persisted to the database. These tags always include any nonstandard tags as well as potentially danger-ous tags such as <SCRIPT> and <APPLET>.

For example, Figure 5–38 shows our sample page based on the Article template, with the content added to the placeholders.

To save the page, click the Save New Page option in the Web Author console. The Save New Page dialog is displayed, as shown in Figure 5–39. This dialog allows us to provide a page name and a page display name. The page name will be used as a part of the hierarchical URL when a user navigates to the page in presentation mode. The page display name is used when a link to this page is provided from other pages on the site; the display name that you specify is used by CMS as text for a link point-ing to this page. You can set the display name to be the same as the page name by clicking the Same As Name button or by simply leaving the dis-play name blank in the Save New Page dialog.

The Display Name is a very useful property—for example, for site navigation—especially if you are implementing a multilanguage site. If your site is going to use a language with a double-byte character set (such as Hebrew), then you can use those characters in the page display name. Since these characters are not valid in a URL, you will not be able to use them in the page name. We will look into site navigation in detail in Chapter 14.

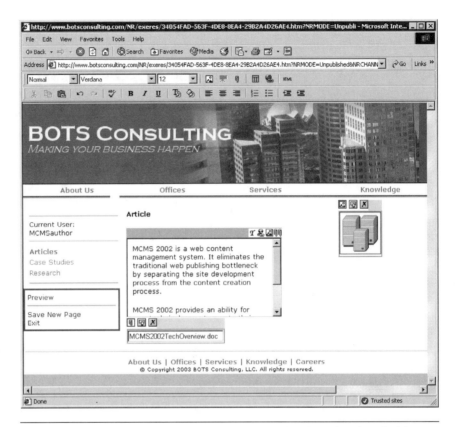

**Figure 5–38** Sample page with the content added to the placeholders

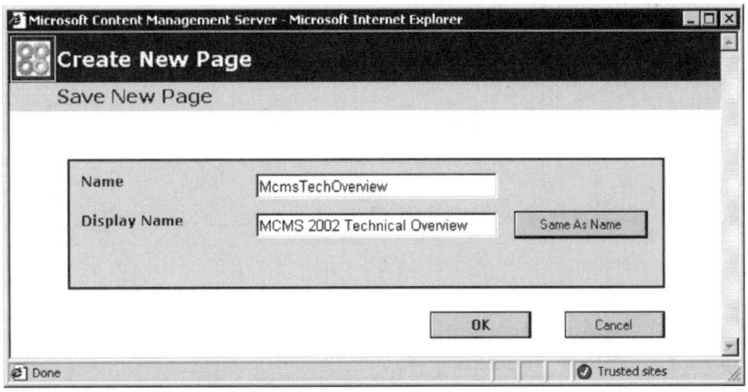

**Figure 5–39** Save New Page dialog

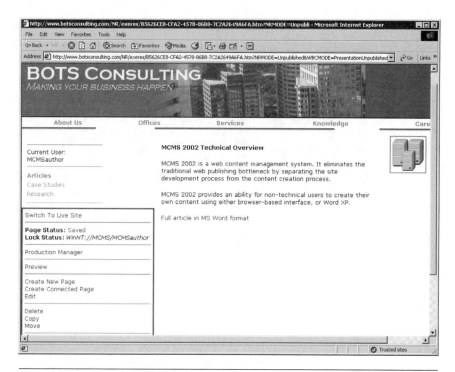

**Figure 5–40**  Saved sample page

After you've clicked OK in the Save New Page dialog, the Web Author displays the page in Edit view, as shown in Figure 5–40; the Page Status in the Web Author console is shown as Saved. Although the page has been saved, it is not yet available on the site; it should go through the publishing workflow to be approved by the editor and the moderator. Only after the page has been approved will it be published. We will focus on this process in the next chapter.

## Setting Up Page Properties

Because CMS pages are dynamic objects that are built at runtime from the templates and the placeholders' content, we can specify page properties that affect when and how the page is displayed on the site. To display the Page Properties dialog, click Page Properties in the Web Author console (Figure 5–41).

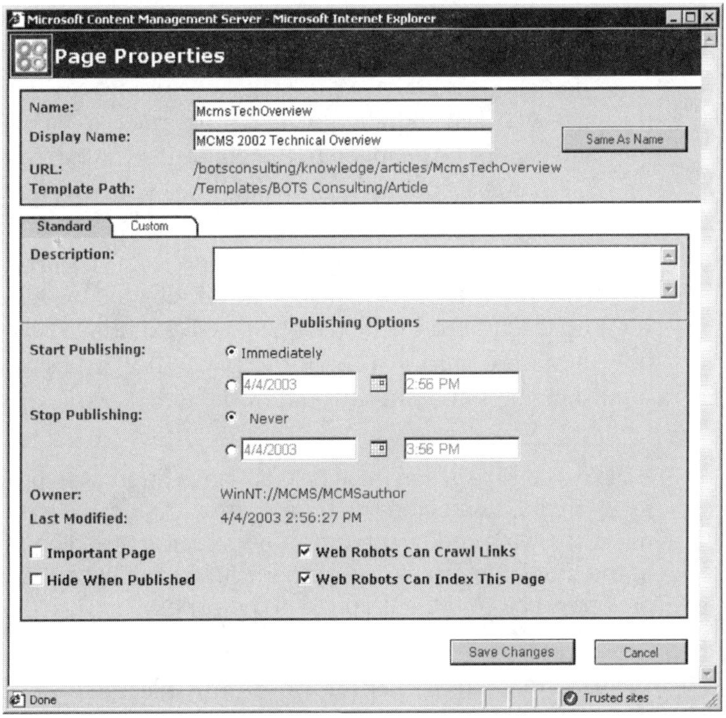

**Figure 5–41**  Page Properties dialog

**NOTE:** Content authors may either set up the page properties themselves or leave them to be set up by the editors and the moderators at a later stage of the publishing workflow. We will discuss this process in detail in the next chapter.

In the top area of the Page Properties dialog box, you can change the name and the display name for the page, and see the hierarchical URL for the page as well as the name and the path of the template on which the page is built. The URL and the template details are displayed for your information only; they cannot be modified.

The Standard tab of the Page Properties dialog provides the ability to set up the publishing schedule for the page. You can specify the start publishing options as either start immediately or start at an exact date and time; and the stop publishing options as either never stop or stop at an exact date and time. The calendar icon provides the ability to select the exact date for the start and the expiry dates; or you can just type the dates in.

The dialog also displays the page owner and the date and time when the page was last modified; these properties are for your information only and cannot be changed in the dialog. At the top of the Standard tab, there is a Description field that allows you to type in the optional description of a page. At the bottom of the Standard tab, there are four check boxes. The Important Page check box sets up a flag that can be used later on by the developers; it is not selected by default, and you only set it up if required by the developers. The Hide When Published check box allows the author to hide the page after it has been approved for publishing; it is also not selected by default.

---

**NOTE:** The Hide When Published option is often used programmatically— for example, to provide linear navigation. An author writing a ten-page news story may not want subscribers to start reading in the middle of the story. Therefore, the author will hide all but the first page and provide a link to the next page in the series.

---

The Web Robots check boxes are selected by default; they allow CMS to generate the HTML META tags that contain information for Web crawlers such as search engines. The Web Robots Can Crawl Links check box allows robots to follow the links from the page; the Web Robots Can Index This Page check box allows robots to index data in the current page.

---

**NOTE:** For details on the robots META tags, refer to Chapter 6.

---

The Custom tab (Figure 5–42) allows us to set up values for the additional custom properties if these are defined in the page template by the template designers. There are two types of custom properties: text and selection. To set up the value for a text custom property, you may type the text in the Current Value column, or use the default value if provided. A selection custom property is displayed as a drop-down list in the Current Value column; you may select the value from the list, or use the default value provided. We will discuss custom properties in detail in Chapter 6.

After you've set up the page properties, click Save Changes to save the properties and return to the page in Edit mode. The page with changed properties needs to be approved before it can appear on the live site.

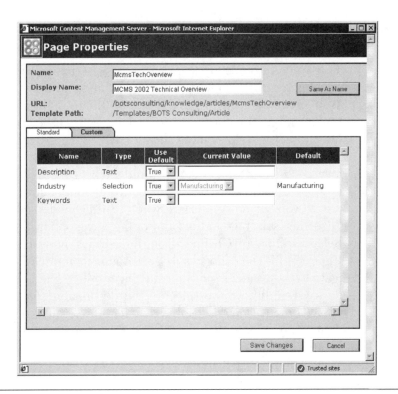

**Figure 5–42**  Page Properties, Custom tab

## Editing the Page

Often, the authors need to edit a page after is has been published. To edit the page, navigate to the page, switch to Edit mode, and click Edit in the Web Author console, as we have already seen in Figures 5–7 and 5–8. The page is displayed with the editable placeholder content inside the placeholders; you can change this content as required. When you've finished editing the content, select one of the two options on the Web Author console: either Save to save your edits and stay on the same page to carry on with editing, or Save And Exit to go to the page in Edit mode. After you've saved the page and exited the template-based authoring, the page status in the Web Author console is changed to Saved; you can change page properties if required. In order to be published, the page needs to be approved by the editor and the moderator; we will discuss this process in the next chapter.

# Copying, Moving, and Deleting Pages

The Web Author console provides options for copying, moving, and deleting pages. To copy or move a page into a different location on your Web site, you need to have the appropriate authoring rights on the source and destination channel. To delete a published page, you need to have authoring rights on the channel that contains the page. To delete a saved page that hasn't been published, either you need to be the page owner—the user who originally saved the page—or you need to have the appropriate administrative rights on the channel that contains the page.

To copy or move a page, switch to Edit mode and navigate to the page; then select either the Copy or the Move option in the console. The Select Destination Channel dialog appears, as shown for page copying in Figure 5–43. The dialog displays the channel hierarchy; you need to navigate to the channel you want the page to be copied or move into, and click OK. After you've selected the destination channel, the page is copied or moved and is displayed in the browser in its new destination in Edit mode. In order to be published, the copied or moved page needs to be approved by the editor or the moderator; the approval process is the subject of the next chapter.

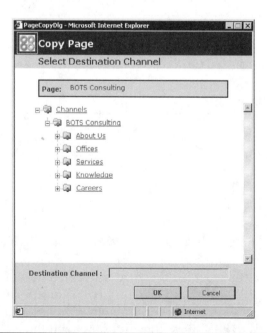

**Figure 5–43** Select channel dialog

**Figure 5–44** Page deletion warning

**NOTE:** The status of a newly copied page is Saved. The status of a moved page depends on whether the original page has already been published. If it hasn't, the status of the moved page is Saved. If you are moving a published page, the status of the moved page is Waitingfor-ModeratorApproval.

To delete the page, switch to Edit mode, navigate to the page, and select the Delete option from the Web Author console. A warning message is displayed, as shown in Figure 5–44; click OK to continue with the page deletion. You cannot restore a page deleted using the Web Author.

# Production Manager

The Production Manager dialog lists all pages that have been created but have not been published on the site. To display the Production Manager dialog (Figure 5–45), select the Production Manager option in the Web Author console.

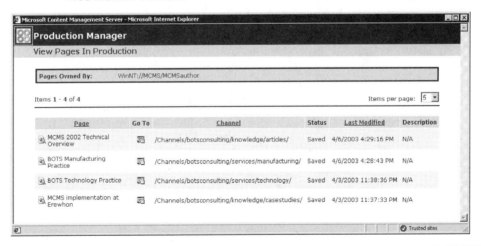

**Figure 5–45** Production Manager

The Production Manager displays the pages in production that are owned by the currently logged-on user. The pages are listed by their display name. The Production Manager allows the page owner to preview the pages by clicking the Preview icon, and to navigate between the pages in production that are in Edit mode by clicking the Go To button (refer to Table 5–4 for the icons' look and functionality). This navigation feature is very useful because the pages in production are not available on the live site; therefore, you are not able to browse to them.

The order of the pages can be sorted by the page display name if you click on the Page link in the header row, or by the containing channel name if you click on the Channel link, or by the last modified date and time if you click on the Last Modified link. The default sorting order is by time; the newer pages appear at the top of the table.

## Summary

The Web Author is an application that enables users to create and manage content, using a Web browser. Content authors can quickly and easily add or modify Web content, without the need to learn a specific HTML authoring tool such as Microsoft FrontPage or Macromedia Dreamweaver. The CMS Web pages are based on templates created by template designers during the site development stage; these templates contain placeholders that provide the ability for content authors to insert their content into the designated page areas. The content may include text, images, hyperlinks, attachments, HTML tags, and XML documents. The type of content for each placeholder is set up by the placeholder's properties. These are assigned at the development stage and indicated by the buttons on the top of the placeholder and the toolbar at the authoring stage.

After the content authors have created or edited a page, the page has to be saved. Saved pages are not immediately available on the live site. In order for them to become available to the site subscribers, the pages need to be approved for publishing. We will concentrate on this workflow process in the next chapter.

# CHAPTER 6

# Publishing Workflow

## Overview

In the previous chapter, we looked into the Web Author and focused on authoring content for a CMS-based Web site. When the CMS pages have been saved, they are persisted to the CMS content repository. However, the saved pages aren't necessarily made immediately available on the live Web site; they may only be visible in Edit mode. Most Web sites require that the pages go through an approval process. In order for the saved pages to be published on the live site, they need to be reviewed and approved for publishing.

CMS provides a three-step publishing process (Figure 6–1), as follows:

1. An author creates and saves a page, and then submits the page to a publishing workflow for approval.
2. An editor approves the page content. The editor can modify the page created by the author. If the editor declines the page, it is returned to the author.
3. A moderator approves the page, and the page is published. If required, the moderator can modify the page display name and the publishing properties, including the publishing schedule, and the publishing flags, such as Important Page, Hide When Published, and two Web Robots flags. If the moderator declines the page, it is returned to the author.

**NOTE:** It is worth mentioning that the steps in the publishing workflow are optional; you don't have to implement the full workflow if you don't need it. Later in this chapter, we will discuss how to reduce the workflow.

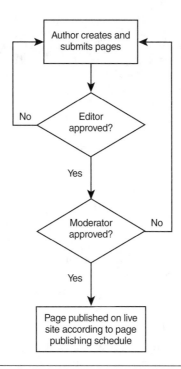

**Figure 6–1** CMS publishing workflow

There are three formal roles defined within CMS for the business users who participate in the publishing process, as follows:

- Authors: Business users who can create, edit, save, and submit content to the channels where they have authoring rights.
- Editors: Business users who can edit and approve the content submitted by the authors in the channels where they have editing rights. The editor role overlaps the author role. As well as doing everything authors do, editors can approve the page content for publication.

    Editors can either approve, or change and approve, or decline the page content. They can ask the author to edit a page, or edit it themselves before approving it.
- Moderators: Business users who can approve how and when a page is displayed in the channels where they have moderating rights. The moderators also have authoring capabilities in the channels they are assigned to.

Moderators can either approve, or change and approve, or decline the page publishing properties, including publishing schedule. Moderators can reject inappropriate pages and can ask for the publishing properties, the page content, or both to be changed. Alternatively, they can revise the page publishing properties before approving the page content.

However, they cannot revise the page content without the editor's approval. Moderators can act as authors on the content, but any changes they submit will go to the editor for approval.

---

**NOTE:** When a moderator acts as an author, they are no different from any other author: All content they create or change must be approved by the editor.

---

Users are assigned their roles by a CMS administrator before they log on for the first time. A user can have more than one role, depending on how the Web site is set up. For example, a user can be an author in one channel and an editor in another channel. CMS user rights are defined by the role, or combination of roles, assigned to the user.

---

**NOTE:** Setting up CMS user rights will be discussed in detail in Chapter 17.

---

Editors and moderators use the Web Author to approve or decline the pages. Depending on the user's rights, different options are available in the Web Author console.

In this chapter, we will concentrate on the CMS publishing workflow. We will begin with the standard three-step publishing process and will walk through all the steps, starting with submitting a page. We will then look into page content approval by the editor and, finally, the moderator's approval and publishing. Later in the chapter, we will discuss the reduced workflow and auto-approval.

## Submitting the Page

As we have seen in Chapter 5, after the author has saved the page, the page status changes to Saved. The page content is now persisted in the CMS database, and the page is available for additional editing if required. When the page has the Saved status, the page is not available on the live site but will be displayed in Edit mode.

The page also becomes locked by its owner—the user who has saved the page. This ensures that multiple authors cannot edit the same page before it has been approved by the editor.

The publishing workflow process is started by submitting the saved page for editor approval. The page is submitted by clicking the Submit option in the Web Author console. After the page has been submitted, it enters the workflow and its status changes to WaitingforEditorApproval (Figure 6–2).

The page can be previewed in Edit mode, but it is not visible on the live site.

---

**NOTE:** When the page content and the page properties are submitted, or posted, the combination is referred to in CMS as a *posting*. Throughout the book, we will be referring to pages and postings interchangeably.

---

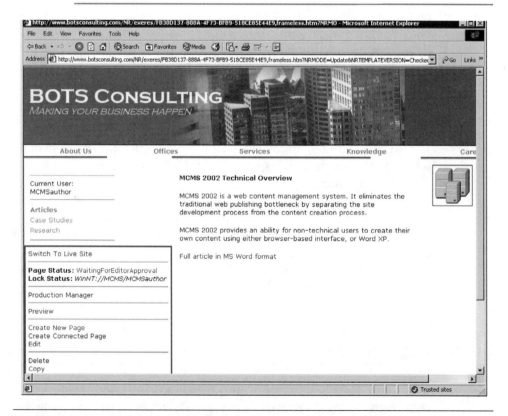

**Figure 6–2** Submitted sample page

# Page Status

Depending on where a page is positioned in the publishing process, CMS assigns different statuses of ongoing publishing activity to the page. When editors or moderators revise the page, approve the page, or decline it, the status of the page changes. The page statuses maintained by CMS are as follows:

- New: The status of a page when an author is inserting content into the placeholders, before the page is saved for the first time.
- Saved: The status of a page after it has been saved, before the page is submitted for approval.
- WaitingforEditorApproval: The status of a page after it has been submitted for approval but has not been approved by an editor. A page usually enters this state from the Saved state.
- WaitingforModeratorApproval: The status of a page after it has been approved by the editor but has not been approved by a moderator. A page usually enters this state from the Waitingfor EditorApproval status, although there are some exceptions, which we will see shortly.
- EditorDeclined: The status of a page after it has been declined by an editor, before it is modified and resubmitted by the page authors.
- ModeratorDeclined: The status of a page after it has been declined by a moderator, before it has been modified and resubmitted.
- Approved: The status of a page after it has been approved for publishing by a moderator but where the current time is less than the publishing start time of the page.
- Expired: The status of a page after it has been approved by a moderator but where the current time is greater than the expiry time of the page.
- Published: The status of a page after it has been approved by a moderator and where the current time is greater than the start time, but less than the expiry time of the page. This is the only state in which a page can be seen by site subscribers.

A page status is displayed in the Web Author console for the current page. Using the Production Manager, page creators can see the status of all pages they own (Figure 6–3).

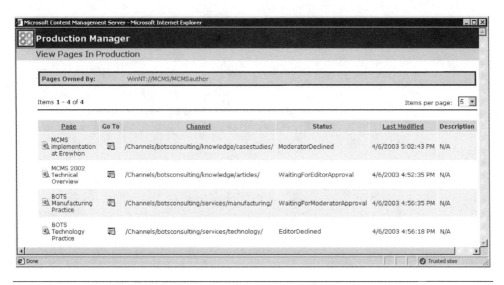

**Figure 6–3** Different page statuses in Production Manager

## Editor's Approval

After an author has submitted a page, a user with editor rights is responsible for checking the page for content accuracy. The editor can either approve, or change and approve, or decline the page. The editor and author roles overlap; an editor can do everything an author can plus approve and decline content.

Before the editor approves the page, they can make changes to the page content and properties. In other words, a user who has editor rights to a channel can create and approve a new page without the page requiring a separate editor approval step. In the three-step CMS publishing workflow, the editor can modify the page content and properties but usually can't approve the page for publication.

When a user with editing rights logs on to a CMS site and switches to Edit mode, they have more options available in the Web Author console than an author. An Approval Assistant link is displayed in the console to the editors on all pages that are located in the channels where they have editing rights. In addition, the pages that have WaitingforEditor Approval status, or are saved by the editor, also have Approve and Decline options available in the console (Figure 6–4).

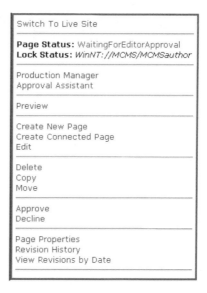

**Figure 6–4**  Web Author default console as displayed to a user with editing rights

Page approval can be performed in one of two ways:

- Using console commands: Pages can be approved or declined individually by using the Approve or Decline options in the Web Author console on each page.
- Using the Approval Assistant: The Approval Assistant displays a list of all pages waiting for editor approval in the channels to which the currently logged-on user has editing rights (Figure 6–5). The pages are listed in a table using their display name. Other information displayed for each page includes the Location field, which shows the channel that contains the page; the page status; the page owner; and the last modified date and time. By default, the sorting order is by time, with the newer pages on the top of the list. You can change the sorting field and order by clicking the heading of the appropriate column, with the exception of the Status column.

**NOTE:** If there are no pages waiting for the editor's approval, the Approval Assistant window displays the message "There are no pages waiting for approval."

**124**    Chapter 6    Publishing Workflow

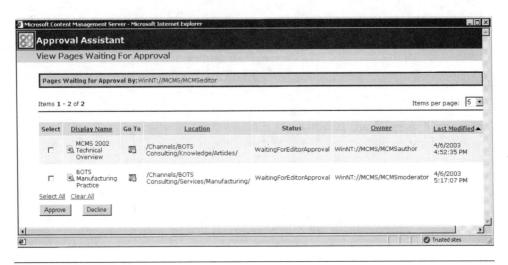

**Figure 6–5** Approval Assistant

The Approval Assistant provides the ability to approve or decline multiple pages as well as to preview a page and navigate to the page. The ability to use the Approval Assistant for navigation between pages submitted for editor approval cannot be underestimated. Using the Approval Assistant may be the only way to browse to these pages. In Edit mode, URLs are not hierarchical, and it's not practical to either type them in or bookmark the page. Often, there are navigational aids within the page template that allow the editor to navigate between the pages in a given channel. However, if this is not the case, then the Approval Assistant provides an easy way to go to the pages awaiting approval.

To approve a page using the Approval Assistant, select the page by clicking the Select check box in the leftmost column, and then click the Approve button at the bottom of the list. To Decline a page, select the page and click the Decline button. You can approve or decline multiple pages by selecting these pages and then clicking the appropriate button. You can also use the Select All and Clear All links to select and deselect all pages in the list.

In addition to creating and editing content, editors can perform the following operations on the pages that are contained in the channel where they have editing rights:

- Approve a page: When an editor approves a page, the page status usually changes to WaitingforModeratorApproval (Figure 6–6).

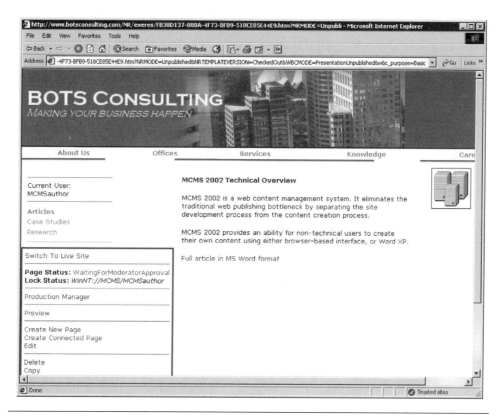

**Figure 6–6**  Sample page approved by an editor

However, there is an exception to this rule when the page status changes directly to Published after the editor's approval. This happens when an author changes the content of existing, published pages. If the content of a published page has been edited by an author and submitted for an editor's approval, then when the editor approves the changes, the new version of the page is published on the live site. In this case, the moderator's approval stage of the publishing workflow is bypassed, because the moderator has already approved the publishing attributes, such as the schedule, for the original published page. These attributes have not been changed, so the moderator's approval is not required.

■ Decline a page: When an editor declines a page, the page status changes to EditorDeclined. The page author will have to check the page status in the Production Manager to find out if the page has been approved or declined; there is no notification mechanism available in CMS out of the box.

- Edit a submitted page and modify the page properties: When an editor changes the page content and/or the page properties, the page has to be saved first. The page status is changed to Saved. Then the editor will need to approve it; it is not approved automatically. There are two ways of approving the page modified and owned by the editor:
  - The editor can resubmit the page; then the page status changes to WaitingforEditorApproval, and the page is listed in the Approval Assistant. The editor can then approve the page either by using the Approve or Decline console commands or by using the Approval Assistant.
  - The editor can approve the page they own directly from the console commands without resubmitting it.
- Submit a page they don't own: If a page has been saved by somebody else but not yet submitted, an editor can submit this page.
- Delete a page they don't own: An editor can delete pages in the channel that are owned by somebody else.

---

**NOTE:** It is possible to extend the publishing workflow to include, for example, an e-mail notification of publishing events, such as the page's being approved or declined. We will look into customizing the workflow in Chapter 31.

---

The editors' main responsibility is the quality of the content. Often, the editors are also responsible for setting up the page custom properties. We mentioned the custom properties in Chapter 5; now let's take a more detailed look at them.

These properties are not shown anywhere on the page. Custom properties for pages are defined in the corresponding page template by the template designers. The template contains the custom property name and type. A type defines how the property values are represented in the Web Author. A custom property may be represented as a drop-down list; the content creators may select the value from the list or use the default value provided by the template. Alternatively, the content creators may be asked to type the text for the property value or use the default value provided. A page can have multiple custom properties. Different pages can have the same custom properties.

Custom properties then can be used programmatically in the template code in a number of ways. For example, custom properties can be used to categorize content. Content authors and editors may select the predefined values for the custom properties when they add or edit content. If you want to use custom properties in this way, then these properties must be defined consistently throughout your site, as follows:

- Each custom property must have the same name and the same type across all page templates.
- If a custom property is represented as a drop-down list, it must have the same set of values.

Typically, the custom properties are used to generate META tags for the search engines, such as Keywords and Description META tags used by the internal and external search engines. Keywords and Description META tags, along with the full text of a page, are the primary sources of information that search engines use to index the page. META tags can be created at runtime; the page template includes code that programmatically retrieves the content stored in the custom properties and inserts it into the HTML <HEAD> container.

**Keywords and Description META Tags**

Keywords defined in the META tags on a page are added to the search engine index as the search keywords for this page, and description text is displayed after the link to your page in the search results page. When the search engine crawler comes to the page with the following META tags, it will use the string "BOTS Consulting is a management consulting firm" to describe the page, and will use the words listed within the content attribute in the second META tag as the search keywords for this page.

```
<META name="Description" content="BOTS Consulting is a management
    consulting firm">
<META name="Keywords" content=" BOTS, BOTS Consulting, consulting,
    consultancy, consultancies, consult, consulting firms, management
    consulting, consultants, consultant ">
```

For example, when the user searches for consulting firms, this page will be returned as a result of the search.

It is a good practice of Web design to provide Keywords and Description META tags for the search engines. It is advisable to provide values for Keywords and Description custom properties on your Web site pages so that the META tags can be generated.

The editor can modify the page properties that are set up by the page author; the editor's settings override the author's settings. For example, as shown in Figure 6–7, our sample page has custom properties for categorization and for the search engines, as follows:

- A custom property called Industry is used for categorization. The use of this property allows us to mark pages on our site that relate to a specific industry; the value for the property is chosen from the list of values set up by the template designers. In our example, the default value is Manufacturing, but the value selected for the current page is Technology. The following META tags will be generated:

```
<META name="Industry" value="Manufacturing">
```

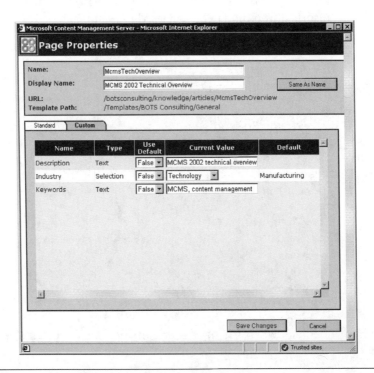

**Figure 6–7** Sample page custom properties

■ Two custom properties called Keywords and Description are used for the search engines. The Keywords property contains the list of the keywords for this particular page; the Description property contains the text that provides a brief description of the page content. The following META tags will be generated:

```
<META name = Keywords content="MCMS, content management">
<META name=Description value="MCMS 2002 technical overview">
```

# Moderator's Approval

The final stage in the CMS workflow process is for a moderator to approve the page. After an editor has approved a page, a user with moderator rights is responsible for publishing the page in a particular channel and verifying the page content and page properties. The moderator controls whether the pages with the WaitingforModeratorApproval status are published to the live site. The pages usually get this status after they have been approved by the editors. However, there are exceptions, including the following:

■ If publishing properties—for example, the publishing schedule or the display name of an existing published page—have been changed, then the page bypasses the editor and gets the Waiting forModeratorApproval status from the Published status after the changes to the properties have been saved.
■ If a page originally was declined by the moderator, and subsequently its publishing properties have been changed by the page author or the page has been resubmitted without changes, then the saved page bypasses the editor and gets the WaitingforModerator Approval status from the ModeratorDeclined status.
■ If a published page has been moved and its content has not been modified, the page status in the new location changes to Waiting forModeratorApproval, bypassing both the Saved status and the WaitingforEditorApproval status.

When a user with moderating rights logs on to a CMS site and switches to Edit mode, they have the same options as an editor available in the Web Author console (Figure 6–4). They can use the Approval Assistant to approve or decline pages, or they can use the Approve and

Decline commands in the console to approve or decline pages individually.

If a moderator modifies the page content, saves the page, and resubmits it, the page status changes to WaitingforEditorApproval. If the moderator changes the page name, description, or values for custom properties and clicks Save Changes in the Page Properties dialog, the page status also changes to WaitingforEditorApproval. The page content, custom properties values, description, and name have to be approved by the editor first; moderators cannot approve their own changes to any of them.

However, if the moderator changes the page display name and the standard properties, such as the page publishing schedule and the Web Robots check boxes, the status of the page stays the same: WaitingforModeratorApproval.

---

**NOTE:** Moderators can change all standard properties except the page description. Changes to the page description property should be approved by the editor.

---

This functionality is implemented in CMS in order to separate the responsibility for the content from the responsibility for page publishing to the live site: Editors are responsible for the content, while moderators are responsible for the publishing. In addition to approving and declining pages, before moderators approve a page for publishing, they can modify the following properties of the page (Figure 6–8):

- Display Name: The Display Name property defines the text for the link pointing to the current page from other locations on the site.
- Page publishing schedule: The publishing schedule defines the period of time when the page is available on the live site in presentation mode, as follows:
  - Start Publishing can be set either to start immediately or to start at an exact date and time. The default is the page's last modified time. The exact date and time can be typed in, or the date can be selected by clicking the calendar icon, as shown in Figure 6–8. When the calendar is displayed, it points to the currently specified date; you can navigate to the desired date.

    The start date of the page can't be earlier than the creation or start date of the containing channel, whichever is earlier. This applies to the whole hierarchy of channels that contain the current channel, which, in turn, contains the current page.

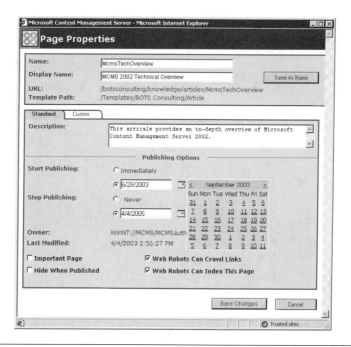

**Figure 6–8** Sample page standard properties

■ Stop Publishing can be set either to never stop or to stop at the exact date and time. The default is Never. As before, the calendar icon provides the ability to select the date for the expiry date; or you can just type in both the date and the time. The expiry date can't be earlier than the start date.

■ Important Page: This check box sets up an additional flag on the page. This flag can be analyzed programmatically—for example, inside a template file. It is not selected by default.

■ Hide When Published: This check box makes the page invisible after it has been published. Once again, this option can be analyzed in the code and changed programmatically at runtime, depending on the business logic implemented by the site designers. This check box is also not selected by default.

■ Two Web Robots settings: These check boxes define whether and how the page should be made available to Web robots. The settings define how the robots META tags for the page are generated at runtime, as follows:

■ The Web Robots Can Crawl Links check box allows Web robots, also referred to as spiders or crawlers, to follow links from the page. If this box is selected, the following META tag is inserted into the HTML <HEAD> container at runtime:

```
<META name="ROBOTS" content="FOLLOW, NOINDEX">
```

- The Web Robots Can Index This Page check box allows Web crawlers to index the page. In this case, the following META tag is inserted at runtime:

```
<META name="ROBOTS" content="INDEX, NOFOLLOW">
```

- If both Web Robots check boxes are selected, as by default, the META tag is as follows:

```
<META name="ROBOTS" content="FOLLOW, INDEX">
```

- Leaving both boxes empty causes the following META tag to be generated:

```
<META name="ROBOTS" content="NOFOLLOW, NOINDEX">
```

---

**NOTE:** In a rare case, you may need to set up a start date that is earlier than the current date. If you try to set up a start date for a page that is earlier than the corresponding date for the containing channels, the Web Author will revert to the original date without warning you.

---

**Web Robots**

Web robots are programs that automatically traverse Web sites. They are also known as spiders or crawlers. An example of a Web crawler is a search engine program that indexes your site for further searches.

Compliance with robots META tags is voluntary. However, most well-known robots will honor robots META tags.

For more information on Web robots, have a look at The Web Robots Pages at http://www.robotstxt.org/wc/robots.html.

After the moderator has approved a page, depending on the page publishing schedule, one of the following three events occurs:

- If the current time is earlier than the page's Start Publishing time, the page status is set to Approved; the page will be available on the live site when the start time is reached.

- If the current time has passed the page expiry date, the page status is set to Expired; the page is not available on the live site.
- If the current time matches the page publishing schedule, the page status is set to Published; it is immediately made available on the live site in presentation mode (Figure 6–9).

---

**NOTE:** An approved page is not locked and is owned by everybody.

---

If a page is declined by the moderator, then the page status changes to ModeratorDeclined, and this is how the page appears in the author's Production Manager. Declined pages will only be displayed in Edit mode and will not be displayed on the live site until the moderator re-approves the page.

This concludes our discussion about the three-step CMS publishing process. However, before we move on to the next section, it is worth mentioning an anomaly in the workflow between editing existing page content and editing existing page publishing properties. If you change the content for a published page, then save and submit the changes, the

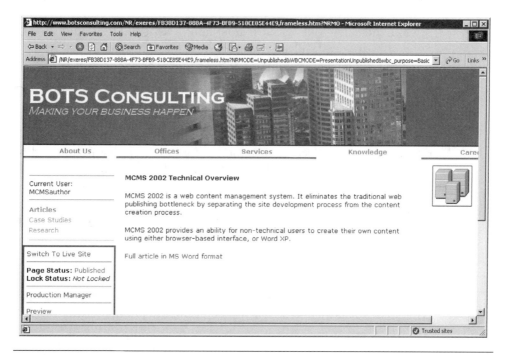

**Figure 6–9**  Published sample page in Edit mode

original version of the page is available on the live site until an editor approves the new content. However, if you take an existing, published page and change its publishing properties, such as the publishing schedule or the display name, then the existing page stops being published until it is approved by a moderator. This behavior may result in the page's disappearing from the live site and then reappearing at a random time. Undoubtedly, it can create problems for your users.

## Auto-approval

Depending on your corporate processes and business needs, the CMS default workflow may not be suitable for your environment. The standard CMS three-step workflow approval process can be reduced if required.

The workflow process stages can be bypassed—for example, if you determine that for a particular site there is no requirement for content editing and/or moderation. This functionality is called auto-approval. It can be achieved by not assigning the workflow roles to a channel, as follows:

- If a channel doesn't have a moderator assigned to it, then an editor's approval will approve the pages for publishing.
- If a channel doesn't have either an editor or a moderator assigned to it, the content author will be able to submit pages live to the Web site.

Another way of reducing the workflow is by combining the workflow roles for the users. If a user with moderator rights also has editing rights, all page content and properties they save and submit are automatically approved. For example, if the user who is creating pages either has administrative permissions on a channel or has multiple publishing roles, such as author, editor, and moderator, the workflow will be significantly reduced because they can create and approve their own content in order to publish it.

**NOTE:** The publishing workflow can also be extended or otherwise customized by the developers. This will be discussed in Chapter 31.

# Page Revisions

Web sites and Web pages are always changing over time; CMS sites and pages are no exception. During a CMS page's lifetime, the page may— and most probably will—be modified many times. Once a new version of the page has been approved, this version is displayed on the live site according to its publishing schedule. CMS doesn't delete the previous approved page version; it is automatically maintained for revision tracking. Any page change that has been approved by an editor is a revision. Each approved change to a page creates a new page version.

Revision tracking is always enabled; page versions are stored by date and time. Page content and properties that have to be approved by the editor are versioned, while page properties that can be changed by a moderator without further editor approval are not versioned. Versioned changes include placeholder content, resource gallery items used on the page, custom properties, and page description. Changes that are not versioned include page name, page display name, publishing schedule, and publishing flags, such as Important Page, Hide When Published, and the two Web Robots flags.

**NOTE:** Code in the template ASPX file is not stored in the database and is not versioned by revision tracking.

CMS archives all approved pages; there is no configurable maximum number for the length of the revision history. Although page versions are maintained by CMS, there is no rollback facility. If you want to go back to an older version, you need to manually copy and paste content from the older page preview into a new version of your page.

**NOTE:** It is possible to purge page revisions using the Site Manager; we will discuss how to do it in Chapter 16.

Revision histories are made available to content creators using Web Author console commands that allow them to compare versions. There are two console commands related to revisions:

- The Revision History command lists all available page revisions and allows content creators to compare any two of them (Figure 6–10).

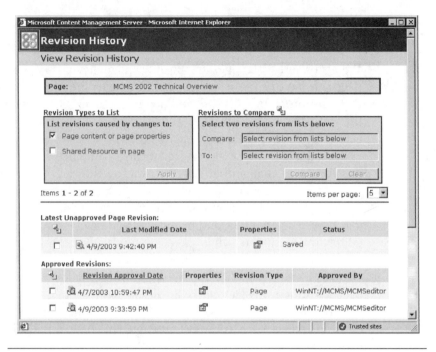

**Figure 6–10** Revision History dialog

For example, when you edit a page, you may need to compare it with the approved version of the page.

■ The View Revisions by Date command provides the ability to view a page revision in presentation mode as it was displayed on the site at the specified date and time. You can either manually specify a date and time for a revision you want to view, or select the date from the calendar provided (Figure 6–11).

When viewing and comparing the page revisions, you need to be aware that they are displayed using the current template file. This is especially important if you are looking at a specific revision by date. Even if the template file has been changed since that date, the revision will be displayed using the current template file, not the original template file as it was on that particular date. As a result, the revision may not be displayed as it was displayed originally. For example, if the template file has had a placeholder removed since that date, the page revision will be based on the current template file and will not display this placeholder and its content.

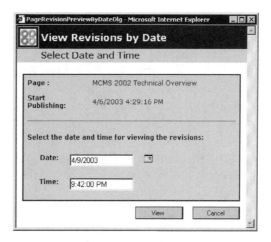

**Figure 6–11**  View Revisions by Date dialog

To compare a particular page's revisions using the Web Author, a currently logged-on user must have authoring or editing rights to the page. Selecting the Revision History command on the console displays the Revision History dialog, shown in Figure 6–10, which provides an interface for comparing the revisions.

Two check boxes under Revision Types to List provide the ability to specify the types of revisions you want to display, as follows:

- Page content or page properties: This option is selected by default.
- Shared Resource in page: This option is not selected by default.

**NOTE:**  Changes to resource gallery items are viewed within the pages that use these items; any approved change to a resource gallery item used in a page creates a new page version.

Depending on the revision types you've specified, the list of revisions that meet the type criteria will be displayed. Different information is listed for the approved page versions versus an unapproved version of the page, as follows:

- The latest unapproved page revision, if it exists:
    - Date and time when the revision was last modified
    - Current page status

- Approved revisions:
  - Revision approval date and time
  - Revision type
  - Name of the user who approved the revision
- Both approved and unapproved revisions:
  - Preview and Properties icons

To compare two versions, select them by clicking the Select box for each of the versions, and then click the Compare button. The changes between two pages are displayed under three comparison tabs (Figure 6–12), as follows:

- The Appearance tab displays differences in the page content.
- The Source tab displays differences in the page HTML.
- The Properties tab compares the versioned page properties and displays changes.

The Appearance and Source tabs display text changes as color-coded: The text that has been added is in one color, and the text that has

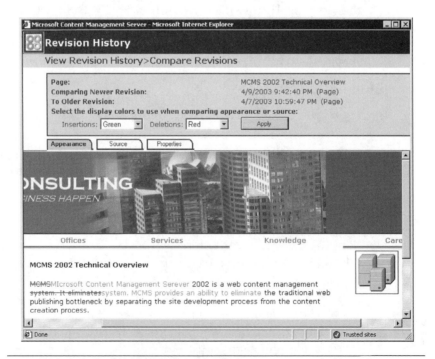

**Figure 6–12**  Compare Revisions interface

been deleted is in a different color with strikethroughs. Changed images in the Appearance tab appear with color borders around them. The default colors are green for additions and red for deletions; you can select other colors from the lists provided for both options.

## Summary

CMS defines a publishing workflow process that ensures the quality of the content published on a CMS Web site. Several CMS publishing roles, such as author, editor, and moderator, can be assigned to individual users, allowing all content to pass through this workflow. Authors, editors, and moderators use the Web Author for creating and approving content. Once the template designers have created templates and the site administrator has assigned user roles, the whole content creation process can occur without any further need for the developers or administrators to be involved.

The publishing workflow includes creating a page by an author, approving the page content by an editor, approving the page publishing schedule by a moderator, and, finally, publishing the page on the live site if approved. In this chapter, we walked through the publishing workflow process and discussed the statuses assigned to a page in different workflow stages.

Depending on your business requirements, the standard three-step workflow can be changed. We discussed the auto-approval process used to reduce the workflow. However, the workflow can be extended or otherwise customized to include various roles if required. We will look into how this can be done in Chapter 31.

In the next chapter, we will focus on CMS content creation using Microsoft Word.

# CHAPTER 7

# Authoring Connector

In Chapters 5 and 6, we looked into content creation and publishing using the Web Author. CMS 2002 also provides the ability for nontechnical content authors to create CMS content directly from Microsoft Word XP. This functionality is achieved by installing and using the CMS Authoring Connector component in addition to Word XP on the content authors' client computers. In this chapter, we'll detail how to use the Authoring Connector and look into its architecture and functionality.

## What Is the Authoring Connector?

The Authoring Connector is a stand-alone tool that doesn't require any other CMS 2002 components to be installed on a client computer. The Authoring Connector provides a new feature in CMS 2002 that enables business users to create and submit content without leaving Word XP. In the previous versions of CMS, document content could only be copied and pasted into the placeholders in the Web Author. Using Word XP with the Authoring Connector, authors can create and update content on the CMS site using a wizard-driven interface. Currently, the Authoring Connector enables content authoring from Word XP only; content from other Office applications, such as Excel, must be manually copied and pasted into the appropriate placeholders, using the Web Author as before.

The Authoring Connector Wizard provides an author with a list of predefined publishing tasks and guides the author through the submitting content to be published. Upon completion of the wizard, the Authoring Connector creates a new posting. The status of the posting is set to WaitingforEditorApproval. For content to become available on the live site, the page has to go through the publishing workflow as usual.

**NOTE:** As we have mentioned previously, in CMS 2002 the terms "page" and "posting" can be used interchangeably.

The publishing tasks for the authors are preconfigured by a site administrator, thus shielding the business users from the detailed understanding of CMS site structure and functionality.

A content author can submit an entire document or a selected part of a document. How the content is inserted into a CMS page is defined by the placeholders within a template on which this page is based. The content can be inserted into the page in one of two ways:

- The content, including text and/or images, is displayed inline as a part of a Web page.
- The entire document is inserted into a page as an attachment.

For example, Figure 7–1 shows a page created from Word XP using the Authoring Connector. The selected text from the Word document is displayed inline, providing the abstract for the full document, which is available for download as an attachment on the same page.

**Figure 7–1** CMS page created from Word XP

**NOTE:** The Authoring Connector targets templates, not placeholders. The content is placed into the placeholders within the template depending on the types of placeholders and their properties defined by the template designers.

Now that we have an idea as to what the Authoring Connector is, let's discuss its architecture and look into how it is used.

## Authoring Connector Components

The Authoring Connector contains both client and server components. A high-level architecture of the Authoring Connector components is shown in Figure 7–2.

The client component is a Word add-on called offcon.dll. The add-on provides additional Word menu options (Figure 7–3) that launch the publishing wizard. When the Authoring Connector client component is installed, the Send to MCMS drop-down menu is added to the File menu. It includes the following options:

- Create New Page
- Update Same Page
- Replace Any Page

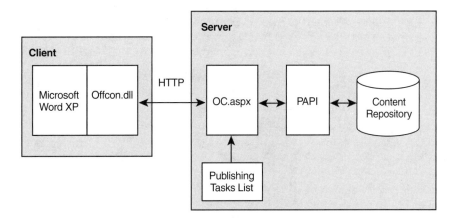

**Figure 7–2** Authoring Connector components

**Figure 7–3** Additional File menu options in Word XP

The client component needs to be installed on each computer that will use the Authoring Connector; Word XP has to be installed on client computers before installation of the Authoring Connector client component.

**NOTE:** The server requires no additional configuration; all software components are installed by default.

If the Macro Security in Word XP is set to High, when Word XP is launched for the first time after the Authoring Connector has been installed, it may give a security warning regarding potential macro viruses (Figure 7–4). To prevent the warning from appearing again, in the warning dialog box click the "Always trust macros from this source" check box, and then click the Enable Macros button. Word adds the Microsoft Corporation certificate to the list of trusted sources (Figure 7–5) and will not display the warning again.

**NOTE:** To review the list of trusted sources for macros in Word XP, select Tools > Options > Security tab, click the Macro Security button, and choose the Trusted Sources tab.

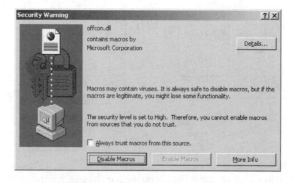

**Figure 7–4** Word XP security warning

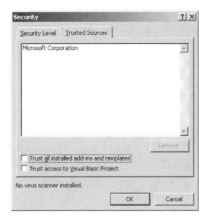

**Figure 7–5** Trusted sources for macros in Word XP

On the server side, the Authoring Connector user interface is contained in the ASP.NET page OC.aspx; this page is essentially a collection of ASP.NET Web forms. The client component communicates with the server component over HTTP; therefore, HTTP connectivity is required between the client and the server. If the OC.aspx file is not available or has been secured on the server, then the Authoring Connector will not be able to submit content.

**NOTE:** The URL pointing to OC.aspx can be modified within the wizard. We will discuss that in the next section in this chapter.

The OC.aspx file is located in the folder *<installation point>*\Server\ IIS_CMS\OfficeWizard. On a CMS site, this folder by default is mapped to the virtual directory /MCMS/CMS/OfficeWizard. The same folder contains the file PublishingTasks.xml, which provides a list of Authoring Connector publishing tasks displayed in the wizard. This file can be modified by a site administrator; we will look into how to do it later in this chapter.

The Authoring Connector Wizard interacts with the OC.aspx file, which in turn interacts with the Publishing API. Upon completion of the wizard, the Authoring Connector creates a new posting and then copies the content from the Word document into the available placeholders defined in the target template.

There are two types of placeholders that a template designer may use within a template specifically for Word content: OfficeHtmlPlaceholder

**Authoring Connector Customization**

The behavior of the Authoring Connector can be customized. For example, you may require a different publishing workflow for Word-based authoring than for browser-based authoring. Another example is a multilingual site, in which additional consideration should be given to the globalization directives (code-pages) for your site and the character sets used on the site, as well as to choosing fonts in Word that match the character set for the language you are using.

For details, refer to the MSDN article located at http://msdn.microsoft.com/library/default.asp?url=/library/en-us/dnmscms02/html/mscms_custauco.asp.

and OfficeAttachmentPlaceholder. In our example in Figure 7–1, the inline abstract text is inserted into the OfficeHtmlPlaceholder, and the full Word document is inserted as an attachment into the OfficeAttachmentPlaceholder.

It is worth mentioning that authors can submit Word content using any template, and into any channel to which they have rights, even if the templates are not designated as Word authoring templates and may not contain OfficeHtmlPlaceholder and/or OfficeAttachmentPlaceholder. In such cases, content is inserted into the first available HtmlPlaceholder, and the source document is uploaded into the first AttachmentPlaceholder. We will focus on how the content is inserted into the placeholders later in this chapter

In the original Word document, the Authoring Connector creates two additional custom properties, as follows:

- The CmsServerUrl property contains the full URL pointing to the location of the OC.aspx file on the CMS server. For example, the value for this property can be set to http://www.botsconsulting.com/MCMS/CMS/OfficeWizard/oc.aspx.
- CmsPostingGuid contains the posting Globally Unique Identifier (GUID).

These document properties allow the Authoring Connector to find the posting that corresponds to where the document content was last submitted for publishing. The next time the author opens the document, the option of updating an existing posting becomes available. The

Authoring Connector updates the existing posting by copying content from Word XP into the available placeholders.

---

**NOTE:** There is no interaction between the Authoring Connector and the template .aspx file. When content is created using the Authoring Connector, the template .aspx file is not run; therefore, any custom code in the template file is not executed.

---

# Using the Authoring Connector

Content authors use the Authoring Connector to submit their content from Word XP. An entire document or a selected part of a document can be submitted. Content authors can create a new page, update an existing page originally created by using the Authoring Connector, or replace an existing page.

## Creating a New Page

The process of creating a new page using the Authoring Connector consists of several steps:

- If you would like to submit part of a Word document, select the content as required. If you are submitting an entire document, don't make any selection.
- Change the URL pointing to the OC.aspx file if you are publishing to a different server or using a different file location.
- Choose a channel where the new page will be published, and a template on which it will be based. These parameters can either be chosen as a publishing task or be specified manually.
- Set up the page properties.
- Preview the page and confirm your choices.

The first step is to select in the Word document the content to be published; alternatively, the entire document will be published. Then, choose the File > Send to MCMS > Create New Page menu option. If the document has not been saved, you will be prompted to save it (Figure 7–6); click Yes. The Authoring Connector Wizard is then launched. If a selection has been made in Word, the Authoring Connector prompts

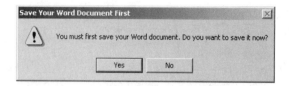

**Figure 7–6** Word XP prompt before the wizard is launched

you to choose whether to publish the selection or the whole document, as shown in Figure 7–7. If no selection has been made, the text in the middle section of the Welcome screen is not displayed (Figure 7–8).

From this screen you can change the URL for the OC.aspx if required. Once the OC.aspx location is set up for a document, it is saved to the CmsServerUrl property in the Word document when the wizard has completed. It does not need to be set up again if there have been no changes. It also becomes the default for any other Word document opened on a client machine that does not already have the CmsServerUrl property defined. In addition, any Word template based on the document with this property will pick up the OC.aspx location. To change the location, select the "Change server name and path" check box and click Next; then specify the new URL (Figure 7–9) and click Next.

The wizard can only be accessed by users who have authoring rights in at least one of the channels on the CMS site. If the current user does

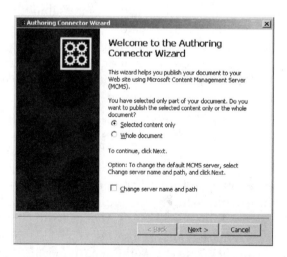

**Figure 7–7** Authoring Connector Wizard Welcome screen, selected text being submitted

**Figure 7–8** Authoring Connector Wizard Welcome screen, entire document being submitted

not have sufficient permissions on the CMS server, an additional login dialog will be displayed (Figure 7–10).

Then, a Publishing Task dialog is displayed, as shown in Figure 7–11. This dialog presents a list of publishing tasks from which an author can choose. Publishing tasks are preconfigured by an administrator. Each

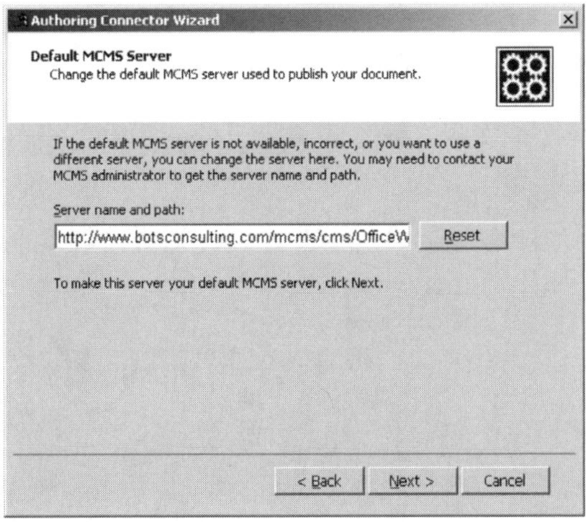

**Figure 7–9** Change the default server and location dialog

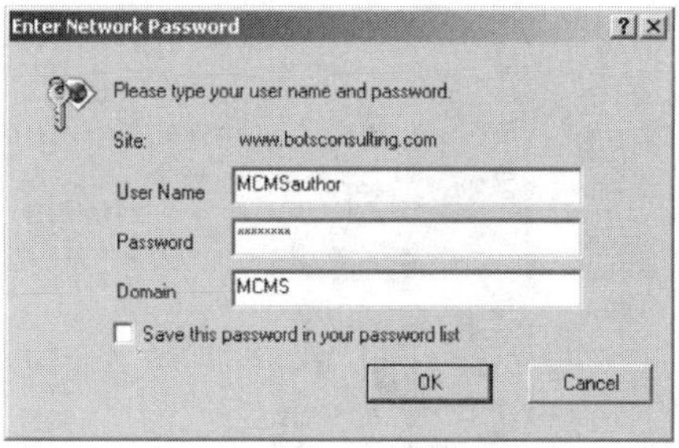

**Figure 7-10**  Login dialog

publishing task is listed by name. This name is an alias for a combination of three parameters, as follows:

- A short description of the task, which is displayed in the dialog when the task has been selected
- A template on which a new page will be based
- A channel where a new page will be published

When content is created using the Web Author, the content author needs to navigate to a channel where the new page will be submitted, select a template on which the new page will be based, and then enter the content into the placeholders. In the Authoring Connector, using publishing tasks allows administrators to preconfigure the channel and

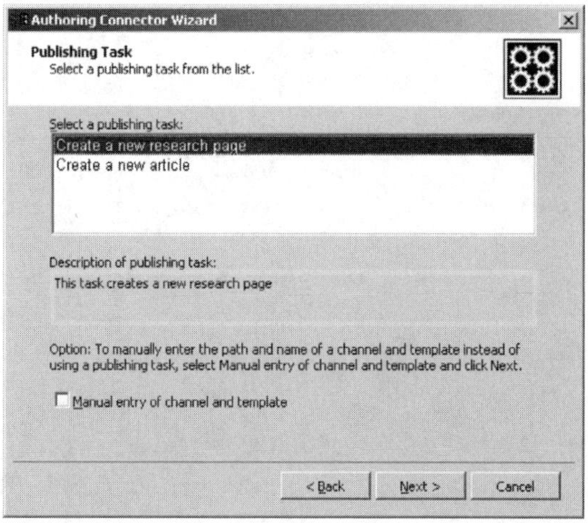

**Figure 7-11**  Publishing Task dialog

the template. Therefore, an author does not require any additional knowledge of the CMS site structure: The document content is uploaded into the preconfigured template and stored in the preconfigured channel based on the parameters defined by a publishing task.

The author only needs to create the document and choose a task; the task guarantees that the appropriate template is selected and the content is submitted for publishing in the appropriate channel, thus reducing the probability of a user error.

The author rights on channels and templates determine which tasks are displayed. Only tasks that contain channels and templates to which the current user has rights are shown. For example, if an author only has access to one channel, then only the tasks related to that channel will be displayed, provided the author has rights to the templates used in these tasks.

The Authoring Connector also provides the ability for an author to override the publishing tasks and manually enter a channel and a template. To achieve this, check the "Manual entry of channel and template" box if it is enabled, and click Next. In the Channel Information dialog, navigate to the required channel, or type the full path from the root channel Channels, as shown in Figure 7–12, and click Next. In the Template Information dialog, navigate to the required template, or type the full path from the root template gallery Templates, as shown in Figure 7–13.

**NOTE:** The template path is based on the template gallery hierarchy and not the physical location of the template file.

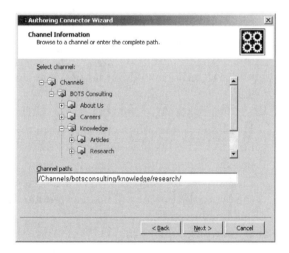

**Figure 7–12** Channel Information dialog

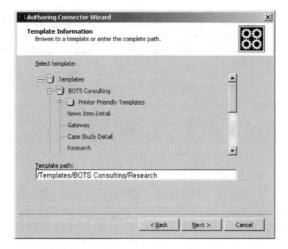

**Figure 7–13**  Template Information dialog

Regardless of whether the template is specified by a publishing task or manually, the Authoring Connector does not provide the ability to target placeholders within the template. The content is inserted into a page depending on the type and number of placeholders defined within a template, as follows:

- If there are one or more OfficeHtmlPlaceholders within the template, the content is inserted into all of them as inline content to be displayed within a page. For instance, if there are two Office HtmlPlaceholders within a template, the content will be inserted into both of them. The content can be either the entire document or a selected part of the document. The properties of each of the OfficeHtmlPlaceholders define what content will be published and how.

  For example, if images are not allowed for a particular Office HtmlPlaceholder, then only text from the Word document will be inserted into this placeholder and displayed on a page; all images will be filtered out. If the same template has another OfficeHtml Placeholder that allows images but no text, then only images from the Word document will be inserted into this placeholder; the text will be filtered out.

- If there are one or more OfficeAttachmentPlaceholders within the template, the entire source document is inserted into all of them as a file attachment; the link to the document is displayed within a page. Regardless of whether part of the document has been selected or not, the entire document will be inserted as an attachment. For example, if there are two OfficeAttachmentPlaceholders within a template, the source document will be inserted into both of them as an attachment in exactly the same way.

If there are one or more OfficeHtmlPlaceholders and Office AttachmentPlaceholders defined within the template, the inline content is inserted into all OfficeHtmlPlaceholders, and the source document is inserted as an attachment into all OfficeAttachment Placeholders.

- If there are no OfficeHtmlPlaceholders in the template, the content will be inserted into the first HtmlPlaceholder defined within a template for inline publishing. If there are no OfficeHtml Placeholders and no HtmlPlaceholders within a template, no inline content will be published on the page.
- If there are no OfficeAttachmentPlaceholders in the template, the document will be inserted as an attachment into the first AttachmentPlaceholder defined within a template. If there are no OfficeAttachmentPlaceholders and no AttachmentPlaceholders within a template, the source document is not inserted as an attachment into the page.

---

**NOTE:** The formatting of text inserted into an OfficeHtmlPlaceholder depends on the properties of the placeholder, the original text formatting in Word, and the mapping of the styles definition within the template to styles in Word. We will look into preserving formatting later in this chapter.

---

The next step is to configure the page properties. First of all, the Authoring Connector displays a Page Information dialog, shown in Figure 7–14, which provides the ability to specify the page name, title, and description. The page name will be used as a part of a URL pointing to the new page. The title sets up the Display Name property as we know it in the Web Author. By default, the Authoring Connector displays the first 128 characters of the text as both the page name and title; this can be changed. The Page Description property allows the author to provide a meaningful description of the page; this property is optional and is limited to 256 characters in length.

Clicking Next displays a Publishing Dates and Times dialog, as shown in Figure 7–15; this dialog allows an author to specify the desired

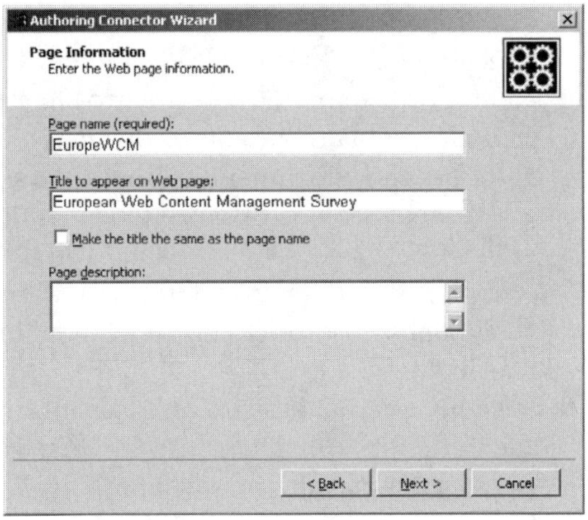

**Figure 7–14** Page Information dialog

publishing schedule for the page. As we have seen in the previous chapter, this schedule can be changed by editors and moderators after the page has been submitted to the publishing workflow.

There is also an "Advanced page properties" check box, which allows the author to display the Advanced Page Properties dialog, shown in Figure 7–16. It provides the ability to set up the page attributes, as well as to specify values for custom properties for a page if they are defined in the template.

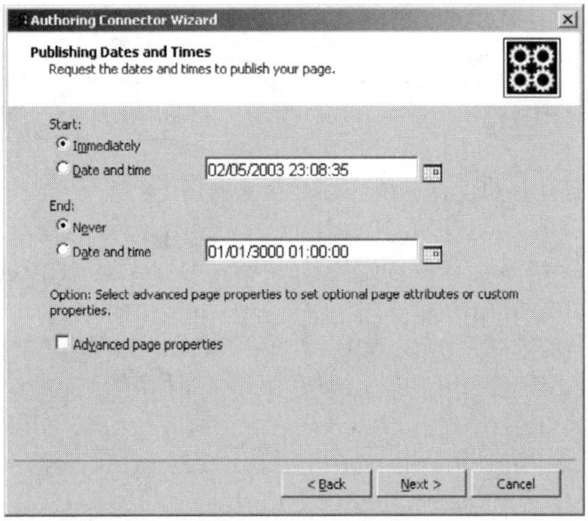

**Figure 7–15** Publishing Dates and Times dialog

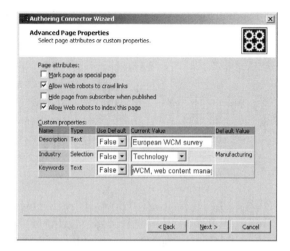

**Figure 7–16** Advanced Page Properties dialog

The page attributes are the same settings as the page publishing properties presented in the Web Author, Page Properties dialog. However, be warned that the names for the settings in the Authoring Connector are very close but not exactly the same as in the Web Author, as follows:

■ Mark page as special page: This setting is the same as Important Page in the Web Author; it is not selected by default.
■ Allow Web robots to crawl links: This is the same as Web Robots Can Crawl Links in the Web Author; it is selected by default.
■ Hide page from subscriber when published: This setting is the same as Hide When Published in the Web Author; it is not selected by default.
■ Allow Web robots to index this page: This is the same as Web Robots Can Index This Page in the Web Author; it is selected by default.

Custom properties are defined by template designers and will therefore be displayed by the same names and provide the same default values in both the Authoring Connector and the Web Author. The author can change the values of the custom properties. If no custom properties are specified in the template, the "Custom properties" table is not displayed in the Advanced Page Properties dialog.

The final step of the wizard allows the author to preview the page, and provides a summary of the configuration in the Page Submission dialog, as shown in Figure 7–17.

A Preview Page button displays the page in a default browser window; the author may be required to log on to the site.

The following items are presented in this screen for reviewing: page name; page display title, which is the same as the Display Name property in the Web Author; channel where the page will be published; and template on which the page will be based. To make changes to any of these items, click Back until you reach the dialog where you need to change the required information.

The Page Submission dialog also provides an indication of how the document content will be inserted into the resulting page: as inline text and images, as an attachment, or both. As we have already seen, these options are not controlled by the author; they are defined within the template by the type of the available placeholders.

Clicking Next in the Page Submission dialog submits the page for publication and then displays the final wizard dialog, shown in Figure 7–18. The final dialog allows you either to finish and go back to Word or to launch the Web Author. The status of the page displayed in the Web Author is WaitingforEditorApproval. In order for the page to become available on the live site, it should be approved for publishing by going through the workflow as configured on the channel where it is submitted.

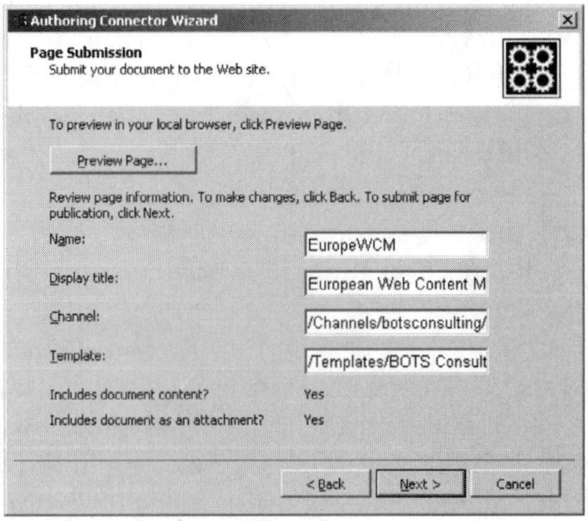

**Figure 7–17** Page Submission dialog

**Figure 7–18** Authoring Connector Wizard final dialog

As we have already mentioned, upon completion of the wizard two properties are added to the Word document: the CmsServerUrl property, which contains the URL pointing to the location of the OC.aspx file on the CMS server; and the CmsPostingGuid, which contains the GUID for the newly created posting (Figure 7–19).

It is worth mentioning that these two properties are available in the Word document regardless of where the document is located. You can

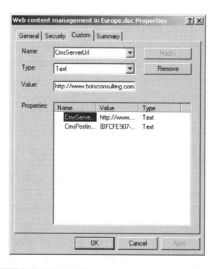

**Figure 7–19** Word XP document properties

copy the Word document or send it in an e-mail. Anyone editing the new copy of the document would be able to publish it to the proper location because of the CMS properties stored in the document.

## Updating a Page

The CmsServerUrl and the CmsPostingGuid properties allow you to update a page that was previously created using Word and the Authoring Connector. In this case, you are not required to specify the channel and template by selecting a publishing task or manually. Instead, the wizard goes straight to the Page Information screen, which provides the ability to modify the page properties.

To update an existing page, in the Word document select the content you'd like to publish, if required, and then choose the File > Send to MCMS > Update Same Page menu option. If you have not yet saved your work, you will be prompted to do so.

After the Authoring Connector Wizard starts, it points to the OC.aspx location as defined in the CmsServerUrl property of the document; click Next.

---

**NOTE:** Whether you submit an entire Word document or a selected part, the submitted content will overwrite all of the inline content in the target page that originates from Word. If there is a Word attachment in the target page, it will be changed to the new version of the document.

---

In the Page Information dialog, change the page properties if necessary, and click Next; in the Publishing Dates and Times dialog, change the publishing schedule if required, and then click Next. In the Page Submission screen, review the page information, and preview the page by clicking Page Preview if desired. Clicking Next submits the page and displays the Completing the Authoring Connector Wizard page, where you can go back to Word or start the Web Author.

---

**NOTE:** If your page includes dynamic navigation, in the page preview you may see two postings listed under the same display name: the original one that you are replacing and the new one that you are submitting. This is only a temporary issue: After you've submitted the page, the original one will be replaced with the new one. If you look at the submitted page in the Web Author, only the new page will be displayed in dynamic navigation.

---

## Replacing a Page

Replacing a page using the Authoring Connector allows you to change the content of any existing page, regardless of whether it was originally created from Word. In this case, the new page will be placed in the same channel and will be based on the same template as the original page. The wizard allows you to navigate to the page and then takes you straight to the Page Information dialog.

To replace an existing page, in the Word document select the content you'd like to publish, if required, and then choose the File > Send to MCMS > Replace Any Page menu option. If you have not yet saved your work, you are prompted to do so.

After the Authoring Connector Wizard starts, it points to the default OC.aspx location; you can change it if required and then click Next. The Authoring Connector Wizard displays the Page to Replace dialog, which allows you to select a page to be replaced (Figure 7–20). In the "Select page" area, expand Channels and navigate to the page to be replaced, or type the full path to the page in the "Web page path" box; then click Next.

---

**NOTE:** As before, the submitted content will overwrite all of the inline content in the target page that originates from Word. If there is a Word attachment in the target page, it will be changed to the new source document.

---

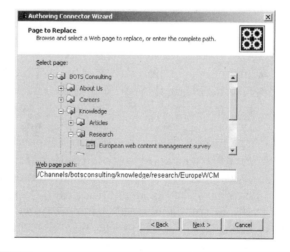

**Figure 7–20**  Page to Replace dialog

In the Page Information dialog, change the page properties if necessary—you are allowed to change the page name and other properties—then click Next. In the Publishing Dates and Times dialog, change the publishing schedule if required, and then click Next. In the Page Submission screen, review the page information and preview the page by clicking Page Preview if desired. As we have seen already, clicking Next submits the page and displays the Completing the Authoring Connector Wizard page, where you can go back to Word or start the Web Author.

---

**NOTE:** As before, if your page includes dynamic navigation, in the page preview you may see two postings listed under the same display name instead of the one you are submitting. However, in the Web Author, only the new page display name will be displayed in dynamic navigation.

---

## Preserving Word Formatting and Styles

Content authors who are used to rich formatting in Word XP may expect the formatting of the content to be preserved in the resulting CMS pages when it is displayed inline. Although it is usually possible to set up the properties of the placeholders in the page templates and/or cascading style sheets to preserve formatting, it has to be pointed out that not all the content on a CMS page will be displayed exactly as it is shown in Word; this may be caused by additional user-defined settings in the client browser options and/or differences in the implementation of cascading style sheets in different browsers.

In Word, there are two types of formatting styles, as follows:

- Inline styles are formatting options stored inline together with the text to which they are applied. For example, font and color applied to the selected section of the document text using Word formatting options represent an inline style. The formatting options that define the style are wrapped around the content and therefore can be represented in HTML.
- Document styles are named formatting options stored in the header of the document; they can be applied and changed globally. For example, Heading 2 represents a document style. Authors can select document styles from the Word styles and formatting toolbar or a side bar. A reference to a style encapsulates the

selected content. However, the style information in the document header is not carried over by the Authoring Connector; therefore, the intended formatting cannot be applied.

A template designer can allow inline styles by setting the Formatting property of an OfficeHtmlPlaceholder to Full Formatting. If other formatting is selected, inline styles may be partially or fully lost when the content is inserted in the placeholder.

Preserving document styles requires more work. A good technique for preserving the document styles is to have a corresponding external cascading style sheet attached to the template. This style sheet has to provide the style definitions for the named styles used within Word documents.

---

**NOTE:** It is also possible to define document styles in an embedded style sheet in the <head> section of a template. In this case, the styles will only be preserved within pages based on this particular template.

---

The name of the style is wrapped around the content published by the Authoring Connector; therefore, if the style is defined within a cascading style sheet, it will be applied within a page. This technique will work just fine for capturing document styles that are used widely within an organization—for example, within corporate templates. However, if an author defines new document styles or updates existing ones in an existing Word document, the change will not be reflected on the site until the cascading style sheet is updated to reflect the changes.

To import a style definition from Word XP, in Word apply a particular style to the selected content, and save the document as Web page, filtered. Open the resulting .htm file in Notepad, go to the <head> section of the document, and locate the <style> container and the relevant style definition. Copy the style definition to an external cascading style sheet. If an embedded style sheet is used, copy the definition into the <style> container in the <head> section of an appropriate tempalte.

In some cases, template designers may be required to disable both document and inline styles. To achieve this, the template designers must set the Formatting property of OfficeHtmlPlaceholder must be set to NoFormatting. In this scenario, all style and formatting information will be stripped from the document content.

# Setting Up Publishing Tasks

Publishing tasks displayed to authors in the Authoring Connector Wizard are defined in a publishing task list that is set up by a site administrator. The publishing task list is an XML file called PublishingTasks.xml, located on the target server. This enables all clients connecting to the server to view the same list of publishing tasks. In order for a specific task list to be displayed in the Authoring Connector Wizard, the author must have rights to the channel and the template that are specified in the PublishingTask.xml document on the server. The default location of the XML document is *<installation drive>*:\Program Files\Microsoft Content Management Server\Server\IIS_CMS\OfficeWizard\Publishing Tasks.xml.

---

**NOTE:** When multiple servers in a Web farm are used for authoring, copy the same PublishingTasks.xml file on all authoring servers to enforce consistency.

---

## Publishing Tasks Document Structure

The XML tasks list document is composed of a root element, <tasks>, and child elements, <task>. Each <task> element should contain four child elements, as follows:

- The <name> element contains the name of the publishing task; it must be less than 132 characters in length.
- The <description> element contains a short description of the publishing task; it must be less than 1,024 bytes in length.
- The <template>, or <templateGuid>, element identifies which template should be used by the Authoring Connector, by the full path or GUID, respectively.
- The <channel>, or <channelGuid>, element identifies in which channel the page should be created, by the full path or GUID, respectively

For example, the following task list defines two publishing tasks, for creating a research page and for creating an article.

```xml
<?xml version="1.0" ?>
<tasks>
  <task>
    <name>Create a new research page</name>
    <description>
      This task creates a new research page
    </description>
    <template>/Templates/BOTS Consulting/Research</template>
    <channel>/Channels/botsconsulting/knowledge/research/</channel>
  </task>
  <task>
    <name>Create a new article</name>
    <description>This task creates a new article</description>
    <templateGuid>
      {ECF2A30B-7FBD-4771-B311-6C9551B2C2CF}
    </templateGuid>
    <channelGuid>
      {B5626CE8-CFA2-4578-86B8-7C2A2649A6FA}
    </channelGuid>
  </task>
</tasks>
```

The schema for the PublishingTasks.xml document is contained in the schema file PublishingTasks.xsd, located by default within the same folder. Each task has to follow the name, description, template, and channel order. The <name> and <description> elements can contain HTML escape markup. However, you need to make sure that all characters are properly escaped; otherwise, the XML document will not be valid.

If any of the required elements are not defined or are defined wrongly, an error will occur and no tasks will be shown in the publishing task list. For example, if the <channel> element refers to a channel that does not exist, the publishing task will not be displayed to the authors.

---

**NOTE:** Searches by GUIDs are faster and require fewer resources on the server. Therefore, it is more efficient from a performance point of view to provide ChannelGUID and TemplateGUID values, rather than the virtual path locations of the channel and the template. Using GUIDs to define channels and templates also ensures that any naming changes to the site do not require modifications to the task list.

---

When you create publishing tasks, ensure that the task names and descriptions clearly define the tasks for the nontechnical users.

## Creating and Modifying the Publishing Tasks

The task list is an XML file that can be created or modified in Notepad or any XML editor. Also, you can download a GUI tool called the Publishing Task Editor from www.microsoft.com. The Task Editor is shown in Figure 7–21; it enables easier creation and modification of the PublishingTasks.xml file.

There are two files that are required for the Task Editor: TaskEditor App.exe and tasklist.xsd. These two files must be located in the same directory. Also, CMS 2002 must be installed on the same computer; otherwise, the Task Editor will not function properly.

---

**NOTE:** The tasklist.xsd file, which is in the same directory as the Task Editor, is not exactly the same as PublishingTasks.xsd. However, both files adhere to the same standards for specified tasks.

---

The Task Editor provides the following functionality:

- Creating, copying, and deleting tasks.
- Selecting a valid channel and template by a path or GUIDs. When the Channel or the Template browse button is clicked in the Task Editor, either the Select a Channel or the Select a Template window appears, which allows navigating to the channel or template, and selecting the format: Path or GUID. For example,

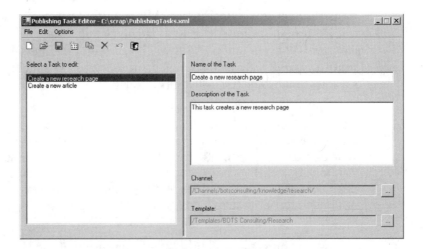

**Figure 7–21** Publishing Task Editor

the Select a Channel window shown in Figure 7–22 has an Articles channel selected, which is specified by GUID.

■ Checking for duplicate task names that are not allowed.

■ Checking length restrictions for elements' values.

■ Validating and saving the XML document. A task file cannot be saved in the Task Editor unless each of the tasks is valid and the generated file is valid.

---

**NOTE:** When you save the file in the Task Editor, the .xml extension is not automatically added; you need to type it in manually.

---

The location of the PublishingTask.xml and PublishingTask.xsd documents can by modified by changing the web.config file in the Authoring Connector Web application. By default, they are located in the same directory as OC.aspx. This directory is mapped to the virtual directory /MCMS/CMS/OfficeWizard. However, for security reasons, it is recommended that you put these two files outside a virtual directory and specify their absolute path in the web.config file. System administrators may also choose to change the names of the files.

The default location of the Authoring Connector's web.config file is *<installation drive>*:\Program Files\Microsoft Content Management Server\Server\IIS_CMS\OfficeWizard. The <appSettings> section within the <configuration> container defines the location and name of the publishing tasks and schema files. If this section is not present, the

**Figure 7–22**  Select a Channel window in the Publishing Task Editor

default location is used. However, the settings can be easily modified; for example:

```
<appSettings>
  <add key="Publishing Tasks XML File Path"
   value="C:\secure\tasks.xml" />
  <add key="Publishing Tasks Schema File Path"
   value="C:\secure\tasks.xsd" />
</appSettings>
```

**NOTE:** The value for the key attribute must be specified exactly as in the preceding code.

## Restricting Authors to Predefined Publishing Tasks

By default, the Authoring Connector allows authors to manually select the template on which the page will be based and the channel into which the page will be posted. However, this manual override feature can be disabled, effectively restricting authors to use of the predefined tasks in the publishing task list.

To disable the manual override option in the Authoring Connector Wizard, you need to make changes to the OC.aspx file.

**NOTE:** The modifications to the OC.aspx file are not supported by Microsoft, which means that changes to the OC.aspx file may be lost when you are applying service packs, hotfixes, or upgrades. Therefore, back up the original and modified version of the OC.aspx file before proceeding with any CMS update. After the update has been completed, you may be able to reapply your modifications in the appropriate sections.

Using Visual Studio .NET or a text editor, open the *<installation drive>*:\Program Files\Microsoft Content Management Server\Server\ IIS_CMS\OfficeWizard\OC.aspx file, and then locate and modify line 145 by adding the keyword `disabled`, so that it reads as follows:

```
<td style="PADDING-TOP: 12px"><asp:checkbox id="chkManualEntry"
    disabled accessKey="M" runat="server" AutoPostBack="True"
    Text="<u>M</u>anual entry of channel and template">
    </asp:checkbox></td>
```

**Figure 7–23** Manual override disabled

After you make this change, the "Manual entry of channel and template" check box in the Authoring Connector Wizard will be disabled, as shown in Figure 7–23.

## Summary

In this chapter, we looked into the architecture, functionality, and usage of the CMS Authoring Connector component. The Authoring Connector enables content creators to create and modify CMS pages without leaving Word XP. After the new page has been created or modified, in order for it to be available on the live site, it has to be approved by the editors and moderators assigned to the channel to which the page has been published.

This chapter completes the Content Authoring and Publishing part of the book. In the next part, we will look into creating and developing a CMS-based Web site. We will start with creating an infrastructure for a new CMS site.

# PART III

# Creating Site Framework

# CHAPTER 8

# Creating a New CMS Site

## Overview

During CMS installation, one of the IIS virtual sites is selected to become a CMS-enabled site. However, after the installation, it is often necessary to create another CMS site on the same machine.

There are several configuration issues to consider before you start creating a new site:

- A CMS site is a Web application. It can be installed at the root of a virtual IIS site and accessed using the root URL http://<*CMS site*>, or it can be installed in a virtual directory off the root and accessed using the nonroot URL http://<*IIS site*>/<*CMS application*>.
- The site information is stored in the Content Repository, which is a SQL database. This database may be dedicated or may be shared between several sites within the same CMS installation.
- CMS allows multiple CMS sites to be hosted on the same machine; each is accessed using its own root URL http://<*CMS site*>. This configuration may require HTTP host headers to be enabled in IIS. All sites share the same database.

Based on the configuration decisions you make, there are different ways to set up a new CMS site.

- The new CMS site will use a dedicated IIS virtual site and a dedicated database; the site will be accessed using the root URL http://<*CMS site*>.

- The new CMS site will be installed as a Web application off the IIS site root; the site will be accessed using the nonroot URL http://*<IIS site>*/*<CMS application>*. If you want this site to be accessed using the root URL, you will have to write a redirection page or configure the redirection on IIS.
- The new CMS site will use a dedicated IIS virtual site but will share the database with other CMS sites; the site will be accessed using the root URL http://*<CMS site>*.
- The new CMS site will share both the IIS virtual site and the database with other CMS sites; the site will be accessed using the root URL http://*<CMS site>*; HTTP host headers identification will be enabled on the IIS site.

In this chapter, we will look into all these configurations. To start with, we will focus on creating a new CMS site with its own dedicated database. In this scenario, a CMS site may have its own dedicated IIS site and be installed at the root of this site, or it may be installed as an off-root Web application; we will look into both possibilities. We will then discuss the installations that allow multiple CMS sites to share resources such as the IIS sites and the database. Let's start.

There are several tasks involved in creating a new CMS site, as follows:

- Creating and configuring a new empty SQL database to be used by CMS
- Setting up an IIS virtual site
- Running the CMS Database Configuration Application (DCA) to point the CMS server to a new database and to populate the database with the CMS schema
- Running the CMS Server Configuration Application (SCA) to configure the CMS server
- Adding virtual directories manually

As far as the sequence of tasks is concerned, the first two are interchangeable; the others need to be performed in sequence. The last task is only required for Web sites with authoring enabled.

# Creating and Configuring a New Database

CMS stores all site content and objects in a dedicated SQL Server 2000 database. Our first task is to create an empty database and configure the CMS system account permissions for this database.

## Creating an Empty Database

To create a database, start SQL Server Enterprise Manager (Start > Programs > Microsoft SQL Server > Enterprise Manager); expand the Microsoft SQL Servers node and navigate to the server where you'd like the database to be created; right-click Databases and select New Database (Figure 8–1). In the Database Properties dialog box, type the name for your new database—for example, MCMS (Figure 8–2). You can use any alphanumeric characters in the database name; just make sure that they are not all numbers. You cannot use any special characters, with the exception of the underscore character. After you've typed the database name, click OK. The empty database is created; it is shown in the Enterprise Manager under the Databases node.

## CMS System Account Permissions on the Database

The CMS server performs database transactions at runtime as well as at design time. The CMS server runs under the CMS system account that is specified during the CMS installation. It is recommended that you use Windows authentication on the SQL server that hosts the CMS database. In order to be able to read and write to the database, the CMS system account must have db_datareader and db_datawriter permissions

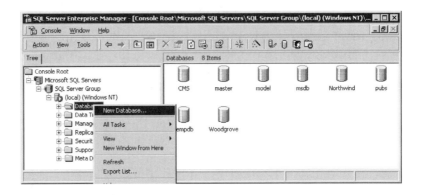

**Figure 8–1** Databases pane

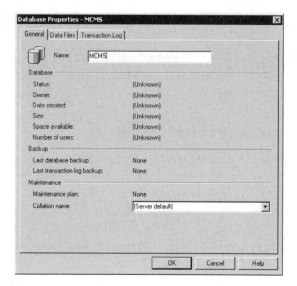

**Figure 8–2** Database Properties dialog box

on the database. If you need to import data for deployment, then the CMS system account also requires db_ddladmin rights.

---

**NOTE:** When a new CMS site is configured, the system account does not require db_ddladmin rights on the CMS database. However, to avoid an error message in DCA later on, you can assign db_ddladmin rights on the CMS database to the system account. You can remove db_ddladmin rights after the CMS site has been created.

---

If SQL Server authentication is used, then the specified SQL Server account is used for all CMS database operations. This account needs appropriate permissions on the CMS database, as follows: db_datareader, db_datawriter, and db_ddladmin. The db_ddladmin permission is only required for importing data.

To grant permissions on the CMS database to the system account, in SQL Server Enterprise Manager, navigate to the server where you've created the CMS database. Expand the Security node and click Logins. In the Logins pane, select the CMS system account, right-click the account, and select Properties (Figure 8–3).

In the SQL Server Login Properties dialog box, select the Database Access tab; in the Permit pane select the CMS database by clicking the check box in the Permit column. After you've selected the database,

**Figure 8–3** Logins pane

the CMS system account name appears in the User column, and a list of roles for this user appears in the Permit in Database Role pane. In the Permit in Database Role list, scroll down and select db_datareader, db_datawriter, and db_ddladmin if required, as shown in Figure 8–4; then click OK.

We have created and configured the database to be used for CMS. You can now exit SQL Server Enterprise Manager.

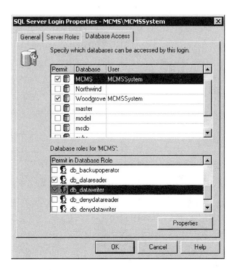

**Figure 8–4** CMS system account rights

# Creating a New Virtual Web Site

Our next task is to create a new IIS virtual Web site that will serve as an entry point to the CMS server. This Web site will get requests from the users and send back responses with dynamically generated CMS pages.

Before you start to create a Web site, decide how you are going to uniquely identify your new site. Each Web site is identified by a combination of three parameters: an IP address, a TCP port number, and a HTTP host header name. The default for a TCP port number is 80; host headers are not enabled by default. For example, in a staging environment you may have several Web sites on a computer with a single IP address and different port numbers (i.e., http://<*server IP address*>:80 and http://<*server IP Address*>:8080). However, this is not a good option in a production environment, because URLs may appear confusing and difficult to memorize for your users. In a production environment, you can either assign different IP addresses to different virtual Web sites running on the same machine, or use a single IP address and identify the sites by using HTTP host headers. In any case, make sure you have a registered DNS name and the IP address for the site.

---

**NOTE:** Refer to Appendix A for reference information on HTTP and the use of HTTP host headers.

---

We need to start with creating a physical directory that will be used as a home directory for the new Web site—for example, C:/CMSsite. We will now create a virtual Web site that uses this directory as its home directory.

To create a new Web site, open the Internet Information Services snap-in (on Windows 2000 select Start > Programs > Administrative Tools > Internet Services Manager, or Start > Programs > Administrative Tools > Computer Management, and expand Services and Applications; on Windows 2003 select Start > Administrative Tools > Internet Information Services (IIS) Manager, or Start > right-click My Computer > Manage, and expand Services and Applications). The next step is slightly different depending on whether you are running Windows 2000 with IIS 5, or Windows 2003 with IIS 6. In IIS 5, navigate to your server, right-click it, select New, and then select Web Site. In IIS 6, expand your server, right-click the Web Sites folder, select New, and then select Web Site. On both platforms, the Web Site Creation Wizard Welcome page appears; click Next. On the Web Site Description page, type a description for the Web site in the Description box—for example, BOTS CMS site—and click Next.

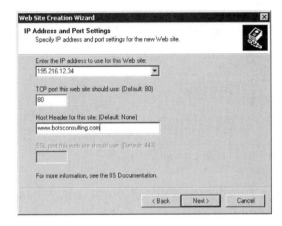

**Figure 8–5** IP address and port settings

On the IP Address and Port Settings page, select the IP address that your site will use; then specify the TCP port number if you are using other than 80. If you are using an HTTP host header, which is the site DNS name, type it in (Figure 8–5).

For example, the new site shown in Figure 8–5 will share an IP address and TCP port number with other sites installed on the same IIS box, but will use the host header name www.botsconsulting.com to be uniquely identified by IIS.

On the Web Site Home Directory page, click Browse and navigate to the directory you'd like to use as the site home directory—for example, C:/CMSsite (as shown in Figure 8–6). Click Next. On the Web

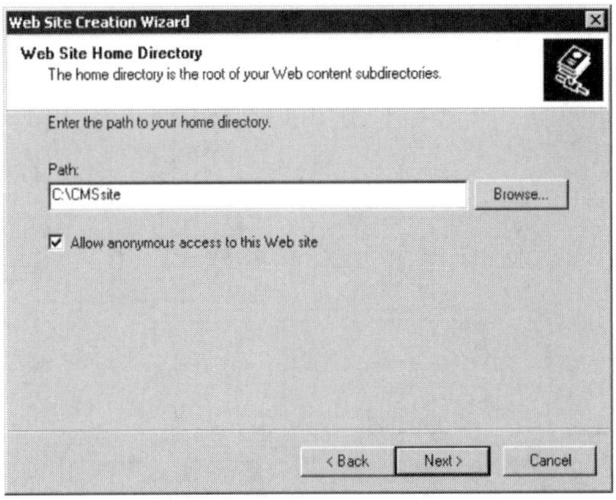

**Figure 8–6** Home directory

**Figure 8–7** New virtual Web site

Site Access Permissions page, accept the defaults and click Next, then click Finish.

The virtual Web site has been created and is shown in the IIS snap-in; it is an empty site with no content (Figure 8–7). Don't close the IIS snap-in yet; we will need it later on.

If you are creating a CMS site that will run from the off-root virtual directory, there are several additional steps you need to perform. First, create the directory on the hard disk that will be a home directory for a Web application that will contain your CMS site. Second, using the IIS snap-in, configure the virtual directory on the existing IIS site to point to this physical directory (right-click the IIS site and select New > Virtual Directory; click Next in the Virtual Directory Creation Wizard Welcome dialog; in the Virtual Directory Alias dialog type the name for your CMS site and click Next; in the Web Site Content Directory dialog, browse to the physical directory you created in the first step and click Next; in the Access Permissions dialog, accept the defaults and click Next; click Finish). Make sure the virtual directory is configured as a Web application starting point; it will be shown in the IIS snap-in. To configure the virtual directory as an application starting point, right-click the directory, select Properties, select the Virtual Directory tab, and in the Application Setting

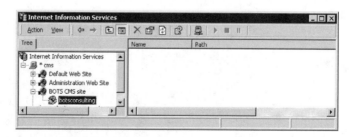

**Figure 8–8** New Web application

section click Create. For example, Figure 8–8 shows the /botsconsulting Web application on the www.botsconsulting.com virtual Web site running on IIS 5.

# Using the Database Configuration Application

Our next task is to configure the CMS server to use the new database. This is done by using the CMS Database Configuration Application. The DCA is a local application; it runs on the machine where the CMS server is installed.

**NOTE:** A user who runs the DCA must have db_owner permissions on the CMS database.

The DCA executable file is called NRDCApplication.exe and is located in the *<installation drive>*/Program Files/Microsoft Content Management Server/Server/bin folder. You can start DCA by using the shortcut Start > Programs > Microsoft Content Management Server > Database Configuration Application.

After you've launched the DCA, click Next in the Welcome screen. In order to perform configuration, the DCA needs to stop the IIS. It displays a "Stop service?" dialog box asking you to confirm the IIS stop (Figure 8–9). If you click No, the DCA will display a Confirm Exit dialog box (Figure 8–10). If you choose No, the DCA will go back to the Welcome screen; if you choose Yes, the DCA will exit.

To carry on with the configuration, select Yes in the "Stop service?" dialog box, shown in Figure 8–9. After the IIS has been stopped, a Select MCMS Database screen is displayed (Figure 8–11). The screen shows the current CMS database in the format *<SQL server name>.<database name>*. To change the database, click Select Database; in the SQL Server Login dialog box, click Options to expand the box, then select the

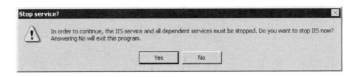

**Figure 8–9** DCA "Stop service?" dialog

**Figure 8–10** DCA Confirm Exit dialog

name of the SQL server hosting the database from the Server drop-down list and the name of the CMS database from the Database drop-down list (Figure 8–12); make sure the correct login ID is listed for the CMS system account; click OK.

After you've clicked OK in the Select MCMS Database screen, the DCA checks whether the CMS system account has db_datareader, db_datawriter, and db_ddladmin rights on the database. If any of these rights are missing, it displays an "error verifying rights" message (Figure 8–13). You can safely OK this message and carry on with the DCA since it does not use the CMS system account for database configuration. Instead, it uses the currently logged-on user account to populate the CMS database. This account must have db_owner rights on the database. However, if you dismiss the "verifying rights" error at this stage, make sure you check that the CMS system account has the appropriate rights on the CMS database; otherwise, your CMS server will not function properly.

After the database has been selected, the DCA checks whether the selected database has already been populated with the CMS schema. If

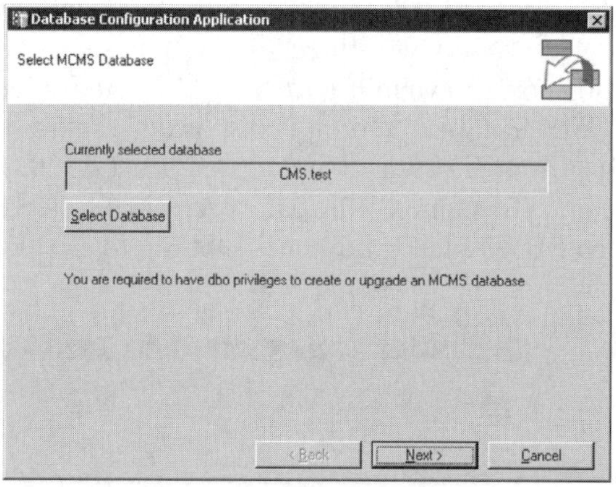

**Figure 8–11** DCA Select MCMS Database screen

**Figure 8–12** DCA SQL Server Login dialog box

it hasn't, the DCA displays the Empty Database dialog box, shown in Figure 8–14. Click OK to confirm the installation of the schema into the database. The Database Population screen is displayed (Figure 8–15); click Next to populate the database with the CMS schema.

**NOTE:** The DCA can be used to switch between CMS databases. For example, in a development environment, you may have two different CMS sites you are working on. Each may have its own database. A CMS server can only work with one database at a time; to switch to another CMS database, you can use the DCA. If the selected database already has the CMS schema installed, the Use Existing Database dialog box (Figure 8–16) is displayed instead of the Empty Database dialog.

**Figure 8–13** DCA "Error verifying rights" message

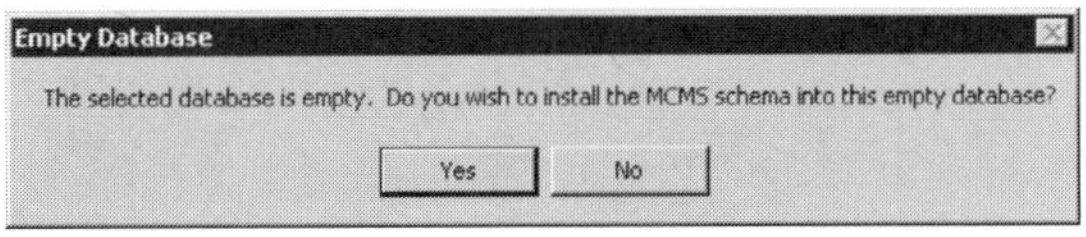

**Figure 8–14** DCA Empty Database dialog

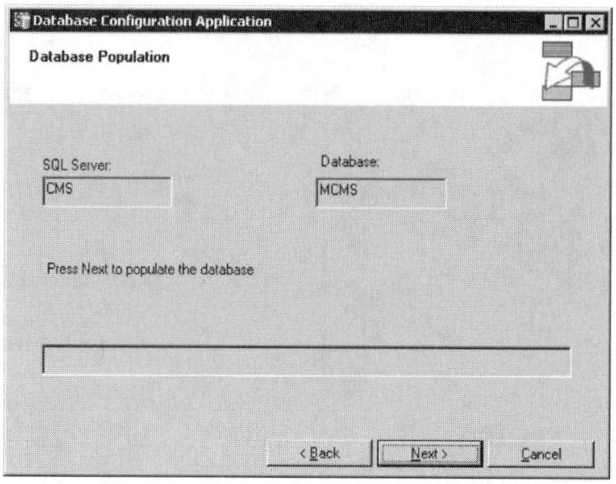

**Figure 8–15** DCA Database Population screen

The next step in the installation is to specify the initial CMS administrator account (Figure 8–17). This account is very important: It is the only account that can log in to the Site Manager and assign CMS user rights to other user accounts after the site has been created. Even the system administrator on the computer running CMS is not allowed to access the Site Manager without being explicitly assigned rights to do so. Additional CMS administrators can be added by the initial administrator using the Site Manager. CMS user rights are discussed in detail in Chapter 17.

**NOTE:** If you are using the DCA to switch to an existing CMS database, then the DCA allows you to create additional CMS administrators (Figure 8–18).

Specify the CMS administrator credentials; the account must be in the format *<domain name>/<user name>*. You need to type it in; there is no browsing available. For example, the CMS administrator account for our site is MCMS/MCMSadministrator (Figure 8–17).

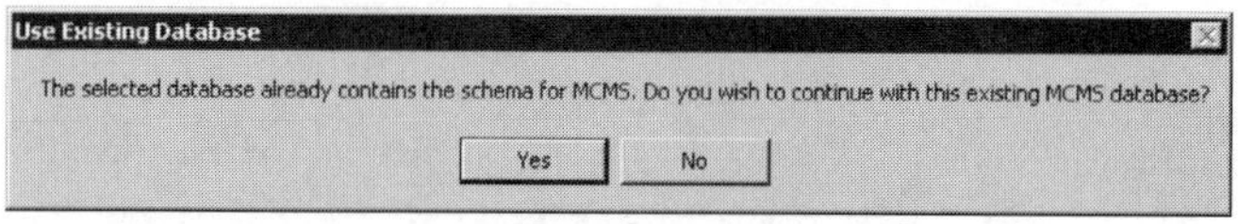

**Figure 8–16** DCA Use Existing Database dialog

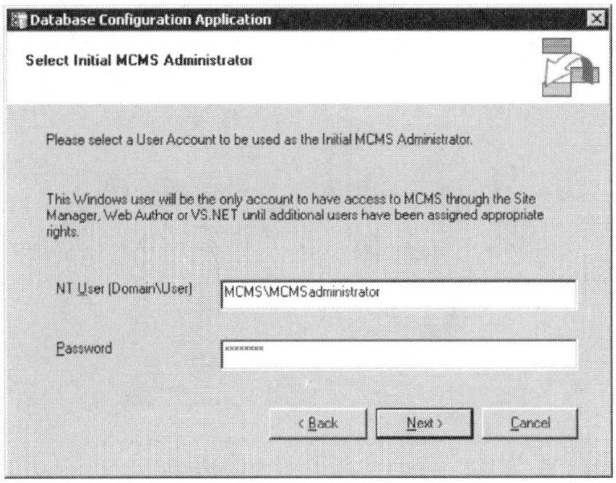

**Figure 8–17** DCA Select Initial Administrator screen

That's all the information required by the DCA. Before finishing, it asks you to confirm the start of SQL Server Agent for background processing jobs (Figure 8–19). The background job configured at this stage is the CMS database purging job called BGP-*<database name>*. You can see it in SQL Server Enterprise Manager if you open *<SQL server>* > Management > SQL Agent > Jobs and then double-click the job name in the right-hand pane (Figure 8–20). Note that the owner of this job is the user account that is currently running the DCA. You can change the job ownership if required.

Click OK in the dialog box to start the SQL Server Agent service. If for any reason you are not willing to let DCA attempt to start the SQL

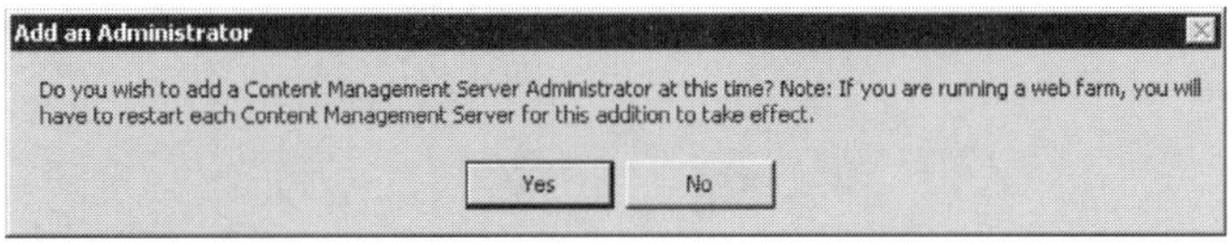

**Figure 8–18** DCA add administrator account dialog

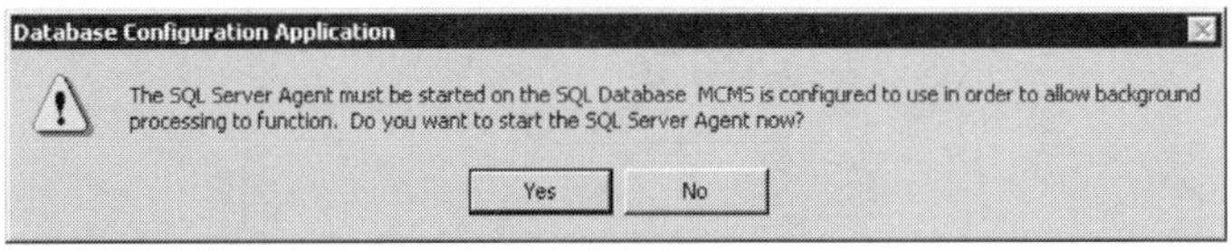

**Figure 8–19** DCA SQL Server Agent dialog

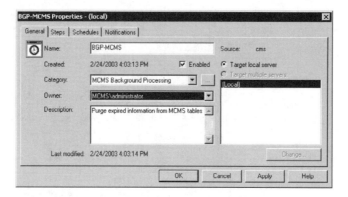

**Figure 8–20** Database purging job properties

Server Agent service, you don't have to. However, you will need to start it manually at a later stage; otherwise, the purging job will not run and the database can grow unnecessarily large, affecting the performance of your CMS site. Regardless of the choice you make, the DCA displays the completion screen (Figure 8–21). If you are ready to proceed to configuring your CMS server using the Server Configuration Application, just click Finish; if you are going to configure the server later, clear the SCA check box and click Finish.

When you click Finish, the DCA restarts the IIS. If it encounters problems with starting IIS sites, it displays the warning shown in Figure 8–22. Click OK, then go to the IIS snap-in, and make sure all IIS

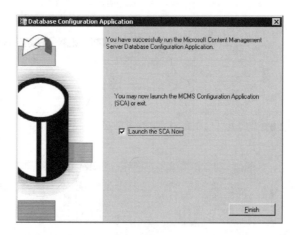

**Figure 8–21** DCA final screen

**Figure 8–22**  Unable to start Web service message

Web sites are up and running. The Web site where the SCA is installed is very often the culprit; you need to start it manually (right-click the site and select Start). However, sometimes all Web sites are up and running, although the warning is still displayed by the DCA. Don't close the IIS snap-in yet; we will use it in the next step.

# Configuring an IIS Site as a CMS-Enabled Site

The next task is to configure the virtual IIS site as a CMS site using the Server Configuration Application. The SCA is a Web-based configuration utility. There are many CMS settings that can be set up using the SCA; these are discussed in granular detail in Chapter 18, Using the Server Configuration Application. We are going to concentrate on how to configure the IIS virtual Web site to become a CMS Web entry point. When an IIS site is configured as a CMS entry point, CMS checks all requests to the site in order to determine whether they are CMS requests. It then processes the CMS requests to generate content; non-CMS requests are processed by IIS as usual.

By default, the SCA is launched automatically after the DCA has completed (Figure 8–23); however, if you cleared the SCA launch check box in the DCA, you can start it manually later on. Locally, the SCA can be started using the Start menu shortcut (Start > Programs > Microsoft Content Management Server > Server Configuration Application); remotely, you can start it from the browser using http://<*SCA installation Web site*>/NRConfig. The SCA screen consists of two panes: The top pane displays information about the current installation that cannot be changed; the bottom pane presents six tabs that contain configuration options.

Select the Web tab (Figure 8–24); the table displayed shows information about all IIS virtual Web sites, such as IP address, TCP port, and host header name if it is set up. The last column is labeled "MCMS?". This column shows whether the site is configured as a CMS site. For

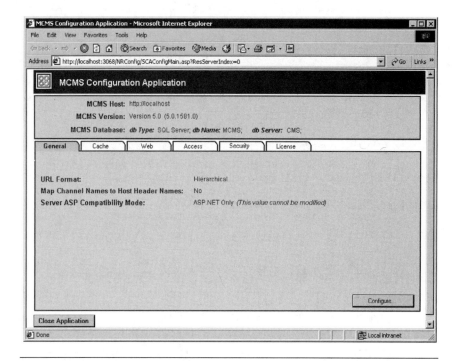

**Figure 8–23** SCA default screen

example, we can see from Figure 8–24 that the BOTS CMS site that we created earlier is shown as not CMS-enabled. We know that this is a newly created IIS site that is currently empty. To set up the site as the CMS entry point, click Configure; in the Web Server Configuration screen, in the MCMS? drop-down list for your site, select Yes - Read Write (Figure 8–25). The SCA displays a dialog box informing you that it will stop and restart the affected Web site; click OK, and then OK again to close the Web Server Configuration screen.

**NOTE:** We are creating a new CMS site with authoring enabled. There-fore, we selected the Read Write setting for the site. After the site has been developed, if you want to disable authoring, you may recon-figure the site to be Read Only.

Go to the IIS snap-in and open the newly configured CMS site. Sev-eral new virtual directories and applications have been configured, as shown in Figure 8–26, for the CMS site on IIS 5. These directories pro-vide CMS functionality as well as cache for the CMS-generated pages.

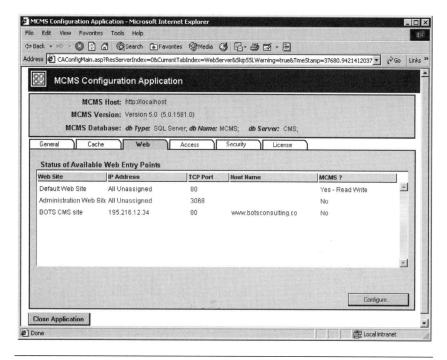

**Figure 8–24**  SCA Web tab

For example, /MCMS/CMS/WebAuthor contains files for the Web Author console.

The next task is to enable guest access to your new site. All access in CMS is authenticated; to provide anonymous access for the site users,

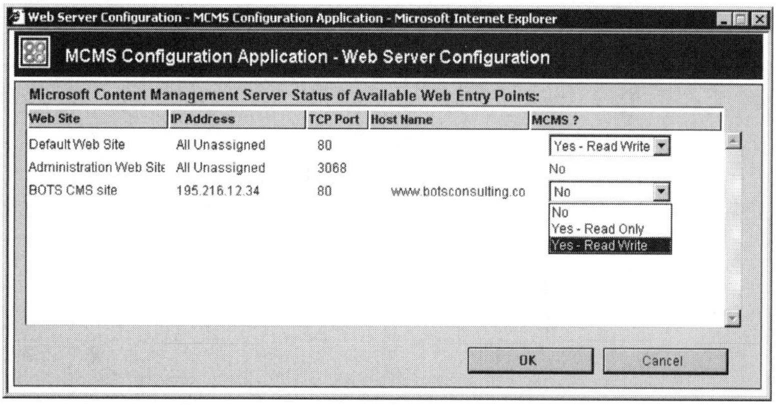

**Figure 8–25**  SCA Web Server Configuration screen

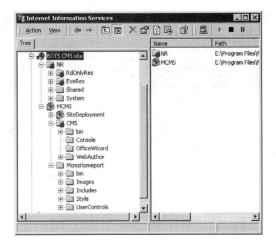

**Figure 8–26** CMS Web entry point structure, as configured by SCA

we need to set up a guest account. To specify the guest account, in the
SCA select the Security tab (Figure 8–27). You can see that there is no
guest account set up as yet. Click Configure; in the Security Configuration window in the Allow Guests On Site drop-down list, select Yes; then

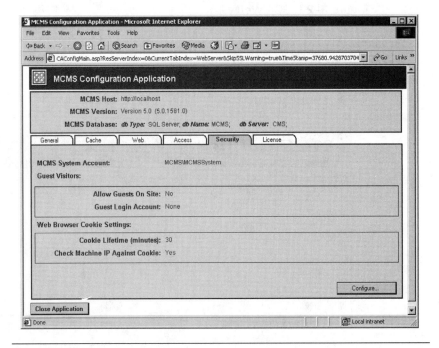

**Figure 8–27** SCA Security tab

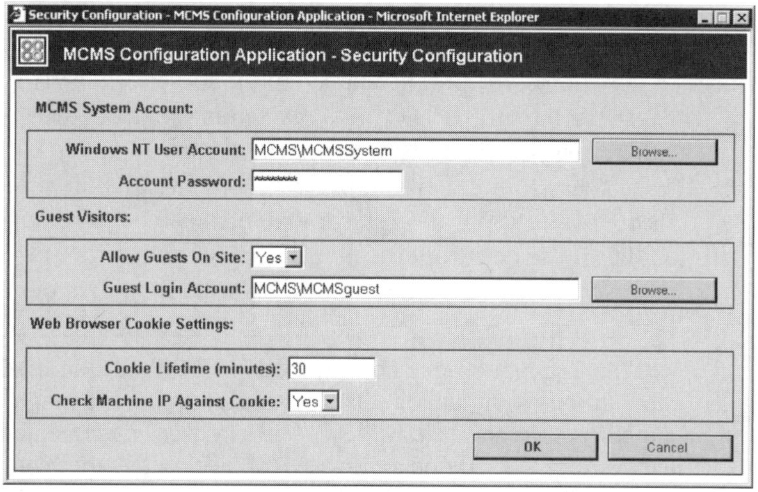

**Figure 8–28** SCA Security Configuration window

either type in the guest account user name in the format *<domain name>/<user name>* (Figure 8–28) or browse to it; then click OK. Notice that the guest login account is now displayed in the Security tab.

# Adding Virtual Directories Manually

There are two virtual directories called CMS and webctrl_client that we need to manually add to our CMS Web site. These directories are required to support Web-based authoring and site development.

The CMS virtual directory must be located inside the Web application that will contain our CMS site. It should point to the physical directory *<CMS installation drive>*/Program Files/Microsoft Content Management Server/Server/IIS_CMS. If you are creating a CMS site installed at the root of the IIS site, then the full name of this virtual directory will be *<CMS site>*/CMS; if you are installing a CMS site as a Web application off root, then it will be *<IIS site>/<CMS application>*/CMS.

To create a CMS virtual directory, in the IIS snap-in right-click the Web site (or the virtual directory containing the site if CMS is installed as an off-root Web application), select New > Virtual Directory and click Next in the Virtual Directory Creation Wizard Welcome screen; type

CMS as the virtual directory alias and click Next; in the Web Site Content Directory screen navigate to *<CMS installation drive>*/Program Files/Microsoft Content Management Server/Server/IIS_CMS and click Next; in the Access Permissions screen select Execute permission in addition to Read and Run Scripts, and click Next; click Finish. After the wizard has completed, in IIS 5 the /CMS virtual directory is configured as a separate application starting point; we need to remove it. Right-click CMS and select Properties; in the Virtual Directory tab in the Application Settings area, click Remove (Figure 8–29); then click OK.

---

**NOTE:** The last step is not required in IIS 6, because IIS 6 does not configure new virtual directories as application starting points by default; therefore, the /CMS virtual directory has been configured as a directory, not an application, which is exactly what we need.

---

The /webctrl_client virtual directory should be located at the root of the IIS site, configured as a CMS Web entry point. It should point to *<IIS installation drive>*/Inetpub/wwwroot/webctrl_client.

To create the /webctrl_client virtual directory, repeat the preceding process, but type webctrl_client as the virtual directory alias, point to *<IIS installation drive>*/Inetpub/wwwroot/webctrl_client, and accept the default permissions. If required, remove the application starting point following the previous instructions.

**Figure 8–29** CMS properties

**Figure 8–30** CMS site structure

The site structure for the new CMS site installed at the root of the IIS site is shown in Figure 8–30; the site structure for the new CMS site installed as the off-root Web application is shown in Figure 8–31 (both figures show the site running on IIS 5).

**Figure 8–31** CMS Web application structure

## Accessing the CMS Site by a Root URL

When the CMS site is installed, you may want to access it by a root URL that contains only the server DNS (or WINS) name (i.e., http://<*CMS site*>). There are additional configuration steps required to make this happen. These steps are different depending on whether your site is installed at the root of the IIS site or off root.

If your new CMS site is at the root of the IIS site, you are likely to expect that your default CMS page will be returned to the user as a result of accessing the URL http://<*CMS site DNS name*>. However, this is not the case; regardless of the IIS default document configuration, to return the default home page, the URL has to specify the name of the default page explicitly (i.e., http://<*CMS site*>/<*home page*>). This is not very user friendly, so let's change it.

To enable the CMS site root requests, we need to configure CMS to enable the host headers mapping. CMS host headers mapping provides the ability to host several CMS Web sites, with different domain names, on the same CMS server. It also enables the CMS site root requests. You don't have to host multiple sites to use the host headers mapping; it can be used in order to enable CMS site root requests for a single site.

---

**NOTE:** CMS host headers mapping doesn't necessarily require HTTP host header identification to be enabled on your IIS site. CMS host headers mapping is implemented as an ISAPI filter. Regardless of your IIS virtual site configuration, you may use the host headers mapping for the CMS site. We will look into CMS host headers mapping in detail in Chapter 18.

---

To configure CMS host headers mapping, perform the following two steps:

■ Using the SCA, enable CMS to map host headers into channel names. To do that, select the General tab (Figure 8–23); click Configure; in the General Configuration window in the Map Channel Names to Host Header Names drop-down list, select Yes (Figure 8–32); click OK.

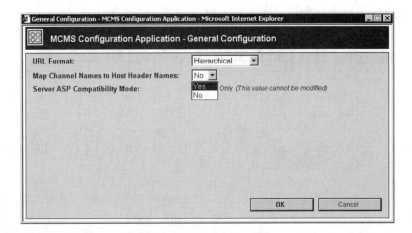

**Figure 8–32** SCA General Configuration window

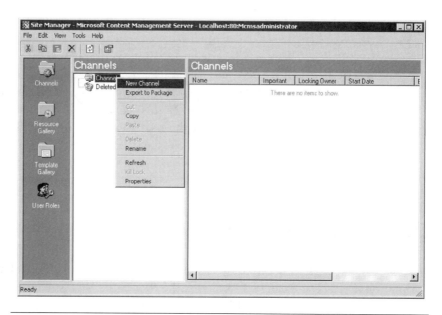

**Figure 8–33** Creating a new top-level channel in the Site Manager

■ Using the Site Manager, create a top-level channel with the same
name as the DNS name of the site (which is the value of the host
header). The default page in this channel will be sent back as a
response to the CMS site root request. To do that, open the Site
Manager (Start > Programs > Microsoft Content Management
Server > Site Manager); type in the initial CMS administrator credentials; right-click the Channels node in the middle pane (Figure 8–33) and select New Channel. In the Name box, type the
DNS name for your CMS site (for example, www.botsconsult-
ing.com), and click OK (Figure 8–34). Close the Site Manager.

**NOTE:** We will look into creating channels in the Site Manager for the
new CMS site in Chapter 9. Refer to Chapter 16 for a detailed discussion about working with channels.

**Figure 8–34** Top-level channel that is mapped to the HTTP host header

We have configured your new CMS site to return the home page to the root URL.

If your new CMS site is an off-root Web application, your default CMS page will be returned to the user as a result of accessing the URL http://<*IIS site*>/<*CMS application*>. This is expected behavior; however, you may want to change it. In this scenario, the request to the root is handled by IIS. If you want the user to access your CMS site by the root URL http://<*IIS site*>, you will have to provide redirection from the root to /<*CMS application*>.

# Creating a CMS Site with Shared Resources

So far we have focused on creating a new CMS site that has its own database. The site can be installed at the root of the Web site or as an off-root Web application. In this configuration, one IP address and one registered DNS name are required.

However, it is sometimes necessary to share the resources, especially in a development environment. For example, you may need to have several independent CMS sites sharing the same IIS site and the same database; or your environment may already have multiple IIS sites that you would like to become CMS sites that share the same database; or it may be required in the development environment that CMS sites share the IIS site, with each site having its own database. All these solutions are possible. We will now determine the setup steps for each of these configurations.

## Multiple CMS Sites Sharing an IIS Site and a Database

You can have several CMS sites sharing the same database and the same IIS site. Each site is identified by an independent URL, http://<*CMS site*>. Each site has its own DNS name; the fact that they share a server infrastructure is transparent to the user. One IP address and several registered DNS names are required; all DNS names point to the same IP address mapped to the IIS site. All sites share the same CMS administrator and guest accounts; they also share the same administration tool and the user groups.

Assuming that the first CMS site is installed at the root of an IIS site and has already been configured using the steps we have discussed, to add a new CMS site, you need to do the following:

- Using the IIS snap-in, add a host header *<CMS site>* to the existing IIS site, as shown in Figure 8–35. (Right-click the IIS site; select Properties; in the Web Site tab in the Web Site Identification section, click Advanced; in the Advanced Multiple Web Site Configuration dialog in the Multiple Identities table, select your IIS site; in the Advanced Web Site Identification dialog, type in the host header name, which is the site DNS name.)
- Using the SCA, verify that Map Channel Names to Host Header Names is set to Yes.
- Using the Site Manager, create a new top-level channel called *<CMS Site>* (Figure 8–36).
- Using Windows Explorer, create a separate subdirectory in the home directory of the IIS site that you will use to store the files for your new site. This step is optional; however, it is highly advisable because it will allow you to separate the site files and avoid confusion in the future.

In this scenario, none of the sites can use Secure Sockets Layer (SSL) because HTTP host headers that identify different sites are included in the encrypted client request, and therefore the mapping cannot take place.

**NOTE:** Refer to Chapter 18 for a full explanation of how this setup works.

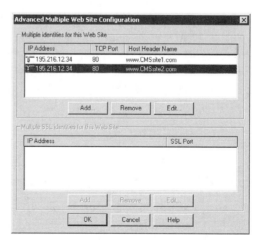

**Figure 8–35** Adding HTTP host headers

**Figure 8–36** Multiple top-level channels mapped to HTTP host headers

Sometimes, a developer working on several CMS projects on one machine may want to move from one project to another without reconfiguring the environment. This is usually achieved by creating several CMS Web applications on one IIS site. Each Web application is installed in the virtual directory off the IIS site root; they all share the same database. Each CMS project is identified by a URL pointing to the separate CMS Web application, http://<IIS site>/<CMS application>. The CMS site name is the name of a Web application hosted by the IIS Web site; each site is a separate Web application.

In this scenario, one IP address and one DNS name for the IIS site are required. You don't have to enable host headers on the IIS site, and the host headers mapping is disabled in CMS.

Assuming that the first CMS Web application is installed off an IIS site root, to create a new CMS site in this way, perform the following tasks:

- Create a directory on the hard disk that will be the home directory for a Web application that will contain your CMS site.
- Configure the virtual directory on the IIS site to point to this physical directory. Make sure it is configured as a Web application.
- Create the /CMS virtual directory under your Web application (i.e., /<CMS application>/CMS, which points to the physical directory <CMS installation drive>/Program Files/Microsoft Content Management Server/Server/IIS_CMS).
- Check that the /webctrl_client virtual directory exists at the root of the IIS Web site; if it doesn't, create it and point it to <IIS installation drive>/Inetpub/wwwroot/webctrl_client.

## Multiple CMS Sites Each Using an Independent Dedicated IIS site, Sharing a Database

You can have multiple CMS sites on the same machine that each use a dedicated IIS site while sharing the same database. Each CMS site is identified by an independent URL, http://<CMS site>. Each IIS site has its own DNS name; it may have its own IP address and port number, or they may be shared. If they are shared, then each site is identified by an HTTP host header. As before, the fact that the sites share a server infrastructure is transparent to the user. Because all sites share the database, the sites share the same CMS administrator and guest accounts; they also share the same administration tool and the user groups.

Assuming that the first CMS site is installed at the root of an IIS site and has already been created using the steps we have discussed, to add a new CMS site, you need to do the following:

- Using Windows Explorer, create a physical directory that will be the home directory for the new site.
- Using the IIS snap-in, create a new virtual IIS site; the home directory for this site should point to a physical directory you've created.
- Using the SCA, configure the new IIS site as a CMS Web entry point. Verify that Map Channel Names to Host Header Names is set to Yes.
- Using the IIS snap-in, add the /CMS and /webctrl_client virtual directories to your IIS site; they should point to the physical directories *<CMS installation drive>*/Program Files/Microsoft Content Management Server/Server/IIS_CMS and *<IIS installation drive>*/Inetpub/wwwroot/webctrl_client, respectively.
- Using the Site Manager, create a new top-level channel called *<CMS Site>*.

## Multiple CMS Sites Sharing an IIS Site, Each Using an Independent Dedicated Database

In a development environment, developers are often required to work on several independent CMS projects. Sometimes, they must have an independent dedicated database for each project. Usually, these requirements come from the organization's security policy.

You can have several independent CMS sites that share one IIS site, with each having its own database. Each site is identified by a URL pointing to the separate CMS Web application, http://*<IIS site>*/*<CMS application>*. The CMS site name is the name of a Web application hosted by the IIS Web site; each site is a separate Web application. CMS can only use one database at a time. Therefore, you will have to switch between the databases using the DCA.

One IP address and one DNS name for the IIS site are required. You don't need to enable HTTP host headers on the IIS site, and host headers mapping is disabled in CMS in this scenario.

To create a new CMS site in this way, perform the following tasks, using the detailed instructions provided at the beginning of the chapter:

- Create a new database and assign permissions to the CMS system account.
- Create the directory on the hard disk that will be the home directory for a Web application that will contain your CMS site. Configure the virtual directory on the IIS site to point to this physical directory. Make sure it is a Web application.
- Run the DCA to configure the database as the CMS database and to assign an initial CMS administrator account.
- Run the SCA to check that the IIS site is configured as a CMS Web entry point with read/write permissions, and to assign a CMS guest account.
- Create the /CMS virtual directory under your Web application (i.e., /<CMS application>/CMS, which points to the physical directory <CMS installation drive>/Program Files/Microsoft Content Management Server/Server/IIS_CMS).
- Check that the /webctrl_client virtual directory exists at the root of the IIS Web site; if it doesn't, create it and point it to <IIS installation drive>/Inetpub/wwwroot/webctrl_client.

## Summary

In this chapter, we looked into the options for creating a new CMS site. To start with, we focused on a CMS site with a dedicated database that can be installed at the root of an IIS site or as an off-root Web application. To create the site, we performed the following tasks: created a new database and configured MCMS system account permissions for this database; set up an IIS site; configured the new database as a CMS database and specified the CMS administrator account; configured the IIS site to become a CMS site, enabled guest access, and specified the CMS guest account; and added virtual directories manually. We also looked into enabling root URL access to our new CMS site so that users can access it by the URL http://<CMS site>.

We created a new empty site that is authoring-enabled. You can use the same process to create read-only sites after you have deployed your content.

We also defined the process for creating CMS sites that share resources, which can be an IIS site and/or a database. These configurations are particularly useful in a development environment.

In the next chapter, we will create the structure for a new site.

# CHAPTER 9

# Setting Up Site Structure

In the previous chapter, we created a new CMS site. In this chapter, we will set up a site structure for the new site, including channels, template galleries, and resource galleries, and then assign permissions for the guest users and the site developers. We will base the CMS site structure on the information architecture of the site.

---

**NOTE:** In this chapter, we will focus on setting up the structure for the new site. Chapters 16 and 17 provide a detailed discussion of all options available for configuration of the CMS publishing environment.

---

A well-planned information architecture is beneficial for both site users and site creators. If the information on the site is well organized, users can understand the site organization effortlessly, even when they access the site for the first time. Even if the content on your site is well written and accurate, your site needs logical organization of information. Users want to find information quickly and easily, and they do not like to get lost in chaotic cross-referenced Web sites. Poor information architectures make users confused and frustrated. Site creators also benefit from a logically organized site; for example, they don't have to change the existing content and site structure to place new content on the site. A CMS site is no exception and will benefit greatly from a well-thought-out information architecture.

## Navigation and Channels

Most Web sites use hierarchical organization schemes—all site content starts from the home page. Information hierarchies provide one of the best ways to organize complex bodies of information. Most users are familiar with the hierarchical approach and find it easy to understand the hierarchical site structure. Effectively employing a hierarchical structure requires a thorough analysis of how to best organize your content.

The information architecture defines your site's navigation. If your site is well organized, it makes it easier for users to navigate their way around it. Navigation is one of the most critical aspects of any Web site. Regardless of how much useful information a site provides and how good it looks, if it doesn't have a logical, easy-to-understand navigation scheme, it will confuse users and may chase them away.

Another critical aspect of any Web site is security. Security requirements must be taken into account when you design your site's architecture since you may require additional structures to deal with security issues.

There are several basic steps in organizing your information. First of all, you need to divide information into logical units; second, you establish a hierarchy of these units and structure the relationships between them. The logical units provide containers for your site's content. In a classic Web site, these containers are virtual directories that provide storage for Web pages; the information architecture is implemented using the virtual directories hierarchy. In a CMS Web site, pages are built dynamically from the data stored in the CMS database; they are not stored in the virtual directories but instead are organized using virtual storage spaces called channels. In CMS, the channel is the most granular object to which security can be applied. Therefore, the channels hierarchy implements the information architecture of your CMS Web site.

Let's consider the BOTS Consulting Web site. The information architecture for the site is shown in Figure 9–1. On the first level, there are five logical units that may contain other logical units and pages:

- About Us
- Offices
- Services
- Knowledge
- Careers

One of the first-level units—Offices—contains pages with information about local offices, while the other four top-level units—About Us, Services, Knowledge, and Careers—contain more logical units. Each of the logical units will become a channel in our site structure; the users will be able to navigate the site using URLs that reflect the hierarchical channels structure. For example, http://www.botsconsulting.com/services would take the user to the services channel, which represents the Services logical unit within our site.

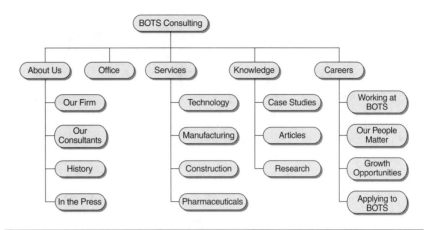

**Figure 9–1** Information architecture diagram for the sample site

Often, we need descriptive text as a link for the logical unit of information represented by a channel. Such text may be too long or otherwise unsuitable to be used as part of the URL. For example, we could use "Pharmaceuticals" for the link and http://www.botsconsulting.com/services/pharma as the URL. To this end, CMS provides two different name properties for a channel: the channel *name* is used as part of the URL, and the channel *display name* provides text for the link to this channel. In our example, "pharma" is the channel name, and "Pharmaceuticals" is the channel display name.

The channels structure that is mapped to the information architecture for the BOTS Consulting site is shown in Figure 9–2. You can see that the

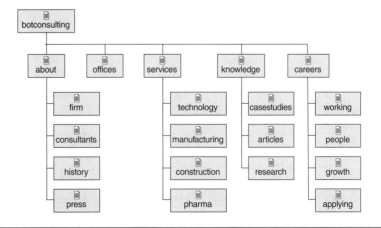

**Figure 9–2** Channels structure for the sample site

**Figure 9–3** Global navigation of the sample site

names of the channels are sometimes different from the names of the logical units in the information architecture diagram in Figure 9–1. The reason is that Figure 9–2 shows channels by their names that are used in the URLs; when a link to a channel is displayed on the site, it is presented using the channel's display name. Each page on the BOTS Consulting site will have a global navigation bar at the top of the page showing links to the first-level channels by their display names (Figure 9–3), and the drop-down menus will further show the structure of each channel.

---

**NOTE:** Creating dynamic navigation for a CMS site is discussed in detail in Chapter 14.

---

Creating channels is the first step in setting up the CMS site structure. To set up the site structure, we will use the CMS Site Manager.

## Using the Site Manager

The Site Manager is a Win32 application called NRclient.exe. It is located at *<installation drive>*:\Program Files\Microsoft Content Management Server\Client\. The Site Manager is launched using the shortcut from the Start menu (Start > Programs > Microsoft Content Management Server > Site Manager).

---

**NOTE:** The shortcut points the Site Manager application on the local machine to the login ASP page on the CMS server box, as follows: *<installation drive>*:\Program Files\Microsoft Content Management Server\Client\NRclient.exe http://*<CMS server name>*:*<port number>*/NR/System/ClientUI/login.asp.

---

The Site Manager can be installed on any computer running Windows 2000/XP. It uses HTTP as the protocol for connecting to the CMS server, so HTTP access is required between the computer where the Site Manager is installed and the CMS server. Although the Site Manager uses HTTP to connect to the CMS server, it doesn't have a browser interface; the HTTP access is implemented by a proxy.

**NOTE:** If the Site Manager cannot be launched on the client, check that the URL http://<*CMS server name*>:<*port number*>/NR/System/ClientUI/login.asp is accessible from the browser on the client machine.

The Site Manager is an administration tool; therefore, only authorized users have access to it. When you start the Site Manager, the authentication dialog is always displayed (Figure 9–4). There are two choices: "Log on as <*user name*>" provides the credentials of the currently logged-on user to the CMS server; "Log on as the following user" requires specifying the domain, user name, and password explicitly.

**NOTE:** The credentials of the currently logged-on Windows user are not sent to CMS automatically; you have to select the first option in the authentication dialog for this to happen.

When you start the Site Manager for the first time after creating a new CMS site, only the CMS administrator account specified in the DCA is authorized to access the Site Manager. As shown in Figure 9–4, you need to type in the CMS administrator credentials and click Start.

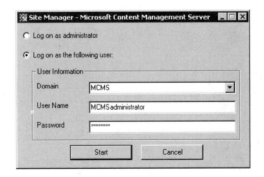

**Figure 9–4** Site Manager authentication dialog

---

**NOTE:** It is a good practice for the CMS administrator account to be different from the system administrator account.

---

The Site Manager window consists of three panes (Figure 9–5). The left pane provides the ability to switch between configuring channels, resource galleries, template galleries, and user roles. Depending on which icon you select in the left pane, the middle and the right pane will show the appropriate information.

When you select the Channels icon, the middle pane shows the channel structure, while the right pane shows the pages within a selected channel. When you start the Site Manager, the channels hierarchy is displayed by default. For each page within a channel, several properties are displayed in the right pane: the page name, whether the page has been flagged as Important, the locking owner, the start date, the expiry date, and the date and time when the page was last modified. When you select the Resource Gallery icon, the middle pane shows the resource galleries structure, while the right pane shows resources within a selected gallery. For each resource, the following properties are displayed: the resource name, the locking owner, the file size, the file MIME type, and when the file was last modified. When you select the Template Gallery icon, the middle pane shows the template galleries structure, while the right pane shows templates within a selected gallery. Each template has the following properties displayed: the template name, the locking owner, and when it was last modified.

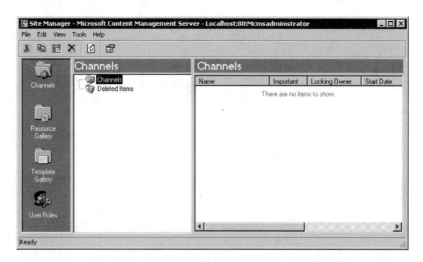

**Figure 9–5** Site Manager window showing a new empty site

Channels and template and resource galleries contain other data; within the CMS environment they are collectively known as *containers*.

The Site Manager interface uses the familiar Windows Explorer-type metaphor. We can cut, copy, paste, and delete objects displayed in the middle and the right panes in the usual way. The first four buttons on the Site Manager toolbar provide shortcuts for the Cut, Copy, Paste, and Delete operations.

The next button on the toolbar is the shortcut for Global Refresh. When we work on the site structure using the Site Manager, the objects and the settings we configure are stored in the CMS database. However, only user rights are updated in the database immediately. All other settings are first put in a cache. This cache resides on the client; it is implemented in the proxy. We actually change the settings on the cached objects; the database is not updated right away. Caching is used to increase Site Manager performance and to prevent the database objects from being locked. However, sometimes when multiple users are creating objects or changing the settings, the cached objects can become out of sync with the database. To synchronize the Site Manager cache with the CMS database, use the View > Global Refresh menu command or the Global Refresh button on the toolbar. You can individually synchronize each object by selecting Refresh from the object's shortcut menu.

**NOTE:** If, for any reason, an individual object is locked in the CMS database, to release the lock you can use the Kill Lock command from the object's shortcut menu. To release the lock for all objects in the CMS database, use the Tools > Kill Lock menu command. The Kill Lock command is available to users with administrative rights, such as CMS administrators and channel managers.

The last button on the toolbar is the Properties button; it displays the properties dialog for an object selected in the middle pane.

**NOTE:** All buttons on the toolbar are available when you select the Channels, Resource Gallery, or Template Gallery icons in the left pane. Only the Global Refresh button is available when you select User Roles.

All objects presented in the Site Manager are uniquely identified within the CMS database by their Globally Unique Identifier (GUID). Object names do not act as unique identifiers; therefore, we can have objects with the same names if required. For example, to provide a seamless consecutive update for a page, you can have two pages with the same name within the same channel. The expiration date of one version of the page should be set as the start date of the other version; both pages have to be approved using the Web Author console.

---

**NOTE:** CMS does not enforce uniqueness for the object names. We will discuss objects with the same names in more detail in Chapter 16.

---

When an object in the middle or the right pane is deleted, it is moved into the Deleted Items container displayed in the middle pane. The channels, resource galleries, and template galleries hierarchies have their own Deleted Items container, which acts as a Recycle Bin for the hierarchy; you can restore objects from there or clear the deleted items.

By default, when a channel is deleted, the Site Manager displays a warning message. If you don't want this warning to be displayed, in the Tools > Options dialog clear the Delete Channel Notice check box (Figure 9–6).

## Creating the Channels Hierarchy

To create a new channel, in the Site Manager, display the channels hierarchy by clicking the Channels icon in the left pane of the Site Manager window; right-click the channel where you'd like the new channel to be created, and select New Channel. Since we are creating the first channel for the site, right-click the root node in the hierarchy called Channels,

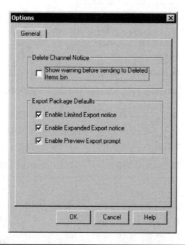

**Figure 9–6** Site Manager Options

and then select New Channel. The New Channel dialog box is displayed, as shown in Figure 9–7. It contains several fields at the top of the dialog and several tabs underneath. Let's look into the Name, Display Name, Description, and Parent Channel fields.

We will start with giving our new channel a name. This name will be used as part of the hierarchical URL for all pages and subchannels in the new channel. When the channel name is used in the URL, it is URL-encoded. If special characters are used in the channel name, the URL can become very user unfriendly. For example, a space character in a channel name is replaced by a plus sign (+) in the URL; therefore, it's a good practice to avoid spaces in channel names.

There are restrictions on what a channel name can contain. These restrictions are listed in the sidebar.

For the sample site, we will name the top-level channel "bots consulting."

---

**NOTE:** Our sample Web site is installed as a Web application in a virtual directory off the root of an IIS virtual Web site. As we discussed in Chapter 8, if you'd like your CMS site to be in the root of a Web site, the top-level channel name should be mapped to the HTTP host header; in our example, it would be www.botsconsulting.com. Both approaches are perfectly viable.

---

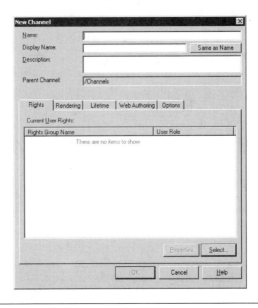

**Figure 9–7** New Channel dialog box

**Naming Channels**

Do:

- Use English letters and numbers [a–z, A–Z, 0–9] as well as four special characters: dash, underscore, and left and right parentheses [–, _, (, )].
- Give channels unique names within a site.

Don't:

- Use non-US-ASCII alphanumeric characters.
- Use the six special characters #, &, %, +, /, |.
- Use long names. A channel name must be less than 100 characters in length.
- Use two consecutive periods.
- Use a period as a last character.
- Use NR for a name—this is a reserved name for the root virtual directory in CMS (the name denotes the origins of CMS as an NCompass Resolution [NR] server).

The Display Name property doesn't have the same restrictions as the Name property. It can contain non-US-ASCII as well as spaces. As we have mentioned already, the display name is a user-friendly alias that is used as text for a link pointing at your channel when the channel is presented to the users—for example, within a navigational structure for your site in a browser, or within the Web Author console or the Authoring Connector. The Display Name property can be set up in any language because it can include non-US characters, including double-byte characters. This is particularly useful for multilingual sites.

If you are happy for the display name to be identical to the channel name, you can click the Same as Name button (Figure 9–7). For the "botsconsulting" channel, we will use the display name BOTS Consulting.

The Description field is an optional field that allows us to provide a meaningful description for the channel. It is not normally used outside the Site Manager and can contain any characters. The only limitation is its size—it should not be more than 255 characters in length.

The Parent Channel field is a read-only field that displays the full path to the parent channel from the root of the channels hierarchy. We are creating the first channel for the site; therefore, the parent channel is the root identified as /Channels. For example, when you create a first-level channel, such as the "knowledge" channel in our sample site, the parent channel will be identified as /Channels/botsconsulting/knowledge.

There are several configuration tabs in the New Channel dialog box: Rights, Rendering, Lifetime, Web Authoring, and Options. We don't need to use them now; after the channel has been created, the same configuration options are available from the Channel Properties dialog box. In this section, we concentrate on creating the channels structure for our site; all channel configuration options are discussed in detail later in the book in Chapter 16.

**NOTE:** If you'd like to know more about channel configuration options now, refer to Chapter 16, and then come back to this chapter.

To save the newly created top-level channel, click OK in the New Channel dialog box. We will carry on with creating the channels hierarchy for our sample site using the names and display names that are listed in Table 9–1.

**NOTE:** When you create multiple subchannels within a channel, by default the subchannels are sorted and displayed in alphabetical order. To change the sorting order within a channel, right-click the channel in the Site Manager, select Properties, choose the Sorting tab, and arrange the subchannels in the required order. This is important for dynamic navigation generation.

After all channels have been created, the channels hierarchy in the Site Manager appears as shown in Figure 9–8.

The channels we have created don't contain any pages. Let's see what is displayed in the browser if we access one of the channels we've just created—for example, Services. Because the sample site has been created as a Web application off the root of the IIS virtual server, this channel is accessible using the URL http://www.botsconsulting.com/botsconsulting/services.

**NOTE:** If the sample site were created in the root of the IIS virtual server, the URL for the services channel would be http://www.botsconsulting.com/services. Refer to Chapter 8 for options for creating CMS sites.

After we've typed the URL in the browser, CMS displays the default authentication page (Figure 9–9).

**Table 9–1** Sample Site Channel Names and Display Names

| First-Level Channel Name | Second-Level Channel Name | Channel Display Name |
|---|---|---|
| about | | About Us |
| | firm | Our Firm |
| | consultants | Our Consultants |
| | history | History |
| | press | In the Press |
| offices | | Offices |
| services | | Services |
| | technology | Technology |
| | manufacturing | Manufacturing |
| | construction | Construction |
| | pharma | Pharmaceuticals |
| knowledge | | Knowledge |
| | casestudies | Case Studies |
| | articles | Articles |
| | research | Research |
| careers | | Careers |
| | working | Working at BOTS |
| | people | Our People Matter |
| | growth | Growth Opportunities |
| | applying | Applying to BOTS |

**NOTE:** The default authentication page is an ASP page called Manual Login.asp, located in the folder *<installation drive>*:\Program Files\ Microsoft Content Management Server\Server\IIS_NR\System\ Access\.

We have to type in the CMS administrator credentials because this account is currently the only one that exists in CMS. Then the CMS default channel page is displayed (Figure 9–10). This page shows the links to the parent channel, the same-level channels, and the child channels for

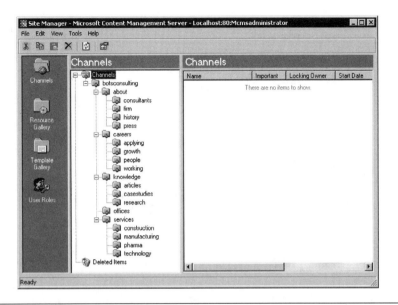

**Figure 9–8**  Channels hierarchy for the sample site

the services channel. The Switch to Edit Site link is displayed because the CMS administrator by default has authoring rights in all channels.

**NOTE:** The channel default page is an ASP page called Cover.asp, located in the folder *<installation drive>*:\Program Files\Microsoft Content Management Server\Server\IIS_NR\Shared\.

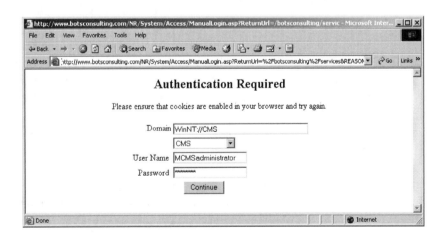

**Figure 9–9**  CMS authentication page

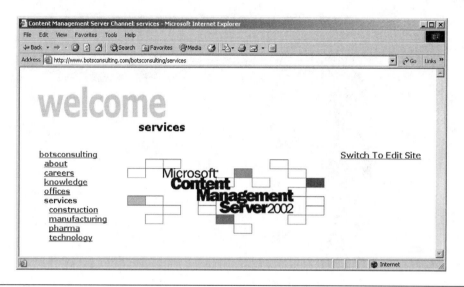

**Figure 9–10**  CMS channel default page

## Creating the Template Galleries Hierarchy

Just as channels provide a way to organize pages, template galleries allow us to organize templates. A template gallery may contain templates and other template galleries. A template galleries hierarchy is an integral part of the CMS site structure. Template galleries can be created in the Site Manager and in Visual Studio .NET (VS.NET); templates are created using VS.NET only.

Usually, site developers create templates and template galleries in VS.NET; we will look into that in the next chapter. However, you may need to create a template gallery using the Site Manager; let's do it.

To create a new template gallery in the Site Manager, click the Template Gallery icon in the left pane to display the template galleries panes; then right-click the gallery where you'd like the new gallery to be created and select New > Gallery. We are creating the first template gallery for the site; therefore, right-click the root node in the tree called Templates and select New > Gallery. The New Template Gallery dialog box appears (Figure 9–11).

Using the New Template Gallery dialog box, we can name the new template gallery and provide a description for it. The name should be easily understood by the content authors. The description is optional and is limited to 255 characters in length. Parent Gallery is a read-only field that shows the full path to the parent gallery from the root of the

**Figure 9–11** New Template Gallery dialog box

template galleries hierarchy. We will talk about the Rights tab later; click OK to create the new gallery.

For our sample site, we have created a template gallery called BOTS Consulting (Figure 9–12).

## Creating the Resource Galleries Hierarchy

A resource gallery provides the ability to organize resources for our site. The resource gallery can contain individual files—for example, images— as well as other resource galleries. A resource galleries hierarchy is part of the CMS site structure. Resource galleries are created using the Site

**Figure 9–12** Template gallery hierarchy for the sample site

Manager but are populated with resources using the Resource Manager in the Web Author.

To create a new gallery, click the Resource Gallery icon in the left pane to display the resource galleries panes; then right-click the gallery where you'd like the new gallery to be created and select New > Gallery. We are creating the first resource gallery for the site; therefore, right-click the root node in the tree called Resources and select New > Gallery. The New Resource Gallery dialog box appears (Figure 9–13).

To name the new gallery, in the New Resource Gallery dialog box type in the Name field. The name should be meaningful for the content authors. The description is optional and, similar to other containers, is limited to 255 characters in length. As with template galleries, Parent Gallery is a read-only field that shows the full path to the parent gallery from the root of the resource galleries hierarchy. We will talk about the Rights tab later; click OK to create the new gallery.

Again, for our sample site, we have created a resource gallery called BOTS Consulting (Figure 9–14).

## User Rights

Channels and template and resource galleries form the structure for the CMS site. However, at the moment, this structure is only accessible to

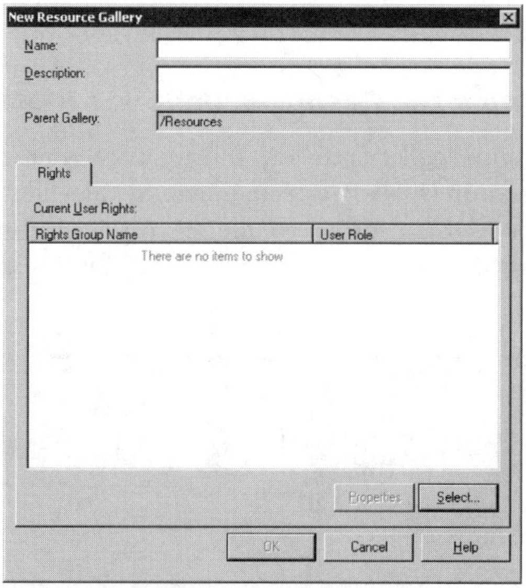

**Figure 9–13** New Resource Gallery dialog box

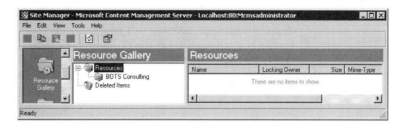

**Figure 9-14** Resource Gallery hierarchy for the sample site

one user—the CMS administrator. This is not sufficient; therefore, we need to assign CMS permissions on our site to other users.

In the CMS environment, there are eight predefined user roles: administrators, channel managers, template designers, resource managers, authors, editors, moderators, and subscribers. We have already come across the subscribers, authors, editors, and moderators roles. For example, in Chapter 6, we have seen the user roles involved in the publishing workflow, such as authors, editors, and moderators. The other four roles—administrators, channel managers, template designers, and resource managers—perform various tasks in site development and administration. Administrators have permissions to perform any tasks in the CMS environment; channel managers are responsible for administration of the channels they are assigned to; template designers develop templates; and resource managers look after resources in the resource galleries they are assigned to.

We will have a detailed discussion focused on user roles and setting up user rights in the CMS environment later in the book, in Chapter 17. However, there are two groups of users that need to have appropriate permissions on the site during the development stage: the subscribers and the template designers. In this section, we will concentrate on assigning rights for these two types of users.

To access the user roles panes in the Site Manager, click the User Roles icon in the left pane (Figure 9–15). Assigning permissions to user accounts involves several steps, which include adding a user account to a CMS rights group within a role and then assigning this group to the appropriate containers.

Let's start with subscribers. Subscribers are ordinary users who are allowed to browse our site. In the CMS environment, there is no anonymous access to the site; all access must be authenticated. In Chapter 8, we have already enabled a guest account to be used for anonymous

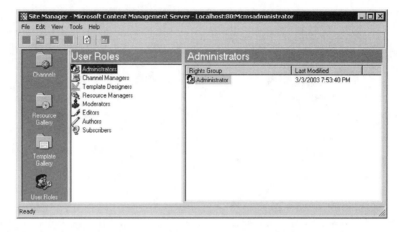

**Figure 9–15** User roles within the Site Manager

access to the site; we now need to provide subscriber permissions for this account.

First of all, we need to create a subscribers rights group. Right-click the Subscribers role in the middle pane and select New Rights Group. The group called New Rights Group is created and is displayed in the right pane; right-click it, select Rename, and give it a meaningful name. For our sample site, we will call the group BOTS Consulting Subscribers (Figure 9–16).

Second, we need to add the CMS guest account to this group. To add the account to the group, right-click the group, select Properties,

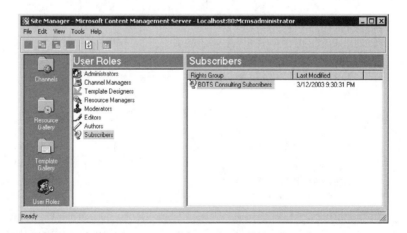

**Figure 9–16** Subscribers rights group for the sample site

and choose the Group Members tab. The Rights Group Members list is currently empty; there are no group members. Click the Modify button; in the Group or User Name field, type the guest account name using the format WinNT://*<domain name>*/*<account name>*—for example, WinNT://MCMS/MCMSguest (Figure 9–17). If you don't want to type a name, you can select a domain from the list called NT Domains, then from the top drop-down list choose Select from a list of all groups and users, and then browse to the guest account. Don't be confused by the label NT Domains. It is inherited from the previous version of CMS; in fact, Windows 2003, 2000, and NT domains are listed. After you've specified the guest account either by typing or by browsing, click Add and then OK. The guest account has been added to the group members list (Figure 9–18).

The third step is to assign permissions to the new group. To assign permissions for multiple containers, we will use the group's Properties > Group Rights tab. The tab displays the containers hierarchies. The red X beside a container name indicates that the group does not have permissions for this container. To assign one container to a rights group, you need to click once the name of the container. The red X beside the container name changes to a green check mark, which means that the group has permissions on the container. The actual permissions are

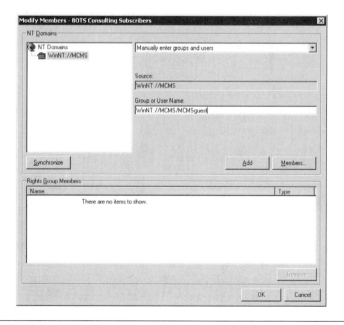

**Figure 9–17** Specifying the group member account

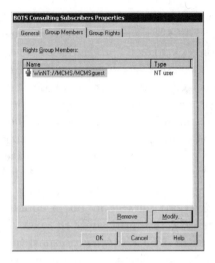

**Figure 9–18**   Guest user membership of the Subscribers rights group

defined by the subscribers role. In order for our users to browse the whole site, they need to be able to view content in all channels and galleries; this means that the subscribers group must be assigned to all containers.

By default, the child containers don't inherit the rights from the parent container. However, you'll be relieved to know that we don't have to change the red Xs to the green check marks for each container individually. Instead, we can assign the permissions to the root containers and propagate them to the rest of the hierarchy. For example, click the Channels root container to assign permissions for it, then right-click the container, and select Propagate Rights to Children. Each red X beside the container and all its children changes to a check mark. Repeat the same process for the Resources and Templates root containers (Figure 9–19); click OK.

**NOTE:** To assign permissions individually for each container, use the Rights tab in the container's Properties dialog box.

We have enabled the users to browse the site without authentication. However, at the moment there is nothing for them to browse, because the site is empty. The content for the new site will be provided by the site authors. In order to be able to provide the content, the site authors need the templates on which to base their pages. The templates

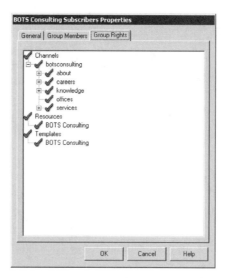

**Figure 9–19** Subscribers group rights for the sample site containers

for our new CMS site must be created by the site developers; without the templates, there will be no content and therefore no site. In order for the developers to be able to create CMS templates, they must be assigned the appropriate permissions. That's what we will do next.

A template designer is a special user role within the CMS environment for the site developers. When a template designers group is assigned to a container, the members of this group can create new containers within this container and assign rights to these new containers, including channels, template galleries, and resource galleries. When a template designers group is assigned to a template gallery, within this gallery the members of the group can create and edit templates as well as delete the templates they own. To test their work, they have the subscribers, authors, editors, moderators, and resource managers permissions within the containers where they have rights.

To assign the permissions for the template designers, create the rights group within the template designers role, add the developers accounts to this group, and then assign the group to the appropriate containers. You can have more than one template designers group with permissions assigned for different site containers.

For our sample site, we will create one group called BOTS Consulting Developers within the template designers role (Figure 9–20), add the developers accounts to it, and then assign the group to all containers within the site (Figure 9–21).

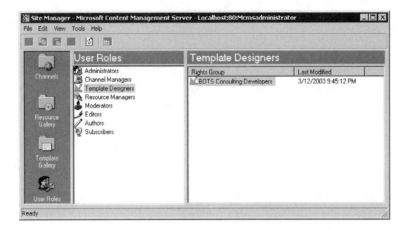

**Figure 9–20**  Template designers rights group for the sample site

**Figure 9–21**  Template designers group rights for the sample site containers

## Summary

In this chapter, we created the site structure for the new CMS site. We started with understanding the information architecture for the site; we then created a channels hierarchy mapped to the information architecture. Channels are virtual containers that provide the ability to organize content for the site; thus, the channels structure allows us to create global navigation for the site.

The site structure is set up using the CMS Site Manager application; we discussed how the Site Manager works. We created a channels hierarchy as well as resource and template galleries hierarchies for the site. Then we assigned permissions for the site users and site developers. This is the minimum set of permissions you are likely to need for the site development stage.

---

**NOTE:** To set up the publishing environment for your users, you need to assign other CMS permissions in addition to those for subscribers and template designers; the full set of CMS user roles and their rights is discussed in Chapter 17.

---

As we have mentioned previously, our site currently doesn't have any content. In order for the site authors to create pages for the new site, the templates for these pages have to be developed. In the next chapter, we will start looking into how to use Visual Studio .NET for CMS development.

# CHAPTER 10

# Developing for CMS Using Visual Studio .NET

## Overview

When CMS 2002 was released, there was one very significant change in the product: direct integration with an integrated development environment (IDE). In this case, the IDE was Visual Studio .NET (VS.NET). This change in the product has had a great and profound effect on the way you develop solutions based on CMS. First and foremost, from a developer's perspective, you have everything you need to create a new site from within the IDE. Very few times will you have to leave the IDE to accomplish a task; and even in those instances when you do leave the IDE, Microsoft has provided access right from Visual Studio. In this chapter, we'll examine how Visual Studio integrates with CMS. In addition, we'll discuss how to create new template galleries and template gallery items (TGIs).

## How Is a CMS Project Different from Regular Web Projects?

Although CMS is based on .NET and uses ASPX pages, CMS projects are different from typical Web projects. Most importantly, the ASPX pages that support a CMS site aren't run as themselves. What we mean by this is that the ASPX pages are run in the context of a posting (a Web page) within your site. When a user looks at a CMS-based site, they're really looking at postings, which are supported by templates. Templates, as we will see, are in part the ASPX files you'll be creating later and in part a template gallery item (covered later in this chapter). As a result of these differences, debugging your projects is a little different as well (we'll learn more about that in Chapter 12). Finally, when you create a new CMS Web application, a user control is automatically added to the project; this user control is the administrative functions provided by CMS and is referred to as the default console.

As we mentioned, CMS projects are not like normal ASP.NET Web applications, primarily because the ASPX pages aren't run directly. In CMS terms, the ASPX pages are essentially the support for *postings* added by a content contributor. Although, in truth, the ASPX pages are processed as they normally would be end users who view a CMS-based site never actually "see" the ASPX file directly. Instead, they see the posting.

For most Web applications, the developer chooses which ASPX page is shown to the end user. ASP.NET Web applications typically have one "container" (an ASPX page), hiding and unhiding controls based on events or operations. In a CMS-based site, content contributors choose which ASPX page (in the form of a template) they want to use when they create a posting. It's the choice of the content contributor which "container" is used to display content or functionality within a site. As a result, a developer has less control over what ASPX page is used and when. When that posting is displayed to some end user, its content is combined with the ASPX page and then rendered to the end user (we'll learn more about this processing in the next chapter). So, unlike a typical ASP.NET application, your CMS project will probably have multiple containers (ASPX pages), each possessing a unique content format or functionality mix. For some of you, this is a pretty big shift in the way that you need to think about developing Web applications. However, understanding this concept is key to creating effective CMS-based solutions.

As a result of this "there but not seen" environment that an ASPX page operates in, debugging is a little different. We'll go through a couple of debugging scenarios in Chapter 12, but it's important to understand that although debugging in VS.NET works just fine, you will start the debugging process differently with CMS projects.

Lastly, a CMS project includes a special user object. Similarly to how a typical ASP.NET Web application has a default webform1.aspx file automatically inserted into the project, CMS projects come with a user control called "defaultconsole." Unlike the generic webform1.aspx file, however, this user control is one of the core components you'll add to almost every template file you create. This user control will be created in a folder in your solution called "console."

In Figure 10–1, you can see what the Solution Explorer shows after we've created our CMS project.

**Figure 10–1** A typical CMS project

# Creating a New CMS Project

Now that you have a little background on how a CMS project is different from a typical ASP.NET application, let's create a new CMS project. Before we begin, make sure that you have the following installed on your development machine:

- Visual Studio .NET
- Content Management Server 2002
- IIS
- Content Management Server 2002 Site Manager

---

**NOTE:** CMS requires a SQL server to house the repository. The SQL server does not have to run on the same server/PC that you're developing on, but you will need access to one.

---

Once you have the components installed and running on your machine, follow these steps to create your new CMS project.

1. Open Visual Studio and click the File menu.
2. From the list of options, pick New and then pick Project.
3. After you've done this, you will see a dialog like the one pictured in Figure 10–2.
4. From the list of project types, click the plus (+) sign next to the Content Management Server type.

5. Under Content Management Server will be the choice of two different project types: one for C# and one for VB.NET. In this book, all examples will be in C# (which is how we created our project). However, you can choose either language.

6. Once you've chosen your language preference, you can choose from one of three types of CMS projects: MCMS Web Application, MCMS Web Service, and MCMS Empty Web Project. All the project types listed are similar to their non-CMS counterparts, except that they automatically include references to the appropriate Microsoft.ContentManagement namespaces and have the defaultconsole user control added, as we discussed earlier. For our project, click the MCMS Web Application.

7. In the Location field, type in the name of your CMS application. In this book, we'll be using "botsconsulting" as the project name.

8. Once you've changed the name of the project in the Location field, click OK.

9. After about 10 to 20 seconds (depending on your machine), your new CMS project will be created.

Now that we have our project, let's examine the various new features that CMS adds to the VS.NET environment.

If you click the Tools menu in VS.NET and you're familiar with VS.NET, you'll notice that there is an entry for Content Management Server. If you choose that option, you'll notice that there are quite a few

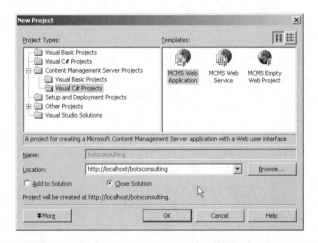

**Figure 10–2** The New Project dialog in VS.NET

tools listed. All the tools listed are external to VS.NET, but having them in the Tools menu provides a very convenient way to get to each of them. Figure 10–3 shows the new tools added to the Tools menu.

In addition to the new tools, there's an important window addition to VS.NET: the Template Explorer window. This new window is one that you will probably use regularly as you develop your CMS solution.

The Template Explorer is one of the views directly into the CMS repository. It shows all the template galleries and template gallery items defined within CMS (we'll learn more about each in this chapter). It is also the way that you can create new template galleries and template gallery items as you need them for your project. To show the Template Explorer window, click the View menu from within VS.NET. Choose the Other Windows option and then MCMS Template Explorer, as shown in Figure 10–4.

Once you've chosen this option, you'll see the Template Explorer window appear in your VS.NET environment (shown in Figure 10–5).

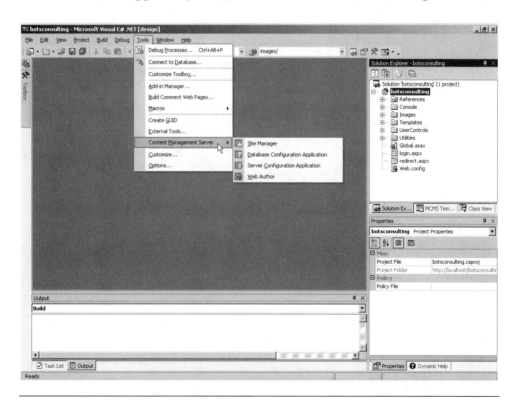

**Figure 10–3** The Tools menu in VS.NET

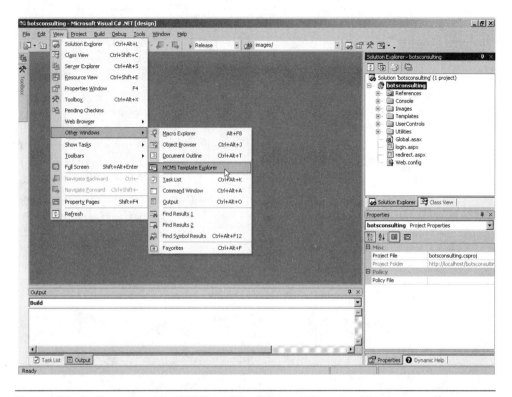

**Figure 10–4**  Choosing the CMS Template Explorer from the View menu

**Figure 10–5**  The CMS Template Explorer window

In our environment, we've docked the Template Explorer window in the same place that our Class View and Solution Explorer live. You may wish to dock the window elsewhere in your VS.NET environment. However, all subsequent screen shots will show the Template Explorer docked with the Solution Explorer and the Class View.

Now that you've created your CMS project and you have your Template Explorer window shown, let's examine template gallery items.

## Template Gallery Items

In CMS 2002, templates are split into two parts. All the information about a template is stored in an object called a template gallery item (TGI), and the physical code is stored in an ASPX file (and the matching code-behind). In this section, we'll examine the TGI and how to change its properties, including adding placeholders and custom properties.

### What Are They?

A TGI, in essence, is a list of all the properties or metadata for a given template. It contains all the information that CMS knows about a template, including the definition for all placeholders in the template, the custom properties, and the location of the physical template file. Further, when your content contributors choose a template, they're actually looking at the list of TGIs that exist within the gallery they've chosen.

## Creating a TGI

To begin the process of exploring TGIs, let's first create a new template gallery and a new TGI. To create your new gallery and TGI, follow these steps.

1. While viewing the Template Explorer, right-click the Templates template gallery.
2. From the context menu, pick New Gallery.
3. After CMS has created the new template gallery, it will highlight the name and allow you to change it. By default, CMS names all new galleries "New Template Gallery." In our examples, we'll be

working on behalf of BOTS Consulting, so our new template gallery will be called "BOTS Consulting."

4. Once you've created your template gallery, right-click it and, from the context menu, pick New Template.

5. As with the new gallery, CMS places a new TGI in your gallery and names it "New Template" by default. You can name your template anything you'd like. For the purposes of this exercise, we're going to call our new template "Generic."

If all has gone well, your Template Explorer should show you something similar to Figure 10–6. Please note that we've installed the sample site on our CMS server, so in addition to our new gallery, you'll see the WoodgroveNet gallery. If you've installed the sample site, you will also have that template gallery.

You'll notice that the names of your new gallery and template are both shown in bold. Also, you'll notice that next to your template is a "broken" icon with a red check mark. We'll discuss the "broken" icon and the check mark later. However, let's address the use of bold now.

The use of bold on each object indicates that neither object has been "saved" to the repository. If you open the Site Manager and look in the template gallery, you'll notice that the objects exist, but their names have not been updated with the values you gave them (you may have to click the circular arrow button—Global Refresh—to see the new objects). In Figure 10–7 you'll see what we're talking about.

**Figure 10–6** The Template Explorer with the new gallery and template added

In order to for your name changes to appear properly in the repository, you must save the changes to the gallery and TGI. To save the changes, simply right-click the object and select Save. Figure 10–8 shows this operation on the TGI. Be sure to perform the same operation on the gallery as well. Once you've saved the changes, you can go back to the Site Manager, click the Global Refresh button, and see the objects with the names you gave them in VS.NET.

Now, remember the check mark and the "broken" icon on your TGI? The check mark indicates that the template is "checked out." A checked-out TGI can be edited by only one person. If you were in a multideveloper environment, this mechanism would allow your colleagues to see the TGI and view its properties, but would not allow them to modify it until you have checked it back in. As for the "broken" icon, it indicates that this TGI does not have a template file associated with it. We'll address that issue in Chapter 13, so for now, your TGI will remain broken.

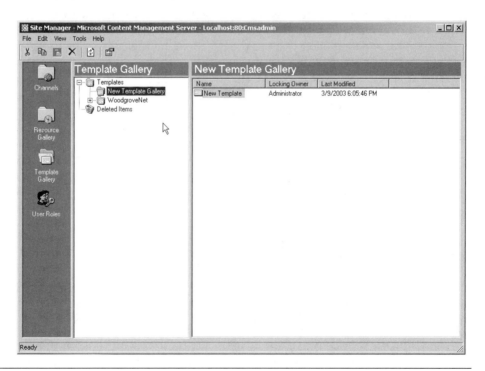

**Figure 10–7** The Site Manager shows the new objects, but without the updated names.

**Figure 10–8** Right-click the object and pick Save to commit the new name to the repository.

---

**NOTE:** In the preceding examples, we demonstrated how to create one template gallery. Ultimately, once you begin developing your CMS site, you'll probably want to create one or more subgalleries to logically group your templates for your content contributors, or create multiple galleries representing the different sites you may potentially run in one CMS implementation. At BOTS Consulting, the development team has created a single gallery for their site. How you choose to set up your galleries will be based on a logical layout for galleries and any security requirements you may have. Since different user groups can be granted access to different galleries, creating various galleries may provide you with the flexibility of creating "advanced" templates, which are offered to only a few content contributors.

---

## Adding Placeholder Definitions to Your TGI

One of the unique elements in all the templates you create will be the template's placeholders. As you inventory your content and analyze the various page types, you should really study the content itself—not just the layout, but the content types (text, images, files) and what attributes are applied to the content (bold, tables, hyperlinks). As content contributors add content to the site, they are actually adding that content to placeholders defined in the TGI. As you study the content, you should be thinking about what kinds of placeholders you'll need in each template that you develop.

As we mentioned, the TGI contains the definitions for all the place-holders in the template. As you create your placeholder definitions, you'll have to decide what kinds of content each placeholder will store and what flexibility that placeholder will allow the content contributor. By flexibility, we mean what kinds of formatting they can apply, as well as what types of content can be contributed to the placeholder itself. For example, Figure 10–9 depicts a press release in the BOTS Consulting Web site. You'll notice that there are primarily two text elements to the release: the body copy and the call-out text. Scanning further, you'll notice that the release does not have any special attributes or HTML constructs (such as tables). In other words, the text is primarily a plain Verdana font with bold applied only in certain areas. From this example, we can gather that we may only need two placeholders, and those place-holders will only need to allow plain text and bold.

Now, if we were to try to create a TGI to match the format and layout of this page, we would have to create placeholders that fit the descriptions we just provided. In Figure 10–10, you'll see the Properties view of a TGI. The Properties view allows you to change the various elements of a

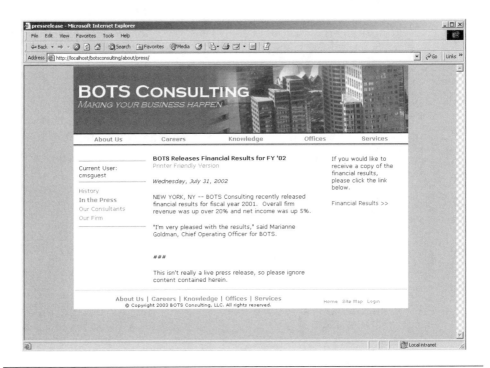

**Figure 10–9**  A BOTS Consulting press release

**Figure 10–10** TGI Properties view in VS.NET

TGI, including the custom property and placeholder definitions, as well as which ASPX page is tied to this TGI. To see the properties of any TGI, simply click the TGI in the Template Explorer view.

In your TGI Properties view, locate the Placeholder Definitions property. This property allows you to get to the designer, where you can define the various placeholder definitions your template will have. Very much as a TGI is the definition of a template and ultimately ties back to an ASPX page, a placeholder definition is the metadata about a placeholder. Once this information is defined, you can then bind a placeholder control within the ASPX file to the definition in the TGI. To create a new placeholder definition, click the Placeholder Definitions property. Then click the ellipsis that appears. Figure 10–11 shows this operation.

Once you've clicked the ellipsis, you get the Placeholder Definition Collection Editor, shown in Figure 10–12.

The Placeholder Definition Collection Editor allows you to create the various placeholder definitions for your template. Native to CMS are six distinct definitions, each providing varying functionality and property sets. The six types are:

- HTML
- XML

- Attachment
- Image
- Office attachment
- Office HTML

**Figure 10–11** You click the ellipsis to define your placeholders.

**Figure 10–12** The Placeholder Definition Collection Editor

When a placeholder control is bound, the definition controls not only the look of the placeholder, but the kind of content that placeholder will accept. We'll discuss each of these placeholders in more depth in Chapter 13. For now, it's important to understand that each of these placeholder types will play a specific role in your templates.

To add a new placeholder definition to your TGI, simply click the Add button in the lower left. Once you've clicked Add, CMS will, by default, add an HTML placeholder definition (if you click the down arrow next to the Add button, you can choose a different placeholder type). Looking immediately to the right of the new definition, you'll see its properties. We'll learn more about each of the properties in Chapter 13 as we discuss placeholders in more depth. However, the complete placeholder definition collection for the BOTS Consulting press release template is shown in Figure 10–13. You'll notice that there are more placeholders in the definition collection than we discussed earlier. As it turns out, the press release *could* contain content other than what we originally identified. As a result, the BOTS IS/IT department decided to add additional placeholders so that content contributors would have more flexibility in the type of content they could contribute.

**Figure 10–13** The BOTS Consulting press release placeholder definitions

# Adding Custom Properties

Another element of a TGI is the custom property definitions. Custom properties allow a developer to assign additional metadata to a template, the values of which can be assigned by the content contributor (or the developer, programmatically). These custom properties can then be used in a number of ways, including creating HTML META tags, determining what content to summarize on a posting, searching for specific postings, and determining what content to display to a subscriber. Your design will largely determine whether you need custom properties and how to use them. In BOTS Consulting's case, custom properties are used in the case studies section to allow subscribers to see case studies of a particular type.

**NOTE:** Although custom properties are a terrific way of providing a flexible tagging structure for content in CMS, searching by them is an expensive transaction. Overuse of custom property searches can seriously impact the performance of your CMS site. Good uses for custom properties might be certain metadata about the page, such as key words or the GUID of a related posting; you would retrieve the value at the posting level and then search on the GUID, which is a very efficient search.

As we mentioned earlier, custom properties allow developers to create custom attributes for postings. In the same way that placeholder definitions define what each placeholder will accept, custom properties define what additional attributes a posting can possess and, in some cases, what values can be applied to those properties. When the content contributors create new postings based on the template, the posting will possess the properties defined in the TGI, and the content contributor assigns the values.

When you create your TGI, you have the option of creating a custom property collection. This collection will hold the custom properties to which you want the content contributor or some automated process to assign values. When you create your properties, you have the choice of two types: selection and text. Each type defines the behavior the content contributor will see when they create a posting based on this template. If you look at Figures 10–14 and 10–15, you can see the ellipsis that you click to call up the Custom Property Definition Collection Editor and the interface itself (similar to the Placeholder Definition Collection Editor).

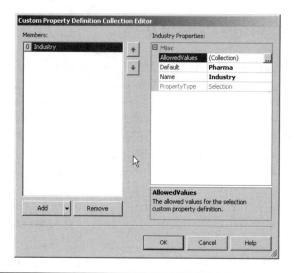

**Figure 10–14** You click the ellipsis to see the custom property definition interface.

The selection custom property allows the developer to create a property and then provide a fixed number of "allowed" values. Essentially, this creates a drop-down list of values that a content contributor can set when they create a new page. The advantage to a selection custom property is the limited number of values the property can hold. This

**Figure 10–15** This is the interface you use to create the custom properties in your template.

is especially useful if you need to search for a posting using a custom property, since you have to search for an exact value match (there's no facility to search "like" with a custom property), or you need to exactly match a property and value pair. The downside to selection custom properties is that the values cannot be updated programmatically; you must change the allowed values through the VS.NET interface. Keep in mind that you must supply a "default" value for the property. By default, CMS chooses the first property you enter.

In Figure 10–16 you can see how the selection custom property appears to the content contributor in the Page Properties dialog. In this case, the Case Study Detail template has one custom property to designate the industry with which the case study is associated. In the BOTS' site, there's only one channel for all case studies, regardless of what practice contributed the study. However, the business users wanted a way to tag each case study so they could visually segment the case studies when being viewed by potential customers.

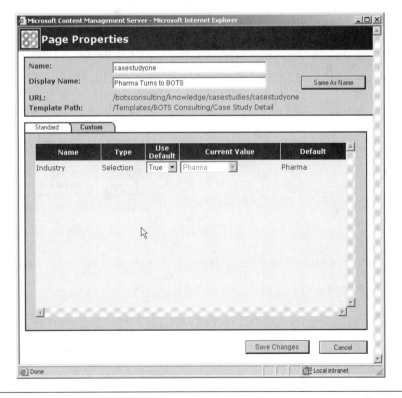

**Figure 10–16** The Page Properties dialog is where content contributors can set the value of custom properties.

The text custom property allows the business user to fill in a free-form value. Text custom properties are useful when there is no specific set of values a property can have. They are especially useful when developers are assigning values to properties programmatically.

With the Generic TGI you created earlier, let's add a custom property to the custom property collection. As shown in Figure 10–14, click the ellipsis. Once you've clicked the ellipsis and you see the Custom Property Definition Collection Editor, click the down arrow next to the Add button (simply clicking the Add button will, by default, create a text custom property). For this example, let's add a selection custom property. After you've completed this step, you should see something like Figure 10–17.

You'll notice that CMS automatically gives the new custom property a name (as it did with the template and template gallery). To change the custom property name, simply click the Name property and change it. In this example, we'll call our new custom property "sample."

Because this is a selection custom property, CMS automatically creates a new item in the collection of values. Similarly to adding a new custom property to the TGI, you also can create new values in the *allowed values* collection. The allowed values collection is the list of values that will fill the property's drop-down list in the Page Properties dialog box. For this example, we'll add two values: Value1 and Value2 (we're not terribly creative). To add the values, click the Allowed Values property and

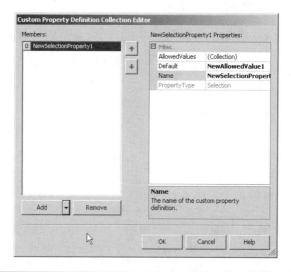

**Figure 10–17** The Custom Property Definition Collection Editor with the new custom property

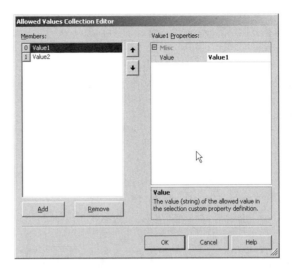

**Figure 10–18** The allowed values you've just added

click the ellipsis to see the Allowed Values Collection Editor (are you seeing a pattern yet?).

You'll notice that there is already one value in the collection. As mentioned earlier, because you selected a selection custom property, CMS automatically fills the allowed values collection with one member. Since one value already exists, simply click the value's property field to the right and change the value to "Value1." To add a new value, simply click the Add button and change the value to "Value2."

Figure 10–18 shows what you should be seeing in VS.NET once you've completed the preceding steps.

## Summary

In this chapter, we've explored creating a new CMS project in VS.NET. We learned that although there are similarities to a standard Web form project, there are some differences, such as the existence of a default user control and how our ASPX pages are treated. As a result, you will have to take additional steps when debugging your projects.

In addition to reviewing how to create a new CMS project, we looked at template gallery items. A TGI is one of two parts of a template within CMS. TGIs define what placeholders and custom properties our template will possess as well as what ASPX file is associated with the template.

Finally, we explored how to create placeholder definitions and custom properties. After we created a TGI called "Generic," we added a new HTML placeholder definition and then added a selection custom property with two allowed values.

# CHAPTER 11

# Template-Based Page Processing

## Overview

In CMS, processing a page request consists of multiple steps and involves several layers. All pages in CMS are dynamically built from the information contained in the page template and the placeholder content contributed by the authors. Template metadata is stored in the CMS database, while the template file is stored in the CMS server file system. In the previous chapter, we looked into creating template gallery items (TGIs) that represent the template metadata in VS.NET. In this chapter, we will discuss how a CMS page is processed, from receiving an HTTP request from the browser to sending the HTTP response back.

---

**NOTE:** We are going to look into ASP.NET-based processing. For ASP-based processing, refer to the CMS 2002 and CMS 2001 product documentation.

---

When authors create a page, they populate the placeholders in the template with the content and then post the page to a channel. The data corresponding to this posting is stored in the database, including the following information:

- The posting Globally Unique Identifier (GUID)
- The template on which the posting is based
- The placeholder content
- The publishing schedule for the posting

The posting properties, placeholder content, and template metadata are stored separately and are brought together to create a page only during the processing of the posting's template ASPX file. The code in ASPX template files makes use of CMS Publishing API (PAPI) objects to read the data from the CMS database and to commit changes to the database. The output of the ASPX template processing is a CMS page that is put in the cache and then sent back to the user.

---

**NOTE:** Template metadata is usually referred to as just a template. As we have discussed in Chapter 10, templates are also known as template gallery items in VS.NET.

---

Depending on whether the CMS page is requested for viewing in presentation mode or for creating and editing content in authoring mode, the HTML for the placeholders within the page will be different. The placeholders are rendered in different modes by the placeholder server controls that are part of the ASPX template. Depending on the mode, the processing is slightly different.

We will start by looking into how the page is processed in presentation mode, and then discuss page processing in authoring mode.

# Page Processing in Presentation Mode

When a page is requested by a user in presentation mode, the placeholder content is rendered as part of the resulting page HTML. The user is not aware that some parts of the page are static and others are generated dynamically; the HTML for the page is assembled on the server using a combination of data from the CMS database and the server file system. This process involves several steps. Figure 11–1 shows the logical architecture of the processing and the steps involved. Let's look into these steps.

## Step 1

The user types a URL, or clicks a link, pointing to a CMS page in a browser—for example, http://www.botsconsulting.com/offices/uk. It is a user-friendly hierarchical URL. The page request arrives at the IIS site—for example:

```
:GET /offices/uk HTTP/1.1
Host: www.botsconsulting.com
```

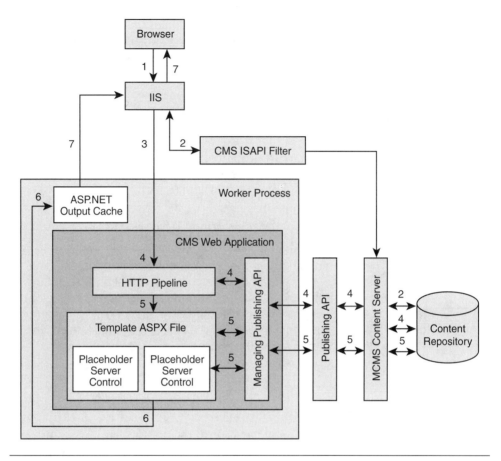

**Figure 11–1** Logical architecture of CMS page processing

## Step 2

IIS has the CMS server installed, and the virtual Web site has been enabled as a CMS Web entry point. Therefore, the request is passed to the CMS ISAPI filter. The filter is called the Resolution filter and can be found at *<installation drive>*\Program Files\Microsoft Content Management Server\Server\bin\ReAuthFilt.dll. The Resolution filter analyzes the URL to identify whether the request is for a CMS page or resource. If not, the request is returned to the IIS for processing.

If the filter has identified the request as a CMS page request, it searches the database for the information that corresponds to the requested posting. It obtains the posting GUID and follows the posting to the metadata for the template associated with it. The template metadata includes a reference to the name and location of the template ASPX file. The filter gets the template ASPX file name and then constructs a new URL that points to the ASPX file and contains the posting GUID as one of the query string parameters. It looks similar to the following example:

```
/botsconsulting/templates/office.aspx?NRMODE=Published&NRNODEGUID=
%7b7DE6CC74-73ED-4EBC-BBC0-04714D6EA80A%7d&<other query string
parameters>
```

In this example, the NRMODE parameter specifies that the published version of the page is requested, and the NRNODEGUID parameter identifies the posting GUID.

The filter then passes the transformed URL back to IIS.

---

**NOTE:** The hierarchical URL in the original request identifies the page location in the channels hierarchy; it is purely a logical path as set up in the CMS server. What the Resolution filter does is convert this logical path to a real URL of a template ASPX file. The query string parameters identify the page-specific content and the processing mode. It is this ASPX file and the query string parameters that CMS server uses to compile the posting for IIS to serve.

---

## Step 3

IIS analyzes the request and passes it to the appropriate worker process for processing. This step is performed differently in IIS 5 and IIS 6 because their architectures are different. In IIS 5, because the request is for an ASPX file, it is passed to the ASP.NET ISAPI filter aspnet_isapi.dll, which in turn passes it to the ASP.NET runtime worker process, aspnet_wp.exe. In IIS 6, depending on the IIS isolation mode, the request is either passed to the Web worker process w3wp.exe in IIS 6 isolation mode (which in turn has an ASP.NET ISAPI filter installed), or the request is run by a worker process within inetinfo.exe in IIS 5 isolation mode.

---

**NOTE:** For information about IIS 6 isolation modes, refer to the IIS 6.0 Architecture section in the IIS 6 product documentation.

---

## Step 4

The worker process deals with the request as with any other ASPX request. First of all, the request goes through the HTTP module pipeline.

An example of an HTTP module pipeline as defined in a machine. config file is shown in the sidebar, together with an explanation of how HTTP modules work. The modules perform various tasks, including cache and state management, and security authentication and authorization.

## HTTP Pipeline

An HTTP pipeline is a sequence of HTTP modules. An HTTP module is a class that implements the System.Web.IHttpModule interface, as follows:

```
:public interface IHttpModule
{
        void Init(HttpApplication context);
        void Dispose();
}
```

For each HttpModule in the pipeline, the worker process calls the module's Init and Dispose methods. Init is called when the module is attached to the HttpApplication object, and Dispose is called when the module is detached from HttpApplication. The Init and Dispose methods allow the module to hook into events exposed by HttpApplication, including the beginning of a request, the end of a request, a request for authentication, and so on.

The HTTP modules in the pipeline are able to modify a request as it goes through.

Here is an example of an HTTP module pipeline contained in the machine. config file.

```
<httpModules>
        <add name="OutputCache"
type="System.Web.Caching.OutputCacheModule"/>
        <add name="Session"
type="System.Web.SessionState.SessionStateModule"/>
        <add name="WindowsAuthentication"
type="System.Web.Security.WindowsAuthenticationModule"/>
        <add name="FormsAuthentication"
type="System.Web.Security.FormsAuthenticationModule"/>
        <add name="PassportAuthentication"
type="System.Web.Security.PassportAuthenticationModule"/>
        <add name="UrlAuthorization"
type="System.Web.Security.UrlAuthorizationModule"/>
        <add name="FileAuthorization"
type="System.Web.Security.FileAuthorizationModule"/>
</httpModules>
```

The CMS site is an ASP.NET Web application, and it has its own web.config file. The HTTP pipeline for the CMS site consists of HTTP modules defined in the machine.config and web.config files; all HTTP modules in machine.config and web.config are initialized when the application starts.

When you create a CMS project in VS.NET, the web.config file is created for you. It includes four CMS-specific HTTP modules, as follows:

```
<httpModules>
     <add type="Microsoft.ContentManagement.Web.Security.
CmsAuthorizationModule, Microsoft.ContentManagement.Web, Version=
5.0.1200.0, Culture=neutral, PublicKeyToken=31bf3856ad364e35"
name="CmsAuthorizationModule" />
     <add type="Microsoft.ContentManagement.Web.
CmsEndRequestModule, Microsoft.ContentManagement.Web, Version=
5.0.1200.0, Culture=neutral, PublicKeyToken=31bf3856ad364e35"
name="CmsEndRequestModule" />
     <add type="Microsoft.ContentManagement.Publishing.Events.
PostingEventsModule, Microsoft.ContentManagement.Publishing,
Version=5.0.1200.0, Culture=neutral, PublicKeyToken=
31bf3856ad364e35" name="CmsPosting" />
     <add type="Microsoft.ContentManagement.Web.Caching.
CmsCacheModule, Microsoft.ContentManagement.Web, Version=
5.0.1200.0, Culture=neutral, PublicKeyToken=31bf3856ad364e35"
name="CmsCacheModule" />
</httpModules>
```

The HTTP modules specified in CMS web.config have the following functionality:

- Microsoft.ContentManagement.Web.Security.CmsAuthorization Module performs the authentication and validates that the requesting user has sufficient rights to requested objects.
- Microsoft.ContentManagement.Web.CmsEndRequestModule makes sure that all resources allocated during the request processing in the CMS Web application are released.
- Microsoft.ContentManagement.Publishing.Events.PostingEvents Module implements CMS publishing events; it is used in conjunction with event handlers in global.asax for extending the publishing workflow.

- Microsoft.ContentManagement.Web.Caching.CmsCacheModule handles CMS cache invalidation and makes sure that only published MCMS content is stored in the output cache.

---

**NOTE:** We will look into CMS security in Chapters 17, 19, and 20, and extending the publishing workflow in Chapter 31.

---

As a result of the request processing by the appropriate CMS-specific HTTP modules, if the request is authorized, the CMS context for ASPX template execution is created. Several CMS PAPI objects are instantiated and initialized:

- CmsHttpContext object
- Posting object
- Template object

Figure 11–2 shows the relationship between the PAPI objects that are used in the CMS Web application for ASPX template processing. We will be discussing these objects and their role in page processing in the next several pages.

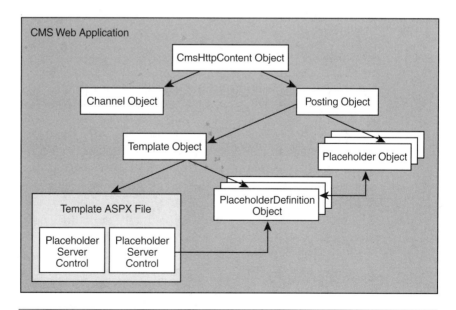

**Figure 11–2** CMS objects and ASPX template processing

The CmsHttpContext object is created for every request, or, to be precise, for every System.Web.HttpContext ASP.NET object, which in turn is created for every request. The CmsHttpContext object serves as an entry point to the PAPI object model; all other objects are retrieved from this class. The template code uses the PAPI object model; therefore, a CmsHttpContext instance must be available when template execution starts. The code in the ASPX template accesses the instance using the CmsHttpContext.Current property.

The CmsHttpContext.Mode property provides a way to determine whether the request is for the published or unpublished version of a page, and whether database updates are required. When a page is requested in presentation mode for viewing, this property is set to Published. The property takes its value from the NRMODE parameter in the query string of the transformed ASPX URL in the request.

---

**NOTE:** We will look into the CmsHttpContext object in detail in Chapter 24.

---

The Posting object corresponds to the requested page. Information about the posting is read from the CMS database using the GUID provided in the query string of the ASPX URL. This process consists of several steps: The CMS content server reads the data from the database and exposes this data to a COM-based PAPI; this data is then exposed to the ASP.NET environment using the Posting object in the managed PAPI layer.

---

**NOTE:** We will look into the Posting object in detail in Chapter 26.

---

The Template object corresponds to the template on which the requested page is based. The template metadata from the CMS database is read and exposed using the Template object in the same way as described earlier for the Posting object. The Template object has various properties that expose the metadata that is required for ASPX template file execution—for example, the placeholder definitions collection (Figure 11–2).

## Step 5

After the HTTP pipeline, the request goes to the ASPX template. The template file (and the code behind) includes static HTML and the server controls. It may also include user controls, JavaScript, or anything else you would put in an ASPX page. If it is the first request for the ASPX file, then it is retrieved from the file system, compiled, and put in the ASP.NET cache; for subsequent requests, it is run from the cache. The worker process instantiates the compiled class and any contained classes, such as server controls and HTML elements, and runs the code.

The placeholder content for a page is rendered by the placeholder server controls. Each placeholder server control is bound to the managed PAPI PlaceholderDefinition object that, in turn, determines the Placeholder object (Figure 11–2). When a placeholder server control runs, it instantiates and initializes a Placeholder object. The Placeholder object obtains the placeholder content from the database and then exposes it to the placeholder server control. After the content for all placeholders has been obtained, the resulting page is assembled and is ready to be returned to the requesting user.

During template execution, Web Author server controls run. If the requesting user has authoring rights, the Switch to Edit Site link is displayed in the resulting page.

---

**NOTE:** We will look into Web Author rendering in the next main section.

---

## Step 6

If ASP.NET output caching is enabled in the template ASPX file, the page is cached by the worker process for use by subsequent requests.

## Step 7

IIS sends the page back to the requesting browser.

---

**NOTE:** In CMS 2001, the resulting page was put in the CMS dynamic cache. By default, this cache was located in the /NR/ExeRes virtual directory on the IIS site that pointed to the physical directory *<installation drive>*\Program Files\Microsoft Content Management Server\Server\exeres. Then a URL that reflected the location of the resulting page in the dynamic cache on the file system was returned to IIS. It looked similar to the following example:

/NR/ExeRes/7DE6CC74-73ED-4EBC-BBC0-04714D6EA80A.htm

In CMS 2002, this virtual directory is also present, but it is not used for dynamic caching, and the resulting pages are not put into it. Instead, the pages are cached in the ASP.NET output cache. However, the same URL format is still being used. It doesn't reflect the actual location of the file; it is just a convention inherited from the previous version of CMS.

The browser gets the page, parses the HTML, and issues additional HTTP requests for the resources that are required to build the page, such as images, cascading style sheets, JavaScript files, or any other files. The processing of these requests differs from what we've discussed so far. Figure 11–3 shows the logical architecture and the steps involved in the processing of CMS resource requests.

## CMS Resource Processing

1. The browser issues a request.
2. IIS gets the request and passes it to the CMS Resolution ISAPI filter. If it is a request for non-CMS content, the request is returned to IIS. If the request is identified as a CMS resource request, the ISAPI filter passes the request to the CMS content server.

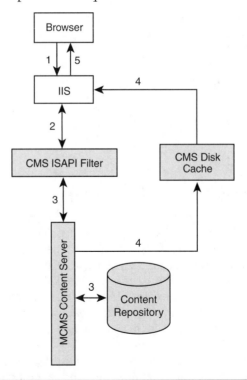

**Figure 11–3** Logical architecture of CMS resource processing

3. The CMS content server verifies the rights, and if the request is authorized, the server checks whether this is the first time the resource has been requested. If this is the case, CMS retrieves the requested resource from the database.

4. The retrieved resource is put in the CMS static cache for use by subsequent requests. By default, the CMS static cache is located in the /NR/RdOnlyRes virtual directory on the IIS site that points to the physical directory *<installation drive>*\Program Files\Microsoft Content Management Server\Server\rdonlyres.

   A URL that reflects the location of the resulting file in the static cache is returned to IIS. It looks similar to the following example:

   ```
   /NR/RdOnlyRes/2206150E-E01C-4473AE7F-D3EDAC2DFE99/0/
   <resource name>
   ```

5. IIS uses the returned URL to retrieve the resource file from the cache and send it back to the requesting browser.

## Page Processing in Authoring Mode

When a page is requested in authoring mode, the placeholders are rendered as authoring controls that provide the ability to create and edit the content within the placeholders. The overall logical processing is similar to presentation mode page processing. However, there are differences in how the placeholder server controls render the content and how the new content is written to the CMS database.

In Chapters 5 and 6, we have discussed CMS content authoring using the Web Author. In order to understand page processing in authoring mode, we need to take into consideration the modes of the Web Author application used for the different stages of the editing process. It is the combination of the publishing mode (specified by the CmsHttpContext.Mode property) and the Web Author mode that defines how the placeholder server controls run and how the placeholders are rendered in the page.

A special class called WebAuthorContext provides a set of properties, methods, and events that are required for the functioning of the Web Author. The current context of the Web Author application is available from the property WebAuthorContext.Current. The current mode of the Web Author is available from the property WebAuthor

Context.Current.Mode. We will discuss the WebAuthorContext class in more detail in Chapter 30 when we look into customizing the Web Author.

As we have already mentioned in the previous main section, when a user with authoring rights requests a page in presentation mode, the Switch to Edit Site link is displayed. When the page is generated in presentation mode, WebAuthorContext.Current.Mode is PresentationPublished. CmsHttpContext.Mode is set to Published.

When the user switches to Edit mode, another page request is sent to the CMS site. In the URL, the query string parameter WBCMODE defines the current mode of the Web Author application. The WebAuthorContext.Current.Mode property takes its value from the WBC MODE parameter in the query string of the URL in the request. In this case, WebAuthorContext.Current.Mode is PresentationUnpublished. The CmsHttpContext.Mode is set to Unpublished.

Let's go through the steps when an author edits an existing page. You may need to refer to Figures 11–1 and 11–2 for the sequence of steps and the relationship between objects.

1. The user clicks Edit in the Web Author console. The request for the page is sent to the CMS site.
2. IIS receives the request and passes it to the CMS Resolution ISAPI filter.
3. The request is passed to the appropriate worker process.
4. The request arrives at the CMS Web application and goes through the HTTP pipeline as defined by HTTP modules contained in the machine.config file and the web.config file. The request is authenticated and authorized, and the CMS context is created. In this case, the CmsHttpContext.Mode property is set to Unpublished. WebAuthorContext.Current.Mode is AuthoringReedit.
5. ASP.NET instantiates the template compiled class and runs the code. The placeholder server controls determine the publishing mode and the Web Author mode, and then render the placeholders in the resulting page as authoring controls. The configuration of these authoring controls is defined by the Placeholder Definition objects contained in the template. For example, an HTML placeholder definition may have the AllowHyperLinks property set to False, which means that authors are not allowed to use <A> tags for hyperlinks in the content of this placeholder. In this example, the authoring control will be rendered without the Hyperlink formatting button.

The placeholders in the resulting page are populated by the existing content obtained from the CMS database by the corresponding Placeholder objects.

During template execution, Web Author server controls check the Web Author mode and render the Web Author console in a resulting page.

6. The resulting page is put in the ASP.NET output cache. Because the page is unpublished, it will never be served from the cache for subsequent requests.
7. IIS returns the page to the requesting browser.

The user edits the page and changes the content of the placeholders, and then clicks Save. Let's look at the steps; once again, you may need to refer to Figures 11–1 and 11–2 for the sequence of steps and the relationship between objects.

1. When the user clicks Save, browser issues a request to CMS.
2. IIS receives the request and passes it to the CMS Resolution ISAPI filter.
3. The request is passed to the worker process that does the initial processing of the request.
4. The CMS context is created as before. In this instance, the CmsHttpContext.Mode property is set to Update. WebAuthor Context.Current.Mode is AuthoringReedit.
5. The template code runs. The placeholder server controls instantiate the corresponding PlaceholderDefinition and Placeholder objects. The properties configured in the placeholder definition are used to validate the new content. For example, if hyperlinks are not allowed for the HTML placeholder, the content in this placeholder is checked for the presence of <A> tags. After the validation, cleanup of invalid content is performed, such as deleting the <A> tags in our example. After the content has been validated and cleaned, it is committed to the CMS database using a Placeholder object. Then, the rest of the code in the template runs, including Web Author server controls, and the resulting page is rendered. The page status in the Web Author console is set to Saved.
6. The resulting page is put in the cache.
7. IIS returns the page to the requesting browser.

## Summary

In this chapter, we looked into CMS page processing. Page processing in CMS is based on ASPX templates. It uses multiple layers, including IIS, ISAPI filters, the worker process, CMS Web application, Publishing API, CMS content server, and CMS database. The CMS Web application initializes and instantiates the CMS context, which provides access to the PAPI objects. The PAPI objects allow us to interact with the CMS database. The template ASPX file and the template metadata define how the placeholder server controls render the content. The content is obtained from and committed to the CMS database by the Placeholder object that corresponds to the placeholder server control. Depending on whether the page is requested in presentation mode or authoring mode, the placeholder server controls execute differently and emit different HTML in the resulting page.

Templates are central to the concepts and execution of CMS. In the next chapter, we will look into designing templates.

# CHAPTER 12

# Designing Templates

## Overview

The basis for all CMS-based sites is templates. In CMS, templates define the look and feel as well as the functionality of your site. The development that you'll do will happen primarily within the context of a template. In Chapter 10 we talked about one half of what makes up a template—a TGI—and in Chapter 11 we explored template-based processing. In this chapter we'll explore the other component, the ASPX page. We will define what a template is, how to classify templates into logical groups, how to create templates, and how to debug them once you've written your code.

## What Is a Template?

Within any Web site, there are patterns of functionality and presentation. For example, in the BOTS Consulting Web site, all press releases share a common design and feature set. If you were to take any press release within the site and remove all of the content—that is, the information that any specific press release is trying to communicate—you would end up with a basic framework upon which any press release can be built. If you were able to reuse this press release framework over and over, you would have in essence developed a basic template.

At a very basic level, a CMS template is a container. The template "contains" components contributed by a designer—namely the visual design of the template—and components that provide functionality contributed by a developer—namely the code that a template may possess.

Lastly, a template is a container of other containers—containers that allow content contributors to enter content into the CMS repository. These containers are editable areas of the page called *placeholders.*

It's likely that you've built template-like HTML files or created systems that dynamically read data from a database and render it within a specific page design, so you may be familiar with the template concept. However, unlike homegrown systems that tend to be geared toward limited-use content entry and display, CMS templates are built based on a flexible framework that allows you to create very robust enterprise Web applications.

The biggest advantage of CMS templates is that they don't require you to code them to a specific scenario. Instead, templates in CMS are generally a collection of reusable components either provided by Microsoft or that you have created. Once the template is created, CMS provides an environment for content contributors to use that template to create pages (postings) within their site. The advantage is that your development and design efforts are limited to a relatively small number of templates. Yet these templates can yield literally thousands of pages within the site. Should you need to make a correction to the site or want to change the design, you simply change a few templates, and all pages based on those templates inherit the changes.

To illustrate our point, let's examine a page type within the BOTS Consulting Web site. For this example, we'll look at a press release (shown in Figure 12–1). You'll notice that you have several elements, such as the branding, the global navigation, the secondary navigation, and then all of the content. Drilling down further within the content, you'll notice that there's a title, a release date, the release itself, and a disclaimer. If you were to contribute a new press release to the BOTS site, you would use a *press release* template to create that new page. This template would define the design of your press release as well as what content belongs or doesn't belong in the release. Each element of content is entered into the placeholders, as defined by the template.

Beyond the components already mentioned, the template also contains an administrative menu, called the *edit console* (also called the *default console* or just the *console*), which provides the interface to the content creation and management features in CMS. The edit console is provided by Microsoft and must be included in all templates that will be used by a content contributor. An excellent characteristic of the edit console is that it is "bright" enough to understand when it should display itself and when it should not. Further, it knows what authority a given user has, and displays only the functionality that user should have (we'll

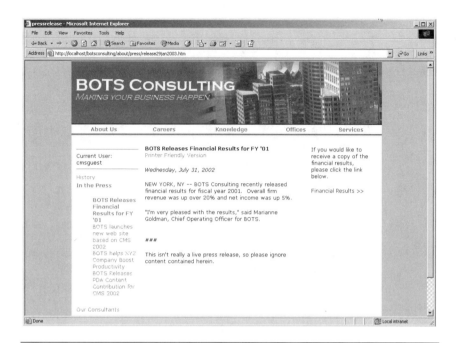

**Figure 12–1** A typical press release in the BOTS Consulting Web site

learn more about this when we discuss security). The sum total of all of these objects represents the template.

So, in short, we can think about a template as the framework for a given page. The framework controls the visual design elements, administrative functions, and sections where end users can enter content. Generically, then, we might refer to a template as a container, which holds all the elements that make up a page. In the BOTS site, for example, the press release template is a collection of objects and containers that define the design and the content structure for all pages based on the press release template.

Now, let's examine what the CMS template might look like when a user is contributing content.

In Figure 12–2 you'll notice that the look of the page has changed only slightly. Unfortunately, because of the size of the page, you can't see the edit console, but you can see the placeholders. Beyond that, you can see the branding image, the main navigation, and the side navigation. At the bottom (not shown), along with the disclaimer is a copy of the main navigation plus three links that take you home, to the site map, and to a login prompt. All these elements are part of the press release template.

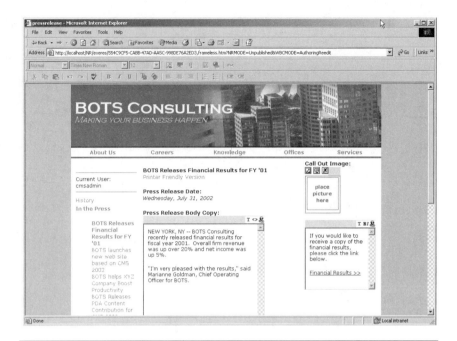

**Figure 12–2** The press release template in the BOTS Consulting Web site

# Basic Template Types

Nowhere in the CMS documentation will you find references to template "types." In CMS, there is truly only one kind of template—referred to simply as "a template." However, logically, there are several different types of page templates. For the purposes of learning how to effectively design templates, we can categorize templates as detail, summary, format, and composite.

## Detail Template

As we mentioned, you'll probably never see a description of any of the template types we just listed in Microsoft's documentation, but you've probably created pages in your own site that mimic each of these types. Take, for example, a press release in the BOTS Consulting site. You'll notice that all of the content on that page is sourced from that page. In other words, with the exception of the navigation, the content on the page doesn't come from anywhere else in the site—the page is the source of its own content. This page could be considered a detail page, since it is the lowest level of the navigation and is the source of content for other portions of the site. In order to create a detail page, you need a *detail* template. In this case, the press release template we discussed earlier is an example of a detail template. (Refer to Figure 12–1 earlier in this chapter for an example of a press release.)

## Summary Template

Now, if you have a number of detail pages, you generally need some mechanism for aggregating all of the content in to a short listing or a summary. A *summary* template is the next type of template that you'll likely create in CMS. In contrast to a detail template, the summary template is the basis for pages that don't have any content of their own. The only purpose for pages based on a summary template is to summarize the content stored in other pages. For example, if you look at the default page for the press release section in the BOTS Consulting Web site (shown in Figure 12–3), you'll notice that it is a simple listing of all of the press releases in that section. The summary lists the date of the press release, a short title, and a link to the release itself. Again, this page

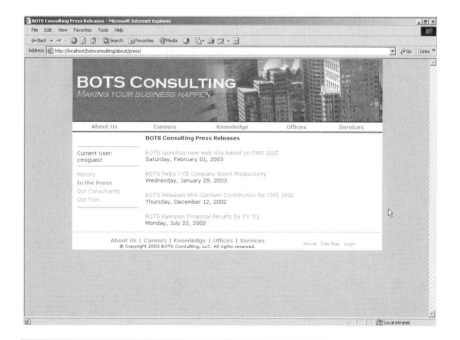

**Figure 12–3**  The press release summary in the BOTS Consulting Web site

doesn't have any content of its own; it simply aggregates content from other pages. In this case, it's exposing the display name, the start date, and the URL properties.

## Format Template

The next type of template is the *format* template. As its name suggests, its purpose is to format or reformat content that was entered in the context of an entirely different template. A format template has two distinguishing features: 1) It is not meant to be used by content contributors, and 2) it reformats the content contained in pages created with a different, but related template. The best example of a format template is a "printer friendly" version of a page. Looking at our BOTS Consulting press release in Figure 12–1, you'll notice that there is a link to a printer-friendly version of the release under the title. If you were to click that link, you would see a version of the release that looks like Figure 12–4.

Creating a printer-friendly version of a page isn't difficult, even without CMS. However, conceptually, format templates provide even greater possibilities. For example, if BOTS Consulting needed to produce a

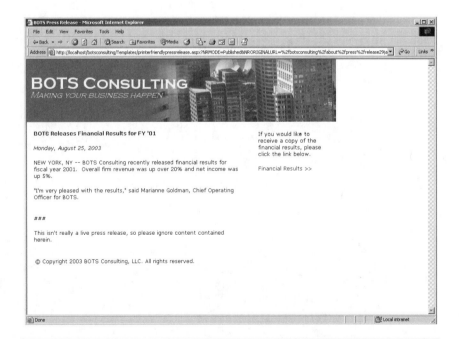

**Figure 12–4** A "printer friendly" version of a press release

version of the press release that complied with Americans with Disabilities Act (ADA) Section 508, they would simply have to create a format template that reformatted the content to conform to that standard. Or if BOTS needed to create a Microsoft Word document version of a press release, they would simply need to create a format template that transformed the press release content in to Word (see the following note). The point is that since CMS stores content separately from presentation, you have the ability to take content entered in the context of one template and display it in the context of a different template. Essentially, you would build specific templates to display content in particular formats—hence a *format* template.

---

**NOTE:** The ability to transform content from HTML to Word is not a feature of CMS. However, Chapter 36 illustrates a technique for this kind of functionality.

---

## Composite Template

The last type of template is what we call a *composite* template. A composite template is really the combination of a detail and a summary template. This type of template typically creates pages that have content summarized from other pages within the site as well as sourcing its own content. In fact, this type of template may create pages that are summarized in summary or composite pages. In the BOTS Consulting site, the best example of a composite page is the home page. The home page contains content summaries from the news and case studies sections, but the underlying home page template has three placeholders to allow content contributors to change the call-out graphic, the title, and the body copy.

As you can see from Figure 12–5, there is some content that is unique to the home page, and there is also content being pulled from the company news section. As we mentioned, composite templates produce pages that are a mix of "original" content and summarized content. If you look at the template through the Web browser (Figure 12–6), you'll notice that there are three placeholders on the page as well as the summary of the news section.

As we mentioned before, the categories of templates we provide here are just a way of thinking about your site and template design. We have found this framework to be useful in developing the various components of a template.

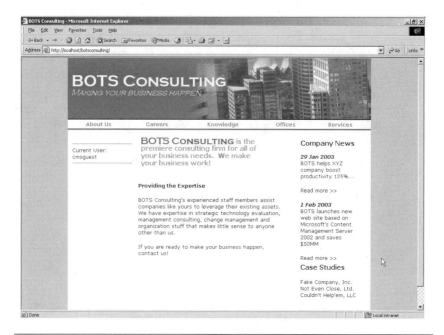

**Figure 12–5** The BOTS Consulting home page is a composite page that summarizes content as well as sourcing its own.

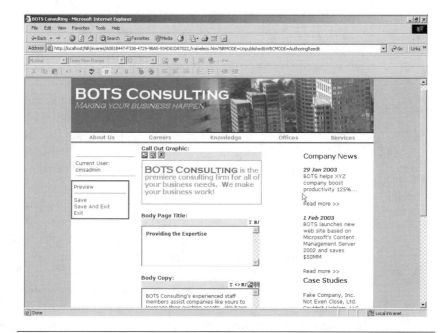

**Figure 12–6** The BOTS Consulting home page

# Planning Your Templates

A very common mistake that new CMS developers make is to trivialize the task of planning their site (or planning application development in general). As you'll probably read in a couple of places in this book, it's one thing to create a CMS-enabled site, but it's another matter entirely to create a *good* CMS-enabled site. Unlike in traditional Web development, you're not creating pages, you're creating templates. When you create pages, you have complete control over every aspect in your site. There are no surprises and there are no "gotchas," because you've been over the entire site and you're building one page at a time. If you encounter a page that doesn't quite fit, you can make slight adjustments so that it renders properly. Unfortunately, as you develop your site and you build more pages, you are "stuck" coding each page; or if you've componentized some portions of the page, you're still coding unique HTML that may only exist on that one page—largely because the content may force changes (images that *have* to be there, but are bigger than you planned on, for example).

Conversely, using CMS, you can more consistently regulate how your site is developed through the use of templates. You're probably familiar with the concept of templates in the context of Word, Dreamweaver, and FrontPage. In each case, the template provides a framework so that you can start entering content or adding functionality. The advantage is that as you create new pages or documents based on this template, you can reduce the repetitive tasks—such as formatting—and you only have to concentrate on the actual tasks of entering the unique content or functionality. In the case of CMS, you'll define how each page within the site will behave by creating the "rules" for how a template should render content given a certain set of circumstances. This kind of development generally leads to reduced maintenance, more consistent site design, and an improved user experience. However, you need to be careful to appropriately plan your new site to realize these benefits (yes, we're repeating ourselves because it's important).

So, how do you start the process of developing your site in this sort of environment? Well, from a template perspective, there are two steps to begin with: analyzing your existing site (or new design) and creating your template framework.

## Analyzing Your Site

After reading the first part of this chapter, you're probably beginning to analyze your own Web project. You're mentally walking through the different page types within your own site, or you may even be "flipping" through your site right now. If you're doing either of these activities, you're on the right track. The trick is to try to understand precisely how your site works, identifying the common elements and varying pages types. Ultimately, this will lead to a general definition of what templates might make up your site. What you'll probably find are a few basic page designs, common across your site. In a very large site, you may have groups of pages with a common design and/or functionality set. As you navigate through your site, take notice of how the navigation appears or doesn't appear. How many content elements make up the page? All these questions will help you better understand the construction of each page, and ultimately the components that you'll have to build.

Later, as you're developing your site, you'll probably find that your initial plan wasn't 100% accurate. Don't be discouraged—it happens to the best of us. The important thing to remember is that the changes you're making will likely improve your site, including details that you probably overlooked in your enthusiasm to begin development.

To begin this process, find a page design that seems to be common to a grouping of content. This design may be common to the whole site—which is ideal—or it may be common to a subset of the content. What we're looking for is something "generic." We want to try to create a template that has no unique elements but contains only those page elements that are common to the set of content you've logically grouped together. In the BOTS Consulting site, you'll notice that the branding image, the global navigation, and the footer always appear the same way, no matter what page is shown. Each of these elements is common to all the pages within the site and therefore can be included in your generic template. Once you've identified common elements, try to identify those elements that may be semiconsistent across your site. For example, in the BOTS Consulting site, you may have noticed that the left-hand navigation appears most of the time within the site. Include these elements in your generic template as well. In the BOTS site example, the left navigation appears about 80% to 90% of the time (we'll deal with the rules for when it doesn't show up later), so we'll include that in our generic template.

Once you've finished assembling the generic template (you can do this all in HTML), load it in a browser and compare it with the rest of your site. You should be able to clearly identify how each page could fit into this template. There may be gaping "holes," which may or may not be filled with content (remember, though, white space is good), but in general you should be able to "see" your site. Figure 12–7 shows the generic template for BOTS.

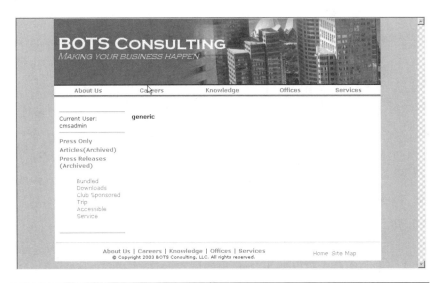

**Figure 12–7** The BOTS Consulting generic template

If you compare this generic template with the pages you've seen earlier in the chapter, you'll notice that all the other pages have the core design elements contained in the generic template. Essentially what we've done is to create the basis for all the other templates, which will then support the site postings. After we've created this generic template, we need to start identifying the components that make up the template. For example, the header is a common element and could be componentized. The same holds true for the footer and navigation. It's this kind of site deconstruction that will help you establish your site framework.

## Creating Your Template Framework

Once you've developed your generic template, start analyzing each page in your site to determine the components that make up each page. Some of these components will be included in the generic template, while others will only be included in specific templates. Remember, a template isn't limited to the visual design; there may be functionality differences as well. Let's return to the BOTS Consulting Web site and take a look at the home page (Figure 12–5). You'll notice that the generic template and the home page share a number of similarities, but the home page contains a news summary, a case study summary, and introduction text. These two elements of a page are a great start in identifying the unique elements in your site.

In Chapter 36, we discuss several methodologies that you can use to help with this process. For example, a content inventory will help you assess all of the content in your site. After the inventory is finished, you'll be in a better position to determine your specific template needs. Once you're ready to start building your templates, the generic template will serve as your foundation, eliminating a lot of the grunt work in developing your templates.

In the case of the BOTS Consulting site, the IS/IT department created several components (user controls) to include in the generic template. One element is the header user control. This user control primarily contained two elements: the branding and the global navigation. In Figure 12–8, you can see the Design view of that control. If you look closely, you'll see that the control simply contains a graphic banner at the top that contains the branding and the photo element. Just below that graphic is the table server control, which will ultimately house the main navigation when the code is executed.

You'll notice that there isn't much to the control. However, this control can be used over and over again across the site. In fact, every template in the site will use this control, since it provides both the branding and the navigation.

As the BOTS Consulting IS/IT department analyzed their site, they ended up creating the following user controls, which are common to all templates:

- Header
- Footer
- Side navigation

**Figure 12–8**  The header user control in the BOTS site

Each of these elements is common to all of their templates. Interestingly, it's possible to further deconstruct their site. For example, the footer contains three distinct elements: a copy of the main navigation, the copyright message, and three global navigation elements. The header contains two distinct elements: the branding image and the main navigation. Finally, the side navigation also displays the currently authenticated user, as well as navigation to sections within the site. Depending on your particular needs, you may choose to create even more granular elements to build your templates. Although BOTS chose to create "larger" components, creating smaller components may have advantages, such as the ability to place the global navigation on a page, without carrying the main navigation and copyright notice. Again, the choice is up to you.

## Creating a Template File

Once you have your framework established, it's time to begin the physical creation of the template file. The template file is where all of your code and controls will be placed—it's the container for the specific site and CMS elements that will make up the physical template. Also, you'll want to create a project structure that helps you organize all the controls and templates you may create for your project. This is not a requirement, but it will make your life easier as you develop your CMS site. In Figure 12–9, you'll see the structure that we're using for our BOTS Consulting project. Your project structure may be different, but we've found that the organization shown works very well.

**Figure 12–9** A basic organizational structure for a CMS project

### ASPX or ASP?

CMS 2002 can use either an ASPX or an ASP file. This book only presents examples using ASPX and .NET. However, if you're upgrading an existing CMS 2001 site or simply wish to use ASP 3.0, you can.

Now that we have some organization to our project, let's create our first template ASPX page. The first step is to select the template folder we have in our project. Simply right-click that folder, pick Add, and then pick Add New Item from the list. The resulting dialog box will have a choice for Content Management Server (shown in Figure 12–10). After clicking the Content Management Server option in the left column, choose the MCMS Template File object type in the right column (it's the only choice). Be sure to change the name of your template in the Name field in the dialog (otherwise, you'll end up with a really unattractive and not terribly descriptive template name). After you click OK, VS.NET will add the new ASPX file to your templates folder in your project.

You've just created your first template file! Now what? To begin, let's review the TGI that we created earlier. When we talked about TGIs in Chapter 10, we created the generic TGI to support the ASPX page that has yet to be created. Now that you have your ASPX page, we should revisit that TGI and fix the "broken" icon.

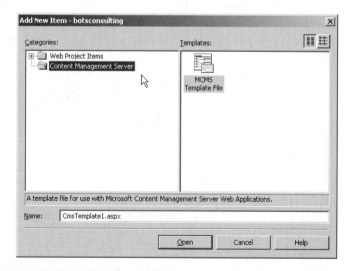

**Figure 12–10**  The Add New Item dialog has a choice for Content Management Server.

The first thing we need to do is to save the new ASPX file and then point the TGI to the ASPX page you've just created. Click the Save icon in the VS.NET toolbar and then open the Template Explorer window (or tab over to it) and find your generic TGI. Once you've located your generic TGI, make sure it's checked out. If the TGI has a red check mark on it, it's checked out. If it's not checked out, just right-click the object and pick Check Out from the context menu. Now, locate the TGI property TemplateFile. If you select this property, you'll see the familiar ellipsis icon appear. This allows you to browse your server to locate the template file. Locate the templates folder you created and then click the template you just created; we called our template "generic" to match the TGI, but you may have used a different name (the choice is up to you). Once you've chosen the template file, simply click OK, and you should end up with a property view similar to Figure 12–11.

Once you've completed this process, the icon next to your TGI should be whole. This indicates that your TGI is tied to a physical template file. Once this is done, it's a good idea to save your TGI by right-clicking the TGI and picking Save from the menu.

## Adding Components to Your Template File

At this point, you may be thinking to yourself, "Besides the association with the TGI, how is a template file different from a typical ASPX

**Figure 12–11**  The TGI property view with the newly selected template file

page?" That's a good question. Fundamentally, there isn't any difference. The real departure from a typical ASPX page is the inclusion of certain standard CMS controls (server and user) that make a typical ASPX page a CMS template file and how the ASPX page is processed at runtime.

So what are the components? The first one is a user control that we saw in Chapter 10 when you created your CMS project. It's the default console (also called the edit console). The console is the interface that your content contributors will be interacting with when they're contributing content, approving content, submitting content for approval, looking at the revision history, or accessing other CMS functionality from within a Web browser. In fact, without the console, your template is useless to your content contributors. Although you might be able to make the template available to your content contributors, they'd never be able to save the content they entered, since that function is on the console!

Adding the console to your template file is pretty easy. In your Solution Explorer, locate the "console" folder. It's included by default in all CMS projects (later in the book, we'll talk about how to customize it, so you can ignore the design of the console for the moment). Once you've located it, just left-click the control and drag it to your template file (be sure to be in the *Design* view). After you've dragged the console to your template, you should see something like Figure 12–12.

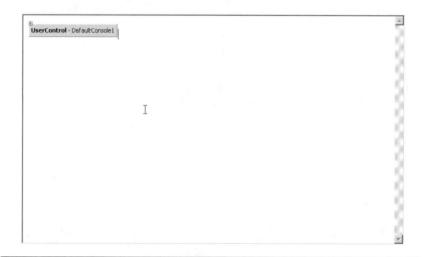

**Figure 12–12**  A blank template file with the edit console

**NOTE:** VS.NET likes to create new ASPX files with the grid layout enabled. Unfortunately, the console doesn't allow for absolute positioning natively. As a result, you'll want to turn off the grid layout. Just remove the MS_POSITIONING="GridLayout" attribute from the BODY tag in the HTML view. If you don't turn off the grid layout, the console may overlap other elements (such as placeholders) when the template is rendered. Using flow layout can also be set as a default in VS.NET.

### Customized Edit Console

There are several customized versions of the standard edit console floating around the Internet. Microsoft's MSDN site contains an article about a floating edit console, and http://www.gotdotnet.com has several downloadable edit consoles.

After you've added the console, you can begin to add placeholder controls. The placeholder controls render as the content entry elements we saw earlier in the chapter. They are also tied to the placeholder definitions you created in your TGI. To add a placeholder control to your template, switch to Design view, open the Toolbox, and look for the Content Management Server section, shown in Figure 12–13.

Notice that there are three server controls. These are the three controls that ship with Content Management Server. Each roughly matches to the major placeholder types we explored briefly when creating the TGI (we talked about six placeholder types—all but the image, XML, and attachment types map to the HTMLPlaceholderControl). In this example, drag an HTMLPlaceholderControl to the template. After you've done this, your template should look roughly like Figure 12–14.

The next step is to bind the placeholder control to the placeholder definition in the TGI. Just click the placeholder control in your template. In the Properties view of the control, locate the property Placeholderto Bind. When you click the property, you'll be given a drop-down list of all available placeholder definitions that are compatible with the placeholder control selected. CMS is smart enough not to present you with an image placeholder definition if you've selected an HTML placeholder control. From the list, select the placeholder definition you added in Chapter 10. Once you've done that, you'll notice that a new design-time element is added to your placeholder control: the placeholder definition name in brackets. This indicates that you have successfully bound the placeholder control to the placeholder definition.

**Figure 12–13** The Content Management Server Toolbox with the three placeholder controls

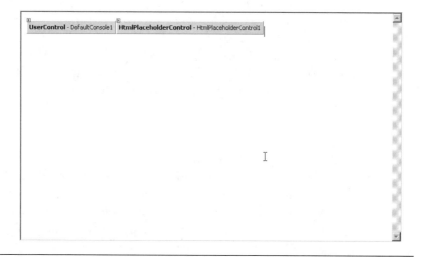

**Figure 12–14** The generic template with the controls added

**NOTE:** If the drop-down list does not show any placeholders, you've either chosen the wrong template file (ASPX) page in your TGI properties, or you haven't committed the changes to the TGI by saving it.

In our example, we've taken the liberty of finishing our generic template. We started by using the basic HTML framework we created earlier. We then created a header control (as we mentioned earlier) as well as a footer and a side navigation control (for in-channel navigation). After creating those controls, we added them to our template, along with our placeholders and console. In Figure 12–15, you can see what the completed template looks like in Design view.

Templates aren't always pretty in Design view. In fact, we very often have to "preview" them to see what they'll look like. Luckily, CMS provides a preview feature for templates in our solution. To preview what your template would look like if it were a page in your site, switch to the Template Explorer window. Locate your template and right-click the TGI. From the context menu, pick Browse In Presentation Mode. Although this view won't show you a fully rendered page with content, it

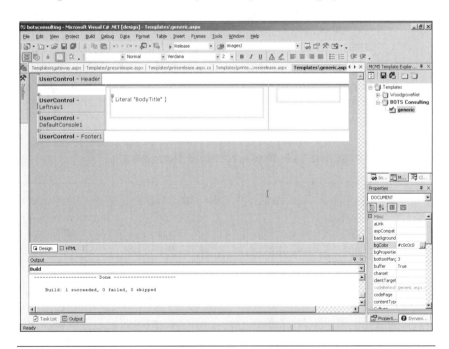

**Figure 12–15** The completed generic template in Design view

will allow you to see what a page, based on this template, might look like in your site.

---

**NOTE:** When CMS renders a template in this way, any navigation you've built will render fictitious channels and postings. This is a feature of CMS that provides a richer view of your template so that you may see what your navigation might look like as well.

---

# Debugging Your Templates

Now that you've created your template, you'll probably want to test it to make sure it works. The preview feature probably works fairly well for the quick "acid test," but it doesn't really give you an accurate indication of whether your template will operate properly in production. As we mentioned earlier in the chapter, debugging CMS projects can be slightly different from debugging typical ASP.NET projects (if you've ever worked with Visual Interdev—and gotten the debugging to work—you're already familiar with one technique). Although templates are ASPX pages, as you learned in Chapter 11, the process of rendering a page involves a few steps. As a result, you have to use one of two techniques for debugging your templates. Depending on your comfort, you may choose to use one technique over another, but they both work equally well.

## Attaching to the ASP.NET Process

Because templates aren't executed directly, you can't simply run the project as you have with other ASP.NET projects. The first technique is attaching to the ASP.NET process. If you have had experience with CMS 2001, this is similar to what debugging was like in Visual Studio 6. Unlike in VS6, this works fairly well.

To begin, you'll want to open a template within your project and set a breakpoint. The easiest way to do that is to click in the left margin, next to the line of code on which you'd like VS.NET to break. In Figure 12–16, you can see what this looks like.

In our example, we're using the BOTS Consulting Press Release Summary template. We've set a breakpoint at the line of code where we're creating a new HTMLAnchor object. Once VS.NET breaks on

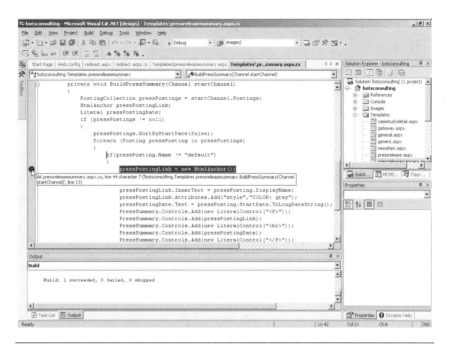

**Figure 12–16**  Setting a breakpoint in your code

that line, we can walk through the rest of the code line-by-line, observing exactly what happens.

Once you've set your breakpoint, you can attach to the ASP.NET process and walk through your code one line at a time. To attach to the ASP.NET process, use the following steps:

1. While in VS.NET, click the Debug menu.
2. From the Debug menu, choose Processes.
3. The Processes dialog will display. In the list of processes, choose aspnet_wp.exe.
4. Click the Attach button.
5. When the list of program types appears, make sure that only the Common Language Runtime is checked.
6. Now click OK, leaving the Processes dialog open (shown in Figure 12–17).

After you've successfully attached to the ASP.NET process, open an Internet Explorer session and browse to your site. In our case, we want to browse to the In the Press section of the site, since the summary

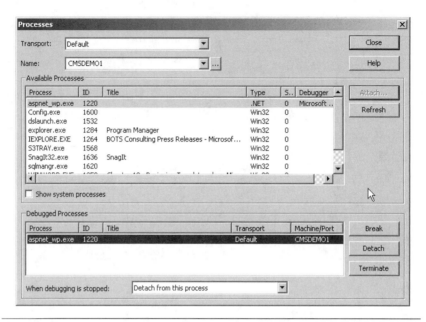

**Figure 12–17** The Processes dialog in VS.NET once you've attached

posting uses our Press Release Summary template. When we navigate to that section, VS.NET will reappear and break the code execution where we set our breakpoint. When this happens, simply close the Processes dialog and step through your code using the F11 key (step into) or F10 (step over). In Figure 12–18, you can see what this process looks like.

In Figure 12–18, in the lower left section of the screen, you can see all the objects that were created as well as all the values of the objects and what system type they are. On the lower right side, you can see all the assemblies that were loaded and their status. In this way, everything that your application is doing is exposed; if a variable is assigned the wrong value or no value at all, you can instantly see that happen as you walk through the code. By far, this is one of the coolest features of VS.NET (it's surprising what excites us, isn't it?). If you've ever had to put in multiple response.write statements in ASP code to see what's going on or had to rely on IIS to tell you what line number failed in your code, you'll appreciate this way of debugging.

## Using a Redirect Page

As we mentioned earlier, there is another technique for debugging. This technique isn't too radically different from a tracing perspective, but it

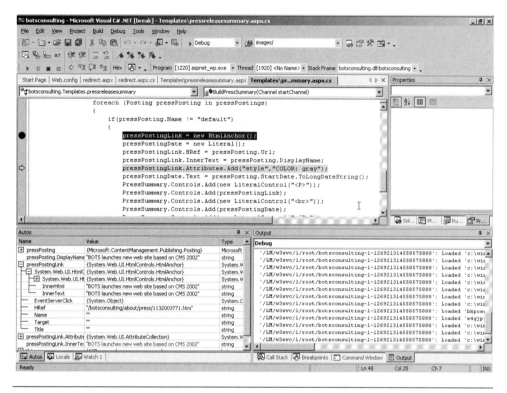

**Figure 12–18** Stepping through code in VS.NET

eliminates the need to attach to the ASP.NET process. The technique is really just creating a redirect page, setting that page as your start page, and using the typical debugging process in VS.NET (pressing F5). The real advantage is that debugging is a bit more "natural."

In the BOTS Consulting site, we created a simple redirect page in the root of the solution. We called the page redirect.aspx (hey, we're developers—name creativity is not our strong suit). In the ASPX page, we have the following code:

```
private void Page_Load(object sender, System.EventArgs e)
{
    Response.Redirect("http://localhost/botsconsulting/");
}
```

Notice there's nothing overly complicated about the code. It simply redirects to the BOTS Consulting root. To create your redirect page, simply right-click your project (or in whatever folder you wish to place the page), pick Add, and then choose Web Form. This creates a standard

**Figure 12–19**  Setting the redirect.aspx page as the start page

ASPX page in your project (you don't have to create a CMS template file). Once the page has been added to your project and you see the Design view, switch to the code-behind and add the redirect code to the Page_Load event.

Once you have your redirect page created, simply set it as your start-up page. To set this page to be the start-up ASPX file, right-click the page in your Solution Explorer. From the context menu, pick Set As Start Page (shown in Figure 12–19). Once you've done that, simply press F5, and VS.NET will rebuild your solution, start Internet Explorer, and run your Web application. When the code execution hits a breakpoint, VS.NET will reappear and allow you to step through your code.

## Summary

In this chapter, we examined what a template is within the context of CMS. A template, in essence, is a framework upon which all pages within a CMS site are built. It contains all the visual and functional elements of a page within the site, without any content. Content contributors can then choose to use a specific template to create a page within the site.

Next, we looked at the various logical template types. Each logical template type is really just a way of looking at your site; it provides a framework for analysis. This framework can be very useful for both new and existing sites. We discussed detail, summary, format, and composite template types as a way of categorizing the types of templates that you might build in your own Web projects. Each logical type has certain unique characteristics that should make their identification easy when you are analyzing your existing site or a site you're in the process of creating.

Once we finished discussing the various logical template types, we examined the high-level process of assembling a simple template. We talked about creating a generic template, which could represent some number of pages within your site. With this generic template, we could begin to identify the various subelements, which in the BOTS site were turned into user controls.

After we developed our generic template in HTML and identified the basic components, we created our first ASPX page. The ASPX page is the second part of the two elements that make up a CMS template; the other is the TGI. We then modified the TGI to point to this new ASPX page, we added our components, and we tied the placeholders to the corresponding placeholder definitions in our TGI.

Finally, we learned how to debug templates with VS.NET. Because templates are run directly as ASPX pages, you have to use one of two techniques: attaching directly to the ASPX process or using a redirect page. Essentially, both techniques work equally well—the one that you use is a personal choice.

# CHAPTER 13

# Working with Placeholders in Visual Studio .NET

## Overview

In Content Management Server, placeholders are a very important part of the content contribution interface. They allow authors to physically contribute content, but also constrain what content can or cannot be contributed. In order to effectively develop a CMS-based solution, you should have a good understanding of each of the placeholder types and how they fit into any potential solution.

In this chapter, we'll explore each of the intrinsic placeholder controls and placeholder definition types, and see how they're used. In addition, we'll talk a little about the best practices, discussing how to effectively use placeholders within your template.

## Placeholder Types

In CMS, there are three intrinsic placeholder controls and six definitions. Each placeholder control has a corresponding placeholder definition. The HTML and attachment placeholder controls can also be bound to the OfficeHtmlPlaceholderDefinition and OfficeAttachment PlaceholderDefinition, respectively. The last placeholder definition type, the XMLPlaceholderDefinition, does not have a corresponding control.

The most common use for this placeholder definition is in the development of custom placeholders. For more information on developing custom placeholders, refer to Chapter 29.

Each placeholder has its own "specialty" when it comes to content. Depending on the solution, one or more of these placeholders may be added to your templates. In the following sections, we'll discuss each of the three intrinsic controls and their corresponding definitions. Because of the overlap between each of the placeholder controls, we're only going to cover the differences between placeholders. For example, we'll cover a lot of background on the HTML placeholder but won't repeat the same information for the other placeholder controls unless there are significant differences.

## HTML Placeholder

If any placeholder could be called the "bread and butter" placeholder, it would be the HTML placeholder. The HTML placeholder is probably the most commonly used placeholder in CMS, since it will generally accept any kind of content—from HTML content (as the name suggests) to attachments (files uploaded to CMS) to images—with no trouble at all.

### General Usage

HTML placeholders can be used in a number of situations. Most commonly, they're used as a "big bucket" for content. In other words, since HTML placeholders can accept any kind of content, they're often used to allow content contributors to contribute a fairly wide variety of content. When template designers don't know the actual structure of the contributed content or feel that the structure is too complex to handle programmatically, they'll often provide one HTML placeholder configured to accept any content. Although this is one approach, we don't recommend it, but it does work in some cases.

In Figure 13–1, we show two HTML placeholders in the BOTS Consulting site. These two placeholders happen to be located on the press release template. If you look at the upper right corner of a placeholder, you should notice different icons. These icons provide a pictorial guide to the type of content that may be added to the placeholder. Each icon represents a specific setting for the placeholder. These settings determine what types of content can be contributed to the placeholder and how that content can be manipulated. For example, the first placeholder, the Press Release Body Copy placeholder, is configured to accept

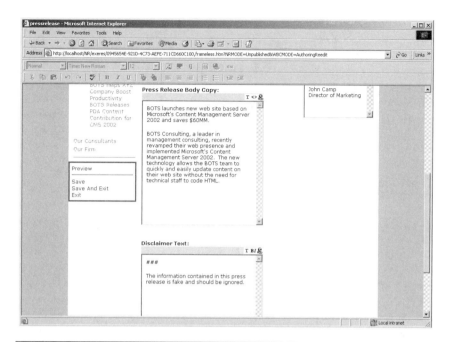

**Figure 13–1**  HTML placeholders in the BOTS press release template

plain text, HTML styles, and hyperlinks. The second placeholder, Disclaimer Text, is configured to accept plain text, text markup, and hyperlinks. Although all placeholders have a version of these icons, the HTML placeholders have the most varied combination of potential icons.

Depending on how the placeholder is configured, HTML placeholders will generally accept any content or formatting. Refer to Figure 13–1 again. Look near the top of the screen shot. Notice the two new toolbars. These toolbars are similar to any Office toolbar you may have seen in the past. These toolbars, for the HTML placeholder, provide the basic formatting options available to the content contributor. If you look closely at Figure 13–1, you'll notice that most of the buttons are grayed out. Based on the settings in the placeholder definition and the placeholder control, CMS will automatically eliminate functionality that is disabled. Now, if we move our cursor to the second placeholder, for the disclaimer text, notice how the toolbar changes in Figure 13–2. Notice that the drop-down list that showed Normal is grayed out now, and the B, I, and U buttons (for bold, italics, and underline) are enabled. Should a contributor add content that has invalid (disallowed) formatting applied (i.e., copying and pasting content), the formatting will be

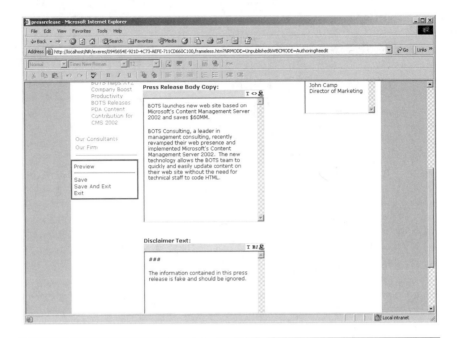

**Figure 13–2** The IE toolbars connected to the HTML placeholder

stripped out during the save operation (although it will initially appear as if the formatting were accepted).

Now, let's take a look at another HTML placeholder that is set up to accept more formatting and content. In Figure 13-3, you'll see the Case Study Detail template. This template has two placeholders, both HTML. Looking at the Case Study Body Copy placeholder, you'll notice that the icons in the upper right corner indicate the additional types of content that can be contributed to this placeholder. The two paperclip icons (yes, they're paperclips) indicate that you can contribute attachments. In other words, a content contributor can upload one or more files to this place-holder. Each file or "attachment" will be displayed as a link. In addition, this placeholder allows images to be contributed in a similar fashion; the placeholder will accept one or more images. Unlike the attachment, when an image is contributed, it will automatically appear inside the place-holder. In Figure 13–4, you can see the same posting with an image and an attachment contributed.

Now that you have a sense of what an HTML placeholder looks like in a template, let's take a closer look at how you set up this particular type of placeholder.

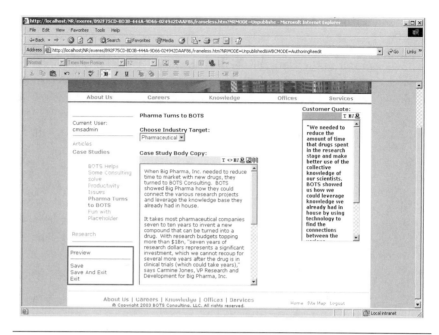

**Figure 13–3** A BOTS Consulting case study with the placeholder exposed

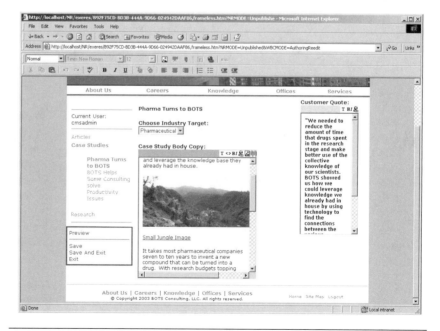

**Figure 13–4** An image and an attachment contributed to the HTML placeholder

## Setup

All placeholders in a template are really two objects: a placeholder definition in the template gallery item (TGI) and a placeholder server control. The setup of a placeholder is a combination of two of these objects (and is generically referred to as simply "a placeholder"). It doesn't matter which element you start with, since you need both for the placeholder to function properly. In our case, we'll review the placeholder control first and then review the placeholder definition.

All placeholder controls are located in the Toolbox in VS.NET. There are only three intrinsic placeholder server controls: HTML, Attachment, and Image. The HTML placeholder control is used with the HTML PlaceholderDefinition and the OfficeHTMLPlaceholderDefintion. In Figure 13–5, you'll see a shot of the Toolbox in VS.NET listing the three controls we just mentioned. Keep in mind that the controls are only visible in the Toolbox if you're in *Design* view when reviewing a template file.

**Figure 13–5** The intrinsic placeholder controls in the VS.NET Toolbox

If we want to add a placeholder to a template, we simply drag and drop that placeholder to the Web form. In doing so, a new object appears on our form. In our example, we created a new template file called "sample" to allow us to play with the placeholders. Once you've added your placeholder control to your template file, you can click it to see the object properties. Figure 13–6 shows the various properties that can be set at the object level, and the following list explains each setting.

- BackColor: Controls the background color of the placeholder. The background color will be applied to each line of text individually.
- BorderColor: Controls the border color of the placeholder.
- BorderStyle: Determines if the placeholder has a border around it and what the border looks like.
- BorderWidth: Determines the width of the border applied to the placeholder. Be careful with this setting. As much as it seems intuitive that the border will not frame the placeholder as a whole, it will actually frame each line of text; the result is not pretty.
- CssClass: At design time or runtime, can be set to a specific CSS class. Keep in mind that authors could potentially override this property setting by changing font attributes during contribution.
- Font: Determines the font that is used in the placeholder. This specific property has subproperties that determine the specific

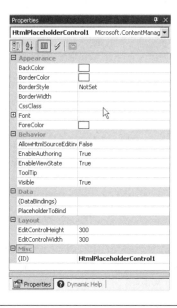

**Figure 13–6** The properties of an HTML placeholder in VS.NET

font attributes that can also be applied. Again, the content contributor could potentially override these settings.

- ForeColor: Controls the color of the text in the placeholder. While you are editing, the chosen color won't be seen, but the font will assume the set color if you preview or save the page and view it in Edit or Live mode.

- AllowHtmlSourceEditing: Allows content contributors to switch to a view of the content that exposes the HTML tags that are written in the background. This property should generally be set to False to prevent nontechnical users from accidentally changing the HTML tags. However, this property may be set to True for more advanced users and where more HTML editing flexibility is needed.

- EnableAuthoring: Allows you to turn off authoring within a placeholder. This property should generally be set to True. One example of where this property may be used is when a developer needs to restrict access to a placeholder's content if the current user isn't an editor (an editorial comments placeholder, for example). The author should be able to read the content in the placeholder but not be able to change it. When an author is editing the posting, the property could be set to False. When the editor edits the posting, the property can be programmatically set to True.

- EnableViewState: Controls whether the .NET view state is enabled.

- ToolTip: Allows you to enter a string that will appear when you roll your mouse over the placeholder border in authoring mode and over the text in Live mode. Because the tooltip appears in Live mode, it may not be appropriate in all cases.

- Visible: Determines whether the placeholder is visible at runtime. This setting affects both authoring and Live mode. Building on the example of a comments placeholder, this property would be useful for hiding the contents entirely when the page is published to the live site.

- DataBindings: Is inherited from the System.Web.UI.Control namespace. For more information on the System namespace, please refer to http://go.microsoft.com/fwlink/?LinkID=9677.

- PlaceholderToBind: Defines to what placeholder definition the placeholder object is bound. The drop-down list for this property will only list compatible placeholder definitions. For example, you can't bind an image placeholder definition to an HTML placeholder object.

- EditControlHeight: Determines the height, in pixels, of the control in authoring mode. This setting does not constrain the content in Live mode.
- EditControlWidth: Determines the width, in pixels, of the control in authoring mode. This setting does not constrain the content in Live mode.
- ID: Is inherited from System.Web.UI.Control. For more information on the System namespace, please refer to http://go.microsoft.com/fwlink/?LinkID=9677.

Now that we know the various object-level settings that we can apply to a placeholder, let's examine the placeholder definition for an HTML placeholder. To begin, switch to the Template Explorer in VS.NET. In our template gallery, we've created a corresponding TGI to match our new sample template. We used the same name for our TGI (sample). Once you've created the new TGI, find the property PlaceholderDefinitions. Click the ellipsis next to that property, and you should see the Place holder Definition Collection Editor, shown in Figure 13–7.

If you've been reading this book from the beginning, you'll likely recognize this interface from Chapter 12. If you haven't been reading from the beginning, then it's new to you. In any event, this interface is the tool that you'll use to create the various placeholder definitions for each of your placeholder objects. You'll end up adding one placeholder definition to the collection for each placeholder control on your template.

**Figure 13–7** The Placeholder Definition Collection Editor

Let's create a placeholder definition for the HTML placeholder we added earlier. To do so, simply click the Add button. Even though there are six placeholder definition types, CMS will create an HTML placeholder definition by default. If you want to create a different type, you can click the down arrow at the right of the Add button. Once you've created your new definition, you should see something like Figure 13–8.

Once you have your new placeholder definition, you can begin to set the various properties for the definition. The settings for the HTML placeholder definition are explained in the following list.

- AllowHyperlinks: Determines whether content contributors are allowed to contribute hyperlinks to the placeholder. Setting this property to False will disable the link icon in the placeholder toolbar. Keep in mind that if you set the placeholder to allow HTML editing, it's possible for the content contributor to manually enter a hyperlink into the placeholder.
- AllowLineBreaks: Determines whether content contributors can insert line breaks in the content. This setting is useful when you want to use a placeholder for a title or you don't want content contributors to press Enter (or Shift-Enter) and insert blank lines in the content.

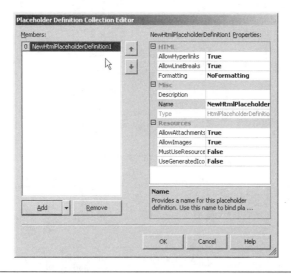

**Figure 13–8** A new placeholder definition in the Placeholder Definition Collection Editor

- Formatting: Provides five options for text formatting.
  - NoFormatting: Does not allow any formatting to be applied to content in the placeholders.
  - FullFormatting: Allows all formatting possibilities to be applied to content in a placeholder. These options include HTML styles, bold, italics, font, font color, background color, alignment, lists (ordered and unordered), indenting, and tables. This is the only option that allows tables.
  - TextMarkup: Allows content contributors to apply basic bold, italics, and underlining to content.
  - HtmlStyles: Allows content contributors to apply HTML styles such as headings (H1, H2, and so on), Formatted, Address, and lists. Most HTML styles are supported. However, tables are not supported as a style.
  - TextMarkupandHtmlStyles: Is a combination of the text markup and HTML styles settings. This gets you pretty close to full control, allowing users to apply HTML styles as well as ad hoc bold, italics, and underline.
- Description: Allows you to provide a description of a placeholder. The text entered into this field will show up as default text within the placeholder when a user creates a posting based on the template.
- Name: Allows you to name the placeholder definition. This name will be the string index in the placeholder collection. Should you need to programmatically retrieve or modify content, you will use this name to access the placeholder object using the Publishing API.
- Type: Returns the placeholder type (HTML, XML, Office, and so on). This is a read-only property.
- AllowAttachments: Determines whether a content contributor can upload files to the placeholder.
- AllowImages: Determines whether a content contributor can upload images to the placeholder.
- MustUseResources: Is related to the AllowImages and Allow Attachments properties. It determines whether attachments or images have to come from a shared resource gallery or whether they can be uploaded from the contributor's local or network drive.
- UseGeneratedIcon: Determines whether uploaded attachments are represented by icons or text links. CMS natively has all the Office icons, but less common files will get a generic icon.

## Design Considerations

HTML placeholders can provide a tremendous amount of flexibility. However, there are several design considerations you should take into account when developing your template.

- Generally, HTML placeholders provide enough flexibility for most authoring situations. Unfortunately, table editing is not a strength. Content contributors can easily create tables of specific column and row depth, but after the initial creation, it's not possible to edit the table definition. In order to edit tables once they've been created, you'll have to turn on HTML editing in the placeholder object or delete the existing table and re-create it.
- Users who contribute images to an HTML placeholder will find they can't exercise enough control over the placement of that image, unless it has been copied and pasted from another source that defined the layout. For example, there's no easy way to add an align attribute to the image tag that's created when the image is contributed. The best way to provide this sort of flexibility is to create several placeholders, each specializing in a particular type of content. Then, arrange the content programmatically, or extract the raw content from the placeholder and "manually" render the values, hiding the placeholder control (set the Visible property to false). Alternatively, create the content in a tool like FrontPage or Dreamweaver, and copy and paste the HTML directly into the placeholder; images will have to be uploaded separately once you've copied the HTML framework over. Also, depending on the content, you can use the Authoring Connector and Word to appropriately format the content before it goes into CMS.
- There's a small gap in authoring flexibility between the TextMarkupandHTMLStyles and the FullFormatting settings. Specifically, you have to set the placeholder to full control in order to allow tables. Your specific design will determine the best way to mitigate this situation, but we've found that it's generally not a huge problem to overcome.
- CMS will strip out placeholder content that isn't allowed by the definition. This is generally a good thing. However, if a content contributor enters content that's outside the scope of a given placeholder, they won't realize that certain formatting or content isn't allowed until after they save. For example, even if you have the placeholder set to TextMarkup, a user could copy and paste a

table from Word. Initially, the placeholder will display the table as it was in Word. When the user saves the content, however, the table will be stripped out. This is largely a training issue, but it can generate a help desk call or two.

---

**NOTE:** If the properties of the placeholder are changed on an existing template and made more restrictive, the original content will continue to be displayed until that page is edited. Once the page is edited, the old content will be displayed for authoring, but on save, the now invalid formatting will be stripped out.

---

## Single Attachment Placeholder

The single attachment placeholder (attachment placeholder) is used to allow content contributors to upload files to a posting. In truth, the attachments may not always be uploaded directly from the contributor's machine to a posting; essentially, the attachment placeholder allows content contributors to display a link to a file within the context of their posting. The actual file could be stored in a resource gallery, or it could have been uploaded from a local source directly to the posting. Either way, the attachment will reside in the CMS repository once it has been contributed (preventing broken links). In Figure 13–9, an attachment placeholder is shown on the attachment template for BOTS Consulting.

### General Usage

The attachment (or single attachment) placeholder is useful in a number of situations. At a very basic level, it's useful for allowing content contributors to upload files to CMS. Unlike the HTML placeholder, however, the attachment placeholder only allows one file per placeholder. However, this is only part of the story. It's also possible to use the attachment placeholder to integrate Flash (Macromedia) into your design. A user can contribute the Flash movie to the placeholder, and then the template will extract the resulting link to integrate with an object tag in the HTML

### Setup

As you saw in Figure 13–9, the attachment placeholder looks quite different from the HTML placeholder. As with the HTML placeholder, a

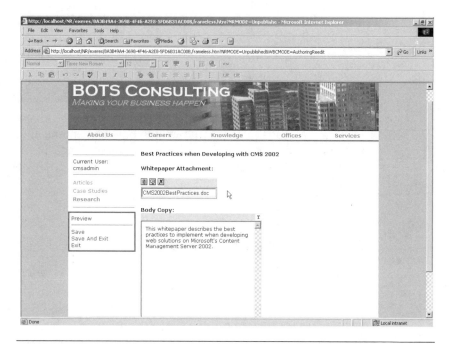

**Figure 13–9** An attachment placeholder on the attachment template in BOTS Consulting

paperclip indicates an attachment, except that in the case of the attachment placeholder, the paperclip is a button in the upper left. This button also allows you to choose the attachment the placeholder will hold. You'll also notice that there are other buttons located in the upper left. The button immediately to the right of the paperclip allows content contributors to set the display name of the attachment, and the last button (the X) allows content contributors to clear the value in the placeholder. Let's switch to VS.NET and explore the attachment placeholder object.

We're using the same sample template we used when talking about the HTML placeholder. In this template, we've now added an attachment placeholder. In Figure 13–10, you can see the template with both the HTML and attachment placeholders added to the Web form. Notice that there isn't any visible difference, except that the label on the control is SingleAttachmentPlaceholder.

The single attachment placeholder shares most of the same properties as the HTML placeholder properties. In fact, the attachment placeholder has fewer properties, since there's much less flexibility to determine display characteristics. Most notably, there aren't any height

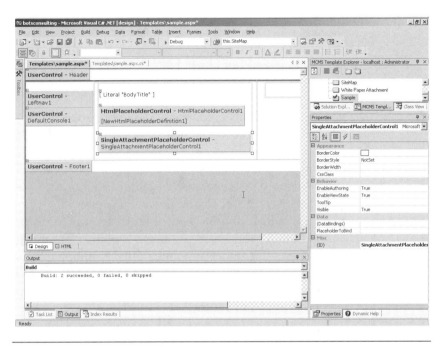

**Figure 13–10** An attachment placeholder on the sample template

and width properties; attachment placeholders are always the same size. However, even though we have a placeholder definition for our HTML placeholder, if you use the drop-down list for the PlaceholderToBind property, you'll notice that the HTML placeholder definition isn't listed. Again, this property will only list compatible types. In the case of the attachment placeholder, the only compatible definition types are Attachment PlaceholderDefinition and OfficeAttachmentPlaceholderDefinition.

Once we've created the new placeholder definition, let's look at each of the properties. The following list provides a brief explanation of each.

- Description: Allows you to provide a description of a placeholder.
- Name: Allows you to name the placeholder definition.
- Type: Returns the placeholder type (HTML, XML, Office, and so on). This is a read-only property.
- MustUseResources: Determines whether attachments or images have to come from a shared resource gallery or can be uploaded from the contributor's local or network drive.
- UseGeneratedIcon: Determines whether uploaded attachments are represented by icons or text links. CMS natively has all the Office icons, but less common files will get a generic icon.

### Design Considerations

The attachment placeholder is a pretty simple animal. However, there are some design considerations that you should be aware of when developing templates with this placeholder type.

- Attachment placeholders, by default, display either the display name of the attachment or an icon. This may be the desired behavior. However, if the only elements on a template are an attachment and a longer description (likely in an HTML placeholder), consider building an attachment redirect template. Code samples and an explanation are provided in Chapter 36.
- If you allow content contributors to use local resources, as opposed to using share resources from the resource gallery, each attachment becomes a unique entity. Even if two files are exactly the same, CMS has no way of knowing and will create a new entity for the duplicate file, thereby doubling the storage requirement for that attachment. Strongly consider using the resource galleries to control what files are used in your site. Not only do resource galleries provide a little more content control, but attachments that are used more than once will not be duplicated, and if the resource changes, the change will cascade across the site.
- If a content contributor uploads a local resource to an attachment and then later deletes it, the orphaned asset will be removed from the database when the nightly CMS cleanup occurs (assuming the SQL agent is enabled on your server).
- If you have to visually represent an attachment placeholder differently from the default behavior, it's very easy to get the URL and display text back from the placeholder, as well as set the icon used for the file programmatically. The AttachmentPlaceholder class in the PAPI provides a granular selection of properties to enable extracting what you need.

## Single Image Placeholder

The image placeholder allows content contributors contribute images to a posting. As with the attachment placeholder, this object is used when you want to have a single object in a container, as opposed to having multiple images or attachments in an HTML placeholder. In Figure 13–11 you can see what a single image placeholder looks like in the BOTS Consulting site. In this case, the image placeholder is used as a call-out image on the General template.

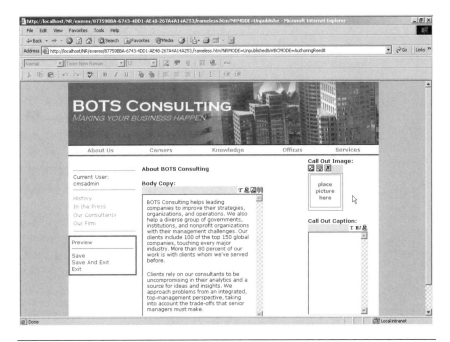

**Figure 13–11**  A single image placeholder in the BOTS Consulting site

### *General Usage*

Overall, single image placeholders are useful when you need to allow a content contributor to provide a single image for an element of a page. This sounds a little obvious, but like the attachment placeholder, this is really the "single" alternative to allowing multiple attachments or images in an HTML placeholder. This is not to suggest that if you have a single image placeholder on a template, you only need one image. In fact, you can effectively have more than one image placeholder on a template. It's very likely that you will prefer this design, since it provides a lot more control over the visual design of your end page.

The single image interface is similar to that of the attachment placeholder. Notice that at the upper left of the placeholder, there are three buttons. The first button indicates that this is an image placeholder (although the "place picture here" default image probably gave it away as well). It also allows you to browse to the image that you want to add to the placeholder, in the same way that the attachment placeholder did. The next two buttons provide the ability to change the ALT attribute for the resulting image tag and to clear the placeholder contents. Let's switch to VS.NET and explore the properties of this placeholder object.

*Setup*

In Figure 13–12, you can see what the image placeholder object looks like in VS.NET.

Again, there isn't any visual difference beyond the label that CMS provides on the object. However, there are some differences with regard to the properties. The image placeholder allows you to size the display height and width. Unlike with the HTML placeholder, these settings don't affect authoring, but they do affect the live site view. In essence, the properties DisplayHeight and DisplayWidth control the scaling of the image; physically, these properties are represented as the height and width attributes of the resulting image tag.

Now, let's look at the single image placeholder definition. Open the Placeholder Definition Collection Editor and create a new image place-holder definition. Remember to use the down arrow next to the Add button to add a definition other than an HTML definition. In Figure 13–13 we've provided a screen shot of the Placeholder Definition Collection Editor.

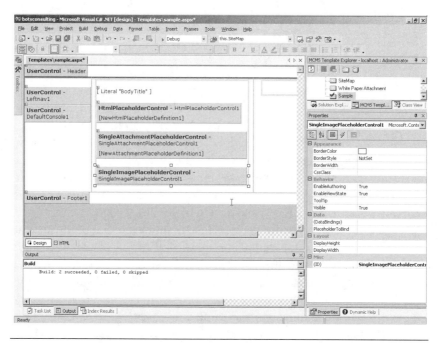

**Figure 13–12** The single image placeholder in the sample template

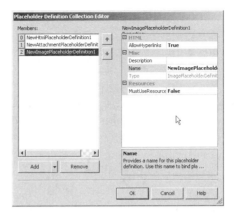

**Figure 13–13** The Placeholder Definition Collection Editor with the new image placeholder definition

In the definition there are several properties of note. The following list provides a brief description of each.

- AllowHyperlinks: Allows you to determine whether you will allow content contributors to provide a hyperlink on the image.
- Description: Allows you to provide a description of a placeholder.
- Name: Allows you to name the placeholder definition.
- Type: Returns the placeholder type (HTML, XML, Office, and so on). This is a read-only property.
- MustUseResources: Determines whether images have to come from a shared resource gallery or can be uploaded from the contributor's local or network drive.

### *Design Considerations*

As with the single attachment placeholder, the single image placeholder is a pretty straightforward control. However, here are some design considerations for when you develop your template.

- During authoring, there's no way to stipulate alignment for an image. In other words, there's no way to specify the align attribute of the image tag that's rendered in presentation (Live) mode. If you want to provide authors with the ability to align images when they contribute them, consider using a custom property on the

template that specifies the image alignment. The value of the custom property can be extracted programmatically and used to provide the alignment value desired. Programmatically, you can simply
set the attributes of the resulting image tag using the Attributes
property.

- If you use the DisplayHeight and DisplayWidth properties of
the image placeholder, keep in mind that the control will scale the
image. It will not resize the image. This behavior could have
undesirable results. However, not stipulating a height and width
for an image tag will cause the browser to take longer to render
the page. One solution would be to set up specific resource galleries that hold images of a particular size. These galleries would
correspond to the image placeholder sizes on your templates.

## Effective Placeholder Use

There are many ways to implement CMS. As a result, there are wide
variations in how developers and designers use placeholders. We've
compiled a short list of best practices for using placeholders within your
templates.

- Try to limit the number of placeholders on your template. There's
sometimes a tendency to add lots of placeholders to account for
the various elements of a page. For example, if you wanted a page
with 20 images and 20 blocks of text, you'd end up with 40 placeholders on a page. Although this is technically possible to do, it
not only presents a poor user interface, it will affect page render
performance. As an alternative, consider creating a detail-summary
relationship. For each image and text block on the page, create a
detail posting. Then create a summary page that consolidates all
of the image/text posting content into one page. Not only will this
improve content contribution, but it will promote content reuse
and improve site performance. To prevent all these postings from
showing up in the navigation, make them hidden postings, or
place them in a hidden channel. Also, consider creating a Web
Author task-based publishing link in the edit console to add additional text/image pair postings. See Chapter 36 for more information on Web Author task-based publishing.

- Don't stick "one big" placeholder on your templates, allowing content contributors to just throw anything in it. Not only does this particular methodology provide the opportunity for poor content practices and poor design, it may be frustrating to your content contributors. Consider componentizing your content into separate placeholders, each with a specific purpose. Allow each placeholder to accept only specific types of content.
- Don't be afraid to access content in placeholders programmatically. A lot of novice template developers think that where the placeholder is situated is where the content should render. This is really not the case. For a whole host of reasons, you may want to render the content differently from the way the placeholders are laid out. For example, if you want to render an image within a block of text, wrapping the text around the image, it may be impractical to place the image placeholder next to the HTML placeholder. Instead, consider placing the image placeholder first and then the HTML placeholder directly underneath. This arrangement makes much more sense from a contributor perspective. Then, when the page renders, hide the actual placeholder controls. You can grab the content and render it programmatically in the way that makes sense for your page.
- Size your placeholders properly. It sounds like a simple guideline, but the size of a placeholder will suggest the amount of content to be contributed. Content contributors will look at a large placeholder and try to contribute a large amount of content. Conversely, a smaller placeholder will suggest that less content should be contributed. One example of this behavior is the use of a placeholder for the title of a page. If you size the title placeholder too large, content contributors think they can provide a lot of content, even though the actual space provided for the content is relatively small.
- Just because you have content on a posting, it doesn't mean that you need a placeholder. Content on a posting could be coming from another posting, a database, or a placeholder. Consider carefully where your content is coming from before you place another placeholder on the template.
- If you have multiple placeholders on a page, make sure that the instructions on the placeholders are clear and concise. It is important that all the authors use the placeholders in a consistent way for future maintenance on the template. Using labels over the placeholders and/or default text will help ensure that authors know what each placeholder is supposed to contain.

## Summary

In this chapter, we examined each of the three placeholder controls and the six placeholder definitions that ship with Content Management Server. We also discussed best practices for effective placeholder use and controlling content. For each placeholder control, we talked about its general usage, how to set it up, and design considerations.

Keep in mind that creating a template in CMS is really an act of creating an interface for content contribution. As a result, you must effectively use the most basic interface element you have available to you. There are several best practices that can be applied to developing templates and using placeholders. We covered a few of them here, but it's likely you'll develop your own as you work more on the platform.

# CHAPTER 14

# Creating Dynamic Navigation

## Overview

By now, you should be pretty comfortable with the basics of template creation and placeholders. The next step is to create a navigation scheme that supports the new site. After implementing CMS, you will find that as content contributors adopt the new technology, it will be literally impossible to keep up with the rate of content additions. Even if you have a relatively small number of content contributors, you're almost guaranteed that they will be able to add more content to your site than you could possibly expect. As a result, the old methodology of manually creating links to the new content has to go. With CMS you can replace that old methodology with *dynamic navigation*. Dynamic navigation is created using the Publishing API (PAPI, discussed more fully in Chapter 23). It will allow you to create a generic navigation scheme for your site, which will automatically update as new content is added to your site. In this chapter, we'll examine how you create dynamic navigation with CMS.

We'll begin by looking at the various components that are needed to build navigation. Specifically, we will examine postings, channels, and administrative functions as they relate to the development of navigation in your site. Next, we'll discuss some of the design considerations you need to take into account when developing navigation. There are definitely good and bad ways to develop navigation within a site. Finally, we will demonstrate how you can create basic navigation using each of these elements and will review how the BOTS Consulting site uses the PAPI to create navigation within the BOTS site. Once the chapter is finished, you should have a solid understanding of how to build navigation in CMS, using the PAPI.

# What Is Navigation in CMS?

Navigation in CMS means using the PAPI to access the structure and content within the repository. Fundamentally, three elements are used to create navigation: postings, channels, and administrative features. At this point, you're probably familiar with all three. However, it's important that you understand each within the context of navigation. Once we have a basic understanding of these elements, we'll take the discussion a little further by introducing specific navigation examples. Unlike with some Microsoft products, you can't simply install CMS and have a useful tool. CMS provides the framework, but it's up to you to use the framework to build your site.

## Postings

Within a traditional Web site, the most simple navigation type is to HTML pages. In CMS, Web pages are represented by the *Posting* object, and therefore simple navigation is always going to lead a content consumer to a posting. A posting is the object that physically holds and/or displays content within your site. As a result, when a content consumer traverses your site, they're really looking for postings.

Consider the types of templates we discussed in Chapter 12. We discussed four: detail, composite, format, and summary. Of the four discussed, it's likely that direct navigation will involve postings created with the detail, summary, and composite template types, since they either hold or display content. The format template will be used in conjunction with the creation of "alternate" forms of the same content; you can find out more about this kind of navigation in Chapter 36. Figure 14–1 shows an example posting navigation scheme and a detail posting in the BOTS Consulting site.

If you look on the left side of the page, you'll notice that the postings for the current channel are listed. Each posting that's added to the In the Press channel will automatically show up in the left navigation. In this way, content contributors can happily add content, and the IT staff tasked with supporting the site doesn't have to worry about editing HTML. One key element to navigation, however, is that nothing shows up that the current user isn't allowed to see. In other words, CMS manages access to all objects within the repository, and only the objects that the current user has access to will appear in navigation. In the same way, CMS prevents content that hasn't been approved from showing up on the live site.

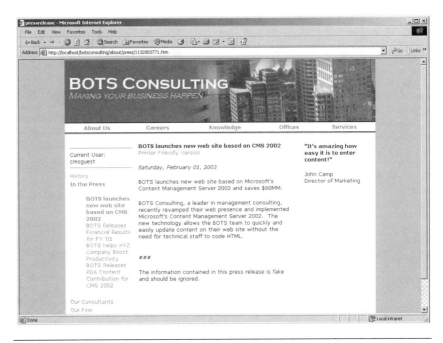

**Figure 14–1** A detail posting showing navigation to other postings in the About Us channel

## Channels

In a traditional Web site, HTML files are stored in file directories. Navigation in these traditional Web sites can point to directories, which contain a collection of files; when a user clicks a link to a directory, they are redirected to a page within that directory and shown the directory contents or are given an error. CMS has a concept similar to a file directory, which it calls *channels*.

When you are creating navigation, channels will usually form the core of your navigation. Because channels hold all of the content in your site, you'll often see channels show up in the main or global navigation. When a user creates a new posting, it's stored in a channel. If a user clicks a link to a channel, CMS tries to redirect the user to a posting. If no posting exists, CMS has a mechanism called a *rendering script* that takes over. In the BOTS Consulting example, if a content consumer clicks the About Us link in the main navigation, they're really navigating to the About Us channel. In the About Us channel, the content consumer will find a listing of the other channels in About Us as well as postings that are stored there. This summary listing is simply a posting

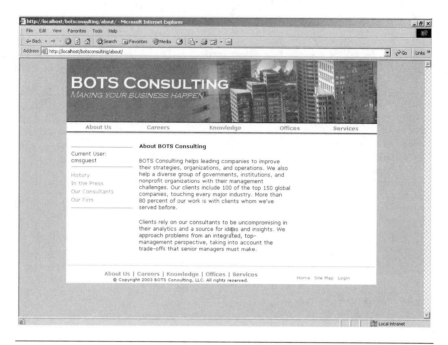

**Figure 14–2** The About Us section of the BOTS Consulting Web site

created using the Press Release Summary template. In Figure 14–2 you can see this navigation behavior in the BOTS site.

Now, if no posting existed in that channel, what would CMS do? As we mentioned earlier, if a posting doesn't exist, CMS will display the channel rendering script. The default rendering script is shown in Figure 14–3. If the WoodgroveNet Bank sample site is installed, content consumers will see something like Figure 14–4. Notice that this rendering script is radically different from the default one provided by Microsoft. You can write your own rendering script for your site and then configure your channels to react in a specific way by changing certain channel properties. For more information on configuring channels, refer to Chapter 16.

## Administrative Features

The last type of element that a content contributor can navigate to is administrative functions. The reason we stipulate content contributor instead of a more general audience is that, for the most part, only content contributors will see administrative navigation. Essentially, administrative navigation includes those links that allow the user to affect the

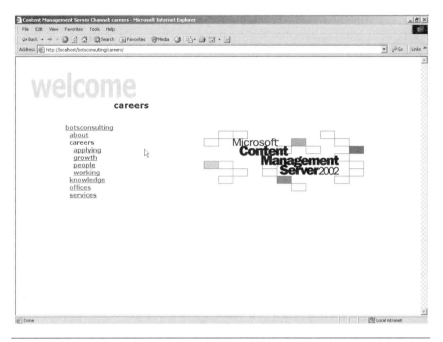

**Figure 14–3**  The default cover page for CMS

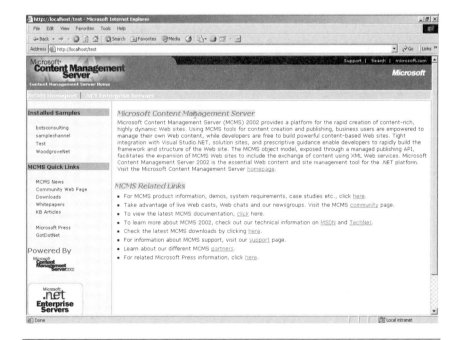

**Figure 14–4**  The WoodgroveNet sample rendering script

site in some way or links that are only shown in Edit mode. The best example of administrative navigation is the edit console. However, the edit console isn't the only administrative navigation that could exist. Beyond the edit console, you could have custom administrative navigation in your site. For example, you could potentially create task-based publishing within the Web Author. Task-based publishing is something that's closely associated with the Authoring Connector for Word. However, it's possible to create the same sort of task-based publishing within the Web Author. In this case, only roles that allow content creation should see the link(s). In Figure 14–5, two types of administrative navigation are shown: task-based publishing and the edit console. The edit console flows into the site just under the left navigation, and the task-based publishing link shows up under the user ID of the current content contributor: in this case, cmsadmin.

As we examine dynamic navigation more deeply, keep all three of these navigation elements in the back of your mind.

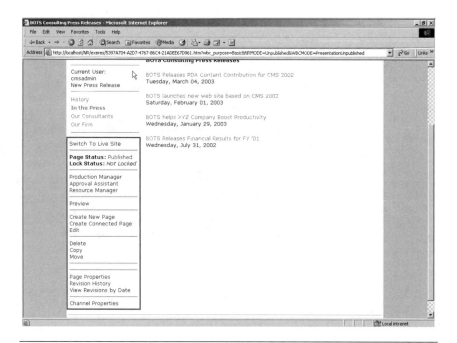

**Figure 14–5**  Administrative navigation in the In the Press section of the BOTS site

# Design Considerations

Now that you've "seen" the basic navigation elements, we should discuss some design considerations that you need to take into account when developing your site. At the most basic level, everyone needs to be able to navigate to where they want to either consume, contribute, or generally affect content (such as setting publishing dates). This sounds trivial, but it's actually more difficult to pull off than you would think. Next, you must remember that navigation is dynamic. Dynamic navigation has a number of challenges that are easily accounted for, but not keeping this in mind will lead to disaster. Finally, are there "unique" situations that you have to deal with in your site? For example, are there some cases where the navigation should not render at all? In the following sections, we'll explore each of these issues and discuss techniques for handling them. Our techniques will not be an exhaustive list, but they should help you as you're developing your site.

## Users Must Be Able to Navigate to Add Content

One of the most important rules about navigation is that a user must be able to navigate to where they want to add, modify, or delete content. Practically, what this means is that there needs to be some mechanism that allows content contributors to navigate to a channel or posting, switch to Edit mode, and perform an operation. This is especially important in a new site, since there are no real postings that can carry the edit console. To some extent, Microsoft handles a new-site situation by providing a default rendering script. However, the rendering script simply provides a basic page response in the event that no posting exists in a channel. In Figure 14–3, we saw the default rendering script, and in Figure 14–4 we saw the sample provided by the WoodgroveNet Bank site. However, when you create your navigation logic, it is possible not to display navigation to a channel or a posting. For various reasons, you may develop code that assumes that your site only has a certain fixed set of levels. If at some point you decide to add levels and don't change your navigation code, content contributors won't be able to add content—they can't navigate to those new channels, so they can't switch to Edit mode and create a new posting. We'll talk a little more about this later, but keep in mind the basic rule: You must be able to navigate to a channel or a posting to perform any action, including content consumption.

## Navigation Is Dynamic

It is possible to build a site, using CMS, that isn't dynamic. In other words, it's possible to hardcode links to channels and postings as you might have done historically with static sites. However, this would eliminate one of the advantages of CMS. One of the great powers of CMS is that it allows you to design logic that is relatively generic but allows for all kinds of site structures. For example, if you look at Figure 14–6, you'll see a posting based on one of the BOTS Consulting site's templates, but it's been created in a non-BOTS channel. The left navigation dutifully creates the appropriate links even though it's not in the "right" channel (meaning the BOTS Consulting site). Not only is this convenient from a development standpoint, but it prevents rendering broken links based on content that may not exist.

Now, dynamic navigation is a very good thing, but it could potentially get away from you if you're not careful. Since you're in an environment that changes as content is created and changed, your navigation is constantly dealing with an ever-changing set of data. As a result, you could experience unexpected results when trying to display navigation elements. One unexpected result could be poor formatting, or it could

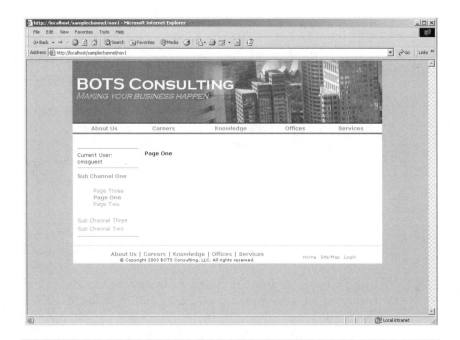

**Figure 14–6**  Left navigation in a non-BOTS channel

be an exceedingly long page. An example of poor formatting can be found in the BOTS site. In Figure 14–8 you can see the length of the page titles could be considered a little too long for the space provided in the left navigation. Also, if we were to add, say, 10 or 15 more postings to this section, the left navigation would become quite long. These are the kinds of issues (as well as others) that will manifest themselves if you don't properly plan your navigation. To help you account for these elements, try some of the following techniques.

- Properly plan how your navigation will appear in your site. Make sure you know how much space is going to be devoted to the various navigation elements. When the BOTS site was created, the developers didn't account for the long display names their authors added. In a "real" production environment, this may be unacceptable. If you have constraints with regard to title size because of your design or page weight, consider setting limits for your content contributors or enforcing limits by developing a mechanism to programmatically check the length of the page title through workflow.

- Set some practical limits on how many elements you can display in your navigation. In traditional Web development, you can always go back and modify the design to accommodate more content or simply remove elements that aren't necessary. With CMS, you still have this opportunity, but since you're no longer in charge of adding content, you may be unaware of what's happening on the site. A little planning about how long pages can be and how many navigation elements your design can support will go a long way. When you create your navigation logic, build in some constraints as to how many elements or levels you'll display. This is definitely easier than it sounds, since it's not a technical problem but a business process issue; getting your contributors to agree to this constraint isn't always easy. Having a complete, detailed information architecture diagram of your site will help you appropriately plan your navigation (a simple site map probably isn't sufficient). Take a look at Chapter 37 for more suggestions about site migration and planning.

- Don't underestimate the potential for someone to break the rules if you don't enforce them. Given the opportunity, a content contributor will ultimately find a way to "break" your site. Consider programmatically enforcing any "unbreakable" rules you establish. This can be done by adding a "wizard" to your site that walks the contributor through the process of creating the posting and places some validation on things like display name to ensure they conform to a certain size. Creating wizards does take more development time, but it may eliminate a whole host of potential problems.

Once you've gotten the hang of creating dynamic navigation that doesn't get away from you and schemes that can adapt to various structures, remember performance. Dynamically assembling navigation is an expensive transaction. CMS is a very solid performer, but if you don't write your code properly or efficiently, you can easily create a very poorly performing site. To avoid creating a sluggish site, consider the following suggestions.

- Use .NET output caching. Output caching can significantly improve the performance of your site by reducing the processing required for rendering your pages. Given the nature of CMS, implementing an appropriate caching scheme is not a trivial effort; but if done properly, it can yield tremendous benefits.
- Use recursion sparingly. We'll show you an example, later in the chapter, of how to create a recursive navigation function. Recursion can be a very useful programming technique, but it tends to consume a fair amount of resources. If you use recursion to build navigation, you should strongly consider implementing some sort of caching scheme.
- Don't use custom properties to build navigation. As temping as it may be to use the Searches class to find postings and channels via a custom property value, it's a *very* expensive transaction. CMS will literally search the entire repository for the object you're looking for (there's no way to constrain the search). Custom properties are good for a lot of things, but building navigation is not one of them.
- Do performance testing on your site. The performance of your site will be based on a number of factors. Don't underestimate the value of properly testing your site. We encourage you to set some basic and reasonable performance metrics and use a testing tool to help establish whether your new site meets the criteria. Visual Studio .NET provides Application Center Test in the Enterprise Architect version for just this reason.
- Consider turning off control view state for controls that don't need it. .NET can potentially add a tremendous amount of data to

your page. Generally, this isn't a problem. However, in some situations, when you're using a number of controls to build various navigation elements on a page, the property bag could get out of hand. At the very least, consider turning off view state for the live site if it's not necessary. This will greatly reduce the size of your pages.

## Dealing with Unique Situations

No matter what site you look at, there are always elements in that site's navigation that require special consideration. For example, in the BOTS site, we always want to display the child channels of the main navigation element on the left side. When we're in one of those child channels, we want to display the postings. However, there are a few cases where we don't want that to happen. Specifically, when a user navigates to a channel with a summary page, it's redundant to display links to summarized postings in the left navigation. In the BOTS In the Press section, there's a summary page as the default posting, so there's no need to repeat that navigation in the left navigation. It's only when we navigate to a specific release that we want to display the other postings in the left navigation. Unfortunately, that rule can't be universally applied. In the Our Consultants section, there isn't a summary page as the default posting, so they do want to list the various consultant profiles in the left navigation; when the site was originally written, that detail escaped the BOTS developers. The result is shown in Figure 14–7.

At first glance, Figure 14–7 appears to be a perfectly formatted BOTS Consulting default channel page. There's introductory text, and the left navigation points you to all the other channels in the About Us section. However, there are two consultant "Day in the Life" postings that also exist in that channel. Unfortunately, you can't see them because the navigation logic in the left navigation did exactly what it was told: Display the postings in the current channel if you're not on a default page (actually any page called "default"). It just so happens that the left navigation operates this way because BOTS didn't want the navigation to repeat in the In the Press section when they were displaying a summary page (thereby thwarting themselves again!). To fix this situation, they added a custom property to each channel that indicated whether to display postings in the left navigation when the default posting is displayed. Once they did that, they ended up with what you see in Figure 14–8.

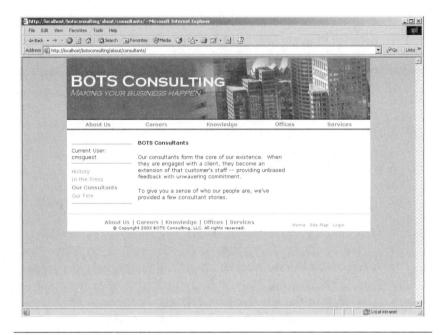

**Figure 14–7**  The flawed left navigation in BOTS

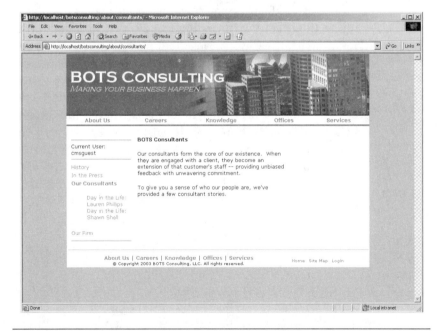

**Figure 14–8**  The corrected left navigation for the Our Consultants section of BOTS

To help you appropriately plan your navigation (and avoid these and other pitfalls), we've listed a few techniques to create navigation that can deal with a number of different situations.

- Plan, plan, plan. We can't stress this enough. It's often difficult to have all the requirements for your site up front. However, trying to gather, solidify, and document as much as you can before you write any code will save you a lot of time.

- Use custom properties to help you set attributes on navigation elements. Now, we're not suggesting you use custom properties to search for channels, but use them as additional attributes to a collection you've already gotten from the PAPI. As you iterate through the collection (or use a .NET control such as a datalist), you can read a custom property to determine how to handle certain conditions. We're also not saying that custom properties will solve every problem. Custom properties, used judiciously, can be a huge help. BOTS was able to implement one custom property to help with the left navigation situation. However, if you find that you're adding custom property after custom property to account for exceptions, you should probably refer back to our first bullet.

- Use naming conventions to help. It may sound like a "hack" to use a channel naming convention, but often the simplest solution is the one you should use. A very common technique with CMS 2001 was to prefix an object name with an underscore character (_). This underscore would let the navigation code know to ignore that object and not list it in the navigation, thereby creating a "hidden" object.

## Creating Navigation Elements

As we mentioned, there are essentially three elements that you can use to create navigation: postings, channels, and administrative functions. To utilize each of these elements, you'll use the PAPI, accessing the specific objects and properties.

## Examine the Objects and Properties Necessary for Navigation

With the exception of administrative functions, all navigation is built with channels or postings. Both channels and postings share common properties for building navigation within your Web site. A list of these properties follows, with a brief explanation of each. Keep in mind that if you closely study the .NET class reference in the CMS documentation, you'll find other properties that may be useful, but the properties listed here are the ones you'll use most frequently.

- Name: Returns the name of the object. The name of the object is what shows up in the URL when an object is requested.
- DisplayName: Returns the display name of the object. The display name usually contains a longer, more descriptive title for the object. Most sites use this display name to allow content contributors to specify what text will show up in the navigation. In the case of multilingual sites, the display name is very useful for providing the language-specific description of the channel or posting, since there are some character restrictions in URLs.
- Url: Returns an unqualified, mode-specific URL to an object. The Url property returns a URL to an object within the context of the current Web Author mode. For example, if the Web Author is in Edit mode (unpublished), a GUID-based URL will be returned with the appropriate query string parameters. If the site is in Live, or Published, mode, the URL will be a friendly URL, like what you're used to seeing.
- UrlModePublished: Forces CMS to provide a non-GUID-based friendly URL to an object. This allows you to retrieve a Live mode URL even if the user is viewing the site in Edit mode.
- UrlModeUnpublished: Forces CMS to provide a GUID-based URL to the object in Unpublished mode. Similar to UrlMode Published, UrlModeUnpublished will always provide the unpublished URL to an object regardless of the current Web Author context mode.
- Parent: Provides a reference to the parent of the object. In either a channel or a posting, the parent property returns a channel item object.

## Creating Basic Navigation

Now that you've familiarized yourself with the general design considerations and components of building navigation, let's examine some basic code samples to show you how to use what you've learned. As a start, let's look at basic channel navigation. By basic channel navigation, we're simply referring to getting a collection of channels from the PAPI and creating HTML that a content consumer can click on to navigate through that collection. Looking at Listing 14–1, you can see the basic traversal of a channel within the current channel.

**Listing 14–1** Basic channel navigation

```
private void createBasicChannelNav(Channel startChannel)
{
    // Get a collection of channels from the startChannel
    ChannelCollection navChannels = startChannel.Channels;

    // Make sure we've gotten a collection back
    if (navChannels != null)
    {

        // Create a new anchor link and iterate through each
        // channel in the collection
        HtmlAnchor navLink;
        foreach(Channel navChannel in navChannels)
        {

            // For each channel in the collection, create new
anchor
            // link and add it to the .NET placeholder control
on
            // on our page
            navLink = new HtmlAnchor();
            navLink.InnerText = navChannel.DisplayName;
            navLink.HRef = navChannel.Url;
            BasicChannelNav.Controls.Add(navLink);
            BasicChannelNav.Controls.Add(new
LiteralControl("<BR>"));
        }
    }
}
```

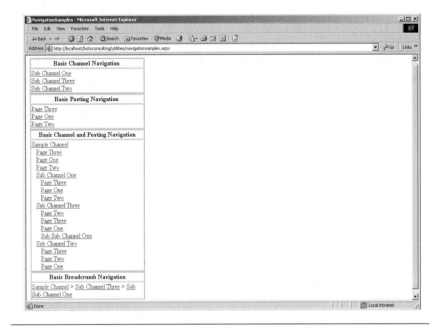

**Figure 14–9**  Basic channel navigation in an ASPX page

In this example, you'll notice that we're using the Channel object and the properties listed in Listing 14–1. We first retrieve a collection of channels in the start channel. Then, we iterate through the collection, pulling out the Url and DisplayName properties. We've created an ASPX page with a .NET placeholder control (note: this is not the CMS placeholder control) to hold the HtmlAnchor controls we're creating in our code (we could have also added the control to the page controls collection). In Figure 14–9 you can see the result of this code (the results of all code samples in this section are shown in this figure).

The next example is basic posting navigation. In Listing 14–2, you'll notice the code is very similar to the channel example. We simply get a collection of postings from the pass-in startChannel object and then iterate through the collection

**Listing 14–2**  Basic posting navigation

```
private void createBasicPostingNav(Channel startChannel)
{
    PostingCollection navPostings = startChannel.Postings;
    if (navPostings != null)
    {
```

```
        HtmlAnchor navLink;
        foreach(Posting navPosting in navPostings)
        {
                navLink = new HtmlAnchor();
                navLink.InnerText = navPosting.DisplayName;
                navLink.HRef = navPosting.Url;
                BasicPostingNav.Controls.Add(navLink);
                BasicPostingNav.Controls.Add(new
LiteralControl("<BR>"));
        }
    }
}
```

Combining both of the prior examples and using recursion to iterate through a whole hierarchy, Listing 14–3 demonstrates mixed channel and posting navigation. Again, this sample builds on the prior two examples, with the exception of the recursive call.

**Listing 14–3** Basic channel and posting navigation

```
private void createBasicChannelPostingNav(Channel startChannel,
string navIndent)
{
    // Retrieve a collection of postings and channels
    PostingCollection navPostings = startChannel.Postings;
    ChannelCollection navChannels = startChannel.Channels;

    // Create an anchor link
    HtmlAnchor navLink = new HtmlAnchor();

    // Write out the link to the start channel and add it
    // to the .NET (not CMS) placeholder control
    navLink.HRef = startChannel.Url;
    navLink.InnerText = startChannel.DisplayName;

    // Add an indent before the channel link; this will be additive
for
    // each recursive call
    BasicChannelPostingNav.Controls.Add(new
LiteralControl(navIndent));

    // Add the link to the .NET placeholder control
    BasicChannelPostingNav.Controls.Add(navLink);
```

```
        BasicChannelPostingNav.Controls.Add(new
LiteralControl("<br>"));

        // Check to see if we got back a collection of postings
        if (navPostings != null)
        {
            foreach(Posting navPosting in navPostings)
            {
                // Write out a link to each posting
                navLink = new HtmlAnchor();
                navLink.InnerText = navPosting.DisplayName;
                navLink.HRef = navPosting.Url;

                // Add an indent to each posting (this will be
additive as
                // we call the function recursively)
                BasicChannelPostingNav.Controls.Add(new
LiteralControl("   "+navIndent));

                // Add the posting link to the .NET placeholder
control
                BasicChannelPostingNav.Controls.Add(navLink);
                BasicChannelPostingNav.Controls.Add(new
LiteralControl("<BR>"));
            }
        }

        // Make sure we got back a collection of channels
        if (navChannels != null)
        {
            foreach(Channel subChannel in navChannels)
            {
                // For each of the sub channels, call the function
recursively

                createBasicChannelPostingNav(subChannel,
navIndent+"   ");
            }
        }

}
```

Our last sample is a very simple breadcrumb example. In Listing 14–4, notice that we use the parent property of the Channel object to "walk" up the hierarchy. Each time, we retrieve the appropriate properties from the channel we're working with and then reset the currentLocation variable to the parent of that channel. This function provides a good opportunity to create an overload for this function that accepts a posting instead of a channel; the basics of this function would remain the same, since the parent property of a posting also returns a channelitem. Although this function was implemented using a conditional loop, it could just easily have been implemented using recursion.

**Listing 14–4** Basic breadcrumb navigation

```
private void createBasicBreadcrumbNav(Channel startChannel)
{
    // Create a variable to hold the start channel object
    Channel myCurrentLocation = startChannel;

    // Make sure you're not already at the "root" of your site
    if (myCurrentLocation.Guid != myBaseChannel.Guid)
    {
        HtmlAnchor navLink;

        // While you're not at your root create a breadcrumb
        while(myCurrentLocation.Guid != myBaseChannel.Guid)
        {
            // Create a new anchor link and set the appropriate
            // values
            navLink = new HtmlAnchor();
            navLink.HRef = myCurrentLocation.Url;
            navLink.InnerText = myCurrentLocation.DisplayName;

            // Add your breadcrumb to the .NET placeholder
control
            BasicBreadcrumbNav.Controls.AddAt(0,navLink);
            BasicBreadcrumbNav.Controls.AddAt(0,new
LiteralControl(" > "));

            // Set the current location to the parent of the
            // current location; we're walking one level up
            myCurrentLocation = myCurrentLocation.Parent;
        }
```

```
        // When the loop exits, create a new anchor object
        // and set the appropriate value to the root of your
        // breadcrumb
        navLink = new HtmlAnchor();
        navLink.HRef = myBaseChannel.Url;
        navLink.InnerText = myBaseChannel.DisplayName;
        BasicBreadcrumbNav.Controls.AddAt(0,navLink);
    }
}
```

## BOTS Consulting Navigation Samples

Reviewing basic examples is nice, but it's always better to see the navigation implemented in "real" sites. BOTS is certainly not a very complicated site, but we thought it was useful to share the main and left navigation code as a way of comparing the basic examples to code that had a few exceptions. Both the left and main navigation code was implemented in a user control that was dropped onto a page for ease of reuse.

In Listing 14–5, you'll notice that we're not taking in a value to start the navigation. In the function, BOTS is grabbing a very specific channel and starting with that. They made the assumption that this code would be used only in their site. This isn't a bad technique, but it does tend to limit reuse. As you can see, there aren't any exceptions in this code; it's really just basic channel navigation with some HTML formatting.

**Listing 14–5**  BOTS Consulting main navigation

```
private void createMainNavigation()
{
    try
    {
        // Retrieve the main BOTS Consulting channel
        Channel NavParentChannel = (Channel)CmsHttpContext.
Current.Searches.GetByPath("/Channels/botsconsulting");
        this.GlobalNav.Attributes.Add("width","100%");
        TableRow GlobalNavRow = new TableRow();

        // Make sure we got the channel back
        if (NavParentChannel != null)
        {
```

```
                    // Get the collection of channels in the BOTS
        Consulting site
                    ChannelCollection NavParentSubChannels =
        NavParentChannel.Channels;
                    HtmlAnchor navLink;

                    // Iterate through the channels in the site
                    foreach(Channel SubChannel in NavParentSubChannels)
                    {
                        navLink = new HtmlAnchor();
                        TableCell newTableCell = new TableCell();
                        newTableCell.Attributes.Add("align",
        "center");
                        navLink.Style.Add("FONT-WEIGHT","bold");
                        navLink.Style.Add("COLOR","gray");
                        navLink.HRef = SubChannel.Url;
                        navLink.InnerText = SubChannel.DisplayName;
                        newTableCell.Controls.Add(navLink);
                        GlobalNavRow.Cells.Add(newTableCell);
                    }
                }
                this.GlobalNav.Rows.Add(GlobalNavRow);
            }

            // Perform some very basic exception "handling"
            catch(Exception errException)
            {
                TableRow GlobalNavRow = new TableRow();
                TableCell NavItem = new TableCell();
                NavItem.Text = "The following exception occurred: "
        +errException.Message + "<br>SOURCE: " + errException.Source;
                GlobalNavRow.Cells.Add(NavItem);
                this.GlobalNav.Rows.Add(GlobalNavRow);
            }
        }
```

In the following listings, we provide various "interesting" sections of the left navigation. The code is somewhat lengthy, so we're listing only certain portions that need to be highlighted.

In Listing 14–6, we've provided the task-based navigation. These few lines of code provide a way to create a new posting based on the Press Release Detail template of the In the Press channel. Notice that there are some conditions wrapped around the link so that a content contributor can't accidentally create a posting with the wrong template or in the wrong channel.

**Listing 14–6** Task-based publishing in the Web Author

```
// Check to see if the posting is in EDIT mode
if ((WebAuthorContext.Current.Mode == WebAuthorContextMode.Presen-
tationUnpublished) &&
    (CmsHttpContext.Current.Channel.Name.ToString() == "press") &&
    CmsHttpContext.Current.Posting.Template.Name == "Press Release
Detail")
{
    // Get the template and channel object for this posting
    Template thisTemplate = CmsHttpContext.Current.Posting.
Template;
    Channel thisChannel = CmsHttpContext.Current.Channel;

    // Create the task link
    HtmlAnchor taskPublishingLink = new HtmlAnchor();

    // Get a URL to a new posting based on the Press Release Detail
template
    taskPublishingLink.HRef = WebAuthorContext.Current.
GetAuthoringNewUrl(thisTemplate,thisChannel);
    taskPublishingLink.InnerText = "New Press Release";
    NewTableCell.Controls.Add(new LiteralControl("<br>"));

    // Add the publishing link to the side navigation table cell
    NewTableCell.Controls.Add(taskPublishingLink);
}
```

In Listing 14–7, we're showing how BOTS handles most of the left navigation, including the channels and postings. Notice the special conditions with regard to the default posting and the custom property setting that determines whether to show postings in the left navigation or not. Again, in some cases they want postings to display and in other they don't. In an effort to make the code more flexible, they're examining a custom property on the channel to determine whether postings should be listed.

**Listing 14–7**  The left navigation logic for BOTS

```
private void BuildLeftNavTable(Channel StartChannel)
{

        // Define the necessary variables for creating the
nav table
        // and the links
        HtmlAnchor NavigationLink;
        TableRow NewTableRow;
        TableCell NewTableCell;
        Literal TextPlaceholder;

        // Get a collection of channels in the pass-in
channel
        ChannelCollection SubChannels = StartChannel.
Channels;

        // Check to make sure we got back a collection
        if(SubChannels != null)
        {

                // Iterate through the collection
                foreach(Channel SubChannel in SubChannels)
                {
                        // Create a new row, cell and anchor link
                        NewTableRow = new TableRow();
                        NewTableCell = new TableCell();
                        NavigationLink = new HtmlAnchor();
                        NavigationLink.HRef = SubChannel.Url;

                        // If the channel we're on matches the
current channel
                        // add bolding to the style
                        if (SubChannel.Guid.ToString() ==
CmsHttpContext.Current.Channel.Guid.ToString())
                        {
    NavigationLink.Attributes.Add("style","FONT-WEIGHT: Bold;
COLOR: gray");
                        }
                        else
                        {
    NavigationLink.Attributes.Add("style","COLOR: gray");
                        }
```

```
                         NavigationLink.InnerText = SubChannel.
DisplayName;
                         NewTableCell.Controls.Add
(NavigationLink);

                         // If the channel we're on matches the
current channel
                         // determine whether we need to display
postings
                         if (SubChannel.Guid.ToString() ==
CmsHttpContext.Current.Channel.Guid.ToString())
                         {

                             // Only display postings if we're
not on the default posting
                             // or the custom property
ShowPostingsOnDefault is set to true
     if((CmsHttpContext.Current.Posting.Name.ToString()!=
"default") ||
     ((CustomProperty)SubChannel.CustomProperties
["ShowPostingsOnDefault"]).Value.ToString() == "True")
                             {
                                 TextPlaceholder = new
Literal();
                                 TextPlaceholder.Text="</UL>";
     NewTableCell.Controls.Add(TextPlaceholder);

                                 // Call the show postings
function
     ShowPostingsInChannel(SubChannel,NewTableCell);
                                 TextPlaceholder = new
Literal();
                                 TextPlaceholder.Text="</UL>"
     NewTableCell.Controls.Add(TextPlaceholder);
                             }
                         }
                         NewTableRow.Cells.Add(NewTableCell);
                         this.LeftNav.Rows.Add(NewTableRow);

                 }
             }
             NewTableCell = new TableCell();
             TextPlaceholder = new Literal();
```

```csharp
                TextPlaceholder.Text = "<hr color='gray' size='1'
width='100%'>";
                NewTableCell.Controls.Add(TextPlaceholder);
                NewTableRow = new TableRow();
                NewTableRow.Cells.Add(NewTableCell);
                this.LeftNav.Rows.Add(NewTableRow);


        }


        private void ShowPostingsInChannel(Channel
CurrentChannel, TableCell PostingTableCell)
        {
                Literal TextPlaceholder;
                HtmlAnchor NavigationLink;
                foreach(Posting SubPosting in CurrentChannel.
Postings)
                    {
                        if(SubPosting.Name.ToLower() !=
"default")
                            {
                                TextPlaceholder = new Literal();
                                TextPlaceholder.Text = "<br>";
                                NavigationLink = new HtmlAnchor();

                                // If the posting we're on is the
current posting
                                // then add bolding to the style
                                if(SubPosting.Guid.ToString() ==
CmsHttpContext.Current.Posting.Guid.ToString())
                                    {
        NavigationLink.Attributes.Add("style","FONT-WEIGHT: bold;
COLOR: gray");
                                    }
                                else
                                    {
        NavigationLink.Attributes.Add("style","COLOR: gray");
                                    }
                                NavigationLink.HRef =
SubPosting.Url;
                                NavigationLink.InnerText =
SubPosting.DisplayName;
```

```
PostingTableCell.Controls.Add(NavigationLink);

PostingTableCell.Controls.Add(TextPlaceholder);
                            }
                    }
            }
```

It is a little more complex than the main navigation, but still uses the concepts we demonstrated in the basic navigation samples. In addition, it accounts for the unique situations within the BOTS site.

## Summary

In this chapter, we reviewed how to build and manage dynamic navigation. We started by providing a basic definition for dynamic navigation in CMS. We then talked about the three core components of all navigation in CMS: postings, channels, and administrative functions. Each of these three elements will be included in most navigation you build.

Once a basic foundation for navigation was laid, we reviewed some of the design considerations when developing navigation. We covered three primary topics: that users must be able to navigate your site, the implications for dynamic navigation, and dealing with unique navigation considerations. In each case, we tried to provide some advice for avoiding common pitfalls.

Finally, we demonstrated how to take what you've learned and put it into practice. We started by creating some fairly basic samples that demonstrated posting navigation, channel navigation, posting and channel navigation, and breadcrumb navigation. After the basic samples were shown, we provided code samples for the navigation actually implemented in the BOTS Consulting site.

# CHAPTER 15

# Connected Postings

## Overview

In this chapter, we'll look at a somewhat unique feature of CMS: connected postings. We'll explain what connected postings are, how they're used in a site, and some best practices. Once we've finished with that, we'll explain how to create connected postings through the Web Author and through the PAPI. Finally, we'll discuss some of the workflow implications of connected postings.

## What Are Connected Postings?

Connected postings are two or more postings that share a common set of content. If one of the postings is edited, the changed content is reflected in all the connected postings.

We could add a bit more of a description as to why, something like this: It may be a requirement of site design that the same content be reused in different areas of the site. If the content is changed in one area of the site, then the change is reflected everywhere this content is displayed. This reuse of content is the reason behind connected postings—that is, a single set of content is included in a number of different postings throughout the site. To allow even greater flexibility, different, connected templates may be used to repost the same content. Having different templates to repost the same content means that the content can have different formatting, the arrangement of placeholders may be different, only a subset of placeholders may be displayed, and so on. If you want to use different templates for connected postings, the templates themselves must be defined as connected. One of the biggest advantages of connected postings is that since each posting is stored in a different channel, you can effectively limit who can see what posting.

Essentially, think of connected postings as separate entities in CMS that both display the same content. Unlike the copy function in the edit console, which duplicates the content, connected postings share one content source; if you change the content in one posting, the resulting change is automatically reflected in the other connected posting. Now, having two postings sharing content is really only half of the story. In order to create connected postings, you must also create a set of connected templates.

---

**NOTE:** It's possible to create a connected posting with only a single template. In some cases this is desirable, because you can deposit the connected postings in different channels for security reasons. However, in most cases, connected postings are likely to use different templates.

---

Connected templates are actually the basis for connected postings. Connected templates are two TGIs that share the same definitions and custom properties. Because they share placeholder definitions, it's possible to ensure that content can be automatically repurposed across postings. In fact, it's not possible to create a connected posting with two templates that aren't connected.

Once the TGIs are connected, they are each pointed to a different template file. What this allows you to do is to share content across two postings with potentially different placeholder controls and/or visual design. Now, there are some rules you need to understand when working with connected postings; the short list follows.

- A connected posting must use the same template as the original posting or a template that's connected to the original posting's template.
- A connected posting cannot be created in the same channel as the original posting if they both use the same template.
- If you change the content in one posting, you change the connected posting's content as well. This has workflow implications, which we will talk about later in the chapter.
- Most of the page properties (excluding custom properties) are not shared between two connected postings. The only properties that are shared are the name and description; every other property is independent, including the display name.

- As a result, changing nonconnected page properties such as the start date won't affect the other posting; in essence, connected postings can have different start dates.
- A content contributor who wishes to create a connected posting must have authoring rights in both the source and the destination channels.
- It's possible to create a collection of connected postings without publishing any of the postings beforehand.
- There is no parent-child relationship between the connected postings; all postings are peers.
- If the original posting is already published, the connected posting will only have to be approved by a moderator (if you have one defined).

Now that you have the basics of connected postings, let's examine how you go about creating connected postings in CMS.

## Creating Connected Postings

There are a few "moving" parts to connected postings. One of the most basic rules for connected postings is that you must have connected templates (or use the same template). The connected templates set up the environment to allow content sharing between the connected postings. In order to create a connected template, you need to use VS.NET to create a template file and a connected TGI, and then bind the TGI to the template file. The new template file does not have to contain the same number of Template objects as the original TGI. However, you cannot add additional placeholder definitions in the connected TGI unless you want the other connected templates to share those same definitions (which may be desirable).

In the following sections, we'll first discuss creating a connected set of templates. We'll show you how to create a connected TGI and wire the placeholder definitions to the various placeholder controls on your new template file. In our demonstration, we'll show how you can have fewer placeholder controls than definitions to allow you to selectively decide what content shows up when you create postings on the new template.

## Creating Connected Templates

As we mentioned, in order to create connected postings, you must first create connected templates. In our example, we're going to create an alternative version of our press release template, which eliminates the call-out caption and call-out image on the right side of the page. To refresh your memory, refer to Figure 15–1 for a screen shot of an existing press release.

As a first step, we should review what placeholders the existing Press Release Detail template contains. In our existing press release template, we have five placeholders: the Calendar placeholder (which is a custom placeholder we will build later in the book), the BodyCopy placeholder, the Disclaimer placeholder, the CallOutImage placeholder, and the Call OutImageCaption placeholder. All the placeholders, except the CallOut Image placeholder, use the HTML placeholder definition. As we mentioned earlier, we want to create a connected template that does not contain the call-out image or caption; the placeholder definitions will still exist; we simply won't connect them to a physical placeholder control.

When we first created the BOTS site, we took the time to create a generic template, which represented the basic structure of all our

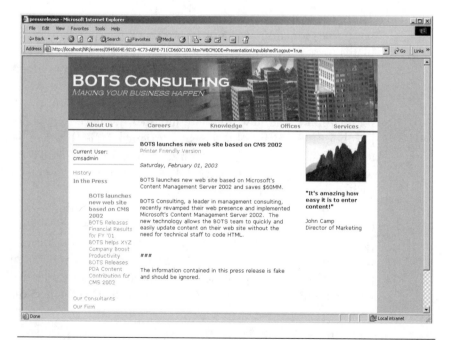

**Figure 15–1**  A press release on the BOTS Consulting Web site

templates (as we mentioned in Chapter 12). Now, we are simply going to copy this generic template file and create our new file. In our example, we're going to call the new template file Press Release sans CallOut.

Once you have your new template file set up, you just need to add the placeholders you want to have. For this example, we want to reproduce three of the five placeholders: the Calendar placeholder, the Body-Copy placeholder, and the Disclaimer placeholder. We'll add the three HTML placeholder controls to our template and give them the same names as our placeholder definitions (they don't have to be named the same; we're doing this for convenience). In Figure 15–2, you can see what our new template looks like.

Now that we have our new template, we need to create our connected TGI. To create a new, connected TGI, open the Template Explorer in VS.NET. If you don't already have the window docked somewhere, you can call it up by going to the View menu, picking Other Windows, and then choosing MCMS Template Explorer. Once you've located the Template Explorer window, find the template you want to connect. In the BOTS site, we're going to use the Press Release Detail template. To make your connected TGI, right-click the TGI in the Template Explorer

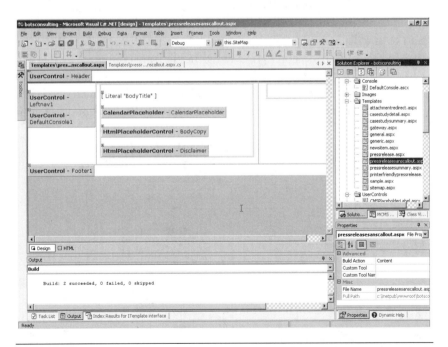

**Figure 15–2** The new Press Release sans CallOut template in the BOTS Consulting site

and choose Create Connected from the context menu. Figure 15–3 shows this operation. You may notice in Figure 15–3 that we have a small chainlike icon on the upper right corner of our TGI. The chain icon indicates that your TGI is connected; our template already happened to have been connected to another template, but it won't make a difference in this operation. Once you've created your connected TGI, your original and connected TGIs will also have the chain icon.

Once we have our TGI and our template file, we simply need to connect the TGI to the template file and the placeholders to the placeholder definitions in the TGI. First, set the TGI TemplateFile property to point to your new template—in our case, the pressreleasesanscallout.aspx file. Next, starting with the Calendar placeholder, we set the PlaceholderTo Bind property of each of the placeholder controls we added earlier to the appropriate definition—Calendar to Calendar, BodyCopy to Body Copy, and Disclaimer to Disclaimer. Once we're finished with that, our new template can now be used by our content contributors to create connected postings. In Figure 15–4, you'll see the completed template file, along with the resulting TGI.

There are a few things for you to be aware of now that you've created your connected TGI. Because connected TGIs share a common set of definitions, if you check out a connected TGI, CMS will warn you that it will lock all other connected TGIs. Although this isn't generally a big problem, it could prevent others from changing aspects of the other TGIs while you have the connected TGI checked out. Further, if you make a change to a connected TGI, the change will cascade to the other connected templates. For example, if you add another definition or a

**Figure 15–3** Creating a connected TGI in the Template Explorer

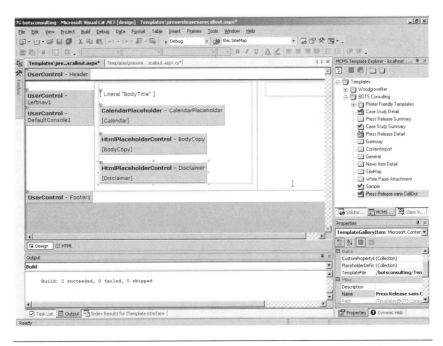

**Figure 15–4**  The finished template with the new, connected TGI

custom property, that definition or custom property will now exist in all
the other TGIs. Also, all the connected templates will be shown in bold
(unsaved changes) until you save the changes or check in the TGI.

## Using the Web Author

Now that you have your connected template, you're ready to create a
connected posting. One of the easiest ways to create a connected posting
is with the Web Author. In the edit console there is a link for Create
Connected Page just below the Create New Page link. Use the following
instructions to create a connected posting.

1. Navigate to the posting that will serve as the original posting.
2. Switch to Edit mode.
3. Click Create Connected Page (shown in Figure 15–5).
4. After clicking the Create Connected Page link, you'll see the
   Create Connected Page Wizard, which allows you to browse
   through the channels in your site to specify the location of your
   connected page (shown in Figure 15–6).

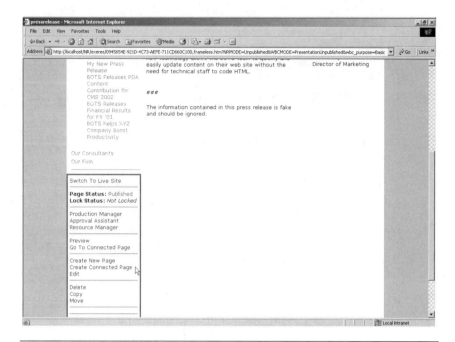

**Figure 15–5**  The Create Connected Page link in the edit console

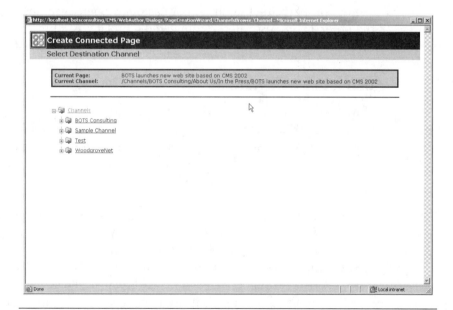

**Figure 15–6**  The Create Connected Page interface to select a new channel

5. After you've chosen your channel, you can select from a list of connected templates. In our case, we have three templates we can choose from: the original template plus two connected templates we've created. We're going to use the template we just created: Press Release sans CallOut (shown in Figure 15–7).

6. After you've chosen the template you wish to use, CMS will redirect you to the new posting, in authoring mode. As expected, only three of the original five placeholders are shown in our new connected page. In Figure 15–8, notice, however, that the placeholders also contain content; this is the content carried over from the original posting. Also make note that the BodyCopy placeholder has a new symbol in the upper right corner of the placeholder. This new symbol, which looks something like two sheets of paper connected by a wire, indicates that this posting is connected and, specifically, that the placeholders are sharing content with another posting.

7. Now, simply save your new posting. When you click Save and Exit, you'll be prompted to enter a new display name. However, the Name property won't be editable, since the name will remain the same as the original posting. We did not provide a figure for this, since you can't tell when the color image is converted to a black-and-white screen shot.

**Figure 15–7** Choosing a connected template

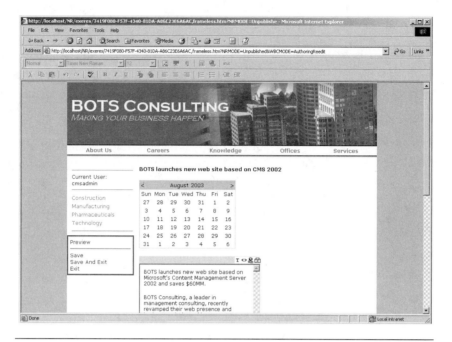

**Figure 15–8**  The new posting in authoring mode

**8.** You have successfully created a connected posting. At this point, you can choose to submit the posting, or if you have the authority, you can approve it on the spot.

As you can see, there isn't much to creating a connected posting using the Web Author. In fact, this is the easiest way of creating alternate versions of postings in your site. If you wanted to run a report to see the other connected postings for this posting, you should notice another edit console menu item, Go to Connected Page. This option will allow you to see the other connected postings, and either preview or navigate directly to them. Figure 15–9 shows the connected posting report.

Now that we know how to create a connected posting in the Web Author, let's examine how you can accomplish the same thing with the PAPI.

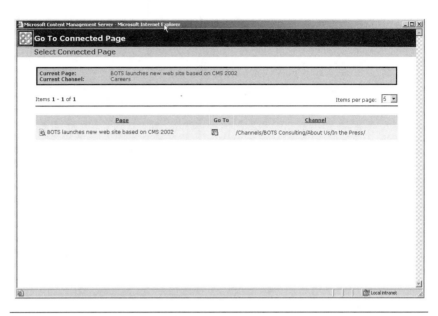

**Figure 15–9** Go to Connected Page report

## Using the PAPI

By now, you should be familiar with the creation of a connected posting in the Web Author. We'd now like to show you how to accomplish the same thing using the PAPI. First, let's review the prerequisites for creating a connected posting.

- The connected posting must use a different, connected template if you create it in the same channel as the original posting.
- If you create the connected posting in a different channel, you can use the same template as the original posting.
- Any operation against the content of any of the connected postings will be reflected across all the postings.
- The authenticated user must have the authority to create postings in both the source and destination channels.

For the purposes of our demo, we're going to create an ASPX page to hold all of the code. We'll name this ASPX page ConntectedPostings. aspx. In actuality, creating an "out of process" ASPX page creates some additional work for us, but it eliminates the need to create a posting based on a template with exactly the same code as our ASPX page; the choice is ultimately yours. An explanation of what we're doing in our ASPX page follows.

- First and foremost, we must be in Update mode in order to affect the repository. If our page were a posting in CMS, we could retrieve the property UrlModeUpdate and redirect to it. Since this is an out-of-process page, however, we need to redirect to the page with NRMODE=Update specified in the query string.
- Once we're in Update mode, we'll need to authenticate as a user who has authority to create postings in the source and destination channels. Because the BOTS site has guest access enabled, when our page starts, CMS will log us in as the guest account. In our code, we're redirecting to the login.aspx page to allow us to authenticate. Once we're authenticated, the login page will return us to our ASPX page automatically.
- Next, we pass a posting and a destination channel. The posting will provide us with a collection of connected templates. Alternatively, we could retrieve the posting's Template object and then get the connected templates, but the way we did it is a bit shorter. With the collection of connected templates, we can create the connected postings using the original posting and the connected templates. The destination channel is where the connected postings will end up.
- Once we have the collection of connected templates, we iterate through each of them and create a connected posting. Normally, you're more likely to create a single connected posting at a time. However, we wanted to demonstrate how you could create a number of connected postings at once.
- As we create each connected posting, we report what template was used to create the posting.
- Once we're finished, we report the operation has completed.

**NOTE:** The BOTS site uses Forms authentication, which allows us to log in to CMS as a user that's different from the current Windows user. If we were using Windows authentication, the current user would need the appropriate permissions to create the connected postings. In that case, we wouldn't use the login page at all; CMS would automatically authenticate us.

In Listing 15–1 you can see the code in our ASPX page. The code is commented to help you match it to the preceding list of bullet items.

**Listing 15–1** The code for ConnectedPostings.aspx

```
protected System.Web.UI.WebControls.PlaceHolder PageOutput;
private CmsHttpContext myContext;

private void Page_Load(object sender, System.EventArgs e)
{
     // Check to see if the NRMODE querystring has been set.  If not
     // redirect back to the page with the parameter set
     if(Request.QueryString["NRMODE"] != "Update")
     {Response.Redirect("/botsconsulting/utilities/
connectedpostings.aspx?NRMODE=Update");}

     // Create a reference to the current context
     myContext = CmsHttpContext.Current;

     // Find the original posting and channel; we've hard coded
paths
     // for demonstration purposes.  Normally you would pass in the
     // beginning values.
     Channel connectedPostingChannel = (Channel)myContext.Searches.
GetByPath("/Channels/botsconsulting/services");
     Posting originalPosting = (Posting)myContext.Searches.
GetByPath("/Channels/botsconsulting/about/press/1132003771");

     // Make sure that we got back both objects
     if (originalPosting != null && connectedPostingChannel !=
null)
     {
          // We got the objects we wanted, so update the PageOutput
server control
          this.PageOutput.Controls.Add(new LiteralControl("Found
both the channel and the posting<br>"));
          this.PageOutput.Controls.Add(new LiteralControl
("Attempting to create the new connected posting(s)<br>"));

          // Call the CreateConnectedPostings function
          CreateConnectedPostings(originalPosting,
connectedPostingChannel);
     }

     // We didn't get back the objects we wanted, so just end.
     else
     {
```

```
        this.PageOutput.Controls.Add(new LiteralControl("Could
not find either the destination channel or original posting<br>"));
        this.PageOutput.Controls.Add(new LiteralControl("The
current user " + myContext.User.ServerAccountName + " may not have
rights<br>"));
        this.PageOutput.Controls.Add(new LiteralControl("or the
objects may not exist<br>"));
    }
}

private void CreateConnectedPostings(Posting startPosting, Channel
destinationChannel)
{

    // Make sure the current user has authoring rights
    // in the source and destination channel
    if (destinationChannel.CanCreatePostings && startPosting.
Parent.CanCreatePostings)
    {
        // Get a list of the connected templates for the passed
in posting
        TemplateCollection myConnectedTemplates = startPosting.
ConnectedTemplates;
        // Check to make sure we got a collection back
        if (myConnectedTemplates != null)
        {
            // Loop through the entire collection and create a
connected
            // posting with each template
            foreach(Template connectedTemplate in
myConnectedTemplates)
            {
                this.PageOutput.Controls.Add(new
LiteralControl("Creating new connected posting based on the "
                    + connectedTemplate.Name + "
template.<br>"));
                            destinationChannel.
CreateConnectedPosting(connectedTemplate,startPosting);

                // Commit the changes to the repository and release any
                // locks on the objects
                myContext.CommitAll;
```

```
            }
            this.PageOutput.Controls.Add(new
LiteralControl("Operation completed successfully.<br>"));
        }
    }
    else
    {

        // If we're not logged in with a user ID that has authority
        // to create connected postings, redirect to the login
        // page.  This will continue to fire until the appropriate
        // credentials are provided.
        Response.Redirect("/botsconsulting/login.aspx?
returnurl=" + HttpUtility.UrlEncode("/botsconsulting/utilities/
connectedpostings.aspx?NRMODE=Update"));
    }

}
```

In the preceding code sample, we were able to create a number of connected postings all at once. The code isn't complex, since CMS takes a lot of the work out of the operation. However, you should be careful to check for locks on the objects. In general, objects that are free of locks will be "owned" by everyone. If the posting you're using to create connected postings is owned by a specific user, it's likely that it's still going through a workflow process or in the midst of an edit.

## Workflow Implications of Connected Postings

So far we've learned what connected postings are and how they operate inside CMS. In addition, we've explored how to create postings using the Web Author and the PAPI. Now we should cover some of the workflow implications of connected postings.

Throughout this chapter, we referred to or hinted at some of the unique workflow characteristics of connected postings. However, we felt it was important to provide you with a consolidated list of workflow implications.

- Connected postings share content, so changes in one posting affect the other connected postings.

- When a content state change in one posting occurs, all connected postings reflect the same status.
- Connected postings will follow the workflow path of the channel where the authoring takes place. For example, in our BOTS site, we created a new press release in our press section. Since we have an editor defined in that channel, when the author submits the content for approval, the state of the posting changes from Saved to WaitingforEditorApproval. Now, suppose we created a connected posting in the Careers channel, which doesn't happen to have editors defined. If, when we created the connected posting, we changed the content and subsequently submitted the change for approval, the posting would immediately go to Waitingfor ModeratorApproval instead of to editor approval. Why? Well, as we mentioned, the Careers channel does not have an editor defined, so the default behavior for content submissions in that channel would be to go to the moderator if page properties need to be defined (as they would with a new posting) or straight to Approved if no moderator approval is necessary. If, however, we didn't make any content changes while we were in the Careers channel and, instead, went to the Press channel to make our changes and then submitted those changes for approval, our posting would go to WaitingforEditorApproval as expected. So, based

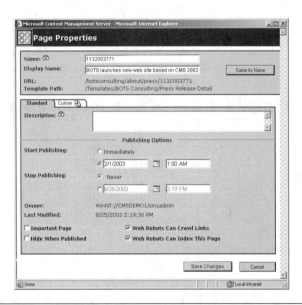

**Figure 15–10** The page properties interface for connected postings

on the channel and the defined groups for that channel, connected postings may follow different workflow paths.

■ Connected postings share certain page properties. In Figure 15–10 we show the page properties interface for two connected postings. The "connected page" icon is shown next to each property that the postings will share. The properties that aren't shared can be changed independently and follow different workflow paths. Shared properties will affect all postings and subsequently affect the page status of each connected posting.

■ If a content contributor edits a posting that has connected postings, all connected postings will be locked by that contributor.

## Summary

In this chapter, we examined connected postings in CMS. Connected postings are one mechanism within CMS to allow repurposing of content across one or more sites run on a single implementation of CMS. We discussed what connected postings are and how they operate within CMS. We talked about the relationship between connected templates and connected postings, explaining that connected postings can only be created using connected templates. We then looked at how to create connected postings using the Web Author and the PAPI. For the PAPI example, we provided a full code example.

Once we covered the basics of connected postings and templates, we reviewed some of the workflow implications. Connected postings, because of their nature, sometimes operate differently from a posting based in a single channel. A collection of connected postings could potentially follow different workflow paths, based on where change content was submitted for approval.

# PART IV

# Site Administration and Security

# CHAPTER 16

# Working with Containers

## Overview

In the previous chapters, we discussed how to create and develop a CMS Web site. We will now concentrate on site administration tasks, starting off by focusing on managing the CMS publishing environment.

In CMS, managing the publishing environment means managing virtual storage. Virtual storage is used to organize pages, templates, and other site resources, such as images and video files. As we have already mentioned, virtual storage spaces are referred to as containers. There are three types of containers.

- A channel container stores pages and subchannels.
- A template gallery container stores templates and other template galleries.
- A resource gallery container stores site resources such as images, video files, and file attachments, as well as other resource galleries.

After the containers have been set up, users are granted rights to these containers. For example, by assigning user rights to a channel, you can specify who can only view pages inside the channel, and who can author, edit, or approve the same pages. When a user browses to a page in a channel, the page is displayed in different ways depending on the user rights. For instance, as we have seen in Chapter 5, the Web Author console is not visible to the site subscribers but is displayed to the users with appropriate rights, such as authors, editors, and moderators. To have rights in a container, a user must be a member of at least one CMS rights group that is assigned to this container. In turn, each rights group belongs to one of the CMS roles, which determines the rights the user will have in that container.

Each object in CMS virtual storage has a Globally Unique Identifier (GUID) assigned to it. All objects are uniquely identified by their GUIDs, not by their names. As a result, it is possible, for example, for two or more channels to have the same name. Because these channels have different GUIDs, they are treated as two independent objects within CMS.

---

**NOTE:** To avoid confusion, make sure the publishing schedules for the channels with the same names do not overlap. This is one of the site administration tasks; we will discuss it later in the chapter.

---

In this chapter, we will concentrate on administering containers; in the next chapter, we will look into setting up user rights. In most cases, the Site Manager is used to perform administration tasks on CMS containers; however, certain tasks can be performed in the Web Author and Visual Studio .NET as well.

# Working with Channels

Channels store pages and provide the hierarchical structure for CMS sites. This structure determines the overall navigation for your site and is similar to a virtual directories structure for IIS-based sites. However, there is an important difference: In CMS, no actual disk directories are used for storage; instead, the content is stored in the SQL Server database and is organized in channels. The Site Manager provides a GUI that allows us to organize and manage the hierarchical channel structure.

---

**NOTE:** Channel hierarchy implements the information architecture of your site. We have created the channel hierarchy for our sample site in Chapter 9.

---

The Site Manager provides the ability to perform usual administration tasks, such as creating, renaming, and deleting channels, as well as CMS-specific channel configuration tasks—for example, setting up channel rendering options and sorting order. Site administrators, channel managers, and template designers can create and administer channels.

To display the channels hierarchy, click the Channels icon in the left pane of the Site Manager window (Figure 16–1).

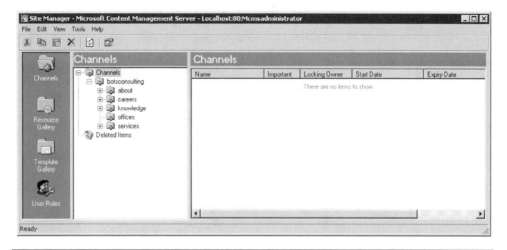

**Figure 16–1** Channels hierarchy

## Configuring Channel Properties

You can configure an existing channel by using the tabs within the Properties dialog box. To display the Properties dialog, right-click the existing channel and select Properties.

---

**NOTE:** Some configuration options can be set up when you create a channel using the New Channel dialog; the tabs in the New Channel dialog provide access to the subset of options accessible via the channel's properties.

---

The Properties > General tab (Figure 16–2) allows us to change the display name of the channel and the channel description. As we have discussed in previous chapters, the display name is a user-friendly alias that is used as text for a link pointing at your channel when the channel is presented to the users—for example, within a navigational structure for your site in a browser. The Display Name property can contain non-US-ASCII and spaces, which is very useful for multilingual sites.

The Description property allows us to provide a meaningful description of the channel content; it is an optional property. The Description field is limited to 256 characters in length and is mainly used for site maintenance. The General tab also shows when the channel was created and by whom, the locking owner, and when and by whom it was last modified; this information is read-only and can't be changed.

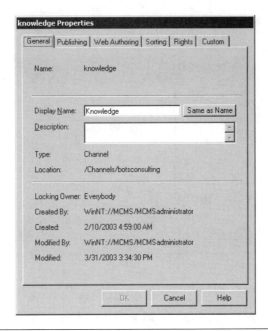

**Figure 16–2** Channel general properties

The name, display name, and the description of a channel can also be changed from the Web Author by using the Channel Properties dialog (Figure 16–3).

The Properties > Publishing tab (Figure 16–4) provides access to the channel rendering and lifetime settings as well as the channel options.

The Options section on the Publishing tab (Figure 16–4) provides access to four channel publishing options; the first two options are also available from the Web Author using the Channel Properties dialog (Figure 16–3).

- The Important Channel check box sets up an additional flag on the channel. This flag can be analyzed programmatically; it is used for all sorts of business reasons. For example, it can be used to denote channels that will be protected by SSL. This flag by default is not selected.
- The Hide When Published check box makes the channel invisible after it has been published. This option can also be analyzed in the code and changed programmatically at runtime depending on the business logic you'd like to implement; by default this option is not

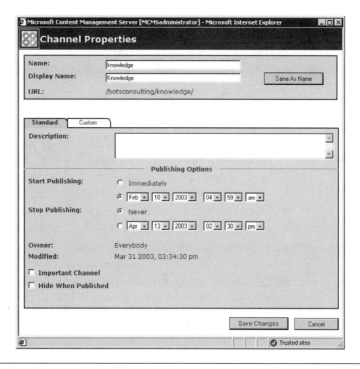

**Figure 16–3** Channel Properties dialog available from the Web Author console

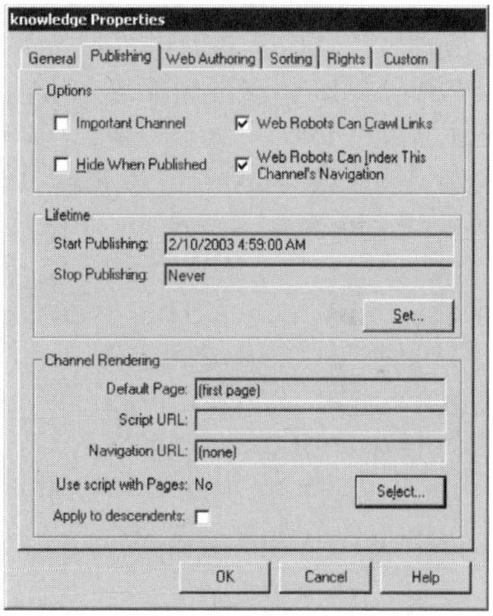

**Figure 16–4** Channel publishing properties

selected. For example, if this flag is set, then the channel will be hidden in the navigation structure displayed on the published site.

- The Web Robots settings define how the robots META tags are generated at runtime for a channel navigation page, whether static or generated by a script.

The Web Robots settings for a channel are only available from the Site Manager, as follows:

- The Web Robots Can Crawl Links check box allows Web robots to follow links from this channel navigation page. A channel navigation page is a page displayed by the channel rendering when the channel is accessed by its URL.
- The Web Robots Can Index This Channel's Navigation check box allows Web crawlers to index the navigation page that is displayed for the channel URL.

---

**NOTE:** Pages within the channel have their own robots META tags (refer to Chapter 6 for details of the robots META tags). These are configured by authors, using Page Properties in the Web Author console or Advanced Page Properties in the Authoring Connector. Automatically, the channel robots META tag configuration settings apply only to the channel rendering. However, programmatically they can be used anywhere in the site—for example, for generating META tags for some or all pages or subchannels within the current channel.

---

The Lifetime section on the Publishing tab (Figure 16–4) defines the channel's publishing schedule. Click the Set button to display the Set Channel Lifetime dialog box (Figure 16–5), where you can set the Start Publishing and Stop Publishing options. The channel's publishing schedule can also be changed from the Web Author by using the Channel Properties dialog, as shown in Figure 16–3.

Start Publishing defines the server date and time when the channel becomes available on the live site. You can define the exact date and time or make the channel visible immediately. If necessary, you can set the start publishing date of the channel to the day of your choice in the past. However, using the Site Manager, you cannot set a start date that is before the installation date of CMS.

---

**NOTE:** You can set a channel start date that is before the installation date of CMS by using the Publishing API. In this case, the Site Manager accepts a new date.

---

**Figure 16–5** Channel lifetime

Stop Publishing defines the server date and time when the channel stops being available on the live site. However, it is not deleted from the Content Repository and remains visible from the Site Manager. The following list describes the Stop Publishing options.

- The Never Stop Publishing option provides permanent availability of the channel on the live site.
- The Interval option defines an amount of time after the channel has been published. The values are 1 day; 1 and 2 weeks; 1, 4, and 6 months; and 1 year. This option is only available in the Site Manager.
- The exact date and time option specifies the expiry date for the channel. The date and time here refer to the date and time on the CMS server computer.

The Channel Rendering section on the Publishing tab defines what is displayed in the browser when the channel is accessed by its URL, without a page name. To configure the options, click Select. The Select Channel Rendering dialog box is displayed, as shown in Figure 16–6. This dialog allows you to specify the page that should be used as the default page for the channel, as well as whether any additional processing should occur on the server. The default page can be defined in one of two ways.

- You can explicitly specify the name of the page to be used as the default. The name should be typed manually; there is no browsing button. The page doesn't have to exist in the channel at the time of configuration; it can be added later. However, if your default page is not present in the published channel on the live site, an error message will be displayed in the browser when a user tries to access the channel URL.

■ You can choose that the first page in the channel be used as its default page. This is the default setting. "First" means any page that is the first item in the list displayed under Properties > Sorting.

In the Channel Rendering section, you can specify a script to be executed when content in the channel is accessed. This script is called a channel rendering script, or just a channel script; it is also referred to as a channel outer script. This setting is optional. The script can be either an ASP or ASPX page for mixed mode sites, and only an ASPX page for ASP.NET sites. The channel script is defined by its location in the IIS virtual site; this location should be typed in manually, there is no browse button. The channel script can perform any processing that is required by the logic of your site—for example, combine pages in a frameset, verify the security credentials, redirect the user to another channel or page, or display a list of all pages in the channel.

The No and Yes radio buttons define whether the channel script is executed only when the channel URL is requested or when the channel URL as well as all page URLs within the channel are requested. For example, if Yes is selected, then the channel script will be run for the channel requests (http://*<site>*/*<channel>*) as well as page requests (http://*<site>*/*<channel>*/*<page>*).

On a framed site, a channel rendering script contains the frameset and must run when a user browses either to a channel or to any page in the channel.

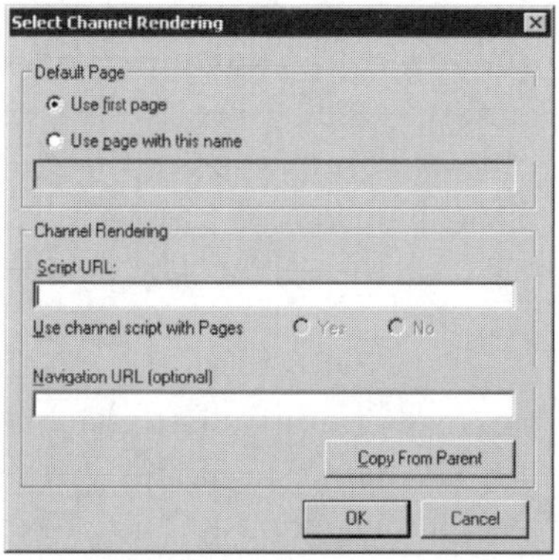

**Figure 16–6** Channel rendering properties

For example, a sample channel script is configured for the root channel node Channels when you create your site. The script is called McmsHomeport.aspx and is located in the folder <installation point>\ Server\MCMS\McmsHomeport\. By default, this folder is mapped to the virtual directory /MCMS/MCMSHomeport on the IIS virtual site that is configured as the CMS Web entry point. It provides an ASPX page that is displayed for an empty CMS site with no pages. The page lists the CMS Web applications on the IIS virtual site and provides a brief description of CMS and the links to support information on the microsoft.com site (Figure 16–7).

A channel may contain no pages—only subchannels. This configuration can be used, for example, to organize the content in channels in a logical way for a site and to provide better navigation through the site's content. However, if a URL points to a channel, we still need to provide a browser with a page to display. The Navigation URL box does exactly that—it specifies what to return to the browser if there are no pages in the channel. Usually, it will be a page that provides links to the content of the channel; therefore, the URL is referred to as the Navigation URL. The Navigation URL can be a frameset. You need to type in the URL

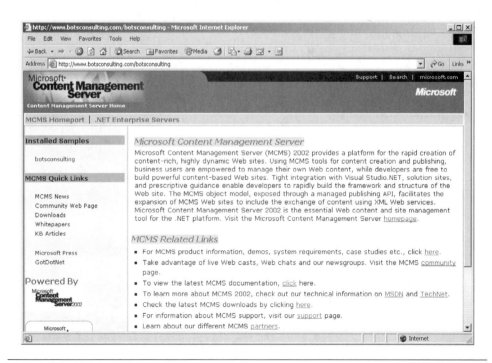

**Figure 16–7** Sample channel rendering script

manually. In effect, this box provides a simulation of HTTP redirection on the server side.

---

**NOTE:** You can also use a channel rendering script to dynamically generate a navigation page for a channel with no stored pages. The Navigation URL is mostly used for compatibility with CMS 2001.

---

If there is no script or Navigation URL configured for a channel without stored pages, then the default channel cover page provided by CMS will be displayed when a browser points to a channel URL. The default page is an ASP page called Cover.asp, located in the folder *<installation point>*\Server\IIS_NR\Shared\. For example, Figure 16–8 shows the channel cover page displayed on our sample site for the top-level channel botsconsulting. If we click the root node Channels, the channel rendering script will be displayed, as shown in Figure 16–7.

For a nonroot channel, the channel rendering properties can be inherited. Click the Copy From Parent button (Figure 16–6) if you want the settings to be the same as for the parent channel. You can apply the channel rendering settings to the subchannels by selecting the "Apply to descendents" check box in the Channel Rendering section on the Publishing tab (Figure 16–4).

**Figure 16–8** Channel cover page

The Publishing > Web Authoring tab allows you to set up the default template and resource galleries for the channel (Figure 16–9).

Both settings are optional. However, it makes sense to assign the default template and resource galleries to the channel since these could be accessed programmatically using the Channel.DefaultTemplate Gallery and Channel.DefaultResourceGallery properties. Using these properties we can, for example, customize the Web Author console. It is worth mentioning that the content authors don't have to use the default gallery; they can select another one if they wish.

Another benefit of assigning the default galleries is that the site administrator can see explicitly who needs rights where. It's a good practice, one of those "nice-to-haves."

A gallery can be a default gallery for more than one channel. Setting up the default galleries is easy: Browse to the gallery that is to become the default gallery by clicking the ellipsis button (Figure 16–10), select it, and click OK. Typing the gallery name in a box is not allowed; you have to browse to it. If you want to clear an entry, use the Clear button.

The Publishing > Sorting tab (Figure 16–11) specifies the order of the items contained within the channel. The items may be pages or channels. The position of an item within the list can be changed using the Up and Down buttons.

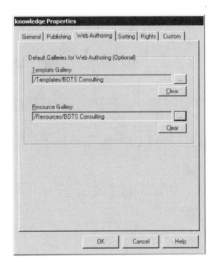

**Figure 16–9** Setting up the default template and resource galleries for a channel

**Figure 16–10** Select Template Gallery dialog box

The purpose of this ordered list is twofold.

- The channel's default page can be configured as the first page in the list.
- It is a standard practice to provide navigation within the channel, which means displaying the channel items as links. This can be accomplished programmatically using the properties of the ChannelItem class; we have seen it in Chapter 14. The navigation links within the channel appear in the order of the channel items

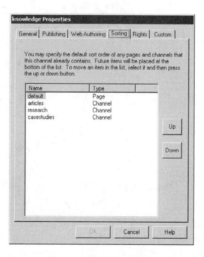

**Figure 16–11** Channel sorting order

within the list in the Sorting tab. It is likely that you will want to change the default order of the items within the channel for meaningful and user-friendly navigation.

The Publishing > Rights tab assigns the CMS rights groups to a channel (Figure 16–12). Make sure you assign at least one subscribers rights group to the channel; otherwise, ordinary users may not be able to view content in the channel on the live site. If you want your channel to have the same group assignment as its parent channel, click Modify and then click Add Parent's Rights. We will focus on setting up user rights in the next chapter.

The Publishing > Custom tab allows you to set up the custom properties for a channel (Figure 16–13). A custom property is a name/value pair associated with a channel. A channel can have multiple custom properties. Different channels and pages can have the same custom properties. After the custom properties have been defined for a channel, their values can be assigned or changed from the Web Author by using the Channel Properties dialog > Custom tab, as shown in Figure 16–14.

---

**NOTE:** Custom properties for CMS pages are defined in their corresponding templates in Visual Studio .NET. The values for custom properties are assigned by content contributors, using the Web Author or the Authoring Connector (refer to Chapters 5 or 7, respectively, for a detailed discussion).

---

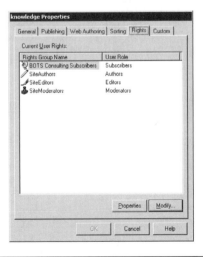

**Figure 16–12** Channel rights

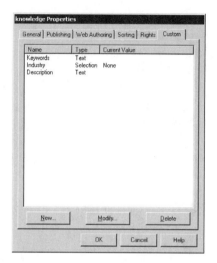

**Figure 16–13**  Custom tab of the Channel Properties dialog in the Site Manager

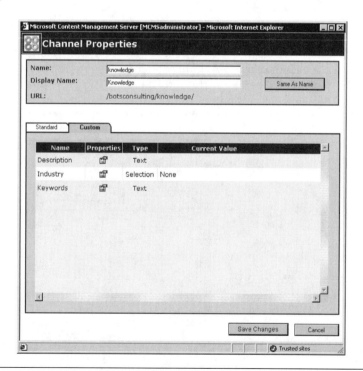

**Figure 16–14**  Custom tab of the Channel Properties dialog in the Web Author

Custom properties can be used programmatically—for example, to present the user with the channels and pages that share a particular property value. If custom properties are created consistently across a number of channels and pages, then you can provide additional functionality for the site. The key here is the word "consistently." Defining custom properties should be part of defining the overall architecture of your site. For example, let's say that we created a custom property for a brief summary of content provided within a channel. We could then use this summary as additional information we present to the user in the navigation structure—for instance, when a user's mouse is over the channel's display name.

**NOTE:** Custom channel properties can be created only using the Site Manager. The current version of the Publishing API does not expose a method to create custom channel properties programmatically. This limitation, combined with the inability to manage user rights programmatically, can hinder efforts to use automated scripts to create large numbers of channels.

Setting up a custom property involves giving it a name, selecting the type of the property, and defining its values. The New button allows you to set up a new custom property; the Modify button provides the ability to change the values of the existing properties; the Delete button deletes the selected property. The custom property name can be up to 45 characters in length.

There are two types of custom properties: text and selection.

- The text custom property value (Figure 16–15) must be a US-ASCII string. The string length is limited to 2,000 characters. The string cannot contain any control characters (ASCII 1–31) other than tab, LF, and CR (ASCII 9, 10, and 13, respectively). The value defined in the Custom tab is a default value for the property. To provide a value, position your cursor in the Current Text Value box and either type or paste the text. The value can be changed by users with the appropriate rights from the Web Author console, using the Channel Properties dialog > Custom tab, by clicking the Properties icon and assigning the value (Figure 16–16).
- The selection custom property has a list of Allowed Values (Figure 16–17). Values are added to the list by clicking the New button and typing the value in the Add Value dialog box. The up and down arrow buttons move the selected value up and down the list.

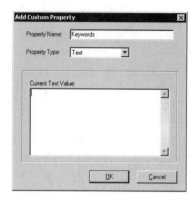

**Figure 16–15** Text custom property

The Set as Current button marks the highlighted value in the list as current. Selection-based custom property values are usually presented in a user interface by drop-down lists. Values are positioned in the drop-down list in the same order as they are positioned in the Allowed Values list in the Custom tab. The value marked as current is selected by default. It is mandatory to set one of the values in the Allowed Values list as current. This value can be changed by users with the appropriate rights from the Web Author console, using the Channel Properties dialog > Custom tab (Figure 16–18).

As we discussed in Chapter 6, custom properties are typically used to generate Keywords and Description META tags for the internal and

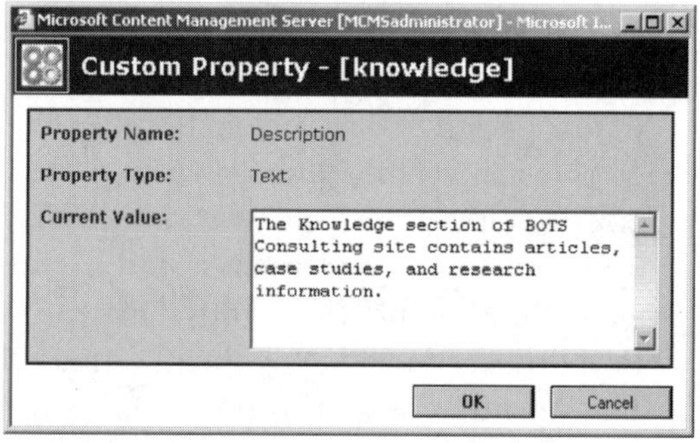

**Figure 16–16** Assigning the value for a text custom property in the Web Author

**Figure 16–17**  Selection custom property

external search engines. Custom properties can also be used to categorize content across the site. Authors apply the values to the predefined custom properties when they add content using the Web Author; the actual META tags are created at runtime programmatically. In the code, developers retrieve the content stored in the custom properties and insert it into the META tags in the HTML header using the Channel.Custom Properties collection.

That's all about creating and configuring channels. The other tasks we need to look into are renaming, moving, copying, and deleting channels, as well as moving, copying, and deleting the pages within the channel. Performing these tasks for the channels inside the Site Manager is like working with folders inside Windows Explorer.

**Figure 16–18**  Assigning the value for a selection custom property in the Web Author

## Renaming a Channel

To rename a channel in the Site Manager, right-click the channel you'd like to rename, select Rename, and type the new name. This name will be used as a part of the URL. If you want to change the channel's display name, you can do it from the Properties > General tab. You can rename all channels, including the default root node Channels.

The Name and Display Name properties for a channel can also be changed from the Web Author console using the Channel Properties dialog (Figure 16–3).

## Moving and Copying a Channel

Right-click the channel you'd like to move or copy, and select either Cut or Copy; then right-click the channel where you want the channel to be moved or copied, and click Paste.

As we have already mentioned, the Site Manager doesn't enforce the uniqueness of channel names. This is because the name of a channel is not used as its unique identifier. Instead, each object in the Content Repository has a GUID assigned to it. Two channels with the same names have different GUIDs; hence they are treated as two independent objects within CMS.

If the publishing schedules of two channels with the same name overlap, both channels will be displayed in the browser. It could be quite confusing for users. Therefore, it is important to rename the channel after you've copied it, or make sure the publishing schedules of channels with the same names do not overlap. The expiration date and time of one of the channels must precede the start date and time of the other channel.

You can dovetail the publishing schedules to make the second channel with the same name available at the same time the first one expires. This technique allows seamless site updates.

## Deleting, Removing, and Restoring a Channel

To delete a channel, right-click the channel and click Delete. Deleted channels are moved to the Deleted Items container. From there, you can either restore the channel or remove it permanently.

To remove the channel permanently, open the Deleted Items container, right-click the channel, and select Delete. To restore the channel, move it from the Deleted Items container to where you'd like it to be restored.

## Moving, Copying, and Deleting Pages in a Channel

To move or copy a page using the Site Manager, right-click the page you'd like to move or copy and select either Cut or Copy; then right-click the channel where you want the page to be moved or copied to, and click Paste.

CMS allows pages with the same names to be stored in a channel. Each page is identified by its own GUID, and is therefore completely independent and has its own set of properties, including the name and the publishing schedules. To avoid confusion, make sure the publishing schedules for pages with the same names do not overlap. You can use the same technique for consecutive updates as for the channels: Set the start date of the new version of the page to the expiration date of the version you'd like to replace.

---

**NOTE:** Pages that are copied or moved individually will have to be approved for publishing in the normal way, using the publishing work-flow configured on their destination channel. If the content of the moved page hasn't been changed, it only requires moderator approval. However, if you move the channel containing the page, then the page does not need reapproval.

---

To delete a page using the Site Manager, right-click the page and click Delete. Deleted pages are moved to the Deleted Items container. From there, you can either restore the page by moving it back in the channels hierarchy, or remove it permanently by right-clicking it and selecting Delete. If you'd like to permanently remove all pages and channels in the Deleted Items container, right-click it and select Clear Deleted Items.

You can move, copy, and delete pages using the Web Author console; we discussed how to do it in Chapter 5. There are some differences in implementation of the functionality between the Site Manager and the Web Author. For example, pages deleted from the Web Author console are not moved to the Deleted Items container and can't be restored.

# Working with Template Galleries

A template gallery is a virtual storage space that provides a way to store and organize template metadata. Template metadata is usually referred to as just a template; it includes references to a template file location, placeholder definitions, and custom property definitions. Templates and template files are created and managed using the Template Explorer within Visual Studio .NET.

---

**NOTE:** Template galleries can be created using the Site Manager as well as the Template Explorer in Visual Studio .NET. User rights to template galleries can be assigned only using the Site Manager.

---

In this section, we will look into working with template galleries using the Site Manager. It is similar to working with folders in Windows Explorer. Site managers, channel managers, and template designers can create and administer template galleries.

To access the template galleries tree, click the Template Gallery icon in the left pane of the Site Manager window (Figure 16–19).

## Renaming, Moving, and Copying a Template Gallery

To rename a template gallery, right-click the template gallery you'd like to rename, select Rename, and type the new name. If you want to change the gallery's description, you can do it from the Properties > General tab (Figure 16–20).

---

**NOTE:** To access the Properties dialog box, right-click the template gallery and select Properties.

---

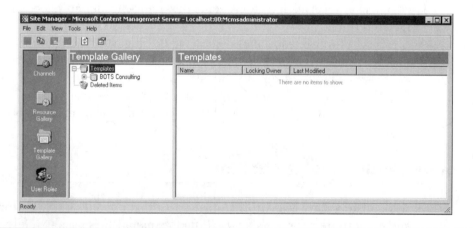

**Figure 16–19** Template gallery hierarchy

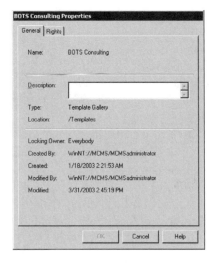

**Figure 16–20**  Template gallery properties

To move or copy a template gallery, right-click the template gallery you'd like to move or copy, and select either Cut or Copy; then right-click the destination gallery where you want it to be moved or copied, and click Paste.

The Site Manager allows galleries with the same name to be stored inside the parent gallery because they have different GUIDs. However, it is a good practice to rename the template gallery immediately after you've copied it into the same gallery as the original; otherwise, it could become very confusing for both authors and administrators of your site.

## Deleting, Removing, and Restoring a Template Gallery

To delete a template gallery, right-click it and click Delete. Deleted template galleries are moved to the Deleted Items container. From there, you can either remove the deleted gallery permanently by right-clicking it and selecting Delete, or restore the gallery by moving it back to the template galleries tree.

## Moving, Copying, and Deleting Templates in a Template Gallery

To move or copy a template, right-click the template you'd like to move or copy and select either Cut or Copy; then right-click the template gallery where you want the template to be moved or copied, and click

Paste. You can also drag and drop the template onto a template gallery in the tree pane.

Templates, and other CMS objects, are identified by GUIDs; therefore, the Site Manager allows templates with the same name to be stored inside a template gallery. You cannot rename the template from the Site Manager, you can rename it only from the Template Explorer in Visual Studio .NET.

To delete a template, right-click the template and click Delete. Deleted templates are moved to the Deleted Items container in the template galleries hierarchy. From there, you can either restore the template by moving it back into a template gallery or remove it permanently by right-clicking it and selecting Delete. If you'd like to permanently remove all templates and template galleries in the Deleted Items container, right-click it and select Clear Deleted Items.

## Reverting a Template

Sometimes, after you have changed a template but haven't approved it, you need to go back to the template that has been previously approved. You can achieve this "rollback" functionality in the Site Manager by right-clicking the template and selecting Revert to Approved. If this option is grayed out, it means that this particular template cannot be reverted.

---

**NOTE:** The Revert to Approved option allows you to revert the template metadata, including placeholder definitions, custom properties definitions, and the template file location. However, this option doesn't control the changes to the template ASPX file. Using the Revert to Approved option, you can revert changes to the metadata, but not the code.

---

## Dependent Report

A template's dependent report shows all pages that are based on this template. To run a dependent report for a template, right-click the template and select Dependent Report. The report is displayed in an Internet Explorer pop-up window, as shown in Figure 16–21.

---

**NOTE:** You can revert templates and run dependent reports only from the Site Manager.

---

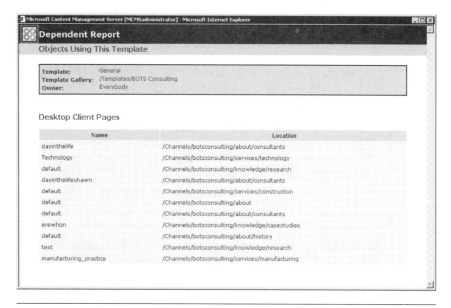

**Figure 16–21** Dependent report

## Assigning Rights to a Template Gallery

Rights to an existing template gallery are assigned using the Properties > Rights tab (Figure 16–22). If you want your template gallery to have the same rights group assignment as its parent gallery, click Modify and then click Add Parent's Rights. We will look into assigning rights in the next chapter.

**Figure 16–22** Template gallery rights

# Working with Resource Galleries

A resource gallery is a virtual storage space that stores resources and other resource galleries. Resources are images, audio and video files, or any other files that can be used as file attachments. Resource galleries can store any Multipurpose Internet Mail Extensions (MIME) type files. Resources are either displayed inline in the browser or presented as a link to the resource file: If the resource is not one of the well-known image or video types, the file is displayed as a link (attachment) within a page. How the linked file is viewed is determined by a client's browser and the applications available on the client computer.

Resources are mainly managed using the Resource Manager in the Web Author console. Resource galleries are managed using the Site Manager. Site managers, channel managers, template designers, and resource managers can create and administer resource galleries.

To access the resource galleries tree, click the Resource Gallery icon in the left pane of the Site Manager window (Figure 16–23). Working with resource galleries using the Site Manager is similar to working with folders in Windows Explorer. Most of the tasks are exactly the same as for the template galleries.

## Adding Resources to a Resource Gallery

Resources can be added to a resource gallery in one of two ways: either using the Resource Manager or using the Site Manager.

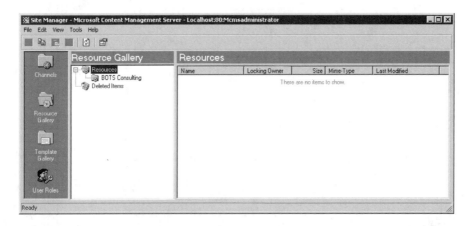

**Figure 16–23**  Resource gallery hierarchy

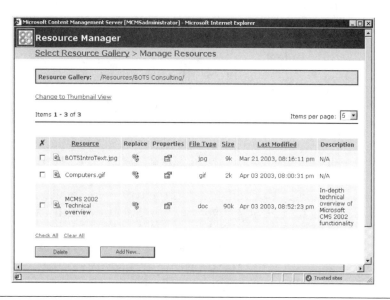

**Figure 16–24**  Manage Resources dialog

If you want to use the Resource Manager, then log on to the site, switch to Edit mode, and from the Web Author console select Resource Manager. In the Resource Manager dialog, navigate to the resource gallery you'd like to import your file into, and select it. In the Manage Resources dialog (Figure 16–24), click the Add New button (you might need to scroll down to find it). In the Add Resource dialog (Figure 16–25), browse to the file you'd like to add, and click Open.

The next task is to assign the MIME type to the newly added resource. Any file in a resource gallery has a MIME type assigned to it. When a new resource is created, if a new file name has an extension, the MIME type is assigned from the extension using the MIME mapping from the registry of the CMS server computer. If there is no MIME type mapping for the extension, then usually the MIME type application/x-octetstring (a binary format) will be assigned to the new resource. If this is not suitable, you'll need to map the appropriate MIME type to the extension in the registry as follows:

- Start the Registry Editor (on the Start menu, click Run, and then type regedit.exe) and expand HKEY_CLASSES_ROOT.
- Determine whether the registry already contains a key for the file extension—for example, .pdf. If the key does not exist, create it—that is, HKEY_CLASSES_ROOT\.pdf.

- Check whether the file extension key contains a value named Content Type. If it does not exist, create the value as a string value.
- To assign the MIME type, double-click the Content Type value and type the MIME type for the file extension in the Value data box—for example, application/pdf (Figure 16–26).

If the name of the file that you are adding to a resource gallery doesn't have an extension, you can select the MIME type from the File Type list. The list is quite limited—only well-known image, video, and document types are listed. If the type of a new file is not listed, carry on without selecting a type. In this case, usually the MIME type application/x-octetstring will be assigned to the new resource. If this is not suitable, rename the file to have an extension, and, if necessary, map the extension to the MIME type in the registry.

A template designer may enable the UseGeneratedIcon property for a single attachment placeholder in a template. This means that an icon representing a resource type must be shown by CMS, together with the attachment's display name, as a link to a resource in the published pages that are based on this template. However, if an application identified by the attachment type is not installed on the CMS server machine, there is no icon available to be generated. To resolve this situation, you can either

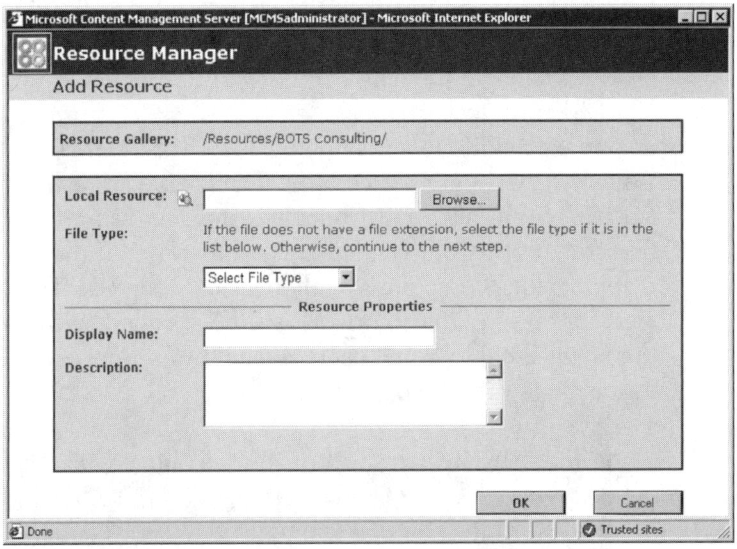

**Figure 16–25** Add Resource in Resource Manager

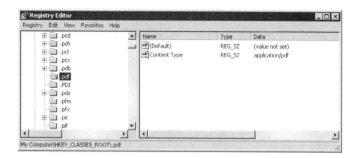

**Figure 16–26**  MIME type mapping in the registry

install the application in question on the CMS server—for example, the Adobe Acrobat viewer for PDF files—or you can define the default application icon in the registry using the path of a file that contains the icon. If you decide to follow the second route, you can obtain the file and the registry settings from the computer where the application is installed. For example, for Microsoft Word XP, you need to do the following:

- Under the HKEY_CLASSES_ROOT\.doc registry key, set the value data for the default value to a name that identifies the application that handles Word documents. You can look up this name on a computer that has Word installed. For Word XP, the name is Word.Document.8.
- Under HKEY_CLASSES_ROOT, create a key named Word. Document.8.
- Under HKEY_CLASSES_ROOT\Word.Document.8, create a key named DefaultIcon.
- Under the DefaultIcon key, set the default value as the path of a file that contains the icon that you want to use, followed by a comma and the number of the icon in the file that is to be used. In this example, the path is to the wordicon.exe file. The complete path on a computer that has Word XP installed is <installation drive>:\WINNT\Installer\{90280409-6000-11D3-8CFE-0050048383C9}\wordicon.exe,1 (Figure 16–27).
- Copy the wordicon.exe file to the location you specified in the previous step.

The last task is to define the display name and description for a resource. It is a good practice to provide both. The display name may be used programmatically to generate a link to a resource; it is a default

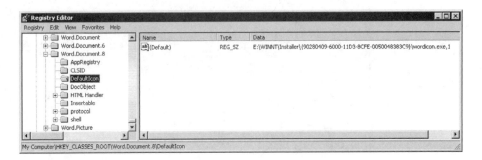

**Figure 16-27** Default icon configuration in the registry

display name that can be overwritten by the authors inserting the resource into their pages. The description appears in the Resource Manager in the resource record and could assist the content authors in selecting the appropriate file. The description is limited in length to 256 characters.

The other method of adding a resource to a gallery is using the Site Manager. To do this, open the Site Manager and navigate to the resource gallery to which you want to add a resource. In Windows Explorer or on the Desktop, select the file you wish to add. Then drag and drop it on the appropriate resource gallery. Make sure you drop it in the resource gallery tree, not in the resources pane. This method makes the display name the same as the file name and leaves the Description property for the new resource empty. You can change these using the Resource Manager by navigating to the resource, selecting the Properties icon for this resource, and modifying the Display Name and Description properties.

### Replacing a Resource in a Resource Gallery

Replacing a resource allows you to automatically change it in all pages and templates that reference this resource. A good example is updating a company's logo. The existing pages and templates that use the logo will automatically display the new one after it has been updated.

Resources are replaced using the Resource Manager. To replace a resource, navigate to the resource and click the Replace icon for the resource (Figure 16-28).

Click the Browse button to select the new resource file, and then click Open. The new resource file can have a different name but must have the same file extension as the old file. The original MIME content

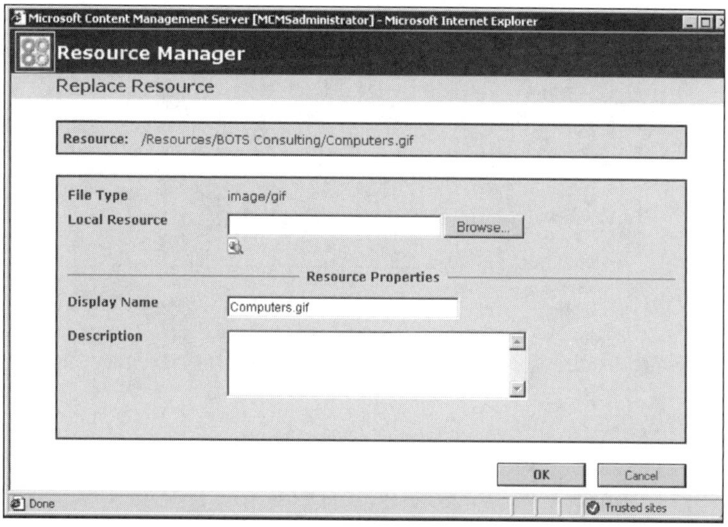

**Figure 16–28** Replacing a resource

type for a resource is preserved. You can't, for example, replace a JPEG image with a GIF. If the extensions, and therefore the MIME types, don't match, an error message is displayed (Figure 16–29), and the replacement process is aborted. If necessary, you can change the display name and description for the replaced resource.

## Renaming, Moving, and Copying a Resource Gallery

To rename a gallery, in the Site Manager right-click the resource gallery you'd like to rename, select Rename, and type the new name. If you want to change the gallery's description, right-click the gallery, select Properties, and then change the Description property from the Properties > General tab. The description is limited to 256 characters in length.

To move or copy a resource gallery, in the Site Manager, right-click the gallery you'd like to move or copy and select either Cut or Copy; then right-click the gallery where you want it to be moved or copied, and click Paste. All links in pages and templates to the resources inside the moved resource gallery will be maintained.

As with other CMS objects, galleries with the same name can be stored inside the parent gallery because they have different GUIDs. However, having two or more resource galleries with the same name is

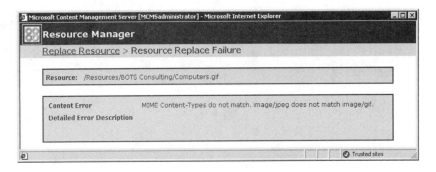

**Figure 16–29** MIME content mismatch error message

very confusing for content authors. It is a good practice to rename the resource gallery immediately after you've copied it.

## Deleting, Removing, and Restoring a Resource Gallery

To delete a resource gallery, right-click it in the Site Manager and click Delete. Deleted resource galleries are moved to the Deleted Items container in the resource galleries tree. From there, you can either remove the deleted gallery permanently by right-clicking it and selecting Delete, or restore the gallery by moving it back to the resource galleries tree.

## Moving, Copying, and Deleting Resources in a Resource Gallery

To move or copy a resource, right-click the file name in the right pane of the Site Manager window you'd like to move or copy, and select either Cut or Copy; then right-click the resource gallery where you want the resource to be moved or copied, and select Paste. You can also drag and drop the resource onto a resource gallery in the tree pane. Moving and reorganizing resources inside the Site Manager doesn't break links in any pages or templates referencing that resource.

**NOTE:** It used to be possible to run resource-dependent reports in CMS 2001. This feature is no longer available in CMS 2002.

Resources are identified by GUIDs in the same way as other CMS objects. This means that you can have, for example, two image files with the same name in the same resource gallery. This is better avoided because it could create problems for content authors.

To delete a resource, right-click the file name and click Delete. Deleted resources are moved to the Deleted Items container in the resource galleries tree. From there, you can either restore the resource by moving it back into a resource gallery or remove it permanently by right-clicking it and selecting Delete. If you'd like to permanently remove all resources and resource galleries in the Deleted Items container, right-click it and select Clear Deleted Items.

You can also delete resources using the Resource Manager in Web Author console. If using the Resource Manager, navigate to the resource you'd like to delete, select the resource by clicking the check box to the left of the resource name, and then click the Delete button. Resources deleted from the Resource manager can't be restored.

## Assigning Rights to a Resource Gallery

Rights to the existing gallery are assigned using the Properties > Rights tab (Figure 16–30). If you want your gallery to have the same rights group assignment as its parent gallery, click Modify and then click Add Parent's Rights. We will look into assigning rights in the next chapter.

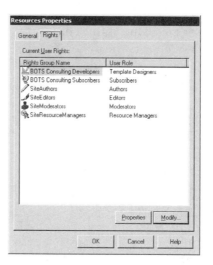

**Figure 16–30** Resource gallery rights

## Killing a Lock

When a user is working on a CMS object, this object is locked to prevent two users from working on the same object at the same time. CMS assigns a short-time session lock to the object when a user modifies it. Other users can work with a locked object in read-only mode; however, administrators and channel managers can override the lock. The objects include channels, pages, template galleries, templates, resource galleries, and individual resources.

**NOTE:** A session lock is different from the ownership lock assigned, for example, when an author creates a page. The author automatically becomes the owner of the page, and the page is locked while it goes through the publishing workflow to prevent other authors from changing it before it has been approved. The lock is removed when the page is published, and the locking ownership is assigned to a CMS pseudo-account called Everybody. A pseudo-account is an internal CMS entity that is not mapped to any Windows account. Setting page locking ownership to Everybody allows all CMS users with appropriate rights to edit the page. However, the short-time session lock does not change the locking ownership.

If a user's machine crashes or is turned off while the user is working with a CMS object, the object may remain locked after the user's machine has been rebooted. If a user is not able to work on an object they have rights to, you may need to remove a session lock placed on an object by CMS.

Administrators and channel managers can use the Kill Lock command, available from the Tools menu in the Site Manager, to end the session lock. You can also right-click an object, such as a channel or a page, and select Kill Lock. Before you use the Kill Lock command, make sure no user is currently working with the page you are killing the lock on; otherwise, the latest edits may be lost.

## Purging Revisions

As we discussed in Chapter 6, CMS stores all approved page, template, and resource revisions. For example, any page change that has been approved by an editor is a revision; each approved change to a page creates a new page version. The number of revisions on your system is limited only by the size of your database; object versions are stored by date and time. There is no option to automatically purge revisions or disable the creation of revisions. Historical revisions, including large resources, remain in your database and take up space.

Administrators can permanently delete all object revisions that are older than a defined time using the Site Manager. CMS purges all revisions in the site database that are older than the date and time specified. It is advisable to back up the CMS database before purging because this operation cannot be undone.

To purge revisions, in the Site Manager from the Tools menu select Clear Revision History. The Clear Revisions dialog box appears, as shown in Figure 16–31; specify the date and time corresponding to the revisions to be purged, and click Clear. A calendar is provided when you click the down arrow button in the date box. Click Yes in the confirmation message (Figure 16–32). All revisions older than the date you specified will be deleted.

**NOTE:** Users may be locked out of the system during the revision purging procedure; therefore, don't purge revisions from your site at times of high usage.

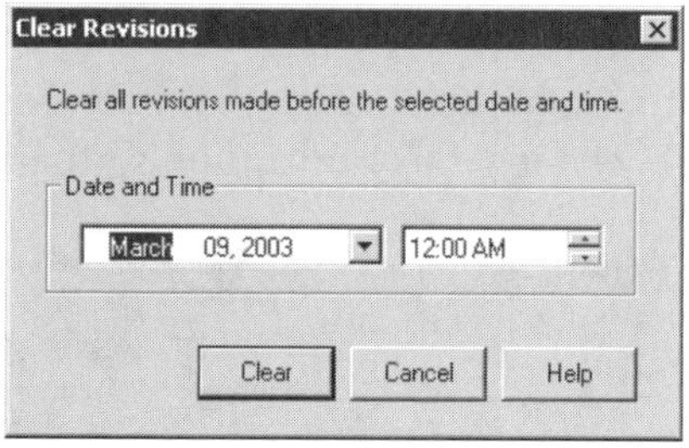

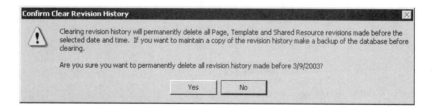

**Figure 16–31** Clear Revisions dialog box

**Figure 16–32** Clear Revision History confirmation message

# Purging the CMS Database

When items are deleted from a Deleted Items container, they are flagged as such in the appropriate tables in the database, and therefore the Site Manager doesn't display them anymore. For the same reason, the deleted items are not accessible from the PAPI. However, the deleted items' data is not actually deleted from the CMS database at this stage.

The deleted items' data is purged from the CMS database tables by a background SQL Server Agent job that is created when you populate the database in the DCA. By default, the job is called BGP-<*CMS database name*> and is scheduled to run daily at 1 AM. To access the job, open SQL Server Enterprise Manager and then open Microsoft SQL Servers > SQL Server Group > <*server name*> > Management > SQL Server Agent > Jobs, as shown in Figure 16–33.

The job consists of four steps performed in the following sequence (Figure 16–34):

1. Process expired pages.
2. Purge content for deleted pages.
3. Update gallery-based resources.
4. Purge data for deleted resources.

The first step deletes the expired postings; it is not enabled by default. To change this and other settings, right-click the job in the

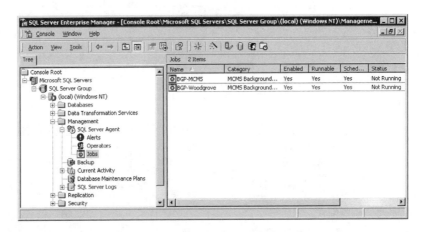

**Figure 16–33** Background purging job

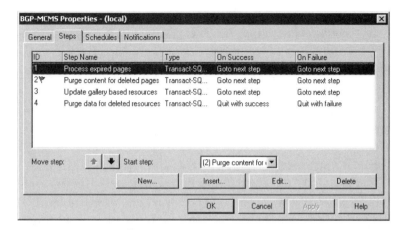

**Figure 16–34** Background purging job default steps

right pane and select Properties, and then go to the appropriate tab, as follows:

- The General tab allows you to the change job's ownership, category, and description. The job is enabled by default; to disable the job, clear the Enable box in the General tab.
- The Steps tab provides the ability to change the sequence of steps, add new steps, or run each step individually if necessary (Figure 16–34).

  To enable the first step—deleting expired pages—select step 1 from the "Start step" list.
- The Schedules tab allows you to modify the default schedule for the job.
- The Notifications tab provides the ability to set up actions to perform on the job's completion.

Background job events are logged in the SQL Server Agent log file *<SQL server installation point>*\MSSQL\LOG\sqlagent.out. You can view the SQL Server Agent error log by right-clicking the SQL Server Agent node and selecting Display Error Log.

**NOTE:** In certain situations, you have to manually start SQL Server Agent. For example, when you stop SQL Server, SQL Server Agent is stopped as well. However, when you restart SQL Server, SQL Server Agent is not restarted automatically. Another example is when SQL

Server is installed on a remote computer. The DCA that is installed locally cannot start SQL Server Agent on a remote machine. In both scenarios, to enable the background purging of the CMS database, you must start SQL Server Agent manually.

# Summary

In this chapter, we looked into administering containers. There are several tools, such as the Site Manager, the Web Author, and Visual Studio .NET, that you can use to perform administrative tasks. Table 16–1 compares the Site Manager with the Web Author and VS.NET, and provides a brief reference to show which tool can be used for which task.

**Table 16–1**  Comparison of Tools for Administrative Tasks

| Object | Task | Site Manager | Web Author | VS.NET |
|---|---|---|---|---|
| Channel | | | | |
| | Create a channel | Yes | No | No |
| | Rename a channel | Yes | Yes | No |
| | Edit channel display name and description | Yes | Yes | No |
| | Edit channel publishing schedule | Yes | Yes | No |
| | Set up publishing flags: | | | |
| | Important channel, Hide when published | Yes | Yes | No |
| | Set up robots flags | Yes | No | No |
| | Edit channel rendering properties | Yes | No | No |
| | Set up default galleries | Yes | No | No |
| | Set up the sorting order for the channel items | Yes | No | No |
| | Assign rights to users | Yes | No | No |

**Table 16–1** Comparison of Tools for Administrative Tasks *(Continued)*

| | | Tools | | |
|---|---|---|---|---|
| Object | Task | Site Manager | Web Author | VS.NET |
| | Set up custom properties | Yes | No | No |
| | Move a channel | Yes | No | No |
| | Copy a channel | Yes | No | No |
| | Delete a channel | Yes | No | No |
| | Restore a channel | Yes | No | No |
| | Kill lock | Yes | No | No |
| Page | | | | |
| | Create a new page | No | Yes | No |
| | Edit a page | No | Yes | No |
| | Move a page | Yes | Yes | No |
| | Copy a page | Yes | Yes | No |
| | Delete a page | Yes | Yes | No |
| | Restore a page | Yes | No | No |
| | Edit page properties | No | Yes | No |
| | Kill lock | Yes | No | No |
| Template gallery | | | | |
| | Create a new template gallery | Yes | No | Yes |
| | Rename a template gallery | Yes | No | Yes |
| | Edit a description property | Yes | No | Yes |
| | Move a template gallery | Yes | No | Yes |
| | Copy a template gallery | Yes | No | Yes |
| | Delete a template gallery | Yes | No | Yes |
| | Restore a template gallery | Yes | No | No |
| | Assign rights to users | Yes | No | No |
| | Kill lock | Yes | No | No |

*continued on page 390*

**Table 16–1**  Comparison of Tools for Administrative Tasks *(Continued)*

| Object | Task | Tools | | |
|---|---|---|---|---|
| | | Site Manager | Web Author | VS.NET |
| Template | | | | |
| | Create a new template | No | No | Yes |
| | Rename a template | No | No | Yes |
| | Edit template properties | No | No | Yes |
| | Check in and check out a template | No | No | Yes |
| | Move a template | Yes | No | Yes |
| | Copy a template | Yes | No | Yes |
| | Delete a template | Yes | No | Yes |
| | Restore a template | Yes | No | No |
| | Run a dependent report | Yes | No | No |
| | Revert to approved | Yes | No | No |
| | Kill lock | Yes | No | No |
| Resource gallery | | | | |
| | Create a new resource gallery | Yes | No | No |
| | Rename a resource gallery | Yes | No | No |
| | Edit a description property | Yes | No | No |
| | Move a resource gallery | Yes | No | No |
| | Copy a resource gallery | Yes | No | No |
| | Delete a resource gallery | Yes | No | No |
| | Restore a resource gallery | Yes | No | No |
| | Assign rights to users | Yes | No | No |
| | Kill lock | Yes | No | No |
| Resource | | | | |
| | Add a resource to a resource gallery | Yes | Yes | No |
| | Replace a resource in a resource gallery | No | Yes | No |

**Table 16–1**  Comparison of Tools for Administrative Tasks *(Continued)*

| | | Tools | | |
| | | Site Manager | Web Author | VS.NET |
| Object | Task | | | |
|---|---|---|---|---|
| | Move a resource | Yes | No | No |
| | Copy a resource | Yes | No | No |
| | Delete a resource | Yes | Yes | No |
| | Restore a resource | Yes | No | No |
| | Kill lock | Yes | No | No |

For tasks that can be performed using different tools, there may be subtle differences in implementation of functionality. These differences have been outlined in the chapter where appropriate.

**NOTE:** Table 16–1 shows the use of VS.NET for administrative tasks; we are not talking here about writing code to modify an object's properties programmatically.

In this chapter, we focused on managing containers such as channels, template galleries, and resource galleries. However, to provide a publishing environment for our site, we need to assign rights groups to these containers. We will concentrate on this task in the next chapter.

# CHAPTER 17

# Setting Up User Rights

Authentication, authorization, and security are paramount issues in our modern world. Content Management Server (CMS) holds the ability to authenticate users and assign them role-based privileges that allow them to perform certain functions, while restricting their ability to perform other functions. User rights are derived from user membership in one or more CMS rights groups; members of each rights group have privileges that are based on predefined CMS roles. In this chapter, we will focus on how to set up role-based user rights in CMS.

## User Roles

In CMS all access is authenticated and mapped to a user role. There are eight user roles in CMS 2002: administrator, channel manager, template designer, resource manager, moderator, editor, author, and subscriber. Each CMS user role has precoded permissions that cannot be changed. It is not possible to create additional user roles. Figure 17–1 shows the eight CMS user roles displayed in the Site Manager.

We have come across the different CMS user roles in previous chapters of the book. For example, when we discussed the publishing workflow in Chapter 6, we looked into three publishing roles: author, editor, and moderator. Now we are going to take a detailed look into all the CMS user roles.

Every CMS user is assigned at least one role. When users browse the site, even anonymous access is enabled via a guest account that has to be mapped to a subscriber role. All CMS content resides in containers: pages in channels, resources in the resource galleries. Depending on the role, or combination of roles, that a user account is mapped to on a container, the user has different rights on this container.

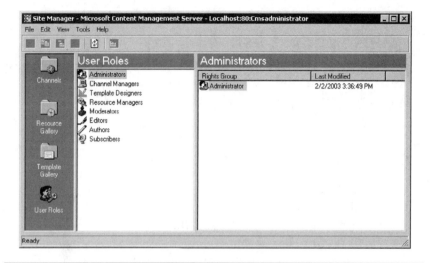

**Figure 17–1**  User roles and Administrator rights group

## Administrator Role

The administrator role is the role of a CMS administrator. Administrators have full administrative and publishing rights to the entire site and can perform any task that any other role can—that is, act as an author, editor, moderator, template designer, resource manager, or channel manager in all channels and galleries.

Administrators can create all containers: channels, template galleries, and resource galleries. Administrators are solely responsible for setting up rights groups for all user roles and assigning members to these groups. Administrators can assign rights groups to all containers, and have subscriber rights to all channels.

## Channel Manager Role

The channel manager role allows CMS administrators to delegate administrative tasks on the parts of the site structure. Channel managers are in effect mini-administrators. They have full administrative and publishing rights to the subset of the site containers they've been assigned rights to: channels, template galleries, and resource galleries. Within the containers that channel managers have rights to, they can:

- Create new containers, such as channels, template galleries, and resource galleries.

- Assign rights groups to containers.
- Act as an author, editor, moderator, template designer, or resource manager.

Channel managers have subscriber rights to all channels they are managing.

## Template Designer Role

Template designers are developers who create templates and template files in VS.NET. If they have rights on a container, within this container they can:

- Create new containers, such as channels, template galleries, and resource galleries.
- Assign rights groups to containers.
- Act as an author, editor, moderator, or resource manager.

Within the template galleries that they have rights to, they can create, edit, and check in templates. They can also edit, check in, debug, and delete templates that they own.

Template designers cannot perform certain tasks on the templates in the template galleries where they have rights; these tasks can only be performed by administrators and channel managers. The tasks are as follows:

- Check in a template that has been checked out by another user.
- Kill lock on templates from within the Site Manager.

Template designer rights on a channel include subscriber rights to this channel.

## Resource Manager Role

Resource managers are responsible for managing resources in the resource galleries. Resources can be added to a page from a local source; however, resource galleries provide a simple way to make common resources available across the site. If resource managers are given rights on a resource gallery, inside this gallery they can view, add, move, replace, and delete resources. Resource managers cannot create any containers, including resource galleries; this is the responsibility of the administrator or the channel manager.

## Author Role

Authors create pages and submit them for approval by editors. They use the Web Author console or Word with the Authoring Connector to author pages. Although they can set the page properties themselves, they are really just suggesting the settings, since editors and moderators can both override these settings.

Authors require access to the following containers:

- Channels. An author creates pages in assigned channels. The channels are accessible from the authoring tools, and when the author creates a new page, the page is saved in the channel. Authors can create, edit, and submit pages to a channel. They can delete pages they own.
- Template galleries. The author needs read access to the appropriate template galleries so that they can select a template for a page they are creating.
- Resource galleries. The author requires read access to resource galleries so that the author is able to add digital assets from these galleries to a page during the authoring process.

Author rights on a channel include subscriber rights to this channel.

## Editor Role

Editors can do everything that authors can, as well as approve page content for publication. Editors can approve or decline pages. They can ask the author to revise the page, or they can do it themselves.

Editors require access to the following containers:

- Channels. An editor needs to able to access pages created by authors and make modifications if required. Editors can create, edit, and submit pages and page content, and approve and decline page content. Editors can edit, submit, approve, decline, and delete pages, regardless of who owns them. Editors cannot approve or decline page publishing properties.
- Template galleries. Since editors are working with pages, they need read access to the appropriate template galleries where the template the current page is based on is located.
- Resource galleries. Editors require read access to resource galleries so that they can add resources to a page.

Editor rights on a channel include subscriber and author rights to this channel.

## Moderator Role

Moderators ensure that page content and page publishing properties are relevant and appropriate for all channels to which they are assigned rights. Page content is approved by the editor; publishing properties, such as the publishing schedule, are approved by a moderator. Moderators can ask for the page publishing schedule to be revised, or can revise it themselves.

Moderators require access to the following containers:

■ Channels. A moderator needs to able to access pages created by authors and approved by editors to be able to approve them for publication. Moderators can create, edit, and submit pages and page content, and approve and decline page publishing properties. Moderators can edit, submit, approve, decline, and delete pages, regardless of who owns them. Moderators cannot approve or decline page content.

■ Template galleries. Since moderators are working with pages, they need read access to the appropriate template galleries where the template the current page is based on is located.

■ Resource galleries. Moderators require read access to resource galleries so that they can add resources to a page.

Moderators have subscriber and author rights on the channel to which they are assigned rights.

## Subscriber Role

Subscribers are those users who just browse the site. They have read-only access to pages published on the site; they do not participate in the publishing process.

In order to be able to view a page, they need to have read access to the channel where the page is located, the template gallery where the template for the page is stored, and the resource gallery where the resources used on the page can be found.

CMS does not provide default anonymous access; in order to view pages published on the site, all users browsing the site must be given subscriber access to the appropriate channels. Even if we allow guest access to the site, we still need to assign a subscriber role to the guest account and give it permissions for the appropriate containers so that users can view the content on our site.

---

**NOTE:** If a user has any rights to a container, they also have subscriber rights on the container, which means they can view items in this container.

---

A user can belong to one or more subscriber groups. On an internal site, for example, the human resources department could only allow a specific group of users to view the company's private content in a secured channel. At the same time, the members of this group have subscriber rights to other parts of the site that are available to all employees. On an external site, all users have subscriber rights to the public parts of your site, while some users can also have subscriber rights to the premier content on the site.

# Rights Groups

In CMS a user cannot be directly mapped to a role. The reason is that roles are tied to containers, and the user can have different roles in different containers. For example, a user can be an author in one channel and a subscriber in another. In order to allow users the ability to perform different roles in different containers, we need to have a unique instance of a role mapped to a container. This is done via *CMS rights groups*. Rights groups allow us to define a unique instance of a role. For example, there is only one author's role, but for different channels we may need to define two distinct author groups.

A CMS rights group must contain one or more user and user group accounts, and usually consists of user groups. In most cases, users and user groups are set up in the Active Directory. However, the accounts can also be NT domain accounts as well as local Windows 2003/2000/NT accounts. Each rights group must have a unique name within each role.

Each rights group belongs to one of the CMS user roles, which determines the rights the members of the group will have in a container. Each role has its own set of rights groups.

A user or user group may belong to many rights groups within the same user role. For example, a user can be an author for two different channels.

A user can have many different roles. For example, the same user can be a subscriber in one channel and a template designer in another. A user's roles can overlap; for example, the user can have both author and editor roles in a channel.

Each role may have one or more rights groups except the administrator role. There is only one rights group within the administrator role. It is called Administrator and is created when CMS is installed (refer back to Figure 17–1). After the installation, this rights group has only one member: the user account set up during the installation to be a CMS administrator account. When you start the Site Manager for the first time, you have to log in with this account. You can then add more members to the Administrator rights group if required. However, to centralize administrative control of your site, it is a good practice to keep the number of members in this group low.

Members of the Administrator rights group have all rights to all containers. Therefore, you don't assign the Administrator rights group to a container. It is always there by default and cannot be removed.

To assign rights on a container to a user, you must perform the following three steps:

1. Create a CMS rights group within a role you'd like the user to have in this container.
2. Add the user account to the CMS rights group.
3. Assign this rights group to the container.

**NOTE:** In CMS, a container is the most granular object on which security can be applied.

Only members of the Administrator rights group within the administrator role can create rights groups and assign members to rights groups. We will now look into this process step-by-step.

**NOTE:** Creating CMS rights groups and assigning members to these groups can only be done by a CMS administrator using the Site Manager. It cannot be done programmatically; there is no API for working with the rights groups.

## Creating a Rights Group

Rights groups are created within a user role. To access user roles, click the User Roles icon in the left pane of the Site Manager window (refer back to Figure 17–1).

Right-click one of the user roles you want to associate the new rights group with; then click New Rights Group. Alternatively, right-click any of the existing groups within the user role and select New Group.

The new rights group is created and displayed in the left pane of the Site Manager window as the last entry in the list. It is called New Rights Group. The icon beside the rights group indicates the role to which the group belongs.

You can create new rights groups for all roles but the administrator. There is only one Administrator rights group that belongs to this role.

To name a new rights group, right-click New Rights Group, select Rename, and then type a name for the new group. The name should be less than 100 characters in length and shouldn't contain non-US-ASCII alphanumeric characters. You can use spaces in the rights group name.

It is a good practice to use self-explanatory names. For example, if the rights group we are creating is for editors who edit content in the Manufacturing channel, we can name it "Manufacturing Editors" (Figure 17–2).

After you have created and named a new rights group, it's a good practice to add a description for this group. The description is optional, but it may help in administering the group in the future if the description

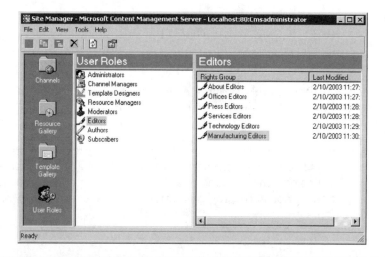

**Figure 17–2**  Adding a new rights group

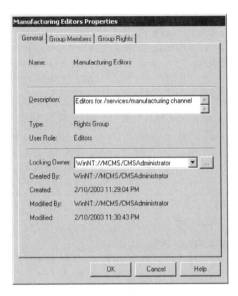

**Figure 17–3** The General tab of Properties

provides useful information about the group—for example, to what containers the group is assigned. To add a description, right-click the rights group, select Properties, and fill in the Description box in the General tab.

As shown in Figure 17–3, the General tab, apart from Description, provides some other useful data about the group, such as when it was created and by whom, when it was last modified and by whom, and who is the locking owner of the group. The ownership lock blocks users from assigning the same rights group concurrently to containers. Provided you have CMS administrative rights, you can change the locking owner.

## Assigning Members to Rights Groups

The next step is to add members to the rights group. A member of a CMS rights groups may be a Windows 2003/2000/NT individual user or a group account. The account may be a domain account or a local account. Managing membership in a CMS rights group is done using the group's Properties > Group Members tab.

To assign the members to the group, on the Group Members tab click the Modify button. The Modify Members dialog box for the rights group opens. In the NT Domains area, select a domain. Don't be confused by the name of this area: All domains, whether Windows 2003, 2000, or NT, are displayed as NT domains; it is just an interface peculiarity.

> **NOTE:** Domains are added to the CMS environment using the Server Configuration Application (SCA). We will look into adding domains in Chapter 18.

After you've selected a domain in the NT Domains section, the domain name, in the format WintNT://<*domain name*>, appears in the Source field. You cannot type in the Source field. If you'd like to add accounts from a domain, but the domain is not shown in the NT Domains section, this domain has to be configured in the SCA first.

> **NOTE:** The CMS system account must have at least read access to Active Directory Users in the Windows domains from which you are adding the users and groups.

To display the domain security groups from the drop-down list, choose "Select from list of all groups," or choose "Select from list of all groups and users" to display both user and group accounts, as shown in Figure 17–4. The accounts are displayed in the Name area. Up to a

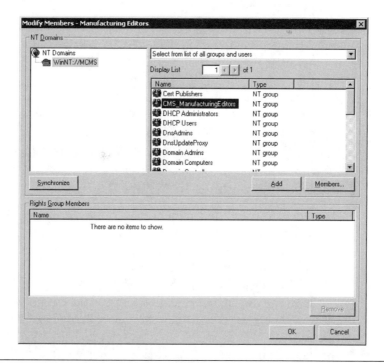

**Figure 17–4**  Modify Members dialog box

thousand accounts may be displayed at one time. A text box called Display List allows you to move between the "pages." The number of pages equals the number of total users/groups in the domain divided by 1,000. For example, if a domain contained 5,010 users/groups, the text box would show that there were six pages overall.

CMS imports user accounts approximately every 10 to 17 minutes. Any valid account is a potential CMS user. If a user or group you want to add doesn't appear in the Name list, click the Synchronize button to force the import and update the list of users and groups in the domain.

To add a Windows security group and all its members to the CMS rights group, select the Windows group account from the Name list and click Add. The group is moved to the Rights Group Members list. Similarly, to add an individual user, select the user account from the list and click Add. Instead of selecting the account and clicking the Add button, to move a user or group account to the Rights Group Members list, you may just double-click the Windows account in the Name list.

If the user or group account is not displayed in the list even after you've synchronized it, make sure that "Manually enter groups and users" is chosen, and then type the Windows user or security group account name from this domain in the Group or User Name field; then click Add. The user or group is moved to the Rights Group Members list.

You can also look in the Windows group membership if you wish and add individual members to the CMS rights group. To choose members of a Windows group, select the group name and click Members. The NT Group Members dialog box appears, as shown in Figure 17–5. To add an

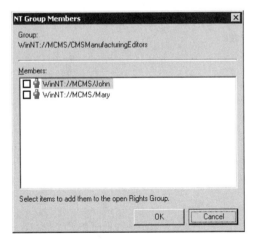

**Figure 17–5** NT Group Members dialog box

account to the rights group, select the check box beside the name of the account; select as many accounts as you need, and click OK.

It is a good practice to assign members to the CMS rights groups on a Windows group basis. Rather than adding Windows user accounts to each CMS rights groups individually, add Windows security group accounts to the CMS rights group. When you add or remove users from the Windows groups, the CMS rights groups will reflect the changes automatically. Organizing the group membership in this way may significantly minimize the administrative overhead of maintaining user rights in CMS.

After you've added all the necessary accounts to the Rights Group Members list, click OK in the Modify Members dialog box. The selected account names appear in the Rights Group Members area on the Group Members tab, as shown in Figure 17–6. You have assigned members to the rights group.

## Removing Members from Rights Groups

To remove an account from a CMS rights group, right-click the group, go to the Properties > Group Members tab, select the account you want to remove, and click Remove.

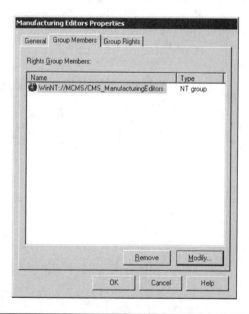

**Figure 17–6** The Group Members tab of Properties

**NOTE:** There is no synchronization between the Active Directory and the CMS database. If a CMS user has been removed from the Windows domain, the user account name still remains in the CMS database. However, the user is no longer able to log on to CMS.

When a user account is deleted from the Active Directory, it still appears in any CMS rights groups the user was a member of. It is necessary to use the Site Manager to manually remove the user from the CMS rights groups to which they were assigned.

This is one of the reasons why it is not advisable to have individual CMS users as members of a rights group. Instead, create a Windows security group, add users to this group, and add the group account to the CMS rights group. For example, John and Mary are going to become editors in the Manufacturing channel. We can now create a Windows security group called CMS_ManufacturingEditors, add John's and Mary's Windows accounts to this group, and then add the CMS_Manufacturing Editors group account to the Manufacturing Editors CMS rights group we have already created (refer back to Figures 17–2, 17–4, and 17–6).

## Assigning a Rights Group to Containers

After a CMS rights group has been created and members have been added to it, the next step is to set up the containers in which the group members will be working. The mapping between a CMS rights group and a container can be done from either the rights group Properties or the container Properties.

To assign a rights group to containers, right-click the rights group and go to the Properties > Group Rights tab. The tab shows the containers hierarchy. Red X marks indicate that the rights group is not assigned to a container; green check marks indicate that the rights group has already been assigned to a container (Figure 17–7). When a rights group is assigned to a container, the members of the group have rights in this container that are defined by the role to which the rights group belongs. For example, you can see from Figure 17–7 that the rights group Manufacturing Editors is assigned to the /botsconsulting/services/manufacturing channel, the resource gallery /BOTS Consulting/general, and the template gallery /BOTS Consulting.

The members of the group can create, edit, and submit pages and page content, and approve and decline page content in the /services/manufacturing channel; they have read access to the resource and template galleries to which they are assigned.

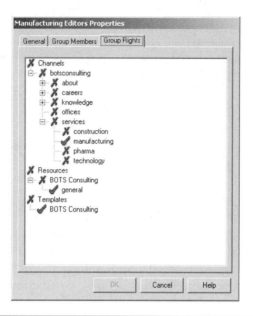

**Figure 17–7** The Group Rights tab of Properties

To assign one container to a rights group, just click once the name of the container you want to assign. The red X beside the container name changes to a green check mark. To assign a container and all its subcontainers, or children, right-click the container and select `Propagate Rights to Children`. Each red X beside the container and all its children changes to a green check mark.

To remove the rights group from the container, click it once, and the green check mark changes to a red X. To remove the rights group from the container and all its subcontainers, right-click the container and select `Propagate Rights to Children`.

Assignment and removal of rights groups to and from containers take effect immediately. Therefore, the Cancel button becomes disabled. To undo your changes, you must reassign rights groups to containers manually.

Containers' hierarchies in the Site Manager provide access to an individual container's configuration. You can see a container description, if it has been set up, when you hover your mouse over its name. You can access the full properties of a container by right-clicking its name and selecting Properties. The Properties > Rights tab on a container shows a list of rights groups already assigned to the container.

You can also assign rights groups directly from a container. To do this, right-click a container name in the Site Manager hierarchy (a channel, a template gallery, or a resource gallery) and choose the Properties > Rights tab. The Current User Rights list shows rights groups that have been assigned to the channel. To add or remove a rights group, click the Modify button; in the Look In box, select a user role and then the name of the rights group within this role, and click Add. The rights group is added to the Selected Rights Groups box. To assign the channel the same rights groups as its parent folder, click Add Parent's Rights, and the rights groups for the parent channel appear in the Selected Rights Groups box.

For example, to assign the authors rights group Manufacturing Authors to the /botsconsulting/services/manufacturing channel, select Authors in the drop-down list, select the Manufacturing Authors rights group you'd like to assign, and then click Add (Figure 17–8).

## Subscriber, Author, Editor, and Moderator Rights

When you assign the subscribers, authors, editors, or moderators rights groups to a channel, don't forget to assign the same rights groups to the

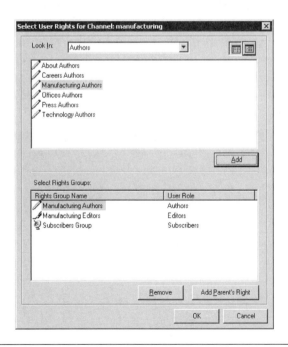

**Figure 17–8** Select User Rights for Channel dialog box

appropriate template galleries and resource galleries. Failure to do that will lead to authors, editors, and moderators being unable to author or edit pages in the channel. Even if you set up the default template and resource galleries for the channel, the rights are not propagated from the channel to the galleries. You need to assign the appropriate rights groups manually.

If a channel only has authors and/or editors rights groups assigned and no moderators, then the pages are published after the page content has been approved by a member of the editors rights group. The publishing details will be approved automatically. When you click OK in the channel Properties > Rights > Selected Rights Groups box, the Site Manager displays the message shown in Figure 17–9, asking you to confirm auto-approval.

When any rights group is assigned to a channel, the members of this group are assigned the subscription rights to the channel. This allows the rights group members to view content published to the channel in their browser.

If your site dynamic navigation has been set up to display the channels structure in the same hierarchical order as the Site Manager, then to view it in a channel, this channel's subscribers should have rights to the channels above it in the channel hierarchy. To this end, you need to make sure that the channel's subscribers have appropriate rights in the hierarchy above this channel. For example, as shown in Figure 17–10, subscribers in the Research channel need the subscription rights in the Knowledge channel if you want them to be able to navigate to it.

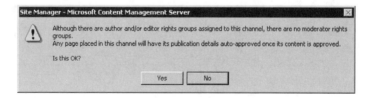

**Figure 17–9** Auto-approval message

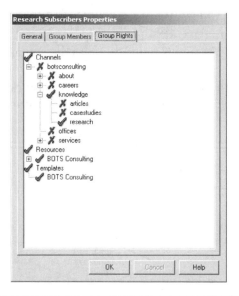

**Figure 17–10** Subscribers rights in channel hierarchy

## Summary

In this chapter, we focused on setting up user rights in the CMS environment. Setting up user rights is an integral step in configuring the publishing environment in CMS. Configuring the publishing environment consists of two stages, as follows:

1. Creating and configuring containers
2. Assigning user rights to these containers

We discussed creating containers in Chapter 9; then, in the previous chapter, we looked into configuring containers. In this chapter, we concentrated on user roles and setting up user rights on containers. In order to set up rights on a container for a user, you need to perform the following three steps:

1. Create a CMS rights group within a role you want to assign to the user on this container.

2. Add the Windows 2003/2000/NT user or security group account to the CMS rights group.
3. Assign this rights group to the container.

In the next chapter, we will continue with site administration and talk about the Server Configuration Application.

# CHAPTER 18

# Using the Server Configuration Application

The Server Configuration Application (SCA) provides a Web-based interface for configuring the content server component in the CMS installation. The SCA is first run during the CMS installation. However, the SCA is independent of the installation and can be run at any time to configure the server. If you are running multiple CMS servers in a clustered environment, then each server must have an SCA.

The SCA can be run locally or remotely. In order to use the SCA, you must be a local administrator on the computer that is running the CMS server.

Two types of parameters can be configured using the SCA.

- Local settings apply to a CMS server running on the same computer as the SCA. A local setting is indicated by an icon of a terminal.
- Global settings apply to all CMS servers in a cluster. A global setting is indicated by a globe icon in the SCA. The global setting is stored in the CMS database and affects all servers in the cluster that point to that database, unless individually overridden with a local setting.

## Launching the SCA

The SCA is an ASP application; its starting page is called SCAConfig Main.asp. The SCA is located in the folder *installation drive*\Program Files \Microsoft Content Management Server\server\NRConfig on a machine where the SCA is installed. On a local machine, you can launch the SCA from the Start menu (Start > Programs > Microsoft Content

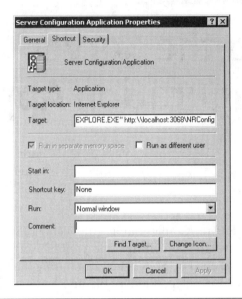

**Figure 18–1** The SCA shortcut properties

Management Server > Server Configuration Application). The icon on the Start menu is just a shortcut that points to the SCA URL http://*<computer name>*:*<port number>*/NRConfig, where *<computer name>*:*<port number>* identify the Web site where the SCA is installed (Figure 18–1). On any machine that has HTTP access to the SCA computer, you can launch it by directly typing the URL. The Web site, and therefore the port number, is selected in the Database Configuration Application (DCA) during CMS installation. By default, the site is the IIS Administration Web Site.

When you launch the SCA, the following checks are performed to determine if CMS exists on a machine.

- At least one of the following registry keys exist: HKEY_LOCAL_MACHINE\SOFTWARE\NCompass\Resolution Content Server\Configuration\0\EntryPoints\*<N>*, where *<N>* is the IIS instance ID of the Web site.

  There is one registry key for every CMS Web entry point (CMS-enabled IIS virtual Web site). For example, the default Web site has an instance ID of 1.
- The Web site with the *<N>* instance ID has an /NR virtual directory. This directory identifies the site as a CMS site.

- Two ISAPI filters are installed in the IIS at the global level:
  - Resolution filter located at *<installation drive>*:\Program Files\Microsoft Content Management Server\Server\bin\ReAuthFilt.dll
  - Resolution HTML Packager located at *<installation drive>*:\Program Files\Microsoft Content Management Server\Server\bin\REHTMLPackager.dll

If any of the checks fail, the SCA will not start.

Since the SCA is a configuration utility, it must be secure and not accessible to anonymous users. During the SCA installation, the /NRConfig virtual directory is created on a selected Web site on a local machine. The IIS Administration Web Site has the most security; therefore, it is the default Web site for SCA installation. The NRConfig virtual directory points to the *<installation drive>*:\Program Files\Microsoft Content Management Server\server\NRConfig local directory where the SCA is located. During the installation, the ACLs are set on this directory to restrict access to local administrators (Figure 18–2).

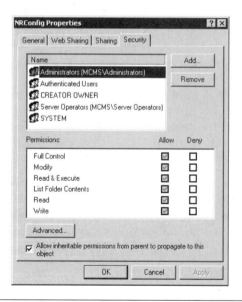

**Figure 18–2** NRConfig directory security

For security reasons, it is not recommended that you install and run the SCA on a Web site if any of the following statements are true.

- The site is a CMS site used for authoring and/or browsing.
- The site uses the default HTTP port 80.
- The site grants access to everyone by default (it should deny access by default and grant access only to explicit IP addresses or domain names).
- The site allows anonymous access.

The best practice to ensure security when the SCA is used remotely is to run it over a Secure Sockets Layer (SSL) connection. You need to use SSL, for example, to protect the user name and password information for a local administrator if it is being passed in clear text over the network. If there is no SSL enabled, when the SCA is first launched it displays a security alert. This alert is displayed only once, on the first run.

---

**NOTE:** Each CMS server must have the SCA installed for configuration purposes. However, once the server has been configured, you can stop the Web site where the SCA has been installed. This will provide an additional security layer for your server.

---

The SCA screen (Figure 18–3) in the top pane displays the current CMS server parameters: the URL of the IIS virtual site that hosts the first CMS site created on the computer where SCA is installed, the CMS version, the name of the CMS database, and the name of the SQL server hosting the database. These are read-only and cannot be changed from the SCA. However, you can change the database name and location using the Database Configuration Application (DCA). Underneath the read-only pane are six tabs that provide access to configuration options: General, Cache, Web, Access, Security, and License. We will now look into the configuration options available in each tab.

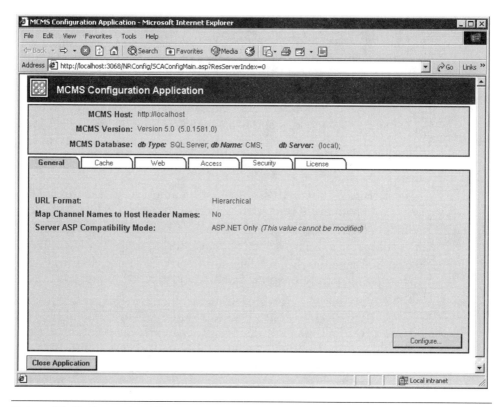

**Figure 18–3**  General settings

# General Settings

The General configuration tab is the SCA default tab (Figure 18–3). It allows configuration of settings that affect how CMS URLs are formed. Basically, this tab sets up how users can browse the CMS Web site.

## URL Format

The URL Format setting allows us to configure how site resources are accessed via a URL in presentation mode. The options are Hierarchical and Unique ID Based.

Hierarchical URLs follow the CMS channel hierarchy; the channel names present the user with a logical way to browse the site. This setting is the recommended option. The URL looks similar to the URLs formed following a virtual directory structure in non-CMS Web sites.

For example, http://www.botsconsulting.com/botsconsulting/about/history points to the /botsconsulting/about/history channel.

When channel names are used in URLs, the special characters in the names are replaced by URL-encoded characters. For example, if you have a channel called About Us, it will appear in a URL as About+Us— that is, http://*<site name>*/About+Us. The space character in the channel name is URL-encoded and becomes a + character. URLs with many URL-encoded special characters can be confusing for users. To prevent this, follow the channel naming conventions outlined in the sidebar in Chapter 9.

Unique ID Based URLs generate numerical URLs to identify pages and channels. These URLs are based on the Globally Unique Identifiers (GUIDs) that are stored in the Content Repository for each CMS object, such as pages and channels. For example, the URL for the /botsconsulting/about/history channel would look similar to http://www.botsconsulting.com/NR/exeres/30895FCA-6899-46FD-94E5-241CB1BC6888.htm.

To change the URL type, click Configure on the General tab (you may need to scroll down in the browser window for this button to be displayed); in the General Configuration window (Figure 18–4), from the URL Format drop-down list, select Hierarchical or Unique ID Based, and click OK. You may need to restart IIS after making this change.

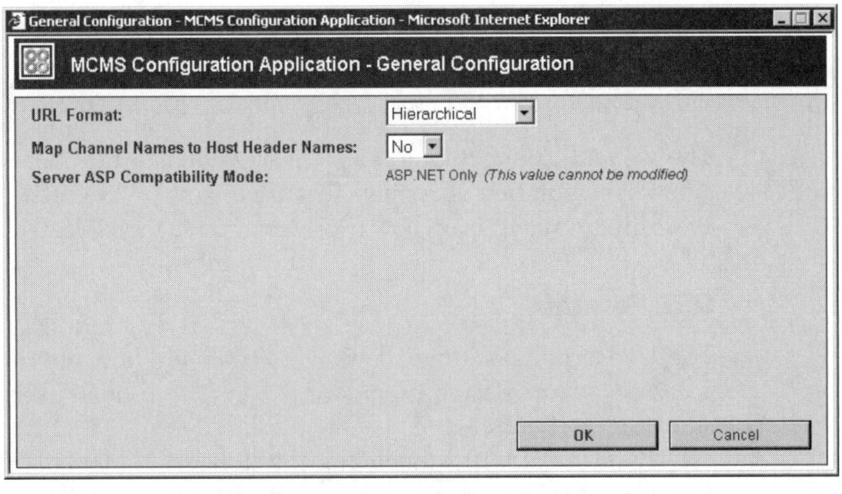

**Figure 18–4** General Configuration window

## Using Host Headers Mapping

The Map Channel Names to Host Header Names setting provides the ability to automatically map top-level channels as the root channels for a URL with a host header name that is identical to the channel name. It is a useful feature that allows us to host several CMS Web sites, with different domain names, on the same CMS server. These sites share the same CMS database.

The cohosting of CMS sites is transparent to users. From the user point of view, they are accessing a separate site, not a shared infrastructure.

Host headers mapping only affects URL generation and parsing in presentation mode. The available settings are Yes or No; the default setting is No. To change the host headers mapping, click Configure on the General tab; in the General Configuration window (Figure 18–4), from the Map Channel Names to Host Header Names drop-down list, select the appropriate option and click OK.

The CMS host headers mapping functionality is implemented as an ISAPI filter that matches the host header of an incoming HTTP request to the top-level channel names. The HTTP host header is the DNS name of a site; a top-level channel must have the same name. If the HTTP host header of the incoming request exactly matches the name of a top-level channel, CMS maps the request to the channel. When this option is enabled, every channel in the root channel becomes a virtual CMS Web site. For example, a top-level channel may be called www.CMSsite1.com (Figure 18–5). When the HTTP request for www.CMSsite1.com comes to the server, the site name in the HTTP host header is mapped to the top-level channel with the same name—for example, www.CMSsite1.com.

---

**NOTE:** Refer to Appendix A for reference information on HTTP host headers.

---

When CMS generates a URL pointing to an item inside the virtual site www.CMSsite1.com, it prefixes the URL with the name of the channel in which it is contained. For example, the URL pointing to the /products channel within the www.CMSsite1.com channel would be http://www.CMSsite1.com/products.

A CMS virtual site name must be a valid DNS name. The DNS name should point to an IP address of the IIS server. Multiple virtual

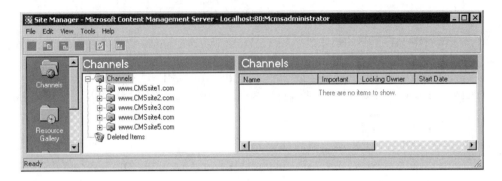

**Figure 18–5**  Channels hierarchy with host headers mapping enabled

CMS site names may point to the same IP address or may use different IP addresses that are assigned to the same IIS server.

It is worth stressing that you don't have to configure HTTP host headers on the IIS server to use the CMS host headers mapping functionality. These options are not hardwired together. In IIS, HTTP host headers are used to provide multihosting. The HTTP host headers identify multiple virtual Web sites that reside on one physical server. In this case, all sites share the same IP address. However, you can also provide IIS multihosting by assigning a unique IP address to each virtual Web site without configuring HTTP host headers. In both cases you can enable CMS host headers mapping.

However, you need to configure the HTTP host headers on the IIS site if a single IP address is used for multiple CMS sites. You don't have to set up separate virtual sites under IIS. Instead, you may use a single IIS site with multiple HTTP host headers configured. If you prefer, you can use multiple IIS sites with a single host header configured for each, or any combination of these methods. Each IIS site must be set up as a CMS Web entry point; it is CMS that does the mapping.

**NOTE:** We will look into CMS Web entry points later in this chapter.

For example, let's consider the hosting of five CMS sites on an IIS server with a single IP address. Each site has its own DNS name, as follows: www.CMSsite1.com, www.CMSsite2.com, www.CMSsite3.com, www.CMSsite4.com, and wwwCMSsite5.com. Figure 18–5 illustrates the top-level channels structure in the Site Manager for a CMS server that is configured for host headers mapping. There are five top-level channels that are the root channels for virtual CMS sites, with the same names as their corresponding sites. Each of the five DNS names may be mapped as a host header name to a separate IIS site (Figure 18–6), or all five DNS names for the virtual sites may be mapped as host header names to a single IIS site using the IIS snap-in (Figure 18–7). In any case, a Web request for the URLs that refer to these sites will be mapped to the appropriate channel.

When you decide whether to use one IIS site or multiple IIS sites with host headers mapping, you need to take into consideration how your CMS sites will run in these different configurations. If you use a single IIS site with multiple host headers, then all CMS virtual sites will run within one Web application. If you use multiple IIS sites, each with a host header enabled, then each CMS virtual site will run as an independent Web application.

However, if you need to apply different settings to multiple CMS sites, then you need to consider setting up multiple IIS virtual sites. For example, you may need to protect one site with SSL, but not the others. In this case, you don't use HTTP host headers to identify the IIS site, but you would need to identify the site with a unique IP address. Another example is having one read-only site on an IP address on the external interface and a read/write site on an internal interface for security reasons. Once again, the sites will be identified by IP addresses; you don't need to configure HTTP host headers on the IIS.

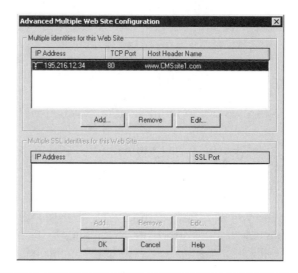

**Figure 18–6** IIS site with HTTP host headers enabled

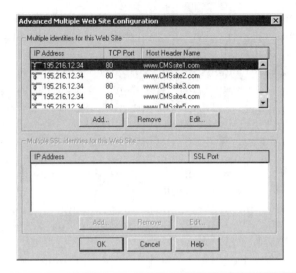

**Figure 18-7** Multiple HTTP host headers configured on a single IIS Web site

When CMS host headers mapping is enabled, you must make sure that every channel directly under the root channel is a virtual Web site. You cannot have a mixture of virtual Web site and normal channels on the same CMS server using the same database. The setting is applicable to all sites sharing the CMS database.

CMS host headers mapping can be used for a single CMS site. When you create your new CMS site as a Web application in the root of a virtual IIS site, you expect to be able to access the default page of the top-level channel by the root URL that contains only the DNS name of the IIS site, such as http://<*CMS site*>. However, for this to happen, you need to enable CMS host headers mapping on your site. Refer to Chapter 8 for step-by-step configuration instructions for accessing your site by the root URL.

Another common requirement is to map multiple DNS names to a single site. For example, you may want the incoming requests for both www.CMSsite.com and CMSsite.com to come to the same CMS site, www.CMSsite.com. In this case, the HTTP host headers in the incoming request will be different depending on the DNS name used. However, it is possible to map different DNS names to a single top-level channel so that different users can reference the same channel, www.CMSsite.com, by using different site names. This functionality can be achieved in several ways—for example:

- Create a custom 404 error page that redirects the incoming request for CMSsite.com to www.CMSsite.com.
- Write an ISAPI filter that modifies the HTTP host header of the incoming request from CMSsite.com to www.CMSsite.com before the CMS ISAPI filter receives the request.

### Compatibility Mode

The last setting shown on the General tab is the Server ASP Compatibility Mode. The available values are Mixed and ASP.NET Only. Mixed mode means that the CMS server supports both ASP and ASP.NET sites; CMS server in ASP.NET Only mode supports only ASP.NET sites. The server compatibility mode is selected during the CMS installation and cannot be changed after the installation.

## Configuring Cache

Content Management Server uses caching to increase the speed of page processing and thus to improve the performance of the Web site. Three types of caching can be used with CMS: disk cache, in-memory object cache, and ASP.NET output cache. Disk cache and in-memory object cache are configured using the SCA Cache tab (Figure 18–8).

**NOTE:** ASP.NET output caching is configured directly in the ASP.NET-based page templates; it cannot be configured in the SCA.

### Disk Cache

The disk cache is a file-based cache for page resources. The location of the cache is configured during the installation of CMS. The default location is <*installation drive*>\Program Files\Microsoft Content Management Server\Server. After the installation, the cache location can be

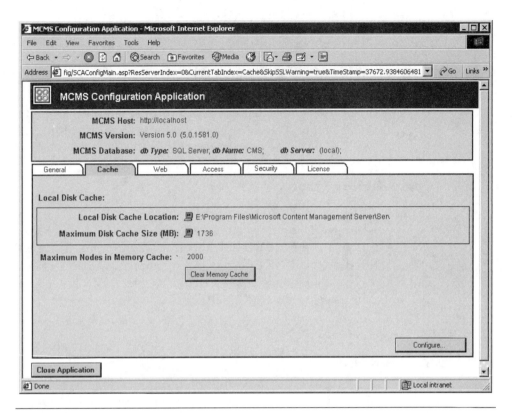

**Figure 18–8** Cache settings

changed using the SCA. Two directories are created under the specified cache location:

- The *<cache location>*\rdonlyres directory provides disk cache for read-only content—for example, images.
- The *<cache location>*\exeres directory provides disk cache for dynamically generated content—for example, pages in ASP-based sites.

These two directories are added to the CMS Web site as the virtual IIS directories under the /NR virtual directory: /NR/rdonlyres and /NR/exeres, respectively. When you change the physical cache location, these virtual directories are reconfigured automatically to point to the newly created directories for the dynamic and the read-only cache.

The cache directories' locations are stored in the registry. The registry key HKEY_LOCAL_MACHINE\SOFTWARE\NCompass\

Resolution Content Server\Configuration\0\Local\Cache contains the values PhysicalExecPrefix and PhysicalReadPrefix, which point to the physical disk location of the dynamic cache and the read-only cache, respectively.

The /NR/exeres directory is used for dynamic caching only in ASP-based sites. In ASP.NET-based sites, dynamically generated pages and user controls are cached in the ASP.NET output cache. However, the ID-based page and channel URLs in both ASP and ASP.NET sites look as if the resulting pages were served from /NR/exeres—for example, http://www.botsconsulting.com/NR/exeres/30895FCA-6899-46FD-94E5-241CB1BC6888.htm. In ASP.NET sites, this is just a convention for how the ID-based URLs are formed; the pages are not cached in the disk-based dynamic cache.

To set up the cache location, click Configure on the Cache tab; in the Cache Configuration window (Figure 18–9), click Browse; in the Disk Cache Location Browser (Figure 18–10), navigate to a folder you want to become the cache location (the currently selected folder will be highlighted in red), and then OK to confirm in the Cache Configuration window.

It is a good practice to put the CMS cache and the IIS log files on different drives, to prevent the log files from accumulating and causing problems with the CMS caching.

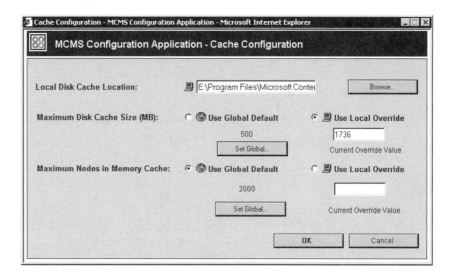

**Figure 18–9** Cache Configuration window

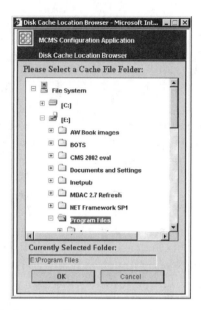

**Figure 18–10** Disk Cache Location Browser

The minimum cache size is 50MB. The maximum cache size is the currently available free space on the cache location drive. The default is 50% of the maximum, up to 2GB. To set up the maximum cache size, in the Cache Configuration window (Figure 18–9), click the top Set Global button to specify the global maximum cache value for the cluster (Figure 18–11), or type the value for the local maximum cache in the bottom Current Override Value box.

## Node Cache

Node cache settings allow us to configure the in-memory object cache. When the CMS server accesses objects stored in the Content Repository,

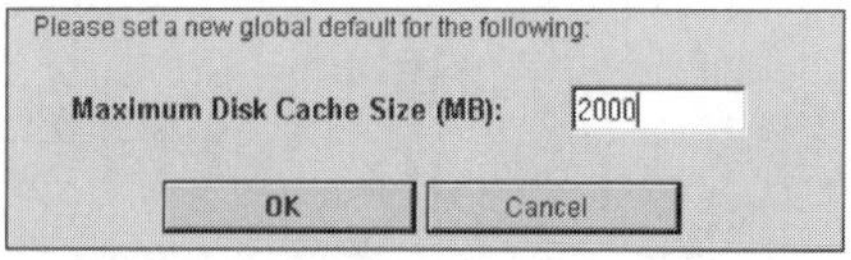

**Figure 18–11** Global Maximum Disk Cache Size

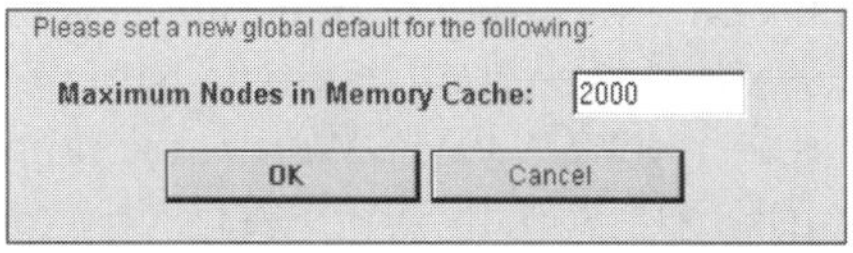

**Figure 18–12**  Global Maximum Nodes in Memory Cache

these objects are referred to as *nodes*. Once the database has been queried, the server caches the resulting objects as nodes in memory to avoid additional database access. Using the SCA, we can:

- Set up the maximum number of nodes to be cached.
- Clear the memory cache.

To set up the maximum number of nodes in memory cache, in the Cache Configuration window (Figure 18–9), click the bottom Set Global button to specify the global maximum number of nodes in memory cache for the cluster (Figure 18–12), or type the value for the local maximum number of nodes in memory cache in the bottom Current Override Value box.

The size of the node cache should be sufficient to store frequently accessed objects but not so large that it has to be stored in virtual memory.

**NOTE:**  You can use the Task Manager to monitor physical memory usage.

Clearing the in-memory node cache provides the ability to force synchronization with the database. If the server appears to be suffering from synchronization problems, click the Clear Memory Cache button on the SCA Cache tab (Figure 18–8). You may notice a minor decline in server performance during the memory clearing operation.

## Setting Up Web Entry Points

Within IIS we usually have multiple virtual Web sites; these sites may be uniquely identified using IP addresses and port numbers as well as HTTP host headers.

When CMS is installed, only one IIS virtual site is configured as the CMS Web site. Since the IIS virtual site points to a CMS server, the IIS sites are referred to as CMS Web entry points. Since the CMS ISAPI filters are installed globally on the IIS site, any of the IIS virtual sites can be an entry point for CMS.

---

**NOTE:** CMS Web sites are entry points into Content Management Server; they are not multiple instances of Content Management Server running on the same machine.

---

The SCA Web tab (Figure 18–13) provides the ability to configure the IIS virtual sites as CMS entry points.

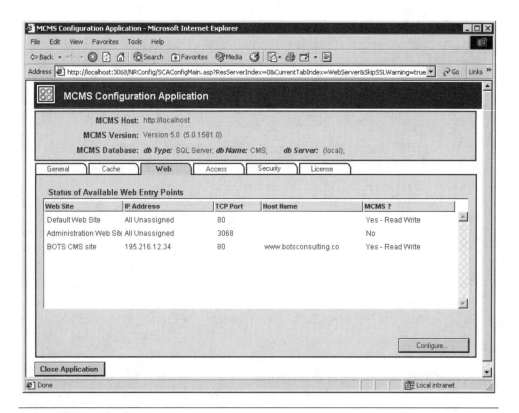

**Figure 18–13** Web entry points

For each of the IIS virtual sites, we can add or remove the CMS entry point. There are three configuration options available in the SCA.

■ Yes—Read Write: The IIS virtual site is configured as a CMS entry point; the CMS site is accessible in both presentation mode and authoring mode.
■ Yes—Read Only: The IIS virtual site is configured as a CMS entry point; the CMS site is only available in presentation mode (which is read-only); it is not accessible in authoring mode. The Switch to Edit Site link is not displayed, because the Web Author client is disabled. The Site Manager session will not be allowed to run either, even for viewing containers.
■ No: The IIS virtual site is not configured as a CMS entry point.

Combining read-only sites with one read/write entry point is very useful for deployment on a Web farm. We will look into it in Chapter 20.

To configure a CMS Web entry point for an IIS virtual site, in the SCA Web tab, click Configure; in the Web Server Configuration window (Figure 18–14), select the appropriate option for the IIS virtual site from the drop-down list in the MCMS? column. For each IIS virtual site running on a machine where the SCA is installed, the Web Server Configuration window lists the site name, IP address, TCP port number, HTTP host header (under the Host Name column), and the CMS entry point setting (under the MCMS? column).

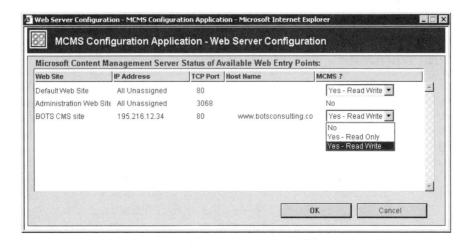

**Figure 18–14** Web Server Configuration window

Once the CMS entry point is added in the SCA, two things are configured.

- The following registry key is created: HKEY_LOCAL_ MACHINE\SOFTWARE\NCompass\Resolution Content Server\ Configuration\0\EntryPoints\<*N*>, where N is the IIS virtual site ID.
- The /NR and /MCMS virtual directories are added to the IIS site.

For the configuration changes to take effect, the IIS site has to be stopped and restarted. When you change the entry point setting, you will receive a warning to this effect, shown in Figure 18–15. The actual configuration takes place when you click OK in the Web Server Configuration window.

---

**NOTE:**  You cannot change the entry point setting for the IIS virtual Web site that hosts the SCA.

---

To remove an entry point from an IIS site, select No from the dropdown list in the MCMS? column for this site. Both the /NR and /MCMS virtual directories will be removed from the site.

---

**NOTE:**  If only one IIS virtual site is configured as a CMS entry point, this entry point cannot be removed.

---

# Adding Domains

In CMS all access is authenticated against Windows user accounts. The SCA Access tab displays a list of domains that will be used to authenticate CMS users (Figure 18–16). Administrators can add domains to this

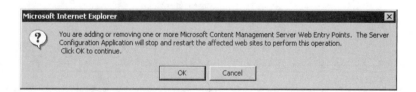

**Figure 18–15**  Web entry point warning

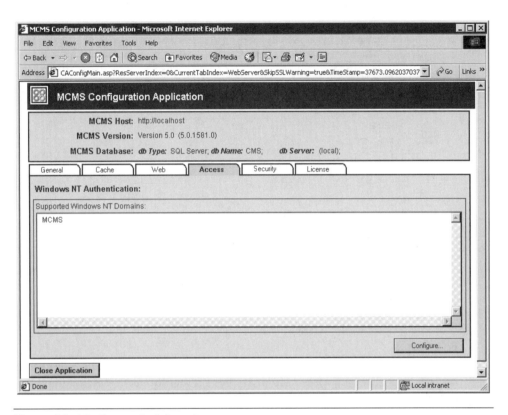

**Figure 18–16** Supported domains

list. When you log in to the Site Manager and when you use the Web Author manual login, only these domains are available. In the Site Manager, only these domains will be listed for selecting accounts to be added as members of the CMS rights groups. By adding domains in the SCA, you make them visible in the CMS environment. You can then increase the number of users from these domains that take part in the publishing workflow.

The SCA Access tab lists Windows 2003, Windows 2000, and Windows NT domains used for authentication under the same heading, Windows NT Authentication, in the Supported Windows NT Domains list (Figure 18–16). The list displays the NetBIOS domain names.

To modify the list of supported domains, in the SCA Access tab click Configure; in the Access window either manually enter the domain name and click the Add button (Figure 18–17), or click the Browse button and select the domain you'd like to add from the list of visible domains, and click OK.

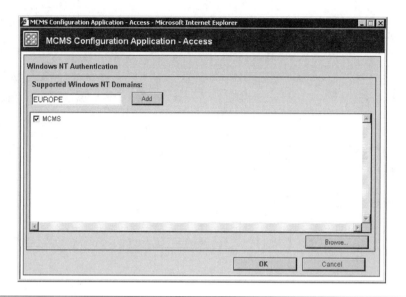

**Figure 18–17**   Access window

The CMS system account is used to browse domains; in order to do so, it must have appropriate privileges on the domains. We will look into the CMS system account in the next section.

# Configuring Security Settings

Security settings such as the CMS system account, CMS guest access, and cookie properties are configured in the SCA Security tab (Figure 18–18).

## CMS System Account

The CMS system account is the Windows account under which Content Management Server is run. This account is set up during the installation. It can be either a domain account or a local account. After the installation, the CMS system account can be modified using the SCA.

It is recommended that you create a dedicated Windows user account to be used as the CMS system account. The account should not be configured as a privileged Windows user, since it only requires limited access. If the CMS system account password is changed, CMS will

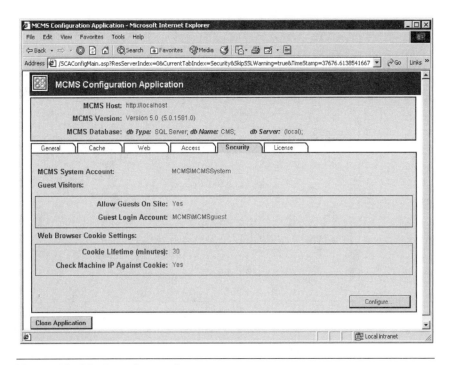

**Figure 18–18** Security settings

not be able to write files to the cache folder and access the CMS database. Therefore, you need to set the password on the account to never expire. It is not recommended that you run CMS under any of the existing user accounts, because users change their passwords from time to time.

However, if the CMS system account credentials have been reset, you can change the system account information when you launch the SCA. Since the SCA is unable to launch, it will give an error message suggesting that you change the system account password (Figure 18–19). Click the Configure button to specify the correct password (Figure 18–20).

CMS uses the system account to connect to the Active Directory (AD) and to access protected resources. For Active Directory access, the system account needs to have sufficient permissions to enumerate and browse any domains, organizational units (OUs), containers, groups, and users that are from CMS-supported domains. It must have at least read permissions on these AD objects. For example, in order to be able to select a user or group from a listed domain to add to a CMS rights group, the CMS system account would need at least read rights in that domain.

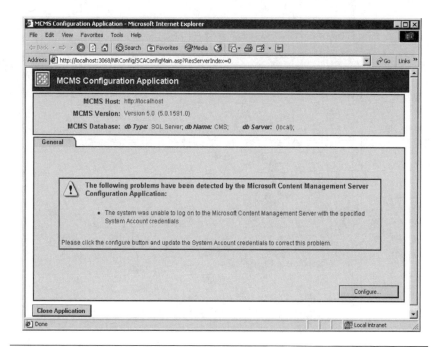

**Figure 18–19** Message to change system account password

As far as accessing resources is concerned, the CMS system account uses an impersonation process to carry out the tasks on behalf of the authenticated user as an agent. The CMS system account must have a "log on locally" right on the computer where CMS is installed. We will look into CMS authentication and authorization in Chapter 19.

If SQL Integrated Security is used, then the CMS system account must have read and write access to the CMS database hosted by SQL. The CMS system account must have the following database roles assigned to it

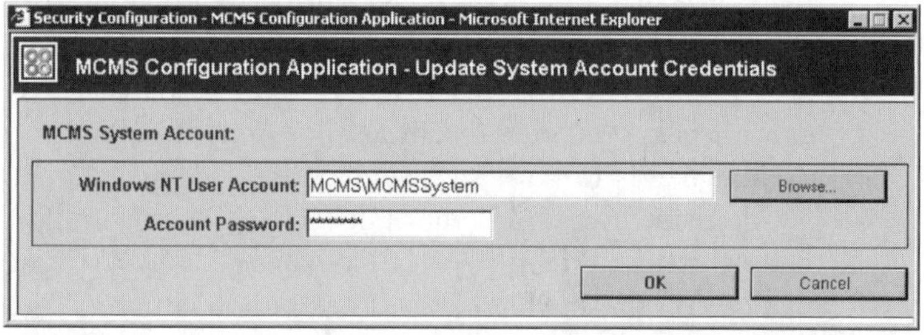

**Figure 18–20** Update System Account Credentials dialog box

on the CMS database: db_datareader and db_datawriter. Using an import function in site deployment also requires the db_ddladmin role.

The setting for the CMS system account is stored in the CMS database. To modify the CMS system account, in the SCA Security tab click Configure; in the Security Configuration window (Figure 18–21), in the MCMS System Account section, either manually enter the account name in the form *<domain>\<user name>*, or click the Browse button to select the domain and the account. If you are using a local account, enter the account name in the form *<local computer>\<user name>*. If you decide to browse to the account, you will be presented with a warning message that the CMS NT browser can take a while to present you with the list of users (Figure 18–22); just click OK; then select a domain from the Windows NT Domain list and an account from the Windows NT Users list (Figure 18–23).

The CMS system account must have a password. A blank password is not allowed. If you leave the password blank, the error message shown in Figure 18–24 will be displayed. After you have selected the account, type in the corresponding password and click OK. If the account credentials cannot be verified against the AD, the warning shown in Figure 18–25 will be displayed.

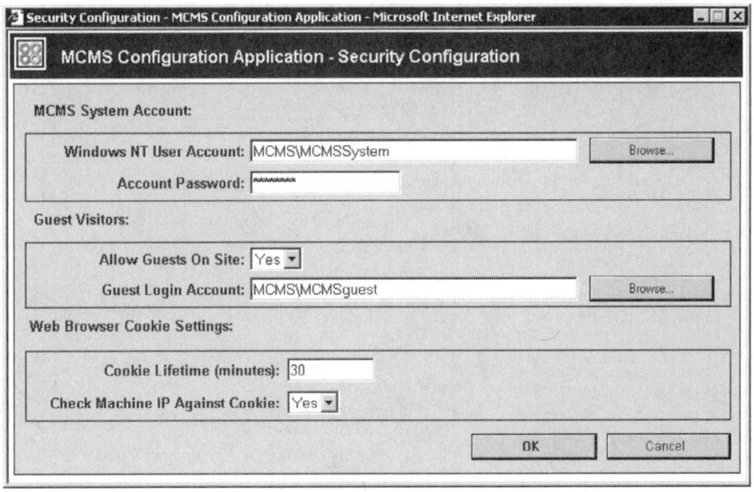

**Figure 18–21** Security Configuration window

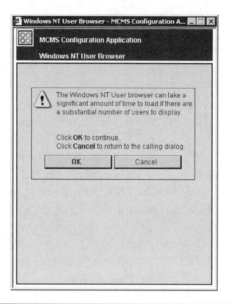

**Figure 18–22**   NT Browser warning

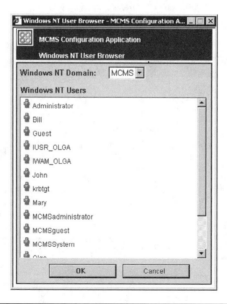

**Figure 18–23**   Windows NT User Browser

**Figure 18–24**  Blank password message

## Guest Access

Guest access enables unauthenticated users to access the CMS site. Since all CMS access must be authenticated, a guest account is used to map anonymous users to a specified account. It can be either a domain account or a local account. In order for anonymous users to be able to view the CMS Web site, the guest account must be added to a subscribers rights group in the Site Manager, and then this rights group must be assigned to the channels and galleries that guest users are allowed to view.

---

**NOTE:** If the guest account is added to any other rights group but the subscribers group, the guest account is still only granted subscriber rights. If the guest account is enabled, guest user rights are added to all other user rights. For example, on a site with guest access enabled, a channel manager has full rights on the channels they are managing and guest rights on the rest of the site.

---

The SCA provides the ability to configure guest access. Guest access is enabled during the CMS installation. After the installation, it can be changed using the SCA. To change whether guest access is allowed, in the SCA Security tab, click Configure; in the Security Configuration window (Figure 18–21), in the Guest Visitors section, in the Allow Guests On Site drop-down list, choose Yes or No; then click OK.

**Figure 18–25**  System account credentials warning

The setting for the CMS guest account is stored in the CMS database. To modify the CMS guest account, in the SCA Security tab, click Configure; in the Security Configuration window (Figure 18–21), in the Guest Visitors section, either manually enter the account name in the form *<domain>\<user name>* or click the Browse button to select the domain and then the account. If you are using a local account, enter the account name in the form *<local computer>\<user name>*. No password is required for the guest account. Click OK to confirm the configuration change.

## Cookie Settings

When a user is authenticated by CMS, the user is assigned a CMS authentication cookie. A user may be an explicitly authenticated user or a guest user. Depending on the CMS authentication configuration, the CMS authentication cookie is either a persistent cookie that is stored on the hard disk on the user's machine, or an in-memory cookie that is maintained in the browser on the client machine and is lost when the browser is closed. This cookie is attached to subsequent requests from the user's machine to the CMS server, which validates the request.

---

**NOTE:** We will look into CMS authentication configuration in different scenarios in detail in Chapters 19 and 20.

---

The Security tab (Figure 18–18) allows us to specify two cookie settings:

- Cookie Lifetime: Cookie lifetime is the amount of time, in minutes, that a cookie is valid. The cookie is valid for a certain amount of time, after which it expires. After the cookie has expired, users are asked to authenticate themselves again. The default is 30 minutes.

  To modify the setting, in the SCA Security tab click Configure; in the Security Configuration window (Figure 18–21), in the Web Browser Cookie Settings section, type the new amount of time in minutes for which you'd like the cookies to be valid.
- Check Machine IP Against Cookie: A CMS cookie contains the IP address of the machine where the first request from an authenticated user came from. If this property is set to Yes, the originating IP address of every subsequent request is validated against the IP address in the cookie, to make sure that subsequent requests

come from the same user's machine as the original authentication request. Although this setting is certainly not bulletproof, it provides an additional security layer.

However, in certain scenarios, if this setting is enabled, your site may appear to be not working properly for certain users. This happens when each HTTP request from the same user may have a different IP address. If this is the case, disable the setting.

To modify the setting, in the SCA Security tab, click Configure; in the Security Configuration window (Figure 18–21), in the Web Browser Cookie Settings section, select Yes or No from the drop-down list for the Check Machine IP Against Cookie setting; click OK.

## Viewing the CMS License

The SCA License tab (Figure 18–26) provides read-only information about the server license. The tab displays the following information:

- User name
- Company name
- Product ID
- License type
- Expiry date (for the evaluation version only)

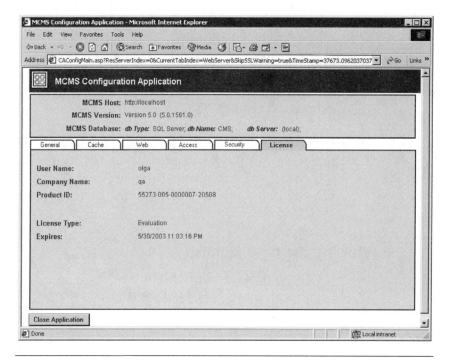

**Figure 18–26** License tab

# Summary

In this chapter, we looked into the CMS server configuration options available via the Server Configuration Application. The available settings include URL formation and parsing, CMS caching, Web entry points, supported domains, security settings (such as system and guest accounts, and cookie properties), and read-only license information.

In the next chapter, we will focus on user authentication and authorization in the CMS environment.

# CHAPTER 19

# Managing User Access

In previous chapters, we created and developed a CMS site, set up the publishing environment for the site, and discussed the server configuration options. Also, in Chapter 11 we had a detailed discussion about CMS page processing. We are now well equipped to look into user authentication and authorization in the CMS environment.

## CMS Authentication and Authorization Process

As we have already seen, CMS processing involves several layers, as follows:

- Browser
- IIS and ISAPI filters
- Worker process (ASP.NET worker process aspnet_wp.exe in IIS 5/ Windows 2000, or Web worker process w3wp.exe in IIS 6/Windows 2003)
- CMS Web application and Publishing API objects
- CMS content server and the Content Repository database

A diagram showing the logical architecture of CMS page processing is shown in Figure 19–1.

---

**NOTE:** For a detailed discussion of CMS page processing in different modes, refer to Chapter 11.

---

As a CMS request passes through multiple layers on the server side, it is authenticated and authorized. Authentication and authorization of a CMS request consists of multiple steps and involves several technologies; it makes use of IIS and ASP.NET security mechanisms. The logical

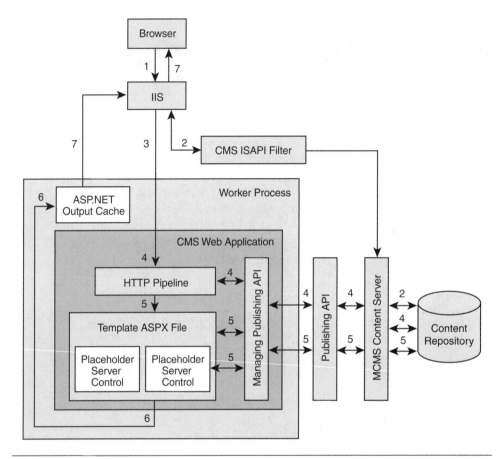

**Figure 19–1** Logical architecture of CMS page processing

sequence of steps involved in CMS authentication and authorization is shown in Figure 19–2.

A browser has a role to play as well. Within the CMS Web application, the authentication state information is stored in a CMS authentication cookie; if cookies are disabled or not supported in the browser, the CMS application may not function properly.

We will look into each layer, starting with reviewing IIS security because the CMS application may rely on IIS for initial authentication of the user. We will then concentrate on the ASP.NET settings for authentication, impersonation, and authorization, and how their use affects the CMS Web application. Then, we will focus on CMS user authentication and authorization, and discuss the configuration required for Windows authentication and forms-based authentication in the CMS Web application.

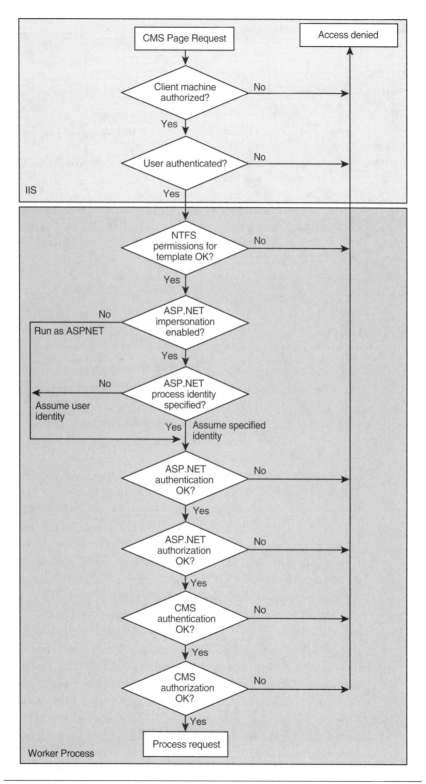

**Figure 19–2** IIS and ASP.NET security mechanisms used in CMS authentication and authorization

**Authentication and Authorization**

Authentication is the process of discovering and verifying the identity of a user—that the user actually is who they claim to be. An authenticated user is typically assigned a token that contains the user's current identity. Authentication only indicates that the user's identity has been verified and does not provide any resource access.

Authorization is the process of determining a user's ability to access specific resources; an authorized user has permissions to a resource. When a user requests access to this resource, the identity of the user is checked against a list of allowed users. Authorization cannot take place without the identity of the user and must follow authentication.

# IIS Security

Any Web server must be secured against unauthorized access; authentication is a requirement of any Web application. The IIS security mechanisms interact with ASP.NET security; Figure 19–1 shows how the CMS page request is typically processed through the IIS security checks and passed on to the worker process that provides the ASP.NET runtime environment.

Security in IIS is set up using the Directory Security tab (in IIS Manager, right-click the Web site and select the Properties > Directory Security tab), as shown in Figure 19–3. Before authenticating a user, IIS performs authorization checks on the client machine's domain name or IP address; these can be configured using the IP Address and Domain Name Restrictions dialog, shown in Figure 19–4 (the dialog is displayed when you click the Edit button in the IP address and domain name restrictions area in the Directory Security tab).

After the client machine has been authorized, IIS attempts to authenticate the user. Every request is authenticated; every request operates in the security context of a user account. There are a number of configurable mechanisms for authenticating users in IIS. When IIS authenticates a user, it creates a worker thread using the user's credentials and then uses that thread to perform the requests. In this way, IIS relies on Windows to provide authorization and enforce security. IIS is a Windows service and runs in the context of the local system account. IIS uses impersonation to control security: When a user makes a request to the server, access to resources is performed as the user and not the trusted

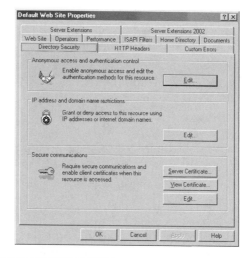

**Figure 19–3**  IIS Directory Security tab

local system account; while the actual InetInfo process runs as System, the worker thread runs in the context of the user.

## Impersonation

Impersonation is the ability of a thread to execute in a security context that is different from the context of the process that owns the thread; it is a term for the adoption of a different security identity. Impersonation is especially useful within server applications to ensure that that user making the request has sufficient permissions to complete the processing. The application impersonates that user and attempts to perform the action; Windows security will either allow or deny the access to a requested resource.

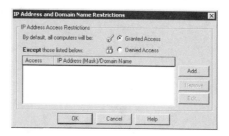

**Figure 19–4**  IIS IP Address and Domain Name Restrictions dialog

IIS 5 and IIS 6 support several methods of authentication:

- Anonymous access
- Basic authentication
- Digest authentication
- Integrated Windows authentication
- Certificate authentication

The Authentication Methods dialog, shown in Figure 19–5, provides the ability to configure the first four methods in the list (the dialog is displayed when you click the Edit button in the authentication control area in the Directory Security tab).

**NOTE:** IIS 6 provides two additional authentication methods: Advanced digest authentication, and Universal Naming Convention (UNC) authentication. To enable these methods, you need to configure the appropriate metabase properties: UseDigestSSP, and UNCUserName and UNCPassword, respectively. For details, refer to the IIS 6 product documentation.

## Anonymous Access

Anonymous access is the default method of authentication for IIS. It is used to provide access to the resource for any user and does not require a user to supply a user name or password. In order to process a request, IIS must use an identity for authorization; by default, IIS

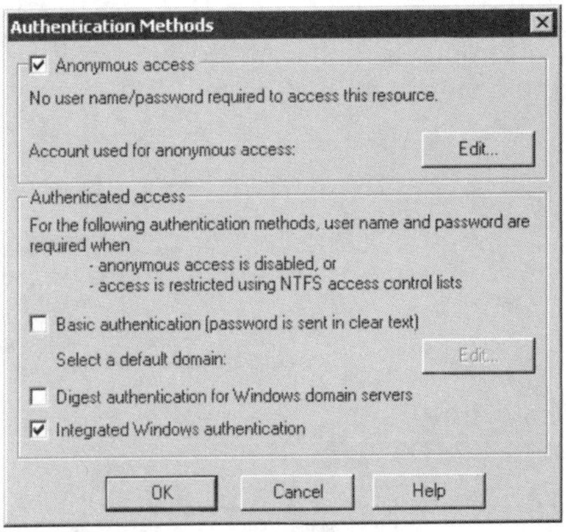

**Figure 19–5** IIS Authentication Methods dialog

impersonates a local account, IUSR_<*machinename*>, to process anonymous requests. You can manually change this account by clicking the Edit button in the anonymous access area of the Authentication Methods dialog (Figure 19–4) and supplying the credentials for a new account.

## Basic Authentication

Basic authentication is part of the HTTP specification. Being a standard mechanism means that it has the widest support among Web browsers and Web servers. With Basic authentication, the browser displays a login dialog to allow a user to enter a user name and password, which are then passed to the Web server via the HTTP headers. The information that the user enters is base-64 encoded before it is sent over the network. This encoding scheme can be easily decoded; therefore, this method of authentication should never be considered secure unless protected by an appropriate encryption such as Secure Sockets Layer (SSL). On the server, the user credentials are authenticated against the Windows security accounts on one of the domains or servers on your network, the user is logged on locally on the Web server, and then IIS impersonates the request to access resources.

Basic authentication works with nearly all browsers and is not affected by proxies or gateways.

## Digest Authentication

Digest authentication is a challenge-response mechanism that sends a password digest, or hash, over the network. The password never crosses the network. The browser encrypts the digest using a password entered by a user and passes it to the server; the server compares the encrypted digest with the one generated from the stored password; if they are the same, then the user is authenticated. Digest authentication is more secure than Basic, but the use of SSL is still recommended.

Digest authentication only works with IE5 and later; it is unaffected by proxies or gateways.

IIS 6 introduced a stronger version of digest authentication called Advanced digest authentication. The difference between the versions is that with Advanced digest authentication the user credentials are stored on the domain controller as a hash, and therefore they cannot be read by anybody with access to the domain controller, even the domain administrator. However, the authentication algorithm used between IIS and the client remains the same.

## Integrated Windows Authentication

Integrated Windows authentication is a challenge-response mechanism that uses either Kerberos v5 or NTLM (NT LAN Manager) authentication. A negotiation process between a client and a server is used to determine which one will be used. If the server is in a nondomain environment, then NTLM authentication will be used; if the server is in an Active Directory domain where a Key Distribution Center (KDC) is available, then Kerberos may be used as an authentication mechanism. The browser will attempt to automatically use the credentials of the currently logged-on user to connect to the Web server; usually, no logon dialog is presented to the user. Both Kerberos and NTLM use strong hashing algorithms, and therefore the Integrated Windows authentication mechanism provides the strongest form of security we've discussed so far.

Integrated Windows authentication requires that clients run IE5 or later in the Windows environment. This mechanism does not work over proxy servers or firewalls; therefore, it performs best in an intranet environment.

## Certificate Authentication

The Certificate authentication mechanism provides the ability to authenticate the user if a recognized certificate is present in the HTTP request. Using the Secure Communications dialog, shown in Figure 19–6, you can configure IIS to require or accept client certificates. By default, they are ignored.

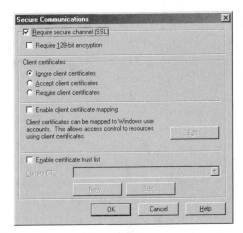

**Figure 19–6** IIS Secure Communications dialog

To enable Certificate authentication, you have to install the server certificate and enable SSL as well as establish the certificate trust list (CTL) that will list the certification authorities (CAs) whose certificates your site will trust.

---

**NOTE:** To use client certificates, user browsers need to have certificates installed and be configured to present certificates as part of the request.

---

Each client certificate will be checked against the CTL as a first step for authentication. For users with accepted certificates, you can then require that they use Basic, Digest, or Integrated Windows authentication, or you can map the client certificates into Windows user accounts. You can map one certificate or multiple certificates to one Windows account.

If you choose to require certificates, then users without certificates will be denied access. For users with certificates, the certificates will be validated against the CTL. If the certificates are valid, either the users are asked to identify themselves using Basic, Digest, or Windows Integrated authentication, or their certificates are mapped to Windows accounts.

If you choose to accept certificates, users with certificates will be authenticated as just described; users without certificates will be required to authenticate using Basic, Digest, or Windows Integrated authentication.

Certificate authentication is the most secure authentication mechanism; it is particularly well suited for business-to-business (B2B) communication over the Internet.

# ASP.NET Security

After IIS has authenticated the user, it passes the request and the user identity to the appropriate worker process. The worker process uses this identity to check the NTFS permissions on the ASPX template files. If the ACLs on template files do not grant at least read access to the user, access is denied.

We will now examine under what identity the request may be processed.

---

**NOTE:** To configure the security settings in the ASP.NET environment, machine.config is used for machine-wide settings, and web.config is used for application-specific settings

---

## ASP.NET Impersonation

By default, ASP.NET runs under a special account identity. This account has a limited number of privileges. In IIS 5, this account is called ASPNET. By default, the worker process will access all resources using this account identity regardless of what identity has been passed by IIS, unlike classic ASP, which uses the identity passed by IIS.

**NOTE:** The default permissions for the ASPNET account are explained in detail in Knowledge Base article 317012.

In certain scenarios, the default account permissions are not sufficient, and we need to configure the worker process to use a different identity for processing requests. This is called ASP.NET impersonation, and the new identity can be set up in several ways:

- On a machine-wide basis for all Web applications (in IIS 5 and in IIS 6 running in IIS 5 isolation mode)
- For an application pool (in IIS 6 running in worker process isolation mode)
- For a particular Web application
- Using the credentials of a user who has made a request

To configure ASP.NET impersonation on a machine-wide basis for IIS 5, you need to edit the <processModel> section of the machine. config file. This section contains user name and password entries for the account credentials used by ASP.NET—for example:

```
<processModel . . . username="MACHINE" password="AutoGenerate" . . . />
```

The default for "username" is MACHINE, which causes ASP.NET to assume the ASPNET account identity; the default for "password" is AutoGenerate, which causes ASP.NET to use a cryptographically strong random password stored in the Local Security Authority (LSA) for that account. The account can be changed to either a named user account or SYSTEM. SYSTEM causes ASP.NET to use the local system account. Although in certain situations you may need to use the SYSTEM account, bear in mind that it has almost unlimited privileges.

If you want to change an ASP.NET runtime identity to a user

account, change the user name and password in the <processModel> section, as follows:

```
<processModel . . . username="domain\user" password="password" . . . />
```

In this scenario, the user name must be qualified with the domain name for the domain account, or the local server name for the local account. The disadvantage is that the user name and password are stored in machine.config in clear-text format.

---

**NOTE:** The Aspnet_setreg.exe utility, available from microsoft.com, provides the ability to encrypt these attributes and store their values in the registry under a secure key. For detailed instructions, refer to Knowledge Base article Q329290.

---

### CMS and Domain Controllers

In general, it is not advisable to run your CMS server on a domain controller, because a compromise of the server is a compromise of the domain. However, if you need to use the Windows 2000 domain controller, you will have to change the default ASP.NET process identity because there is a known problem with using the ASPNET identity on Windows 2000 domain controllers. ASPNET is configured as a local account; it is a member of a built-in Users local group. However, on a domain controller, all user accounts are domain accounts and are not local machine accounts. As a result, on domain controllers, ASP.NET fails to start because it cannot find a local account named <localmachinename>\ASPNET. The solution is either to create a new account with the same permissions as ASPNET, which is recommended, or to use a local system account. In any case, you need to change the <processModel> section of the machine.config file accordingly. Full information about this bug is provided in Microsoft Knowledge Base article 315158.

In IIS 6, the worker process identity in IIS 5 isolation mode is configured using the processModel element in exactly the same way as in IIS 5.

However, in worker process isolation mode, the worker process identity is configured in a different way, using the application pool properties. By default, in IIS 6 a worker process runs as a Network Service. To change the worker process identity, right-click the application pool you would like to configure, select Properties, and click the Identity tab.

Then, you can select either Predefined or Configurable options. The Predefined option allows you to select Network Service or Local Service, or Local System identities. The Configurable option allows you to explicitly specify the account name and password under which you want your worker process to run.

If you wish to configure impersonation for the CMS Web application, you need to edit the <identity> element in the web.config file.

---

**NOTE:** The web.config file for the CMS Web application is created by Visual Studio .NET when you create a CMS project in VS.NET; it is located at the root of your CMS Web application.

---

There are three settings for the <identity> element that you can use.

- `<identity impersonate="false"/>`: This is the default setting. It turns off impersonation and causes the worker process to use the default identity.
- `<identity impersonate="true"/>`: This setting causes the worker process to adopt the identity of the user making a request within the CMS Web application. This is the identity that is passed on by IIS. If IIS uses Anonymous authentication, then this identity will be IUSR_<*machinename*>; if IIS uses any other authentication mechanism, it will be an authenticated Windows user identity. All processing for the request will be performed under this identity.
- `<identity impersonate="true" name="domain\user" password="password"/>`: This setting provides the ability to specify the account to be used by ASP.NET within the CMS Web application. Once again, the user name must be qualified with the domain name for the domain account, or the local server name for the local account; and the password is stored in web.config in clear-text format.

---

**NOTE:** As before, you can encrypt the "username" and "password" attributes and store their values in the registry under a secure key using the Aspnet_setreg.exe utility, available from microsoft.com.

---

## ASP.NET Authentication

ASP.NET provides its own authentication systems that we can use within the CMS Web application; these systems are called ASP.NET authentication providers.

ASP.NET authentication providers are implemented as HTTP modules that are defined within the HTTP pipeline in machine.config. These modules contain the code necessary to authenticate user credentials; they are identified in the <httpModules> section of the machine.config file, as follows:

```
<httpModules>
. . .
            <add name="WindowsAuthentication"
type="System.Web.Security.WindowsAuthenticationModule"/>
            <add name="FormsAuthentication"
type="System.Web.Security.FormsAuthenticationModule"/>
            <add name="PassportAuthentication"
type="System.Web.Security.PassportAuthenticationModule"/>
. . .
</httpModules>
```

The use of authentication providers within ASP.NET allows us, for example, to implement anonymous access for IIS and pass all requests from IIS through to the application for authentication. This approach is particularly well suited for public access Internet sites.

ASP.NET authentication will always occur in the HTTP runtime, after IIS authentication. ASP.NET authentication is configured using the <authentication> element within the web.config file. There are four possibilities.

- None: This mode specifies that ASP.NET doesn't perform any authentication, but provides the ability for the ASP.NET runtime to accept every request that is passed on from IIS. This mode is specified using the <authentication mode="None"/> element in web.config.
- Windows authentication: This mode is designed to be used in conjunction with IIS authentication; it validates users against Windows security accounts. It is the default authentication mode; for CMS projects, it is configured when VS.NET creates a web.config file for the project. Windows authentication is useful when you want to use impersonation; it retains the user account identity

passed on from IIS. You can use it with the Basic, Digest, and Integrated Windows authentication methods in IIS. If IIS is configured for anonymous access, this mode will verify that the IUSR_<*machinename*> account is valid.

This mode is specified using the <authentication mode= "Windows"/> element in web.config.

As we discussed in the previous section, in order to provide impersonation, you need to use the <identity impersonate = "true"/> element in web.config. If you enable impersonation, then resources accessed by your application—such as files, folders, registry keys, and Active Directory objects—are accessed with the user identity. If you don't enable impersonation, which is disabled by default, then your application uses the default worker process identity to access resources. However, the user identity is used in both cases—with or without impersonation—to access the ASPX files and other ASP.NET files; the difference is in accessing resources programmatically from the code at runtime.

- Forms authentication: This method uses HTML forms, client-side redirection, and authentication tickets stored in cookies. If IIS is configured for anonymous access, all authentication is handled by ASP.NET. Forms authentication relies on a WebForm interface and therefore is not dependent on any specific client-side features or functionality; all modern browsers support the HTML <form> tag. This is how it works:

1. The user requests a page.
2. Since the user does not have a valid authentication ticket, access to the resource is denied.
3. The request is redirected to a login page, as defined in web.config.
4. The user enters credentials in the login page, and they are sent to the server.
5. The login page verifies the credentials. You can verify against Windows security accounts, or you can verify against your own list of users and their credentials. This can be in any form—for example, a SQL database, an XML document, or even a text file.
6. The user is given an ASP.NET Forms authentication cookie, which identifies the user as authenticated. Subsequent requests from the browser automatically include the cookie. If the cookie is passed from the browser, ASP.NET accepts the

request as authenticated; if there is no cookie in the request, or it has expired or is otherwise invalid, then the user is redirected to the logon page.

The Forms authentication mode is specified by setting the <authentication> element to Forms mode in web.config—for example:

```
<authentication mode="Forms" >
    <forms loginUrl="login.aspx" name="MyCookie"  path="/"
    protection="All" timeout="30"/>
</authentication>
```

The <forms> element in our example defines the name and location of the login page; the name of the form that will become the name of the authentication cookie; the cookie lifetime in minutes; the path of the cookie to be set on the client; and the level of cookie protection set to "All," which instructs ASP.NET to both encrypt and validate authentication cookies.

To make sure the user credentials are not intercepted, you are strongly advised to protect the login page with SSL. In this case, all data transmitted between the browser and the server will be encrypted, including the user credentials.

■ Passport: This mode performs authentication using the Microsoft Passport service. Microsoft Passport allows Internet users to establish a single centralized storage for a set of credentials that can be used on any Passport-compliant Web site. Passport authentication uses a ticketing scheme: Once the user logs on to any Passport-compliant site, the central Passport service provides a ticket in an in-memory cookie. The Passport authentication provider within ASP.NET checks whether a ticket is present in the request; if it's not present or is invalid, then the user is redirected to the Passport login. Passport verifies the user credentials, issues a ticket, and redirects the user back to the originally requested page.

The authentication mode is an application-wide setting that can only be set in the application root web.config file. You cannot use forms-based authentication in one part of your application and Windows authentication in another.

## ASP.NET Authorization

Authentication mechanisms allow us to verify the user's identity; but to determine what they can do, we need authorization. Authorization is set up in web.config using the <authorization> element. This element defines the list of users and groups that are permitted or denied access to the CMS Web application.

---

**NOTE:** When referring to groups, in the ASP.NET environment the term "roles" is used. When using Windows authentication, roles and groups mean the same thing; however, for Forms authentication the meaning is different.

---

The authorization settings are contained within the <authorization> element; they consist of <allow> and <deny> elements that allow and prohibit access. There are special characters for anonymous users and all users; for example <deny users="?"/> denies anonymous users; <allow users="*"/> allows all users. The <allow> and <deny> elements are evaluated in sequence; those that match the user identity are applied.

The authorization entries in web.config differ depending on the authentication provider you use, as follows:

- Authorization for Windows authentication: The user and group names must match the security accounts in the Windows account database; for domain accounts, the user and group names must be prefixed with the domain name. Let's look at the following example:

```
<authorization>
    <deny users="?"/>
    <deny users="CMS/UserNotAllowed"/>
    <allow roles="CMS/administrators"/>
    <deny users="*"/>
</authorization>
```

In this example, anonymous access is blocked, as well as the access for a user named UserNotAllowed from the CMS domain. Access for the administrators group from the CMS domain is allowed, and, finally, all other users are denied access. The sequence is important: If UserNotAllowed was a member of the administrators group, the user would be denied access because the directive for UserNotAllowed occurs first.

■ Authorization for Forms authentication: With Forms authentication, there is no concept of a domain; user names are just the names we pass on from the login page. ASP.NET checks the authorization section in web.config before it redirects the request from the login page to determine their permissions.

As far as groups are concerned, if you want to use them you may need to add some code to the AuthenticateRequest event in global.asax. This event is raised when the authentication provider attempts to authenticate a user, even if authentication fails. Your code needs to establish group membership at runtime. The names of the groups you create in the code must match the roles defined in web.config. For example, in your code you may read the group names from the database.

Let's look at an example of an <authorization> element for Forms authentication:

```
<authorization>
   <deny users="?"/>
   <allow users="administrator"/>
   <allow roles="PremierUsers"
   <deny users="*"/>
</authorization>
```

In this example, anonymous users are denied access, while a user named "administrator" and a group called PremierUsers are allowed access.

## CMS Authentication and Authorization

CMS authentication and authorization is layered on top of IIS and ASP.NET security. Web.config in the CMS Web application contains security settings for authentication and authorization, with both Windows and Forms authentication modes supported. The authentication based on these settings is handled by ASP.NET authentication providers as usual. We will look into the steps for creating web.config elements for both methods shortly. However, before we do that, we need to understand how CMS handles authentication and authorization after ASP. NET has authenticated and authorized the request.

## CMS Authorization Module

After ASP.NET has authenticated and authorized the user based on the settings in web.config, the request is passed to the CMS Authorization HTTP module, called CmsAuthorizationModule. The CMS Authorization module is defined as part of the HTTP module pipeline that is defined in web.config for the CMS application, as follows:

```
<httpModules>
     <add type="Microsoft.ContentManagement.Web.Security.
CmsAuthorizationModule, Microsoft.ContentManagement.Web, Version=
5.0.1200.0, Culture=neutral, PublicKeyToken=31bf3856ad364e35"
name="CmsAuthorizationModule" />

     . . .

 </httpModules>
```

The CMS Authorization module gets the user identity from ASP. NET; it then passes the credentials to the CMS content server, which in turn determines CMS rights groups membership and thus the CMS permissions for the user. All CMS access, including guest access, must be authenticated against a Windows account, regardless of the ASP.NET authentication method used. CMS user rights can only be assigned to Windows security accounts, so any form of authorization must involve a domain account.

---

**NOTE:** Refer to Chapter 17 for a detailed discussion on setting up CMS user rights.

---

It is worth stressing that the CMS Authorization module in web. config is run before the template file is processed.

If no user credentials are supplied with the request, depending on whether the CMS guest access is enabled, one of the following two things happens:

- If guest access is enabled, CMS authenticates the request using the configured guest account, and permissions are defined on the rights groups that the guest account has been made a member of.
- If guest access is disabled, the CMS Authorization module will return an access denied error.

---

**NOTE:** Guest access is set up using the SCA; refer to Chapter 18 for details of the configuration steps.

---

Once CMS has authenticated the request, a CMS authentication ticket is issued to the browser. The ticket contains account information to indicate that a user has been successfully authenticated, as follows:

- User identity and access rights
- Date and time of issue
- IP address of the client

The ticket is encrypted using the CMS server machine key and put in a cookie called CMSAUTHTOKEN. Figure 19–7 shows an example of a CMS authentication cookie sent to the browser.

As we discussed in Chapter 18, the CMS authentication cookie's settings are configured using the SCA. You can set up the cookie's lifetime and whether the originating IP address of the client should be checked against the IP address contained in the cookie (Figure 19–8).

When CMS is deployed in a Web farm, it is important that all servers be configured with the same cookie encryption key. If the encryption keys differ between the servers, then a server will not be able to accept the CMS authentication cookie issued by another server, and therefore the user will be prompted for authentication again.

In this scenario, you need to use a tool provided by CMS called Managekey. It enables you to synchronize the encryption keys between the servers in a cluster; and it allows you to export the encryption key from the first server into a file and then import it into all the other servers in the cluster (Figure 19–9). The tool is located in the folder

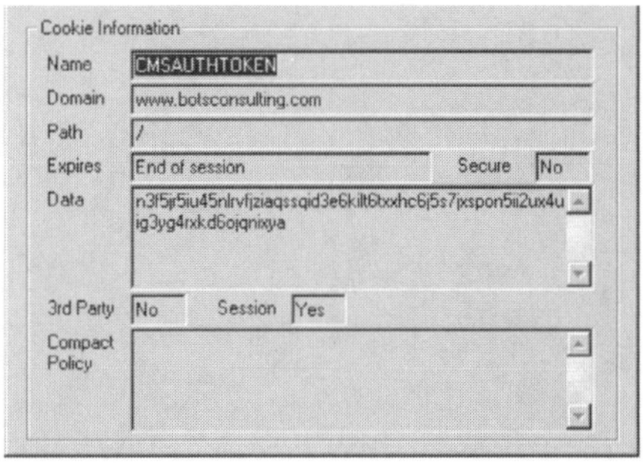

**Figure 19–7** CMS authentication cookie

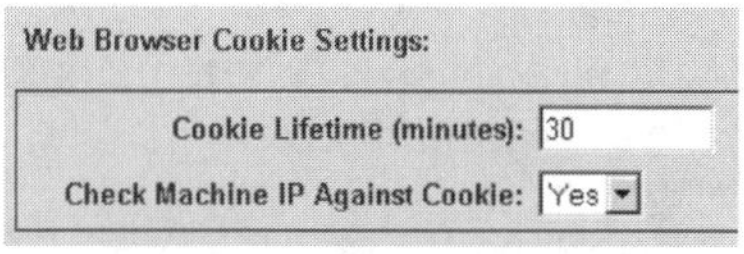

**Web Browser Cookie Settings:**

Cookie Lifetime (minutes): 30

Check Machine IP Against Cookie: Yes

**Figure 19–8**  Cookie settings in the SCA

*<installation drive>*\Program Files\Microsoft Content Management Server\Server\bin.

**NOTE:** CMS is not doing any impersonation of the user. That is, it matches the user name in the ticket against the user rights on the targeted CMS asset, but it is not changing the thread context of the request.

## CMS Authentication Methods

As we mentioned already, the method of authentication used by the CMS Web application is defined in the web.config file. The methods of authentication that can be used by CMS are Windows and Forms. We will now look into configuration and development steps for each method.

### Windows Authentication in CMS

In Windows authentication, the ASP.NET runtime uses the credentials obtained by IIS. The request is authenticated by IIS, and the credentials

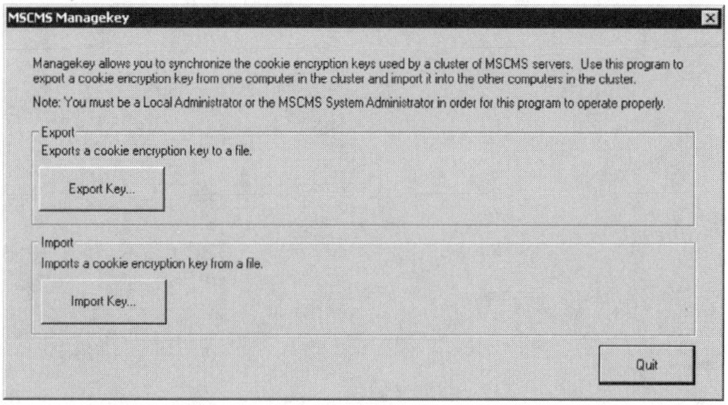

MSCMS Managekey

Managekey allows you to synchronize the cookie encryption keys used by a cluster of MSCMS servers. Use this program to export a cookie encryption key from one computer in the cluster and import it into the other computers in the cluster.

Note: You must be a Local Administrator or the MSCMS System Administrator in order for this program to operate properly.

Export
Exports a cookie encryption key to a file.

Export Key...

Import
Imports a cookie encryption key from a file.

Import Key...

Quit

**Figure 19–9**  Managekey utility

are passed to ASP.NET and then to the CMS Authorization module to determine the user permissions.

To configure CMS for Windows authentication, perform the following steps:

1. Configure IIS authentication using either Basic, Digest, or Integrated Windows authentication.

   > **NOTE:** For additional security, you can use client certificates with Windows authentication. We will look into this configuration in Chapter 20.

2. Edit the web.config file to enable ASP.NET to use Windows authentication and to impersonate the user account that IIS authenticates before handing the request off to ASP.NET. To do this, set the authentication mode to Windows, and set the impersonation element to "true," as shown in the following example:

   ```
   <authentication mode="Windows"/>
   <identity impersonate="true"/>
   ```

   > **NOTE:** You don't have to enable impersonation to make sure that the user identity passed from IIS is used to access the ASPX templates on an NTFS file system—this will be done in any case. You need to enable impersonation to make sure that the user identity, and not the ASP.NET process identity, is used when resources such as files, folders, registry keys, and Active Directory objects are accessed programmatically from the code at runtime.

3. Edit web.config to ensure that the ASP.NET authorization settings deny anonymous access, as follows:

   ```
   <authorization>
      <deny users"?"/>
   </authorization>
   ```

4. Depending on your requirements, either enable or disable guest access in the SCA.
5. Check the NTFS permissions on the ASPX template files to make sure that your users have appropriate permissions for the

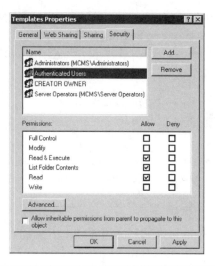

**Figure 19–10** NTFS permissions for the folder storing ASPX template files

ASPX files. The Read permissions are required for template files. For example, if all your template files are stored within a folder called Templates, in the Security tab of this folder's Properties, add the Authenticated Users group if it's not there already, and ensure that this group has at least read permissions (Figure 19–10).

### Forms Authentication in CMS

Forms authentication requires the CMS user to enter credentials using form fields on a Web login page rather than using the standard mechanisms of IIS. The web.config file contains an entry for the location of this login page in the <forms> element.

No default login pages are provided in CMS; you need to develop your own. The login page must perform the following tasks:

- Authenticate and authorize the user
- Issue an ASP.NET Forms authentication cookie
- Issue a CMS authentication cookie

Please note that two cookies will be issued during the CMS authentication and authorization process. The first cookie will be used by the

ASP.NET Forms Authentication module; the second one will be used by the CMS Authorization module. These cookies must share the same timeout value; otherwise, the user will be prompted to reauthenticate when either of the cookies expires.

To help you with the login page development, the CMS Publishing API provides classes that are used for authentication and authorization in the CMS environment.

- CmsFormsAuthentication is a class that wraps the functionality of forms-based login tasks. This class's methods authenticate the user against Windows domains; there are also methods that provide management of both the CMS authentication ticket and the ASP.NET Forms authentication ticket.
- CmsAuthenticationTicket is a class that contains the CMS authentication ticket that we discussed in the previous section.
- CmsAuthorizationModule is an HTTP module that we discussed in the previous section.
- CmsSecurityException provides access to security exceptions raised when your code is executed.

These classes are defined within the Microsoft.ContentManagement. Web.Security namespace. When you develop a custom login page, you use the methods of the CmsFormsAuthentication class as shown in Table 19–1.

---

**NOTE:** When developing ASP.NET forms-based authentication login pages, you use the FormsAuthentication class. This class manages the logon process and handles the issuing of cookies containing ASP.NET authentication tickets. The CmsFormsAuthentication class provides similar functionality to the FormsAuthentication class, but it issues both the ASP.NET and CMS cookies.

---

When a nonauthenticated user requests a CMS page, the user is redirected to the login page. When the user enters the credentials in the form fields in the login page and clicks the Submit button, the Submit event handler in your code within the login page code behind will start with generation of a CMS authentication ticket. Once that is created, a CMS authentication cookie containing the ticket, as well as an ASP.NET Forms authentication cookie, must be returned to the client browser,

**Table 19–1** CmsFormsAuthentication Methods

| Method | What It Does |
|---|---|
| RedirectFromLoginPage | Redirects an authenticated user back to the originally requested URL; issues both a CMS authentication cookie and, optionally, an ASP.NET Forms authentication cookie for an authenticated user |
| SetAuthCookie | Creates both a CMS authentication cookie and, optionally, an ASP.NET forms authentication cookie for an authenticated user and puts them in the outgoing response |
| GetAuthCookie | Creates a cookie corresponding to a supplied CmsAuthenticationTicket, but does not set the cookie as part of the outgoing response |
| AuthenticateAsUser | Validates the supplied name and password for a Windows account, and creates a CmsAuthenticationTicket corresponding to that account |
| AuthenticateAsCurrentUser | Creates a CmsAuthenticationTicket corresponding to the current Windows user |
| AuthenticateAsGuest | Creates a CmsAuthenticationTicket corresponding to the CMS guest account |
| AuthenticateUsingWindowsToken | Creates a CmsAuthenticationTicket corresponding to a Windows account token |

and then the browser should be redirected to the originally requested page. Your code will be similar to the following example:

```
CmsAuthenticationTicket Ticket =
CmsFormsAuthentication.AuthenticateAsUser(Fullname, Password);
if(Ticket !=null)
{
      CmsFormsAuthentication.RedirectFromLoginPage(Ticket,true,
false);
}
else
{
      //Render a message that username/password are not valid
}
```

In this example, the AuthenticateAsUser method authenticates the user credentials against the Windows security accounts, authorizes the user, and returns the CMS authentication ticket. The RedirectFrom LoginPage method redirects based on the contents of the ReturnUrl parameter in the query string; if it doesn't exist, it redirects to default. aspx. This method has three parameters.

- AuthenticationTicket contains a CmsAuthenticationTicket representing an authenticated user.
- SetASPNetCookie defines whether the ASP.NET Forms authentication cookie should be set in addition to the MCMS cookie; if true, the ASP.NET cookie is created.
- createPersistantCookie defines the type of CMS authentication cookie to issue; if true, a persistent cookie will be issued; if false, an in-memory cookie will be created.

To configure CMS for Forms authentication, perform the following steps:

1. Configure IIS for anonymous access.
2. Create a login page and save it in the virtual directory on your server. For public access Internet sites, to provide security, your login page should be located in a directory protected by SSL. We will look into this configuration in Chapter 20.
3. Edit the web.config file to enable ASP.NET to use Forms authentication and to point to the location of the login page. To do this, set the authentication mode to Forms, and specify the login page details in the <forms> element, as shown in the following example:

```
<authentication mode="Forms">
   <forms loginUrl="LoginPage.aspx" name="MyFormCookie"
path="/" protection="All" timeout="30"/>
</authentication/>
```

**NOTE:** The cookie lifetime specified in the "timeout" attribute of the <forms> element applies to the ASP.NET Forms authentication cookie only; the CMS cookie lifetime is set up using the SCA.

**4.** Make sure that the authorization settings in web.config allow access, as follows:

```
<authorization>
    <allow users="*"/>
</authorization>
```

**5.** Depending on your requirements, either enable or disable guest access in the SCA.

**6.** Verify the NTFS permissions on the ASPX template files to make sure that the ASP.NET process identity account has appropriate rights on the the template files. The default ASPNET account is a member of the local Users group; if you use the default account, check that the Users group has at least read permissions on your templates.

When CMS is deployed in a Web farm, all CMS servers should be able to recognize each other's CMS authentication cookies and ASP.NET Forms authentication cookies. To enable this, you need to synchronize several encryption keys between the servers in the cluster.

To synchronize the encryption keys used for CMS authentication cookies between the servers, you need to use the Managekey utility that we discussed earlier in this chapter.

To synchronize the keys for encryption and validation of the ASP.NET Forms authentication cookies, you need to edit the <machineKey> element in the machine.config file on all servers in the cluster. Before we discuss the <machineKey> element, let's look into how Forms authentication cookies' encryption and validation are defined. Whether encryption and validation are enabled is defined by the value of the "protection" attribute in the <forms> element in web.config. If the "protection" attribute is set to All, the cookies are encrypted and validated, which is the best level of protection and the recommended approach. Other values include Encryption and Validation, for enabling either only the encryption or only the validation of the cookies.

If the keys for validation and encryption on servers in the cluster are not synchronized, the user will be asked to reauthenticate each time a server in the cluster gets a request previously authenticated by another server.

The <machineKey> element defines those keys. For each server, the <machineKey> element and its attributes need to be specified in the machine.config file. The settings must be the same for all servers in the cluster. The syntax of this element is as follows:

```
<machineKey validationKey="AutoGenerate|value"
            decryptionKey="AutoGenerate|value"
            validation="SHA1|MD5|3DES" />
```

The validationKey attribute defines the key used to validate the cookie. The default value is AutoGenerate. This is not suitable to our environment, because the generated values will be different on different servers. Therefore, we need to supply the value for this key manually. The recommended key length is 128 hexadecimal characters (64 bytes). The decryptionKey attribute defines the key used for the cookie's decryption. Again, the default value is AutoGenerate, which is not suitable for Web farms; therefore, we need to supply the value for this key manually. Once again, the recommended key length is 128 hexadecimal characters (64 bytes). The "validation" attribute defines the hashing algorithm: MD5, SHA1, or 3DES. The hash is computed from the cookie data using an algorithm defined in the "validation" attribute with the validation key, and is then sent to the client with the cookie data. Both the data and the hash are encrypted. When the cookie is returned, the server decrypts it and then validates it by reapplying the hashing algorithm using the validation key.

### User Identity

As we have seen in this chapter, the user identity in CMS depends on a combination of settings within IIS, ASP.NET, and CMS itself. Table 19–2 lays out the resulting identities for permutations of the key security settings in CMS, as follows:

- Worker process identity: You can get this identity programmatically using the WindowsIdentity.GetCurrent method.
- User account authorized in the CMS content server for the current HTTP request: This account identity is available programmatically from the CmsHttpContext.Current.User.ServerAccountName property.
- User account identity within the CMS ASP.NET Web application for the current HTTP request: This account identity is available programmatically from the HttpContext.Current.User.Identity.Name property.

**Table 19-2** CMS and ASP.NET Identities

| web.config Authentication Mode Setting | Is CMS guest access enabled? | Is IIS anonymous access enabled? | web.config Impersonate Setting | Windows Identity. GetCurrent | CmsHttpContext. Current.User. Server AccountName | HttpContext. Current. User.Identity. Name |
|---|---|---|---|---|---|---|
| Windows | Yes | Yes | true | IUSR_<machinename> | <CMS guest> | blank |
| Windows | Yes | Yes | false | ASPNET | <CMS guest> | blank |
| Windows | Yes | No | true | <Windows user> | <Windows user> | <Windows user> |
| Windows | Yes | No | false | ASPNET | <Windows user> | <Windows user> |
| Windows | No | Yes | true | <Windows user> | <Windows user> | <Windows user> |
| Windows | No | Yes | false | ASPNET | <Windows user> | <Windows user> |
| Windows | No | No | true | <Windows user> | <Windows user> | <Windows user> |
| Windows | No | No | false | ASPNET | <Windows user> | <Windows user> |
| Forms | Yes | Yes | true | IUSR_<machinename> | <CMS user> | <CMS user> |
| Forms | Yes | Yes | false | ASPNET | <CMS user> | <CMS user> |
| Forms | Yes | No | true | <Windows user> | <CMS user> | <CMS user> |
| Forms | Yes | No | false | ASPNET | <CMS user> | <CMS user> |
| Forms | No | Yes | true | IUSR_<machinename> | <CMS user> | <CMS user> |
| Forms | No | Yes | false | ASPNET | <CMS user> | <CMS user> |
| Forms | No | No | true | <Windows user> | <CMS user> | <CMS user> |
| Forms | No | No | false | ASPNET | <CMS user> | <CMS user> |

In Table 19–2, *<Windows user>* refers to the currently logged-on Windows user account, *<CMS guest>* refers to the CMS guest account, and *<CMS user>* refers to the Windows account authorized in CMS when the forms-based login is used.

# Summary

Authentication and authorization of a CMS request is layered on top of IIS and ASP.NET security. To understand how to manage user access in CMS, it is necessary to understand the authentication, impersonation, and authorization mechanisms for both of these technologies. CMS authentication and authorization is performed by the CMS Authorization module. There are two different authentication mechanisms supported in CMS: Windows authentication and forms-based authentication; the former is more suitable for internal sites, while the latter is best suited for external sites. Authorization in CMS is based on the CMS rights groups that the user is a member of. Each rights group belongs to the role that defines this group's permissions; a user can be a member of more than one group; the user permissions are defined by the combination of the group's permissions.

In the next chapter, we will apply our understanding of how to manage user access to several CMS deployment scenarios, and will look into securing CMS sites.

# CHAPTER 20

# Securing a CMS Site

Security is an extremely important aspect of your Web site. Securing a CMS site means preventing unauthorized access to the site while allowing authorized access. CMS site security is not something to be taken lightly; securing the CMS environment takes time and requires planning because there are multiple layers and variables to consider. CMS page processing involves IIS, ASP.NET, the CMS content server, and the CMS database. This means that, in addition to internal CMS security mechanisms, CMS uses the security of these technologies. Depending on whether your site is internal or external as well as on your selected model for CMS site security and your company security policy, the settings you need to configure will be different.

In this chapter, we will look into the different options that may be used for securing a CMS installation and then go through the security settings for different CMS scenarios, including CMS intranet, Internet, and extranet sites.

## CMS Installation Security

Security spans multiple layers in a CMS installation, from the operating system to the CMS Web application. Configuring security for a CMS site involves many configuration options on different levels. In this section, we will consider the settings that contribute to the security of the CMS installation. These settings apply to all CMS sites.

## Hardening Your Servers

CMS servers, especially production servers, must be hardened to protect them from potential attack. When you build them, consider applying the following:

- Windows 2000 high security template: There is a CMS version of a high security template that can be installed from the CMS installation CD. If you use a standard Windows 2000 high security template, after the template has been applied, make sure you manually grant the account that the ASP.NET worker process runs under rights to the %temp% folder. For example, the Publishing API relies on this account's rights to the %temp% folder.
- CMS-customized version of the IIS Lockdown Tool and URLScan: To customize the IIS Lockdown Tool for CMS, replace the iislockd.ini and urlscan_cms.ini files in the IIS Lockdown Tool with the files with the same names that are provided on the CMS installation CD. The CMS version of the IIS Lockdown Tool removes support for File Transfer Protocol (FTP), Simple Mail Transport Protocol (SMTP), and Network News Transfer Protocol (NNTP). It disables the following services: Index Server Web Interface, server side includes, Internet Data Connector, Internet Printing, HTR Scripting, and Web Distributed Authoring and Versioning (WebDAV). It also removes MSADC, IIS Admin, and IIS Help.

  The CMS IIS Lockdown Tool enables URLScan. URLScan screens HTTP requests and can reject them based on specific criteria, thus reducing the exposure to possible attacks.
- Microsoft Baseline Security Analyzer (MBSA): MBSA is a general tool that scans your system for common security configuration problems, missing patches, and hotfixes. It is not CMS-specific.

## Enabling IPSec

A CMS installation usually involves multiple servers communicating with each other. A simple example is when the CMS server and the SQL server hosting the CMS database are installed on different machines (Figure 20–1).

If you are using multiple machines, consider enabling Internet Protocol Security (IPSec) to encrypt traffic between them. Using IPSec does not require any changes to existing applications; IPSec provides IP-level security and is therefore transparent to applications.

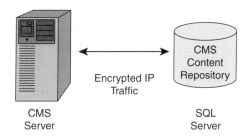

**Figure 20–1** Using IPSec

## Using SSL and Obtaining Certificates

If you want parts of your site to be HTTPS-enabled, you need to obtain certificates to be installed on the server side. For intranet sites, the certificates may be obtained from an internal certification authority (CA); for Internet sites, the certificates must be obtained from a globally recognized CA; for extranet sites, the CA may be internal, but it must be recognized by other partner companies that participate on the extranet.

You need to install a server certificate on IIS, enable SSL on port 443, and then enable secure communications for directories where you need HTTPS. The SSL-enabled CMS site should use a separate Web entry point.

## CMS System Account

As we discussed in Chapter 18, the CMS system account is used for Active Directory (AD) communication and for accessing data stored in SQL Server, on the file system, and in the registry. Because CMS services run under the CMS system account, any problems that this account encounters may, and probably will, cause a disruption in CMS services.

The CMS system account may be a domain account or a local account. The best practice is to use an account with the least privileges. Don't use a domain administrator account or an IIS anonymous account as the CMS system account. Refer to Chapter 18 for instructions on setting up the CMS system account.

The CMS system account must have:

- Read rights for the AD domains where members of CMS rights groups are located.

- The db_datareader and db_datawriter database roles assigned on the CMS database. Using an import function in site deployment also requires a db_ddladmin role. In this case, SQL trusted authentication is used.

---

**NOTE:** For CMS database access, you can use either SQL trusted authentication or SQL authentication. It is recommended that you use SQL trusted authentication so that the CMS database is accessed with the CMS system account security context. However, in certain scenarios, your company policy may prohibit propagation of a security context between applications installed on different machines and separated by a firewall. If this is the case, you need to specify the SQL server account to be used with the CMS database.

---

If you use a local account as the CMS system account, then you must ensure that there is a matching local account on the SQL machine with a synchronized password. It is this local account, not the CMS system account, that requires permissions on the CMS database. In this case, SQL authentication is used. It is not advisable to use this account on any other databases on the same SQL server. On the SQL server machine, this local account must have the following privileges:

- Access this computer from the network
- Log on as a batch job

If your CMS site is deployed in a Web farm (Figure 20–2) and you want to avoid using a domain account as a CMS system account, make sure that each machine has identical local accounts, with synchronized passwords, set up as the CMS system account. In turn, this account must match the local account on the SQL machine.

## Setting Up Web Entry Points

To minimize the surface of a potential attack, consider separating the CMS production sites from the authoring site. On the production sites, configure the IIS virtual site as a read-only CMS Web entry point. On the authoring site, configure the IIS virtual site as a read/write CMS Web entry point.

If your authoring and production sites share the same machine, consider using two network interfaces. For example, the production site can

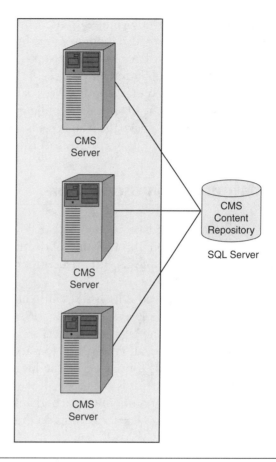

**Figure 20–2** CMS Web farm

be installed on the IIS site using an external interface with an external IP number, while the authoring site can be installed on the IIS site using an internal interface with an internal IP number. The first site should be configured as a read-only CMS Web entry point, and the second site as a read/write CMS Web entry point. You can also consider using a port other than 80 for a read/write CMS Web entry point. Refer to Chapter 18 for details on configuring CMS Web entry points.

## Removing Components

To minimize the surface of a potential attack even more, consider removing unnecessary authoring and management CMS components from the production servers as follows: Web Author, Authoring Connector, Site

Manager, and Site Deployment. To uninstall these components, run the setup program and remove them from the list on the Custom Setup page.

We discussed in Chapter 18 that each CMS server must have the SCA installed for configuration purposes. However, once the server has been configured, you can stop the Web site where the SCA has been installed. When you need to change configuration settings using the SCA, restart this Web site, make the changes, and then stop it once again.

# Authentication and Authorization

In CMS, every user is associated with a Windows account. The identity of a user is verified through authentication, and then access to the requested site resources is authorized according to the rights associated with the user's account.

As we have already discussed, authentication and authorization in CMS spans multiple layers, including IIS, ASP.NET, and CMS server. Figure 20–3 shows the high-level logical architecture of the CMS authentication and authorization process for accessing Content Repository objects. Access rights for objects on the file system are defined by NTFS permissions; this process is not shown in Figure 20–3 for simplicity.

When setting up authentication and authorization for your site, you need to consider the security settings on the following layers:

- IIS security: Considerations include IIS authentication mechanisms and use of SSL. We discussed IIS authentication mechanisms in the previous chapter; in this chapter we will focus on their use in different scenarios.
- ASP.NET security: Considerations include ASP.NET authentication, authorization, and impersonation settings and their configuration at different levels. Once again, we discussed ASP.NET security mechanisms in the previous chapter; in this chapter we will concentrate on using them in different ways in different scenarios.
- CMS content server security: Considerations include enabling or disabling guest access to the site, creating CMS rights groups within CMS roles, adding members to these rights groups, and assigning the rights groups to the site containers.

    After a user has been authenticated, CMS right groups membership defines user access to containers such as channels,

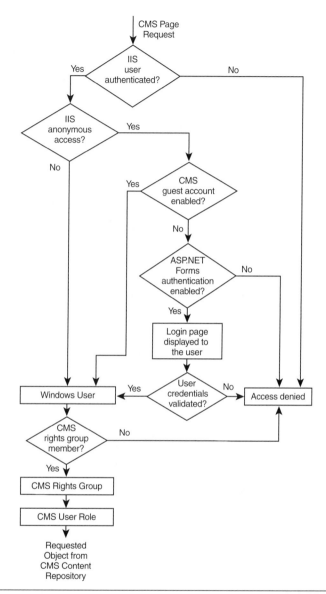

**Figure 20–3**  CMS authentication and authorization process

template galleries, and resource galleries. Refer to Chapter 17 for a detailed discussion of setting up user rights.

In ASP.NET-based sites, the CMS Authorization HTTP module enables CMS Web applications to use CMS content server authentication and authorization.

- NTFS permissions: Considerations include setting up access to site files such as ASPX template files and static site files—for example, images, cascading style sheets, and client-side JavaScript files.

  Depending on the combination of IIS authentication configuration and ASP.NET authentication and impersonation settings, the ASPX files must have at least read permissions for either the default worker process account or the IIS impersonation account IUSR_ *<machinename>*, or the appropriate Windows user accounts.

  For static site files, you need to consider setting up permissions in a different way, simply because these files are not processed by ASP.NET. Depending on whether anonymous access is enabled in IIS, the static site files that are not stored in the CMS resource galleries must have read permissions for either the IIS impersonation account IUSR_*<machinename>* or the appropriate Windows user accounts.

  We looked into CMS user identities and the necessary NTFS permissions in the previous chapter; in this chapter, we will see examples of assigning these permissions to different accounts.

We will now look into setting up security for CMS sites in different scenarios, as follows:

- Intranet site with Windows authentication
- Intranet site with forms-based authentication
- Internet site with full public access
- Internet site with public access and private areas that use an external authentication source
- Extranet site with forms-based authentication
- Extranet site with certificate-based authentication

---

**NOTE:** When we discuss the authorization and authentication of a user request in these scenarios, you may need to refer back to Figure 20–3.

---

## Intranet Sites

A CMS intranet site is only accessible by users within a company's corporate network. The site may be very simple, or it may be big and complex. In an intranet environment, all users have Active Directory accounts, and it is usually possible to assume that everyone uses a common browser standard. It is also a common assumption that users can be authenticated using their Windows credentials.

---

**NOTE:** For CMS internal sites, it is a good practice to use AD groups to organize and manage CMS users according to their roles in the publishing process as well as their rights to parts of the site.

---

There are different authentication mechanisms that can be used for internal sites. If there are no firewalls for internal traffic on your company network, and you can control the installation of IE on users' Desktops, then IIS Integrated Windows authentication may be the authentication method best suited for your environment. Windows authentication provides a high level of security, and because of the automatic logon feature in IE, users will not be prompted to enter their credentials if they are already logged on. Authentication credentials are maintained for the browser session; therefore, the only way to log off is to close the browser; there is usually no logon/logoff link on the site.

However, in certain scenarios in an intranet environment, Windows authentication is not suitable—for example:

- You have a variety of browsers in your organization.
- You have a complex network topology that spans multiple sites and uses firewalls, even for internal traffic.
- The security policy in your company requires separation of the operating system logon from an application logon.

If any of these apply to you, then instead of Windows Authentication, you can use either IIS Basic authentication over SSL, or IIS Certificate authentication, or ASP.NET forms-based authentication over SSL. The most frequently used method is ASP.NET forms-based authentication— for several reasons.

Basic authentication is supported by all browsers; it is widely used and easy to configure. However, if you want to use Basic authentication on your site, you have to enable SSL because otherwise user credentials are sent unencrypted from the browser to the server. With Basic authentication, SSL must be enabled on all site resources. This creates overhead and leads to performance degradation because all traffic between the client and the server is encrypted for all site resources.

Certificate authentication requires that all users have their certificates issued and installed in their browsers. This means, among other things, that your company must have a Public Key Infrastructure (PKI) environment that issues, renews, and revokes user certificates. PKI companywide systems are quite costly to maintain and manage, and they are not very widely used. Although server-side certificates are commonplace and are used everywhere in a corporate environment, client-side certificates are usually issued only when business needs require enhanced security; not all company employees who are likely to use the CMS intranet site will have them.

Forms-based authentication is the most flexible authentication mechanism. It does not require certificates on the client side, and it requires SSL only for the login page itself so that user credentials are encrypted for transfer between the browser and the server. You may of course use SSL for the rest of the site for additional protection if required.

This leaves us with two authentication mechanisms widely used on CMS intranet sites: Windows authentication, and forms-based authentication.

Configuring security for a CMS intranet site includes configuration and settings on multiple layers. The authentication method defines some of them, but not all. Let's look into how to configure CMS intranet site security for each of the authentication methods.

## Internal Sites with Windows Authentication

To set up security for your internal site using Windows authentication, consider the following steps.

1. IIS authentication: Configure IIS for Integrated Windows authentication. Disable anonymous access.
2. ASP.NET security:
   a. Authentication: Configure ASP.NET for Windows authentication. To do this, open the web.config file from the root on the CMS Web application and make sure that the following is configured in the authentication section:

   ```
   <authentication mode="Windows"/>
   ```

   b. Authorization: Configure ASP.NET to deny anonymous access. Make sure that the following element is added to the web.config authorization section:

   ```
   <authorization>
      <deny users="?"/>
   <authorization/>
   ```

**c.** Impersonation: Decide how you want the CMS application to access resources such as files, registry keys, and the Active Directory: as an IIS authenticated user, with the default worker process identity, or with a fixed process identity that is different from the default (refer to Chapter 19 for details on ASP.NET impersonation). Depending on your decision, configure ASP.NET impersonation in web.config—for example:

```
<impersonate="true"/>
```

3. NTFS permissions: Set up read permissions for Active Directory user accounts on site files, including template files and static files, such as images, cascading style sheets, and client-side JavaScript.
4. CMS guest access: Using the SCA, disable guest access to CMS.
5. CMS system account permissions: Verify that the CMS system account has permissions to view the tree in the AD domains to which the site users belong. If the intranet site is companywide, the CMS system account needs to have enumeration rights on all AD domains that maintain user accounts.
6. CMS user rights:
   a. Create CMS rights groups: Using the Site Manager, create CMS rights groups within CMS roles; add Active Directory user and group accounts to these rights groups.

      It is a good practice to create AD security groups for CMS-specific roles, add user accounts to these groups, and then add these groups as members of the CMS rights groups. This approach allows you to use only AD for maintenance of user rights in the CMS environment.

      For example, create an AD security group called Cms-GeneralUsers and add to it all groups and user accounts that are allowed to browse the general areas of the site; if you want all employees to be able to browse the general areas of the site, add a Domain Users group for all AD domains. Then, create an AllSiteSubscribers rights group within the CMS subscriber role, and add the CmsGeneralUsers AD group as a member of the AllSiteSubscribers CMS rights group.

      Create another group called CmsFinanceUsers and add accounts of all employees who work in the finance department. Then create a FinanceSubscribers rights group and add the CmsFinanceUsers AD group as a member of the FinanceSubscribers CMS rights group.

If you want to change who is allowed to browse the general area of the site, you only need to change the membership of the AD group CmsGeneralUsers. Similarly, if you want to change who is allowed to browse specific financial areas on the site, you only need to change the membership of the AD group CmsFinanceUsers.

Although this approach requires some planning for mapping between CMS rights groups and AD groups, this is only a one-off effort. After the initial stage, the management of such an environment is much easier and cleaner than managing multiple individual users' AD accounts within the CMS rights groups.

You may need to set up different groups for production, authoring, and development sites.

For production sites, you need to set up at least one subscribers group. Depending on the business requirements for the site, you may need to set up more than one subscribers group so that you can grant different group rights to different parts of the site.

For content authoring sites, you need to set up the publishing workflow for the site. Depending on your environment, you will need one or more authors, editors, moderators, resource managers, and channel managers groups. You will also need a subscribers group for full site testing so that, for example, authors can see the parts of the site to which they don't have authoring rights.

For development sites, you need at least one template designers group and a subscribers group for testing.

**b.** Assign rights groups to the site containers: After you've created the CMS rights groups, you need to assign them to containers, such as channels, template galleries, and resource galleries. User rights are defined by the role to which the group belongs.

Continuing with our example, you will need to assign the AllSiteSubscribers rights group to the parts of the site that provide general information available to all intranet users, and the FinanceSubscribers rights group to the part of the site that contains information for the finance department only.

On a CMS site that is configured following these steps, processing of a page request includes the following authentication and authorization sequence:

- IIS authenticates the client request using Integrated Windows authentication; the user credentials are passed to the worker process.
- The CMS Web application is configured to use ASP.NET Windows authentication; therefore, the user credentials from IIS are used for template file authorization and then are passed to the CMS Authorization module.
- The CMS Authorization module calls the CMS content server, which authenticates the user and defines the CMS rights group membership for this user. If, based on the role permissions for the groups the user is a member of, the user is authorized, then access is granted to the resource, and a CMS authentication cookie is attached to the HTTP response. Otherwise, an access denied error is returned to the Web application and then to the user.

## Internal Sites with Forms-Based Authentication

With forms-based authentication, some of the security settings are similar to those for Windows authentication. However, others are quite different. To set up security for your internal site using forms-based authentication, consider the following steps.

1. IIS security:
   a. Configure IIS for anonymous access; enable Integrated Windows authentication as well. Anonymous access will be used for page processing and forms-based authentication. However, static site files, such as cascading style sheets or images, are not processed by ASP.NET. Therefore, we need to enable Windows-based security for these files.
   b. Install the server certificate and enable SSL on port 443 on your server.
   c. Create a virtual directory on your server—for example, /secure—and enable SSL for this directory. After you've enabled SSL, all files in this directory are available only using HTTPS. For example, if there is a file called test.htm in the /secure directory, to obtain a page, the following URL should be used: https://<*server name*>/secure/test.htm.

2. ASP.NET security:
   a. Authentication:
      1) Create a login page that authenticates the user against AD security accounts—for example, by using the Cms FormsAuthentication.AuthenticateAsUser(*AccountName*; *AccountPassword*) method with the user-supplied credentials and verifying that the returned CmsAuthentication Ticket is not null. Refer to Chapter 19 for the sample code.
      2) Save the login page in the HTTPS-enabled virtual directory—for example, as /secure/LoginPage.aspx.
      3) Edit the web.config file to enable ASP.NET to use Forms authentication and to point to the location of the login page. To do this, set the authentication mode to Forms, and specify the login page details in the <forms> element, as shown in the following example:

```
<authentication mode="Forms">
   <forms loginUrl=" https://<server
   name>/secure/LoginPage.aspx" name="MyFormsCookie"
   path="/" protection="All" timeout="30"/>
</authentication/>
```

   b. Authorization: Configure ASP.NET to allow access. Make sure that the following element is added to the web.config authorization section:

```
<authorization>
   <allow users="*" />
<authorization/>
```

3. NTFS permissions:
   a. Verify the NTFS permissions on the ASPX template files to make sure that the worker process identity account has at least read permissions on the templates.
   b. Set up permissions for AD users on the static site files that are not stored in the resource galleries—for example, cascading style sheets and JavaScript files. That's why we enabled Integrated Windows authentication on IIS in step 1, so that the NTFS permissions are used for authorization of access to these files.

4. CMS guest account: Using the SCA, enable guest access and specify the guest account. This account will be used for browsing the general areas of your site available to all users.

5. CMS system account permissions: These settings are the same as before. Verify that the CMS system account has permissions to view the tree in the AD domains to which the site users belong. If the intranet site is companywide, the CMS system account needs to have enumeration rights on all AD domains that maintain user accounts.

6. CMS user rights:

    **a.** Create CMS rights groups: Using the Site Manager, create CMS rights groups within CMS roles; add Active Directory user and group accounts to these rights groups. As before, it is advisable to create AD security groups for CMS-specific roles and add user accounts to these groups; then add the AD group to the CMS rights group. This approach allows you to maintain the membership of CMS rights groups within the Active Directory, by adding or deleting user accounts to or from the AD security groups. However, with forms-based authentication, you don't have to create a companywide group for all site users; you can use the CMS guest account instead.

    You may need to set up different groups for production, authoring, and development sites.

    For production servers, set up a subscribers group and add a CMS guest account to this group. Depending on the business requirements for the site, set up another subscribers group for protected areas of your site.

    For content authoring servers, you need to set up the publishing workflow for the site. Depending on your environment, you will need one or more authors, editors, moderators, resource managers, and channel managers groups. Make sure you set up a subscribers group with a CMS guest account for site testing.

    For a development environment, you need at least one template designers group and a subscribers group containing a CMS guest account for testing.

    **b.** Assign rights groups to the site containers: After you've created the CMS rights groups, you need to assign them to containers, such as channels, template galleries, and resource galleries. Assign the subscribers group with the CMS guest account to all containers; assign other groups to containers as appropriate.

On a CMS site that is configured following these steps, processing of a page request includes the following authentication and authorization sequence:

- IIS receives the page request. Since anonymous access is enabled, IIS passes the IUSR_<*machinename*> identity to the worker process. The ASP.NET authentication mode in the CMS Web application is set to Forms; therefore, the identity passed from IIS is not used for authentication.
- ASP.NET checks to see whether a valid Forms authentication cookie is attached to the request. If not, it tries to pass the worker process default account identity (ASPNET) to the CMS Authorization module. The CMS Authorization module checks whether guest access is enabled and attempts authorization of the CMS guest account. If the requested page is available to all users, the request will be authorized and the page returned to the user, with a CMS authentication cookie attached to the response.
- If there is a valid Forms authentication cookie, the request is passed to the CMS Authorization Module, which checks whether a valid CMS authentication cookie is attached to the request. If both cookies are valid, the CMS Authorization module checks the user rights, and if the user is authorized, access is granted to the resource. Otherwise, an access denied error is returned to the application.
- If either of the cookies is not found or is invalid, the user is redirected to the login page using an HTTPS URL, where the user enters the required credentials.
- The login page verifies the credentials against the AD domains and the CMS server, and if they are authenticated, it attaches two cookies: an ASP.NET Forms authentication cookie and a CMS authentication cookie. If authentication fails, an access denied error is returned to the login page, which displays a message to the user, usually within the login page itself—for example, "Invalid user name/password. Please re-enter your credentials."

# Internet Sites

A CMS Internet site is an external site that is available to any user for browsing. In this environment, we need to cater to various browsers; a common browser standard cannot be guaranteed.

Depending on whether all areas of the site are open to all users, we can distinguish between two types of sites:

- Full public access sites: In a full public access site, all users have the same level of access; there is no need for users to log on.
- Public access sites with private areas: In this scenario, not all areas of the site are available to all users; there are areas that require a user to log on, for example, to view premier content.

Authentication and authorization mechanisms for these types of sites are significantly different. For a public access CMS site, only one user account for guest access and one CMS rights group are required. If the site has private areas, user authentication and authorization requires careful planning; in most cases, external authentication is used. Let's have a look at the settings for both scenarios.

## Full Public Access Sites

With publicly available CMS Internet sites, any user can see the full site. No authentication is necessary; there is no logon/logoff link.

Configuring security in this scenario involves several layers.

1. IIS authentication: Configure IIS for anonymous access; disable all other authentication mechanisms.
2. ASP.NET security: Use the default settings for authentication, authorization, and impersonation, as created by VS.NET in the web.config file at the root of the CMS Web application. No additional configuration is required.

   The default setting in web.config for authentication is as follows:

```
<authentication mode="Windows"/>
```

The default settings for authorization and impersonation are usually inherited from machine.config. These settings are as follows:

```
<authorization>
    <allow users="*"/>
<authorization/>
<impersonate="false"/>
```

3. NTFS permissions: The template files and static site files must have at least read permissions set up for the IIS impersonation account IUSR_*<machinename>;* other resources that are accessed from the template code must have read permissions for the default worker process account, such as the local ASPNET account in IIS 5.

   To provide this configuration, no additional setup is usually required, since the default file access control lists (ACLs) include read permissions for the Everyone group by default.

4. CMS guest accounts: Using the SCA, enable guest access to CMS and specify the guest account. It may be a domain account or a local account. If you use a local account, define it as *local-computer\<account name>*.

   If your CMS site is deployed in a Web farm (Figure 20–2) and you want to avoid using a domain account as a CMS guest account, make sure that each machine has local accounts with identical names set up as the CMS guest accounts. For example, you can create the local account MCMSguest on all computers in the farm.

5. CMS user rights: Create a CMS rights group within a subscribers role and add a CMS guest account to this group; then assign this group to all containers, such as channels, template galleries, and resource galleries.

6. CMS Web entry points: Using the SCA, configure the CMS Web entry point for production servers to be read-only.

---

**NOTE:** Only the authoring/staging server connected to the internal network should have a Web entry point configured as read/write. It will be used to import content into the CMS database.

---

7. CMS authentication cookie encryption keys: If CMS is deployed in a Web farm, all CMS servers should be able to recognize

each other's CMS authentication cookies. You need to use the Managekey utility to synchronize the cookie encryption keys between the servers. Refer to Chapter 19 for an explanation of the Managekey utility.

---

**NOTE:** Since there is no authentication and no requirement to authorize requests, you may consider removing the CMS Authorization module for the HTTP pipeline in web.config to provide additional performance for the site.

---

On a CMS site that is configured following these steps, processing of a page request includes the following authentication and authorization sequence:

- IIS receives the page request. Since anonymous access is enabled, IIS passes the IUSR_*<machinename>* identity to the worker process.
- The CMS Web application is configured to use ASP.NET Windows authentication; therefore, the IUSR_*<machinename>* user credentials from IIS are used for template file authorization. ACLs on the template files include the Everyone group; therefore, file access is authorized. After file authorization, the IUSR_ *<machinename>* user credentials for an anonymous request are passed to the CMS Authorization module.
- The CMS Authorization module gets the anonymous request credentials and checks with the CMS content server whether guest access is enabled. Because guest access is enabled, the server authenticates the user as a guest and defines the CMS rights group membership for the CMS guest account. Because the CMS guest account belongs to the subscribers group that is assigned to all site containers, the request for a page in presentation mode is authorized. Then, a CMS authentication cookie with the guest user ID is attached to the HTTP response.

## Public Sites Using an External Authentication Source

A public site with an external authentication source is an Internet public site with private areas that uses an external system for authenticating users. There are sections of the site that are available to any Internet user, as well as premier content sections that are available only to registered users. Registered users are able to browse the public parts of the site, but to access premium content, they need to provide their credentials; therefore, the logon/logoff link is required. The authentication mechanism best suited for this scenario is ASP.NET forms-based authentication. However, it is unlikely that registered users will have Windows user accounts on your system.

Since any Internet user may register on the site, you don't want to maintain millions of user accounts in your Active Directory domain, but you still need to validate the submitted credentials. The solution is to use an external authentication source. For example, you may maintain user account credentials such as user name and password in the SQL database; or you may maintain user account credentials using your company's customer relationship management (CRM) system; or you may decide to use Microsoft Passport or any other external source that is required by your business needs and is deemed appropriate by your company security policy. The external authentication source may also be used for user profiling.

As we know, CMS requires a Windows user account for authentication and authorization of any request; CMS user rights can be assigned to a Windows account only, not to an external source account. Therefore, we need to provide mapping of externally authenticated users to Windows accounts. This mapping will be many-to-one (Figure 20–4)—many external accounts will be mapped to one Windows account that will define the CMS permissions. The mapped Windows account may be a

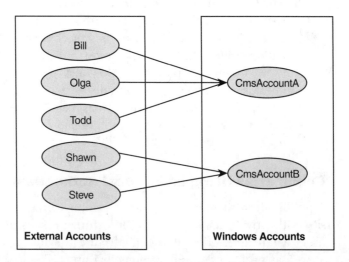

**Figure 20–4** Mapping of external accounts to Windows accounts

domain account or a local account. The number of Windows accounts required depends on the different types of access you need to provide on your site; each Windows user represents one type of access.

The mapping algorithm depends on your business requirements. For example, you can have a mapping list that maps external users to Active Directory accounts. Because the list actually names the AD accounts, it should be secured. You will probably host it on your CMS site, not the external authentication site. In any case, you will need to define procedures for maintenance of the mapping list—that is, how you add new mappings, how you make sure that changes to Windows accounts are reflected in the mapping list, and so on.

Another possibility is to use a type instead of a mapping list, as shown in Figure 20–5. In this case, a flag is specified for each type of access to your site. You then need to map this type flag to a Windows account programmatically. The type flag provides the ability to group the external user accounts together depending on the access these users require to your site. Then, you map any member account of the group to a predefined Windows account on your system. This approach is more flexible than using a mapping list. It saves management overhead in maintaining the mapping list and doesn't expose your Windows

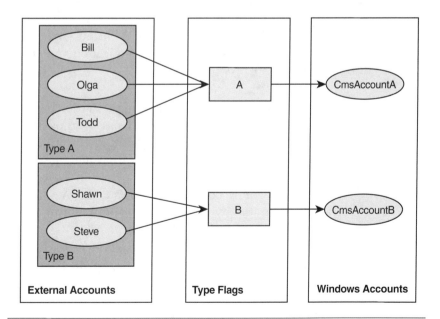

**Figure 20–5** Mapping of external accounts to Windows accounts using user types

accounts. The type flag is usually stored on the external authentication site as a property in the account information. For example, the type flag may be returned to you as an additional user attribute with the validation confirmation from an external source.

In any case, the mapping code will have to be written; it will differ depending on the external authentication source you use. Depending on the source, the user credentials may vary—for example, an e-mail address and password; or a user name and password; or a user name, password, and an answer to a specific question; or just an e-mail address if you are not that concerned about security of access, but want to collect data for user profiling.

The good news is that the CmsFormsAuthentication.Authenticate AsUser method allows us to use both the user-supplied user name and the mapped Windows account credentials to create a unique CMS authentication cookie for this particular user. The syntax is as follows:

```
CmsFormsAuthentication.AuthenticateAsUser( ServerAccountName,
ServerAccountPassword, ClientAccountName, ClientAccountType )
```

where ServerAccountName and ServerAccountPassword are Windows account credentials, ClientAccountName is the user account identifier supplied by the user, and ClientAccountType is the type of user account that we assign in the code according to our business logic.

The runtime logic of the CMS authentication and authorization in this scenario is as follows:

1. Get the user credentials. For example, a user authenticates himself as the user michael with the password pwd123.
2. Validate the user credentials against the external authentication authority. For example, the external authentication authority may be your CRM.
3. Assign a client account type—for example, A.
4. Based on the type, map the external user to a Windows account—for example, CmsAccountA.
5. Retrieve the Windows account password—for example, A-pwd.
6. Authenticate the user to Microsoft Content Management Server, using

```
CmsFormsAuthentication.AuthenticateAsUser(
ServerAccountName, ServerAccountPassword,
ClientAccountName, ClientAccountType )
```

and then verify that the returned CmsAuthenticationTicket is not null.

In our example, ServerAccountName is `CmsAccountA`; ServerAccountPassword is `A-pwd`; ClientAccountName is `michael`; and ClientAccountType is `A`.

To implement this logic, you will need to write code in the login page, usually using event handlers. The event handler implements procedures for authentication against an external source, as well as mapping an externally authenticated user type to a Windows account and obtaining the account's password. You will need to write your own code for the event handler; it will be a general ASP.NET event handler and not CMS-specific. For example, you can write code for an event handler in global.asax—that is, the AuthenticateRequest event handler. You may consider writing your own authentication HTTP module as well.

---

**NOTE:** For an example of event handler structure, refer to Chapter 3 of the online book *Integration Techniques and Strategies for CMS 2002*, available from http://msdn.microsoft.com/library/default.asp?url=/servers/books/cms/integration.asp.

---

To set up security for a CMS Internet site using forms-based authentication mapped to a custom external source, consider the following steps.

1. Windows mapped accounts: Create one account, either domain or local, for each type of access to your site's premier content.

    For example, your business needs require that one group of users is able to see section A of the site's premier content, and another group of users is able to see section B of the premier content. To provide this functionality, you need to create two Windows user accounts: one for the first type of access (for example, CmsAccountA) and another for the second type of access (for example, CmsAccountB). The settings for this example are listed in Table 20–1; the first four columns show mapped accounts by type of access.

2. IIS security:

    a. Configure IIS for anonymous access.

    b. Make sure that the server certificate from a globally recognized CA is installed on your server and that SSL is enabled on port 443.

   **c.** Create a virtual directory on your server that will store the login page, and enable SSL for this directory—for example, /login.

**3.** ASP.NET security:

   **a.** Authentication:

     **1)** Create a login page that implements the logic we discussed. In our example, the code in the login page will use an event handler that validates the user against an external source and provides the mapping of all externally authenticated accounts of type A to the Windows account CmsAccountA, and accounts of type B to the Windows account CmsAccountB. The type flags and the corresponding mapped accounts are shown in Table 20–1.

     **2)** Save the login page in the HTTPS-enabled virtual directory—for example, as /login/LoginPage.aspx.

     **3)** Edit the web.config file to enable ASP.NET to use Forms authentication and to point to the location of the login page. To do this, set the authentication mode to Forms, and specify the login page details in the <forms> element, as shown in the following example:

```
<authentication mode="Forms">
   <forms loginUrl=" https://<server
   name>/login/LoginPage.aspx" name="MyFormsCookie"
   path="/" protection="All" timeout="30"/>
</authentication/>
```

   **b.** Authorization: Configure ASP.NET to allow access. Make sure that the following element is added to the web.config authorization section:

```
<authorization>
   <allow users="*" />
<authorization/>
```

**4.** NTFS permissions:

   **a.** Verify the NTFS permissions on the ASPX template files to make sure that the worker process account has at least read permissions on the template files.

   **b.** Verify that the IUSR_<machinename> account has read permissions on the static site files that are not stored in the resource galleries.

5. CMS guest account: Using the SCA, enable guest access and specify the guest account. It can be a domain account or a local account. This account will be used for browsing the general areas of your site available to all users.

6. CMS system account permissions: If you use AD mapped accounts, verify that the CMS system account has permissions to view the tree in the AD domain where you set up the mapped accounts for the site users.

7. CMS user rights:

   a. Create CMS rights groups: Using the Site Manager, create subscribers rights groups for each type of users that will be supplying their credentials to view sections of premium content. Add Windows mapped accounts to these rights groups—one account to one group.

   Create another subscribers group for your anonymous site users and add a CMS guest account to this group.

   Continuing with our example, you will need to create two subscribers rights groups in CMS—for example, Subscribers TypeA, and SubscribersTypeB; then add the Windows mapped account CmsAccountA to the SubscribersTypeA group, and the second Windows mapped account CmsAccountB to the SubscribersTypeB group. You will also need to create a third subscribers rights group for anonymous site users—for example, SubscribersAnonymous. Table 20–1 shows the mapped accounts and the associated subscribers groups in columns 4 through 6.

   b. Assign the rights groups to the site containers: Assign the subscribers groups you've created to site containers, such as channels, template galleries, and resource galleries, as appropriate for the user type each subscribers group represents. Assign the subscribers group with the CMS guest account to the channels and other containers that can be viewed by all users.

   In our example, you will need to assign the Subscribers TypeA rights group to the channels and other containers that provide information for section A, and assign the Subscribers TypeB group to the channels and other containers that provide information for section B. Then, assign the Subscribers Anonymous rights group to the channels and other containers that do not require authentication. Table 20–1 lists the subscribers groups and their rights to containers in columns 6 and 7.

**Table 20–1** Mapped Accounts and CMS Rights

| User Authentication | Parts of Site Where Access Is Required | Type Flag | Windows Mapped Account | CMS User Role | CMS Rights Group | Rights to Containers |
|---|---|---|---|---|---|---|
| 1 | 2 | 3 | 4 | 5 | 6 | 7 |
| Externally authenticated | Premier content, section A | A | CMS AccountA | Subscribers | Subscribers TypeA | Channels in section A; template galleries and resource galleries required to view content in section A |
| Externally authenticated | Premier content, section B | B | CMS AccountB | Subscribers | Subscribers TypeB | Channels in section B; template galleries and resource galleries required to view content in section B |
| Anonymous | Publicly available | — | *<CMS guest account>* | Subscribers | Subscribers Anonymous | Public channels; template galleries and resource galleries required to view content in public channels |

8. CMS Web entry points: Using the SCA, configure the CMS Web entry point for production servers to be read-only.

9. CMS authentication cookie encryption keys: If CMS is deployed in a Web farm, all CMS servers should be able to recognize each other's CMS authentication cookies. You need to use the Managekey utility to synchronize the CMS cookie encryption keys between the servers. Refer to the previous chapter for an explanation of the Managekey utility.

10. ASP.NET Forms authentication cookie encryption and validation keys: If CMS is deployed in a Web farm, all CMS servers should be able to recognize each other's ASP.NET Forms authentication cookies. You need to edit the <machineKey> element in the machine.config files on all servers to synchronize the ASP.NET Forms authentication cookie encryption and validation keys. Refer to the previous chapter for an explanation of the <machineKey> element and its attributes.

On a CMS site that is configured following these steps, processing of a page request includes the following authentication and authorization sequence:

- IIS receives the page request. Since anonymous access is enabled, IIS passes the IUSR_<*machinename*> identity to the worker process. The ASP.NET authentication mode in the CMS Web application is set to Forms; therefore, the identity passed from IIS is not used for authentication.

- ASP.NET checks whether a valid Forms authentication cookie is attached to the request. If not, it tries to pass the worker process default account identity to the CMS Authorization module. The CMS Authorization module checks with the CMS content server whether guest access is enabled and attempts authorization for the CMS guest account. If the requested page is available to all users, the request will be authorized and the page returned to the user, with a CMS authentication cookie attached to the response.

- If there is a valid ASP.NET Forms authentication cookie, the request is passed to the CMS Authorization Module, which checks whether a valid CMS authentication cookie is attached to the request. If both cookies are valid, the CMS Authorization module checks the mapped Windows user account rights, and if the Windows user is authorized, access is granted to the resource. Otherwise, CMS returns an access denied error to the application.

- If either of the cookies is not found or is invalid, the request is redirected to the login page using an HTTPS URL, where the user enters the required credentials.
- The login page verifies the credentials against the external source—for example, using an event handler in global.asax. If authentication fails, an access denied error is returned to the login page, which displays a message to the user, usually within the login page itself—for example, "Sorry, your login failed. Please re-enter your credentials." If the user credentials are successfully authenticated, the mapping to the Windows account takes place. The login page then authenticates and authorizes the Windows account in CMS, redirects the user to the originally requested page, and attaches two cookies to the outgoing response: an ASP.NET Forms authentication cookie and a CMS authentication cookie.

# Extranet Sites

A CMS extranet site is an external site that is available to predefined users only. All users must be authenticated; there is no anonymous or guest access. For example, an extranet site can be used by your company and its preferred business partners, but will be closed to anybody else. Although it is an external site, only authorized employees of your company and the partner companies are able to use it. Because we cannot control other companies' environments, a common browser standard cannot be guaranteed.

We will start with looking into the security settings for an extranet site with forms-based authentication; we will then concentrate on an extranet site with certificate-based authentication.

## Extranet Sites with Forms-Based Authentication

This form of authentication is normally used for CMS production servers on an extranet. A CMS production server in an extranet environment must explicitly authenticate all users; there is no guest access. Because an extranet CMS site usually needs to serve a variety of clients, the most flexible authentication mechanism is forms-based authentication over SSL.

It is likely that all extranet users will have Windows accounts; therefore, your login page will use the CmsFormsAuthentication. AuthenticateAsUser(*AccountName*; *AccountPassword*) method with the user-supplied credentials for authentication

However, if the extranet users do not have Windows accounts—for example, because of your company security policy restrictions—you may be required to map the extranet user credentials into Windows accounts that are created to reflect the type of users. These accounts are sometimes referred to as role-based accounts because we create one Windows account for each type of user based on the role they can play on our site. Usually, the user credentials are held in a dedicated SQL database. In this case, you will need to write event handlers to authenticate the users against the SQL-held data, and then, if they are authenticated, map the request to a Windows account based on the user role on the site. The user role must be held in the SQL database as well. Then, the login page will use the CmsFormsAuthentication.AuthenticateAs User (*ServerAccountName, ServerAccountPassword, ClientAccountName, ClientAccountType*) method with the mapped account credentials, the user-supplied user name, and the user role extracted from the database.

As always in CMS, configuring security for a production site involves several layers.

1. IIS security:
   a. Configure IIS for anonymous access.
   b. Install the server certificate and enable SSL on port 443 on your server. The certificate must be issued by a CA that will be recognized by all companies using the site.
   c. Create a virtual directory on your server—for example, /login—and enable SSL for this directory.
2. ASP.NET security:
   a. Authentication:
      1) Create a login page that authenticates the user using the CmsFormsAuthentication.AuthenticateAsUser method and verifying that the returned CmsAuthenticationTicket is not null.
      2) Save the login page in the HTTPS-enabled virtual directory—for example, as /login/LoginPage.aspx.
      3) Edit the web.config file to enable ASP.NET to use Forms authentication and to point to the location of the login page—for example:

```
<authentication mode="Forms">
  <forms loginUrl=" https://<server
  name>/secure/LoginPage.aspx" name="MyFormsCookie"
  path="/" protection="All" timeout="30"/>
</authentication/>
```

**b.** Authorization: Configure ASP.NET to allow access. Make sure that the following element is added to the web.config authorization section:

```
<authorization>
  <allow users="*" />
<authorization/>
```

3. NTFS permissions:
    **a.** Verify the NTFS permissions on the ASPX template files to make sure that the worker process identity account has at least read permissions on the templates.
    **b.** Verify that the IUSR_*<machinename>* account has read permissions on the static site files that are not stored in the resource galleries.
4. CMS guest account: Using the SCA, disable guest access.
5. CMS system account permissions: Verify that the CMS system account has permissions to view the tree in the AD domain where the AD accounts for either the site users or mapped user roles, in the case of mapped authentication, are defined.
6. CMS user rights:
    **a.** Using the Site Manager, create subscribers rights groups for each type of user access to the site.

    If your users have AD accounts, create an AD group for each type of access and add these groups to the appropriate subscribers groups.

    If you are using AD mapped accounts, add these accounts to the appropriate subscribers groups—one account to one group.
    **b.** Assign the subscribers groups you've created to site containers, such as channels, template galleries, and resource galleries, as appropriate for the user type each subscribers group represents.
7. CMS authentication cookie encryption keys: If CMS is deployed in a Web farm, use the Managekey utility to synchronize the CMS authentication cookie encryption keys between the servers.

8. ASP.NET Forms authentication cookie encryption and validation keys: If CMS is deployed in a Web farm, synchronize the
   settings in the <machineKey> element in each server's machine.
   config file.

On a CMS site that is configured following these steps, processing of
a page request includes the following authentication and authorization
sequence:

- IIS receives the page request. Since anonymous access is enabled,
  IIS passes the IUSR_<*machinename*> identity to the worker
  process. The ASP.NET authentication mode in the CMS Web
  application is set to Forms; therefore, the identity passed from IIS
  is not used for authentication.
- ASP.NET checks whether a valid Forms authentication cookie
  is attached to the request. If it is, the request is passed to the
  CMS Authorization Module, which checks whether a valid CMS
  authentication cookie is attached to the request. If both cookies
  are valid, the CMS Authorization module checks the user rights,
  and if the user is authorized, access is granted to the resource.
  Otherwise, an access denied error is returned to the application.
- If either of the cookies is not found or is invalid, the user is redirected to the login page using an HTTPS URL, where the user
  enters the required credentials.
- The login page verifies the credentials, and if they are authenticated, attaches two cookies to the response: an ASP.NET Forms
  authentication cookie and a CMS authentication cookie. If authentication fails, an access denied error is returned to the login page,
  which displays a message to the user, usually within the login page
  itself—for example, "Invalid user name/password. Please re-enter
  your credentials."

## Extranet Sites with Certificate-Based Authentication

This form of authentication is used when CMS authoring servers are
accessible using an extranet. So far, we have seen content authoring
done on an internal network. However, often content authors and editors are required to submit content over the Internet. Sometimes, to
save costs, production and content authoring environments may be combined and run on the same servers. More frequently, they run on different machines but share the same database.

An externally accessible CMS authoring server usually has security settings similar to those of an extranet production server. The IIS security settings, ASP.NET security settings, NTFS permissions, and CMS system account permissions are the same; and CMS guest access should be disabled as for a production server.

However, the CMS user rights are different. For content authoring servers, you need to set up the publishing workflow. Depending on your environment, you may need to create one or more of authors, editors, moderators, resource managers, and channel managers rights groups and assign them to appropriate containers to reflect your user privileges on the site. You may also need to create at least one subscribers group so that the content authors are able to test their work.

There are scenarios where additional security is required for content authoring servers. It usually happens in a business-to-business (B2B) environment, where a publishing workflow break-in represents a serious security threat for both companies involved. If this is the case, then Certificate authentication can be used.

With such high security requirements, all authorized users must either have their own Windows accounts or be mapped to Windows accounts. User certificates can be mapped to Windows accounts on either a one-to-one or a many-to-one basis (many certificates to a single account). In order to be able to map certificates, you need to have a copy of all the certificates the users are going to use when connecting to your server. If you don't want to map certificates, or if you are required to provide two-step authentication—both by a certificate and by a user entering their credentials—then instead of certificate mapping, you can enable Basic authentication in IIS. In this case, each user must have a security account; user credentials are validated against this account.

To configure a CMS server for Certificate authentication, consider the following steps:

1. IIS authentication:
   a. Install the server certificate and enable SSL on port 443 on your server. The certificate must be issued by a CA that will be recognized by all companies using the site.
   b. For the directory that hosts your CMS Web application, enable secure communications, and specify that client certificates are required.
   c. You may need to enable a certificate trust list (CTL) to define the certification authorities from which you accept certificates.

    **d.** If you need two-step authentication, configure IIS for Basic authentication.

       If you don't need two-step authentication, enable certificate mapping and map the certificates to the Windows accounts.

**2.** ASP.NET security:

    **a.** Authentication: Configure ASP.NET for Windows authentication. To do this, open the web.config file from the root on the CMS Web application and make sure that the following is configured in the authentication section:

```
<authentication mode="Windows"/>
```

    **b.** Authorization: Configure ASP.NET to deny anonymous access. Make sure that the following element is added to the web.config authorization section:

```
<authorization>
   <deny users="?"/>
<authorization/>
```

    **c.** Impersonation: Depending on your requirements, you may need to configure ASP.NET impersonation in web.config—for example:

```
<impersonate="true"/>
```

**3.** NTFS permissions: Set up read permissions for the appropriate Windows accounts on the template files and the static site files.

**4.** CMS guest access: Using the SCA, disable guest access to CMS.

**5.** CMS system account permissions: Verify that the CMS system account has permissions to view the tree in the AD domains where either the user accounts or the accounts mapped to the certificates are maintained.

**6.** CMS user rights:

    **a.** Using the Site Manager, create CMS rights groups within CMS roles to reflect your publishing workflow.

    **b.** Assign the CMS rights groups you've created to the appropriate containers.

**7.** Cookie encryption keys: If the CMS site is deployed in a Web farm, use the Managekey utility to synchronize the CMS authentication cookie encryption keys between the servers. To synchronize the ASP.NET Forms authentication cookie encryption and validation keys, use the settings in the <machineKey> element in each server's machine.config file.

On a CMS site that is configured following these steps, processing of a page request includes the following authentication and authorization sequence:

- IIS authenticates the request using the client certificate. If the client does not present a valid certificate issued by a CA listed in the CTL, the request is denied.
  If the certificate is accepted, then one of two things happens:

  - If Basic authentication is enabled, the user supplies a user name and password; then IIS authenticates the user credentials against a Windows account.
  - If certificate mapping is enabled, the user certificate is mapped to a Windows account.
  The user identity is passed to the worker process.

- The CMS Web application is configured to use ASP.NET Windows authentication; therefore, the user credentials from IIS are used for the template file authorization and then are passed to the CMS Authorization module.
- The CMS Authorization module calls the CMS content server to authenticate the user and to define the CMS rights group membership for this user. If, based on the role permissions for the groups the user is a member of, the user is authorized, then access is granted to the resource, and a CMS authentication cookie is attached to the HTTP response. Otherwise, an access denied error is returned to the Web application and then to the user.

## Summary

There are many variables to consider when you are securing a CMS site. Security in CMS spans multiple layers, from the operating system to the CMS Web application. Depending on whether your site is internal or external and whether the site has general-access parts, the site security configuration will be different.

In this chapter, we looked into security settings in several common scenarios for intranet sites, Internet sites, and extranet sites. Depending on your business needs and your company security policy, your requirements may be different from the examples we looked into. However, you can use our scenarios as a starting point for your specific implementation.

In the next two chapters, we will look into how to deploy CMS sites from development to production.

# PART V

# Site Deployment

# CHAPTER 21

# Site Deployment Manager

## Overview

Site Deployment Manager (SDM) is an important component of CMS. It provides administrators and developers with a mechanism to move content and CMS-based assets from one implementation to another. Site Deployment Manager can be used either in an interactive mode, through Site Manager, or through programmatic methods, using VBScript.

In this chapter, we'll explore SDM, covering the basics of deployment through Site Manager and how to script automated updates between CMS servers. We'll start by discussing Site Deployment Manager in general. Then we'll show you how to use the interactive interface in Site Manager to import and export Site Deployment Object (SDO) files. Next, we'll demonstrate how to script an incremental deployment process. Finally, we'll provide a brief explanation of how to automate the deployment script execution through the Windows Task Scheduler.

It's important to understand that both the interactive interface for Site Deployment Manager and the COM-based interface are used to move CMS-based assets only. Deploying your site from one environment to another involves moving both the CMS-based assets and the file-based assets (template files, images, controls, and so on). Chapter 22 discusses several deployment scenarios. In this chapter, we're focusing on deploying CMS-based assets only.

## Using Site Deployment Manager

Site Deployment Manager is a utility that ships as a part of CMS. SDM is used to import and export CMS-based assets. Exported assets are placed in a Site Deployment Object file, also referred to as a "package." When you are importing, the SDO file is processed by SDM, and the objects contained in the package are placed in the destination repository.

The interactive user interface for SDM is contained within Site Manager. This interface allows channel managers to export content and administrators to import or export content. Figure 21–1 shows the user interface for the import operation, and Figure 21–2 shows the export user interface.

Keep in mind that SDM is meant for CMS-based assets. SDM packages cannot include assets that are stored external to CMS. For example, all the template ASPX files are stored externally to CMS. As a result, when you deploy a CMS site, you'll have to create an SDO file for the CMS-based assets and then move the non-CMS based assets, placing them both on the destination server. Microsoft recommends using Application Center Server to handle moving the file-based assets. However, you may choose to use other methods—perhaps a scripted FTP or other such method. There are no specific requirements for moving non-CMS based files, so the choice is yours.

---

**NOTE:** When moving a CMS application from one server to another for the first time, you must create a virtual directory on the destination server. When you create a new project through VS.NET, a virtual directory in your solution called CMS is automatically created. When moving your application to a new server, you must manually create this virtual directory under your application directory. The new virtual directory should be mapped to X:\program files\Microsoft Content Management Server\Server\IIS_CMS. This virtual directory contains the JavaScript code and certain assemblies for the Word Authoring Connector and the edit console. Also, you must remove the new application created for the new virtual directory; this virtual directory should inherit the application settings from your CMS application.

---

### Creating Packages

There are two methodologies for processing packages in SDM: manual and scripted. If you choose to manually process packages, you will be

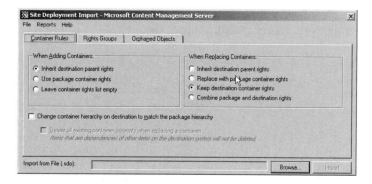

**Figure 21–1**  The SDM import interface

using the interactive Site Manager interface. If you choose to use scripts, you'll end up using VBScript (VBS), which uses a COM-based API (yes, COM). Either methodology will work, and it's likely you'll use a combination, depending on the situation.

In the following sections, we'll discuss both the creation and the consumption of SDO files. We'll first start by showing you how you can create and consume SDO files using the interactive interface. After that,

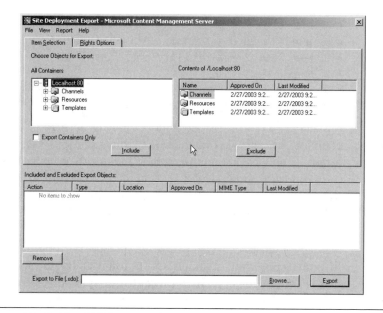

**Figure 21–2**  The SDM export interface

we'll walk you through the process of creating script files to allow you to incrementally deploy content from CMS.

---

**NOTE:** It's not possible to perform a full deployment through a script, and it's not possible to perform an incremental deployment through the interactive interface. In most cases, you'll end up using both methods at different times, based on the operation you need to perform. In addition, there may be some cases where it's simply easiest to back up and restore the entire SQL database. The drawback to this method is that you also carry the CMS settings specific to the source environment. We would recommend using an SQL backup/restore if you're moving a very large CMS database from one environment to another, similar environment. Use Site Deployment Manager for ongoing deployments.

---

### Manually through Site Manager

Once of the easiest ways to process SDO files is using the manual interface in Site Manager. This interface will allow you to both export and import. The only restriction to processing SDO files is that only administrators can import content. However, channel managers have the ability to export content from their channels.

#### Export

To begin, you have to start Site Manager. Click the File menu in Site Manager. Now, choose Package and then Export. In Figure 21–3 you can see how this is done.

Once you've started SDM, you'll be provided with an interface that allows you to choose which objects you'd like to export (shown in Figure 21–4). You'll immediately notice on the left side of the dialog box a complete listing of all containers in the system. To choose an item for export, simply click it and then click Include. This will place the object in the export list, just below the All Containers element. For our example, we've decided to export the BOTS Consulting site. So, we've chosen the botsconsulting channel and clicked Include to add it to the list of objects to be exported. When you chose a container, SDM will export that container and all its children. Since we picked the botsconsulting channel, SDM will export all channels and postings contained in the hierarchy of that channel. However, if you want to export a single posting object, you can simply select that single object. In our example, for each category

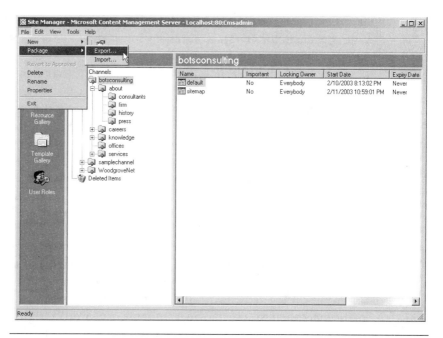

**Figure 21–3**  Starting SDM from Site Manager

**Figure 21–4**  SDM set to export the BOTS Consulting site

of object (channels, templates, and resources), we've selected all the relevant containers for BOTS Consulting. In addition, we've supplied a file name in the Export to File field. In Figure 21–4, you can see what our export interface looks like now that we've added all the containers we want.

Once you're ready to export your objects, just click Export. SDM will prompt you either to continue or to run a preexport report. If you choose to run a preexport report, SDM will simulate the export process to determine what will be exported and if any errors will occur. This same report can also be generated after the actual export process if you so choose. In our case, we've checked the option box that disables this prompt, and our export occurs immediately.

When you export objects, SDM will dutifully export all the objects you've specified, in addition to all dependent objects. For example, if a posting links to a resource that's in the resource gallery, the resource gallery item will automatically be moved, even though you didn't specifically include it in the export; in this way CMS prevents objects from "breaking" in the new environment. The only downside to this behavior occurs when you're moving content "backward" from production to development for testing. Since a posting needs a template to run, SDM will drag the templates for each posting along with the postings themselves. When you import the SDO in your development environment, the development templates will be overwritten with the ones from production. To avoid this problem, you should export your templates in development first, import your SDO from production, and then reimport your original development templates.

The length of time SDM takes to run depends entirely on the number and size of the objects it has to export. If your site is mostly HTML, is relatively flat, and doesn't have too many postings and/or resources, SDM could be done in a matter of seconds. If your site is very large, has a complex channel structure, and/or has lots of binary files, SDM may take longer to run. Once SDM finishes, you'll end up with one SDO file, which you can transfer to the other implementation of CMS to import. In Figure 21–5, we've provided a screen shot of one portion of the export report for our BOTS export exercise. As you can see, the report shows not only the channels, but the postings it exported.

Now, let's go back to our export process and explore a few of the options available to you. The following is a list of options and functions in SDM and a brief explanation of each.

- Exclude: As its name suggests, it's the opposite of the Include option. Exclude allows you to specify particular objects to be

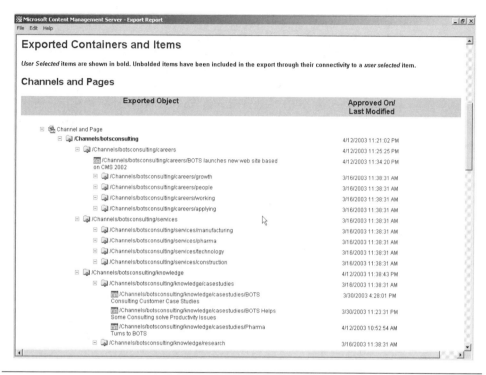

**Figure 21–5** The SDM export report

excluded from the SDO. This is useful if you want to grab most of the objects in a given container but not all of them.

■ Export Containers Only: Use this option if you simply want to export the selected containers but not the objects within them. For example, if you just wanted to transfer a channel structure, resource galleries, or template galleries to a destination CMS server, you could use this option to quickly move an existing structure. This is most commonly used when you are moving containers from a development server to a staging or production server, where the developers want to move a new navigation or gallery structure, but don't want to move any of the objects inside the containers (like test postings or resources).

■ Report/Export Preview: This allows you to run an export preview report manually. This report will tell you exactly what will and won't be moved during an export process. It will also alert you to any potential errors.

■ Report/Dependency: This allows you to run a dependency report on any object in the repository. For a given object, this report tells you what other objects may depend on it. For example, a template may have many postings that use it.

- File/Save Export Profile: This allows you to create an export profile. We'll learn more about profiles later in this chapter.
- Rights Options: If you want to back up and restore the groups and/or users associated with an object, you can use this option to create an SDO that includes this information. Backing up the user groups and rights is especially useful if you need to back up and restore the entire CMS database from one environment to another. You would first back up the rights groups from the destination, restore a database from a development source, and then import the rights groups back in to restore permissions.

### Import

Now that you've walked through a manual export process, let's look at the import process. The import interface is started in a similar way to the export interface. First, start Site Manager, and pick the File menu and then Package. From the submenu choose Import. This will start SDM in import mode. Figure 21–6 shows this choice on the File menu.

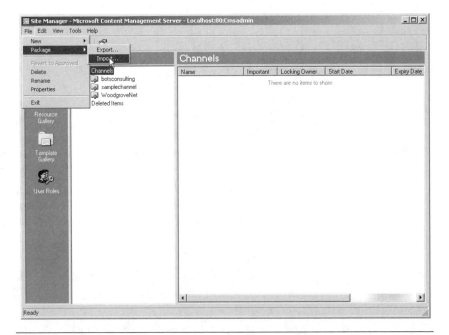

**Figure 21–6** Choosing Import from the Package menu

Once you've started SDM in import mode, let's open the SDO we created earlier and perform an import. Click the File menu and choose Open Package. Once you've done that, your SDO package will be listed at the bottom of the interface, in the Import from File (.sdo) field. Figure 21–7 shows the import interface with our BOTSConsultingSite. SDO chosen.

As you can see, the import interface has a few more choices. In a lot of cases, it's likely you can simply perform the import with the default settings. However, let's review each of the options in the interface, described in the following list, before we proceed. When Adding Containers:

- Inherit destination parent rights: This will reset the permissions that may be stored in the SDO and replace them with the destination container parent's rights. For example, if you were importing a channel into the root channel (Channels) and the root channel allowed anonymous access, the new channel would also allow anonymous access.

- Use package container rights: This option will import the rights group assigned to the imported containers. Essentially, you're going to retain whatever rights were assigned to the containers in the source system.

- Leave container rights list empty: This option imports the containers in the SDO with no rights assigned.

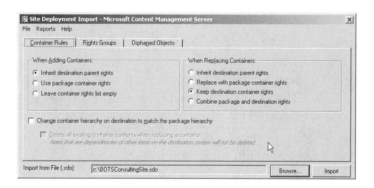

**Figure 21–7** The SDM import interface with our SDO selected

When Replacing Containers:

- Inherit destination parent rights: This option specifies that replaced containers are to inherit the users assigned to the parent container on the destination server.
- Replace with package container rights: Choose this option if you want to use the source container permissions.
- Keep destination container rights: This option replaces the imported container's permissions with the permissions specified on the corresponding container in the destination server; essentially, you're leaving the destination server's permissions on replaced containers intact.
- Combine package and destination rights: This option will combine the rights from the source and destination servers.
- Change container hierarchy on destination to match the package hierarchy: This option will restructure the destination container to match the SDO package.

  Delete all existing container contents when replacing a container: When you select the "Change container hierarchy . . ." option, you can also select an option for SDM to delete containers in the destination machine that don't have a corresponding object in the SDO. This option is useful for "resetting" a destination server to match the source (such as moving a site from staging to production for the first time).
- Reports/Import Preview: This generates a report similar to the report we saw in the export process. The report will show you what objects were imported, replaced, and/or deleted. Further, should there be any potential problems, the report will show you those as well.

---

**NOTE:** Templates will not be deleted if pages based on the template still exist in the destination server.

---

At this point, we should be set up for a basic import. To begin the import process, simply click the Import button. Once the import completes, SDM will give you a success or failure message and the opportunity to see the import report. In Figure 21–8, you can see a portion of our import report. If you refer back to Figure 21–5, you will see the corresponding section of the export report; the two should match.

So, now you should be familiar with the basics of importing and

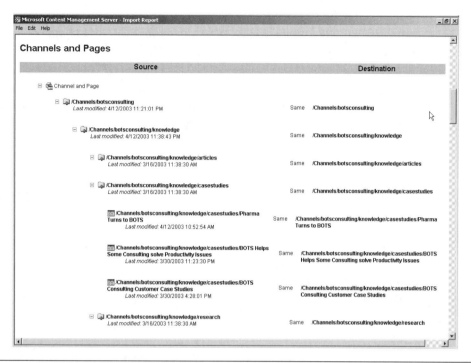

**Figure 21–8** A portion of the import result report

exporting objects. The interactive interface of SDM is a pretty easy tool to use and is quite handy. However, manually importing and exporting objects is not the best methodology if you have to continually move content between environments. As a result, Microsoft provides a COM-based interface to allow you to script an incremental import and export process. This COM-based interface can completely automate the process of importing and exporting content so that you can perform scheduled updates between, say, a development and staging environment or an authoring and production environment with little or no human interaction. In the next section, we'll show you how to create these incremental deployment scripts.

### Deploying Content through the COM Interface

Although the interactive interface of SDM is convenient for the ad hoc movement of CMS objects from one environment to another, any regularly scheduled incremental import/export should be automated. Microsoft provides a COM-based interface that allows you to create scripts that can be used to export and import objects on some regularly scheduled basis.

**NOTE:** The COM interface will only export content that's changed. However, it will import anything in the source SDO file.

The COM interface is broken into two parts—client and server—and then two subcomponents—import and export. Both the client and the server interfaces are the same from a functionality standpoint. The server object set is used to act on a local machine, and the client object is used for performing import or export tasks remotely. For example, if you were creating an export package on a source server, you'd use the server components. Once you've created the SDO package on the source server using the server component, you would transfer the SDO to the destination and use the client component on the source server to start a remote import process on the destination. In our examples, we're going to use the server object to export a package and then use the client object to perform the import. Both the server and the client deployment objects have virtually the same properties and methods.

### Export

To begin, we're going to create an incremental export script to perform an incremental export of our BOTS Consulting site. In our example, we're going to use a VBS file. However, the COM objects can be used from within an ASP page or a .NET script (using the COM Interop). We chose a VBS file because it was convenient and it allowed us to easily create a task in the Task Scheduler (covered at the end of this chapter).

In our VBS file, we start by creating an export object from the Cms DeployServer library. The export object will handle all aspects of the export process on the server. To create the CmsServerExport object, use the following code:

```
Set myCmsServerDeployment =
Wscript.CreateObject("CmsDeployServer.CmsDeployExport.1")
```

Next, you'll need to authenticate on the server. Remember, you can export content as a channel manager or an administrator. In our example we've embedded the user ID and password of our administrator for demonstration purposes. You could also pass in the credentials as parameters to the VBS file. The object model also provides an Authenticate AsCurrentUser method, which will use the current Windows user credentials, or the "run as" credentials if you use the Task Scheduler; choose the option that's appropriate for your environment.

```
Call myDeployObject.
AuthenticateAsUser("WinNT://CMSSERVER/admin","password")
```

Once you've authenticated on the server, you can stipulate your export options by setting the ExportOptions properties in the CmsDeploy Export object. There are only two options when exporting and they're both related to the export of security information. The IncludeRights Groups property allows you to determine whether you're going to export the rights groups in the SDO, and the IncludeCreatedBy property determines whether you're going to export the CreatedBy information (see Listing 21–1).

**Listing 21–1** Setting the export options in our VBS file

```
Set myExportOptions = myDeployObject.Options
If ( Err.Number <> 0 ) Then
        Call Msgbox(Err.Description, vbCritical, "Export Problem
Authenticating User")
     Set myDeployObject = Nothing
     Set myExportOptions = Nothing
     Exit Sub
End If


' Include Rights groups and their members.
'
' IncludeRightGroups:    (1) Do not export rights groups or users (default)
'                                     (2) Export rights groups
without members
'                                     (3) Export rights groups with
members
'
' IncludeCreatedBy:    (1) Do not include created by information
'                                  (2) Include created by
information (default)
'

myExportOptions.IncludeRightsGroups = 3
myExportOptions.IncludeCreatedBy = 2
```

Once you've set the export options, you can start the export. In our example, we added some additional code for stipulating the export package we wanted to create. The export returns a URL to an export report. In a noninteractive mode, you may want to simply redirect the output to a file for review later. In our example, we're starting a browser session to show the report immediately. Listing 21–2 shows our code.

**Listing 21–2** Setting the SDO file name and beginning the export process

```
Dim strPackageFileName, sdoDateQualifier
Dim strReportUrl


' Create a date qualifier for creating unique export names
sdoDateQualifier =  day(now()) & month(now()) & _
year(now()) & hour(now()) & minute(now()) & second(now())


' Set a string with the name and path of the SDO file
strPackageFileName = "C:\BOTSConsultingSite" & sdoDateQualifier & ".sdo"


' Start the deployment
' The first option specifies the name of the export file
' The second option specifies the time interval.  A value
' of 0 specifies to export all objects that have changed since
' the last export regardless of time.  A value of 1 or greater
' specifies the age of objects to be exported.  For example,
' a value of 200 stipulates that all objects that have changed in
' the last 200 minutes should be exported.
' The last option specifies the channel to export.  If no value
' is provided, the entire repository will be evaluated.  All objects
' from the specified channel and below will be evaluated if a value
' is provided.
strReportUrl =
myDeployObject.Export(strPackageFileName,0,"/Channels/botsconsulting")


If ( Err.Number <> 0 ) Then
     Call Msgbox(Err.Description, vbCritical, "Export Problem creating SDO
File")
     Set myDeployObject = Nothing
     Set myExportOptions = Nothing
     Exit Sub
End If
```

Now, to finish out our script, we've included some basic messages back to the administrator. Again, we're using the Msgbox object to indicate the status. However, in a noninteractive mode, you'll want to remove these references. In Listing 21–3, we've provided the complete script from beginning to end.

**Listing 21–3** The complete export script

```
Call ExportCMSObjects()

Sub ExportCMSObjects
      Dim myDeployObject
      Dim myExportOptions

      On Error Resume Next

      Set myDeployObject =
Wscript.CreateObject("CmsDeployServer.CmsDeployExport.1")

      If ( Err.Number <> 0 ) Then
            Call Msgbox(Err.Description, vbCritical, "Export Problem Creating
Deployment Object")
            Set myDeployObject = Nothing
            Exit Sub
      End If

      ' Server side call to authenticate as current user.
      Call
myDeployObject.AuthenticateAsUser("WinNT://DOMAIN/cmsadmin","password")
      'Call myDeployObject.AuthenticateAsCurrentUser()

      If ( Err.Number <> 0 ) Then
            Call Msgbox(Err.Description, vbCritical, "Export Problem
Authenticating the Admin User")
            Set myDeployObject = Nothing
            Exit Sub
      End If

      Set myExportOptions = myDeployObject.Options
      If ( Err.Number <> 0 ) Then
            Call Msgbox(Err.Description, vbCritical, "Export Problem
Authenticating User")
            Set myDeployObject = Nothing
            Set myExportOptions = Nothing
```

```
        Exit Sub
    End If


    ' Include Rights groups and their members.
    '
    ' IncludeRightGroups:    (1) Do not export rights groups or users
(default)
    '                                            (2) Export rights groups
without members
    '                                            (3) Export rights groups with
members
    '
    ' IncludeCreatedBy:    (1) Do not include created by information
    '                                      (2) Include created by
information (default)
    '


    myExportOptions.IncludeRightsGroups = 3
    myExportOptions.IncludeCreatedBy = 2

Dim strPackageFileName, sdoDateQualifier
Dim strReportUrl

' Create a date qualifier for creating unique export names
sdoDateQualifier =  day(now()) & month(now()) & _
        year(now()) & hour(now()) & minute(now()) & second(now())

' Set a string with the name and path of the SDO file
strPackageFileName = "C:\BOTSConsultingSite" & sdoDateQualifier & ".sdo"

' Start the deployment
' The first option specifies the name of the export file

' The second option specifies the time interval.  A value
' of 0 specifies to export all objects that have changed since
' the last export regardless of time.  A value of 1 or greater
' specifies the age of objects, in minutes, to be exported.
' For example, a value of 200 stipulates that all objects that
' have changed in the last 200 minutes should be exported.

' The last option specifies the channel to export.  If no value
' is provided, the entire repository will be evaluated.  All objects
' from the specified channel and below will be evaluated if a value
' is provided.
```

```
strReportUrl =
myDeployObject.Export(strPackageFileName,0,"/Channels/botsconsulting")

If ( Err.Number <> 0 ) Then
      Call Msgbox(Err.Description, vbCritical, "Export Problem creating SDO
File")
      Set myDeployObject = Nothing
      Set myExportOptions = Nothing
      Exit Sub
End If

      ' Create a scripting host shell to provide feedback to the user
      ' and start a browser session for the export report.
      dim winShell
      Set winShell = Wscript.CreateObject("Wscript.Shell")

      ' Show the export report in a web browser
      Call Wscript.Echo("Export has completed successfully.")
      Call Wscript.Echo("Starting browser session to display the export
report.")
      Call winShell.run("http://localhost" & strReportUrl)

      ' Dispose of the objects
      Set myDeployObject = Nothing
      Set myExportOptions = Nothing
      Set winShell = Nothing

End Sub
```

If you use the code we've provided, be sure to specify your domain name when authenticating as well as the appropriate export channel. Other than those two changes, the script should operate as described.

**NOTE:** One last mention—automated scripting is meant for incremental exports only; it's not meant to provide a mechanism for moving the entire repository. If you want to export the entire repository, you can use a SQL backup and restore or use the interactive SDM interface in Site Manager.

## Import

Once you've completed your export, it's time to import the content. As we mentioned in the export section, we're going to use the client object to perform the import. This will allow us to remotely connect to a CMS server to perform the import.

For the most part, the import process is very similar to the export. For the sake of brevity, we provide the following list of the general operations performed in the import process, and we share the script code in Listing 21–4.

- Create the client-side import object.
- Authenticate with the remote CMS server. As in the export example, we specify the credentials explicitly; you could authenticate as the current Windows user instead.
- Set the import options (the various settings are in the comments of our code example).
- Start the import process, pointing to the SDO file you want to process. The path has to be fully qualified.
- Show success and the import report.

**Listing 21–4** The import code example

```
Call ImportCMSObjects()

Sub ImportCMSObjects()

     Dim myDeployObject, myImportOptions
     Dim winShell

     On Error Resume Next

     Set myDeployObject =
WScript.CreateObject("CmsDeployClient.CmsDeployImport.1")

     If ( Err.Number <> 0 ) Then
           Call MsgBox(Err.Description, vbCritical, "Import Problem Creating
Import Object")
           Set myDeployObject = Nothing
           Exit Sub
     End If
```

```
      ' Authenticate against the remote server, either by stipulating the
credentials
      ' or using the current Windows user credentials.  These calls are
similar to the
      ' authentication methods for the export process, except you must also
provide
      ' the URL to the remote system.  Both methods are shown below.
      Call
myDeployObject.AuthenticateasUser("http://localhost/","WinNT://cmsdemo1/cmsad
min","password")
      'Call myDeployObject.AuthenticateAsCurrentUser("http://localhost/")

      If ( Err.Number <> 0 ) Then
            Call MsgBox(Err.Description, vbCritical, "Import Problem
Authenticating Admin User")
            Set myDeployObject = Nothing
            Exit Sub
      End If

      Set myImportOptions = myDeployObject.Options

      If ( Err.Number <> 0 ) Then
            Call MsgBox(Err.Description, vbCritical, "Import Problem Creating
Import Options")
            Set myDeployObject = Nothing
            Set myImportOptions = Nothing
            Exit Sub
      End If

      ' Set the import options
      ' IncludeCreatedBy            (1) This will set CreatedBy property of
all imported objects
      '                                 as the user running the
script (default)
      '                             (2) Retain the CreatedBy properties
of the origin objects.  If
      '                                 the original user does not
exist in the destination, set the
      '                                 CreateBy property to the user
executing the import.
      '
      ' RightsOnAdd                 (1) For objects that do not currently
exist in the destination
```

```
'                                          repository, leave all rights
blank.
'                                          (2) Inherit rights from the parent
container (default)
'                                          (3) Use the rights specified in the
SDO
'
'   RightsOnReplace       (1) Keep the existing destination container
rights. (default)
'                                          (2) Use the rights in the SDO file.
'
'   IncludeRightsGroups   (1) Do not import any rights groups or users
'                                          (2) Import rights groups without
users.  If the group already
'                                                   exists, keep the user list
intact
'                                          (3) Import groups and users
included in the SDO file.  If the
'                                                   rights group exists in the
destination, replace the user
'                                                   list with the one supplied in
the SDO file. (default)

    myImportOptions.IncludeRightsGroups = 2
    myImportOptions.RightsOnAdd = 3
    myImportOptions.RightsOnReplace = 2
    myImportOptions.IncludeCreatedBy = 1

    Dim strReportUrl

    ' Start the import operation
    strReportUrl =
myDeployObject.Import("c:\BOTSConsultingSite134200315235.sdo")

    If ( Err.Number <> 0 ) Then
        Call MsgBox(Err.Description, vbCritical, "Import Problem
Importing SDO")
        Set myDeployObject = Nothing
        Set myImportOptions = Nothing
        Exit Sub
    End If

    ' Provide message that operation completed successfully and open
    ' a browser to display the report
```

```
Set winShell = WScript.CreateObject("WScript.Shell")
Wscript.Echo("Import operation completed successfully.")
Wscript.Echo("Start a web browser to display import report.")
Call winShell.Run("http://localhost" & strReportUrl, 7)

' Dispose of the objects
Set myDeployObject = Nothing
Set myImportOptions = Nothing
Set winShell = Nothing
```

End Sub

Once you've completed your script, you should have a fully functional import process!

## Creating Profiles

When using SDM in an interactive mode, you may want to preserve certain predetermined settings for a deployment. For example, if you periodically need to export a specific set of objects, like new templates from development to production, you may want to create a profile. A profile allows you to preset deployment options and save them in a file, which can be used over and over again to perform a predetermined deployment.

There are two types of profiles in SDM. An export profile stores all settings for a predetermined export process. Conversely, an import profile stores all the settings for a predetermined import process. Creating profiles for semiregular export/import operations will ultimately save you time. Since we've covered a lot of ground in this chapter with regard to deployment, we're combining the creation of an export and an import profile in a more generic description of creating a profile; both operations are similar enough that they don't require separate explanations.

The first step in creating a profile is to start SDM interactively through Site Manager. Be sure to start SDM in the appropriate mode for the profile you wish to create. For example, if you want to create an export profile, start SDM in export mode. If you're creating an export profile, select all the objects you wish to export. In an import profile, you simply have to set how the import process occurs. Once you've finished making all the setting changes and/or selecting the objects, click the File menu. Next, click Save Import/Export Profile (Import or Export based on the mode you're in). Now, just browse to the directory where you want to save the profile, provide the profile with a name, and click OK.

When you're ready to use your profile, begin by opening SDM in interactive mode through Site Manager. When SDM appears, click the File menu and choose Open Import/Export Profile. Once the profile has loaded, SDM will automatically configure itself based on the settings in the profile. Now, just click the Import/Export button.

## Automating Package Processing

The scripts we provided in the previous sections give you the opportunity to automate the deployment process. However, to truly automate the deployment process, you need to be able to schedule running those scripts on some timed basis. We'll provide you with a brief explanation of using the Task Scheduler to help you with this process.

The Task Scheduler is a utility that ships with Windows 2000/2003. It allows you to schedule jobs to run on the server without human intervention. In the case of our deployment, we want to be able to schedule the export and import scripts to run without our having to start them every time; in reality, you may end up combining the two scripts into one to provide more seamless deployment. Here is a list of instructions for scheduling our export task.

1. Open the task schedule by choosing Start > Programs > Accessories > System Tools > Scheduled Tasks. If the option is not listed, it may not have been installed on your server. You can install the utility through the Windows installation routine.
2. In Figure 21–9, you'll see the Task Scheduler interface. Double-click the Add Scheduled Task icon to start the Scheduled Task Wizard.
3. When the wizard appears, click Next.
4. Click the Browse button when prompted for the application to run. Browse to the directory where your VBS files are stored, and select the VBS file you wish to run (Figure 21–10). Click Open when you've made your selection.
5. Type a name for your task. The default is the name of the file you've selected.
6. Select the reoccurrence. In our case, we've chosen to run the script daily (Figure 21–11). However, you should choose the period that makes sense for you and click Next.

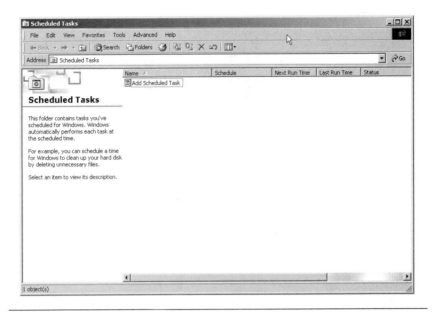

**Figure 21–9**  The Task Scheduler

7. Since we've chosen Daily, we're asked to provide the time and start date of this daily task (Figure 21–12). Once you've made your selection, click Next.

8. Now, choose the credentials under which your job will run (Figure 21–13). If you're using AuthenticateAsUser in your script, you only need to provide credentials for a user with authority to

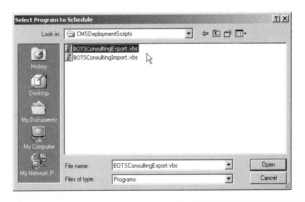

**Figure 21–10**  Select your VBS file

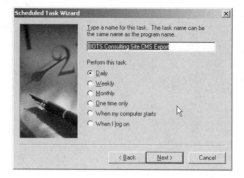

**Figure 21-11** Name your task and provide the timing

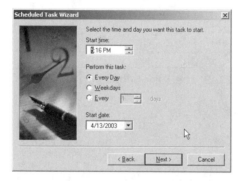

**Figure 21-12** Choosing the time of day and the start date

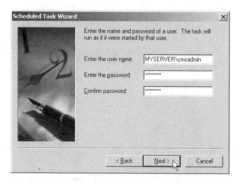

**Figure 21-13** Entering credentials for the scheduled job

run jobs on your server. If you used AuthenticateAsCurrent User, you'll have to provide the credentials of a user who is either a channel manager or an administrator.

9. Finally, you'll be prompted to finish the configuration (Figure 21–14). Just click Finish.

After your job has been scheduled, it will show up in the list of scheduled jobs, shown in Figure 21–15.

**Figure 21–14** The final confirmation prompt before adding the job

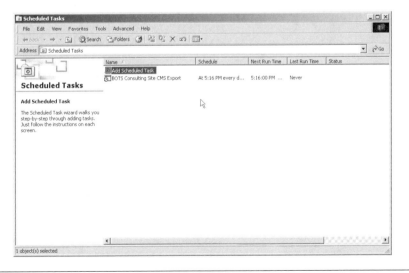

**Figure 21–15** Our task has been added to the scheduled jobs on the server.

## Summary

In this chapter we discussed how to deploy CMS packages. CMS provides a utility called Site Deployment Manager, which allows you to interactively import or export content. This utility also allows you to create profiles to eliminate the somewhat tedious tasks of reconfiguring a reoccurring import/export operation.

In addition to the interactive SDM interface, CMS provides a rich deployment API. This COM-based API allows you to script incremental deployments. Once the scripts have been created, you can schedule those scripts through the Task Scheduler in Windows.

# CHAPTER 22

# Deployment Scenarios

## Overview

Depending on the kind of application you're building with Content Management Server, it can be deployed in a number of ways. We'll start by discussing the various environments that may exist in any scenario. Then, we'll discuss how to combine the various environments for either an intranet or an Internet deployment. Finally, we'll discuss several guidelines for deploying your CMS site.

Before deploying your CMS application, make sure that you fully analyze your requirements. In addition to this book, another resource is Microsoft, which provides best practices in its product documentation and informational articles on http://msdn.microsoft.com or on the Web at http://msdn.microsoft.com/library/en-us/deploymt/htm/cms_de_deploy_hcte.asp.

## Environments and Deployment

It is a common practice in many firms to create separate environments within their infrastructure. Essentially, an environment is the collection of hardware, software, and staff to support your site at a given stage in the development cycle. The reason for this separation is to allow each environment to satisfy the needs of a specific audience or application without affecting any other. For example, a *development* environment would contain the hardware, software, and staff to support your developers and the creation or modification of functionality within your CMS-based Web application. This development environment typically has very early versions of code and/or components that are likely to be unstable or ill suited for a public or semipublic application. Since the hardware and software components in this environment are constantly changing, potentially breaking some features or functions while fixing others, the development environment is the domain of the development staff only.

In this section we'll discuss various environments you may consider implementing as part of a typical deployment. One deployment could be made up of one or more environments discussed here.

## Environment Guidelines

Overall, your particular deployment strategy will be unique to your organization. In addition, a deployment may be different based on the audience that will be using the application. However, there are some basic guidelines that can be used in various forms to create an overall deployment strategy for your CMS application.

- To begin, let's explore some of the questions you should ask as you plan your CMS deployment. Who is the primary audience of your application? Are the users of your application internal to your company (and your network), are they external, or are they a mix? Public facing applications have additional security requirements and should be more "locked down" than applications that are completely internal. An example would be a public Internet site verses an intranet application.

- How many content contributors will you have? How many content consumers will you have? These questions will help you determine the number of CMS servers you'll need for a given environment. For more information on capacity planning, refer to Chapter 35.

- Will you be hosting the CMS server internally or externally? If you're hosting CMS servers externally, you may want to limit the number of "moving" parts at the hosting provider. In other words, you probably only want to have one environment at the hosting provider and house all other environments internally. Also, most hosting services don't provide support for application servers like CMS, so it's a good idea to make sure that any environment that lives at a hosting provider be as clean as possible.

- Is the development of your CMS application done internally or externally? If it is primarily done externally, it may not be necessary to create a formal development environment; the group or firm performing the development will handle this environment. However, you may still want to have a quality assurance (QA) environment to allow your staff to properly test the application in your environment.

■ Is there a need to "test" content? Some organizations need to provide an extra review of the site, even beyond the typical workflow that CMS provides. If you have this requirement, you may need a content QA environment (sometimes called a staging environment). This environment will allow various members of your organization to review the complete Web site before it's published to the production environment.

■ How many developers are working on your site? The more developers you have, the more you need a technical QA environment where all the developers can contribute their code for testing. A technical QA environment will allow a group, other than the developers, to test all the components that have been written by the various developers. This environment could also be called "system test" since you're really doing a complete test of the application, as opposed to the component-level testing that a developer will typically perform. Another advantage of this environment is that it allows developers on the team to get the latest copies of code they're not writing.

■ How often does your content change? If your content changes frequently, you may want to create a content authoring environment. This environment will contain one or more CMS servers that are set up primarily to accept content from contributors.

## Creating Environments

In this section we'll briefly describe and show different environment types as they relate to CMS. Later, when we talk about specific deployment scenarios, we'll reference these environments to build a particular deployment.

The most basic environment is a development environment. The development environment, as discussed earlier, is where your developers will primarily work. This environment is made up of a central server and all the development workstations your developers will be using. The central development server will run a copy of CMS and SQL. Both tools can be loaded on one physical box or they can be separate; the choice is up to you. This central CMS server will hold the "master" copy of all the templates and controls that make up your application. Because it's not possible to perform "remote" development on CMS (i.e., you can't remotely connect to a CMS server using VS.NET), each developer workstation will have its own copy of CMS, along with VS.NET. Each of the developer workstations will then connect to the central SQL server so that they can share TGIs and postings. In this environment, each developer can develop their component of the application on their individual workstation. Once they're done, they either copy the component to the central server or simply check it in to the source control utility of their choice. The development environment will likely be configured to use Windows authentication and have guest access disabled. Figure 22–1 shows a logical diagram of what this environment might be like.

Depending on the complexity of your application, you may also want a QA environment. This environment will consist of one or more servers that can simulate your production environment. The QA environment may or may not have production content, but it will certainly have all the "final" templates, user controls, or other components. Ideally, you will test all aspects of functionality and performance to determine if the application performs acceptably. If this environment is configured exactly the same as your production environment, you should be able to

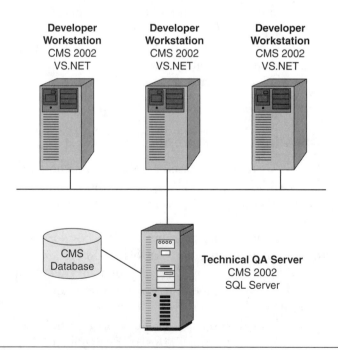

**Figure 22–1** A CMS development environment

accurately predict the application's behavior once it's been moved to your production environment. CMS, in this environment, will likely be configured for Forms authentication to allow your QA staff to test the different user roles. A picture of a QA environment is provided in Figure 22–2. Keep in mind, when we cover the production environment, you should be able to see similarities in the logical configuration without some of the physical network security.

Authoring in CMS does place a certain load on a CMS server and provides the ability to create content. As a result, Microsoft recommends that you have one or more CMS servers dedicated to content

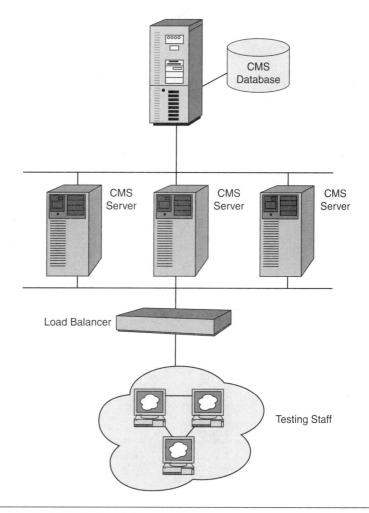

**Figure 22–2** A CMS QA environment

contribution. This environment not only reduces the load on the production environment, but also provides additional security by removing unnecessary entry points to CMS. This environment will consist of one or more authoring servers running a server edition of Windows in addition to one or more servers running SQL Server. CMS, in this environment, will likely be configured for Windows authentication without guest access enabled. Depending on the number of content contributors you have, the authoring environment may or may not be load balanced. In Figure 22–3 we've provided a picture of an authoring environment; we show a load balanced environment, even though it's not required.

Some firms want to perform additional quality tests to ensure proper application function. Although the code should have already been tested

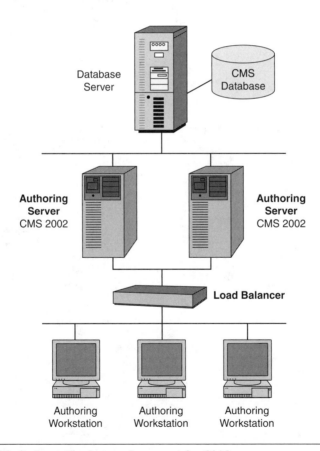

**Figure 22–3** An authoring environment for CMS

in earlier QA phases, a *staging* environment allows content-specific testing. This environment will allow you to perform additional quality tests on the site as it might look in production. Unlike the earlier QA environment, which may not contain production content, this environment will have both production content and a copy of all of the production code. As long as you do not need to perform additional load or performance testing, it's unlikely that you'll need more than one server, running both SQL and CMS. There may be some confusion between this environment and the QA environment we discussed earlier, since they seemingly accomplish the same thing. However, unlike the QA environment, the staging environment is primarily for taking one last look at the content that's been contributed and pushing the content, templates, and code to production; think of the staging environment as the last stop before your application goes live. The staging environment, like the QA environment, will likely use Forms authentication to allow the content to be viewed by the various user roles that may be visiting your site.

**NOTE:** The staging environment is logically set up similarly to the QA environment we've discussed here, so we didn't provide a figure.

The last environment you need to create is the production environment. This environment will serve your site to all content consumers. You should have at least one database server and one CMS server. We would always recommend load balancing two CMS servers for any site, regardless of traffic; load balancing makes maintaining your Web servers easier by allowing you to take one down to install patches or software updates. In addition, load balancing provides application integrity by reducing downtime caused by hardware failure. You may also want to consider database server clustering.

Depending on the kind of production environment you need, you could have one of several different authentication methodologies, such as Passport, Windows, or Forms; in an intranet environment, it's likely you'll use either Forms or Windows. For an Internet deployment, you'll probably use Passport or Forms, and you'll also enable guest (anonymous) access, whereas in an intranet environment, guest access will probably not be enabled. In Figure 22–4 we've provided a logical diagram of a typical production environment.

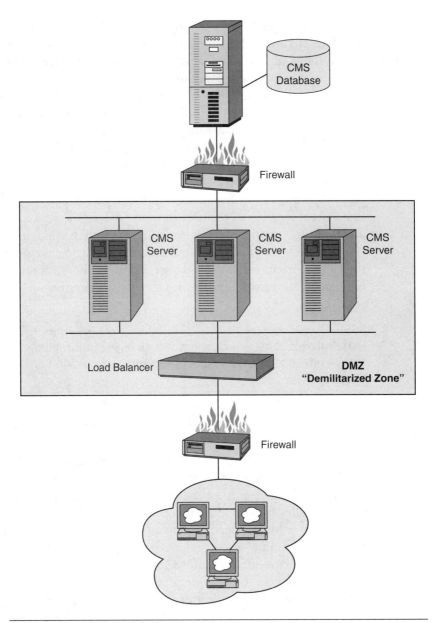

**Figure 22–4**  A production CMS environment

**Can You Combine the Authoring and Production Environments in One Physical Environment?**

There are various opinions on whether the authoring environment and the production environment can be the same. Microsoft generally recommends that the authoring environment and the production environment be separate for performance and security reasons. It is technically possible to combine both logical environments into one physical environment, but we would not recommend this configuration in a public site, although it may be appropriate for an intranet application. The primary reason, beyond security, not to combine the environments is performance—as you contribute content, you defeat your cache, thereby affecting performance (to what extent depends on your application). To determine the optimal configuration for your organization, you should consult network and software architects to review your specific requirements.

# Deployment Scenarios

Now that we've had a chance to discuss the various environments, we can begin to put them together for specific deployment scenarios. Each of these deployment scenarios will describe a generic application focus, such as an intranet or an Internet deployment. These deployment scenarios are meant to provide some guidance when you are deploying your application. However, you should always consult network and application architects to evaluate your specific needs.

**NOTE:** Extranet deployments share similarities with both intranet and Internet applications. However, extranets should generally be deployed similarly to Internet applications, since they technically serve users outside your physical network.

## Intranet Deployment

An intranet deployment describes how you might deploy a CMS-based application to a set of internal users. This application will also receive content from contributors inside your organization. One of the reasons you probably picked CMS for your intranet is that there are frequent content updates and/or you wanted to distribute the management of the intranet to the various groups that may own each of the microsites. Of the environments we discussed earlier, an intranet deployment typically includes a development environment, an authoring environment, and a production environment. In Figure 22–5 we've provided a somewhat abstracted "swim lane" drawing, which shows the flow of templates and content from the different environments that may exist for an intranet deployment.

In Figure 22–5 you can see the basic flow from one environment to another. From the development environment to the authoring environment, you use Site Deployment Manager (SDM) manually to move TGIs and channels as well as galleries. In addition, you would move the template files and other file-based assets, such as images and user controls. Microsoft recommends using Application Center Server to move file-based assets. However, you can simply copy the files using XCOPY.

Once the application-related components are copied to the authoring environment, content contributors can create content. As content is contributed, it is simultaneously deployed back to the development environment as well as to the production environment. Pushing content

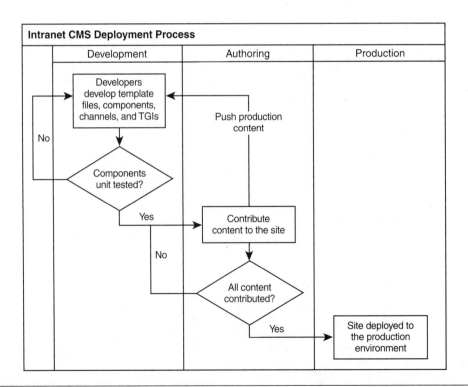

**Figure 22–5** A typical intranet deployment

back to the development environment (a manual operation) allows the developers to work with production content, simulating how the site looks in production. Be careful when you move content from authoring to development, because SDM will also try to move the templates associated with each deployed posting. The best way to handle this situation is to create an SDO file with your TGIs and galleries. Then, import the new postings from the authoring environment and reimport the original TGIs you exported in the first step.

After all of the content has been created, the production content and templates are deployed to the production environment. This is the last step in the process, where you're actually "publishing" both the application code and the content produced in earlier stages. The production environment, unlike the other environments, will be configured with only one read-only entry point (see Chapter 18 for more information on creating entry points). Unlike moving templates or postings between development and authoring, moving content to production will likely be automated using an incremental script. For more information on scripted deployments, refer to Chapter 21.

## Internet Deployment

An Internet deployment of CMS involves a few more steps than the intranet scenario. The Internet deployment and the intranet deployment share the development and authoring environments. However, given the public visibility of an Internet site, we would recommend adding some additional environments to properly test your application. In Figure 22–6 we provide a swim lane diagram that shows the progression of code and content in an Internet deployment.

You should immediately notice the additional environments added to the Internet deployment, the first of which is a QA environment. By adding a specific QA environment we're not suggesting that testing is less important in an intranet deployment. In fact, we're simply suggesting that Internet applications tend to be more complex, and because Internet sites are public, more testing may be necessary. This QA environment will allow a separate group of individuals to perform load and performance testing as well as full functionality testing. Unlike an intranet application, which has a predictable consumption audience, with a presumably standard set of software (e.g., browser version, utilities), an Internet site has a somewhat unpredictable traffic level, with users who have varied browser versions, desktop operating systems, and utility software.

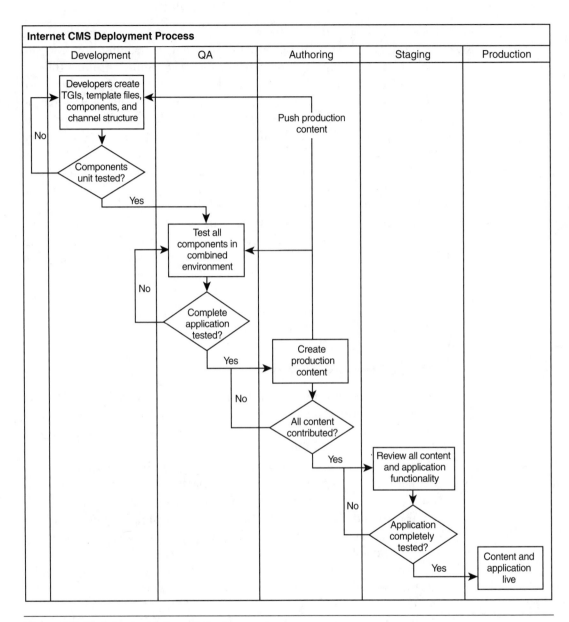

**Figure 22–6** A typical Internet deployment

In addition to the QA environment, the Internet deployment has a staging environment. The staging environment will provide an additional testing environment, which includes not only finalized code, but all production content. Just as the earlier QA environment provided the opportunity for rigorous testing of the application, the staging environment provides the same kind of environment for reviewing the content. You may be thinking that the QA environment theoretically takes care of content testing. However, traditional QA environments are primarily focused on application testing, not content testing. As a result, a real quality process isn't performed. For example, the staging environment will serve departments like marketing or legal, which may need to see "final" content in the context of the site before its deployment to the production environment.

In addition to providing a final QA environment for content, the staging environment is the "launch pad" for deployment to the production environment. Depending on the size of your site and the amount of content changes, having a staging environment provides a virtually dedicated environment to deploying content to the production environment. The staging environment may run not only CMS, but Application Center Server for deploying file assets. In this way, you can be assured that all necessary objects for deploying to production are in one place. Further, any load that deployment places on equipment doesn't affect environments that are heavily active, like authoring.

## CMS and Firewalls

In this section, we'll provide a brief overview of the firewall issues as they relate to CMS. Obviously, this discussion could entail an entire book since firewall security is a highly complex and exhaustive area of study. So we don't claim this discussion is exhaustive; rather, we are trying to point out some of the more basic considerations when it comes to deploying CMS on the Internet as it relates to your firewall structures.

As for any external Web site, one of the biggest issues is the network topology required to support the CMS infrastructure. An example network topology for a CMS Internet site infrastructure is shown in Figure 22–7.

In this example, there are two firewalls used to separate the production environment from the Internet and from the internal network.

### First Firewall

The first firewall separates the production CMS servers from the Internet originating traffic. It must have port 80 open for HTTP traffic, and if your site uses HTTPS, it must also have port 443 open for SSL. The production servers are clustered for scalability, with a network load balancer

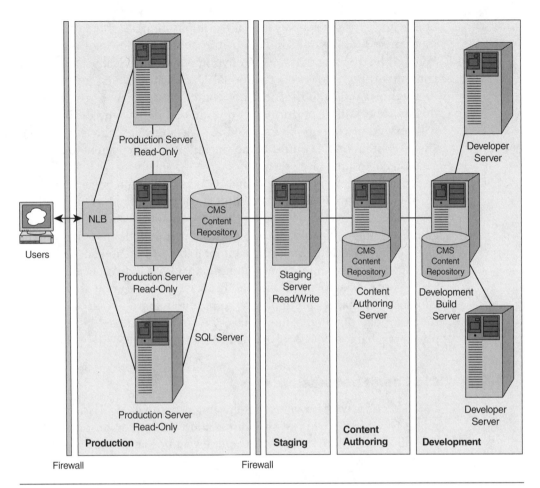

**Figure 22-7** CMS Internet site infrastructure

(NLB) that directs traffic to the servers to provide high availability and performance. Only the NLB IP address is exposed to the Internet. The advantage of NLB is that the clustered servers can all be accessed by a URL from the Internet.

---

**NOTE:** You can learn more about NLB by referencing the white paper *Understanding Network Load Balancing* from Microsoft.

---

Microsoft Application Center can be used for deployment of CMS assets, such as ASP.NET files and registry settings, from the staging environment to the production environment. If you are using Application

Center, you need to configure every production server in the cluster to use specified restricted TCP ports for DCOM.

> **NOTE:** By default, DCOM can use any TCP port from 1024 to 65535. This is not a firewall-friendly configuration, because leaving such a wide range of ports open presents a big security hole. To this end, we need to restrict the number of DCOM ports.

It is recommended that you use ports in the range above 5000 and allocate 15 to 20 ports. To set up DCOM port restrictions, using regedit32.exe create the registry key HKEY_LOCAL_MACHINE\ Software\Microsoft\Rpc\Internet, add a value named Ports with the data type REG_MULTI_SZ, and specify the data value as 5000 to 5020.

### Second Firewall

The second firewall separates the production environment from the internal network, which hosts the CMS development environment as well as the content authoring and staging environments. The site is deployed to the CMS production cluster from the staging environment. CMS Site Deployment uses port 80. If you plan to use the SCA on a production server, you will need to open port 443.

If you use Application Center for deployment, there are additional ports you need to open. Application Center requires that TCP ports 4243 and 4244 are open for data transfer, and TCP port 4242 is open for remote administration. You also need to open the DCOM ports that you configured on the production servers—for example, 5000 to 5020. In a DCOM environment, clients discover the port associated with a particular object by connecting to and using the services provided by DCOM's Service Control Manager (SCM). The SCM always operates at a fixed network port on every computer; this is always port 135 for both TCP and UDP.

Depending on your company security policy, you may consider changing the network topology discussed in our example. For instance, you may use an additional firewall in the production environment to separate CMS production servers and the SQL server hosting the CMS Content Repository (Figure 22–8). For simplicity, only one SQL server is shown; however, for resilience, high availability, and scalability, SQL servers may be clustered.

The second firewall in Figure 22–8 requires additional ports to be open for communication with the SQL server. By default, the SQL

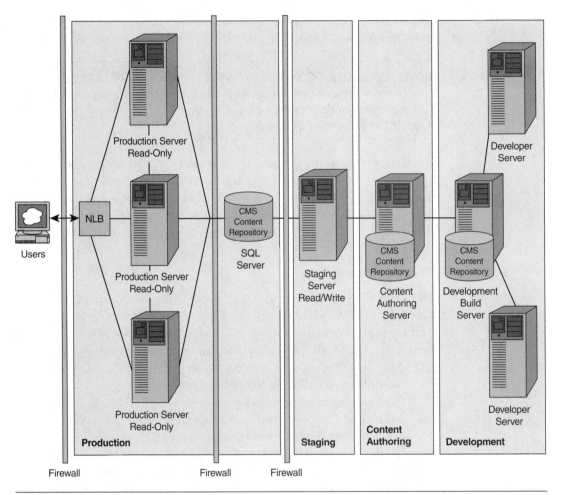

**Figure 22–8** CMS Internet site infrastructure, with production servers and SQL server separated by the firewall

server uses TCP port 1433 to receive data; this can be changed if required. The firewall should be configured to forward the production server IP address through the default port 1433 or through another TCP port configured for the SQL server to receive data. The SQL server uses UDP port 1434 to establish communications links from applications; therefore, the firewall should also be configured to forward requests for UDP port 1434 on the same IP address.

Once again, if you are using Application Center for deployment to the CMS production cluster using TCP, ports 4243 and 4244 need to be open for data transfer, port 4242 for remote administration, ports 5000 to 5020 for DCOM, and port 135 (both TCP and UDP) for SCM.

---

**NOTE:** If you wish to provide a full user acceptance testing (UAT) environment for your CMS site, you need to replicate the firewall configuration using a separate perimeter network.

---

How many firewalls to use in your environment must be defined based on the anticipated security risks and your company security policy.

## Deployment Guidelines

Regardless of the deployment scenario you're working with, there are some basic guidelines for deploying a CMS site.

- Create deployment profiles. Creating deployment profiles in SDM will eliminate the manual selection of objects to deploy and will reduce human error. You'll probably create several profiles for the manual deployments between environments.
- Use scripted incremental deployments for moving content to production. As content is added to the final environment, it can be moved automatically to production on a scheduled basis.
- Make sure to move file-based assets to an environment before using SDM to move CMS-based assets. Moving CMS-based assets to an environment before the file-based assets can cause errors. For example, if a TGI is moved to an environment before the template file, all postings dependent on that TGI will "break."
- Use a SQL backup and restore to initially move a CMS database. Especially for large repositories, using a SQL backup and restore will be faster than using SDM. However, if you're moving a database between environments that use different Active Directory structures, you'll have to manually reconfigure the destination CMS environment so that it uses the appropriate tree and user IDs.
- All environments up to production should use a common Active Directory structure. In an intranet deployment, all environments, including production, will likely use the same Active Directory structure. In an Internet deployment, however, the production environment will probably use a separate Active Directory structure. Keep this in mind when you've moving TGIs, channels, or

templates between environments. For most environments, you'll need to move groups and users along with the content. However, when moving content from production, you may or may not need to move groups and users.

## Summary

In this chapter we discussed how to deploy CMS. We started by discussing various environments that may make up a deployment scenario. These include a development environment, an authoring environment, and a production environment. After we provided the basic explanation for each environment, we discussed how to combine these environments into a deployment scenario. We specifically discussed deployment for an intranet and an Internet site. Finally, we provided some deployment guidelines to help you avoid some common pitfalls.

# Publishing API

# CHAPTER 23

# Introducing PAPI

There have been many APIs to grapple with over the years. We progressed from Win32 to Microsoft Foundation Classes (MFC) to Component Object Model (COM) to Application Template Library (ATL) to the .NET Framework. OK, we skipped a few; but sometimes you could get away with just a cursory understanding of the API. Not so with CMS.

Rarely will anyone implement a CMS solution without interfacing with the CMS Publishing API, commonly referred to as PAPI. Fortunately, Microsoft created a .NET-based version of the PAPI in the latest CMS release. PAPI now exposes nearly every facet of the underlying CMS engine. As with the .NET Framework, Microsoft even exposes the underlying base classes from which the CMS classes are derived.

In this chapter, we will discuss the principal objects of PAPI and how they relate, and we will touch on the base classes and namespaces from which they derive. In addition, we introduce the concept of Context, the primary topic of the next chapter.

Understanding the core CMS building blocks like channels, galleries, templates, postings, and placeholders will be very helpful as we progress through these chapters. These concepts are covered in depth in previous sections in this book. There is much to learn, so let's get started.

## Who Will Need PAPI

Since you are reading this book, it is most likely you. However, not everyone on a CMS project team will care about PAPI. Most of the predefined security roles, such as administrators, channel managers, resource managers, moderators, editors, authors, and subscribers, won't even be aware that PAPI exists. However, template designers, Web site engineers, application architects, and perhaps even information architects and operations personnel will be the key consumers of PAPI. If you have

VS.NET on your desktop and are planning on coding using CMS, you will want to understand this API.

Unlike many of Microsoft's products, CMS does not have many wizards or shortcuts. Although it is true that CMS integration into VS.NET makes an excellent template-building environment, for advanced CMS work, you will have to rely on PAPI. For example, PAPI will be required to construct site navigation, summary templates, custom placeholders, and much more.

## .NET-Based versus COM-Based APIs

Previous versions of CMS only had a COM-based API. However, Microsoft recommends using the .NET-based PAPI version discussed in this book for all new site development. If you have an existing CMS site that you want to migrate to the current release of CMS, the COM-based API will be helpful for this transition and has been enhanced to interact with the content stored in the newest CMS database schema. We briefly describe the COM-based API here.

The COM-based API included in the current release of CMS is primarily for backward compatibility with existing CMS 2001 Web sites and ASP development in the current release of CMS. The COM-based API is divided into the two groups of objects that follow:

- **Publishing objects:** All previously available functionality can be found in the Publishing group of COM components. However, a few methods and properties previously available in the Publishing group have been marked as deprecated. In all cases, newer methods and properties exist and provide developers with more control than the deprecated ones.
- **Site Deployment objects:** This new group can be used to automate incremental deployment of CMS Web sites from a development environment to a production environment or more generally from any source environment to one or more target environments.

---

**NOTE:** The COM-based API is only discussed briefly in this section of our book. Although the CMS Site Deployment functionality is only exposed through the COM-based API, most other references in this book are to .NET-based PAPI. There is a complete set of documentation about the COM-based API on MSDN.

---

Even though parts of the .NET-based PAPI are currently just a veneer (APIs available in previous versions of CMS are merely wrapped versions of the equivalent COM-based APIs, while the new APIs are managed code throughout), anyone doing new development is encouraged to use these interfaces because they will be carried forward in future releases of CMS, whereas the COM-based API will not. Microsoft wrapped the COM-based code using the .NET-based managed-code programming paradigm so that programmers could more easily use the future interfaces in VS.NET and languages like ASP.NET, VB.NET, and C#. The .NET-based PAPI sports a clean, new object model. As we see in the next section, all objects in that model are accessed through one entry point called a Context.

## Context as the Entry Point to PAPI

A Context is the entry point into PAPI from which all interrelated publishing objects exist and can be accessed and manipulated.

**NOTE:** In previous versions of CMS, what we refer to as Context was called Autosession. Autosession is still available in CMS when you are using an ASP-based solution. We will be covering the ASP.NET-based solution.

In a Web site, when an ASPX page runs, a Context instance is established by CMS using the intrinsic credentials and mode of the Http Request found in the query string. From that Context every other object can be immediately accessed. These interrelated objects do not need to be created in order to be used, because CMS will have already initialized and instantiated all the objects within the Context of the Posting or Channel we requested. The specific type of Context created by CMS on an ASP.NET Web site is a CmsHttpContext.

We cannot create an instance of CmsHttpContext, but we can get a handle to the instance that CMS created for our HttpRequest using the Current property. Since only one CmsHttpContext is allowed per running HttpRequest, Current either will return the instance that CMS created or it will create, initialize, and return a Context instance if it does not yet exist.

Unlike previous versions of CMS, the current release also allows for the creation of a Context in a stand-alone solution potentially outside the confines of IIS. Using the CmsApplicationContext class, we can instantiate a Context using the credentials of our choosing in the mode of our choosing. Although most of the objects in the model can be accessed in much the same way as they are within a CmsHttpContext, the concept of a current Posting and a current Channel don't make sense and therefore aren't available. Specific Channels and Postings can certainly be located and manipulated using the Searches property.

---

**NOTE:** The next chapter covers `CmsHttpContext` and `CmsApplication Context` in depth. The Searches property is covered in detail in Chapter 28.

---

Once we have a Context, we can access the objects in the object model. So, let's discuss what we have at our disposal.

# Principal Objects

The PAPI object model illustrated in this chapter primarily focuses on the objects that are most commonly used. Objects in the model that correspond to the following entities in CMS are referred to as principal objects: Context, Channel, Posting, Template, TemplateGallery, Resource, ResourceGallery, Placeholder, and PlaceholderDefinition. These are all discussed in detail from an API perspective in the chapters that follow. Principal objects are the tangible objects that are frequently accessed in an ASPX code-behind in template files. For instance, dynamic navigation and breadcrumbs are typically generated using the channel hierarchy and Posting collections on nearly every page of most sites.

We have also included in the object model the following support objects in CMS, referred to as auxiliary objects: CustomProperty, Custom PropertyDefinition, Searches, SessionSettings, User, and various collections (most of which are covered in the illustrated model).

Some objects are not depicted in our PAPI object model. These objects implement a wide range of concepts in the current release of CMS but don't fit easily into a graphical representation. These include publishing events (which enable code-based customization of workflow), the Web Author, caching of whole and partial Web pages, limited security, and processing exceptions.

# PAPI Object Model

The .NET-based PAPI object model includes all the traditional classes that CMS has always supported and some new classes as well. For instance, Templates are now accessible from the API.

Although the root of all CMS objects is the Context in which the request was made, things can get a bit confusing because objects can contain collections of objects that in turn can contain collections of objects ad infinitum. These collections contain objects that have objects that point back to the containing collection and potentially even the Context. The cyclical nature of the object model can be somewhat daunting and difficult to illustrate. So, we break it into eight separate related submodels.

Object models typically show objects and collections of objects, and their relationship to one another. PAPI is represented in this way in Figures 23–1 through 23–8. To concisely represent the infinite possibilities of this model, we use markers to reference common objects found within the model. Table 23–1 shows which marker represents each PAPI object.

So, we give you the PAPI object model, starting with Context (Figure 23–1).

As stated earlier, Context is the entry point into the CMS object model. As illustrated, we can access the current Channel or the current Posting. Remember, the CmsHttpContext object is instantiated and

**Table 23–1** PAPI Objects and Their Object Model Markers

| PAPI Object | Object Model Marker |
| --- | --- |
| Channel | C |
| Posting | P |
| ResourceGallery | RG |
| TemplateGallery | TG |
| Template | T |
| Placeholder | PH |
| Searches | S |

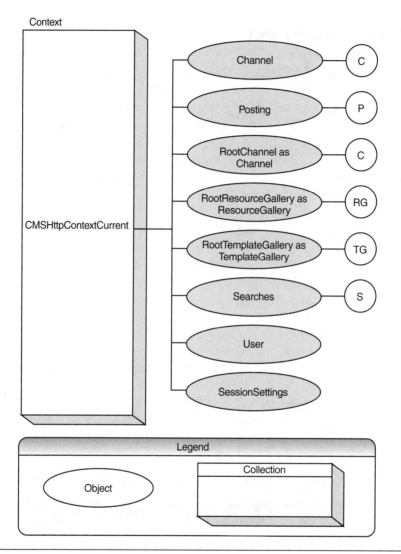

**Figure 23–1** PAPI object model—Context

initialized in the ASP.NET DLL before an ASPX template file is run. In contrast, the CmsApplicationContext object is instantiated manually by the developer, and it provides access to a subset of objects that is nearly the same as the set of objects that are accessible through Cms HttpContext.

There is a polymorphic object (not illustrated in Figure 23–1) that provides access to the ChannelItem, which, depending on the current state of the request or the requested asset, will provide access to the current Posting, if available, or to the current Channel.

There are references to the root object for each of the three hierarchies: RootChannel, RootResourceGallery, and RootTemplateGallery. Be aware that the roots will always be the built-in CMS objects called Channels, Resources, and Templates. So, if the Posting being viewed was in the leaf Channel of a hierarchy like this—/MyChannel/Cool Channel/SubChannel—the RootChannel of SubChannel would be the built-in Channels Channel rather than MyChannel. So, a better representation would look like this—/Channels/MyChannel/CoolChannel/SubChannel. This is similar to a hard drive, where C:\ is the root directory rather than one of the subdirectories.

Searches is a powerful, if potentially expensive, property that can be used to locate specific objects. We describe the Searches objects in Figure 23–8 and give example code for each property in Chapter 28.

The User object is very weak in this release of CMS. There isn't very much that can be done programmatically with the User object outside of a couple of names and whether the user is in the Everybody group.

Lastly, the Context includes a SessionsSettings object that determines things like the automatic filtering of hidden items in collections and what locale an internationalized site will use.

A Channel (Figure 23–2) in a CMS Web site is the conceptual equivalent of folders (directories) in a Windows file system. Channels serve as containers for Postings and other Channels. Since a Channel can contain other Channels, the Parent property is the Channel that the referencing Channel is contained within. So, if we had a Channel hierarchy like this—/MyChannel/CoolChannel/SubChannel—the parent of SubChannel would be CoolChannel, the parent of CoolChannel would be MyChannel, and the parent of MyChannel would be the built-in Channels object. The parent of the built-in Channels object is null.

---

**NOTE:** We will explore all aspects of the Channel object in the API in Chapter 25.

---

On a Windows file system, a subdirectory can contain other subdirectories and/or files. Similarly, Channels can contain other Channels or Postings. So, not surprisingly, there is a potential collection of Channel objects and a potential collection of Posting objects in every Channel. CMS also provides an all-encompassing collection called AllChildren that contains all the members of both the Channels and the Postings collections.

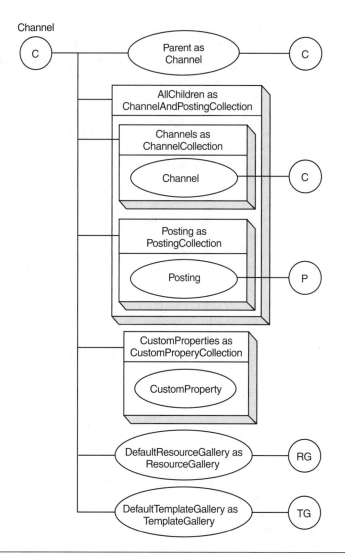

**Figure 23–2** PAPI object model—Channel

---

**NOTE:** All CMS collections can be iterated using the .NET Framework's foreach syntax.

---

Each Channel has a potential collection of name/value pairs called CustomProperties. Some people use a CustomProperty to capture the constraints on an object. Each CustomProperty has an associated Custom PropertyDefinition.

**NOTE:** We cover the use of channel custom properties in Chapter 16.

The DefaultResourceGallery and the DefaultTemplateGallery for a Channel contain the Resource objects and Template objects that authors are encouraged to use when creating new Postings in that Channel. However, authors are not limited to using only the default gallery; they can use any gallery that they have access to. If our code references either of these objects, and they have not previously been set to a value, CMS will throw a trappable error.

A Posting (Figure 23–3) in a CMS Web site is a particular instance of a Template, combined with content for each of its Placeholders. Just as with a Channel, the Parent property of a Posting is the Channel that the referenced Posting is contained within. So, a Posting's Parent property has all the members that a Channel object has.

**NOTE:** We will explore all aspects of the Posting object in the API in Chapter 26.

A ConnectedPosting shares Placeholder content with the referenced Posting. So, there is a potential collection of ConnectedPostings. Checking the IsConnected property of a Posting will establish whether there are ConnectedPostings or not. Likewise, there is a potential collection of ConnectedTemplates. A ConnectedTemplate represents the various ways that a given Posting's content can be rendered.

Like the Channel object, each Posting object has a potential collection of name/value pairs called CustomProperties.

**NOTE:** We cover the use of posting custom properties in Chapter 5.

Every Posting will likely have one or more Placeholders in which content contributors put their content. So, naturally, there is a potential collection of Placeholder objects.

Every Posting is based upon a specific Template, so just as naturally, there is a specific Template object for the referenced Posting.

Postings can be changed over time. It is possible that the current Posting is not yet approved or published. So, PAPI provides the WorkingRevision Posting object as a way to get to an unpublished version of a Posting object in code.

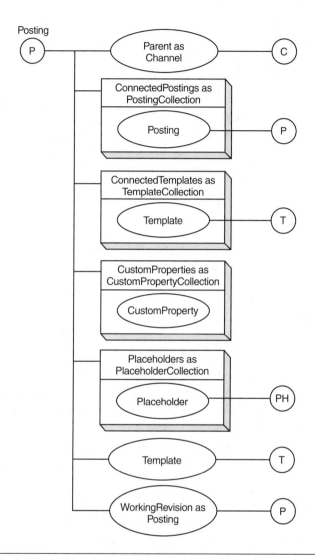

**Figure 23–3** PAPI object model—Posting

A ResourceGallery (Figure 23–4) is a container for Resources and other ResourceGalleries in the CMS Resource hierarchy. It is a hierarchical structure that has parents and children, much like the Channel object that we discussed earlier in this chapter. However, a Resource-Gallery object contains multimedia Resource objects (including images) used to create Templates and Postings rather than the Postings themselves. Resources are basically content stored in the CMS Content Repository that are referenced by URLs from CMS Postings.

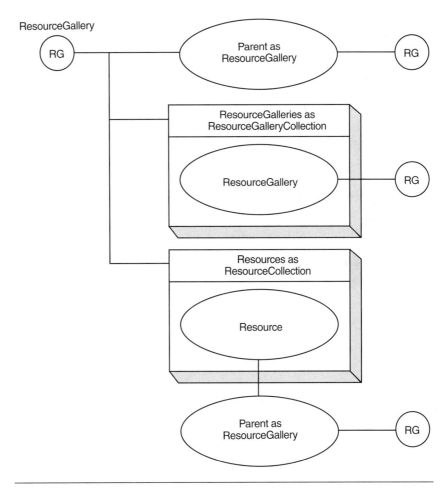

ResourceGallery

**Figure 23–4** PAPI object model—ResourceGallery

Since a ResourceGallery can contain another ResourceGallery, the Parent property is the ResourceGallery that the referenced Resource Gallery is contained within. So, if we had a ResourceGallery hierarchy like this—/MyResourceGallery/CoolResourceGallery/SubResourceGallery— the parent of SubResourceGallery would be CoolResourceGallery, the parent of CoolResourceGallery would be MyResourceGallery, and the parent of MyResourceGallery would be the built-in Resources object. The parent of the built-in Resources object is null.

**NOTE:** We will explore the use of a resource gallery in Chapter 9.

There wouldn't be much use for a ResourceGallery without a collection of Resource objects. It isn't surprising that a referenced Resource object has a Parent property that identifies the ResourceGallery in which that Resource object is located.

A TemplateGallery (Figure 23–5) is a container for Templates and other TemplateGalleries in the CMS Template hierarchy. It has parents and children much like the Channel object that we discussed earlier in this chapter. However, a TemplateGallery contains Template objects used to create Postings rather than the Postings themselves.

Since a TemplateGallery can contain another TemplateGallery, the Parent property is the TemplateGallery that the referenced Template Gallery is contained within. So, if we had a TemplateGallery hierarchy like this—/MyTemplateGallery/CoolTemplateGallery/SubTemplateGallery— the parent of SubTemplateGallery would be CoolTemplateGallery, the parent of CoolTemplateGallery would be MyTemplateGallery, and the parent of MyTemplateGallery would be the built-in Templates object. The parent of the built-in Templates object is null.

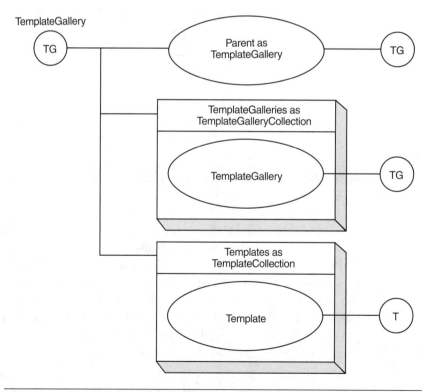

**Figure 23–5** PAPI object model—TemplateGallery

**NOTE:** We will explore the use of a template gallery in Chapter 9.

There wouldn't be much use for a TemplateGallery without a collection of Template objects. We illustrate the Template object in Figure 23–6.

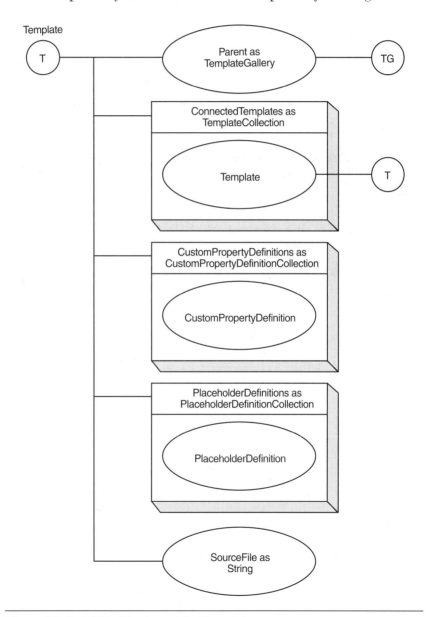

**Figure 23–6** PAPI object model—Template

A Template is the logical representation of a physical template file upon which one or more Postings may be based. Each Template object has a Parent property that indicates in which TemplateGallery the referenced Template object can be found.

The Parent object of a Template is the TemplateGallery that the referenced Template object is contained within. So, a Template's parent property has all of the members that a TemplateGallery object has.

Each Template has a potential collection of ConnectedTemplates. Checking the IsConnected property of a Template will establish whether there are ConnectedTemplates or not.

Similar to the Channel object, each Template object has a potential collection of custom values called CustomPropertiesDefinitions.

---

**NOTE:** We cover the use of templates in Chapter 12 and template custom properties in Chapter 10.

---

Every Template will likely have one or more PlaceholderDefinitions that describe the structure of the template file. So, naturally, there is a potential collection of PlaceholderDefinition objects. We illustrate the Placeholder object in Figure 23–7.

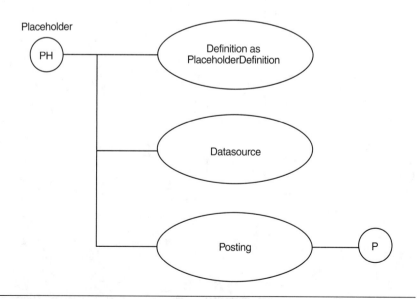

**Figure 23–7** PAPI object model—Placeholder

A Placeholder object polymorphically encapsulates a particular type of content in a CMS Posting. A Posting orchestrates the displaying of content in a collection of Placeholders based upon the positioning and style dictated by an underlying Template (and template file), using PlaceholderDefinition objects as a logical reference to the physical placeholder controls found in the file system. The following is a list of the various placeholder types that come with CMS: AttachmentPlaceholder, HtmlPlaceholder, ImagePlaceholder, InvalidPlaceholder, Office AttachmentPlaceholder, OfficeHtmlPlaceholder, and XmlPlaceholder. A developer can create a custom Placeholder to handle unique content.

---

**NOTE:** We will explore all aspects of the Channel object in the API in Chapter 25, and the Searches object in the API in Chapter 28. We explored the use of Placeholders in Chapter 13.

---

As important as Placeholders are to CMS, the object model for them isn't very complex. Logically, each Placeholder has an associated PlaceholderDefinition object.

A Datasource object allows a Placeholder object to use a source other than CMS to save and load its data. Cool.

The referenced Placeholder will belong to a specific Posting, so there is a Posting object with all the members of a posting. This behaves much the same way you would expect a Parent property (which isn't available) would behave.

The Searches method enables you to search for Channels, Postings, Templates, TemplateGalleries, Resources, and ResourceGalleries that match specific criteria. As you can see depicted in the object model (Figure 23–8), most searches return a collection of objects, but there are three that return a single polymorphic object.

The results of a search will typically need to be cast as a specific data type in order for the object to be assigned to a variable. The following two lines of code both are equally effective at casting the search result as a posting:

```
myPosting = CmsHttpContext.Current.Searches.GetByGuid(sGuid) as
Posting;
myPosting = (Posting) CmsHttpContext.Current.Searches.GetByGuid
(sGuid);
```

The code in this book typically casts objects using the "as" keyword followed by the data type because it is easier for the code to flow to

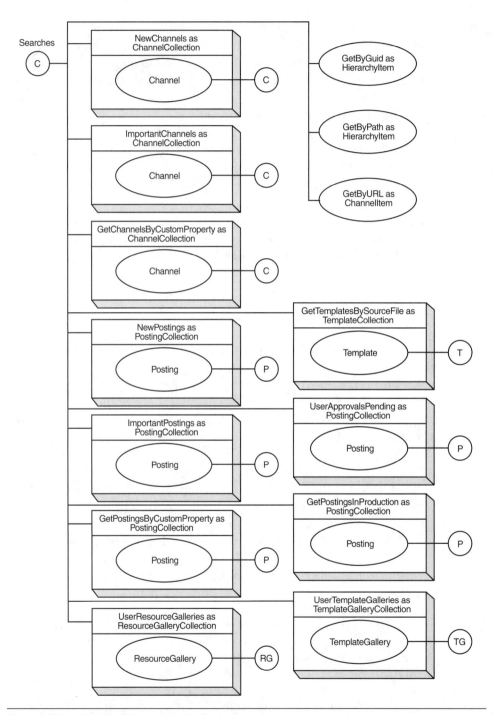

**Figure 23–8** PAPI object model—Searches

multiple lines, which is good for displaying code in a limited-width book. However, preceding the cast object with the data type in parentheses works just as well in VS.NET.

Like most CMS objects, the Searches object automatically takes into consideration the rights and privileges of the User, the current Mode, and the possibility that multiple versions of an object exist when performing a search. Deleted items are never returned.

# Relationship between Principal Objects

With a little thought, we can mostly infer relationships between the principal objects from the object model.

Relationships written as business rules (similar to the cardinality and optionality that might be captured for a database model) follow:

- A CmsHttpContext has one and only one current Channel.
- A CmsHttpContext may have zero or one current Posting.
- A CmsApplicationContext has no current Channel.
- A CmsApplicationContext has no current Posting.
- Any Context has one and only one RootChannel.
- Any Context has one and only one RootResourceGallery.
- Any Context has one and only one RootTemplateGallery.
- Any Context has one and only one Searches engine.
- Any Context has one and only one User.
- Any Context has one and only one SessionSettings.

If a Channel includes the following objects—Channel, RootChannel, Parent as Channel, and member of a ChannelCollection—then the following rules apply:

- A Channel may have zero or one Parent as Channel.
- A Channel may have zero or one collection of Channels.
- A Channel may have zero or one collection of Postings.
- A Channel may have zero or one collection of CustomProperties.
- A Channel may have zero or one DefaultResourceGallery.
- A Channel may have zero or one DefaultTemplateGallery.

If a Posting includes the following objects—Posting, WorkingRevision, and member of a PostingCollection—then the following rules apply:

- A Posting has one and only one Parent as Channel.
- A Posting may have zero or one collection of ConnectedPostings.
- A Posting may have zero or one collection of ConnectedTemplates.
- A Posting may have zero or one collection of CustomProperties.
- A Posting may have zero or one collection of Placeholders.
- A Posting has one and only one Template.
- A Posting may have zero or one WorkingRevision as Posting.

If a ResourceGallery includes the following objects—Resource Gallery, RootResourceGallery, Parent as ResourceGallery, Default ResourceGallery, and member of a ResourceGalleryCollection—then the following rules apply:

- A ResourceGallery may have one or zero Parents as Resource Gallery.
- A ResourceGallery may have zero or one collection of Resource Galleries.
- A ResourceGallery may have zero or one collection of Resources.
- A Resource has one and only one ResourceGallery.

If a TemplateGallery includes the following objects—Template Gallery, RootTemplateGallery, Parent as TemplateGallery, Default TemplateGallery, and member of a TemplateGalleryCollection—then the following rules apply:

- A TemplateGallery may have one or zero Parents as Template Gallery.
- A TemplateGallery may have zero or one collection of Template Galleries.
- A TemplateGallery may have zero or one collection of Templates.

If a Template includes the following objects—Template and member of a TemplateCollection—then the following rules apply:

- A Template has one and only one Parent as TemplateGallery.
- A Template may have zero or one collection of Connected Templates.
- A Template may have zero or one collection of CustomProperty Definitions.

- A Template may have zero or one collection of Placeholder Definitions.
- A Template has one and only one SourceFile.

If a Placeholder includes the following objects—Placeholder and member of a PlaceholderCollection—then the following rules apply:

- A Placeholder has one and only one Definition as Placeholder Definition.
- A Placeholder has one and only one DataSource.
- A Placeholder has one and only one Posting.

Searches will be discussed at length in Chapter 28.

# Base Classes

As previously mentioned, in the .NET-based PAPI, Microsoft has exposed the underlying base classes from which the CMS classes are derived. These classes are typically not intended to be instantiated. They are exposed for the purpose of highlighting class inheritance as an important aspect of the .NET programming paradigm.

Let's put the CMS Context classes into context (Figure 23–9). The items with dotted lines are discussed in other chapters in this book.

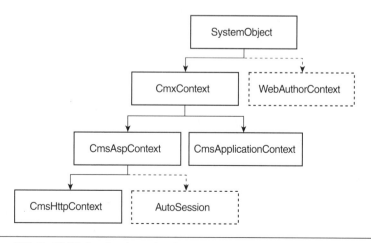

**Figure 23–9** CMS Context context

The System.Object class is the ultimate superclass of all classes in the .NET Framework. As such it supports all classes in the .NET Framework class hierarchy and provides low-level services to classes derived from it. System.Object is the root of the .NET type hierarchy.

CMS derives CmsContext, the base class for all classes that allow you to access PAPI, from System.Object. The CmsContext class provides the base properties and methods common to CmsHttpContext (the context of a CMS Web page), CmsApplicationContext (the context when there is no posting URL involved, as is the case in Web Services, stand-alone applications, and Web pages that need a context other than the one handed them by CMS), and Autosession (the context used in older versions of CMS and in ASP pages for the current release of CMS). We discuss the first two of these contexts separately in Chapter 24.

Interestingly, Microsoft has included one additional level of abstraction called CmsAspContext. This intermediate class inherits a lot of its functionality from CmsContext but adds critical functionality for accessing channel- and posting-specific content common to both CmsHttp Context and Autosession (this COM-based component is included for backward compatibility with previous versions and for ASP-based CMS development). So, CmsAspContext and CmsApplicationContext are on the same level in the class hierarchy, but we will never interact directly with CmsAspContext.

The HierarchyItem class provides the base functionality for dealing with all three CMS hierarchies. ChannelItem, ResourceGalleryItem, and TemplateGalleryItem all provide the unique functionality common for their respective hierarchy.

Similarly, the CmsCollection class provides the base functionality for dealing with CMS collections. CmsManagedCollection, HierachyItem Collection, and ChannelItemCollection then provide the various specific collections with the unique functionality common for their respective collections.

Placeholder and PlaceholderDefinition provide the base functionality for dealing with CMS Placeholders, while LegacyPlaceholder provides functionality for placeholder types used in previous versions of CMS.

CMS has nine types of exceptions that all inherit their base functionality from the CmsException and CmsPublishingException base classes.

# Exploring Namespaces

Although this concept is not necessarily new, the .NET Framework adopted the concept of a namespace. Think of a namespace as a way to categorize classes so that they are easy to find. For the same reason you use meaningful subdirectory names in a file system rather than keeping all your files in the root, CMS classes are organized into ten meaningful namespaces (generally referred to as PAPI).

## .Publishing Namespaces

The CMS .Publishing namespaces are by far the largest group of classes, referencing nearly every aspect of a CMS site. They are subdivided into the four groups that follow:

- **Microsoft.ContentManagement.Publishing namespace:** This group contains the core classes used to interact with CMS, such as obtaining Context (Chapter 24), traversing channels (Chapter 25), managing postings (Chapter 26), and locating assets (Chapter 28). These and other classes are all accomplished through this namespace.
- **Microsoft.ContentManagement.Publishing.Events namespace:** This group contains classes used for reacting to things that are happening when users are interacting with CMS. Extending the default CMS publishing workflow (Chapter 31) and responding to workflow and events (Chapter 6) are key tasks that can be accomplished using classes in this namespace.
- **Microsoft.ContentManagement.Publishing.Extensions.Placeholders namespace:** This group contains classes used for manipulating placeholder definitions (for placeholder controls see the .WebControls namespace). There are classes for each distinct type of content, including HTML, images, XML, and attachments. Classes specifically for MS Word are found in the final .Publishing namespace.
- **Microsoft.ContentManagement.Publishing.Extensions.Placeholders.Office namespace:** This group contains classes used for manipulating placeholder definitions populated by the Authoring Connector (Chapter 7). There are classes for Office HTML and Office attachments.

## .Web Namespaces

The CMS .Web namespaces are automatically used for working with ASP.NET Web applications and are subdivided into the three groups that follow:

- **Microsoft.ContentManagement.Web namespace:** This group contains classes used for ensuring that CMS-enabled Web applications properly release resources, extending the ASP.NET Output Cache directive to support caching by several new VaryByCustom attributes: CmsPosting, CmsControl, CmsRoles, CmsUser, and so on. This namespace is referenced by VS.NET by default and should not be removed unless you intend to handle caching and authentication in a proprietary way.

- **Microsoft.ContentManagement.Web.Caching namespace:** This group contains classes used for registering a cache validation callback for the current posting, not caching unpublished content, and spoiling the cache when changes are made within the CMS server.

- **Microsoft.ContentManagement.Web.Security namespace:** This group contains classes used to ensure that all users are authenticated, for managing both CMS and ASP.NET authentication tickets (cookies).

## .WebControls Namespaces

The CMS .WebControls namespaces automatically manage placeholder controls, helper controls, and console controls. They are subdivided into the three groups that follow:

- **Microsoft.ContentManagement.WebControls namespace:** This group contains classes used for manipulating intrinsic and custom placeholder controls (Chapters 13, 27, and 29), including retrieving saved content and saving new content, and managing authoring, presentation, and error mode containers. This namespace is referenced by VS.NET by default and should not be removed.

- **Microsoft.ContentManagement.WebControls.Console Controls namespace:** This group contains classes used for manipulating and responding to console-specific controls and events, dictating what you want to happen when a posting is published, and automatically naming the creation of a new posting.

- **Microsoft.ContentManagement.WebControls.Design name-space:** This group contains classes used to provide the user inter-face for design-time editing of PlaceholderToBind property values in VS.NET. CMS uses this class to manage the user inter-face that you see when you are setting up a placeholder definition. This is the namespace you would override to change the default design-time interface for this editor. This is not a common need.

If you have spent any time working with the .NET Framework, you probably already know about referencing namespaces. Similarly to the way header files in C++ or Project References in legacy VB are handled, VS.NET first needs to be able to find the appropriate DLLs that contain the classes you want to use in your project.

To reference a namespace in a VS.NET project, expand the built-in References folder from the Solution Explorer window, and you will see the DLLs that VS.NET includes in the project by default. PAPI .Pub-lishing, .Web, .WebControls, and many others should be listed. Right-click the built-in References folder and select Add Reference (Add Web Reference is for referencing Web Services) from the pop-up menu (Fig-ure 23–10).

A quick browse through the list of .NET assemblies in the resulting Add Reference dialog may still leave you wondering where the CMS

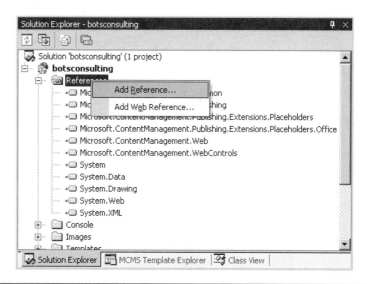

**Figure 23–10** Add Reference in VS.NET

DLLs live. Click the Browse button and navigate to the following default installation directory (if CMS is installed in another directory, you will need to use that installation path to find them): C:\Program Files\Microsoft Content Management Server\Server\bin\*.dll (Figure 23–11).

Notice that many of the DLLs have exactly the same name and a one-to-one correspondence with their namespace. Nice. Some namespaces have been consolidated into a single DLL. That is OK too. The DLLs that you will most commonly reference are .Common.dll, .Publishing.dll, .Publishing.Extensions.Placeholders.dll, .Web.dll, and .WebControls.dll.

Now that the VS.NET project knows where to find the DLLs that contain the namespaces starting with Microsoft.ContentManagement, we can reference them independently in each of our Web Form (ASPX) and Web Control (ASCX) pages. At the top of the code-behind file for these pages, where we need to use a class from any of the ten namespaces that we discussed earlier, we simply include a statement using that namespace. So, for instance, if we wanted to get the CMS current Context (Figure 23–12), we would include the following statement:

```
using Microsoft.ContentManagement.Publishing
```

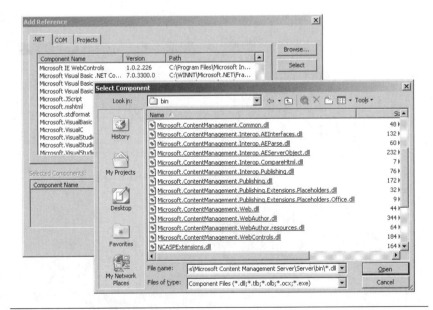

**Figure 23–11** Selecting CMS DLLs

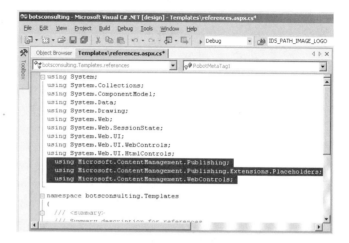

**Figure 23–12** Namespaces used in CMS Template

## Summary

We covered a lot of ground to become familiar with the foundations of PAPI. In this chapter we established that nearly every CMS project will need to use PAPI. We discussed the need for a new .NET-based PAPI, and we touched on the legacy COM-based API. We introduced the concept of Context and its importance to the CMS infrastructure. We discussed the details about significant objects found in the PAPI object model, the principal objects among them, and their relationship to one another. We talked about the base classes (common functionality) and namespaces (class organization) used by PAPI. In the next chapter, we delve deep into CMS Context, the key to accessing all other CMS objects.

# CHAPTER 24

# Obtaining Context

Now that we've been introduced to PAPI, let's dig in a little deeper. In order to interact with PAPI, we will need to gain access to a CMS entry point commonly referred to as a CMS Context. The dictionary defines "context" as the interrelated conditions in which something exists or occurs. CMS defines Context as *the* entry point into PAPI from which all interrelated publishing objects exist and can be accessed and/or manipulated. Said another way, Context is the only way to programmatically get to CMS functionality.

## CMS Context

Figure 24–1 depicts the boundaries of a CMS Context.

From the CMS Context we can, given sufficient user rights, access and manipulate all channels, including the current channel (if there is one); access and manipulate all postings, including the current posting (if there is one) and the placeholder objects that they contain; access and manipulate both the template gallery and the resource gallery, including everything that they contain; and access and manipulate templates and their placeholder definitions. We can only access a few characteristics about the current user, and, unfortunately, we cannot manipulate the CMS security structure.

**NOTE:** We cover setting up user rights in detail in Chapter 17.

It is also possible to create temporary PlaceholderControls, but template files cannot be permanently altered through PAPI.

The two types of Context we explore in this chapter are CmsHttp Context and CmsApplicationContext.

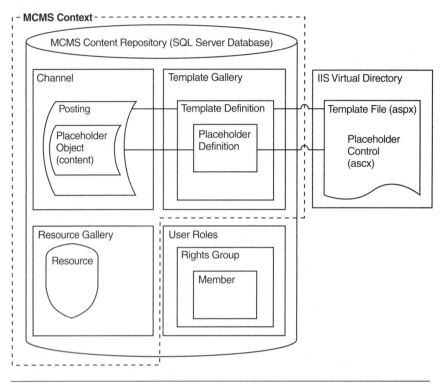

**Figure 24-1** CMS Context

---

**Scratchpad**

You are going to need a way to see the results of the code we write throughout Part VI. Sometimes it helps to simplify the environment so that you know everything that went into its creation. Most of what we do in these chapters will be the equivalent of using a scratchpad to do math problems. In the end, it isn't what is on the scratchpad that has any value; it is the principles that you learned from what you did on the scratchpad. Anything that is done of any consequence can be readily ported to your real project.

Steps for creating the Scratchpad posting used throughout Part VI:
Create a new channel. (See Chapter 16 for help with creating channels.)

1. Using Site Manager as a CMS administrator, create a new channel called Scratch. Just take all the defaults.
2. In the Properties of the new Scratch channel, select the Publishing tab and remove all text, if any, from the Script URL text box in the Channel Rendering section.

Create a new VS.NET project. (See Chapter 10 for help with creating projects.)

3. Using VS.NET, create a new C# project called http://localhost/vs Scratchpad using the MCMS Web Application template.
4. When prompted, authenticate as a CMS administrator.

Create a new template file. (See Chapter 12 for help with creating a template file.)

5. Using the VS.NET Solution Explorer, add a New Item called Scratch-padTemplate.aspx using the MCMS Template File template.
6. In the Properties of the new ScratchpadTemplate.aspx, change the page-Layout from GridLayout to FlowLayout.
7. Drop the following Web Form controls onto the ScratchpadTemplate.aspx Design palette: TextBox, Label, ListBox, and Button.
8. Use the Enter key after each control to place each control on its own line.
9. Change the width of the TextBox, Label, and ListBox to 600px.
10. Drop the DefaultConsole.ascx from the Console directory onto the Scratch padTemplate.aspx Design palette after the Web Form Button control.
11. Double-click the Web Form Button control to create the Button1_Click function in the code-behind window.

Create a new template definition. (Again, see Chapter 12 for help with creating a template definition.)

12. Using the VS.NET MCMS Template Explorer, create a new template called ScratchpadTemplate.
13. In the TemplateFile property of the new ScratchpadTemplate, enter the text "/vsScratchpad/ScratchpadTemplate.aspx" or select the Scratchpad Template.aspx file.
14. Select Build Solution from the VS.NET Build menu.

Create a new posting based upon the new template in the new channel. (See Chapter 5 for help with creating a posting.)

15. Using Internet Explorer, browse to the Scratch channel: http://local host/Scratch.
16. When prompted, authenticate as a CMS administrator. If you get the Home-port page instead of the channel Welcome page, you forgot to remove the Script URL in step 2 when creating the channel. You can do it now.
17. Click the Switch to Edit Site link, click the Create a New Page link, click the Templates link under the Template Gallery column, and select the ScratchpadTemplate.

**18.** Click the Save New Page link.

**19.** In the resulting dialog, enter "Pad" into the Name text box and click the OK button.

**20.** Click the Approve link and then close Internet Explorer.

Open Internet Explorer and browse to http://localhost/Scratch/Pad to see the Pad posting (Figure 24–2) we created. You may be required to authenticate.

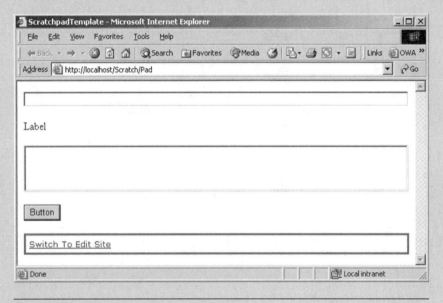

**Figure 24–2** Scratchpad in Internet Explorer

Now we can repeatedly enter code into the Button1_Click function of the underlying template file, refresh the browser, and see the results of that code in this posting. Sweet.

# CmsHttpContext

CmsHttpContext is an object that represents the ASP.NET entry point into PAPI. It is instantiated by CMS on our behalf when we are interacting with a CMS-aware Web application. CMS gets the four pieces of information it needs to create a CmsHttpContext primarily through the QueryString:

- Authenticated user
- Publishing mode

- Channel
- Posting

In a Web application, either the user is authenticated by the application using Integrated Windows security, Forms-based authentication, propriety authentication, IIS anonymous access using the ASP.NET and IUSR_ Machinename users, or guest access is enabled and CMS authenticates the user using the guest account. There are variations on each of these security approaches, but in all cases the user is authenticated as a specific user.

---

**NOTE:** Unless guest access is enabled, on pages where the user has not yet authenticated (like a typical login form), the CmsHttpContext will return an access denied error.

---

The URL QueryString usually specifies a specific posting in a specific channel for CMS to retrieve. It will also typically contain the publishing mode for CMS to create the Context in. If a publishing mode is not provided, the mode defaults to Published.

---

**NOTE:** In previous versions of CMS, what we refer to as Context was called Autosession. Autosession is still available in CMS when you are using an ASP-based solution. We will be covering the ASP.NET-based solution.

---

Perhaps a code sample is the best way to explain.

Open VS.NET to any project you can code in, or follow the steps in the Scratchpad sidebar. Although it is not the best programming practice, we will leave references to all elements as the default names the VS.NET IDE gives to them. In essence, we need to create a template file with the following ASP.NET Web Form controls—TextBox, Label, ListBox, and Button—using their default properties plus the default console, of course. It should look something like Figure 24–2. We will be repeatedly replacing the contents of the Button1_Click function.

Double-clicking the Web Form Button control in the Design palette will create the Button1_Click function in the code-behind of the template file. Replace the entire function with the following code:

```
private void Button1_Click(object sender, System.EventArgs e)
{
  //1. Grab the current CMS context
  CmsHttpContext cmsContext = CmsHttpContext.Current;
```

```
//2. Populate the label with the Publishing Mode
Label1.Text = cmsContext.Mode.ToString();
}
```

At the top of the code window is a list of namespaces in use. If there isn't a line that looks like the following, you will need to add it:

```
using Microsoft.ContentManagement.Publishing;
```

Choose Build Solution from the VS.NET Build menu (Ctrl-Shift-B) or from the drop-down menu that results from right-clicking the solution name. When the build is done, the text

```
Build: 1 succeeded, 0 failed, 0 skipped
```

should be displayed at the bottom of the VS.NET Output window. Compile errors, if any, will need to be addressed before you proceed. VS.NET does a pretty good job of providing feedback when things aren't quite right.

Open Internet Explorer and browse to http://localhost/Scratch/Pad. Click the Button, and the label will display Published (Figure 24–3) in place of its default value of Label.

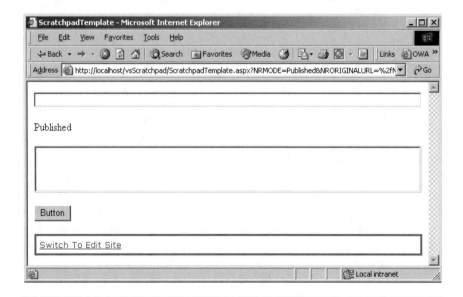

**Figure 24–3** Current Context publishing mode

Click the Switch to Edit Site link, and then click the Button again. This time the label displays Unpublished. Cool.

Let's take a closer look at that code. The first executable line looks like this:

```
CmsHttpContext cmsContext = CmsHttpContext.Current;
```

We are declaring a variable named cmsContext (this can be any name we choose), using CmsHttpContext as the data type and immediately assigning it to the Current property of the existing CmsHttp Context that CMS creates for us using the IIS ISAPI filter when the posting is requested. Notice that there is not a new constructor but a declarative assignment statement instead. Current is declared by the CmsHttpContext class as Static, so it does not require the "new" keyword to instantiate it. Because there is only one CmsHttpContext allowed per HTTP request, the Current property controls access, ensuring that additional instances are not created. The CmsHttpContext class cannot be inherited or created by any other class.

The second executable line looks like this:

```
Label1.Text = cmsContext.Mode.ToString();
```

Position your cursor just after the cmsContext variable name and type a period. An Intellisense window (Figure 24–4) should appear.

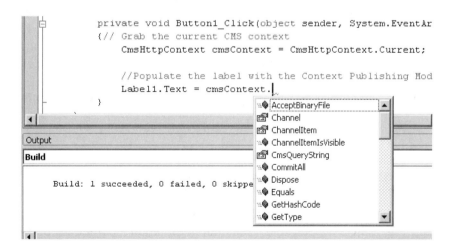

**Figure 24–4** Exploring CmsHttpContext Intellisense

Take a close look at the items in the list. Compare it with Table B-1 in Appendix B. Choose any property (preceded by an icon of a hand pointing to a paper) and type ".ToString( );" after it. For instance, if we used the first property in the list, Channel, the resulting assignment statement would look like this:

```
Label1.Text = cmsContext.Channel.ToString();
```

Build the solution and then browse to or refresh the posting in Internet Explorer. Click the Button, and the label will display the value of the current channel rendered as a string. Since we didn't choose a specific property (characteristic) of the Channel object, like `cmsContext.Channel.DisplayName.ToString()`, .NET just shows us what type of object it is. So, Label displays the text

```
Microsoft.ContentManagement.Publishing.Channel.
```

Spend some time just toying with the different items in the Intelli sense list. The worst that you could do is end up with syntax errors. Remember, every change made in the code window will only be reflected in the browser after a successful VS.NET build.

---

**NOTE:** The first attempt to browse a recently compiled page will require a just in time (JIT) compilation of the changes so it will consequently take longer than subsequent requests.

---

But we have a problem—we can't use the CmsHttpContext if we need to access CMS with a different set of credentials than were provided by the user, or when we need to use a different mode than the posting is in (although it is possible to redirect the user to another publishing mode, we may not want to), or when we aren't in a posting at all. For situations where the CmsHttpContext isn't available or isn't what we need, we use the CmsApplicationContext.

## CmsApplicationContext

Unlike previous versions of CMS, the current release allows the creation of a Context in a stand-alone situation—potentially outside the confines of IIS. For instance, console-based applications, Web Services, or WinForm applications, to name a few, can benefit from the use of a CmsApplicationContext. CmsApplicationContext is the entry point into

PAPI for applications when there is no URL involved. It can also be very useful in a Web application when the current CmsHttpContext isn't what we need. CMS needs the following two pieces of information to fully hydrate a CmsApplicationContext object:

- Authenticated user
- Publishing mode

There is no URL, so channel and posting are not provided. This type of Context is never automatically created for us, so we create an instance of this object using a constructor. The CmsApplicationContext provides four methods for authenticating the Context (discussed in detail later in this chapter) as a specific user in a specific publishing mode. So, we can instantiate a Context using the credentials of our choosing in the mode of our choosing. Outside of the constructor and authentication methods, the functionality of the CmsApplicationContext is inherited from the same base class as CmsHttpContext. So, aside from not having a current Channel object or a current Posting object, the CmsApplicationContext works much the same way that the CmsHttpContext did. Specific Channel and Posting objects can certainly be located and manipulated using root hierarchy properties or the Searches property.

**NOTE:** The Searches property is discussed at length in Chapter 28.

Also, all three hierarchies (channel, resource gallery, and template gallery) are available using the CmsApplicationContext class.

Because we control the creation of CmsApplicationContext, the number of instances that we can create is limited only by the hardware. But like the CmsHttpContext class, the CmsApplicationContext cannot be inherited by any other class.

When we are using CmsApplicationContext, it is possible to expend a large amount of time between an object's modification and the commitment or abandonment (rollback) of that modification. Because other users may be blocked from accessing areas of the site while these transactions are in an uncommitted state, CommitAll should be called swiftly after any modification. As always, is not recommended that you wait for a response from the user before calling CommitAll.

**NOTE:** When you are using a CmsApplicationContext to alter an object, users can be blocked from using portions of CMS if alterations are not swiftly committed. Also, transactions must be committed one at a time.

The "new" keyword must be used when you are declaring the CmsApplicationContext Context. For instance, earlier we used the following code to get a handle to the CmsHttpContext in our template file:

```
CmsHttpContext cmsContext = CmsHttpContext.Current;
```

But to get a handle to the CmsApplicationContext in a stand-alone situation, we would use something similar to the following code:

```
CmsApplicationContext cmsContext = new CmsApplicationContext();
```

Next we need to use one of the four authentication methods of the CmsApplicationContext class; otherwise, this new Context doesn't know what credentials or mode to use, and we won't be able to access or manipulate anything. If we skip this step, we will receive one of those verbose .NET error pages that basically says, Login required. The requested action can only be performed after a successful login has been completed. The current session is not logged in.

The four authentication methods are:

- AuthenticateAsUser
- AuthenticateAsGuest
- AuthenticateAsCurrentUser
- AuthenticateUsingUserHandle

## AuthenticateAsUser

In our initial example, we will use the AuthenticateAsUser method to authenticate to CMS. This method requires, at a minimum, the programmer to provide values for a user name, password, and publishing mode (Update, in this example). The values for the user name and password could be hardcoded, but we are going to use the ClientAccount Name of the current user and a password entered into the TextBox on our posting. The mode will be hardcoded to Update. This implies that the account we log in with must have sufficient security rights to update the posting. If we log in with an invalid user, or, more likely, we forget to type our password into the TextBox, we will receive one of those verbose .NET error pages that basically says, Login attempt failed. Access is denied.

Replace the Button1_Click function of our Scratchpad template with the following code:

```
private void Button1_Click(object sender, System.EventArgs e)
{
  //1. Grab an Application Context
  CmsApplicationContext cmsContextApp =
    new CmsApplicationContext();
  //2. Log in to CMS
  //   Use User ID used to authenticate to Posting
  //   Use password in TextBox
  //   Put the created Context into Update mode
  cmsContextApp.AuthenticateAsUser(
    cmsContextHttp.Current.User.ClientAccountName,
    TextBox1.Text,
    PublishingMode.Update);
  //3. Populate the label with the user name and mode
  Label1.Text = "<b>UserName:</b>" +
    cmsContextApp.User.ToString() +
    " <b>AppMode: </b>" + cmsContextApp.Mode.ToString();
}
```

The comments should adequately explain what the code is doing. Build the solution and then browse to or refresh the posting in Internet Explorer. Type your password into the TextBox and click the button labeled Button. The page should reload, and the Label should display the following (Figure 24–5):

**UserName:** WinNT://Machinename/UserName **AppMode:** Update

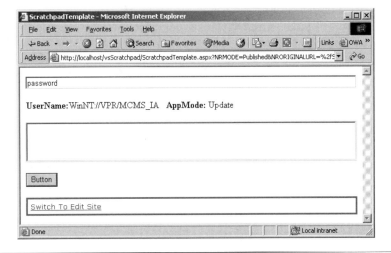

**Figure 24–5** AuthenticateAsUser

where Machinename will be the name of your PC, assuming it is hosted on localhost, and UserName will be the user name you used to authenticate to the application.

If you forget to enter your password or the password isn't for the user in cmsContextHttp.User.ClientAccountName, you will receive one of those verbose .NET error pages that basically says, Login attempt failed. Access is denied.

## AuthenticateAsGuest

Next we will use the AuthenticateAsGuest method to authenticate to CMS. This method requires the programmer to simply provide the publishing mode (Update, in this example) with which the guest user will be authenticated. The built-in guest account will be used to authenticate. If the guest account hasn't been enabled and configured by the CMS Server Configuration Application (SCA), we will get one of those verbose .NET error pages when we run this code that basically says, The current user does not have rights to the requested item.

---

**NOTE:** Using the Server Configuration Application is discussed at length in Chapter 18.

---

This implies that the account we log in with must have sufficient security rights to update the posting. If we log in with an invalid user, we will receive one of those verbose .NET error pages that basically says, Login attempt failed. Access is denied.

Replace the Button1_Click function of our Scratchpad template file with the following code:

```
private void Button1_Click(object sender, System.EventArgs e)
{
  //1. Grab an Application Context
  CmsApplicationContext cmsContextApp =
    new CmsApplicationContext();
  //2. Log in to CMS as Guest
  //   Will only work if Guest Access is enabled in the SCA
  cmsContextApp.AuthenticateAsGuest(PublishingMode.Update);
  //3. Populate the label with the user name and mode
  Label1.Text = "<b>UserName:</b>" +
    cmsContextApp.User.ToString() +
    " <b>AppMode: </b>" + cmsContextApp.Mode.ToString();
}
```

The comments should adequately explain what the code is doing. The only difference between this code sample and the previous one is the way in which we are authenticating the CmsApplicationContext. Build the solution and then browse to or refresh the posting in Internet Explorer. The only visible change in the output is the user name displayed, and, of course, no password was required in the text box (Figure 24–6).

## AuthenticateAsCurrentUser

Next we will use the AuthenticateAsCurrentUser method to authenticate to CMS. This method requires the programmer to simply provide the publishing mode (Update, in this example) with which the CmsApplicationContext will be authenticated. The current user will be used to authenticate.

---

**NOTE:** Be aware, AuthenticateAsCurrentUser may not work as you expect within an ASPX page. IIS has its own set of users (like ASPNET, IUSR_Machinename, and IWAM_Machinename) that it uses to perform things while processing a Web request. It will also behave in different ways depending on the impersonation settings in the web.config and machine.config files. Authentication modes selected for the CMS virtual directory in IIS can also have an impact.

---

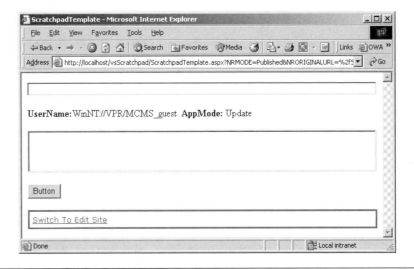

**Figure 24–6** AuthenticateAsGuest

If the guest account is enabled and configured by the CMS Server Configuration Application, it will be used to authenticate, and we will see the actual IIS user being used in the resulting posting. Alternatively, the ASP.NET user (usually ASPNET) could be configured by Site Manager with sufficient security rights to update the posting. However, if one of these options isn't implemented, we will receive one of those verbose .NET error pages that basically says, Login attempt failed. Access is denied.

Replace the Button1_Click function of our Scratchpad template file with the following code:

```
private void Button1_Click(object sender, System.EventArgs e)
{
  //1. Grab an Application Context
  CmsApplicationContext cmsContextApp =
    new CmsApplicationContext();
  //2. Log in to CMS as Guest
  //   Will only work if Guest Access is enabled in the SCA
  cmsContextApp.AuthenticateAsCurrentUser(PublishingMode.Update);
  //3. Populate the label with the user name and mode
  Label1.Text = "<b>UserName:</b>" +
    cmsContextApp.User.ToString() +
    " <b>AppMode: </b>" + cmsContextApp.Mode.ToString();
}
```

The comments should adequately explain what the code is doing. The only difference between this code sample and the previous one is the way in which we are authenticating the CmsApplicationContext. Build the solution and then browse to or refresh the posting in Internet Explorer. The only visible change in the output is the user name displayed (Figure 24–7).

### AuthenticateUsingUserHandle

Finally, we will use the AuthenticateUsingUserHandle method to authenticate to CMS. This method requires the programmer to provide a WindowsIdentity token along with the publishing mode (Update, in this example). The user associated with that WindowsIdentity token (the actual current Windows user, in this example) will be used to authenticate in that mode.

The guest account must be enabled and configured by the CMS Server Configuration Application to use this mode. The Windows user must also be configured by Site Manager with sufficient security rights

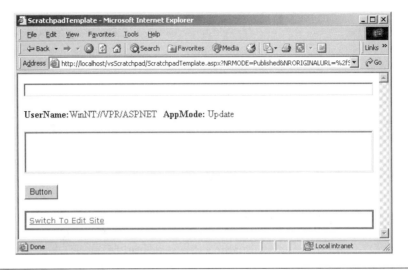

**Figure 24–7** AuthenticateAsCurrentUser

to update the posting. Also, the IIS Web site must be configured using Windows authentication.

---

**NOTE:** Setting up IIS security is covered in Chapter 19.

---

As previously stated, these conditions must all be met, or we will receive one of those verbose .NET error pages that basically says, Login attempt failed. Access is denied.

Replace the Button1_Click function of our Scratchpad template file with the following code:

```
private void Button1_Click(object sender, System.EventArgs e)
{
  //1. Grab an Application Context
  CmsApplicationContext cmsContextApp =
    new CmsApplicationContext();
  //2. Assign current Windows User to a WindowsIdentity variable
  //   This will only work if IIS is set to Windows Authentication
  //   and Guest Access is enabled in the SCA
  System.Security.Principal.WindowsIdentity identCurrentUser =
    System.Security.Principal.WindowsIdentity.GetCurrent();
  //3. Log in to CMS
  //   Use the currently authenticated Windows User for credentials
```

```
//   Put the created Context into Update mode
cmsContextApp.AuthenticateUsingUserHandle(
   identCurrentUser.Token, PublishingMode.Update);

//4. Populate the label with the user token and mode
Label1.Text = "<b>UserToken:</b>" +
   identCurrentUser.Token.ToString() +
   " <b>AppMode: </b>" + cmsContextApp.Mode.ToString();
}
```

The comments should adequately explain what the code is doing.
The second line of code is key; it retrieves the token that we use to seed
this authentication method. Build the solution and then browse to or
refresh the posting in Internet Explorer. The only visible change in the
output is the user name displayed (Figure 24–8).

When you are using Windows authentication, the identity of the
current user under CmsApplicationContext can be affected by the value
of the identity tag in the web.config and/or machine.config files. The
current user will not be the authenticated Windows user unless you
enable impersonation—<identity impersonate="true" />—in one of the
.config files.

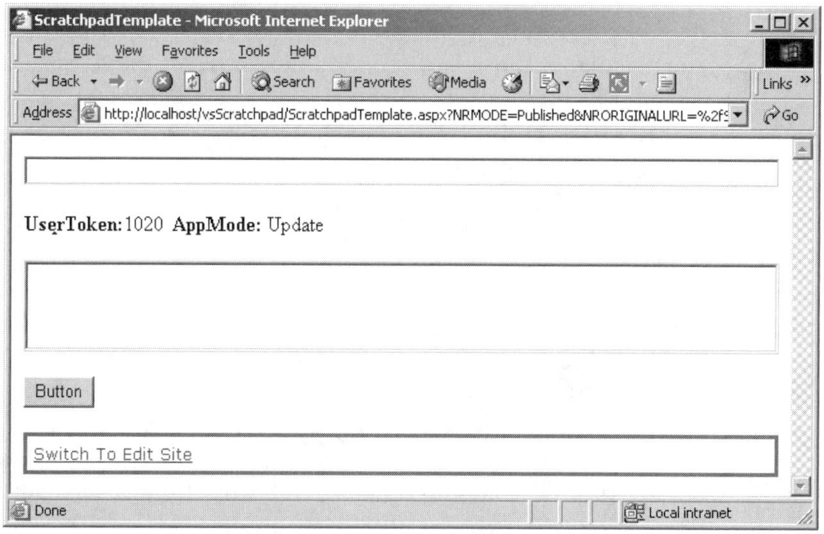

**Figure 24–8** AuthenticateUsingUserHandle

## Context Publishing Modes

In the coding examples we used to authenticate to the CmsApplication-
Context, we hardcoded the CMS Update publishing mode.

There are four publishing modes that we can use:

- *Published mode* presents the live site to the user. Only published
  objects are visible, and updating is not allowed.
- *Unpublished mode* lets the user view the live site plus any unpublished objects, but updating is still not allowed.
- *Update mode* lets the user see unpublished and preview objects,
  and, as the name implies, update objects in the model.
- *Staging mode* is used by the CMS Site Stager when staging a site,
  and updating is not permitted.

By default, the published version of a posting, if there is one, is
returned in both Published mode and Staging mode. The unpublished
version of a posting, if there is one, is returned in both Unpublished and
Update modes. In the event that there isn't an unpublished posting, a
copy of the published version is returned ready for alteration.

If we are going to the trouble of creating a Context, we will likely use
Update mode. However, it is feasible that Published and Unpublished
modes could be helpful in some circumstances.

**NOTE:** Web Author mode has a refinement of the publishing mode and is
discussed at length in Chapters 5 and 30.

## Summary

Let's put this chapter in "context." We discussed when we would anticipate using each of the various CMS Contexts. We defined the properties
and methods of CmsHttpContext and CmsApplicationContext as well
as the constructor for CmsApplicationContext. We coded some simple
scratchpad examples to see these CMS Contexts at work, including all the
ways we can authenticate a CmsApplicationContext. Last, we discussed
the Context publishing modes. Next, we take our newfound CMS Context knowledge and traverse the CMS hierarchies: channels and galleries.

# CHAPTER 25

# Traversing Channels

Now that we've got context, we can begin to organize and exercise the assets in our Web Property. In this chapter we discuss one of the three primary hierarchies of CMS: the channel.

Hierarchies abound. They are used all around us to help us understand and interact with large, potentially complex groups of items. Grocery stores, department stores, hardware stores, stores of all kinds organize their wares hierarchically (see the Hierarchies in Our Lives sidebar).

---

**Hierarchies in Our Lives**

Hierarchies are used all around us. For example, grocery stores organize general areas of the store first by groups like produce, meats, refrigerated goods, frozen goods, dry goods, canned goods, bread, dairy, health, and beauty. Within each group, the store organizes products by labeled aisles of similar products, and within each aisle by product type. For instance, in the bread aisle we will find a section for white bread, another for wheat bread, another for rye and odd breads, still another for hot dog and hamburger buns, and perhaps even an area for day-old bread. Within each section, we will likely find different manufacturers and maybe even different sizes from the same manufacturer. This is done to help us quickly locate a given item within the vast array of items they offer.

Restaurants typically organize their menus hierarchically, first dividing the offered items by sections like appetizer, sandwich, meal, dessert, beverage, and bar. Then within a given section, like beverage, there may be groups like carbonated, coffee, milk, tea. Even within a given group, like milk, there may be further subdivision, like skim, 2%, and whole.

Perhaps the best example of a hierarchy is the military; a corps is made up of divisions, a division of brigades, a brigade of regiments, a regiment of battle groups, a battle group of battalions, a battalion of squadrons, a squadron of companies, a company of batteries, a battery of troops, a troop of platoons, a platoon of detachments, a detachment of sections, a section of squads, a squad of teams, a team of crews, and a crew is made up of various soldiers, airmen, and/or seamen. Within each of these is a specific hierarchical chain of command, and within that a separation of duties by specialty.

CMS capitalizes on the ubiquitous nature of this concept.

---

Many other hierarchy examples could be given (sports, your house, animals, government, religion, and transportation systems, to name a few), but to the point: Hierarchies do make it easier to understand and interact with the objects that they organize. One of the key hierarchies available in CMS is the channel. A CMS channel is used to organize, store, retrieve, and manage postings within our Web Property.

**NOTE:** In the next chapter, we explore postings at length. For now, think of a posting as a collection of information that we want someone to understand and potentially interact with.

In many ways a channel provides functionality similar to a virtual directory in a traditional Web site. It can be used not only to organize information but also to limit access to it. As with all hierarchies, there is one single, master RootChannel called Channels from which every other channel gets its genesis.

However, unlike a directory, Channel objects can have properties, can be easily sorted using multiple keys, can be moved or renamed in part or in whole without breaking links in the site, can be easily traversed both up (using the Parent Channel property) and down (using foreach on the contained Channel objects collection) the hierarchy, are typically used to generate dynamic navigation to their contents, and can even be deleted in code. In fact, all of this functionality is available from within the PAPI Context.

**NOTE:** The ability to move a channel (or a posting) to a new location without any broken links is a feature of CMS called Managed Links. Links are not stored in the database as links but instead as object references. Location is just a characteristic of the object. So, moving an object to a new location simply changes that characteristic, and any link reference will render to the current location.

All code in this chapter will refer to a posting based upon a template with the following ASP.NET Web Form controls—TextBox, Label, ListBox, and Button—using their default properties plus the default console, of course. Follow the steps in the Scratchpad sidebar, in Chapter 24, to re-create exactly the same results shown here, or use your own channels, templates, and postings and just apply the concepts. We will be repeatedly replacing the contents of the Button1_Click function.

**Figure 25–1**  Scratch channel hierarchy

Also, since we will be working with the channel hierarchy, it will be very helpful to have a structure to traverse. Figure 25–1 shows the structure of the potentially familiar hierarchy as viewed in the CMS Site Manager. This structure will be created later in this chapter in the Creating and Deleting Objects in a Channel section. The structure will be used with the other examples in this chapter.

**NOTE:** Using Site Manager to create channels is covered in depth in Chapter 9.

Initially, the only channel that has a posting in it is the Scratch channel.

## Checking Channel User Rights

It is typically desirable to verify that the current user is allowed to perform an action rather than handling the access denied exception that occurs if we allow them to try to do something when they don't have sufficient rights.

### Sufficient Rights

CMS help files outline the specific rights that a user must have to be considered sufficient for virtually any task. Since the goal of this chapter isn't about securing your site, this is left to other areas of the book. (See Chapter 17 for more information on how to set up user rights in Site Manager, and Chapters 19 and 20 for best practices on securing your CMS site.)

That said, most of the code in this part of the book assumes that the user logged in to CMS has sufficient rights to manipulate all the assets in the hierarchy. The easiest way to ensure that insufficient rights are not a problem while you are testing your site locally is to authenticate using the CMS administrator credentials or add the user that you log in to Windows with to the CMS Administrator group using Site Manger, and set IIS to use Integrated Windows authentication for your CMS site.

Alternatively, use the AuthenticateAsUser method of the CmsApplication Context, passing in the user name and password of the CMS administrator, rather than using the CmsHttpContext, as shown in most of the code examples. This way you can always dictate the user and Context PublishingMode. (See Chapter 24 for more information on using the AuthenticateAsUser method of CmsApplicationContext.)

Knowing what the user is allowed to do and not allowed to do can be helpful in dynamically generating navigation. It can be desirable to proactively leave off functionality that the current user isn't allowed to perform. It can also be desirable to visually indicate areas where the user is allowed to perform certain functions (such as by showing a certain icon in front of a link where the user is allowed to perform a given function). This can easily be accomplished using the user rights properties of the Channel object displayed in the following code.

The simple error handling in the code throughout these code samples isn't meant to be the model for how to handle CMS exceptions; there is an application code block from Microsoft on how to do exception handling in .NET. These functions also assume the presence of both a ListBox1 and a Label1 to provide visual feedback to the user, which certainly won't typically be normal, but it works for our purposes.

Replace the Button1_Click function of our Scratchpad template file (see the Scratchpad sidebar in Chapter 24 for details) with the following code:

```
private void Button1_Click(object sender, System.EventArgs e)
{
```

```
try
{
  //1. Grab the current CMS Context
  CmsHttpContext cmsContext = CmsHttpContext.Current;

  //2. Populate the label with the name of the Channel, the
  //   PublishingMode, and an anchor tag to the Update Mode URL
  //   (if the user clicks this, the page will repost in CMS
  //   Update Mode for the current Posting)
  Label1.Text = "<b>Channel: </b>" +
    cmsContext.Channel.Name.ToString() +
    "<br><b>PublishingMode: </b>" + cmsContext.Mode.ToString() +
    "<br><a href=" + cmsContext.Channel.UrlModeUpdate +
    ">Link to Update Mode</a>";

  //3. Populate the ListBox with values for the various
  //   user rights
  ListBox1.Items.Add( "CanDelete: " +
    cmsContext.Channel.CanDelete.ToString()
    );
  ListBox1.Items.Add( "CanCreateChannels: " +
    cmsContext.Channel.CanCreateChannels.ToString()
    );
  ListBox1.Items.Add( "CanCreatePostings: " +
    cmsContext.Channel.CanCreatePostings.ToString()
    );
  ListBox1.Items.Add( "CanSetProperties: " +
    cmsContext.Channel.CanSetProperties.ToString()
    );
}
catch(Exception eError)
{
  //4. Provide error feedback to the developer
  Label1.Text = "<b>Error: </b>" + eError.Message.ToString();
}
}
```

Build the solution and then refresh the Scratchpad posting in Internet Explorer, or browse to it and click the Button. The page should reload and look similar to Figure 25–2.

As you can probably surmise from the preceding example, CMS allows us to programmatically create, alter, and delete channels and

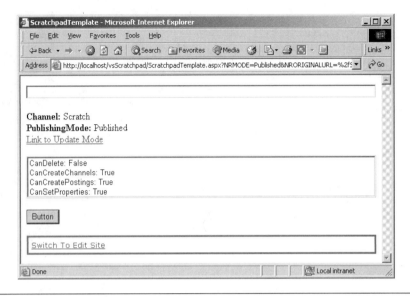

**Figure 25–2** Channel user rights

create postings and connected postings in a referencing Channel object. What may not be self-evident is that the creation, alteration, and deletion of a channel do not have to be submitted or approved to take place. If the user has the authority to alter a channel and that change is committed, that change is live. These Channel properties will help us determine whether we could allow the current user access to this functionality.

The Boolean result of each property is strictly an indicator of the user's rights rather than the proper Context PublishingMode to perform the function. This way, we can provide a visual indication in the dynamic navigation of the user's ability or lack thereof to perform these functions regardless of the mode of the current Context. Therefore, just because one of these properties returns true, that doesn't automatically mean that any attempt to modify an object will succeed. To that end, it is always wise to place the verification that a user has sufficient rights and the actual modification within a .NET try/catch block.

Also, all the following Channel properties cannot be read for objects after they have been deleted and always return false for historical revisions of a Channel object.

A more representative coding example follows in the next main section of this chapter, Creating and Deleting Objects in a Channel.

### CanDelete (Inherited from HierarchyItem)

The CanDelete property indicates whether the authenticated user can delete the referencing Channel object. This property will return true if the authenticated user has sufficient rights (see the Sufficient Rights sidebar) to delete the channel.

This property will return false if the authenticated user does not have sufficient rights or if the channel contains any children (channels or postings). In the preceding code example, CanDelete will always be false because we are asking if the user can delete the channel that this posting is in. Of course they can't; this channel has at least one child: the posting in which the code is running. Also, the CanDelete property will always return false if the referencing Channel object is the RootChannel. The RootChannel is a built-in entity and therefore can't be deleted by anyone.

### CanCreateChannels

The CanCreateChannels property indicates whether the authenticated user can create channels within the referencing Channel object. This property will return true if the authenticated user has sufficient rights (see the Sufficient Rights sidebar) to create a channel within the referencing Channel object.

This property will return false if the authenticated user does not have sufficient rights.

### CanCreatePostings

The CanCreatePostings property indicates whether the authenticated user can create postings within the referencing Channel object. This property will return true if the authenticated user has sufficient rights to create a posting within the referencing Channel object.

This property will return false if the authenticated user does not have sufficient rights.

### CanSetProperties (Inherited from HierarchyItem)

The CanSetProperties property indicates whether the authenticated user can indeed alter the properties of the referencing channel object. This requires the same sufficient rights as creating and deleting a channel.

This property will return true if the authenticated user has sufficient rights and false if they do not have sufficient rights.

# Creating and Deleting Objects in a Channel

To programmatically build the hierarchy illustrated in Figure 25–1, we will use the CreateChannel method of the current channel that our posting is in. We will then create a posting in one of the created channels. We will discuss, but not illustrate, the creation of a ConnectedPosting using the CreateConnectedPosting method. Using Site Manager, we will view our hierarchical masterpiece. And finally, we will delete the entire hierarchy.

## CreateChannel

To successfully use the CreateChannel method, the CanCreateChannels property must return true for the referencing Channel object, and the PublishingMode must be set to Update. Ensuring that CanCreate Channels returns true isn't too difficult (see the Sufficient Rights side-bar). Getting the referencing Channel object into Update Publishing Mode requires a little more work. If we skip this step, we will receive a verbose .NET error page that basically says, You must be in Update mode to do this.

Although it may sound a little more challenging at first, we will use the second approach in the Getting into Update PublishingMode side-bar for the examples that follow. It is a universal solution that can be applied in many places in the code to follow.

The next two code listings will help us break the task of creating a channel hierarchy into manageable, potentially reusable functions.

The first function will return an authenticated CmsApplication Context to the calling method. In Listing 25–1 we are using the AuthenticateUsingUserHandle authentication method, but you can use your preferred CmsApplicationContext authentication method. By encapsulating this functionality, we can simply call the GetAuthenticated CmsApplicationContext function, passing it the PublishingMode we want it to have, and we can be confident that we will successfully get a valid CmsApplicationContext in the specified mode. The comments should adequately explain what the code is doing.

**NOTE:** Authentication methods of the CmsApplicationContext are covered in detail in Chapter 24.

**Listing 25–1** Function to get authenticated CmsApplicationContext

```
private CmsApplicationContext GetAuthenticatedCmsApplicationContext
  (PublishingMode cmsMode)
//******************************************************************
//Create a new CmsApplicationContext and authenticate it
//Pass the created Context back to the calling method
//******************************************************************
{
  //1. Declare a Context variable
  CmsApplicationContext cmsContextApp = null;
  try
  {
    //2. Grab a new Application Context
    cmsContextApp = new CmsApplicationContext();

    //3. Assign current Windows User to a WindowsIdentity variable
    //   This will only work if IIS is set to Windows
    //   Authentication and Guest Access is enabled in the SCA
    System.Security.Principal.WindowsIdentity identCurrentUser =
      System.Security.Principal.WindowsIdentity.GetCurrent();

    //4. Log in to CMS
    //   Use the currently authenticated Windows User credentials
    //   Put Context into the PublishingMode passed to the function
    cmsContextApp.AuthenticateUsingUserHandle(
      identCurrentUser.Token, cmsMode);

    //5. Return the Authenticated Context
    return cmsContextApp;
  }
  catch(Exception eError)
  {
    //6. Provide error feedback to the developer
    Label1.Text = "<b>Error: </b>" + eError.Message.ToString();

    //7. Return the null Context in the event of an error
    return cmsContextApp;
  }
}
```

The second function, in Listing 25–2, creates a Channel object and returns it to the calling method. By encapsulating this functionality, we

### Getting into Update PublishingMode

There are at least two ways to get a CMS Context into Update PublishingMode:

1. Navigate or redirect the posting to the URL that puts the authenticated user's CmsHttpContext into an Update PublishingMode. In an earlier example in this chapter, we included an unexplained anchor tag called Link to Update Mode. We constructed the link using a Channel property called UrlModeUpdate that we talk about later in this chapter. Run that sample and try clicking that link, and then click the Button. You will see that the PublishingMode changes from Published to Update. Alternatively, redirection could be used to put the CmsHttpContext into Update PublishingMode. See the following code for an example of how this might be accomplished (the Woodgrove sample uses this approach):

```
if(cmsContext.Mode != PublishingMode.Update)
{
  Response.Redirect(cmsContext.Channel.UrlModeUpdate, true);
}
else
{
  // Create Channel here
}
```

2. Use the CmsApplicationContext to authenticate into a stand-alone Context in Update PublishingMode, as we did in Chapter 24. However, the CmsApplicationContext will not be privy to the current channel, so an extra step will be required to position this stand-alone Context on the channel where we want to create our new channel. The steps in this approach include creating and authenticating a new CmsApplication Context in Update PublishingMode, positioning the CmsApplication Context to the current CmsHttpContext Channel, creating our Channel(s), committing our changes, and disposing of the CmsApplication Context.

It is good to understand both methods, but standardizing on a single method and using it consistently across the entire site is wise.

can simply call the CreateNewChannel function, passing it the Channel object in which we want the new channel created, along with the name we want the new channel to have, and we can be confident that, assuming sufficient user rights exist, we will successfully get back the created Channel object. The comments should adequately explain what the code is doing.

If the CreateNewChannel function fails for any reason, the Channel object passed back will simply be null.

**Listing 25–2** Function to create a new channel

```
private Channel CreateNewChannel
  (Channel parentChannel, string newChannelName)
//****************************************************************
//Create a new Channel in the parentChannel using the
//newChannelName both passed to the function
//Pass the created Channel back to the calling method
//****************************************************************
{
  //1. Declare a Channel variable
  Channel cmsNewChannel = null;

  try
  {
    //2. Determine if the user has sufficient rights to create
    // a Channel from the would-be parent Channel
    if(parentChannel.CanCreateChannels)
    {
    //3. Create the Channel
    cmsNewChannel = parentChannel.CreateChannel();

    //4. Validate successful creation
    if(cmsNewChannel != null)
    {
      //5. Give it the Name passed to the function
      cmsNewChannel.Name = newChannelName;

      //6. Provide visual feedback of Channel creation in Listbox1
      ListBox1.Items.Add(newChannelName + " Channel created in " +
        parentChannel.Name.ToString() + " Channel"
        );
    }
    else
```

```
{
  //7. Provide visual feedback of creation failure in Listbox1
  ListBox1.Items.Add(newChannelName +
    " Channel creation failed");
}
}
else
{
//8. Provide nonerror feedback to the developer
Label1.Text = "<b>User NOT allowed to create Channels";
}

//9. Return the created Channel
return cmsNewChannel;
}
catch(Exception eError)
{
  //10. Provide error feedback to the developer
  Label1.Text = "<b>Error: </b>" + eError.Message.ToString();

  //11. Return the null Channel in the event of an error
  return cmsNewChannel;
}
}
```

A new channel is not saved to the database until the CommitAll method is called on the Context. The default values for properties are either empty, inherited from the parent channel (including rights), or intuitive. Also, CMS allows the creation of duplicate channels even though this can lead to a situation where ambiguous objects in the hierarchy are created. Of course, they will have different GUIDs, so CMS won't get confused, but it may be confusing to users. So it may be wise to prevent duplicates programmatically.

Now let's use these two functions, along with some elementary PAPI code, to create the channel hierarchy depicted in Figure 25–1. Ensure that the code from Listings 25–1 and 25–2 is entered above the Button1_Click function of our Scratchpad template file.

Replace the Button1_Click function of our Scratchpad template file with the following code:

```
private void Button1_Click(object sender, System.EventArgs e)
{
```

```
try
{
  //1. Grab the current CMS Context
  CmsHttpContext cmsContextHttp = CmsHttpContext.Current;

  //2. Grab an Authenticated Context in Update PublishingMode
  //    using the GetAuthenticatedCmsApplicationContext function
  //    from Listing 25-1
  CmsApplicationContext cmsContextApp =
    GetAuthenticatedCmsApplicationContext(PublishingMode.Update);

  //3. Position the Application Context to the current
  //    CmsHttpContext Channel using its GUID (the most efficient
  //    Searches method)
  //    Cast the result of the Searches object as a Channel
  Channel currentChannel =
    cmsContextApp.Searches.GetByGuid(cmsContextHttp.Channel.Guid)
    as Channel;

  //4. Populate the label with the name of the Application
  //    Context Channel and PublishingMode
  Label1.Text = "<b>Channel: </b>" +
    currentChannel.Name.ToString() +
    "<br><b>PublishingMode: </b>" +
    cmsContextApp.Mode.ToString();

  //5. Create the Channel hierarchy depicted in Figure 25-1
  //    using the CreateNewChannel function from Listing 25-2
  Channel FamilyChannel;
  Channel ParentChannel;
  Channel ChildChannel;
  familyChannel = CreateNewChannel(currentChannel, "Brady");
  parentChannel = CreateNewChannel(familyChannel, "Alice");

  parentChannel = CreateNewChannel(familyChannel, "Carol");
  childChannel  = CreateNewChannel(parentChannel, "Jan");
  childChannel  = CreateNewChannel(parentChannel, "Marsha");
  childChannel  = CreateNewChannel(parentChannel, "Cindy");
```

```
    parentChannel = CreateNewChannel(familyChannel, "Mike");
    childChannel  = CreateNewChannel(parentChannel,  "Greg");
    childChannel  = CreateNewChannel(parentChannel,  "Peter");
    childChannel  = CreateNewChannel(parentChannel,  "Bobby");

    //6. Commit of all changes. If not explicitly called, the
    //   disposition of changes will be based upon
    //   RollbackOnSessionEnd
    cmsContextApp.CommitAll();

    //7. Dispose of the stand-alone Application Context
    cmsContextApp.Dispose();
  }
  catch(Exception eError)
  {
    //8. Provide error feedback to the developer
    Label1.Text = "<b>Error: </b>" + eError.Message.ToString();
  }
}
```

---

**NOTE:** The Searches method of a CMS Context is covered in detail in Chapter 28.

---

Build the solution and then refresh the Scratchpad posting in Internet Explorer, or browse to it and click the Button. The page should reload and look similar to Figure 25–3.

Scroll down the ListBox to see all the channels created. Open Site Manager or choose Global Refresh from the Site Manager View menu if it is already open. The channel hierarchy as depicted in Figure 25–1 should be displayed.

## CreatePosting

Hierarchies don't do us a lot of good unless we can put postings in them. Channel hierarchies are designed to house postings. To successfully use the CreatePosting method, the CanCreatePostings property must return true for the referencing Channel object, and the PublishingMode must be set to Update. Ensuring that CanCreatePostings returns true isn't too difficult. Remember, you must be in Update Mode to do this (see the Getting into Update PublishingMode sidebar).

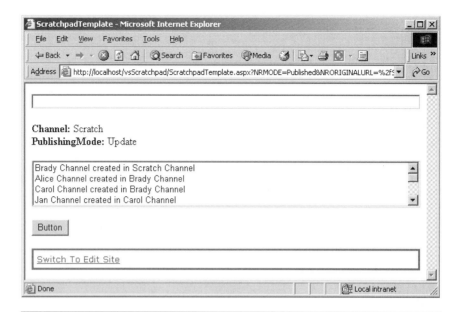

**Figure 25–3**  Create channel hierarchy

A new posting is not saved to the database until the CommitAll method is called on the Context. The default values for properties are either empty or intuitive. Also, CMS allows the creation of duplicate postings. This can lead to a situation where ambiguous objects in the hierarchy are created. Of course, they will have different GUIDs, so CMS won't get confused, but it may be confusing to users. So it may be wise to prevent duplicates programmatically.

Similar to the CreateNewChannel function in Listing 25–2 is the CreateNewPosting function in Listing 25–3. We can simply call the CreateNewPosting function, passing it the Channel object in which we want the new posting created, the name we want the new posting to have, as well as the template we want to base the new posting on, and we can be confident that, assuming sufficient user rights exist, we will successfully get back the created Posting object. The comments should adequately explain what the code is doing. If the CreateNewPosting function fails for any reason, the Posting object that is passed back will simply be null.

**Listing 25–3** Function to create a new posting

```
private Posting CreateNewPosting
  (Channel parentChannel, string newPostingName,
   Template cmsTemplate)
//****************************************************************
//Create a new Posting in the parentChannel using the
//newPostingName based upon the cmsTemplate all passed to the
//function. Pass the created Posting back to the calling method
//****************************************************************
{
  //1. Declare a Posting variable
  Posting cmsNewPosting = null;

  try
  {
    //2. Determine if the user has sufficient rights to create
    //   a Posting from the would-be parent Channel
    if(parentChannel.CanCreatePostings)
    {
      //3. Create the Posting using the Template passed to
      //   the function
      cmsNewPosting = parentChannel.CreatePosting(cmsTemplate);
      //4. Validate successful creation
      if(cmsNewPosting != null)
      {
        //5. Give it the Name passed to the function
        cmsNewPosting.Name = newPostingName;
        //6. Provide visual feedback of Posting creation
        ListBox1.Items.Add( newPostingName +
          " Posting created in " +
          parentChannel.Name.ToString() + " Channel"
          );
      }
      else
      {
        //7. Provide visual feedback of creation failure
        ListBox1.Items.Add(newPostingName +
          " Posting creation failed"
          );
      }
    }
    else
```

```
      {
        //8. Provide nonerror feedback to the developer
        Label1.Text = "<b>User NOT allowed to create Postings";
      }

      //9. Return the created Posting
      return cmsNewPosting;
    }
    catch(Exception eError)
    {
      //10. Provide error feedback to the developer
      Label1.Text = "<b>Error: </b>" + eError.Message.ToString();

      //11. Return the null Posting in the event of an error
      return cmsNewPosting;
    }
}
```

Next we will create a posting named Sam based upon our Scratch-pad template file from the Root TemplateGallery called Templates in the Alice channel (/Channels/Scratch/Brady/Alice) of the channel hierarchy created in the previous code example. Ensure that the code from Listings 25–1 and 25–3 is entered above the Button1_Click function of our Scratchpad template file and that the channel hierarchy from the previous code example is visible in Site Manager. Thus far, our posting doesn't have any placeholders to be troubled with.

Replace the Button1_Click function of our Scratchpad template file with the following code:

```
private void Button1_Click(object sender, System.EventArgs e)
{
  try
  {
    //1. Grab the current CMS Context
    CmsHttpContext cmsContextHttp = CmsHttpContext.Current;

    //2. Grab the Template to create a Posting using its path
    //   Cast the result of the Searches object as a Template
    Template scratchpadTemplate =
      cmsContextHttp.Searches.GetByPath(
        "/Templates/ScratchpadTemplate")
      as Template;
```

```
//3. Grab an Authenticated Context in Update PublishingMode
//   using the GetAuthenticatedCmsApplicationContext function
//   from Listing 25-1
CmsApplicationContext cmsContextApp =
  GetAuthenticatedCmsApplicationContext(PublishingMode.Update);

//4. Grab the Channel to create a Posting using its path
//   Cast the result of the Searches object as a Channel
Channel cmsAliceChannel =
  cmsContextApp.Searches.GetByPath(
    "/Channels/Scratch/Brady/Alice")
  as Channel;

//5. Create a new Posting called Sam in the Alice Channel
//   based upon the Scratchpad Template using the
//   CreateNewPosting function from Listing 25-3
Posting cmsPosting = CreateNewPosting(cmsAliceChannel,
  "Sam",
  scratchpadTemplate);

//6. If Posting was successfully created it will not be null
if(cmsPosting != null)
{
//7. Populate the label with the name of the Application
//   Context Channel, then name of the created Posting,
//   and PublishingMode
Label1.Text = "<b>Channel: </b>" +
  cmsAliceChannel.Name.ToString() +

  "<br><b>Posting: </b>" +
  cmsPosting.Name.ToString() +

  "<br><b>PublishingMode: </b>" +
  cmsContextApp.Mode.ToString();
}
//8. Commit of all changes. If not explicitly called, the
//   disposition of changes will be based upon
//   RollbackOnSessionEnd
cmsContextApp.CommitAll();

//9. Dispose of the stand-alone Application Context
cmsContextApp.Dispose();
}
```

```
catch(Exception eError)
{
  //10. Provide error feedback to the developer
  Label1.Text = "<b>Error: </b>" + eError.Message.ToString();
}
}
```

Build the solution and then refresh the Scratchpad posting in Internet Explorer, or browse to it and click the Button. The page should reload and look similar to Figure 25–4.

Open Site Manager or choose Global Refresh from the Site Manager View menu if it is already open. Drill into the channel hierarchy until you can highlight the Alice channel. The new Sam posting should be visible in the pane to the right, as shown in Figure 25–5.

## CreateConnectedPosting

Sometimes it makes sense for postings to share content. We will explore this concept in detail in the next chapter. For now, just be aware of the rules: To successfully use the CreateConnectedPosting method, the CanCreatePostings property and the CanSetProperties property must both return true for the referencing Channel and Posting objects, respectively. As always, the PublishingMode must be set to Update. A new Connected Posting is not saved to the database until the CommitAll method is called

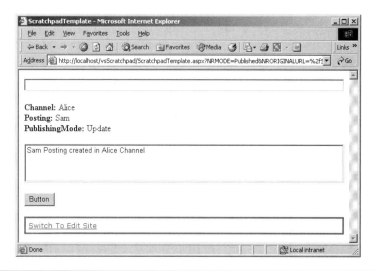

**Figure 25–4** Create posting

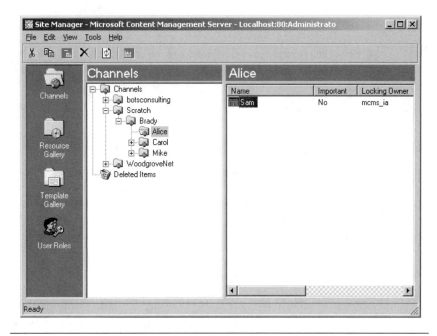

**Figure 25–5**  Created posting in Site Manager

on the Context. The default values for properties are either empty or intuitive; however, the following properties are shared between Connected Posting objects: Description, Name, Placeholders, and CustomProperties. CMS allows the creation of ConnectedPosting objects with duplicate names. There is also a material limit of 15 distinct Template objects for a pool of ConnectedPostings to share. Attempting to go beyond that limit will result in an exception. It may be wise to create a CreateNew ConnectedPosting function to encapsulate that functionality.

The state of the newly created ConnectedPosting is dependent on the state of the existing posting and sometimes whether the channel has a moderator or not. Table 25–1 provides the matrix of state values.

### Delete (Inherited from HierarchyItem)

We've created a channel hierarchy using PAPI; let's delete that hierarchy in like manner. To successfully use the Delete method, the CanDelete property must return true for the referencing HierarchyItem (Channel or Posting). See the rules for CanDelete earlier in this chapter. As before, the PublishingMode must be set to Update.

**Table 25–1** Initial ConnectedPosting State

| Existing Posting State | Channel Moderator | New ConnectedPosting State |
|---|---|---|
| New | Yes or No | New |
| Saved | Yes or No | Saved |
| Waiting For Editor Approval | Yes or No | Waiting For Editor Approval |
| Editor Declined | Yes or No | Editor Declined |
| Waiting For Moderator Approval | No | Approved, Published, or Expired |
| Moderator Declined | No | Approved, Published, or Expired |
| Approved | No | Approved, Published, or Expired |
| Published | No | Approved, Published, or Expired |
| Expired | No | Approved, Published, or Expired |
| Waiting For Moderator Approval | Yes | Waiting For Moderator Approval |
| Moderator Declined | Yes | Waiting For Moderator Approval |
| Approved | Yes | Waiting For Moderator Approval |
| Published | Yes | Waiting For Moderator Approval |
| Expired | Yes | Waiting For Moderator Approval |

Calling the Delete method merely marks an item for deletion. The item isn't actually deleted from the database until CommitAll on the Context is called. Even after a CommitAll, the item isn't actually deleted from any in-memory collection in which it existed before deletion. Interaction with a deleted item before CommitAll will return read-only values; interaction with a deleted item after CommitAll will cause an exception. Unlike with Site Manager, deletion of an item after a Commit All cannot be undone. The item is not moved into a Deleted Items folder. It is possible to undo a delete before a CommitAll by calling a RollbackAll. Any attempt to delete an item that is being edited by another user will cause an exception.

In Listing 25–4 is a function called DeleteAllChildrenFrom. We can use it to delete all the postings and channels for the Channel object passed to the function. The child channels must be empty for CMS to delete them. So, it is implied that any postings and channels of any decedents will also be deleted. We will call this function recursively to accomplish this task.

**Listing 25–4** Function to delete all children from a channel

```
private void DeleteAllChildrenFrom(Channel cmsChannel)
//****************************************************************
//Delete all Postings and Channels from the cmsChannel
//passed to the function. If a child Channel has children, this
//function is called recursively
//****************************************************************
{
  try
  {
    //1. Iterate each Channel in the Channels collection
    foreach (Channel cmsChildChannel in cmsChannel.Channels)
    {
      //2. Check to see if a child Channel has children
      if(cmsChildChannel.AllChildren.Count > 0)
      {
        //3. Call this function recursively
        DeleteAllChildrenFrom(cmsChildChannel);
      }

      //4. Check if the user has sufficient rights to delete
      if(cmsChildChannel.CanDelete)
      {
        //5. Delete empty Channel
        cmsChildChannel.Delete();

        //6. Provide visual feedback of Channel deletion
        ListBox1.Items.Add( cmsChildChannel.Name +
          " Channel was deleted from " +
          cmsChannel.Name.ToString() + " Channel "
          );
      }
    }
    //7. Iterate each Posting in the Postings collection
    foreach (Posting cmsChildPosting in cmsChannel.Postings)
```

```
      {
        //8. Check if the user has sufficient rights to delete
        if(cmsChildPosting.CanDelete)
        {
          //9. Delete the Posting
          cmsChildPosting.Delete();

          //10. Validate successful deletion
          if(cmsChildPosting.IsDeleted)
          {
          //11. Provide visual feedback of Posting deletion
          //    Notice that the Name of a deleted item can be
          //    referenced as read-only
          ListBox1.Items.Add( cmsChildPosting.Name +
            " Posting was deleted from " +
            cmsChannel.Name.ToString() + " Channel"
            );
          }
        }
      }
    }
    catch(Exception eError)
    {
      //12. Provide error feedback to the developer
      Label1.Text = "<b>Error: </b>" + eError.Message.ToString();
    }
}
```

Next we'll delete the entire channel hierarchy we created earlier in this section (posting and all), leaving the original Scratch channel and the single Pad posting.

Replace the Button1_Click function of our Scratchpad template file with the following code:

```
private void Button1_Click(object sender, System.EventArgs e)
{
  try
  {
    //1. Grab the current CMS Context
    CmsHttpContext cmsContextHttp = CmsHttpContext.Current;

    //2. Grab an Authenticated Context in Update PublishingMode
    //   using the GetAuthenticatedCmsApplicationContext function
```

```
//   from Listing 25-1
CmsApplicationContext cmsContextApp =
  GetAuthenticatedCmsApplicationContext(PublishingMode.Update);

//3. Grab the Channel to expunge
//   Cast the result of the Searches object as a Channel
Channel cmsBradyChannel =
  cmsContextApp.Searches.GetByPath("/Channels/Scratch/Brady")
  as Channel;

//4. Populate the label with the name of the Application
//   Context Channel and PublishingMode
Label1.Text = "<b>Channel: </b>" +
  cmsBradyChannel.Name.ToString() +

  "<br><b>PublishingMode: </b>" +
  cmsContextApp.Mode.ToString();

//5. Delete all Channels (and their descendants) and Postings
DeleteAllChildrenFrom(cmsBradyChannel);

//6. Check if the user has sufficient rights to delete
if(cmsBradyChannel.CanDelete)
{
  //7. Delete empty parent Channel
  cmsBradyChannel.Delete();

  //8. Provide visual feedback of Posting creation in Listbox1
  ListBox1.Items.Add( cmsBradyChannel.Name +
    " Channel was deleted from " +
    cmsBradyChannel.Parent.Name.ToString() + " Channel "
    );
}
//9. Commit of all changes. If not explicitly called the
//   disposition of changes will be based upon
//   RollbackOnSessionEnd
cmsContextApp.CommitAll();

//10. Dispose of the stand-alone Application Context
cmsContextApp.Dispose();
}
catch(Exception eError)
{
```

```
    //11. Provide error feedback to the developer
    Label1.Text = "<b>Error: </b>" + eError.Message.ToString();
  }
}
```

Build the solution and then refresh the Scratchpad posting in Internet Explorer, or browse to it and click the Button. The page should reload and look similar to Figure 25–6.

Scroll down the list box to see all the channels and postings deleted. Open Site Manager or choose Global Refresh from the Site Manager View menu if it is already open. The entire channel hierarchy as depicted in Figure 25–1 should be expunged. Notice that you don't even find it in the Deleted Items hive.

Of course, create and delete functionality is typically the domain of a CMS administrator. This PAPI functionality would naturally be manifest in custom administration pages or Web Author customizations.

**NOTE:** See Chapter 30 for details on customizing the Web Author.

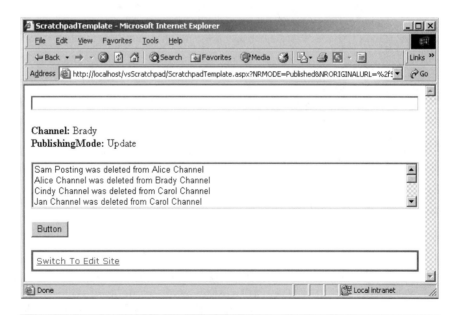

**Figure 25–6** Delete channel hierarchy

## Working with Channel Members

Channels have a vast store of characteristics to be tapped by the developer using PAPI. Some can be changed in code, while others are for retrieval only. We focus on the read-only members first. We start with a comprehensive code example, then an alphabetical list of read-only members specific to Channel objects, followed by an alphabetical list of read-only members inherited for use by Channel objects.

Then we focus on read/write members. Again, we start with a comprehensive code example, then an alphabetical list of read/write members specific to Channel objects, followed by an alphabetical list of read/write members inherited for use by Channel objects.

There are some common facts and concepts about CMS dates that will help us throughout the list of members (see the CMS Dates sidebar for details).

---

**CMS Dates**

All date and time fields use Coordinated Universal Time. The time can be converted to local time using the ToLocalTime method like this:

```
x = CmsHttpContext.Channel.ChangeDate.ToLocalTime;
```

ToLocalTime can also be used in client-side JavaScript so that the time zone on the browsing PC is used rather than the time zone on the server.

To indicate that a ChannelItem object never expires, set the date and time property to January 01, 3000. If the date property is January 01, 3000, this property is displayed using the string "Never" in the corresponding user interfaces. Similarly, script should be written so that a date of January 01, 3000 is displayed by your code as the string "Never".

Table 25–2 summarizes the five channel date and time fields and how they relate to one another.

---

After a channel has been deleted but before it is committed, all properties become read-only. However, even after a deleted channel is committed, it may still reside in an in-memory collection. IsDeleted is one of the few properties that can still be read after a deletion and before a commit. Most other properties will cause an exception if they are referenced.

**Table 25–2** Channel Date and Time Fields

| Created Date | ChangeDate | StartDate | ExpiryDate | LastModified Date | RevisionDate |
|---|---|---|---|---|---|
| Date created. Never changes. | Date of implicit change. Equal to most recent date greater than today: LastModified Date, StartDate, or ExpiryDate. | Date object becomes visible. Always less than ExpiryDate. Within range of parent StartDate and ExpiryDate. | Date object ceases to be Visible. Always more recent than StartDate. Within range of parent StartDate and ExpiryDate | Date of explicit change. Always more recent than or equal to CreatedDate. | Date of most recent ChangeDate for revisions, if any. If January 01, 3000, there is not a historical revision. |

Historical revisions of a channel don't typically keep the value that was associated with the revision when it was the current version. The following properties are the only ones that can be different across all revisions: ChangeDate, CreatedBy, CreatedDate, Description, and Revision Date. All other properties represent the value of the current revision regardless of the value when the historical revision was the current revision. Attempting to assign a value to these properties for a historical revision will result in an exception.

## Read-Only Members

The code to see all the read-only Channel object members is presented comprehensively. Sometimes it just helps to see the output of a property to better understand it, but we don't want to mess with a million code examples.

Replace the Button1_Click function of our Scratchpad template file with the following code:

```
private void Button1_Click(object sender, System.EventArgs e)
{
    //1. Put current Channel into variable
    Channel cmsChannel = CmsHttpContext.Current.Channel;
```

```
//2. Populate the label with read-only properties of a Channel
Label1.Text =
  "<br><b>IsRoot: </b>" + cmsChannel.IsRoot.ToString() +
  "<br><b>Channel: </b>" + cmsChannel.Name.ToString() +
  "<br><b>ChangeDate: </b>" + cmsChannel.ChangeDate.ToString() +
  "<br><b>CreatedBy: </b>" + cmsChannel.CreatedBy.ToString() +
  "<br><b>CreatedDate: </b>" +
    cmsChannel.CreatedDate.ToString() +
  "<br><b>DisplayPath: </b>" +
    cmsChannel.DisplayPath.ToString() +
  "<br><b>GetHashCode: </b>" +
    cmsChannel.GetHashCode().ToString() +
  "<br><b>GetType: </b>" + cmsChannel.GetType().ToString() +
  "<br><b>Guid: </b>" + cmsChannel.Guid.ToString() +
  "<br><b>IsDeleted: </b>" + cmsChannel.IsDeleted.ToString() +
  "<br><b>IsDescendantOf: </b>" +
    cmsChannel.IsDescendantOf(cmsChannel.Parent).ToString() +
  "<br><b>IsWorkingRevision: </b>" +
    cmsChannel.IsWorkingRevision.ToString() +
  "<br><b>LastModifiedBy: </b>" +
    cmsChannel.LastModifiedBy.ToString() +
  "<br><b>LastModifiedDate: </b>" +
    cmsChannel.LastModifiedDate.ToString() +
  "<br><b>OwnedBy: </b>" + cmsChannel.OwnedBy.ToString() +
  "<br><b>Path: </b>" + cmsChannel.Path.ToString() +
  "<br><b>QueryString: </b>" +
    cmsChannel.QueryString.ToString() +
  "<br><b>QueryStringModeUnpublished: </b>" +
    cmsChannel.QueryStringModeUnpublished.ToString() +
  "<br><b>QueryStringModeUpdate: </b>" +
    cmsChannel.QueryStringModeUpdate.ToString() +
  "<br><b>RevisionDate: </b>" +
    cmsChannel.RevisionDate.ToString() +
  "<br><b>Url: </b>" + cmsChannel.Url.ToString() +
  "<br><b>UrlInner: </b>" + cmsChannel.UrlInner.ToString() +
  "<br><b>UrlInnerPlain: </b>" +
    cmsChannel.UrlInnerPlain.ToString() +
  "<br><b>UrlModePublished: </b>" +
```

```
        cmsChannel.UrlModePublished.ToString() +
    "<br><b>UrlModeUnpublished: </b>" +
        cmsChannel.UrlModeUnpublished.ToString() +
    "<br><b>UrlModeUpdate: </b>" +
        cmsChannel.UrlModeUpdate.ToString();
}
```

Build the solution and then refresh the Scratchpad posting in Internet Explorer, or browse to it and click the Button. The page should reload and look similar to Figure 25–7.

### Read-Only Members Specific to Channels
#### IsRoot
The IsRoot property is the only read-only member of the Channel object that is not inherited from another class. As discussed at the beginning of this chapter, there can only be one RootChannel, and it is built in to CMS. It is always called /Channels. If the Channel represented by the object is the built-in CMS RootChannel, it will return true; otherwise, it will return false.

This member can be useful for determining when we are at the top of the channel hierarchy when dynamically building navigation or a breadcrumb display. It is essentially a shortcut for determining if the current object equals the RootChannel.

### Read-Only Members Inherited for Use by Channels
#### ChangeDate (Inherited from ChannelItem)
The ChangeDate property retrieves the date and time of the latest implicit change. It has the standard characteristics of a CMS date and time field described and summarized with the other dates at the beginning of this section. This date can change without any user interaction. The passage of time could bring a ChannelItem to its StartDate or its ExpiryDate, resulting in a change in ChannelItem status. The date of these implicit changes is recorded here. So, this date will be equal to the most recent LastModifiedDate, StartDate, or ExpiryDate that is greater than today.

This member can be useful for identifying fresh content on a Web Property.

**Figure 25–7** Show read-only members

## CreatedBy (Inherited from HierarchyItem)
The CreatedBy property retrieves a User object indicating the user that created the referencing ChannelItem.

This member can be useful for showing a few characteristics about the user that created the ChannelItem.

### CreatedDate (Inherited from HierarchyItem)

The CreatedDate property retrieves the date and time that the Channel Item was created. It has the standard characteristics of a CMS date and time field described and summarized with the other dates at the beginning of this section.

This member can be useful for showing the date and time that the ChannelItem was created or identifying aged information still found on a Web Property.

### DisplayPath (Inherited from ChannelItem)

The DisplayPath property retrieves the fully qualified path using the DisplayName rather than the Name of the ChannelItems involved. The DisplayPath begins, ends, and is delimited with a forward slash ("/"). The RootChannel is concatenated sequentially with the name of each ChannelItem in the object's ancestry.

This member can be useful for showing the full path to this Channel Item but can be used as input to the Searches method of a Context or for dynamically constructing a URL.

### GetHashCode (Inherited from CmsObject)

The GetHashCode method retrieves the hash code for the object.

This identifier is not frequently used by the developer.

### GetType (Inherited from System.Object)

The GetType method retrieves the name of the namespace for the instance that the object represents. For example, Channel objects will always return Microsoft.ContentManagement.Publishing.Channel.

This member can be useful for determining what kind of object is represented by an item in the AllChildren Collection, the ChannelItem property of a CmsHttpContext, or the result of Context Searches.

### Guid (Inherited from HierarchyItem)

A GUID property by definition contains a globally unique identifier. This is generated when the object is created and committed into the CMS Repository, and it never changes. Effectively a candidate key, the GUID is alphanumeric, 32 characters long, separated by dashes, generated in part by the hardware on which the code is running, and guaranteed to be unique across the globe forever.

When a new ChannelItem has been created but has yet to be committed, a temporary, all zero GUID is used.

This member can be especially useful for searching for a Channel Item in a Context. This property was employed in the code example for creating a new ChannelItem earlier in this chapter. Since the assigned GUID doesn't change (like Name and therefore Path can), an object's GUID is a good candidate to be held in application state (query string, form element, view state, and cookie, to name a few), used to dynamically construct URLs (it contains no special characters), or used to index a custom collection.

### IsDeleted (Inherited from HierarchyItem)

The IsDeleted property retrieves a Boolean value that indicates whether the referencing ChannelItem has been deleted or not. It will be true if the referencing ChannelItem has been deleted.

This member can be useful to check through a collection when a user wants to undo a deletion before a commit. After a committed delete, this member is obviously useful to determine whether a specific object in a collection has been deleted or not. If it has, we avoid accessing any other method so as not to invoke an exception. This property was employed in the code example for creating and deleting the Channel Item hierarchy earlier in this chapter.

### IsDescendantOf (Inherited from HierarchyItem)

The IsDescendantOf method determines whether the referencing ChannelItem is an eventual child of another ChannelItem object. This is the only ChannelItem member that requires a parameter. We must indicate what object we want to verify is the referencing ChannelItem's ancestor.

This member can be useful for dynamically creating navigation and breadcrumbs.

### IsWorkingRevision (Inherited from HierarchyItem)

The IsWorkingRevision property retrieves a Boolean value that indicates whether the referencing ChannelItem is a working revision (work in progress) rather than a historical revision. It will be true if it is a working revision. Working revisions can be edited, whereas historical revisions cannot.

This member can be useful to determine if an edit will, regardless of user rights, even be possible.

### *LastModifiedBy (Inherited from HierarchyItem)*

The LastModifiedBy property returns a User object indicating the user that created the referencing ChannelItem. It is the same as the Created By property if the referencing ChannelItem has never been modified.

This member can be useful for showing a few characteristics about the user that last modified the ChannelItem.

### *LastModifiedDate (Inherited from HierarchyItem)*

The LastModifiedDate property has the standard characteristics of a CMS date and time field described and summarized with the other dates at the beginning of this section.

This member can be useful for showing the date and time that the ChannelItem was last modified or for identifying aged/fresh information found on a Web Property.

### *OwnedBy (Inherited from HierarchyItem)*

The OwnedBy property returns a User object indicating the user that currently owns an object. When a user begins updating properties for a ChannelItem, they become the OwnedBy user unless someone else is making changes. Only one person at a time is allowed to make changes to a ChannelItem, so there is a kind of automatic checkout process to prevent users from concurrently updating the same object. In communist states, this property can return a value of Everybody. When that happens, the ChannelItem becomes community property—edit at will, comrade.

This member can be useful to find out who is currently editing the object that we want to edit. If code isn't calling CommitAll quickly enough, this can wreak havoc on a busy site.

### *Path (Inherited from HierarchyItem)*

The Path property retrieves the fully qualified path using the Name property of the ChannelItems involved. The Path begins and ends with and is delimited by a forward slash ("/"). The RootChannel is concatenated sequentially with each ChannelItem in the object's ancestry.

This member can be useful for searching for a ChannelItem using the GetByPath Context Searches method when using a GUID is impractical.

### *QueryString, QueryStringModeUnpublished, QueryStringModeUpdate (All Inherited from ChannelItem)*

All three of these properties retrieve the URL query string parameters used to view the referencing ChannelItem. The QueryString property will present the parameters to use the same mode as currently in use, while the QueryStringModeUnpublished and QueryStringMode Update will present the parameters that could be used to navigate to the referencing ChannelItem in Unpublished or Update PublishingMode, respectively.

These members can be useful to redirect the user to the same ChannelItem in a different mode or to dynamically create a link.

### RevisionDate (Inherited from HierarchyItem)

The RevisionDate property has the standard characteristics of a CMS date and time field described and summarized with the other dates at the beginning of this section.

This member can be useful for showing the date and time that the ChannelItem was last revised or for identifying aged/fresh information found on a Web Property.

### Url (Inherited from ChannelItem)

The Url property retrieves the root relative URL for the referencing ChannelItem that will execute the OuterScriptFile (see the OuterScript File property in the Read/Write Members section later in this chapter), if any.

This member can be useful to redirect the user to the same Channel Item in the same mode or to dynamically create a link.

### UrlInner (Inherited from ChannelItem)

The UrlInner property retrieves the root relative URL for the referencing ChannelItem that will not execute the OuterScriptFile (see the OuterScriptFile property in the Read/Write Members section later in this chapter), if any.

This member is not frequently used.

### UrlInnerPlain (Inherited from ChannelItem)

The UrlInnerPlain property retrieves the root relative URL for the referencing ChannelItem that will not execute the OuterScriptFile (see the OuterScriptFile property in the Read/Write Members section later in this chapter), if any, nor will it propagate any query string parameters from the current request.

This member is not frequently used.

*UrlModePublished, UrlModeUnpublished, UrlModeUpdate
(All Inherited from ChannelItem)*

All three of these properties retrieve a root relative URL for the referencing ChannelItem based upon site configuration. Hierarchy-based sites will retrieve a path-based URL, while Node-ID-based sites will retrieve a GUID-based URL. Both URL versions accomplish the same function. The UrlModePublished, UrlModeUnpublished, and UrlMode Update will present the URL that could be used to navigate to the referencing ChannelItem in Published, Unpublished, or Update Publishing Mode, respectively.

These members can be useful to redirect the user to the same ChannelItem in a specific mode or to dynamically create a link to that mode.

## Read/Write Members

As before, the code to see all the read/write Channel object members is presented comprehensively. All these members can be assigned a value in code or through various other user interfaces. However, none of these changed values will become permanent until CommitAll is called on the Context. Uncommitted changes can be discarded by calling RollbackAll. If neither method is explicitly called when the Context in which the change is made is destroyed (goes out of scope or is disposed of), the disposition of the changes will be decided by the value of the RollbackOn SessionEnd property. By default, this property is false, so all changes are committed. In general, the properties of historical revisions can't be altered.

It is highly recommended that template file developers validate any date set to be sure that it is within the acceptable range for that property. Otherwise, CMS will have to alter it to be within the acceptable range when the change is committed. No message is generated when CMS changes the date, so the user could be surprised by the change. This problem can easily be avoided by validating dates before committing them.

As we discovered earlier, a user must have sufficient rights to make changes to any property, and the Context must be in an Update Publishing Mode (see the Getting into Update PublishingMode sidebar earlier in this chapter). It is always wise to place the verification that a user has sufficient rights and the actual modification of a property within a .NET try/catch block.

### Avoid Hack by Using HtmlEncode

Users will likely be allowed by your Web Property to enter free-form text in properties like the Channel Name, DisplayName, and Description. In the likely event that those properties are rendered back to the user's browser on a posting, the template file developer should be aware of the following underlying risk.

Typical users will simply enter the text that was intended, and everything will work as smoothly as planned. But it is possible for the user to enter any text into those properties, including HTML or even script. A malicious or misguided user could enter values that might be undesirable or even hazardous. Consider the following benign examples.

The user enters the following text in the channel description:

Really cool <a href=http://homepage.com>home page</a>.

When the channel description is rendered, the browser evaluates the text and displays

Really cool *home page.*

where "home page" is a clickable link.

Or worse, the user enters the following text in the channel description:

Really <script language=VBScript>Function body_onclick() Msgbox ('Gotcha') End Function</script> cool Channel.

When the channel description is rendered, the browser evaluates the text and displays

Really cool Channel.

Assuming that the HTML body tag (or some other tag) has an "id=body", which anyone could discover by simply viewing the source sent to their browser, when the user clicks anywhere on the body of the page, they will get a pop-up dialog containing the message "Gotcha".

This out-of-sight hack could go undetected for a long time. A creative user could really wreak havoc, running potentially malicious scripts in windows that open behind the main page as the page is loading, or worse.

To prevent this kind of attack, we recommend that the template developer use the HtmlEnode method of System.Web.HttpUtility to prevent the browser from interpreting the text in the property.

So, rather than coding like this:

```
x = CmsHttpContext.Current.Channel.Description;
```

protect yourself and code like this:

```
x = HttpUtility.HtmlEncode(CmsHttpContext.Current.Channel.Description);
```

An ounce of prevention, you know.

The read/write properties we can set in code using PAPI can also be set using the Site Manager interface.

Replace the Button1_Click function of our Scratchpad template file with the following code:

```
private void Button1_Click(object sender, System.EventArgs e)
{
  //1. Put current Channel into variable
  Channel cmsChannel = CmsHttpContext.Current.Channel;

  //2. Populate the label with read/write properties of a Channel
  Label1.Text =
    "<br><b>ApplyOuterScriptToPostings: </b>" +
      cmsChannel.ApplyOuterScriptToPostings.ToString() +
    "<br><b>DefaultPostingName: </b>" +
      HttpUtility.HtmlEncode(
        cmsChannel.DefaultPostingName.ToString()) +
    "<br><b>OuterScriptFile: </b>" +
      cmsChannel.OuterScriptFile.ToString() +
    "<br><b>Description: </b>" +
      HttpUtility.HtmlEncode(cmsChannel.Description.ToString()) +
    "<br><b>DisplayName: </b>" +
      HttpUtility.HtmlEncode(cmsChannel.DisplayName.ToString()) +
    "<br><b>ExpiryDate: </b>" + cmsChannel.ExpiryDate.ToString() +
    "<br><b>IsHiddenModePublished: </b>" +
      cmsChannel.IsHiddenModePublished.ToString() +
    "<br><b>IsImportant: </b>" + cmsChannel.IsImportant.ToString() +
    "<br><b>IsRobotFollowable: </b>" +
      cmsChannel.IsRobotFollowable.ToString() +
    "<br><b>IsRobotIndexable: </b>" +
      cmsChannel.IsRobotIndexable.ToString() +
    "<br><b>Name (HtmlEncoded): </b>" +
      HttpUtility.HtmlEncode(cmsChannel.Name.ToString()) +
    "<br><b>SortOrdinal: </b>" + cmsChannel.SortOrdinal.ToString() +
    "<br><b>StartDate: </b>" + cmsChannel.StartDate.ToString();
}
```

Lines 3 and 4 in the code are necessary because the default galleries may not have been set and would return a null value. If we try to retrieve the Name property of a null value, we will receive an exception. So, we check for this condition and capture the name only if the gallery reference exists; otherwise, we show an empty string.

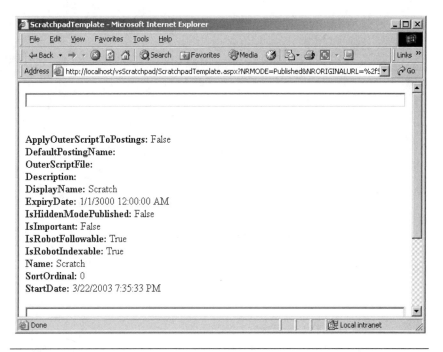

**Figure 25–8** Show read/write members

Build the solution and then refresh the Scratchpad posting in Internet Explorer, or browse to it and click the Button. The page should reload and look similar to Figure 25–8.

As you can see, many of the read/write property values are not set by default for a Channel object.

### Read/Write Members Specific to Channels
*ApplyOuterScriptToPostings*
The ApplyOuterScript property holds the Boolean value that indicates whether the OuterScriptFile (see the OuterScriptFile property later in this section) will or will not be executed when a posting is requested by URL. The OuterScriptFile is always executed when a channel is requested by URL. The property will be true if the referencing Channel object will execute the OuterScriptFile when a posting is requested by URL. The default value for this property is false.

As a Boolean, this property can only be set to true or false. It must be set to true for frames to work correctly.

This member can be useful to specify whether to run the OuterScriptFile when a posting is requested by URL.

*DefaultPostingName*

The DefaultPostingName property holds the case-insensitive name of the posting that will be shown if a user requests the referencing channel without specifying a posting. This is similar to the default document in an IIS virtual directory. However, unlike in IIS, there can only be one default posting specified, and if the posting specified is not found, CMS will either display the first posting in the channel or the CMS Welcome screen if there isn't a first posting. Since CMS does not prevent duplicate posting names, it is possible that this property could refer to an ambiguous name. However, CMS uses the SortOrdinal (see the SortOrdinal property later in this section) to choose which one to display. CMS will display the default posting for the appropriate PublishingMode requested.

CMS will automatically trim leading and trailing spaces and truncate the length to 100 characters for any string assigned to this property. Typical alphanumeric characters are allowed, but we recommend against using spaces in posting names.

This member can be useful to specify which posting to show by default when a channel is requested without a posting.

*OuterScriptFile*

The OuterScriptFile property holds the virtual path (IIS virtual directory and ASPX file name) to the script file executed when a channel, and perhaps when a posting (see the ApplyOuterScriptToPosting property earlier in this section), is requested by URL.

CMS will automatically trim leading and trailing spaces and truncate the length to 2000 characters for any string assigned to this property. Typical alphanumeric characters are allowed, but we recommend against using spaces. CMS does not validate the virtual path provided against IIS for accuracy but does require that it begin with a forward slash ("/"). The virtual path must specify the frameset for frames to work correctly.

This member can be useful to specify the virtual path and name of the outer script file.

### Read/Write Members Inherited for Use by Channels
*Description (Inherited from HierarchyItem)*

The Description property holds the free-form text description (see the Avoid Hack by Using HtmlEncode sidebar) for the referencing ChannelItem.

CMS will automatically trim leading and trailing spaces and truncates the length to 500 characters for any string assigned to this property. Typical alphanumeric characters are allowed.

This member can be useful for setting and showing a verbose description of the ChannelItem that the user is using.

### DisplayName (Inherited from ChannelItem)

The DisplayName property holds the free-form text of the long name or business name for the referencing ChannelItem intended for display purposes (see the Avoid Hack by Using HtmlEncode sidebar). If this property is empty or has never been set, the value in the Name property will be used instead. Unlike the Name property, the DisplayName is never used to construct URLs and doesn't indicate the Path to the Channel Item. It is the default sort order for any ChannelCollection.

CMS will automatically trim leading and trailing spaces and truncate the length to 250 characters for any string assigned to this property. Typical alphanumeric characters are allowed.

This member can be useful for setting and showing a user-friendly description of the ChannelItem that the user is using. This is especially useful for constructing aesthetic dynamic navigation.

### ExpiryDate (Inherited from ChannelItem)

The ExpiryDate property holds the date value for when a ChannelItem will no longer be visible in Published PublishingMode. It has the standard characteristics of a CMS date and time field described and summarized with the other dates at the beginning of this section.

This member can be useful for showing the date and time that the ChannelItem will expire. It can be an excellent field on which to sort ChannelItems in a collection. It could also be useful to proactively provide a warning to users about content that is about to expire.

### IsHiddenModePublished (Inherited from ChannelItem)

The IsHiddenModePublished property holds the Boolean value that indicates whether the referencing ChannelItem will or will not be included in any ChannelItem collection when the Context is in Published or Staging PublishingMode. It will be true if it should be excluded from the collection and false if it should be included in the collection. This does not restrict access to the hidden object; it just removes it from the collection. The default value for this property is false.

If the AutoFilterHidden property of the Context SessionSettings is set to false the setting in this property is ignored, and all ChannelItems are displayed in all collections in all PublishingModes.

As a Boolean, this property can only be set to true or false.

This member can be useful to control what is visible when developers are dynamically constructing site navigation.

### IsImportant (Inherited from ChannelItem)

The IsImportant property holds the Boolean value that indicates whether the referencing ChannelItem is important or not. It will be true if the ChannelItem is important and false if it isn't. Importance of a ChannelItem is determined entirely by the user. The default value for this property is false.

As a Boolean, this property can only be set to true or false.

This member can be useful in classifying ChannelItems into two categories, important and not important. That might be useful for generating some kinds of dynamic navigation.

### IsRobotFollowable, IsRobotIndexable
### (Both Inherited from ChannelItem)

The IsRobotFollowable and IsRobotIndexable properties hold the Boolean values that together indicate whether the referencing ChannelItem allows robots (search engine programs that crawl sites) to follow links and index the site or not. It will be true if robots are allowed to follow links or index, respectively, and false if they aren't. In either case, an appropriate ROBOT META tag is generated to advise the search engine of our preference. However, a META tag can't enforce the preference, just encourage or discourage it. The default value for these properties is true.

As Booleans, these properties can only be set to true or false.

These members can be useful for instructing search engines whether we want our Web Property to be indexed or not, and if indexed, whether we want links to be followed or not.

### Name (Inherited from HierarchyItem)

The Name property holds the free-form text of the actual name for the referencing ChannelItem. This name is not intended for display (see the Avoid Hack by Using HtmlEncode sidebar) per se but is visible to the user in the URL and Path. This property is not allowed to be empty but can be nonunique (not recommended). Changing the value of the Name property actually changes the value of the read-only Path property.

CMS will automatically trim leading and trailing spaces and truncate the length to 100 characters for any string assigned to this property. Typical alphanumeric characters are allowed, but we recommend against using spaces in ChannelItem names. In fact, it frequently makes sense to let the user set the value of the DisplayName and to systematically set the name of a new ChannelItem for them.

This member can be useful for setting and showing a system-oriented description of the ChannelItem. This is especially useful for constructing the links used in dynamic navigation.

### SortOrdinal (Inherited from ChannelItem)

The SortOrdinal property holds the custom sort sequence number for the referencing ChannelItem—that is, the user-defined sequence that this ChannelItem would display relative to other ChannelItems at the same level in a collection.

For example, if there were three ChannelItems named A, B, and C and we wanted them to show in C, A, B order, we may give C a SortOrdinal of 30, A a SortOrdinal of 20, and B a SortOrdinal of 10. In this way we achieve a custom sort sequence, highest to lowest. As you can see, not every value is needed to order the ChannelItems relative to one another. Leaving gaps can potentially make inserting a new value easier, although duplicate values are allowed. We use descending numbers because new ChannelItems are given a SortOrdinal of zero (0).

Only numeric values are allowed.

This member can be useful for custom sorts but also for deciding which of two identically sorted items to show first. Since a series of sort methods applied to a ChannelCollection or PostingCollection behave like a multikey sort, when duplicate values occur, we can use SortOrdinal as a consistent tiebreaker.

### StartDate (Inherited from ChannelItem)

The StartDate property holds the date value for when a Channel Item will first be made visible in Published and Staging publishing modes. It has the standard characteristics of a CMS date and time field described and summarized with the other dates at the beginning of this section.

This member can be useful for showing the date and time that the ChannelItem will become live. It can be an excellent field on which to sort ChannelItems in a collection. It could also be useful to proactively provide a warning to users about content that is about to go live.

## Working with Channel Objects

Thus far we have seen the properties and methods of a Channel that use intrinsic data types. This section will explore CMS-specific objects and collections of objects that are available from a Channel. These are the principal objects graphically modeled in Figure 23–2, PAPI object model —Channel.

---

**NOTE:** The PAPI object model is covered in detail in Chapter 23. The objects covered in this section will be covered in the same order as they are illustrated in Figure 23–2.

---

These objects require some special processing and consideration. As before, there are some common facts and concepts that will help us in this section.

After a Channel object has been deleted but before it is committed, all properties become read-only. However, even after a deleted Channel object is committed, it may still reside in an in-memory collection. All Channel child objects must be removed before a Channel object can be deleted. Even if they still reside in memory, Channel child objects cannot be read once the Channel object has been deleted and committed.

Historical revisions of a channel don't typically keep the value that was associated with the revision when it was the current version. Properties typically represent the value of the current revision regardless of the value when the historical revision was the current revision. Attempting to assign a value to these properties for a historical revision will result in an exception. This concept is extended to the child objects for historical revisions of a channel, including the collections (Channels, Postings, All Children, and CustomProperties) whose contents are based upon the revision date and time of the channel. Channel objects and Posting objects are only included in these collections if they have a corresponding revision date and are currently contained in the referencing Channel object. Otherwise, they are left out.

### Parent (Inherited from ChannelItem)

The Parent property of a Channel object or Posting object returns the Channel object that contains it. The specific Channel object returned depends on the current PublishingMode, the user rights, and potentially the StartDate and ExpiryDate. If the referencing object is contained within the built-in RootChannel, then the RootChannel is returned. Since the RootChannel has no containing Channel, its Parent returns a null, so it is wise to check the IsRoot property (discussed earlier in this chapter) before accessing the Parent property.

Replace the Button1_Click function of our Scratchpad template file with the following code:

```
private void Button1_Click(object sender, System.EventArgs e)
{
  //1. Put current Channel into variable
  Channel cmsChannel = CmsHttpContext.Current.Channel;

  //2. Make sure that the current Channel isn't the root
  if (!cmsChannel.IsRoot)
  {
    //3. Populate the label with the current Channel and its parent
    Label1.Text =
      "<br><b>Current: </b>" + cmsChannel.Name.ToString() +
      "<br><b>Parent:  </b>" + cmsChannel.Parent.Name.ToString();
  }
  else
  {
    //4. Provide nonerror feedback to the developer
    Label1.Text = "Current Channel is the RootChannel";
  }
}
```

Build the solution and then refresh the Scratchpad posting in Internet Explorer, or browse to it and click the Button. The page should reload and look similar to Figure 25–9.

This member can be useful, even essential, in the construction of dynamic navigation, including the infamous breadcrumbs.

---

**NOTE:** Although briefly mentioned later in this chapter, dynamic navigation and breadcrumbs are covered in depth in Chapter 14.

---

## Channels

The Channels collection property of Channel objects depends on the current PublishingMode, the user rights, potentially the IsHiddenMode Published property, StartDate, and ExpiryDate of each Channel in the

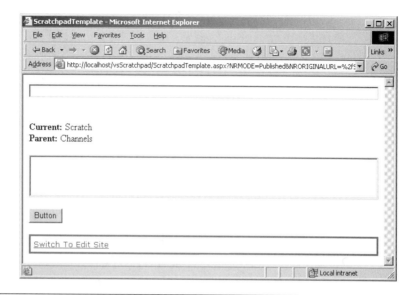

**Figure 25–9**  Show Channel Parent

collection (all three properties are discussed earlier in the Read/Write Members section of this chapter), and potentially the AutoFilterHidden property of the Context.

The Channel objects in the collection will be ordered, by default, first by their SortOrdinal value (discussed earlier near the end of the Read/Write Members section of this chapter) and within that, alphabetically by Name. However, this sort order can be overridden. The Channel Collection contains a large number of built-in sorts, which can be applied to the list. The ChannelCollection sort members are as follows:

- SortByChangeDate (inherited from ChannelItemCollection)
- SortByDisplayName (inherited from ChannelItemCollection)
- SortByDisplayPath (inherited from ChannelItemCollection)
- SortByExpiryDate (inherited from ChannelItemCollection)
- SortByImportance (inherited from ChannelItemCollection)
- SortByLastModifiedDate (inherited from HierarchyItemCollection)
- SortByName (inherited from HierarchyItemCollection)
- SortByOrdinal (inherited from ChannelItemCollection)
- SortByOwner (inherited from HierarchyItemCollection)
- SortByPath (inherited from HierarchyItemCollection)
- SortByRevisionDate (inherited from HierarchyItemCollection)
- SortByStartDate (inherited from ChannelItemCollection)

Each sort method can be applied successively to the Channels collection to create a multikey sort. This can be beneficial if duplicate values are expected in the collection and we want to iterate a consistent sequence of values (as is often the case in dynamically generating navigation for a site). For example, sorting the collection using SortByDisplay Name followed by SortByOwner would yield a list of Channels grouped by Channel Owner in Channel DisplayName sequence. To start the sort sequence over again, we would need to get another instance of the Channels property.

Be cautious about overusing this functionality because sorting is always a CPU-intensive activity, and repeatedly sorting a large list or a large number of small lists could become a resource drain. If most pages in your site require a specific sequence, consider manually ordering items using their SortOrdinal so that they will be sorted correctly when the collection is initially accessed. Remember, by default, new Channels added to the list will have a SortOrdinal of zero (0) and therefore sort to the bottom of the list.

This collection is not self-updating. If new Channel objects are added to the Web Property or existing Channel objects are deleted, the collection in memory will not be updated. It is good programming practice to get the property and use it swiftly. In busy sites, if some time has passed since the property was first acquired, it would typically be better to get the property again rather than use the one previously in memory.

The Channels collection has a Count property that can be used to determine whether the list contains any items. The items in the collection can be iterated using the common foreach statement or directly using the string Name for the item or its zero-based ordinal index.

There is also a Union method for the Channels collection. It can be combined with another collection to create a superset of all the objects in both collections.

Some of these concepts are demonstrated in the following code example. It uses the Scratch channel hierarchy created in the Creating and Deleting Objects in a Channel section earlier in this chapter.

Replace the Button1_Click function of our Scratchpad template file with the following code:

```
private void Button1_Click(object sender, System.EventArgs e)
{
  try
  {
    //1. Grab the current CMS Context
    CmsHttpContext cmsContext = CmsHttpContext.Current;
```

```
//2. Grab the Brady Channel
Channel cmsBradyChannel =
  cmsContext.Searches.GetByPath("/Channels/Scratch/Brady")
  as Channel;

//3. Populate the label with informational text
Label1.Text = "Working with " +
  cmsBradyChannel.DisplayName.ToString() +
  " Channel's Channels collection";

//4. Change sort from Name within SortOrdinal to DisplayName
cmsBradyChannel.Channels.SortByDisplayName();

//5. Apply secondary sort of Owner to the DisplayName sort
//    Duplicate values for Owner will retain the
//    DisplayName sequence
cmsBradyChannel.Channels.SortByOwner();

//6. Iterate the Channels in the Brady Channel
foreach (Channel cmsChannel in cmsBradyChannel.Channels)
{
  //7. Add the DisplayName of each Channel into the ListBox
  ListBox1.Items.Add("Using implicit reference: " +
    cmsChannel.DisplayName.ToString()
    );
}
//8. Check to be sure that there are items in the collection
if (cmsBradyChannel.Channels.Count > 0)
{
  //9. Add the DisplayName of the first Channel into the
  //    ListBox. This is a risky approach.
  ListBox1.Items.Add("Using EXPLICIT reference: " +
    cmsBradyChannel.Channels[0].DisplayName.ToString()
    );
  //10. Add the DisplayName of a the Mike Channel into the
  //     ListBox. This is a very risky approach.
  ListBox1.Items.Add("Using EXPLICIT reference: " +
    cmsBradyChannel.Channels["Mike"].DisplayName.ToString()
    );
}
}
```

```
catch(Exception eError)
{
    //11. Provide error feedback to the developer
    Label1.Text = "<b>Error: </b>" + eError.Message.ToString();
}
}
```

Build the solution and then refresh the Scratchpad posting in Internet Explorer, or browse to it and click the Button. The page should reload and look similar to Figure 25–10.

You'll have to scroll down to see the second explicit reference. If the explicit references to the item in the code under comments 9 and 10 do not find a Channel, an exception ("Object reference not set to an instance of an object") will occur. In general, we want to avoid using an explicit reference to an item in a collection anyway. Believe it or not, using one of the Searches (discussed in Chapter 28) like GetByGuid (ideally), GetByPath, or GetByUrl will likely actually outperform an explicit reference to an item. This is because explicit references require the entire collection to be inflated to access the single entry, whereas the search just hydrates the single instance.

This member collection can be useful, even essential, in the construction of dynamic navigation, including the infamous breadcrumbs.

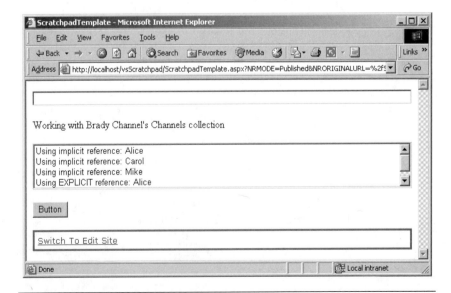

**Figure 25–10**  Working with a Channels collection

## Postings

The Postings collection property of a Posting object is similar to the Channels collection property. Its contents also depend on the current PublishingMode, the user's rights, potentially the IsHiddenMode Published property (discussed earlier in the Read/Write Members section of this chapter), StartDate, and ExpiryDate of the Postings in the collection, and potentially the AutoFilterHidden property of the Context.

The Posting objects in the collection will be ordered, by default, first by their SortOrdinal value (also discussed earlier near the end of the Read/ Write Members section of this chapter) and within that, chronologically by LastModifiedDate.

The same sorting capabilities and cautions that apply to the Channels property apply to the Postings property. The tendency for the collection to get stale, the access methods, and the ability to form a union with other collections are the same too.

Since we have only one posting at this point, only a brief coding example will be shown. Postings are covered in depth in the next chapter.

Replace the Button1_Click function of our Scratchpad template file with the following code:

```
private void Button1_Click(object sender, System.EventArgs e)
{
  try
  {
    //1. Put current Channel into variable
    Channel cmsChannel = CmsHttpContext.Current.Channel;

    //2. Populate the label with informational text
    Label1.Text = "Working with " +
      cmsChannel.DisplayName.ToString() +
      " Channel's Postings collection";

    //3. Change the sort to DisplayName
    cmsChannel.Postings.SortByDisplayName();

    //4. Iterate the Postings in the current Channel
    foreach (Posting cmsPosting in cmsChannel.Postings)
    {
      //5. Add the DisplayName of each Posting into the ListBox
      ListBox1.Items.Add(cmsPosting.DisplayName.ToString());
    }
  }
```

```
catch(Exception eError)
{
  //6. Provide error feedback to the developer
  Label1.Text = "<b>Error: </b>" + eError.Message.ToString();
}
}
```

As with the Channels collection property, explicit references to an item in the collection members are allowed, just not illustrated and not recommended.

Build the solution and then refresh the Scratchpad posting in Internet Explorer, or browse to it and click the Button. The page should reload and look similar to Figure 25–11.

This member collection can be useful, even essential, in the construction of dynamic navigation.

## AllChildren

The AllChildren collection property of Channel and Posting objects (ChannelItem objects) is simply a union of the Channels collection property and the Postings collection property, both discussed just before this property in this section of this chapter. Its contents depend on the contents of those two collections for the given user in the given context.

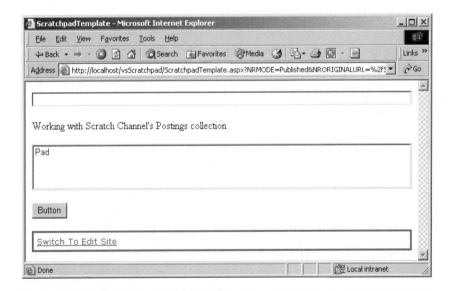

**Figure 25–11** Working with a Postings collection

The ChannelItem objects in the collection will be ordered, by default, first by their SortOrdinal value (discussed earlier near the end of the Read/Write Members section of this chapter) and within that, alphabetically by ChannelItem Name.

The same sorting capabilities and cautions that apply to the other two properties apply to the AllChildren property. The tendency for the collection to get stale, the access methods, and the ability to form a union with other collections are the same too.

Again, a brief coding example is shown to give a flavor of how this is similar to and how it is different from the other two collection properties.

Replace the Button1_Click function of our Scratchpad template file with the following code:

```
private void Button1_Click(object sender, System.EventArgs e)
{
  try
  {
    //1. Put current Channel into variable
    Channel cmsChannel = CmsHttpContext.Current.Channel;

    //2. Populate the label with informational text
    Label1.Text = "Working with " +
      cmsChannel.DisplayName.ToString() +
      " Channel's AllChildren collection";

    //3. Change the sort to DisplayName
    cmsChannel.AllChildren.SortByDisplayName();

    //4. Iterate the Postings in the current Channel
    foreach (ChannelItem cmsChannelItem in cmsChannel.AllChildren)
    {
      //5. Add the CMS type followed by the DisplayName for each
      //   ChannelItem into the ListBox
      ListBox1.Items.Add(
        cmsChannelItem.GetType().ToString() + " " +
        cmsChannelItem.DisplayName.ToString()
        );
    }
  }
  catch(Exception eError)
  {
    //6. Provide error feedback to the developer
    Label1.Text = "<b>Error: </b>" + eError.Message.ToString();
  }
}
```

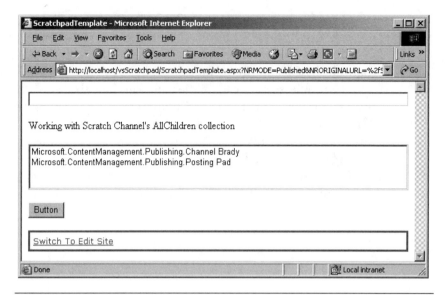

**Figure 25–12** Working with an AllChildren collection

The biggest difference is the casting of the children in the collection as the generic ChannelItem type in the code under comment 4. As with the other two collection properties, explicit references to an item in the collection members are allowed, just not illustrated and not recommended.

Build the solution and then refresh the Scratchpad posting in Internet Explorer, or browse to it and click the Button. The page should reload and look similar to Figure 25–12.

This member collection can be useful, even essential, in the construction of dynamic navigation, including the infamous breadcrumbs.

## CustomProperties (Inherited from ChannelItem)

The CustomProperties collection of CustomProperty objects is predictably used as a catch-all for capturing Channel object characteristics that were not thought of by Microsoft but that we want to have for our Channel objects. These user-defined name/value pairs can be used for nearly anything that we can dream up. They include an optional domain list of allowed values (default values are only allowed on Posting objects). It's like having an intelligent, built-in dictionary object for each Channel object.

For instance, we could set up all channels to have a CustomProperty called IsBottomNavChannel with an allowed values list of true or false.

As we iterate through the Channels collection to dynamically build our navigation, we could check the CustomProperty to see which channels we should include in the bottom navigation and which ones we should leave out.

However, CustomProperties for a channel must be created using Site Manager; the Web Author and PAPI can only be used to add allowed values and update the value of existing CustomProperty objects. This can be a big disadvantage. Some CMS pundits contend that creating a hidden posting in the channel with a collection of placeholders yields the same name/value pair (placeholder/content pair) concept. This is potentially a better solution since new placeholders can be created in code, and we have all the capabilities of a template and code-behind to exploit. Consistency across channels can also be maintained using a template, but this must be done manually by an administrator in Site Manager. For example, if we want to add a new CustomProperty to all of our channels, it must be manually added through Site Manager to each channel, one channel at a time. For a site with lots of channels, the task could be daunting and fraught with potential human error and inconsistency.

That said, CustomProperties are part of CMS and may require our attention. Table 25–3 lists the primary properties and their description for a CustomProperty object.

**Table 25–3** CustomProperty Member Descriptions

| Public CustomProperty Properties | Description |
| --- | --- |
| AllowedValues | Gets a collection of allowed values defined for a target Custom-Property object. |
| DefaultValue | Gets the default value of the target CustomProperty as a string, or as a null reference (Nothing, in Visual Basic) if the Custom-Property does not have a default value. |
| Name | Gets the name of this CustomProperty. |
| UsesDefaultValue | Indicates whether a CustomProperty is using the DefaultValue. |
| Value | Gets and sets a value for this CustomProperty object. |
| ResetToDefault | Resets the target instance of the CustomProperty class to derive its current value from its default value, if a default value exists. |

Unlike the channel itself, each CustomProperty must have a unique Name within the CustomProperties collection for each channel. The Name is essentially the key and is used as the ascending, alphabetical sort order for the collection. Each CustomProperty must also have a value. Unlike postings (discussed in the next chapter), Channel Custom-Property objects do not have an associated template and therefore are not allowed to have default values (these are set up for postings in the template using VS.NET, and there isn't an equivalent capability in Site Manager for channels). So, the CustomProperty UsesDefaultValue property is always set to false, the DefaultValue property always returns null, and the ResetToDefault method has no effect.

To demonstrate this concept, assume that we want our channels to have the CustomProperty previously described, IsBottomNavChannel, with an allowed values list of true or false. Using the Scratch channel hierarchy created in the Creating and Deleting Objects in a Channel section earlier in this chapter, we use Site Manager (our only option) to create the CustomProperty for each channel in the hierarchy. Use the following steps to complete this setup task:

1. Open Site Manager and authenticate as a CMS administrator.
2. Expand each channel so that you can see the entire hierarchy.
3. Start with the Scratch channel.
4. Right-click the channel and choose Properties from the pop-up menu (Figure 25–13).
5. On the resulting Scratch Properties dialog, choose the Custom tab, on the far right.
6. Click the New button, on the bottom left.
7. On the resulting Add Custom Property dialog (Figure 25–14), enter the following values.
8. Enter IsBottomNavChannel into the Property Name text box.
9. Choose Selection from the Property Type drop-down (the section inside of the frame below will change from a single multi-row text box for entering the Current Text Value to a set of controls that allow the creation of the allowed values list).
10. Click the New button to add the first value to the list.
11. On the resulting Add Value dialog, enter "true" into the Value text box and click the OK button.
12. Click the New button again to add a second value of "false".
13. While false is still highlighted, click the Set as Current button to assign the IsBottomNavChannel a value of "false" for the Scratch channel.

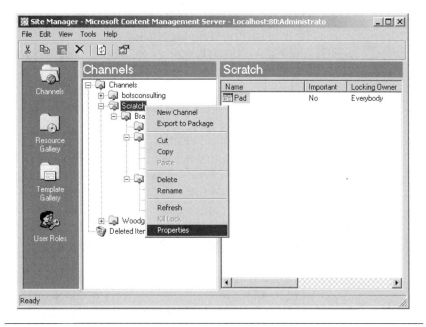

**Figure 25–13**  Choose Properties from pop-up menu

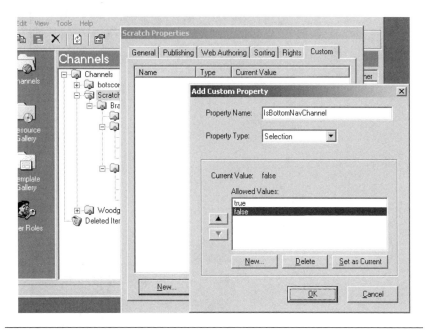

**Figure 25–14**  Add Custom Property dialog

**14.** This will enable the OK button; click the OK button to dismiss the Add Custom Property dialog.

**15.** You will see the IsBottomNavChannel custom property we just added listed on the Custom tab of the Scratch Properties dialog (Figure 25–15).

**16.** Click OK to dismiss the Scratch Properties dialog.

From Site Manager select the Brady channel and repeat steps 4 through 16 in exactly the same way. One at a time, select each of the channels—Alice, Carol, Cindy, Jan, Marsha, Mike, Bobby, Greg, and Peter—and repeat steps 4 through 16 in exactly the same way except for Alice, Carol, and Mike. In step 13, when the Set as Current button is clicked, choose true rather than false. We want these three to be listed in our fictitious bottom navigation. Yes, it is tedious and potentially fraught with error.

When all of the channels have been given our new CustomProperty, you can exit Site Manager and open VS.NET to the Scratchpad template file. We are going to be traversing the channel hierarchy searching for channels with the IsBottomNavChannel custom property set to true (basically looking for Alice, Carol, and Mike from the work we just

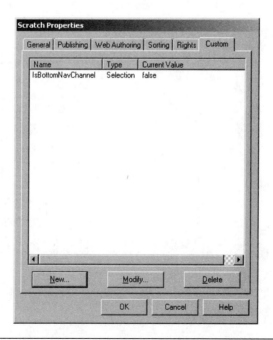

**Figure 25–15** Scratch Properties dialog with custom property listed

completed). The easiest way to traverse the hierarchy is recursively. So, just above the Button1_Click function that we have been replacing throughout this chapter, enter the following code:

```
private void ShowChannelsWithCustomProperty(Channel cmsChannel,
  string nameCustomPropertyToShow,
  string valueCustomPropertyToShow)
//******************************************************************
//Search all Channels from the cmsChannel passed to the function
//for the nameCustomPropertyToShow CustomProperty Name
//with the valueCustomPropertyToShow CustomProperty Value
//If a child Channel has children, this function is called
//recursively
//******************************************************************
{
  try
  {
    //1. Iterate the Channels collection
    foreach (Channel cmsChildChannel in cmsChannel.Channels)
    {
      //2. Iterate the CustomProperties collection
      foreach (CustomProperty cmsChannelProperty
                 in cmsChildChannel.CustomProperties)
      {
        //3. Is it the CustomProperty we are looking for?
        if (cmsChannelProperty.Name == nameCustomPropertyToShow)
        {
          //4. Does it have the correct value?
          if (cmsChannelProperty.Value ==
              valueCustomPropertyToShow)
          {
            //5. Then show it in the ListBox
            ListBox1.Items.Add(cmsChildChannel.Name.ToString());
          }
        }
      }
      //6. Check to see if a child Channel has children
      if(cmsChildChannel.AllChildren.Count > 0)
      {
        //7. Call this function recursively to visit every Channel
        ShowChannelsWithCustomProperty(cmsChildChannel,
          nameCustomPropertyToShow, valueCustomPropertyToShow);
```

```
          }
        }
      }
    catch(Exception eError)
    {
      //8. Provide error feedback to the developer
      Label1.Text = "<b>Error: </b>" + eError.Message.ToString();
    }
  }
}
```

As the comments indicate, this function will recursively traverse all the channels and child channels in a given root channel looking for a CustomProperty with a given Name set to a given Value. Now we just need to seed this function with the channel, CustomProperty name to search for, and the CustomProperty value to select.

Replace the Button1_Click function of our Scratchpad template file with the following code:

```
private void Button1_Click(object sender, System.EventArgs e)
{
  try
  {
    //1. Grab the current CMS Context
    CmsHttpContext cmsContext = CmsHttpContext.Current;

    //2. Populate the label with the root Channel name
    Label1.Text = cmsContext.Channel.Name.ToString() +
      " Channel " +
      "with IsBottomNavChannel CustomProperty set to true";

    //3. Call function to show all Channels in the ListBox with
    //    the IsBottomNavChannel CustomProperty set to true
    //    CustomProperties can only hold strings so true is
    //    in quotes
    ShowChannelsWithCustomProperty(cmsContext.Channel,
      "IsBottomNavChannel", "true");
  }
  catch(Exception eError)
  {
    //4. Provide error feedback to the developer
    Label1.Text = "<b>Error: </b>" + eError.Message.ToString();
  }
}
```

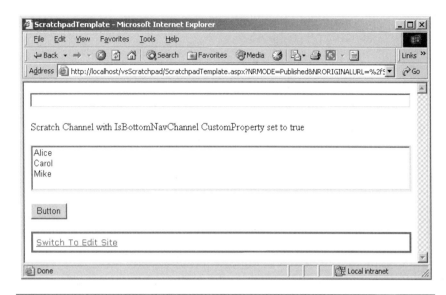

**Figure 25–16**  Channels with true IsBottomNavChannel

Build the solution and then refresh the Scratchpad posting in Internet Explorer, or browse to it and click the Button. The page should reload and look similar to Figure 25–16.

### DefaultResourceGallery, DefaultTemplateGallery

The DefaultResourceGallery and DefaultTemplateGallery properties refer to the resources and templates that authors are encouraged to use when creating new postings in the referencing Channel object. If these properties are not set (no reference to a gallery exists) or the user doesn't have sufficient rights to the referenced gallery, CMS will return a null. Any use of gallery properties and methods will result in an exception if that object is null.

In Site Manager, these two properties can be found in the Default Galleries for Web Authoring section on the Web Authoring tab of the Channel Properties dialog for each channel. Although Site Manager facilitates the setting of these properties, they are not directly used by CMS for any purpose. They are, however, exposed for use within PAPI.

The following code example reuses the GetAuthenticatedCms ApplicationContext function from Listing 25–1. So we need to ensure the code from Listing 25–1 is entered above the Button1_Click function of our Scratchpad template file.

Replace the Button1_Click function of our Scratchpad template file
with the following code:

```
private void Button1_Click(object sender, System.EventArgs e)
{
  try
  {
    //1. Grab the current CMS Context
    CmsHttpContext cmsContextHttp = CmsHttpContext.Current;

    //2. If either gallery is not set, go into update mode
    //    and set it
    if (cmsContextHttp.Channel.DefaultResourceGallery == null |
        cmsContextHttp.Channel.DefaultTemplateGallery == null)
    {
      //3. Grab an Authenticated Context in Update PublishingMode
      //    using the GetAuthenticatedCmsApplicationContext function
      //    from Listing 25-1
      CmsApplicationContext cmsContextApp =
        GetAuthenticatedCmsApplicationContext(
          PublishingMode.Update);

      //4. Position the Application Context to the current Channel
      //    using its GUID (the most efficient Searches method)
      //    Cast the result of the Searches object as a Channel
      Channel cmsChannelApp =
        cmsChannelApp.Searches.GetByGuid(
          cmsContextHttp.Channel.Guid)
        as Channel;

      //5. If Current Channel DefaultResourceGallery is not set
      if (cmsChannelApp.DefaultResourceGallery == null)
      {
        //6. Set it to the root
        cmsCurrentApp.DefaultResourceGallery =
          cmsContextHttp.RootResourceGallery;
      }

      //7. If Current Channel DefaultTemplateGallery is not set
      if (cmsChannelApp.DefaultTemplateGallery == null)
      {
```

```
        //8. Set it to the root
      cmsChannelApp.DefaultTemplateGallery =
        cmsContextHttp.RootTemplateGallery;
    }

    //9. Commit all changes
    cmsContextApp.CommitAll();

    //10. Populate the label with the names of the default
    //    galleries using the CmsApplicationContext Channel
    Label1.Text = "From CmsApplicationContext" +
      "<br><b>DefaultResourceGallery: </b>" +
      cmsChannelApp.DefaultResourceGallery.Name.ToString() +
      "<br><b>DefaultTemplateGallery: </b>" +
      cmsChannelApp.DefaultTemplateGallery.Name.ToString();

    //11. Dispose of the stand-alone Application Context
    cmsContextApp.Dispose();
  }
  else
  {
    //12. Use Current Channel from Http Context
    Channel cmsChannelHttp = cmsContextHttp.Channel as Channel;
    //13. Populate the label with the names of the default
    //    galleries using the CmsHttpContext Channel
    Label1.Text = "From CmsHttpContext" +
      "<br><b>DefaultResourceGallery: </b>" +
      cmsChannelHttp.DefaultResourceGallery.Name.ToString() +
      "<br><b>DefaultTemplateGallery: </b>" +
      cmsChannelHttp.DefaultTemplateGallery.Name.ToString();
  }
}
catch(Exception eError)
{
  //14. Provide error feedback to the developer
  Label1.Text = "<b>Error: </b>" + eError.Message.ToString();
}
}
```

Build the solution and then refresh the Scratchpad posting in Internet Explorer, or browse to it and click the Button. The page should reload and look similar to Figure 25–17.

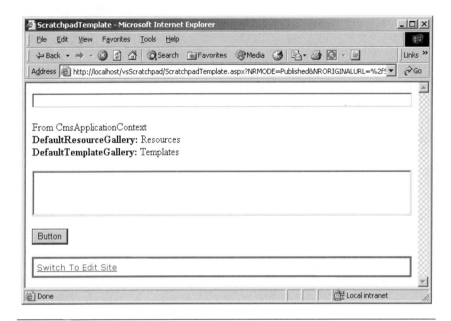

**Figure 25–17**  Show channel default galleries

Of course, these properties can be set to any valid ResourceGallery object or TemplateGallery object, respectively, in CMS. Setting these to the root of the current channel is just a certainty for the sake of the example. Conversely, setting this property to null removes the reference to the default gallery.

This member can be useful to specify the default gallery as described. It could be valuable to use this value if you were creating a custom set of admin screens for the creation of a posting.

### GetByRelativePath (Inherited from ChannelItem)

As previously described, the Channel object's Path property retrieves the fully qualified path using the Name property of the channels involved. The GetByRelativePath method provides a means to get a Channel object or Posting object relative to the current channel's Path. Of course, we can only retrieve objects that the user has appropriate rights to.

This concept and syntax is similar to the relative referencing used in HTML and DOS. The current object is represented with a period ("."), its parent is represented by two periods (".."), and each channel name is separated by a forward slash ("/"). Unlike the channel Path, the relative path string must not begin with a forward slash.

Using the hierarchy given at the beginning of this chapter, consider the following examples.

The Greg channel's path is /Channels/Scratch/Brady/Mike/Greg. With Greg as the current channel, we could use the GetByRelativePath method with the following relative path: "../../.." (Greg's parent's parent's parent). That would retrieve an object that we could cast as a Channel object, and we would have our Scratch channel.

Again, with Greg as the current channel, we could use the GetByRelativePath method with the following relative path: "../../Carol" (Greg's parent's parent's child channel Carol). That would retrieve an object that we could cast as a Channel object, and we would have the Carol channel.

Last, with the Carol channel as the current channel, we could use the GetByRelativePath method with the following relative path: "./Marsha" (Carol's child channel Marsha). That would retrieve an object that we could cast as a Channel, and we would have the Marsha channel.

Let's see these three examples in code.

Replace the Button1_Click function of our Scratchpad template file with the following code:

```
private void Button1_Click(object sender, System.EventArgs e)
{
  try
  {
    //1. Grab the current CMS Context
    CmsHttpContext cmsContext = CmsHttpContext.Current;

    //2. Populate the label with static text
    Label1.Text = "Get Channel Path using GetByRelativePath";

    //3. Remove any previous entries from the ListBox
    ListBox1.Items.Clear();

    //4. Grab the Greg Channel from the Context
    //   Cast the result of the Searches object as a Channel
    Channel cmsGregChannel =
      cmsContext.Searches.GetByPath(
        "/Channels/Scratch/Brady/Mike/Greg")
      as Channel;

    //5. If our search for the Greg Channel was successful
    if (cmsGregChannel != null)
    {
```

```
//6. Add the Channel path to the ListBox
ListBox1.Items.Add
  ("Greg Path: " + cmsGregChannel.Path.ToString());

//7. Grab the relative Scratch Channel using the Greg Channel
Channel cmsScratchChannel =
  cmsGregChannel.GetByRelativePath("../../..")
  as Channel;

//8. If our relative search for Scratch Channel
//   was successful
if (cmsScratchChannel != null)
{
  //9. Add the Channel path to the ListBox
  ListBox1.Items.Add
    ("Scratch Path: " + cmsScratchChannel.Path.ToString());
}
else
{
  //10. Provide nonerror feedback to the developer
  ListBox1.Items.Add ("Scratch Channel not found");
}


//11. Grab the relative Carol Channel using the Greg Channel
Channel cmsCarolChannel =
  cmsGregChannel.GetByRelativePath("../../Carol")
  as Channel;

//12. If our relative search for Carol Channel
//   was successful
if (cmsCarolChannel != null)
{
  //13. Add the Channel path to the ListBox
  ListBox1.Items.Add
    ("Carol Path: " + cmsCarolChannel.Path.ToString());

  //14. Grab the relative Marsha Channel using the
  //    Carol Channel
  Channel cmsMarshaChannel =
    cmsCarolChannel.GetByRelativePath("./Marsha")
    as Channel;

  //15. If our relative search for Marsha Channel
  //    was successful
```

```
        if (cmsMarshaChannel != null)
        {
          //16. Add the Channel path to the ListBox
          ListBox1.Items.Add
            ("Marsha Path: " + cmsMarshaChannel.Path.ToString());
        }
        else
        {
          //17. Provide nonerror feedback to the developer
          ListBox1.Items.Add ("Marsha Channel not found");
        }
      }
      else
      {
        //18. Provide nonerror feedback to the developer
        ListBox1.Items.Add ("Carol Channel not found");
      }
    }
    else
    {
      //19. Provide nonerror feedback to the developer
      ListBox1.Items.Add ("Greg Channel not found");
    }
  }
  catch(Exception eError)
  {
    //20. Provide error feedback to the developer
    Label1.Text = "<b>Error: </b>" + eError.Message.ToString();
  }
}
```

Build the solution and then refresh the Scratchpad posting in Internet Explorer, or browse to it and click the Button. The page should reload and look similar to Figure 25–18.

This member can be useful for searching for a Channel object or Posting object relative to the current channel or posting. However, searching for objects using their path is potentially fraught with error. If the reference is to an ambiguous item (duplicates are not prevented by CMS), one that does not exist, one that is in a different publishing mode, or one that the user doesn't have rights to, a null value is returned. Also, since the Path consists of the names of channels and postings and users can change those names, the Path can change, potentially rendering the code invalid. There can be performance issues as well.

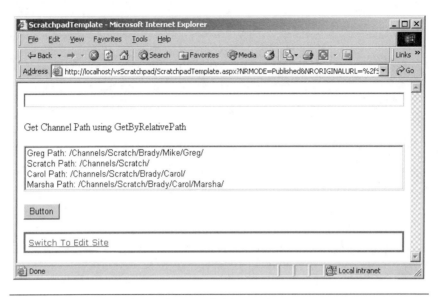

**Figure 25-18** Show GetByRelativePath results

# Constructing Dynamic Navigation and Displaying Breadcrumbs

Most CMS sites dynamically generate their navigation based around the channel and posting structure, the current user's rights, the Publishing Mode that user is working in, and relevant properties of the Context, Postings, and Channels surrounding the content being viewed. Special properties like DisplayName and IsHiddenModePublished aid in the delivery of this navigation. Usually this code is placed into a user control so that it can be used on templates throughout the Web Property.

**NOTE:** Although briefly mentioned here, dynamic navigation and breadcrumbs are covered in depth in Chapter 14.

The beauty of this model is that as the site grows and users change the content and structure, your navigation, which is based on the channel hierarchy and postings within it, immediately reflects the changes to the site. Entire sections of the site can be moved or renamed, and the site navigation will adjust. No more broken links.

Navigation can be created so that it is role specific or based upon the presence or absence of a specific condition or value. It can be as static or dynamic as the site requires.

Things can get a little bit more difficult on a mixed (ASP and ASP.NET) site or one that requires some non-template-based pages. However, these obstacles can also be overcome.

Because dynamic site navigation requests so many objects for each posting served, it can potentially degrade performance. To improve the performance of templates that contain dynamic navigation, the developer should enable output caching. Also, a common rule of thumb is when the number of channels and postings in a given channel exceeds a few hundred, performance issues when rendering navigation may arise. It would be better to have your information architects restructure the site to better accommodate the actual use.

One common technique of presenting the location of the current content within the hierarchy is the use of something called breadcrumbs. Basically, the idea is to show the successive parent of any content until a top-level channel is reached. Traversing the ancestry of a posting can be done both sequentially and recursively. These two methods are the final coding example explored in this chapter.

Ensure that the following two functions, which fundamentally perform the same function, are entered above the Button1_Click function of our Scratchpad template file. First enter the function to build the breadcrumb sequentially:

```
private string SequentialBreadcrumb(Channel cmsLeafChannel,
  string crumbSeperator)
{
  try
  {
    //1. String variable to hold the breadcrumb as it is built
    string growingBreadcrumb = null;

    //2. Declare a Channel variable to hold the current Channel
    //   and initially populate it with the leaf channel
    Channel cmsChannel = cmsLeafChannel;

    //3. Loop until we get to the Top Channel
    while(!cmsChannel.IsRoot)
    {
      //4. Concatenate an anchor tag including the name of this
      //   Channel to the beginning of the growing string
```

```
      growingBreadcrumb = "<a href='" + cmsChannel.Url + "'>" +
        cmsChannel.DisplayName.ToString() + "</a>" +
        growingBreadcrumb;

      //5. Check if the next channel is the Top Channel
      if(!cmsChannel.Parent.IsRoot)
      {
        //6. If not, include the separator
        growingBreadcrumb = crumbSeperator + growingBreadcrumb;
      }
      //7. Set the current Channel to its own parent
      cmsChannel = cmsChannel.Parent;
    }
    //8. Return the completed breadcrumb string
    return growingBreadcrumb;
  }
  catch(Exception eError)
  {
    //9. Provide error feedback to the developer
    Label1.Text = "<b>Error: </b>" + eError.Message.ToString();

    //10. Return the empty breadcrumb string
    return string.Empty;
  }
}
```

Then enter the function to build the breadcrumb recursively:

```
private string RecursiveBreadcrumb(Channel cmsChannel,
  string crumbSeperator)
{
  try
  {
    //1. We have reached the top ancestor
    if(cmsChannel.Parent.IsRoot)
    {
      //2. Pop an anchor tag including the name of the Top Channel
      return "<a href='" + cmsChannel.Url + "'>" +
        cmsChannel.Name.ToString() + "</a>";
    }
    else
    {
      //3. Call this function recursively, on the way back
      //   pop an anchor tag including the name of this Channel
```

```
      //  concatenated to the end of the growing string
      return RecursiveBreadcrumb(cmsChannel.Parent,
        crumbSeperator) +
        crumbSeperator + "<a href='" + cmsChannel.Url + "'>" +
        cmsChannel.Name.ToString() + "</a>";
    }
  }
  catch(Exception eError)
  {
    //4. Provide error feedback to the developer
    Label1.Text = "<b>Error: </b>" + eError.Message.ToString();

    //5. Return the empty breadcrumb string
    return string.Empty;
  }
}
```

Replace the Button1_Click function of our Scratchpad template file with the following code:

```
private void Button1_Click(object sender, System.EventArgs e)
{
  try
  {
    //1. Grab the current CMS Context
    CmsHttpContext cmsContext = CmsHttpContext.Current;

    //2. Grab the Channel for which to display a breadcrumb
    //   from the fully qualified path in the TextBox
    //   Cast the result of the Searches object as a Channel
    Channel cmsChannel =
      cmsContext.Searches.GetByPath(TextBox1.Text)
      as Channel;

    //3. If the Channel was successfully found it will not be null
    if(cmsChannel != null)
    {
      //4. Populate the Label with the results of both the
      //   recursive function and the sequential function
      Label1.Text = "<b>Sequential: </b>" +
        SequentialBreadcrumb(cmsChannel, " > ") +
        "<br><b>Recursive: </b>" +
        RecursiveBreadcrumb(cmsChannel, " > ");
```

```
    }
    else
    {
      //5. Provide nonerror feedback to the developer
      Label1.Text = "<b>Channel not found </b>";
    }
  }
  catch(Exception eError)
  {
    //6. Provide error feedback to the developer
    Label1.Text = "<b>Error: </b>" + eError.Message.ToString();
  }
}
```

Build the solution and then refresh the Scratchpad posting in Internet Explorer, or browse to it, type the full path to any valid channel in your CMS site into the text box (we use /Channels/Scratch/Brady/Alice/ based upon the channel hierarchy created earlier in this chapter) and click the Button. The page should reload and look similar to Figure 25–19.

Each of the nodes in the breadcrumb represents a clickable URL.

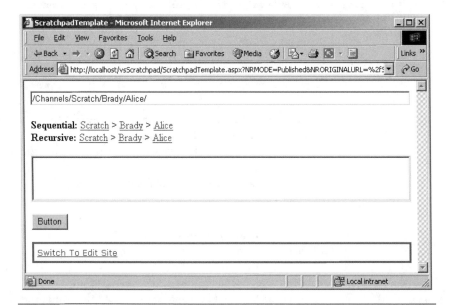

**Figure 25–19** Breadcrumb display

# Summary

We began our discussion about Channel objects in PAPI by describing how important hierarchies are in our lives and in CMS. But using Channel objects must be controlled, so we covered the various user rights and the concept of sufficient rights to accomplish tasks in CMS.

Digging into each individual property and method, starting with the read-only members and followed by the read/write members of a Channel object, we unearthed the usefulness of each member. We showed comprehensive and individual, sometimes reusable, code examples of all members. The various child objects described in the PAPI object model from Chapter 23—including the Parent, Postings, Channels, AllChildren, and CustomProperties—were covered in depth, along with code examples.

Dynamic navigation was touched on, and we ended with a simple breadcrumb code example.

In the chapter that follows, we will cover very similar content in a similar manner for the Posting object.

# CHAPTER 26

# Managing Postings

We have explored CMS Context (see Chapter 24). We understand how to organize, store, retrieve, and manage our assets hierarchically using CMS channels (see Chapter 25). We can create templates using VS.NET (see Chapter 12). Next, we need a way to manage postings based upon those templates housed within those channels in our Web Property.

---

**NOTE:** Although templates do not have a chapter dedicated to them, they are accessible via PAPI. Most of the exact same methods and properties available for postings are available for templates (certainly anything inherited from HierarchyItem). We briefly discuss the unique template members later in this chapter.

---

In many ways, a posting provides functionality similar to a traditional Web page in a data-based Web site. Both are dynamically created at run-time from information that is kept within a repository. Both serve fresh content, which could potentially be cached, every time. Navigation is often included on every page as a separate, uniform set of code. Specific information on the page can be restricted for view and/or update based upon the current user's role.

However, unlike a Web page, postings come with some very convenient built-in capabilities. Although most Web pages are a singular, proprietary work of art, postings are rubber stamps. They are always based upon templates, which can be instantly used to generate new, similar postings with exactly the same functionality. CMS automatically updates posting references when the templates or resources are moved or renamed. Postings also come with a built-in structure for managing who can see them and when, which they inherit from the channel in which they are posted. Since postings have a start date, they can be placed onto the actual production system for users with appropriate rights to interact with before being made available to the general public or a specific group of users. Connected postings allow multiple views of the same set of content. The creation of new postings and the alteration of existing ones can be managed by the built-in CMS workflow engine, which gives users in specific roles the ability to approve changes all the way into the production environment. Indeed, these and other capabilities give postings an edge over the traditional Web page.

All code in this chapter will refer to a posting based upon a template with the following ASP.NET Web Form controls—TextBox, Label, List Box, and Button—using their default properties plus the default console, of course. Follow the steps in the Scratchpad sidebar, found in Chapter 24, to re-create exactly the same results shown here, or use your own channels, templates, and postings and just apply the concepts. We will be repeatedly replacing the contents of the Button1_Click function.

# Checking Posting User Rights

It is typically desirable to verify that the current user is allowed to perform an action rather than handling the access denied exception that occurs if we allow them to try to do something when they don't have sufficient rights (see the Sufficient Rights sidebar in Chapter 25).

Since navigation is frequently created at runtime, it can be desirable to proactively leave off functionality that the current user isn't allowed to perform or visually indicate areas where the user is allowed to perform certain functions. This can easily be accomplished using the Posting "user right" properties. The following code will display the Boolean values for each of these properties.

The simple error handling in the code throughout these code samples isn't meant to be the model for how to handle CMS exceptions; there is an application code block from Microsoft on how to do exception handling in .NET. These functions also assume the presence of both a ListBox1 and a Label1 to provide visual feedback to the user, which certainly won't typically be normal, but it works for our purposes.

Replace the Button1_Click function of our Scratchpad template (see the Scratchpad sidebar in Chapter 24 for details) with the following code:

```
private void Button1_Click(object sender, System.EventArgs e)
{
  try
  {
    //1. Grab the current CMS Context
    CmsHttpContext cmsContext = CmsHttpContext.Current;
```

```
//2. Populate the label with the name of the Posting,
//   and the PublishingMode
Label1.Text = "<b>Posting: </b>" +
  cmsContext.Posting.Name.ToString() +
  "<br><b>PublishingMode: </b>" + cmsContext.Mode.ToString();

//3. Populate the ListBox with values for various user rights
ListBox1.Items.Add( "CanApprove: " +
  cmsContext.Posting.CanApprove.ToString()
  );
ListBox1.Items.Add( "CanDelete: " +
  cmsContext.Posting.CanDelete.ToString()
  );
ListBox1.Items.Add( "CanMove: " +
  cmsContext.Posting.CanMove.ToString()
  );
ListBox1.Items.Add( "CanSetProperties: " +
  cmsContext.Posting.CanSetProperties.ToString()
  );
ListBox1.Items.Add( "CanSubmit: " +
  cmsContext.Posting.CanSubmit.ToString()
  );
}
catch(Exception eError)
{
  //4. Provide error feedback to the developer
  Label1.Text = "<b>Error: </b>" + eError.Message.ToString();
}
}
```

Build the solution and then refresh the Scratchpad posting in Internet Explorer, or browse to it and click the Button. The page should reload and look similar to Figure 26–1.

We increased the height of the ListBox on the template for this example so that Figure 26–1 would show all five entries. You may need to scroll down to see the current value for CanSubmit.

As you can probably surmise from the preceding example, CMS allows us to programmatically approve/decline, delete, move, alter, and submit Posting objects in a referencing Channel object. These Posting properties will help us determine if we should allow the current user to have access to this functionality.

The Boolean result of each property is strictly an indicator of the user's rights rather than the proper Context PublishingMode to perform

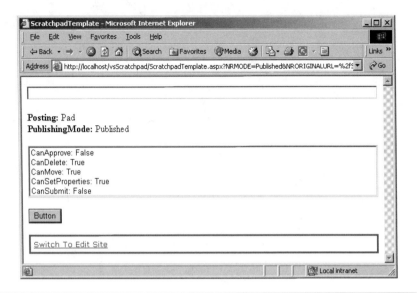

**Figure 26–1** Posting user rights

the function. This way, we can provide a visual indication in the dynamic navigation of the user's ability or lack thereof to perform these functions regardless of the mode of the current Context. Therefore, just because one of these properties returns true doesn't automatically mean that any attempt to modify an object will succeed. To that end, it is always wise to place the verification that a user has sufficient rights and the actual modification within a .NET try/catch block.

Also, all the following Posting properties cannot be read for objects after they have been deleted and always return false for historical revisions of an object.

A more representative code sample follows in the next main section of this chapter: Managing Postings.

## CanApprove

The CanApprove property indicates two things: that the authenticated user has sufficient rights to approve/decline the posting and that the posting requires approval. It will return true if both of these conditions are met and false if they are not met or if the user cannot implicitly acquire ownership.

There are several complex scenarios that determine whether a user has sufficient rights. All of them revolve around the current state of the posting, the rights on the containing channel, and the group membership of the current user.

This property is useful primarily for indicating to the user which postings they have the right to approve.

### CanDelete (Inherited from HierarchyItem)

The CanDelete property indicates whether the authenticated user can delete the referencing Posting object. This property will return true if the authenticated user has sufficient rights to delete the posting from the channel.

This property will return false if the authenticated user does not have sufficient rights or if the user cannot implicitly acquire ownership.

### CanMove

The CanMove property indicates whether the authenticated user can move the referencing Posting object. This property will return true if the authenticated user has sufficient rights to move the posting from the channel.

This property will return false if the authenticated user does not have sufficient rights or if the user cannot implicitly acquire ownership.

### CanSetProperties (Inherited from HierarchyItem)

The CanSetProperties property indicates whether the authenticated user can indeed alter the properties of a posting. This requires the same sufficient rights as for managing postings.

This property will return true if the authenticated user has sufficient rights and false if they do not have sufficient rights or if the user cannot implicitly acquire ownership.

### CanSubmit

The CanSubmit property indicates two things: that the authenticated user has sufficient rights to submit the posting and that the posting could be promoted to a Submitted state. It will return true if both of these conditions are met and false if they are not met or if the user cannot implicitly acquire ownership.

This property is useful primarily for indicating to the user which postings they have the right to submit.

## Managing Postings

There are many ways to manage a posting from PAPI. We will cover the brunt of them in this section. We will start with Submit, Approve, and Decline; then proceed to AcquireOwnership and ReleaseOwnership, CopyTo and MoveTo, and Delete; and end with ValidateChangeToken. Of course, users will need sufficient rights to interact with these methods.

Predictably, all the methods in this section will require that the Context be in Update mode (see the Getting into Update PublishingMode sidebar in Chapter 25). We will be using the function introduced in Listing 25–1 to get an authenticated CmsApplicationContext in Update PublishingMode. If we skip this step, we will receive a verbose .NET error page that basically says, You must be in Update mode to do this.

As always, after a posting has been deleted, attempting to call any of these methods will cause an exception. Also, attempting to call any of these methods on a Historical Revision will cause an exception.

In general, the OwnedBy property (discussed in Chapter 25) is implicitly changed to the current user so that other authors cannot concurrently update the posting or any of its ConnectedPostings. All changes only become permanent and ownership released (if appropriate) once the Context CommitAll method is called. Calling the Context Rollback All method before CommitAll will return the posting to its previously committed condition.

Before we start, to learn about the Submit, Approve, and Decline methods, you need a detailed understanding of a posting's state lifecycle.

---

**NOTE:** Chapter 6 contains an in-depth discussion about page status as it relates to the publishing workflow. Page status is a logical superset of the physical posting state.

---

First we'll discuss the two different names CMS uses for the logical page status and the physical posting state, and then how a posting moves through those posting states. Page status is a simplified logical superset of the actual physical posting state. Table 26–1 outlines the relationship between these two lists.

As you can see, some of the physical posting states have been consolidated and some (Deleted, Historical, and None) are not represented logically at all. Using the Submit, Approve, or Decline methods on a posting will have the same effect as if the authorized user within the same CMS Context

**Table 26–1**  Relationship between Page Status and Posting State

| Page Status | Logical Description | Posting State | Physical Description |
|---|---|---|---|
| New | A new page has been created, but has not yet been saved for the first time. | New | The posting has not been stored permanently by the CMS server. It may be a new posting or a new unapproved version of an existing approved posting. A posting enters this state when it is first created or when a user modifies an existing posting that has only an Approved version. |
| Saved | The page has been saved, but has not yet been submitted for approval. | Saved | The posting has been permanently stored by the server, but has not been submitted or approved. A posting enters this state when it is first saved. |
| Waiting for Approval | The page has been submitted for approval, but has not yet been approved. | WaitingFor Editor Approval | The posting has been saved and submitted. It is waiting for editor approval. |
| | | WaitingFor Moderator Approval | The posting has either been approved by an editor or does not require editor approval. The posting version is now waiting for moderator approval. |
| Approved | The page has been approved. | Approved | The posting has been approved by both an editor and a moderator, or it did not require approval by one or both. The property StartDate is greater than the current date, so the posting is not yet visible on the site in Published mode. |

*(continued)*

**Table 26–1** *(Continued)*

| Page Status | Logical Description | Posting State | Physical Description |
|---|---|---|---|
| Declined | The page has been declined (did not meet approval) and must be resubmitted after modification. | Editor-Declined | The posting has been saved and submitted, but an editor has declined it. |
| | | Moderator-Declined | The posting has been approved by an editor or did not require editor approval, but a moderator has declined it. |
| Expired | The approved page has expired (exceeded the expiration time specified in the publishing schedule for the page). | Expired | The posting has been approved by both an editor and a moderator, or it did not require approval by one or both. The property Expiry Date is less than the current date, so the posting is not visible on the site in Published mode. |
| Published | The page has been published on the live site. | Published | The posting has been approved by both an editor and a moderator, or it did not require approval by one or both. The current date is between the properties StartDate and ExpiryDate, so the posting is visible on the site in Published mode. |
| | | Deleted | The posting has been marked as deleted. |
| | | Historical | The posting is a historical revision. |
| | | None | The posting is in an incorrect state. |

had interactively used the Web Author console to accomplish the task. In fact, the Web Author console uses these methods to accomplish its work.

A posting can be promoted through the various physical posting states as illustrated by the UML transition diagram in Figure 26–2.

A Submit will stop for approval based on the following conditions (assuming CanSubmit is true for the submitting user):

- If at least one editor rights group has been assigned (in Site Manager User Roles) to the containing channel. The posting is only promoted to WaitingForEditorApproval State, unless the submitting user has Editor rights themselves.
- If at least one moderator rights group has been assigned (in Site Manager User Roles) to the containing channel. The posting is only promoted to WaitingForModeratorApproval State, unless the submitting user has Moderator rights themselves.

It is possible, although not depicted, to submit or approve a posting that is in a New state. The default Web Author console requires a posting to be saved first.

As depicted, a Submit or Approve can promote a posting to Approved, Published, or Expired status, depending upon where today falls in relation to the posting's StartDate and ExpiryDate.

A posting can actually be approved by a user with sufficient rights directly from Saved state, EditorDeclined state, and ModeratorDeclined state. Assuming CanApprove is true for the submitting user, the same rules apply as if it had been approved from WaitingForEditorApproval.

When a posting is copied, its state doesn't change, but the state of the copied posting is set to the Saved state. If a posting is moved from any state other than Published, it is promoted to the Saved state. As depicted, if it is moved by a user with moderator rights (including an administrator) it remains in Published state.

Attempts to set posting properties or call posting methods will fail after a posting is marked as submitted, approved, or declined but before CommitAll has been called. CommitAll should be called as quickly after marking a posting as possible.

So, let's see some code using these methods.

## Submit

To successfully use the Submit method, the CanSubmit property must return true for the referencing Posting object. See the rules for Can Submit earlier in this chapter. Also, the PublishingMode must be set to

**Typical Posting State Lifecycle**

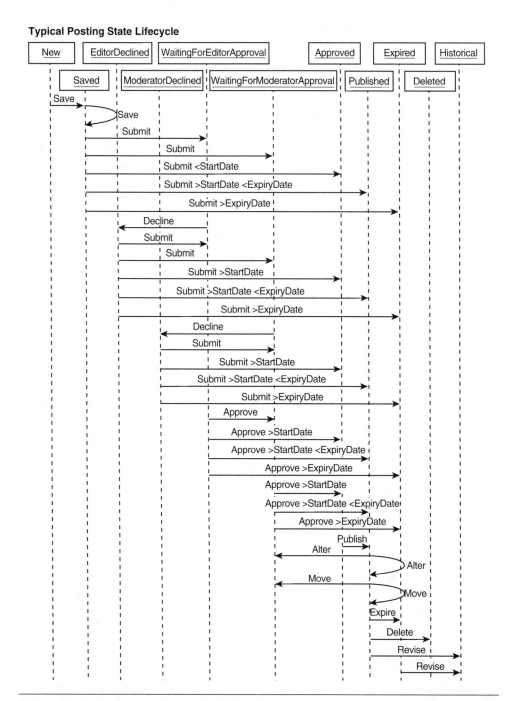

**Figure 26–2** Typical posting state lifecycle

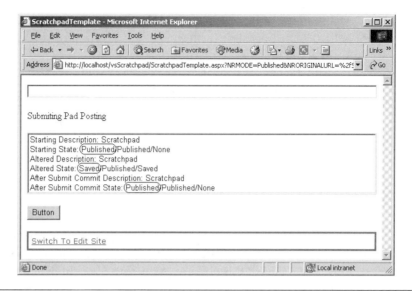

**Figure 26–3** Submitting a posting

Update. Once again, we will be using the function introduced in Listing 25–1 to get an authenticated CmsApplicationContext in Update PublishingMode.

The result of calling the Submit method (Figure 26–3) will depend on the current state of the posting, the current user's rights, and the configuration of user roles for the containing channel. Assuming all goes well, the posting state will change to WaitingForEditorApproval, WaitingFor ModeratorApproval, Approved, Published, or Expired.

The OwnedBy property is updated.

It doesn't make any sense to use Submit on a posting when its state is Approved, Published, Expired, Deleted, or Historical. Attempting to do so will fail or have no effect.

### Approve

To successfully use the Approve method, the CanApprove property must return true for the referencing Posting object. See the rules for CanApprove earlier in this chapter. As before, the PublishingMode must be set to Update (see Listing 25–1).

The result of calling the Approve method (Figure 26–3) will depend on the current state of the posting, the current user's rights, and the configuration of user roles for the containing channel. Assuming all goes well, the posting state will change to WaitingForModeratorApproval, Approved, Published, or Expired.

The OwnedBy property is released if there are no outstanding changes in this posting or any ConnectedPosting(s).

It doesn't make any sense to use Approve on a posting when its state is Approved, Published, Expired, Deleted, or Historical. Attempting to do so will fail or have no effect.

Later in this chapter, we will look at the Approvers collection of users that can approve postings.

## Decline

To successfully use the Decline method, the CanApprove property must return true for the referencing Posting object. See the rules for Can Approve earlier in this chapter. As before, the PublishingMode must be set to Update (see Listing 25–1).

The result of calling the Decline method (Figure 26–3) will depend on the current state of the posting. A posting in WaitingForEditor Approval state will be promoted to EditorDeclined state. A posting in WaitingForModeratorApproval state will be promoted to Moderator Declined state.

The OwnedBy property remains the same so that the user that submitted the posting can change it without an explicit AcquireOwnership (discussed next).

It doesn't make any sense to use Decline on a posting when its state is New, Saved, EditorDeclined, ModeratorDeclined, Approved, Published, Expired, Deleted, or Historical. Attempting to do so will fail or have no effect.

Remember, the following code sample requires Listing 25–1 from the Chapter 25 to work.

Replace the Button1_Click function of our Scratchpad template with the following code:

```
private void Button1_Click(object sender, System.EventArgs e)
{
  try
  {
    //1. Grab the current CMS Context
    CmsHttpContext cmsContextHttp = CmsHttpContext.Current;
```

```
//2. Grab an Authenticated Context in Update PublishingMode
//   from Listing 25-1
CmsApplicationContext cmsContextApp =
  GetAuthenticatedCmsApplicationContext(PublishingMode.Update);

//3. Position the Application Context to the Current Posting
Posting cmsCurrentPosting =
  cmsContextApp.Searches.GetByGuid(cmsContextHttp.Posting.Guid)
  as Posting;

//4. Populate the label with informational text
Label1.Text = "Submiting " +
  cmsCurrentPosting.DisplayName.ToString() + " Posting";

//5. Add the Description value to the ListBox
ListBox1.Items.Add("Starting Description: " +
    cmsCurrentPosting.Description.ToString()
  );

//6. Add the Posting State values to the ListBox
ListBox1.Items.Add("Starting State: " +
  cmsCurrentPosting.State.ToString()
  + "/" + cmsCurrentPosting.StateApprovedVersion.ToString()
  + "/" + cmsCurrentPosting.StateUnapprovedVersion.ToString()
  );

//7. Check that the current user has sufficient rights
if(cmsCurrentPosting.CanSetProperties)
{
  //8. Change the Description
  cmsCurrentPosting.Description = "Scratchpad";

  //9. Commit change
  cmsContextApp.CommitAll();
}
else
{
  //10. Provide nonerror feedback to the developer
  Label1.Text = cmsContextApp.User.ToString() +
    " has insufficient rights to Set Properties";
}
```

```
//11. Check that the current user has sufficient rights
//    CanApprove will be false unless a change has been made
//    that requires approval
if(cmsCurrentPosting.CanApprove)
{
  //12. Add the Description value to the ListBox
  ListBox1.Items.Add("Altered Description: " +
    cmsCurrentPosting.Description.ToString()
    );

  //13. Add the Posting State values to the ListBox
  ListBox1.Items.Add("Altered State: " +
    cmsCurrentPosting.State.ToString()
    + "/" + cmsCurrentPosting.StateApprovedVersion.ToString()
    + "/" + cmsCurrentPosting.StateUnapprovedVersion.ToString()
    );

  //14. Submit the Altered unpublished Posting
  cmsCurrentPosting.Submit();

  //15. Commit change
  cmsContextApp.CommitAll();

  //16. Add the Description value to the ListBox
  ListBox1.Items.Add("After Submit Commit Description: " +
    cmsCurrentPosting.Description.ToString()
    );

  //17. Add the Posting State values to the ListBox
  ListBox1.Items.Add("After Submit Commit State: " +
    cmsCurrentPosting.State.ToString()
    + "/" + cmsCurrentPosting.StateApprovedVersion.ToString()
    + "/" + cmsCurrentPosting.StateUnapprovedVersion.ToString()
    );
}
else
{
  //18. Provide nonerror feedback to the developer
  Label1.Text = cmsContextApp.User.ToString() +
    " has insufficient rights to Approve";
}
```

```
    //19. Dispose of the stand-alone Application Context
    cmsContextApp.Dispose();
  }
  catch(Exception eError)
  {
    //20. Provide error feedback to the developer
    Label1.Text = "<b>Error: </b>" + eError.Message.ToString();
  }
}
```

---

**NOTE:** The Searches method of a CMS Context is covered in detail in Chapter 28.

---

Build the solution and then refresh the Scratchpad posting in Internet Explorer, or browse to it and click the Button. The page should reload and look similar to Figure 26–3.

We increased the height of the ListBox on the template for this example so that Figure 26–3 would show all six entries. You may need to scroll down to see the last two.

In this example, the current posting's Description starts out as an empty string and ends up with a value of Scratchpad. Note the circled values in Figure 26–3. Before any changes were made, the current posting was in Published state; after the committed change, it was promoted to Saved state; after the Submit was committed, it was promoted to Published state again.

The reason the state didn't become WaitingForEditorApproval or WaitingForModeratorApproval is that we are using an administrator account to submit the change, and an administrator is allowed to approve, so our changes are automatically promoted to the next state in the posting lifecycle. We also don't have an editor user role or a moderator user role assigned to the Scratch channel; so even if we didn't use a CMS administrator, as long as the user that we did use could submit the posting, it would have bypassed both Waiting For Approval states. Since the Start Date for the posting was before now, and the ExpiryDate is set to Never (01/01/3000), the next state would be Published.

The coding for Approve and Decline would be very similar. We would use CanApprove (for both) rather than CanSubmit, and, of course, the posting acted on would need to be in a state that required approval.

## AcquireOwnership, ReleaseOwnership

The AcquireOwnership method sets the OwnedBy property's Server AccountName property for a posting and its ConnectedPostings, if any, to the current user after a Context CommitAll is called. It can only be used if the current user has CanSetProperties rights. See the rules for CanSetProperties earlier in this chapter. As before, the PublishingMode must be set to Update (see Listing 25–1).

If used, this property can optionally block other users from implicitly or explicitly taking ownership and can optionally check out the posting, potentially changing it to a Waiting for Moderator Approval state. A non-blocking reassignment of the OwnedBy property implicitly happens whenever writable properties or modifier methods are used on a posting. The posting's OwnedBy property is automatically set to the current user until the implicit modification is complete. If the OwnedBy property is set to the built-in Everybody value, no one currently owns it and anyone can acquire ownership.

However, there are times in a multiuser environment when we may want to block others from taking ownership of a posting while we are working with it. So, we can explicitly call AcquireOwnership with an optional first parameter indicating that we want to explicitly take exclusive ownership. Subsequent requests by anyone else to make changes to this posting will fail until we explicitly call ReleaseOwnership. It is possible for blocked users with sufficient rights to ignore the block and use ReleaseOwnership or AcquireOwnership exclusively on the posting so that they can manipulate it. However, this requires an overt action on their part.

Ownership is released when ReleaseOwnership is called, when another user acquires ownership (implicitly by modifying the posting or explicitly using AcquireOwnership), or when the posting goes into an Approved state.

Remember, the following code sample requires Listing 25–1 from Chapter 25 to work.

Replace the Button1_Click function of our Scratchpad template with the following code:

```
private void Button1_Click(object sender, System.EventArgs e)
{
  try
  {
    //1. Grab the current CMS Context
    CmsHttpContext cmsContextHttp = CmsHttpContext.Current;
```

```
//2. Grab an Authenticated Context in Update PublishingMode
//   from Listing 25-1
CmsApplicationContext cmsContextApp =
  GetAuthenticatedCmsApplicationContext(PublishingMode.Update);

//3. Position the Application Context to the Current Posting
Posting cmsCurrentPosting =
  cmsContextApp.Searches.GetByGuid(cmsContextHttp.Posting.Guid)
  as Posting;

//4. Check that the current user has sufficient rights
if(cmsCurrentPosting.CanSetProperties)
{
  //5. Populate the label with informational text
  Label1.Text = "Acquiring/Releasing Ownership of the " +
    cmsCurrentPosting.DisplayName.ToString() + " Posting";

  //6. Add the OwnedBy ServerAccountName value to the ListBox
  ListBox1.Items.Add("Before Acquisition: " +
    cmsCurrentPosting.OwnedBy.ServerAccountName.ToString());

  //7. Explicitly acquire ownership
  cmsCurrentPosting.AcquireOwnership();

  //8. Commit change
  cmsContextApp.CommitAll();

  //9. Add the OwnedBy ServerAccountName value to the ListBox
  ListBox1.Items.Add("After Committed Acquisition: " +
    cmsCurrentPosting.OwnedBy.ServerAccountName.ToString());

  //10. Explicitly release ownership
  cmsCurrentPosting.ReleaseOwnership();

  //11. Commit change
  cmsContextApp.CommitAll();

  //12. Add the OwnedBy ServerAccountName value to the ListBox
  ListBox1.Items.Add("After Committed Release: " +
    cmsCurrentPosting.OwnedBy.ServerAccountName.ToString());

  //13. Add the OwnedBy IsEverybody value to the ListBox
  ListBox1.Items.Add("Value of OwnedBy IsEverybody: " +
    cmsCurrentPosting.OwnedBy.IsEverybody.ToString());
```

```
    }
    else
    {
      //14. Provide nonerror feedback to the developer
      Label1.Text = cmsContextApp.User.ToString() +
        " has insufficient rights to set properties";
    }
    //15. Dispose of the stand-alone Application Context
    cmsContextApp.Dispose();
  }
  catch(Exception eError)
  {
    //16. Provide error feedback to the developer
    Label1.Text = "<b>Error: </b>" + eError.Message.ToString();
  }
}
```

For what its worth, the code under comment 13 demonstrates that the posting OwnedBy property (really any User property) has an IsEverybody property that returns true if the User is currently set to the built-in Everybody value.

Build the solution and then refresh the Scratchpad posting in Internet Explorer, or browse to it and click the Button. The page should reload and look similar to Figure 26–4.

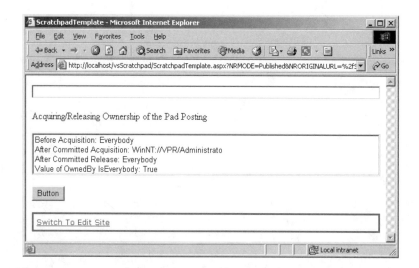

**Figure 26–4** AcquireOwnership of posting

## CopyTo, MoveTo

The CopyTo and MoveTo methods do exactly what you think that they would. CopyTo creates a new Posting object just like the referencing Posting object (ConnectedPostings just become regular Posting objects) in the destination channel. It requires that the current user have sufficient rights to create a new posting in the destination channel.

MoveTo changes the location of the referencing Posting object to the destination channel. The unapproved version of a posting is used, if any; otherwise, the approved version is used. It requires that CanMove be true on the Posting object to be moved and the current user have sufficient rights to create a new Posting object in the destination channel. See the rules for CanMove earlier in this chapter. As before, the PublishingMode must be set to Update (see Listing 25–1).

In both cases the destination posting state is promoted to Saved. As you would expect, these destination posting properties are also changed to intuitive values: CreatedBy, CreatedDate, LastModifiedBy, Last ModifiedDate, OwnedBy, and Parent.

Posting copies are always made from the committed values in the database.

Remember, the following code sample requires Listing 25–1 from the Chapter 25 to work.

Replace the Button1_Click function of our Scratchpad template with the following code:

```
private void Button1_Click(object sender, System.EventArgs e)
{
  try
  {
    //1. Make sure that the user entered something into the TextBox
    //   We will use this entry as the name for the new Posting
    if(TextBox1.Text.Length > 0)
    {
      //2. Grab the current CMS Context
      CmsHttpContext cmsContextHttp = CmsHttpContext.Current;

      //3. Grab an Authenticated Context in Update PublishingMode
      //   from Listing 25-1
      CmsApplicationContext cmsContextApp =
        GetAuthenticatedCmsApplicationContext(
          PublishingMode.Update);
```

```
//4. Position the Application Context to the Current Posting
Posting cmsCurrentPosting =
  cmsContextApp.Searches.GetByGuid(
    cmsContextHttp.Posting.Guid)
  as Posting;

//5. Populate the label with informational text
Label1.Text = "Copying " +
  cmsCurrentPosting.DisplayName.ToString() + " Posting";

//6. Check that the current user has sufficient rights
if(cmsCurrentPosting.CanSetProperties)
{
  //7. Copy the current Posting to the current Channel
  //    creating a new Posting
  Posting cmsNewPosting =
    cmsCurrentPosting.CopyTo(cmsContextHttp.Channel);

  //8. Commit change
  cmsContextApp.CommitAll();

  //9. Change the name of the new Posting to the value in
  //    the TextBox
  cmsNewPosting.Name = TextBox1.Text.ToString();

  //10. Submit the altered, unpublished Posting
  //     Since we authorized as a CMS administrator, Submit
  //     will approve the new Posting too
  cmsNewPosting.Submit();

  //11. Commit change
  cmsContextApp.CommitAll();

  //12. Add new Posting link to the label
  Label1.Text += "<br><a href=" +
    cmsNewPosting.UrlModePublished.ToString() +
    ">Click link to New Posting</a>";

  //13. Add the DisplayName value and URL to the ListBox
  ListBox1.Items.Add("New Posting Display Name: " +
    HttpUtility.HtmlEncode(
      cmsNewPosting.DisplayName.ToString())
    );
```

```
          ListBox1.Items.Add("New Posting URL: " +
            cmsNewPosting.UrlModePublished.ToString()
            );
        }
        else
        {
          //14. Provide nonerror feedback to the developer
          Label1.Text = cmsContextApp.User.ToString() +
            " has insufficient rights to Set Properties";
        }
        //15. Dispose of the stand-alone Application Context
        cmsContextApp.Dispose();
      }
      else
      {
        //16. Provide nonerror feedback to the developer
        Label1.Text = "Enter name for new Posting into the TextBox";
      }
    }
    catch(Exception eError)
    {
      //17. Provide error feedback to the developer
      Label1.Text = "<b>Error: </b>" + eError.Message.ToString();
    }
}
```

Build the solution and then refresh the Scratchpad posting in Internet Explorer, or browse to it and click the Button. The page should reload and look similar to Figure 26–5.

After this code is run, there will physically be a new posting (in this case, called TestPosting) in the same channel as the current posting. We've included a link to the new posting. If you want, open Site Manager, or choose Global Refresh from the Site Manager View menu if it is already open. You can view (or even delete) this new posting from the channel in which it was created.

Next, we will delete this copied posting.

## Delete (Inherited from HierarchyItem)

To successfully use the Delete method, the CanDelete property must return true for the referencing Posting object. See the rules for Can Delete earlier in this chapter. As before, the PublishingMode must be set to Update (see Listing 25–1).

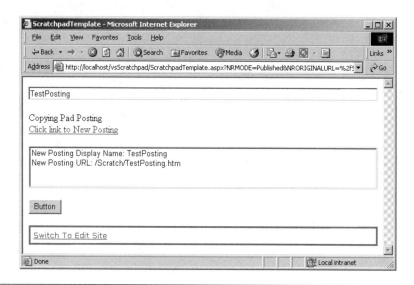

**Figure 26-5**  Copy posting to current channel with new name

Calling the Delete method merely marks an item for deletion. The item isn't actually deleted from the database until CommitAll on the Context is called. Even after a CommitAll, the item isn't actually deleted from any in-memory collection in which it existed before deletion. Interaction with a deleted item before CommitAll will return read-only values; interaction with a deleted item after CommitAll will cause an exception. Unlike in Site Manager, deletion of an item after a CommitAll cannot be undone. The item is not moved into a Deleted Items folder. It is possible to undo a delete before a CommitAll by calling a RollbackAll. Any attempt to delete an item that is being edited by another user will cause an exception.

Replace the Button1_Click function of our Scratchpad template with the following code:

```
private void Button1_Click(object sender, System.EventArgs e)
{
  try
  {
    //1. Make sure that the user entered something into the TextBox
    //   We use this entry as the path to the Posting to delete
    if(TextBox1.Text.Length > 0)
    {
```

```
//2. Grab an Authenticated Context in Update PublishingMode
//   from Listing 25-1
CmsApplicationContext cmsContextApp =
  GetAuthenticatedCmsApplicationContext(
    PublishingMode.Update);

//3. Grab the Posting to expunge
//   Cast the result of the Searches object as a Posting
Posting cmsPosting =
  cmsContextApp.Searches.GetByPath(TextBox1.Text.ToString())
  as Posting;

//4. Check if the user has sufficient rights to delete
if(cmsPosting.CanDelete)
{
  //5. Populate the label with informational text
  Label1.Text = "Deleting " +
    cmsPosting.DisplayName.ToString() + " Posting";

  //6. Delete Posting
  cmsPosting.Delete();

  //7. Provide visual feedback of Posting deletion
  ListBox1.Items.Add( cmsPosting.Name +
    " Posting was deleted from " +
    cmsPosting.Parent.Name.ToString() + " Channel"
    );

  //8. Commit changes
  cmsContextApp.CommitAll();
}
else
{
  //9. Provide nonerror feedback to the developer
  Label1.Text = "<b>User NOT allowed to delete Posting";
}

//10. Dispose of the stand-alone Application Context
cmsContextApp.Dispose();
}
else
{
//11. Provide nonerror feedback to the developer
```

```
      Label1.Text = "Enter the path of the Posting to delete " +
        "into the TextBox";
    }
  }
}
catch(Exception eError)
{
  //12. Provide error feedback to the developer
  Label1.Text = "<b>Error: </b>" + eError.Message.ToString();
  }
}
```

Build the solution and then refresh the Scratchpad posting in Internet Explorer, or browse to it and click the Button. The page should reload and look similar to Figure 26–6.

Open Site Manager, or choose Global Refresh from the Site Manager View menu if it is already open. The posting should be expunged. Notice that you don't even find it in the Deleted Items hive.

## ValidateChangeToken

The ValidateChangeToken method confirms that no other user has changed the posting since it was last retrieved. When a Posting object is hydrated by CMS, a ChangeToken property value is populated and kept

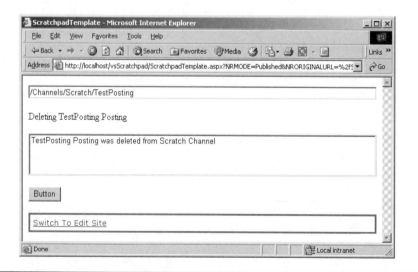

**Figure 26–6**   Delete posting

with the posting. We can pass that token to CMS for this posting to see if anything has happened to the posting since we retrieved it.

However, this method only works in Update PublishingMode and requires that the authenticated user have rights to edit the posting as defined by CanSetProperties (discussed earlier in this chapter). It should be used on the working revision of a posting and then only if there is the possibility that other users may have changed the posting since it was read by the current process.

This method will typically be used just before calling CommitAll. Calling this method successfully will leave the posting locked by the current user until an explicit CommitAll or RollbackAll method is called or an implicit call is made based upon the RollbackOnSessionEnd property of the Context.

Replace the Button1_Click function of our Scratchpad template with the following code:

```
private void Button1_Click(object sender, System.EventArgs e)
{
  try
  {
    //1. Grab the current CMS Context
    CmsHttpContext cmsContextHttp = CmsHttpContext.Current;

    //2. Grab an Authenticated Context in Update PublishingMode
    //   from Listing 25-1
    CmsApplicationContext cmsContextApp =
      GetAuthenticatedCmsApplicationContext(PublishingMode.Update);

    //3. Position the Application Context to the Current Posting
    Posting cmsCurrentPosting =
      cmsContextApp.Searches.GetByGuid(cmsContextHttp.Posting.Guid)
      as Posting;

    //4. Check that the current user has sufficient rights
    if(cmsCurrentPosting.CanSetProperties)
    {
      try
      {
        //5. Check to see if anything has changed since the Posting
        //   was read
        cmsCurrentPosting.ValidateChangeToken
          (cmsCurrentPosting.ChangeToken);
```

```
      //6. Populate the label with informational text. The code
      //   will not get to this line if the previous line fails
      Label1.Text = cmsCurrentPosting.DisplayName.ToString() +
        " Posting not altered by anyone since it was last read";
    }
    catch(Exception eError)
    {
      //7. Provide error feedback to the developer
      Label1.Text = "<b>Bad Token: </b>" +
        eError.Message.ToString();
    }
  }
  else
  {
    //8. Provide nonerror feedback to the developer
    Label1.Text = cmsContextApp.User.ToString() +
      " has insufficient rights to Set Properties";
  }
  //9. Dispose of the standalone Application Context
  cmsContextApp.Dispose();
}
catch(Exception eError)
{
  //10. Provide error feedback to the developer
  Label1.Text = "<b>Error: </b>" + eError.Message.ToString();
}
}
```

Build the solution and then refresh the Scratchpad posting in Internet Explorer, or browse to it and click the Button. The page should reload and look similar to Figure 26–7.

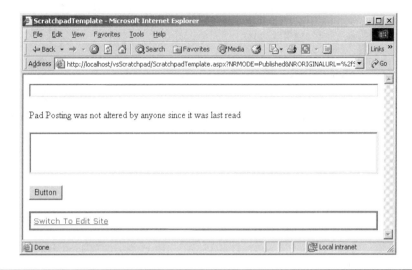

**Figure 26–7** ValidateChangeToken

## Working with Posting Members

Postings have a vast store of characteristics to be tapped by the developer using PAPI. Some can be changed in code, while others are for retrieval only. We focus on the read-only members first. We start with a comprehensive code sample, and then we provide an alphabetical list of read-only members specific to postings. Since channel and posting both inherit functionality from ChannelItem and HierarchyItem, all read-only members inherited for use by postings have already been covered in depth in Chapter 25.

Then we focus on read/write members. Again, we start with a comprehensive code sample followed by an alphabetical list of read/write members specific to postings. Again, the read/write members inherited for use by postings are covered in depth in Chapter 25. Exceptions are noted where necessary.

Likewise, the common facts and concepts that will help us throughout the list of members are the same as those given in the Working with Channel Members section of Chapter 25. This applies to date and time fields, the recommended use of ToLocalTime, the use of January 01, 3000, as an indicator that a date is set to never expire, the rules regarding deleted items and the use of the IsDeleted property, and the rules regarding historical revisions. See the Working with Channel Members section of Chapter 25 for details.

## Read-Only Members

The code to see all the read-only posting members is presented comprehensively. Sometimes it just helps to see the output of a property to better understand it, but we don't want to mess with a million code samples.

Replace the Button1_Click function of our Scratchpad template with the following code:

```
private void Button1_Click(object sender, System.EventArgs e)
{
  //1. Put current Posting into variable
  Posting cmsPosting = CmsHttpContext.Current.Posting;

  //2. Populate the label with read-only properties of a Posting
  Label1.Text =
    "<br><b>ChangeDate: </b>" + cmsPosting.ChangeDate.ToString() +
    "<br><b>ChangeToken: </b>" +
      cmsPosting.ChangeToken.ToString() +
    "<br><b>CreatedBy: </b>" + cmsPosting.CreatedBy.ToString() +
    "<br><b>CreatedDate: </b>" +
      cmsPosting.CreatedDate.ToString() +
    "<br><b>DisplayPath: </b>" +
      cmsPosting.DisplayPath.ToString() +
    "<br><b>GetHashCode: </b>" +
      cmsPosting.GetHashCode().ToString() +
    "<br><b>GetType: </b>" + cmsPosting.GetType().ToString() +
    "<br><b>Guid: </b>" + cmsPosting.Guid.ToString() +
    "<br><b>HasInaccessibleConnectedPostings: </b>" +
      cmsPosting.HasInaccessibleConnectedPostings.ToString() +
    "<br><b>IsConnected: </b>" +
      cmsPosting.IsConnected.ToString() +
    "<br><b>IsDeleted: </b>" +
      cmsPosting.IsDeleted.ToString() +
    "<br><b>IsDescendantOf: </b>" +
      cmsPosting.IsDescendantOf(cmsPosting.Parent).ToString() +
    "<br><b>IsWorkingRevision: </b>" +
      cmsPosting.IsWorkingRevision.ToString() +
    "<br><b>LastApprovedDeclinedBy: </b>" +
      cmsPosting.LastApprovedDeclinedBy.ToString() +
```

```
      "<br><b>LastModifiedBy: </b>" +
        cmsPosting.LastModifiedBy.ToString() +
      "<br><b>LastModifiedDate: </b>" +
        cmsPosting.LastModifiedDate.ToString() +
      "<br><b>OwnedBy: </b>" + cmsPosting.OwnedBy.ToString() +
      "<br><b>Path: </b>" + cmsPosting.Path.ToString() +
      "<br><b>QueryString: </b>" +
        cmsPosting.QueryString.ToString() +
      "<br><b>QueryStringModeUnpublished: </b>" +
        cmsPosting.QueryStringModeUnpublished.ToString() +
      "<br><b>QueryStringModeUpdate: </b>" +
        cmsPosting.QueryStringModeUpdate.ToString() +
      "<br><b>State: </b>" + cmsPosting.State.ToString() +
      "<br><b>StateApprovedVersion: </b>" +
        cmsPosting.StateApprovedVersion.ToString() +
      "<br><b>StateUnapprovedVersion: </b>" +
        cmsPosting.StateUnapprovedVersion.ToString() +
      "<br><b>Url: </b>" + cmsPosting.Url.ToString() +
      "<br><b>UrlInner: </b>" + cmsPosting.UrlInner.ToString() +
      "<br><b>UrlInnerPlain: </b>" +
        cmsPosting.UrlInnerPlain.ToString() +
      "<br><b>UrlModePublished: </b>" +
        cmsPosting.UrlModePublished.ToString() +
      "<br><b>UrlModeUnpublished: </b>" +
        cmsPosting.UrlModeUnpublished.ToString() +
      "<br><b>UrlModeUpdate: </b>" +
        cmsPosting.UrlModeUpdate.ToString();
}
```

Build the solution and then refresh the Scratchpad posting in Internet Explorer, or browse to it and click the Button. The page should reload and look similar to Figure 26–8.

### Read-Only Members Specific to Postings
#### ChangeToken
The ChangeToken property is a numeric value assigned to a posting when it is hydrated from the database. Its primary purpose is to be used with the ValidateChangeToken method (described earlier in this chapter) to determine if anyone else has committed changes to the posting since it was retrieved. If not, any changes that are about to be committed will not be overwriting someone else's changes. A code sample was included with the ValidateChangeToken method.

**Figure 26–8**  Show read-only members

### HasInaccessibleConnectedPostings, IsConnected

The IsDeleted property retrieves a Boolean value that indicates whether the referencing Channel object has been deleted or not.

The HasInaccessibleConnectedPostings property retrieves a Boolean value that indicates, typically to scripts, whether the referencing Posting object has ConnectedPostings that the current user does not have access to. It will be true if the referencing Posting object has one or more postings that the current user cannot access, but obviously "true" does not tell the calling code how many are inaccessible. On the other hand, it will be false if the user has access to all ConnectedPostings even if there are none. Use the IsConnected property to determine whether there are ConnectedPostings or not.

The related IsConnected property retrieves a Boolean value that indicates whether there are ConnectedPostings or not. It will be true if the referencing Posting object has one or more ConnectedPostings, but, obviously, "true" does not tell the calling code how many there are. On the other hand, it will be false if there are no ConnectedPostings.

These properties are useful to determine whether a posting shares its content with ConnectedPostings and whether the user has access to all of them or not.

### LastApprovedDeclinedBy

The LastApprovedDeclinedBy property retrieves the User object associated with the last user to approve or decline a posting, if any.

### State, StateApprovedVersion, StateUnapprovedVersion

The State property retrieves the unique two-character code that the USPS has designated to represent each of the 50 regions that make up the United States. Wrong. The State property really retrieves the current physical page status for the current posting, as represented and discussed earlier in this chapter. Table 26–1 lists all the values that State can hold and their relationship to the page status, and Figure 26–2 depicts how a posting can transition from one state to another.

The StateApprovedVersion property retrieves the current physical page status for the Approved version of the current posting. If there isn't an Approved version, the State will be None.

The StateUnapprovedVersion property retrieves the current physical page status for the Unapproved version of the current posting. If there isn't an Unapproved version, the State will be None.

All three states were included in the first code sample in this section. Review Figure 26–3 and the discussion leading up to that figure.

### Read-Only Members Inherited for Use by Postings

The following members have the same functionality as described for Channel object's read-only members in Chapter 25:

- CreatedBy (inherited from HierarchyItem)
- CreatedDate (inherited from HierarchyItem)

- DisplayPath (inherited from ChannelItem)
- GetHashCode (inherited from CmsObject)
- GetType (inherited from System.Object)
- Guid (inherited from HierarchyItem)
- IsDeleted (inherited from HierarchyItem)
- IsDescendantOf (inherited from HierarchyItem)
- IsWorkingRevision (inherited from HierarchyItem)
- LastModifiedBy (inherited from HierarchyItem)
- LastModifiedDate (inherited from HierarchyItem)
- OwnedBy (inherited from HierarchyItem)
- Path (inherited from HierarchyItem)
- QueryString (inherited from ChannelItem)
- QueryStringModeUnpublished (inherited from ChannelItem)
- QueryStringModeUpdate (inherited from ChannelItem)

### ChangeDate (Inherited from ChannelItem)

The ChangeDate property retrieves the date and time of the latest implicit change. The Posting object's ChangeDate is only different from the Channel object's ChangeDate because it includes the StartDate and ExpiryDate for its Parent, whereas the Channel object's ChangeDate does not.

### Url, UrlInnerPlain, UrlModePublished, UrlModeUnpublished, UrlModeUpdate (All Inherited from ChannelItem)

All Url property rules for Posting objects are less complicated than they are for Channel objects. If there is a reference to an OuterScriptFile and the ApplyOuterScriptToPostings is true, the URL retrieved will execute the OuterScriptFile. Otherwise, it will execute the script referenced by the template. The definition about what the different Url properties return is the same as it is for Channel objects.

## Read/Write Members

As before, the code to see all the read/write Posting object members is presented comprehensively. All these members can be assigned a value in code or through various other user interfaces. However, none of these changed values will become permanent until CommitAll is called on the Context. Uncommitted changes can be discarded by calling RollbackAll. If neither method is explicitly called when the Context in which the change is made is destroyed (goes out of scope or is disposed of ), the disposition of the changes will be decided by the value of the Rollback OnSessionEnd property. By default, this property is false, so all changes are committed when the session ends. In general, the properties of historical revisions can't be altered.

It is highly recommended that template file developers validate any date set to be sure that it is within the acceptable range for that property. Otherwise, CMS will have to alter it to be within the acceptable range when the change is committed. No message is generated when CMS changes the date, so the user could be surprised by the change. This problem can easily be avoided by validating dates before committing them.

As we discovered earlier, a user must have sufficient rights to make changes to any property, and the Context must be in an Update PublishingMode (see the Getting into Update PublishingMode sidebar in Chapter 25). It is always wise to place the verification that a user has sufficient rights and the actual modification of a property within a .NET try/catch block.

There are some properties that the user will be allowed to put free-form text into. We should use the HtmlEncode method of the .NET System.Web.HttpUtility object when displaying what the user has entered to prevent any issues that could arise out of that (see the Avoid Hack by Using HtmlEncode sidebar in Chapter 25).

When any change is made to a posting through any property or method, the posting and all its ConnectedPostings will become owned by the current user. Only one person at a time is allowed to make changes to a ChannelItem. So, there is a kind of automatic checkout process to prevent users from concurrently updating the same object. Also, if the changes are made and committed for an Approved posting, the state of that posting will potentially change to WaitingForModeratorApproval, and the changes will only be visible after approval is given. If there are no channel moderators or if the current user has sufficient rights to approve the change, the state will not change.

Once a posting is marked for submission, approved, or declined, changes to that posting's properties will fail. The properties can only be changed again after a CommitAll or RollbackAll has been called.

The read/write properties that we can set in code using PAPI can also be set using the Site Manager interface.

---

**NOTE:** We discuss using Site Manager in detail in Chapter 9.

Replace the Button1_Click function of our Scratchpad template with the following code:

```
private void Button1_Click(object sender, System.EventArgs e)
{
  //1. Put current Posting into variable
  Posting cmsPosting = CmsHttpContext.Current.Posting;
  //2. Populate the label with read/write properties of a Posting
  Label1.Text =
    "<br><b>Description (HtmlEncoded): </b>" +
      HttpUtility.HtmlEncode(cmsPosting.Description.ToString()) +
    "<br><b>DisplayName (HtmlEncoded): </b>" +
      HttpUtility.HtmlEncode(cmsPosting.DisplayName.ToString()) +
    "<br><b>ExpiryDate: </b>" + cmsPosting.ExpiryDate.ToString() +
    "<br><b>IsHiddenModePublished: </b>" +
      cmsPosting.IsHiddenModePublished.ToString() +
    "<br><b>IsImportant: </b>" + cmsPosting.IsImportant.ToString() +
    "<br><b>IsRobotFollowable: </b>" +
      cmsPosting.IsRobotFollowable.ToString() +
    "<br><b>IsRobotIndexable: </b>" +
      cmsPosting.IsRobotIndexable.ToString() +
    "<br><b>Name (HtmlEncoded): </b>" +
      HttpUtility.HtmlEncode(cmsPosting.Name.ToString()) +
    "<br><b>SortOrdinal: </b>" +
      cmsPosting.SortOrdinal.ToString() +
    "<br><b>StartDate: </b>" + cmsPosting.StartDate.ToString();
}
```

Build the solution and then refresh the Scratchpad posting in Internet Explorer, or browse to it and click the Button. The page should reload and look similar to Figure 26–9.

### Read/Write Members Specific to Postings

There are none.

### Read/Write Members Inherited for Use by Postings

The following members have the same functionality as described for the Channel object's read/write members in Chapter 25:

- Description (inherited from HierarchyItem)
- DisplayName (inherited from ChannelItem)
- ExpiryDate (inherited from ChannelItem)

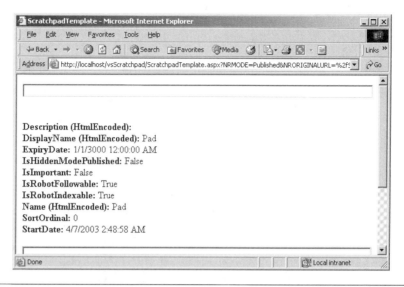

**Figure 26–9**  Show read/write members

- IsHiddenModePublished (inherited from ChannelItem)
- IsImportant (inherited from ChannelItem)
- IsRobotFollowable (inherited from ChannelItem)
- IsRobotIndexable (inherited from ChannelItem)
- Name (inherited from HierarchyItem)
- SortOrdinal (inherited from ChannelItem)
- StartDate (inherited from ChannelItem)

## Working with Posting Child Objects

Thus far we have seen the properties and methods of the Posting object that use intrinsic data types. This section will explore CMS-specific objects and collections of objects that are available from a Channel object. These are the principal objects graphically modeled in Figure 23–3, PAPI object model—Posting.

**NOTE:** The PAPI object model is covered in detail in Chapter 23. The objects covered in this section will be covered in the same order as they are illustrated in Figure 23–3.

These objects require some special processing and consideration. As before, there are some common facts and concepts that will help us in this section.

After a channel has been deleted but before it is committed, all properties become read-only. However, even after a deleted Channel object is committed, it may still reside in an in-memory collection. All Channel child objects must be removed before a Channel object can be deleted. Even if they still reside in memory, Channel child objects cannot be read once the Channel object has been deleted and committed.

Historical revisions of a channel don't typically keep the value that was associated with the revision when it was the current version. Properties typically represent the value of the current revision regardless of the value when the historical revision was the current revision. Attempting to assign a value to these properties for a historical revision will result in an exception. This concept is extended to the child objects for historical revisions of a channel, including the collections (Channels, Postings, All Children, and CustomProperties), whose contents are based upon the revision date and time of the channel. Channel objects and Posting objects are only included in these collections if they have a corresponding revision date and are currently contained in the referencing Channel object. Otherwise, they are left out.

Often it is valuable to iterate through an ordered collection. But the default sequence may not be well suited for the task at hand. So, collections come with some built-in sort options. In Chapter 25, in the Working with Channel Objects section, we listed the available sort members for collections.

Each sort method can be applied successively to the Channels collection to create a multikey sort. This can be beneficial if duplicate values are expected in the collection and we want to iterate a consistent sequence of values (as is often the case in dynamically generating navigation for a site). For example, sorting the collection using SortByDisplayName followed by SortByOwner would yield a list of channels grouped by channel owner in channel DisplayName sequence. To start the sort sequence over again, we would need to get another instance of the Channels property.

Several Posting child objects can only be used if the posting has placeholders. See the Adding Placeholders to Scratchpad sidebar for instructions on adding a couple of placeholders to our posting before we start.

## Adding Placeholders to Scratchpad

Since postings in the real world will typically have placeholders, we will add two HtmlPlaceholderControls to our physical Scratchpad template file and relate them, respectively, to the two HtmlPlaceholderDefinitions already in our logical Scratchpad template. (Working with placeholders in VS.NET is covered in depth in Chapter 13.)

Although it's typically not the best programming practice, just leave the default names and properties for all four entries (Figure 26–10).

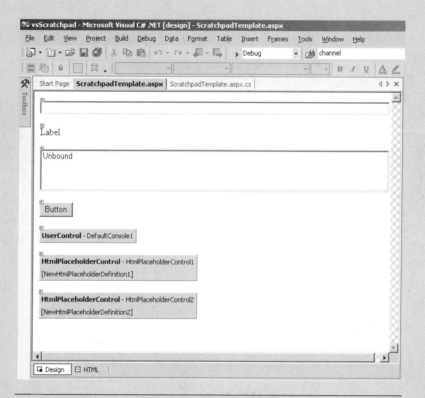

**Figure 26–10** Scratchpad template file in VS.NET

Next, let's give those two new placeholders some values in our Scratchpad posting. Build the solution and then refresh the Scratchpad posting in Internet Explorer or browse to it. (The Web Author console used in the steps that follow is covered in Chapter 5.)

While viewing the Scratchpad posting in Internet Explorer, use the following steps to complete this setup task:

1. Click the Switch to Edit Site link in the Web Author console.
2. Click the Edit link in the Web Author console.
3. Enter the literal string "one" into the first placeholder (you may have to scroll down to see it).
4. Enter the literal string "two" into the second placeholder.
5. Click the Save and Exit link in the Web Author console.
6. Click the Approve link in the Web Author console.
7. Click the Switch to Live Site link in the Web Author console.

The resulting Scratchpad posting should look similar to Figure 26–11.

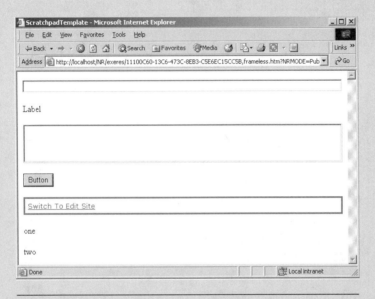

**Figure 26–11** Placeholders with content

Since postings must exist within a channel hierarchy, it will also be very helpful to have a hierarchy to post into. Figure 25–1 in Chapter 25 shows the structure of the potentially familiar hierarchy as viewed in the CMS Site Manager. This channel hierarchy can be created using the code in the Creating and Deleting Objects in a Channel section of Chapter 25 just preceding Figure 25–3. This channel hierarchy will be used with the examples in this chapter. Initially, the only channel that has a posting in it is the Scratch channel.

Note that building the simple Scratchpad template file (illustrated earlier), populating it using the Web Author console, and running the code to create the channel hierarchy described earlier should take no more than three or four minutes to complete. But if you prefer, you can just apply the concepts discussed here to your own channels, templates, and postings.

## Parent (Inherited from ChannelItem)

The Parent property of a Posting object returns the Channel object that contains it. This concept was covered in detail in Chapter 25 regarding a channel and is identical for a posting. See the Working with Channel Objects section near the end of Chapter 25 for details and a code sample.

### ConnectedPostings, ConnectedTemplates

The ConnectedPostings and ConnectedTemplates collection properties of Posting and Template objects, respectively, share the same placeholder content and PlaceholderDefinitions, again respectively, as the referencing Posting object. The IsConnected property, discussed earlier, should be used to determine if this collection contains objects, because both collections' content is dependent on the current PublishingMode, the user's rights, and the state of each ConnectedPosting. In either case, an empty collection does not necessarily mean that there are no Connected Postings. The referencing Posting object or posting template, respectively, is never included in the collection. A Historical Revision Posting object will return ConnectedPostings and ConnectedTemplates that were connected when it was the Approved posting.

ConnectedPostings can be created using the Web Author console, are usually saved in different channels from the current channel, and are typically used to provide different user groups with a view of the same data. The ConnectedPosting is related to the posting template or can use a ConnectedTemplate.

ConnectedTemplates can be created using VS.NET and can be related to a unique template file (ASPX). However, they must be related to the posting template, and they are typically used to present the user with a different look and feel of the content. A common need is for a posting to be shown in a different form for printing than it is for typical viewing. A ConnectedTemplate would be one way to accommodate that need.

---

**NOTE:** Chapter 15 covers ConnectedPostings and ConnectedTemplates in depth, including a detailed code sample.

---

Assuming the user has sufficient rights, any posting can be presented using any of its ConnectedTemplates. This takes the place of the error-prone URLUsingAlternateTemplate (aka Template Switching) used in previous versions of CMS.

## CustomProperties (Inherited from ChannelItem)

The CustomProperties collection of CustomProperty objects for a Posting object is used as a catch-all for capturing characteristics that were not thought of by Microsoft. This concept was covered in detail in Chapter 25 regarding a channel and is similar for a posting. See the Working with Channel Objects section near the end of Chapter 25 for details and a code sample.

All the concepts are the same, and, as with a Channel object, a Posting object's CustomProperty can be maintained and manipulated using the Web Author and PAPI. However, we use VS.NET instead of Site Manager to create a CustomProperty (Figure 26–12).

This means that the number of people who can physically create these is much smaller. This can be a huge disadvantage. The interface is

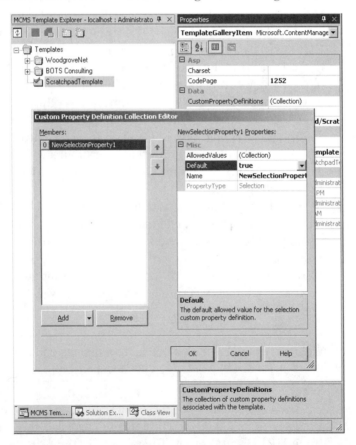

**Figure 26–12** Custom Property Definition Collection Editor

similar to the Site Manager-based version but just different enough to be weird. The same capabilities of creating a Text-based CustomProperty or Selection-based CustomProperty with an allowed values list exist.

The only other difference is the ability to define a default value in VS.NET or in code. So, the UsesDefaultValue property will return true or false, the DefaultValue property will return the value selected in the dialog, and the ResetToDefault method will obviously reset the Value to the DefaultValue.

## WorkingRevision

The WorkingRevision is either the Approved or the Unapproved version of the posting. A posting is typically referred to as a single entity; however the reality is that at any point in time there could be as many as seven concurrent conceptual types of postings (Figure 26–13):

- An in-memory Working Revision Posting object that represents either:
  - A data-based Unapproved posting
  - A data-based Approved posting (which can coexist)
- An in-memory Preview Posting object
- An in-memory historical revision that represents any number of:
  - Data-based historical revisions (postings that were previously in the Approved state)
- A ConnectedPosting fully reliant upon the referencing Posting object's placeholder content

The Context PublishingMode will determine which posting, if any, will occupy the in-memory Working Revision Posting object. Entering a Published Context (aka Live Site in the Web Author console) or Staging PublishingMode hydrates the Approved Committed Posting object into the Working Revision. Entering an Unpublished Context (aka Edit Site in the Web Author console) or Update PublishingMode hydrates the Unapproved Committed Posting object into the in-memory Working Revision. We realize that the Web is inherently stateless so CMS Server Memory is imprecise (more like application state); however, it seems to help people understand the concept of posting revisions, so we left it in.

A posting in the process of being initially created is the first possible in-memory Working Revision and has a State of New until it is initially committed to the database. New is never a State that is physically found in the database and once an Unapproved posting row is created in the

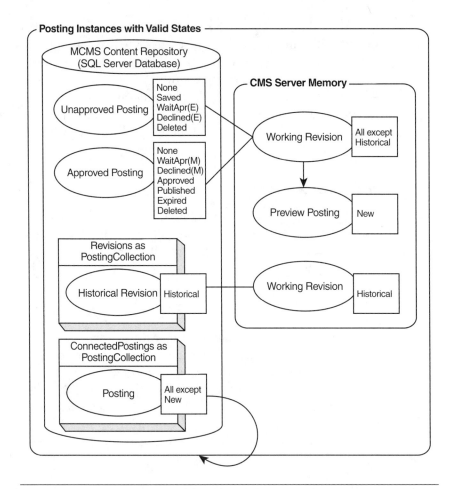

**Figure 26–13**  Posting instances with valid states

database it has a State of Saved. Since there is not an Approved posting in the database, its logical State is None. The in-memory Working Revision now represents that Unapproved posting.

The only physical table in the database is Node, and its contents are managed through a series of indicator fields and business rules, but the logical representation of that physical structure includes Unapproved postings, Approved postings, and Past Approved postings (aka Historical Revisions). However, Working Revision is always a reference to the currently in-memory version of an Unapproved or Approved posting based upon the PublishingMode of the Context that the current user used to obtain the posting.

The user can continue with this now Saved, still Unapproved, in-memory Working Revision or abandon it. If at a future time the user enters an Unpublished Context and retrieves the posting, the Unapproved posting will again become the in-memory Working Revision. However, a subscriber user cannot enter a Published Context and view this posting, because there isn't an Approved version yet.

With the Unapproved posting represented in the in-memory Working Revision, assume the CMS Administrator marks the in-memory Working Revision as Approved and calls CommitAll on the Context. Also assume the Start and Expiry dates are such that it becomes Published. Yes, we are skipping the Submitted step and the Waiting For Approval States as well as the possibility of a Declined posting, but they all use the in-memory Working Revision in the same way any Unapproved posting uses it—basically as the representation of the posting that can be manipulated in-memory until it is committed. Upon Approval however, the Unapproved posting row in the database is changed to Approved with a State of Published. There is no Unapproved posting in the database, so its logical State is None. The in-memory Working Revision now represents that Approved posting, and the CMS Context is switched to Published.

The user can continue with this now Published and Approved in-memory Working Revision or abandon it. If at a future time the user enters a Published Context and retrieves the posting, the Approved posting becomes the in-memory Working Revision. If the user enters an Unpublished Context and attempts to view this posting, they will get a New Unapproved version (based upon the Approved version) that has no associated database row until CommitAll is called. Making changes to this and saving them will create a second physical row in the database, and the process starts over again, but now there is both a current Approved version in the database and a current Unapproved version in the database. With the second still Unapproved revision of the posting represented in the in-memory Working Revision, the CMS Administrator marks the in-memory Working Revision as Approved and calls CommitAll on the Context.

The initially Approved posting row in the database becomes the first Previously Approved posting (aka Historical Revision). Aside from its state changing from Published (could have been Approved or Expired) to Historical, the ChangeDate reflecting today, the RevisionDate reflecting today, and the RevisionCause property reflecting the posting approved, its other properties remain unchanged and can never again be changed. The Unapproved posting row in the database is changed to Approved with a state of Published. Again, there is no Unapproved posting in the database so its logical state is None. The Revisions Collection of the posting (discussed next) now contains two entities (the current Approved and the single Historical Revision).

The IsWorkingRevision Posting object property will return true for any in-memory Working Revision. If at any time the user Previews a posting, the values from the in-memory Working Revision are used to hydrate the read-only in-memory Preview posting. The Web Author console is not rendered. This is not an in-memory Working Revision because it cannot be revised. This posting will display the values that were in the Working Revision for IsWorkingRevision and state, but effectively it is only allowed to have a state of New. An in-memory Working Revision and an in-memory Preview posting can both be instantiated simultaneously. Any uncommitted changes to the in-memory Working Revision are not reflected in the Preview. The IsWorkingRevision Posting object property will return false for the in-memory Preview posting

A new Historical Revision is created every time an Unapproved posting is successfully Approved. If at any time the user views a Historical Revision, the database values for the posting that existed when it became the newest Previously Approved Revision will be used to hydrate the read-only in-memory Historical Revision posting. The Web Author console is not rendered. This read-only posting is only allowed to have a state of Historical. An in-memory Working Revision and an in-memory Historical Revision Posting object can both be instantiated simultaneously. The IsWorkingRevision Posting object property will return false for the in-memory Revision History posting.

With an Unapproved posting represented in the in-memory Working Revision, assume the CMS Administrator marks the in-memory Working Revision as Deleted and calls CommitAll on the Context. Deleted is not a state that is physically found in the database except when Site Manager moves items into Deleted Items before it actually removes them from the database. The Unapproved posting row is physically removed from the table upon a successful delete. The Approved posting row and any Previously Approved posting row (aka Historical Revisions) are untouched. The in-memory Working Revision now represents the Approved posting, if any. Otherwise, the user is taken to the default page in the channel.

With an Approved posting represented in the in-memory Working Revision, the CMS Administrator marks the in-memory Working Revision as Deleted and calls CommitAll on the Context. The Approved posting row is physically removed from the table upon a successful delete. The Unapproved posting row, if any, and any Previously Approved posting rows (aka Historical Revisions) are also deleted. The in-memory Working Revision cannot be rendered, so the user is taken to the default page in the channel.

ConnectedPostings can be modeled similarly to Historical Revisions except that each ConnectedPosting can have all conceptual types of posting, whereas a Historical Revision can only be a Historical Revision. Again, see the graphical representation in Figure 26–13.

## Revisions, RevisionCause, RevisionForDate

The Revisions collection property of a Posting object contains the current Approved posting and all Historical Revisions (previously Approved) versions of the posting. The property takes two optional Boolean parameters that both default to true. The first parameter specifies whether the collection should include Historical Revisions caused by a posting being Approved (most common cause for a Historical Revision) or not. The second parameter specifies whether the collection should include Historical Revisions caused by changes to shared resources.

The RevisionCause property will either return the posting or the resource that was the catalyst for the revision's creation. The Revision-ForDate can be used to retrieve a Historical Revision for a specific point in time. The Historical Revision that was created closest to and/or before the date and time specified will be returned.

The Posting objects in the Revisions collection will be ordered, by default, in reverse chronological order by RevisionDate (most recent first). However, as with all collections, the default sort order can be overridden using the built-in sorts (see Chapter 25 for available sort options) that can be applied to the list.

Be cautious about overusing this functionality, because sorting is always a CPU-intensive activity, and repeatedly sorting a large list or a large number of small lists could become a resource drain. This collection is not self-updating. If new revisions are added to the Web Property or existing channels are deleted, the collection in memory will not be updated. It is good programming practice to get the property and use it swiftly. In busy sites, if some time has passed since the property was first acquired, it would typically be better to get the property again rather than use the one previously in memory.

The Channels collection has a Count property that can be used to determine whether the list contains any items. The items in the collection can be iterated using the common foreach statement or directly using the string Name for the item or its zero-based ordinal index.

There is also a Union method for the Channels collection. It can be combined with another collection to create a superset of all the objects in both collections.

The coding concepts are very similar to the code sample provided for the Channel Postings collection in Chapter 25.

## Placeholders

The Placeholders collection property of a Posting object contains all the Placeholder objects. Placeholders are covered in depth in Chapter 27. This collection cannot be sorted.

Some of the concepts demonstrated in the following code sample use the modified Scratchpad posting created earlier in this chapter.

Replace the Button1_Click function of our Scratchpad template (see the Adding Placeholders to Scratchpad sidebar in this chapter and the Scratchpad sidebar in Chapter 24 for details) with the following code:

```
private void Button1_Click(object sender, System.EventArgs e)
{
  try
  {
    //1. Put current Posting into variable
    Posting cmsPosting = CmsHttpContext.Current.Posting;

    //2. Populate the label with informational text
    Label1.Text =
      HttpUtility.HtmlEncode(cmsPosting.DisplayName.ToString()) +
      " Placeholders";

    //3. Iterate through the collection of Placeholders
    foreach(Placeholder cmsPlaceholder in cmsPosting.Placeholders)
    {
      //4. Put the Name of each Placeholder into the ListBox
      ListBox1.Items.Add(cmsPlaceholder.Name.ToString());
    }

  }
  catch(Exception eError)
  {
    //5. Provide error feedback to the developer
    Label1.Text = "<b>Error: </b>" + eError.Message.ToString();
  }
}
```

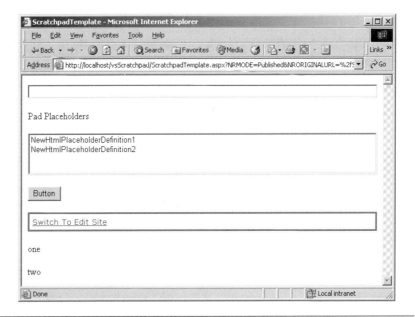

**Figure 26–14** Working with a Posting Placeholders collection

Build the solution and then refresh the Scratchpad posting in Internet Explorer, or browse to it and click the Button. The page should reload and look similar to Figure 26–14.

## Template

The Template property provides access to the underlying Template object (aka TGI or TemplateGalleryItem) used to render the referencing Posting object. A user with sufficient rights can gain a wealth of information using this object. A TGI inherits the same members of the HierarchyItem, and they have exactly the same functionality of the Posting object members described in this chapter; these include CanDelete, CanSetProperties, CreatedBy, CreatedDate, Delete, Description, Guid, IsDeleted, IsDescendantOf, IsWorkingRevision, LastModifiedBy, Last ModifiedDate, Name, OwnedBy, Path, and RevisionDate.

The following template members have very similar functionality to the similarly named Posting object members also described in this chapter: AcquireOwnership/ReleaseOwnership, CanMove (inherited from TemplateGalleryItem), CanSubmit, ChangeToken/ValidateChange Token, ConnectedTemplates, CopyTo, GetByRelativePath (inherited from TemplateGalleryItem), GetHashCode (inherited from CmsObject),

**Table 26–2** Template Members

| Member | Description |
| --- | --- |
| CreateCustomPropertyDefinition | Creates a new custom property definition for this template. |
| CreatePlaceholderDefinition | Creates a new placeholder definition for this template by copying a provided placeholder definition or using a provided type of PlaceholderDefinition. |
| CustomPropertyDefinitions | Gets a collection of CustomProperty Definition objects that have been configured for the template. |
| PlaceholderDefinitions | Gets a collection of PlaceholderDefinition objects that have been configured for this template. |
| SourceFile | Provides the file name, including the virtual path, of the template file. |
| UrlAsPosting | Simulates the appearance of a posting created from the template without the need to create a new posting to preview the template. |

GetType (inherited from System.Object), HasInaccessibleConnected Templates, IsConnected, MoveTo (inherited from TemplateGalleryItem), Parent (inherited from TemplateGalleryItem), State, and Submit.

However, the template members described in Table 26–2 are unique to Template objects.

Replace the Button1_Click function of our Scratchpad template with the following code:

```
private void Button1_Click(object sender, System.EventArgs e)
{
  try
  {
    //1. Put current Posting into variable
    Posting cmsPosting = CmsHttpContext.Current.Posting;

    //2. Populate the label with informational text
    Label1.Text =
```

```
        HttpUtility.HtmlEncode(cmsPosting.DisplayName.ToString()) +
        " Template: " +
        cmsPosting.Template.Name.ToString();

    //3. Iterate through the collection of Placeholders
    foreach(PlaceholderDefinition cmsDefinition
            in cmsPosting.Template.PlaceholderDefinitions)
    {
        //4. Put the Name of each Placeholder into the ListBox
        ListBox1.Items.Add(cmsDefinition.Name.ToString());
    }
}
catch(Exception eError)
{
    //5. Provide error feedback to the developer
    Label1.Text = "<b>Error: </b>" + eError.Message.ToString();
}
}
```

Build the solution and then refresh the Scratchpad posting in Internet Explorer, or browse to it and click the Button. The page should reload and look similar to Figure 26–15.

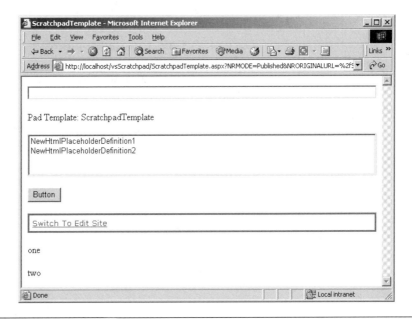

**Figure 26–15** Working with a posting Template property

---

**NOTE:** Figure 26–15 represents only a brief sample showing how to access the Template property of a posting. Templates are covered in depth in Chapters 9, 10, 11, 12, and 16, and make many other cameo appearances throughout the book.

---

## Approvers

The Approvers collection property of a Posting object contains the list of users that could potentially approve the posting. If the optional parameter is passed as true, all users and the members of all NT groups that have rights to approve the referencing Posting object will be included. But if the optional parameter is passed as false or isn't passed at all, only the users and groups (not their members) will be included. Obviously, the list of editors or moderators that have rights to approve the referencing Posting object will depend on the posting's state. When a posting is in WaitingForEditorApproval state, the users from the editor rights group will populate the list. When a posting is in WaitingForModerator Approval state, the users from the moderator rights group will populate the list. Although CMS administrators, template designers, or channel managers are allowed to approve the posting, they are not included in the list.

This property is useful to proactively notify the appropriate users when a posting's state changes. To see the Approvers, the posting will need to be in a Waiting For Approvers state; otherwise, it will return an empty collection.

Replace the Button1_Click function of our Scratchpad template with the following code:

```
private void Button1_Click(object sender, System.EventArgs e)
{
  try
  {
    //1. Put current Posting into variable
    Posting cmsPosting = CmsHttpContext.Current.Posting;

    //2. Populate the label with informational text
    Label1.Text =
      HttpUtility.HtmlEncode(cmsPosting.DisplayName.ToString()) +
      " Placeholders";

    //3. Iterate through the collection of Placeholders
    foreach(Placeholder cmsPlaceholder in cmsPosting.Placeholders)
```

```
    {
      //4. Put the Name of each Placeholder into the ListBox
      ListBox1.Items.Add(cmsPlaceholder.Name.ToString());
    }

  }
  catch(Exception eError)
  {
    //5. Provide error feedback to the developer
    Label1.Text = "<b>Error: </b>" + eError.Message.ToString();
  }
}
```

Build the solution and then refresh the Scratchpad posting in Internet Explorer, or browse to it and click the Button. The page should reload and look similar to Figure 26–16.

## GetByRelativePath (Inherited from ChannelItem)

The GetByRelativePath property of a posting provides a means to get a channel or posting relative to the current posting's Path. This concept

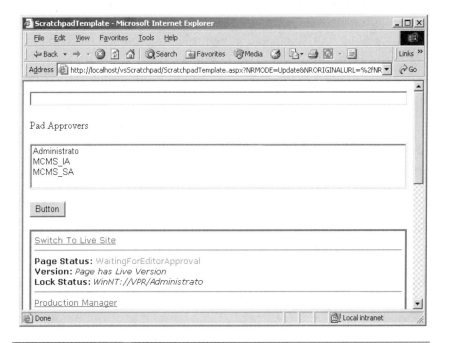

**Figure 26–16** Posting Approvers

was covered in detail in Chapter 25 regarding a channel and is identical for a posting. See the Working with Channel Objects section near the end of Chapter 25 for details and a code sample.

# Summary

Managing postings is a nontrivial undertaking, but PAPI gives us a lot of tools to complete the job. Once again we started by exploring the parentage of a posting and giving a high-level description of all the posting members. We discussed the user rights and how we could proactively determine what the user was allowed to do. Then we cleared up the relationship between page status and posting state.

In the Managing Postings section, we discussed the three ways to mark a posting—Submit, Approve, and Decline—and then proceeded to AcquireOwnership and ReleaseOwnership. We discussed file management, using methods such as CopyTo, MoveTo, and Delete, and ended the management section with ValidateChangeToken.

In the Working with Posting Members section, we dug into each property and method, starting with the read-only members and followed by the read/write members. Members that were inherited from the same roots as channel were previously detailed in Chapter 25.

In the Working with Posting Child Objects section, we talked about how to add placeholders to our template. Our discussion led to the Parent property as well as ConnectedPostings and ConnectedTemplates. CustomProperties for postings are as impractical as they were for channels; however, they are created using a different paradigm. We had a very detailed discussion about the various kinds of posting revisions that CMS supports.

We touched on the Placeholders and Template properties, gaining access to the PlaceholderDefinitions in both, and lastly we talked about Approvers.

In the next chapter, we dig even further into placeholders. They are not as consistent as postings are with channels and templates.

# CHAPTER 27

# Manipulating Placeholders

The leaves on the hierarchy that we discussed when we introduced galleries in Chapter 25 are called placeholders. Galleries can contain other galleries and eventually postings, each posting is based upon a template, and templates typically contain one or more placeholders into which content is captured and later rendered.

## Placeholder Context

Figure 27–1 provides an illustration of a placeholder within the CMS Context. There are three forces at work within a CMS placeholder:

- A placeholder definition identifies the characteristics of information that can be captured. This content type is stored in the CMS Repository database as part of a specific template definition.
- A placeholder control governs, based upon the current Web Author mode, the appearance and interaction of the rendered user content. It is stored in the file system and is generic for all template placeholders.

**NOTE:** The Web Author is covered in depth in Chapter 5 and further explored in Chapter 30. Details about placeholders themselves are examined for each placeholder type in Chapter 13.

- A Placeholder object contains the specific instance of the placeholder being rendered, including the user content. It is hydrated with user content stored in the CMS Repository database for a specific posting's placeholder.

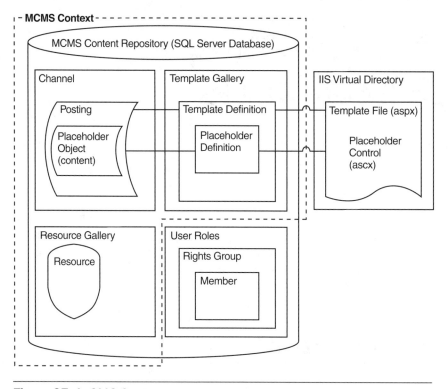

**Figure 27–1** CMS Context

In CMS, a TemplateDefinition must be related to one and only one template file. A PlaceholderDefinition within the TemplateDefinition identifies the characteristics of content that can be captured, and may be related typically one-to-one with an ASP.NET-based Web server control (see the ASP.NET Control Options sidebar) positioned on the associated template file.

---

**ASP.NET Control Options**

ASP.NET provides several different controls that can be used to piece together a Web page. Out of the box, the .NET Framework supports all of the following:

- **Traditional HTML**: HTML tags like `<form><input type="text" id="TextBox1" /></form>` are still available.

■ **HTML server controls**: Tags that relate one-to-one with traditional HTML tags but that the Web server is aware of. They can manipulate, bind, populate, respond to, and render in browser-specific traditional HTML tags, including JavaScript if necessary. These typically look like `<form runat= "server"><asp:TextBox id="TextBox1" runat="server"></asp: TextBox></form>`. Tags that have both the asp: and runat="server" tokens are characteristically built-in HTML server controls and are automatically handled by the .NET Framework. These tags must be within a <form> tag with runat="server". Each page class can only have one <form> tag with runat="server".

■ **Web server controls**: Tags associated with a class that is used to generate its output. These are typically more abstract and complex than HTML server controls. In a Win32 fat client environment, these would be the equivalent of an OCX control. They are self-contained, compiled components that can be dropped onto any ASPX page. They contain the display logic for their user interface and can also sport properties, methods, and even events. ASP.NET has some built-in controls, like the DataGrid and Calendar, that qualify as Web server controls but can be accessed in the same way that HTML server controls are accessed. However, custom Web server controls require an @ Register directive with a unique TagPrefix that is used by the custom tag to relate the control with the class that will be used to render it. An @ Register directive looks something like `<%@ Register Tag Prefix="myCtrl" Namespace="MyNamespace" Assembly="MyName spaceOrAssemblyName"%>`. The tag for this custom Web server control would look something like `<myCtrl:ClassNameWithinNamespace id="NameForUseInCode" runat="server" CustomProperty="1"> </myCtrl:ClassNameWithinNamespace>`. These tags must also be within a <form> tag with runat="server".

■ **Validation controls**: Tags associated with one of the previous two types of server control. These are used to test input that a user enters into the control. This is typically done client-side, but on downlevel browsers this validation might be done on the server. The control detects this and generates the necessary code for the given situation.

■ **Web user controls**: A Web user control can have everything that a Web Form can have. In fact, removing the <html>, <head>, <body>, and <form> elements from a Web Form (these must be in the hosting page) and saving the result as an ASCX in the same project as the hosting ASPX page is normally the way a Web user control is created. These are typically used for creating reusable page elements like menus and toolbars.

Additional documentation is available for each type of ASP.NET control on MSDN or in VS.NET help.

The Web server controls in a template file are called CMS place-holders, and they provide the user interface in both the authoring and presentation modes of the Web Author. For instance, in authoring mode, an HTML placeholder is rendered as an object that looks like a fancy text box allowing a user with sufficient rights to edit the contained content, but in presentation mode, the contained content is simply rendered surrounded with <span/span> tags only allowing the user to view the content. This is all managed at runtime by a Placeholder object that is instantiated and hydrated with the contained content typically from the CMS Repository.

The @ Register directive used by a CMS placeholder server control looks something like the following:

```
<%@ Register TagPrefix="cms"
Namespace="Microsoft.ContentManagement.WebControls""
Assembly="Microsoft.ContentManagement.WebControls,
Version=5.0.1200.0, Culture=neutral,
PublicKeyToken=31bf3856ad364e35" %>
```

The placeholder tag looks something like this:

```
<cms:HtmlPlaceholderControl id="HtmlPlaceholderControl1" runat=
"server" PlaceholderToBind="NewHtmlPlaceholderDefinition1">
</cms:HtmlPlaceholderControl>
```

where cms: relates back to the @ Register directive with a TagPrefix equal to "cms", HtmlPlaceholderControl is the built-in CMS class that will be used within the Microsoft.ContentManagement.WebControls namespace (found in the Microsoft.ContentManagement.WebControls.dll referenced by the VS.NET project), HtmlPlaceholderControl1 is the name that code would use to reference this control, and New HtmlPlaceholderDefinition1 is the name of the PlaceholderDefinition that this control will be related to in the template that is related to this template file. Web user controls are typically used to create the header, footer, and navigation sections of a template file.

The CMS placeholder construction is somewhat analogous to the way that XSL is used to transform XML into HTML. Consider that an element within an XSD identifies the characteristics of information that can be captured, and may be related one-for-one with an HTML element positioned on the document to be rendered. Those HTML elements provide the user interface at runtime for the XML hydrated with the contained content. XSL is like CMS, XSD is like a PlaceholderDefinition,

HTML is like the placeholder control, and the XML is like the Placeholder object.

Placeholders keep the part of the page that can be edited by users separate from the page design. Formatting and presentation for whatever content is ultimately provided is determined in advance by the template and hence the template file on which the page is based. Placeholders can contain HTML, XML, images, or attachments, but, if needed, custom definitions can also be created. When the posting runs, the placeholder is rendered on the page using the associated content from the CMS Repository.

A Placeholder object is inherited from CmsObject, but the PlaceholderDefinition is inherited from CustomReflectableObject. The result is a very different parentage from that of a channel or a posting. For instance, both objects have constructors. The following sections explore the structure of the Placeholder object class followed by the structure of the PlaceholderDefinition class, and then the unique properties of each type of placeholder.

## Creating and Deleting Placeholders and PlaceholderDefinitions

Predictably, all the methods in this section will require that the Context be in Update mode (see the Getting into Update PublishingMode sidebar in Chapter 25). We will be using the function introduced in Listing 25-1 to get an authenticated CmsApplicationContext in Update Publishing Mode. If we skip this step, we will receive a verbose .NET error page that basically says, You must be in Update mode to do this.

As always, after an object has been deleted, attempting to call any of its methods will cause an exception. Also, attempting to call any of these methods on a historical revision will cause an exception.

In general, the OwnedBy property (also discussed in Chapter 25) is implicitly changed to the current user so that other authors cannot concurrently update the Posting object or any of its ConnectedPostings. All changes only become permanent and ownership released (if appropriate) once the Context CommitAll method is called. Calling the Context RollbackAll method before CommitAll will return the Posting object to its previously committed condition.

The simple error handling in the code throughout these code samples isn't meant to be the model for how to handle CMS exceptions; there is an application code block from Microsoft on how to do exception handling in .NET. These functions also assume the presence of both a List Box1 and a Label1 to provide visual feedback to the user, which certainly won't typically be normal, but it works for our purposes.

The first thing we will tackle in code is the creation of a new PlaceholderDefinition. Like the CmsApplicationContext covered in Chapter 24, PlaceholderDefinitions are created using a constructor.

---

**NOTE:** Protected members are outside the scope of this chapter and are covered in the context of creating a custom placeholder in Chapter 29.

---

## PlaceholderDefinition Constructor, CreatePlaceholder

The PlaceholderDefinition constructor creates a new instance of a PlaceholderDefinition within a given template. The new Placeholder Definition will need to be of a specific PlaceholderDefinition constructor because the .NET Framework will not let us create an instance of an abstract class; so we will use the HtmlPlaceholderDefinition constructor in our example.

The steps that we would need to go through to create a Placeholder Definition in a template manually are similar to the steps that we need to follow programmatically:

1. We would start out in VS.NET by selecting a specific Template Definition to add our new PlaceholderDefinition into.
2. In the Placeholder Definition Collection Editor, for the PlaceholderDefinitions property we would add a specific type of PlaceholderDefinition (in this sample, an HtmlPlaceholder Definition).
3. We would then replace the default Name given by VS.NET with the Name that we want to use and set any other properties for the PlaceholderDefinition (we take the defaults for the other properties).
4. We click OK to dismiss the Editor and save our changes.

After we have a PlaceholderDefinition, we create an in-memory Placeholder object based upon that new definition. Once again, we will be using the function introduced in Listing 25–1 of Chapter 25 to get an authenticated CmsApplicationContext in Update PublishingMode.

Replace the Button1_Click function of our Scratchpad template file (see the Scratchpad sidebar in Chapter 24 for details) with the following code:

```
private void Button1_Click(object sender, System.EventArgs e)
{
  try
  {
    //1. Check to be sure a new PlaceholderDefinition name was
    //   entered. Note that there is no checking for name validity
    if (TextBox1.Text.Length > 0)
    {
      //2. Grab the current Template
      Template cmsCurrentTemplate =
        CmsHttpContext.Current.Posting.Template;

      //3. Check to see if the user has sufficient rights
      if (cmsCurrentTemplate.CanSetProperties)
      {
        //4. Grab an Authenticated Context in Update PublishingMode
        //   from Listing 25-1
        CmsApplicationContext cmsContextApp =
          GetAuthenticatedCmsApplicationContext(
            PublishingMode.Update);

        //5. Find the current Template in the Update Context in
        //   which to create the PlaceholderDefinition
        //   Cast the result of a Searches object as a Template
        Template cmsUpdateTemplate =
          cmsContextApp.Searches.GetByGuid(cmsCurrentTemplate.Guid)
          as Template;

        //6. Create HtmlPlaceholderDefinition object using
        //   a constructor
        HtmlPlaceholderDefinition cmsDefinition =
          new HtmlPlaceholderDefinition();

        //7. Replace the default name with the value in
        //   the TextBox
        cmsDefinition.Name = TextBox1.Text.ToString();

        //8. Create the PlaceholderDefinition in the
        //   Update Template
```

```
HtmlPlaceholderDefinition cmsCreatedDefinition =
  cmsUpdateTemplate.CreatePlaceholderDefinition(
    cmsDefinition)
  as HtmlPlaceholderDefinition;

//9. Check if the PlaceholderDefinition create
//   was successful
if (cmsCreatedDefinition != null)
{
  //10. Create Placeholder using new PlaceholderDefinition
  HtmlPlaceholder cmsCreatedPlaceholder =
    cmsCreatedDefinition.CreatePlaceholder()
    as HtmlPlaceholder;

  //11. Check if the Placeholder Object create
  //     was successful
  if (cmsCreatedPlaceholder != null)
  {
    //12. Populate the label with Template Name
    Label1.Text = "<b>Update Template Name: </b>" +
      HttpUtility.HtmlEncode(
        cmsUpdateTemplate.Name.ToString());

    //13. Add to label the New PlaceholderDefinition Name
    Label1.Text +=
      "<br><b>New PlaceholderDefinition Name: " +
      "</b>" + HttpUtility.HtmlEncode(
        cmsCreatedDefinition.Name.ToString());

    //14. Add to the label the New Placeholder Object Name
    //     Because this is only an in-memory Placeholder it
    //     does not have a Datasource, a Name, etc.
    Label1.Text +=
      "<br><b>New Placeholder Object Type: </b>" +
      cmsCreatedDefinition.GetType().ToString();
  }
  else
  {
    //15. Provide nonerror feedback to the developer
    Label1.Text = "HtmlPlaceholder create failed";
  }
}
else
{
```

```
          //16. Provide nonerror feedback to the developer
          Label1.Text = "PlaceholderDefinition create failed";
        }

        //17. Commit all changes
        cmsContextApp.CommitAll();

        //18. Dispose of the stand-alone Application Context
        cmsContextApp.Dispose();
      }
      else
      {
        //19. Provide nonerror feedback to the developer
        Label1.Text = "User does not have CanSetProperties rights";
      }
    }
    else
    {
      //20. Provide nonerror feedback to the developer
      Label1.Text = "TextBox must be a PlaceholderDefinition name";
    }
  }
  catch(Exception eError)
  {
    //21. Provide error feedback to the developer
    Label1.Text = "<b>Error: </b>" + eError.Message.ToString();
  }
}
```

At the top of the code window is a list of namespaces in use. If there isn't a line that looks like the following, you will need to add it:

```
using Microsoft.ContentManagement.Publishing.Extensions.Placeholders;
```

Build the solution and then refresh the Scratchpad posting in Internet Explorer; or browse to it, type the name for a new Placeholder Definition (we used TestPlaceholderDefinition), and click the Button. The page should reload and look similar to Figure 27–2.

When we close the browser or the posting goes out of scope, the in-memory Placeholder object will be expunged, but the Placeholder Definition is a permanent part of our template definition.

Open the PlaceholderDefinitions collection property for the Scratch Template in VS.NET, and we can see the PlaceholderDefinition that was created in our code at the bottom of the list in the Editor (Figure 27–3). It may be necessary to right-click the templates TemplateGallery and

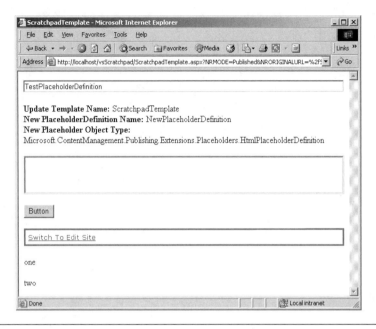

**Figure 27–2** Create PlaceholderDefinition and Placeholder object

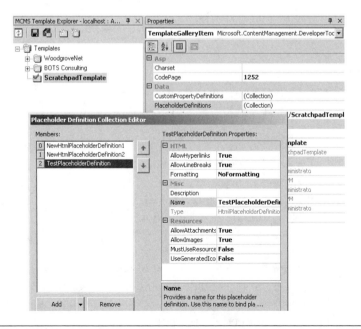

**Figure 27–3** PlaceholderDefinition in VS.NET

select Refresh before VS.NET will requery the database to see the change.

If in line 7 we hadn't altered the Name of the created Placeholder Definition or if the name that we gave had already existed, CMS would have given the default name of NewPlaceholderDefinitionX, where X is a sequential number incremented by one until a unique name is found.

We also could have provided an alternate Datasource when we created our in-memory Placeholder object, and then we could have put in content and later retrieved that content. However, there is an example of how to do this in Chapter 29.

## Clone

The Clone method is an alternative way of creating a new Placeholder Definition in the same or a different template. It works exactly the same as the previous example, except that line 6:

```
//6. Create HtmlPlaceholderDefinition with a Constructor
HtmlPlaceholderDefinition cmsDefinition =
    new HtmlPlaceholderDefinition();
```

would be changed to get a clone of an existing definition (we'll clone the PlaceholderDefinition that we created in the last example):

```
//6. Create HtmlPlaceholderDefinition as a read-only Clone
//   of the TestPlaceholderDefinition previously created
HtmlPlaceholderDefinition cmsDefinition =
    cmsCurrentTemplate.PlaceholderDefinitions
        ["TestPlaceholderDefinition"].Clone()
    as HtmlPlaceholderDefinition;
```

We can optionally pass in a Boolean parameter that if true would make the created PlaceholderDefinition read-only. The default value of this parameter is false. Of course, then we couldn't modify any of the PlaceholderDefinition's properties.

## Delete

The Delete method is used to remove unwanted PlaceholderDefinitions. However, there are some rules. The PlaceholderDefinition must be retrieved via the PlaceholderDefinitions collection of the template rather than the Definition property of a specific placeholder. The user must have sufficient rights—in this case, CanSetProperties rights—and as always the Context must be in Update mode. Deleting a Placeholder Definition may change the state of the template.

Let's remove the TestPlaceholderDefinition that we created in the earlier example.

Once again, we will be using the function introduced in Listing 25–1 of Chapter 25 to get an authenticated CmsApplicationContext in Update PublishingMode.

Replace the Button1_Click function of our Scratchpad template file with the following code:

```
private void Button1_Click(object sender, System.EventArgs e)
{
  try
  {
    //1. Grab the current Template
    Template cmsCurrentTemplate =
      CmsHttpContext.Current.Posting.Template;

    //2. Check to see if the user has sufficient rights
    if (cmsCurrentTemplate.CanSetProperties)
    {
      //3. Grab an Authenticated Context in Update PublishingMode
      //    from Listing 25-1
      CmsApplicationContext cmsContextApp =
        GetAuthenticatedCmsApplicationContext(
          PublishingMode.Update);

      //4. Find the current Template in the Update Context
      //   Cast the result of the Searches object as a Template
      Template cmsUpdateTemplate =
        cmsContextApp.Searches.GetByGuid(cmsCurrentTemplate.Guid)
        as Template;

      //5. Populate the ListBox with the Names of all the
      //    PlaceholderDefinitions in the collection
      foreach(PlaceholderDefinition cmsDefinition in
        cmsUpdateTemplate.PlaceholderDefinitions)
      {
        ListBox1.Items.Add("Before: " +
          cmsDefinition.Name.ToString());
      }
```

```
//6. Grab the PlaceholderDefinition to delete, must be
//   referenced thru the PlaceholderDefinitions collection
PlaceholderDefinition cmsDoomedDefinition =
  cmsUpdateTemplate.PlaceholderDefinitions
    [TextBox1.Text.ToString()]
  as PlaceholderDefinition;

//7. Check to see if we found the PlaceholderDefinition
if (cmsDoomedDefinition != null)
{
  //8. Populate the label with PlaceholderDefinition Name
  Label1.Text = "<b>PlaceholderDefinition To Delete: </b>" +
    HttpUtility.HtmlEncode(
      cmsDoomedDefinition.Name.ToString());

  //9. Delete the PlaceholderDefinition
  cmsDoomedDefinition.Delete();

  //9. Commit all changes
  cmsContextApp.CommitAll();

  //10. Populate the ListBox with the Names of all the
  //    PlaceholderDefinitions that remain
  foreach(PlaceholderDefinition cmsDefinition in
    cmsUpdateTemplate.PlaceholderDefinitions)
  {
    ListBox1.Items.Add("After: " +
      cmsDefinition.Name.ToString());
  }

  //11. Dispose of the stand-alone Application Context
  cmsContextApp.Dispose();
}
else
{
  //12. Provide nonerror feedback to the developer
  Label1.Text = "Didn't find the PlaceholderDefinition";
}
}
else
{
  //13. Provide nonerror feedback to the developer
  Label1.Text = "User does not have CanSetProperties rights";
```

```
      }
   }
   catch(Exception eError)
   {
      //14. Provide error feedback to the developer
      Label1.Text = "<b>Error: </b>" + eError.Message.ToString();
   }
}
```

Build the solution and then refresh the Scratchpad posting in Internet Explorer; or browse to it, type the name for a PlaceholderDefinition to delete (we used TestPlaceholderDefinition), and click the Button. The page should reload and look similar to Figure 27–4.

We increased the height of the ListBox on the template for this example so that Figure 27–4 would show all five entries. You may need to scroll down to see the last one.

## Serialize, DeserializeObject

The Serialize method removes all the state (property values) from the specified PlaceholderDefinition into either an XML string or an Xml Writer. In the example that follows, we place that XML string into the label so we can see it.

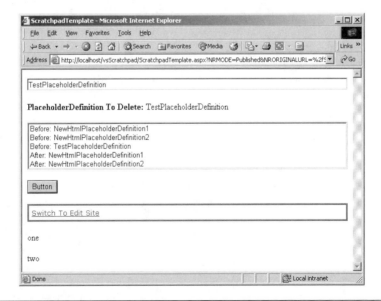

**Figure 27–4**  Delete PlaceholderDefinition

The DeserializeObject method does just the opposite. It takes a previously serialized PlaceholderDefinition as represented by an XmlNode and hydrates a PlaceholderDefinition object from that XML.

Replace the Button1_Click function of our Scratchpad template file with the following code:

```
private void Button1_Click(object sender, System.EventArgs e)
{
  try
  {
    //1. Grab the current Template
    Template cmsTemplate =
      CmsHttpContext.Current.Posting.Template;

    //2. Grab the HtmlPlaceholderDefinition to serialize
    HtmlPlaceholderDefinition cmsDefinition =
      cmsTemplate.PlaceholderDefinitions[TextBox1.Text.ToString()]
      as HtmlPlaceholderDefinition;

    //3. Check to see if we found the PlaceholderDefinition
    if (cmsDefinition != null)
    {
      //4. Show the name of the original PlaceholderDefinition
      ListBox1.Items.Add("Original: " +
        cmsDefinition.Name.ToString());

      //5. Serialize the PlaceholderDefinition XML into the label
      Label1.Text = HttpUtility.HtmlEncode(
        cmsDefinition.Serialize());

      //6. Declare and initialize an XmlDocument object
      System.Xml.XmlDocument xmlDocument =
        new System.Xml.XmlDocument();

      //7. Populate the xmlDocument with PlaceholderDefinition XML
      xmlDocument.InnerXml = cmsDefinition.Serialize();

      //8. Declare and initialize an XmlNode object with the XML
      System.Xml.XmlNode xmlDefinition =
        xmlDocument.DocumentElement;

      //9. Use the XmlNode to hydrate a new PlaceholderDefinitnion
      HtmlPlaceholderDefinition cmsDeserializedDefinition =
```

```
    HtmlPlaceholderDefinition.DeserializeObject(xmlDefinition)
    as HtmlPlaceholderDefinition;

  //10. Show the name of the hydrated PlaceholderDefinition
  ListBox1.Items.Add("Deserialized: " +
    cmsDeserializedDefinition.Name.ToString());
  }
  else
  {
    //11. Provide nonerror feedback to the developer
    Label1.Text = "Didn't find the PlaceholderDefinition";
  }
}
catch(Exception eError)
{
  //12. Provide error feedback to the developer
  Label1.Text = "<b>Error: </b>" + eError.Message.ToString();
}
}
```

Build the solution and then refresh the Scratchpad posting in Internet Explorer; or browse to it, type the name for a PlaceholderDefinition to serialize (we used NewHtmlPlaceholderDefinition1), and click the Button. The page should reload and look similar to Figure 27–5.

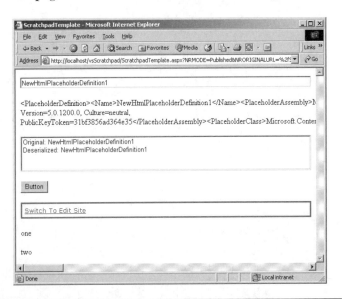

**Figure 27–5** Serialize and Deserialize PlaceholderDefinition

### PropertyChanged

The PropertyChanged event for a PlaceholderDefinition is fired whenever changes are made to the PlaceholderDefinition through a public property setter.

# Working with Placeholder Members

We will focus on the read-only members first (there are only a few). We start with a comprehensive code sample and then provide an alphabetical list of read-only members specific to a Placeholder object. Then we focus on read/write members. Again, we start with a comprehensive code sample followed by an alphabetical list of read/write members specific to a Placeholder object.

### Read-Only Members

The code to see all the read-only placeholder members is presented comprehensively. Sometimes it just helps to see the output of a property to better understand it.

Replace the Button1_Click function of our Scratchpad template file with the following code:

```
private void Button1_Click(object sender, System.EventArgs e)
{
  //1. Put current Posting into variable
  Posting cmsPosting = CmsHttpContext.Current.Posting;

  //2. Grab the first Placeholder to view
  Placeholder cmsPlaceholder = cmsPosting.Placeholders[0]
    as Placeholder;

  //3. Check to see if we found the specified Placeholder
  if (cmsPlaceholder != null)
  {
    //4. Populate the label with the read-only properties
    Label1.Text =
      "<b>GetHashCode: </b>" +
        cmsPlaceholder.GetHashCode().ToString() +
      "<br><b>GetType: </b>" +
        cmsPlaceholder.GetType().ToString() +
```

```
"<br><b>Name: </b>" +
   cmsPlaceholder.Name.ToString();
   }
}
```

Build the solution and then refresh the Scratchpad posting in Internet Explorer, or browse to it and click the Button. The page should reload and look similar to Figure 27–6.

### Read-Only Members for a Placeholder
#### GetHashCode
The GetHashCode method retrieves the hash code for the object. Notice that the actual number returned is different each time.

This identifier is not frequently used by the developer.

#### GetType
The GetType method retrieves the name of the namespace for the instance that the object represents.

This member can be useful for determining what kind of placeholder is in use.

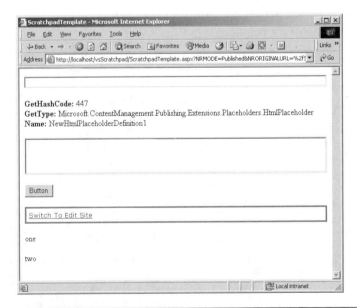

**Figure 27–6**  Show read-only placeholder members

*Name*

The Name property holds the actual name for the referencing place-holder. However, this Name is different from other names we have encountered. It is read-only rather than read/write. So it is not as big a risk for the display hack (see the Avoid Hack by Using HtmlEncode sidebar in Chapter 25). This property must be unique. The value of the Name property is set at runtime and defaults to the name of the place-holder on which it is based.

The maximum length is 100 characters for any string displayed in this property. Typical alphanumeric characters are allowed, but we recommend against using spaces in any Names.

This member can be useful for getting the name of the specific Placeholder object so that it can be used in other searches.

## Read/Write Members for a Placeholder

BeginWrite, EndWrite, RetrieveContent, and SaveContent are all protected members that are accessed from the placeholder-specific classes on our behalf. Suffice it to say that altering members for a Placeholder object requires the implementation and calling of the BeginWrite method to start the process and validate that the user has sufficient rights to update the placeholder. Saving a modified Placeholder object requires the implementation and calling of the EndWrite method. Likewise, retrieving and saving content requires that the RetrieveContent and SaveContent methods be called.

### *Datasource, Datasource.RawContent*

The Datasource property and its singular RawContent property will not likely be used unless you are creating a custom control. It is recommended that you use the specific placeholder property that returns the content in a format specific to that placeholder rather than using its raw format. It is very uncommon to need to iterate through the placeholders on a template. Typically, we want to interact with a specific placeholder of a specific type. It is typically best to cast a Placeholder object and its PlaceholderDefinition as specifically as we can.

If a Placeholder object is temporary, as in the placeholder creation example, calling the protected methods is not necessary, because a transaction isn't needed to keep the Datasource in sync.

A very simple example of accessing the DataSource RawContent property follows.

Replace the Button1_Click function of our Scratchpad template file with the following code:

```
private void Button1_Click(object sender, System.EventArgs e)
{
  //1. Put current Posting into variable
  Posting cmsPosting = CmsHttpContext.Current.Posting;

  //2. Grab the first Placeholder to view
  HtmlPlaceholder cmsPlaceholder = cmsPosting.Placeholders[0]
    as HtmlPlaceholder;

  //3. Check to see if we found the specified Placeholder
  if (cmsPlaceholder != null)
  {
    //4. Populate the label with the RawContent of the Placeholder
    Label1.Text = "<b>RawContent: </b><p>" +
      cmsPlaceholder.Datasource.RawContent.ToString();
  }
}
```

Build the solution and then refresh the Scratchpad posting in Internet Explorer, or browse to it and click the Button. The page should reload and look similar to Figure 27–7.

**Figure 27–7** RawContent

Again, you would be ill advised to use this polymorphic property, because it could be changed in any release of CMS, and the code written against the raw format could fail.

# Working with PlaceholderDefinition Members

We will use the same approach with PlaceholderDefinition that we took with Placeholder: read-only members first followed by nonprotected read/write members.

## Read-Only Members

The code to see all the read-only PlaceholderDefinition members is presented comprehensively.

Replace the Button1_Click function of our Scratchpad template file with the following code:

```
private void Button1_Click(object sender, System.EventArgs e)
{
  //1. Put current Template into variable
  Template cmsTemplate = CmsHttpContext.Current.Posting.Template;

  //2. Grab the first PlaceholderDefinition to view
  PlaceholderDefinition cmsDefinition =
    cmsTemplate.PlaceholderDefinitions[0]
    as PlaceholderDefinition;

  //3. Check to see if we found the specified PlaceholderDefinition
  if (cmsDefinition != null)
  {
    //4. Populate the label with the read-only properties
    Label1.Text = "Read Only PlaceholderDefinition Members";

    //5. Add to label info about GetAttributes
    if (cmsDefinition.GetAttributes() != null)
      if (cmsDefinition.GetAttributes().Count > 0)
        Label1.Text += "<br><b>GetAttributes[0] TypeID: </b>" +
          cmsDefinition.GetAttributes()[0].TypeId.ToString();
      else
        Label1.Text += "<br><b>GetAttributes Count: </b>" +
          cmsDefinition.GetAttributes().Count.ToString();
```

```
else
  Label1.Text += "<br><b>GetAttributes: </b>none";

//6. Add to label info about GetClassName
Label1.Text += "<br><b>GetClassName: </b>" +
  cmsDefinition.GetClassName().ToString();

//7. Add to label info about GetComponentName
Label1.Text += "<br><b>GetComponentName: </b>" +
  cmsDefinition.GetComponentName().ToString();

//8. Add to label info about GetConverter
Label1.Text += "<br><b>GetConverter: </b>" +
  cmsDefinition.GetConverter().ToString();

//9. Add to label info about GetDefaultEvent
if (cmsDefinition.GetDefaultEvent() != null)
  Label1.Text += "<br><b>GetDefaultEvent DisplayName: </b>" +
    cmsDefinition.GetDefaultEvent().DisplayName.ToString();
else
  Label1.Text += "<br><b>GetDefaultEvent: </b>none";

//10. Add to label info about GetDefaultProperty
if (cmsDefinition.GetDefaultProperty() != null)
  Label1.Text += "<br><b>GetDefaultProperty: </b>" +
    cmsDefinition.GetDefaultEvent().ToString();
else
  Label1.Text += "<br><b>GetDefaultProperty: </b>none";

//11. Add to label info about GetClassName
if (cmsDefinition.GetEvents() != null)
  if (cmsDefinition.GetEvents().Count > 0)
    Label1.Text += "<br><b>GetEvents[0] DisplayName: </b>" +
      cmsDefinition.GetEvents()[0].DisplayName.ToString();
  else
    Label1.Text += "<br><b>GetEvents Count: </b>" +
      cmsDefinition.GetEvents().Count.ToString();
else
  Label1.Text += "<br><b>GetEvents: </b>none";

//12. Add to label info about GetHashCode
Label1.Text += "<br><b>GetHashCode: </b>" +
  cmsDefinition.GetHashCode().ToString();
```

```
//13. Add to label info about GetProperties
if (cmsDefinition.GetProperties() != null)
  if (cmsDefinition.GetProperties().Count > 0)
    Label1.Text += "<br><b>GetProperties[0] DisplayName: " +
      "</b>" + cmsDefinition.GetProperties()[0].DisplayName
      .ToString();
  else
    Label1.Text += "<br><b>GetProperties Count: </b>" +
      cmsDefinition.GetProperties().Count.ToString();
else
  Label1.Text += "<br><b>GetProperties: </b>none";

//14. Add to label info about GetType
Label1.Text += "<br><b>GetType: </b>" +
  cmsDefinition.GetType().ToString();

//15. Add to label info about IsReadOnly
Label1.Text += "<br><b>IsReadOnly: </b>" +
  cmsDefinition.IsReadOnly.ToString();
  }
}
```

Build the solution and then refresh the Scratchpad posting in Internet Explorer, or browse to it and click the Button. The page should reload and look similar to Figure 27–8.

### Read-Only Members for a PlaceholderDefinition

All of the following properties are inherited from the CustomReflection Object:

- GetAttributes
- GetClassName
- GetComponentName
- GetConverter
- GetDefaultEvent
- GetDefaultProperty
- GetEvents
- GetProperties

*GetHashCode, GetType*
The same as Placeholder.

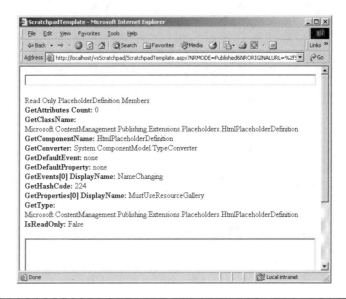

**Figure 27-8** Read-only PlaceholderDefinition members

*IsReadOnly*

The IsReadOnly property retrieves the Boolean value that indicates whether the PlaceholderDefinition can be modified or not. If it returns true, the PlaceholderDefinition is read-only, and any attempt to set a property will result in an exception.

A PlaceholderDefinition can become read-only if it is cloned with the optional parameter set to true.

## Read/Write Members

As before, the code to see all the read/write PlaceholderDefinition members is presented comprehensively. All these members can be assigned a value in code or through various other user interfaces. However, none of these changed values will become permanent until CommitAll is called on the Context. Uncommitted changes can be discarded by calling RollbackAll. If neither method is explicitly called when the Context in which the change is made is destroyed (goes out of scope or is disposed of), the disposition of the changes will be decided by the value of the RollbackOnSessionEnd property. By default, this property is false, so all changes are committed. In general, the properties of deleted or marked-for-delete PlaceholderDefinitions and historical revisions can't be altered.

Properties can only be altered when the PlaceholderDefinition is retrieved from the PlaceholderDefinitions collection property of a Template object rather than the Definition property of a Posting object's Placeholder property. Of course, the user must have sufficient rights (the Posting object's CanSetProperties property must return true), and the mode must be in Update PublishingMode.

Setting a property may change the state of a template and any ConnectedTemplates.

Replace the Button1_Click function of our Scratchpad template file with the following code:

```
private void Button1_Click(object sender, System.EventArgs e)
{
  //1. Put current Template into variable
  Template cmsTemplate = CmsHttpContext.Current.Posting.Template;

  //2. Grab the first PlaceholderDefinition to view
  PlaceholderDefinition cmsDefinition =
    cmsTemplate.PlaceholderDefinitions[0]
    as PlaceholderDefinition;

  //3. Check to see if we found the specified PlaceholderDefinition
  if (cmsDefinition != null)
  {
    //4. Populate the label with the read-only properties
    Label1.Text = "Read Write PlaceholderDefinition Members";

    //5. Add to the label with PlaceholderDefinition Description
    Label1.Text += "<br><b>Description: </b>" +
      HttpUtility.HtmlEncode(cmsDefinition.Description.ToString());

    //6. Add to the label with PlaceholderDefinition Name
    Label1.Text += "<br><b>Name: </b>" +
      HttpUtility.HtmlEncode(cmsDefinition.Name.ToString());
  }
}
```

Build the solution and then refresh the Scratchpad posting in Internet Explorer, or browse to it and click the Button. The page should reload and look similar to Figure 27–9.

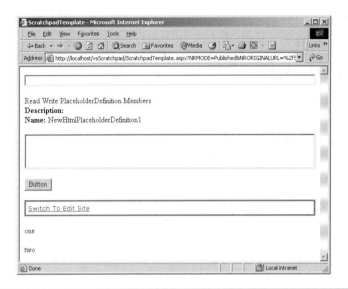

**Figure 27-9**   Read/write PlaceholderDefinition members

### Read/Write Members for a PlaceholderDefinition

As with Placeholders, BeginWrite, EndWrite, and BeginRead are all protected members that are accessed by the PlaceholderDefinition-specific classes on our behalf. Suffice it to say that altering members for a PlaceholderDefinition object requires the implementation and calling of the BeginWrite method to start the process and validate that the user has sufficient rights to update the PlaceholderDefinition. To save a modified PlaceholderDefinition object requires the implementation and calling of the EndWrite method. BeginRead should be implemented and called whenever a PlaceholderDefinition property is read.

The OnCloned method can be implemented to create a proprietary solution when a PlaceholderDefinition is cloned. If this method is implemented, it overrides the default behavior discussed earlier in this chapter.

### Description (Inherited from HierarchyItem)
The Description property holds the free-form text description (see the Avoid Hack by Using HtmlEncode sidebar in Chapter 25) for the referencing PlaceholderDefinition.

CMS automatically trims leading and trailing spaces and truncates the length to 500 characters for any string assigned to this property. Typical alphanumeric characters are allowed.

This member can be useful for setting and showing a verbose description of the PlaceholderDefinition that the user is using.

### Name (Inherited from HierarchyItem)

The Name property holds the free-form text of the actual name for the referencing PlaceholderDefinition. This name is not intended for display (see the Avoid Hack by Using HtmlEncode sidebar) per se but is visible to the user in the URL and Path. This property is not allowed to be empty and must be case-insensitive unique within the collection.

CMS automatically trims leading and trailing spaces and truncates the length to 100 characters for any string assigned to this property. Typical alphanumeric characters are allowed, but we recommend against using spaces in PlaceholderDefinition names.

This member can be useful for setting and showing the Name of the PlaceholderDefinition.

# Working with Placeholder Child Objects

There are two child objects of the Placeholder object. We have already covered both of them exhaustively.

## Definition

The Definition is the PlaceholderDefinition that we covered throughout this chapter. This is an in-memory reference to the actual definitions found in the PlaceholderDefinitions collection of a template. It is meant for reference only.

## Posting

This is the Posting object to which the Placeholder object belongs. Once we have a reference to this, assuming sufficient rights, we can do anything that we discussed in Chapter 26.

## Custom Placeholders

We have talked about the six built-in placeholders that CMS comes with. What if you need to host content that doesn't fit easily into one of the provided containers? Maybe a drop-down list or a Calendar control, perhaps a Flash object or a PDF. Fortunately, this entire infrastructure is extensible. We go through an entire example of creating a drop-down list based upon an XmlPlaceholder in Chapter 29.

## Summary

We started this chapter talking about the three forces at work within a CMS placeholder. We covered the Placeholder object and the PlaceholderDefinition quite extensively. Unfortunately, there are limits on what can be done on the physical side of things in CMS today. We still need a "hands-on" developer to create that initial template file for CMS to do its work. Programmatically manipulating the physical ASPX template file and its placeholder controls is very limited. Only in-memory changes can be made, and they cannot be saved or committed.

We did discuss the various controls available to the .NET developer, and then we delved into the various structures that CMS has borrowed from .NET to make placeholders work.

We created a new Placeholder and a new PlaceholderDefinition and then deleted them. PlaceholderDefinitions can be created and kept, but Placeholder objects are for in-memory use only. We then saw several examples of the various read-only and read/write members of both Placeholder and PlaceholderDefinition objects.

We touched briefly on the Definition and Posting child objects of the placeholder and introduced the concept of creating your very own placeholder types.

Next we explore all the capabilities of a method that we have already used in many of our previous examples: the Context Searches method. It is a very powerful, if potentially resource-intensive, tool.

# CHAPTER 28

# Searching for CMS Assets

There are times, especially when using the CmsApplicationContext in a stand-alone setting or in Update PublishingMode from a posting, when you want to locate a specific object or collection of objects, regardless of the current location. For those times, both the CmsHttpContext and the CmsApplicationContext provide a method called Searches. It provides direct access to an individual object or collections of objects with specific characteristics. For many of the code samples throughout this book to work, we need to use some of the Searches property's methods. We will use all of those methods in this chapter.

## Exploring Searches

The Searches method of a CMS context enables us to search for assets like channels, postings, template definitions, template galleries, resources, and resource galleries. Uses of the Searches method can be broadly grouped into two main categories: searching for a single asset or searching for a collection of assets. Searching for a collection of assets can be further categorized by the type of asset retrieved: Channel objects, Posting objects, Template objects, or Gallery objects.

Searches automatically take into consideration the rights and privileges of the authenticated context user, the context mode, and multiple versions of an asset (if they exist) when returning assets. However, user subscription settings are not considered when we are searching for channels and postings except for the NewChannels and NewPostings methods. Subscribed channels or postings can be determined by checking the Channel.IsSubscribed property and the Posting.Parent.IsSubscribed property. Be aware, deleted items are never returned from a search.

The results of a search will typically need to be cast as a specific data type in order for the object to be assigned to a variable. The following two lines of code both are equally effective at casting the search result as a posting:

```
cmsPosting1 = cmsContext.Searches.GetByGuid(sGuid) as Posting;
cmsPosting2 = (Posting)cmsContext.Searches.GetByGuid(sGuid);
```

The code in this book typically casts objects using the "as" keyword followed by the data type because it is easier for the code to flow to multiple lines, which is good for displaying code in a limited-width book. Preceding the cast object with the data type in parentheses works just as well in VS.NET.

# Searching for a Single Asset

Frequently, we will know precisely which asset we need. It could be a hard-coded reference, a reference input by the user, a reference retrieved from the database, or a reference to an asset related to something in the current context. However, searching for an asset that doesn't exist (or can't be found), is not visible in the current publishing mode, or the user doesn't have sufficient rights to view will return a null reference. Since CMS doesn't require the use of unique names when we are creating assets, it is possible to make a request for more than one asset with the same name. Ambiguous searches also result in a null reference.

The GetByGuid method is the most efficient search, and an asset's GUID is always unique (even historically). Since CMS doesn't require the use of unique names when we are creating assets, the path and URL are not guaranteed to resolve to a unique asset. An asset's GUID does not change if the object is moved to a different container in the hierarchy. If possible, GetByGuid should be used instead of the GetByPath or GetByUrl methods.

## Returning a Single Asset

The following sections cover how the GetByGuid, GetByPath, and Get ByUrl methods can be used to return a single asset.

### GetByGuid

Since our Scratchpad (see the Scratchpad sidebar in Chapter 24 for details) has only a limited set of assets at this point, the first Searches example is something of a self-fulfilling prophecy. It does demonstrate that we can search for an asset given that we know its GUID and that GUIDs are assigned to all assets we create. We will be searching for a posting, but we could just as easily search for a channel, a template, a template gallery, a resource, or a resource gallery. We only need to know the GUID of the asset we want, and GUID is an available read-only property on all assets. Be aware, the GUID string must include braces, hyphens, 32 characters grouped in five alphanumeric sections (8-4-4-4-12), and generally uses the following format: {xxxxxxxx-xxxx-xxxx-xxxx-xxxxxxxxxxxx}.

Replace the Button1_Click function of our Scratchpad template file with the following code:

```
private void Button1_Click(object sender, System.EventArgs e)
{
  //1. Grab the current CMS Context
  CmsHttpContext cmsContext = CmsHttpContext.Current;

  //2. Find this Posting using the Context current Posting's GUID
  //   We must cast the result of a Searches object as a Posting
  Posting cmsPostingFound =
    cmsContext.Searches.GetByGuid(cmsContext.Posting.Guid)
    as Posting;

  //3. Check if Posting was found
  if(cmsPostingFound != null)
  {
    //4. Check if the current Posting is equal to Posting found
    if(cmsContext.Posting.Equals(cmsPostingFound))
    {
      //5. Assign the display name of the Posting
      Label1.Text = "<b>Posting Found by GUID:</b> " +
        cmsPostingFound.Path.ToString();
    }
  }
}
```

The second line of code actually does the search. It looks for a CMS asset that has the same GUID as the current Posting object, casts the object search result as a Posting object, and assigns it to a variable called cmsPostingFound, which is declared as a Posting object. We are referencing the current Posting object's GUID so we can be sure that the formatting of the GUID will be correct, but this value is just a string and can be provided in many other ways.

Build the solution and then refresh the Scratchpad posting in Internet Explorer, or browse to it and click the Button. The page should reload and look similar to Figure 28–1.

### GetByPath

Locating an asset with the GetByPath method is very similar to using the GetByGuid method. In fact, we will only alter the second line in the code from our first example. However, there are several factors to consider when using this method. GetByPath is less efficient than Get ByGuid and may degrade site performance. Unlike with GetByGuid, if an asset is moved to a different container in the hierarchy (the path changes), the search will no longer find the asset. It is also possible to make a request that has an ambiguous search result (two assets with exactly the same path), resulting in a null reference.

This method requires us to provide a root relative or absolute path to an asset; relative paths will result in an exception. An asset's path always begins with a slash mark (the root), followed by the containers it is in (if any) separated by slash marks (/), and ending with its name. Containers can optionally contain a slash mark at the end of the path. So, as we saw in the result of the first example, the path to our Scratchpad posting should be /Channels/Scratch/Scratchpad. If we were just looking for the channel, we could use either /Channels/Scratch or /Channels/Scratch/.

Note that the user only needs read rights to the requested asset for Searches to find it. Assets that the asset itself contains may not be available to the user.

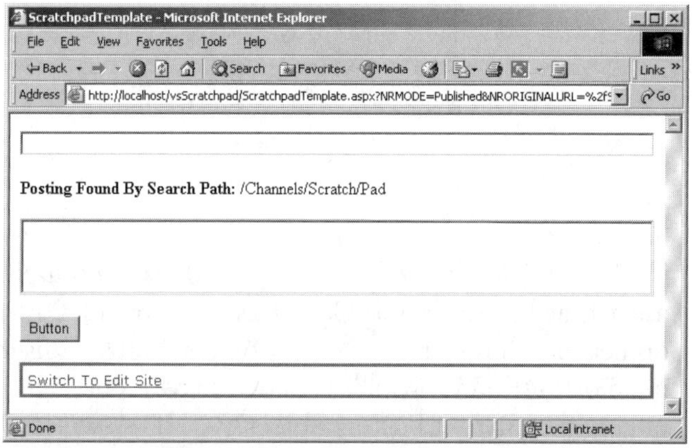

**Figure 28–1** Find current posting Searches example

If an invalid path string is given, an exception will result.

Replace the Button1_Click function of our Scratchpad template file with the following code:

```
private void Button1_Click(object sender, System.EventArgs e)
{
  //1. Grab the current CMS Context
  CmsHttpContext cmsContext = CmsHttpContext.Current;

  //2. Find this Posting using the Context current Posting's Path
  //   We must cast the result of a Searches object as a Posting
  Posting cmsPostingFound =
    cmsContext.Searches.GetByPath(cmsContext.Posting.Path)
    as Posting;

  //3. Check if Posting was found
  if(cmsPostingFound != null)
  {
    //4. Check if the current Posting is equal to the Posting found
    if(cmsContext.Posting.Equals(cmsPostingFound))
    {
      //5. Assign the display name of the Posting
      Label1.Text = "<b>Posting Found By Search Path:</b> " +
        cmsPostingFound.Path.ToString();
    }
  }
}
```

Yeah, that was like cheating. Replacing line 2 with either of the following code snippets should also yield the same result:

```
Posting cmsPostingFound =
  cmsContext.Searches.GetByPath("/Channels/Scratch/Pad")
  as Posting;
```

or let the user type the path into the TextBox:

```
Posting cmsPostingFound =
  cmsContext.Searches.GetByPath(TextBox1.Text.ToString())
  as Posting;
```

Build the solution and then refresh the Scratchpad posting in Internet Explorer, or browse to it and click the Button. The page should reload and look the same as Figure 28–1. We just arrived at the same Posting object that was returned using a different Searches method.

### GetByUrl

The GetByUrl method can only retrieve URL-based assets: Posting objects and Channel objects. CMS can reference these assets using two different types of URLs.

- **Hierarchical URLs**: The hierarchical URL to our Scratchpad posting looks like this: /Scratch/Scratchpad.htm. The possibility of using short, simple URLs is a differentiator for CMS in the marketplace. Most CMS systems require long URLs that are very difficult for users to type and remember. Note the use of the ".htm" suffix in the URL. Since our template is an ASPX page and the posting content is in a SQL Server database, when the request is made of IIS, the CMS ISAPI filter is working behind the scenes to transform this hierarchical URL into the GUID-based Query String we see in the address bar of the browser when the posting it represents is rendered.
- **GUID-based URLs**: The GUID-based URL to our Scratchpad posting looks something like this: /NR/exeres/xxxxxxxx-xxxx-xxxx-xxxx-xxxxxxxxxxxx. Of course, the actual alphanumeric values of the GUID would be used instead of the x's shown here. The braces that were required in formatting the GUID for retrieval using the GetByGuid method are noticeably absent.

It is evident why this method is not very efficient and only intended to be used by search engines and site-indexing software. URLs must be resolved by the CMS engine before the assets can be retrieved. Hence, as you might expect, hierarchical URLs can only return a Channel object or a Posting object that is in a Published state, whereas GUID-based URLs can return a Channel object or a Posting object regardless of its publishing state. It is also probably evident that GetByGuid and GetByPath can retrieve some assets that GetByUrl can't. To get a template, a template gallery, a resource, or a resource gallery, we must use a Searches method other than GetByUrl.

Replace the Button1_Click function of our Scratchpad template file with the following code:

```
private void Button1_Click(object sender, System.EventArgs e)
{
```

```
//1. Grab the current CMS Context
CmsHttpContext cmsContext = CmsHttpContext.Current;


//2. Find this Posting using the Context current Posting's URL
//   We must cast the result of a Searches object as a Posting
Posting cmsPostingFound =
  cmsContext.Searches.GetByUrl(cmsContext.Posting.Url)
  as Posting;


//3. Check if Posting was found
if(cmsPostingFound != null)
{
  //4. Check if the current Posting is equal to Posting found
  if(cmsContext.Posting.Equals(cmsPostingFound))
  {
    //5. Assign the display name of the Posting
    Label1.Text = "<b>Posting Found by URL:</b> " +
      cmsPostingFound.Path.ToString();
  }
}
}
```

Replacing line 2 with either of the following code snippets should also yield the same result:

```
//Hierarchical URL
  Posting cmsPostingFound =
    cmsContext.Searches.GetByUrl("/Scratch/pad.htm")
    as Posting;
```

or:

```
//GUID-based URL (use the actual URL for your Scratchpad posting)
  Posting cmsPostingFound =
    cmsContext.Searches.GetByUrl(
      "/NR/exeres/D8D8026A-8F0B-4804-BBC6-69387182BEA3")
    as Posting;
```

Build the solution and then refresh the Scratchpad posting in Internet Explorer, or browse to it and click the Button. The page should reload and look the same as Figure 28–1. Again, we just arrived at the same Posting object that was returned using a different Searches method.

# Searching for a Collection of Assets

As previously mentioned, searching for a collection of assets can be further categorized by the type of asset retrieved: Channel objects, Posting objects, Template objects, or Gallery objects. These Searches methods are different from our previous searches in several ways. These methods return a collection of assets rather than just a single asset. If no assets are found, the method returns an empty collection rather than a null reference. There isn't a Boolean operator, so multiple, separate searches must be performed, and the results can be combined using the Union method. In certain publishing modes, assets with IsHiddenModePublished equal to true will automatically be removed from the collection.

## Returning a Collection of Channels

The following sections cover how the GetChannelsByCustomProperty, NewChannels, and ImportantChannels methods can be used to return a collection of Channel objects.

### *GetChannelsByCustomProperty*

This method can be called with just the name of the CustomProperty to find or the name and the value (up to 300 characters) of the Custom Property to find. But we don't currently have a CustomProperty on our Scratch channel to search for. Creating CustomProperties and entering their values is done very differently for channels than it is for postings. What follows are brief instructions to help you create a couple of custom properties to search for. If you have a channel that already has custom properties, feel free to use it in the code sample instead.

---

**NOTE:** We illustrate creating and manipulating custom properties for a channel in Chapter 25.

---

First, create CustomProperties for the Scratch channel by following these steps:

1. Log in to Site Manager as the CMS Administrator.
2. Right-click the Scratch channel in the channels hierarchy and choose Properties from the drop-down menu, resulting in the Scratch Properties dialog.

3. Click the Custom tab.
4. Click the New button.
5. Enter customPropertyOne into the Name text box.
6. Enter the word "One" into the Current Text Value text box.
7. Click the OK button.
8. Click the New button again.
9. Enter customPropertyTwo into the Name text box.
10. Leave the Current Text Value text box empty.
11. Click the OK button.
12. Click the OK button to dismiss the Scratch Properties dialog.
13. Close Site Manager.

Next, enter values for each CustomProperty on the Scratch channel by following these steps:

1. Refresh the Scratchpad posting in Internet Explorer or browse to it.
2. Click the Switch to Edit Site link on the Scratchpad posting in the CMS default console.
3. Click the Channel Properties link in the CMS default console, resulting in the Page Properties dialog.
4. Click the Custom tab.
5. Leave the customPropertyOne CustomProperty value defaulting to the value "One". It is defaulting to the literal string "One" because we set the value while we were in Site Manager.
6. Enter the literal "Two" into the text box under the Current Value column for the customPropertyTwo CustomProperty.
7. Click the Save Changes button.
8. Click the Switch to Live Site link in the CMS default console.

Now we can search for channels with a CustomProperty with a given Name.

Replace the Button1_Click function of our Scratchpad template file with the following code:

```
private void Button1_Click(object sender, System.EventArgs e)
{
    //1. Check to be sure a value was entered.
    //   Note that there is no checking for value validity
    if (TextBox1.Text.Length>0)
    {
```

```
//2. Grab the current CMS Context
CmsHttpContext cmsContext = CmsHttpContext.Current;

//3. Find all the channels that have a CustomProperty
//    with a property name equal to the string provided
ChannelCollection cmsChannelsFound =
   cmsContext.Searches.GetChannelsByCustomProperty(
   TextBox1.Text.ToString())
   as ChannelCollection;

//4. Empty the ListBox of all previous entries
ListBox1.Items.Clear();

//5. List the name of every channel returned by the search
foreach(Channel cmsChannel in cmsChannelsFound)
{
   ListBox1.Items.Add(cmsChannel.Name.ToString());
}

//6. If the collection is empty, show No Channels Found
if (cmsChannelsFound.Count==0)
{
   ListBox1.Items.Add("No Channels Found");
}
}
else
{
   //7. Provide nonerror feedback to the developer
   Label1.Text = "TextBox must contain a value";
}
}
```

Build the solution and then refresh the Scratchpad posting in Internet Explorer; or browse to it, enter the name of one of the custom properties that we created (like customPropertyOne) into the text box, and click the Button. The page should reload and look similar to Figure 28–2.

If we type a custom property name that doesn't exist, the Scratchpad posting should reload, adding the literal "No Channels Found" to the ListBox.

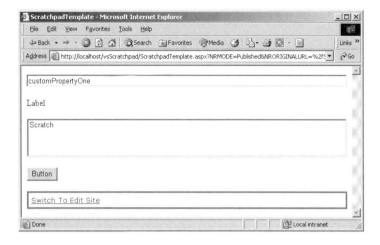

**Figure 28–2**  Find collection of channels

If we change the third line of code to the following, we can also search for the value of a CustomProperty:

```
//3. Find all the channels that have a CustomProperty
//    with a CustomProperty name equal to customPropertyOne and
//    a value equal to the string provided in the TextBox
ChannelCollection cmsChannelsFound =
  cmsContext.Searches.GetChannelsByCustomProperty(
  "customPropertyOne",
  TextBox1.Text.ToString())
  as ChannelCollection;
```

Build the solution and then refresh the Scratchpad posting in Internet Explorer; or browse to it, enter the value of the first custom property that we created (we gave it a value of "One") into the text box, and click the Button. The page should reload and look similar to Figure 28–2.

### NewChannels

This Searches method retrieves a collection of CMS channels based upon when they were last modified. If the Channel object's ChangeDate property is within the last seven days (or a user-specified number of days), it will be retrieved. Since we just added two CustomProperties (in the GetChannelsByCustomProperty section) to the Scratch channel, the change date should be within the time period to be classified as a "New" channel.

Replace the Button1_Click function of our Scratchpad template file with the following code:

```
private void Button1_Click(object sender, System.EventArgs e)
{
  //1. Grab the current CMS Context
  CmsHttpContext cmsContext = CmsHttpContext.Current;

  //2. Find all Channels with their ChangeDate <= three
  //   days from the current date
  ChannelCollection cmsChannelsFound =
    cmsContext.Searches.NewChannels(3)
    as ChannelCollection;

  //3. Empty the ListBox of all previous entries
  ListBox1.Items.Clear();

  //4. List the name of every channel returned by the search
  foreach(Channel cmsChannel in cmsChannelsFound)
  {
    ListBox1.Items.Add(cmsChannel.Name.ToString());
  }

  //5. If the collection is empty, show No Channels Found
  if (cmsChannelsFound.Count==0)
  {
    ListBox1.Items.Add("No Channels Found");
  }
}
```

Build the solution and then refresh the Scratchpad posting in Internet Explorer, or browse to it and click the Button. The page should reload and look similar to Figure 28-2.

### ImportantChannels

This Searches method retrieves a collection of CMS Channel objects whose Important Channel property is checked. This property can be checked at design time in the Options area on the Publishing tab of the Channel Properties dialog in Site Manager. Or it can be checked at runtime in the Publishing Options area on the Standard tab of the Channel

Properties dialog launched from the CMS default console. Check the box to the left of Important Channel in order for the channel to be considered Important and subsequently returned by this search.

Replace the Button1_Click function of our Scratchpad template file with the following code:

```
private void Button1_Click(object sender, System.EventArgs e)
{
  //1. Grab the current CMS Context
  CmsHttpContext cmsContext = CmsHttpContext.Current;

  //2. Find all Channels marked as Important
  ChannelCollection cmsChannelsFound =
    cmsContext.Searches.ImportantChannels()
    as ChannelCollection;

  //3. Empty the ListBox of all previous entries
  ListBox1.Items.Clear();

  //4. List the name of every channel returned by the search
  foreach(Channel cmsChannel in cmsChannelsFound)
  {
    ListBox1.Items.Add(cmsChannel.Name.ToString());
  }

  //5. If the collection is empty, show No Channels Found
  if (cmsChannelsFound.Count==0)
  {
    ListBox1.Items.Add("No Channels Found");
  }
}
```

Build the solution and then refresh the Scratchpad posting in Internet Explorer, or browse to it and click the Button. The page should reload and look similar to Figure 28–2.

Uncheck the box to the left of Important Channel and rerun the search. The Scratch channel should no longer show in the ListBox.

## Returning a Collection of Postings

The following sections cover how the GetPostingsByCustomProperty, NewPostings, ImportantPostings, UserApprovalsPending, and User PostingsInProduction methods can be used to return a collection of Posting objects.

### GetPostingsByCustomProperty

We don't currently have a CustomProperty on our Scratchpad posting to search for. Creating custom properties and entering their values is done very differently for postings than it is for channels. Although custom properties are exposed to PAPI, they must be created in CMS Site Manager for channels and VS.NET for templates (upon which postings are based). PAPI can only update the current value of an existing Custom Property property. So, to see this Searches method in action, we need to do a little prework. What follows are brief instructions to help you create a couple of custom properties to search for. If you have a posting that already has custom properties, feel free to use it in the code sample instead.

---

**NOTE:** We illustrate creating and manipulating custom properties for a posting in Chapter 26.

---

First, create custom properties for the Scratchpad template definition by following these steps:

1. From the VS.NET CMS Template Explorer Window browse to the ScratchTemplate template definition that we created in Chapter 23.
2. If it is not checked out, right-click the ScratchTemplate template definition and select Check Out.
3. In the Properties window, click the ellipsis to the right of the CustomPropertyDefinitions property.
4. In the resulting Custom Property Definition Collection Editor dialog, click the Add button twice to place two TextCustom PropertyDefinitions into the Members collection.
5. On the second property added, change the Value to "Second."
6. Click the OK button.
7. Right-click the ScratchTemplate template definition and select Check In.
8. Choose Save All from the File menu.

Next, enter values for each custom property on the Scratchpad posting by following these steps:

1. Refresh the Scratchpad posting in Internet Explorer or browse to it.

2. Click the Switch to Edit Site link on the Scratchpad posting in the CMS default console.
3. Click the Channel Properties link in the CMS default console, resulting in the Page Properties dialog.
4. Click the Custom tab.
5. Choose False in the drop-down list under the Use Default column for the NewTextProperty1 CustomProperty.
6. Enter the literal "First" into the text box under the Current Value column.
7. Leave the NewTextProperty2 CustomProperty value defaulting to the value "Second". It is defaulting to the literal string "Second" because we set the value property in the second Text CustomPropertyDefinition member in the VS.NET Scratch Template template definition collection of CustomProperty Definitions while we were in VS.NET.
8. Click the Save Changes button.
9. Click the Approve link on the Scratchpad posting in the CMS default console.
10. Click the Switch to Live Site link in the CMS default console.

Now we can search for postings with specific CustomProperty characteristics.

Replace the Button1_Click function of our Scratchpad template file with the following code:

```
private void Button1_Click(object sender, System.EventArgs e)
{
  //1. Check to be sure a value was entered.
  //   Note that there is no checking for value validity
  if (TextBox1.Text.Length>0)
  {
    //2. Grab the current CMS Context
    CmsHttpContext cmsContext = CmsHttpContext.Current;

    //3. Find all Postings that have a CustomProperty
    //   with a property name equal to the string provided
    PostingCollection cmsPostingsFound =
      cmsContext.Searches.GetPostingsByCustomProperty(
      TextBox1.Text.ToString())
      as PostingCollection;

    //4. Empty the ListBox of all previous entries
    ListBox1.Items.Clear();
```

```
//5. List the name of every Posting returned by the search
foreach(Posting cmsPosting in cmsPostingsFound)
{
  ListBox1.Items.Add(cmsPosting.Name.ToString());
}

//6. If the collection is empty, show No Postings Found
if (cmsPostingsFound.Count==0)
{
  ListBox1.Items.Add("No Postings Found");
}
}
else
{
//7. Provide nonerror feedback to the developer
Label1.Text = "TextBox must contain a value";
}
}
```

Build the solution and then refresh the Scratchpad posting in Internet Explorer; or browse to it, enter the default name of one of the custom properties that we created (like NewTextProperty1) into the text box, and click the Button. The page should reload and look similar to Figure 28–3.

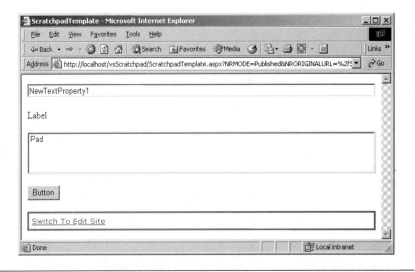

**Figure 28–3** Find collection of postings

If we change the third line of code to the following, we can also search for the value of a custom property:

```
//3. Find all the postings that have a CustomProperty
//   with a property name equal to NewTextProperty1 and a
//   CustomProperty value equal to the string provided
PostingCollection cmsPostingsFound =
  cmsContext.Searches.GetPostingsByCustomProperty(
  "NewTextProperty1",
  TextBox1.Text.ToString())
  as PostingCollection;
```

Build the solution and then refresh the Scratchpad posting in Internet Explorer; or browse to it, enter the value of the first custom property that we created (we gave it a value of "First") into the text box, and click the Button. Again, the page should reload and look similar to Figure 28–3.

### NewPostings

This Searches method retrieves a collection of CMS postings based upon when they were last modified. If the Posting object's ChangeDate property is within the last seven days (or a user-specified number of days), it will be retrieved. Since we just added two CustomProperties (in GetPostingsByCustomProperty section) to the Scratchpad posting, the change date should be within the time period to be classified as a "New" posting.

Replace the Button1_Click function of our Scratchpad template file with the following code:

```
private void Button1_Click(object sender, System.EventArgs e)
{
  //1. Grab the current CMS Context
  CmsHttpContext cmsContext = CmsHttpContext.Current;

  //2. Find all Postings with their ChangeDate <= three
  //   days from the current date
  PostingCollection cmsPostingsFound =
    cmsContext.Searches.NewPostings(3)
    as PostingCollection;

  //3. Empty the ListBox of all previous entries
  ListBox1.Items.Clear();
```

```
//4. List the name of every Posting returned by the search
foreach(Posting cmsPosting in cmsPostingsFound)
{
  ListBox1.Items.Add(cmsPosting.Name.ToString());
}

//5. If the collection is empty, show No Postings Found
if (cmsPostingsFound.Count==0)
{
  ListBox1.Items.Add("No Postings Found");
}
}
```

Build the solution and then refresh the Scratchpad posting in Internet Explorer, or browse to it and click the Button. The page should reload and look similar to Figure 28–3.

### ImportantPostings

This Searches method retrieves a collection of CMS postings whose Important Posting property is checked. This property can only be checked at runtime in the Publishing Options area on the Standard tab of the Posting Properties dialog launched from the CMS default console. Check the box to the left of Important Posting in order for the posting to be considered Important and subsequently be returned by this search. Changes to this property do not change the state of the posting.

Replace the Button1_Click function of our Scratchpad template file with the following code:

```
private void Button1_Click(object sender, System.EventArgs e)
{
  //1. Grab the current CMS Context
  CmsHttpContext cmsContext = CmsHttpContext.Current;

  //2. Find all Postings marked as Important
  PostingCollection cmsPostingsFound =
    cmsContext.Searches.ImportantPostings()
    as PostingCollection;

  //3. Empty the ListBox of all previous entries
  ListBox1.Items.Clear();

  //4. List the name of every Posting returned by the search
  foreach(Posting cmsPosting in cmsPostingsFound)
```

```
  {
    ListBox1.Items.Add(cmsPosting.Name.ToString());
  }

  //5. If the collection is empty, show No Postings Found
  if (cmsPostingsFound.Count==0)
  {
    ListBox1.Items.Add("No Postings Found");
  }
}
```

Build the solution and then refresh the Scratchpad posting in Internet Explorer, or browse to it and click the Button. Again, the page should reload and look similar to Figure 28–3.

Uncheck the box to the left of Important Posting and rerun the search. The Scratchpad posting should no longer show in the ListBox.

### UserApprovalsPending

To obtain a collection of the postings that are shown when the Approval Assistant link is clicked in the CMS default console, we would use the Searches UserApprovalsPending method. For our Scratchpad posting to show up, we need to alter something that would require approval. One easy thing to change is the current value of the NewTextProperty1 CustomProperty on the Custom tab of the Page Properties dialog launched from the CMS default console. Save the changes and notice that the Approve link is now showing in the CMS default console. Don't click it yet. Depending on how your permissions are set, you may need to click the Submit link. If the posting state doesn't go all the way to Published, the following code sample will produce the correct result.

Replace the Button1_Click function of our Scratchpad template file with the following code:

```
private void Button1_Click(object sender, System.EventArgs e)
{
  //1. Grab the current CMS Context
  CmsHttpContext cmsContext = CmsHttpContext.Current;

  //2. Find all Postings with UserApprovalsPending
  PostingCollection cmsPostingsFound =
    cmsContext.Searches.UserApprovalsPending()
    as PostingCollection;
```

```
//3. Empty the ListBox of all previous entries
ListBox1.Items.Clear();

//4. List the name of every Posting returned by the search
foreach(Posting cmsPosting in cmsPostingsFound)
{
  ListBox1.Items.Add(cmsPosting.Name.ToString());
}

//5. If the collection is empty, show No Postings Found
if (cmsPostingsFound.Count==0)
{
  ListBox1.Items.Add("No Postings Found");
}
}
```

Build the solution and then refresh the Scratchpad posting in Internet Explorer; or browse to it, click the Switch to Edit Site link in the CMS default console to put the context into the correct mode, and click the Button. Again, the page should reload and look similar to Figure 28–3.

Leave the Unpublished posting unapproved until the UserPostings InProduction section is complete.

### UserPostingsInProduction

To obtain a collection of the postings that are shown when the Production Manager link is clicked in the CMS default console, we would use the Searches UserPostingsInProduction method. Our modified Scratchpad posting should show up because we haven't yet approved the changes.

Replace the Button1_Click function of our Scratchpad template file with the following code:

```
private void Button1_Click(object sender, System.EventArgs e)
{
  //1. Grab the current CMS Context
  CmsHttpContext cmsContext = CmsHttpContext.Current;

  //2. Find all Postings with UserPostingsInProduction
  PostingCollection cmsPostingsFound =
    cmsContext.Searches.UserPostingsInProduction()
    as PostingCollection;
```

```
//3. Empty the ListBox of all previous entries
ListBox1.Items.Clear();

//4. List the name of every Posting returned by the search
foreach(Posting cmsPosting in cmsPostingsFound)
{
  ListBox1.Items.Add(cmsPosting.Name.ToString());
}

//5. If the collection is empty, show No Postings Found
if (cmsPostingsFound.Count==0)
{
  ListBox1.Items.Add("No Postings Found");
}
}
```

Build the solution and then refresh the Scratchpad posting in Internet Explorer; or browse to it, click the Switch to Edit Site link in the CMS default console to put the context into the correct mode, and click the Button. Again, the page should reload and look similar to Figure 28–3.

Click the Approve link in the CMS default console to publish the CustomProperty changes. Browse to the Scratchpad posting again, click the button labeled Button, and the Scratchpad posting should reload, adding the literal "No Postings Found" to the ListBox.

## Returning a Collection of Templates

The GetTemplatesBySourceFile method is the only means to return a collection of Template objects. The next section covers this in detail.

### GetTemplatesBySourceFile

This Searches method retrieves a collection of CMS template definitions based upon the value of their TemplateFile property. When we initially created the template definition in VS.NET, we set the TemplateFile property (Figure 28–4).

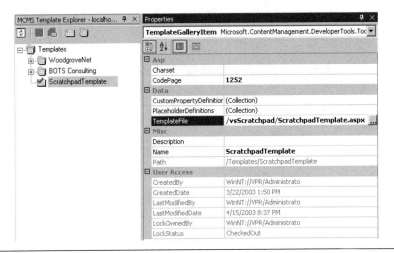

**Figure 28-4** The TemplateFile property

Replace the Button1_Click function of our Scratchpad template file with the following code:

```
private void Button1_Click(object sender, System.EventArgs e)
{
  //1. Check to be sure a value was entered.
  //   Note that there is no checking for value validity
  if (TextBox1.Text.Length>0)
  {
    //2. Grab the current CMS Context
    CmsHttpContext cmsContext = CmsHttpContext.Current;

    //3. Find all Templates with a specific TemplateFile using
    //   GetTemplatesBySourceFile
    TemplateCollection cmsTemplatesFound =
      cmsContext.Searches.GetTemplatesBySourceFile(
      TextBox1.Text.ToString())
      as TemplateCollection;

    //4. Empty the ListBox of all previous entries
    ListBox1.Items.Clear();

    //5. List the name of every Template returned by the search
    foreach(Template cmsTemplate in cmsTemplatesFound)
    {
      ListBox1.Items.Add(cmsTemplate.Name.ToString());
    }
```

```
   //6. If the collection is empty, show No Templates Found
   if (cmsTemplatesFound.Count==0)
   {
     ListBox1.Items.Add("No Templates Found");
   }
 }
 else
 {
   //7. Provide nonerror feedback to the developer
   Label1.Text = "TextBox must contain a value";
 }
}
```

Build the solution and then refresh the Scratchpad posting in Internet Explorer; or browse to it, enter the name of the TemplateFile to search for into the text box, and click the Button. The page should reload and look similar to Figure 28–5.

## Returning a Collection of Galleries

The following sections cover how the UserResourceGalleries and User TemplateGalleries methods can be used to return a collection of objects.

### UserResourceGalleries

To obtain a collection of ResourceGalleries and the Resource objects they contain, we use the Searches UserResourceGalleries method.

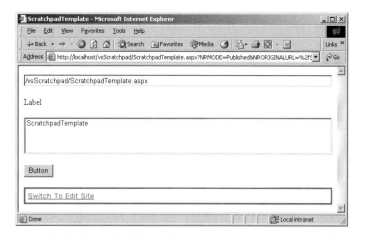

**Figure 28–5** Find collection of templates

Replace the Button1_Click function of our Scratchpad template file with the following code:

```
private void Button1_Click(object sender, System.EventArgs e)
{
  //1. Grab the current CMS Context
  CmsHttpContext cmsContext = CmsHttpContext.Current;

  //2. Find all ResourceGalleries available to the user
  ResourceGalleryCollection cmsGalleriesFound =
    cmsContext.Searches.UserResourceGalleries()
    as ResourceGalleryCollection;

  //3. Empty the ListBox of all previous entries
  ListBox1.Items.Clear();

  //4. List the name of every ResourceGallery returned
  foreach(ResourceGallery cmsGallery in cmsGalleriesFound)
  {
    ListBox1.Items.Add(cmsGallery.Name.ToString());

    //5. List the name of every Resource in each Gallery found
    //   Prefix the name with dashes
    foreach(Resource cmsResource in cmsGallery.Resources)
    {
      ListBox1.Items.Add("----" + cmsResource.Name.ToString());
    }
  }

  //6. If the collection is empty, show No ResourceGallery Found
  if(cmsGalleriesFound.Count==0)
  {
    ListBox1.Items.Add("No ResourceGallery Found");
  }
}
```

Build the solution and then refresh the Scratchpad posting in Internet Explorer, or browse to it and click the Button. The page should reload and look similar to Figure 28–6.

We increased the height of the ListBox on the template file for this example so that Figure 28–6 would show ten entries. You may need to scroll down to see all the entries. Most of these are coming from the Woodgrove and BOTS Consulting sites. Remember, this is one of the CMS sitewide searches.

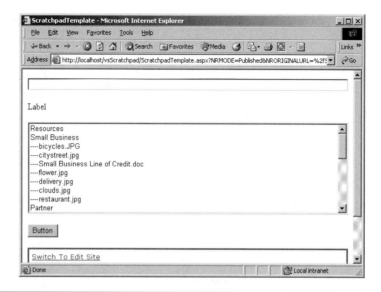

**Figure 28–6**  Find collection of resource galleries

### *UserTemplateGalleries*

Similarly, to obtain a collection of TemplateGalleries and the Template objects they contain, we use the Searches UserTemplateGalleries method.

Replace the Button1_Click function of our Scratchpad template file with the following code:

```
private void Button1_Click(object sender, System.EventArgs e)
{
  //1. Grab the current CMS Context
  CmsHttpContext cmsContext = CmsHttpContext.Current;

  //2. Find all TemplateGalleries available to the user
  TemplateGalleryCollection cmsGalleriesFound =
    cmsContext.Searches.UserTemplateGalleries()
    as TemplateGalleryCollection;

  //3. Empty the ListBox of all previous entries
  ListBox1.Items.Clear();

  //4. List the name of every TemplateGallery returned
  foreach(TemplateGallery cmsGallery in cmsGalleriesFound)
  {
    ListBox1.Items.Add(cmsGallery.Name.ToString());
```

```
//5. List the name of every Template in each Gallery found
//   Prefix the name with dashes
foreach(Template cmsTemplate in cmsGallery.Templates)
{
    ListBox1.Items.Add("----" + cmsTemplate.Name.ToString());
}
}


//6. If the collection is empty, show No TemplateGallery Found
if(cmsGalleriesFound.Count==0)
{
    ListBox1.Items.Add("No TemplateGallery Found");
}
}
```

Build the solution and then refresh the Scratchpad posting in Internet Explorer, or browse to it and click the Button. The page should reload and look similar to Figure 28–7.

We increased the height of the ListBox on the template file for this example so that Figure 28–7 would show ten entries. You may need to scroll down to see all the entries. Most of these are coming from the Woodgrove and BOTS Consulting sites. Remember, this is one of the CMS sitewide searches.

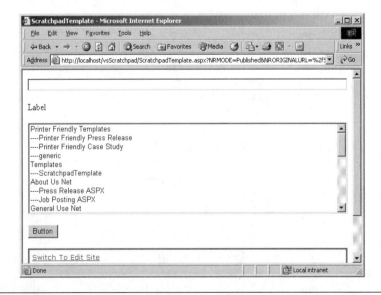

**Figure 28–7**  Find collection of template galleries

# Efficient Searching for CMS Assets

As your Web Property grows and the number of assets gets larger, the ability to search for assets with specific characteristics becomes even more compelling. However, we must be careful with how we implement the Searches property because searching may require a great deal of system resources. Performance can certainly become a concern if searches are too wide or are used too often.

The following Searches methods must iterate the entire CMS Content Repository to retrieve the objects requested and should be used sparingly:

- GetChannelsByCustomProperty
- GetPostingsByCustomProperty
- GetTemplatesBySourceFile
- ImportantChannels
- ImportantPostings
- NewChannels
- NewPostings
- UserApprovalsPending
- UserPostingsInProduction
- UserResourceGalleries
- UserTemplateGalleries

These searches should only be used when the business needs demand that the entire Repository be searched. If the search can be localized, it should be done.

It is wise to use GetByGuid rather than GetByPath or GetByUrl when you are looking for a specific object. Searching for assets that could be moved or could have duplicates can pose an additional hurdle to using the Searches methods effectively. It can also help to organize the hierarchies in the Web Property such that the number of child containers doesn't exceed 15, the number of items in a container doesn't exceed 300, and the number of levels of depth doesn't exceed ten. CMS will allow you to exceed these thresholds, but the consequences could be a less responsive site, especially when searching for assets.

One exception to the limited use of Searches has to do with accessing a specific item within a known collection. When the Item property of a collection is requested, CMS must hydrate the entire collection to return just the single instance. However, using a Searches method results in the hydration of just the individual instance. So, in this case performance will actually be improved by using a Searches method.

If the resulting search doesn't result in the collection of assets that are needed, it may be helpful to combine the results of more than one search using the Union method, creating a unified custom collection of assets to manipulate.

## Summary

Searching is one of those features that won't probably be used extensively, but when it is needed, it is really needed. So, we coded examples of every kind of search possible in CMS. That completes our exploration of PAPI and brings Part VI to a conclusion.

In Part VII we discuss various ways that CMS can be extended—from developing your own custom controls to customizing the Web Author, and extending the publishing workflow to multilingual sites, dynamic data, and Web Services.

# Extending CMS

# Developing Custom Controls for CMS

## Overview

CMS 2002 is a very powerful tool for managing Web sites. However, what makes it powerful is not limited to the out-of-the-box functionality. Rather, it's a combination of out-of-the-box functionality and the open architecture that CMS provides.

In this chapter, we'll explore developing custom controls for CMS. When we talk about custom controls, we're specifically talking about creating server or user controls that take advantage of CMS functionality—controls that make use of the PAPI or build on intrinsic CMS controls that you can inherit. For example, we'll show you how to create a new kind of placeholder and how to develop a useful user control for labeling placeholders when the user is contributing content. Keep in mind that our examples, while useful, are certainly not an end in and of themselves; they demonstrate some of the possibilities that are available to you.

## User Controls

User controls are created visually in VS.NET. Generally, user controls are created by dragging and dropping server controls onto what almost appears as a Web form. Once you've added the server controls you want, you can create new, unique functionality by adding additional code to the control. By now, you're already familiar with the user control supplied by CMS, the edit console, which is a collection of CMS console controls. The edit console is used on almost every template to provide content contribution functionality. But what if you wanted to create your own controls?

Creating your own user controls can be a very good way to extend functionality in your templates. Also, because you can create user controls visually, the process of creating new controls is relatively easy. Let's take, for example, the need in the BOTS Consulting site to add labels over each placeholder. These labels will serve as a cue to the content contributor, indicating what content goes in a particular placeholder. Since this is something you'll have to do over and over again, a user control may make a great deal of sense, since it is easy to create and is reusable.

To begin, let's take a closer look at the problem for a moment. In the BOTS site, we want to make sure that each placeholder has a label above it. This label would ensure that content contributors know what content to put in each placeholder. However, we only want these labels to show in certain cases—specifically, when placeholders are visible. If this is a one-time event, it's probably better to use an existing control and wrap it in some conditional logic. However, if you have multiple placeholders across multiple templates, it's probably better to create a control. In this case, we're going to create a user control.

Start by creating a new user control in your project. To create the control, right-click the folder in your project where you want to create the control. From the context menu, choose Add, then Add New Item. In the next dialog that appears, choose Web Project Items and then click (once) the Web User Control type. In the "name" field, type "CMS PlaceholderLabel". As we mentioned before, we've created a special folder in the BOTS Consulting project for user controls—called User-Controls (we told you we're not that creative when it comes to names); in Figure 29–1 you'll see our new user control in that folder.

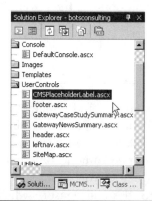

**Figure 29–1**  CMSPlaceholderLabel in the UserControls folder

Once you have your new user control, you'll need to add other controls and code. In this example, we want to create a control that displays text within your Web page selectively, based on the Web Author context. In our example, we're going to add a literal control to our user control. The literal control will allow us to place any sort of text on the page we like (and it doesn't add <SPAN> tags to the HTML as label controls do). Just drag a literal control from the Toolbox directly onto your control (in Design view). Now, name the control OutputText. The actual name of your object doesn't have to match what we've defined, but the code in this section will reflect our name. In Figure 29–2, you'll see the Design view of VS.NET with the new literal control added and with the Name property set.

Now that you have the literal added to your user control, you'll have to add the appropriate namespace references. For this example, all we need to add is the Microsoft.ContentManagement.WebControls namespace.

```
using System;
using System.Data;
using System.Drawing;
using System.Web.UI;
```

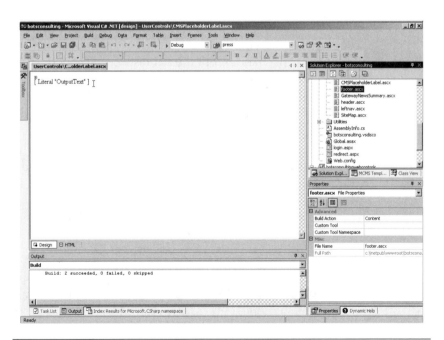

**Figure 29–2** The literal control added to the user control

```
using System.Web.UI.WebControls;
using System.Web.UI.HtmlControls;
using Microsoft.ContentManagement.WebControls;
```

Next, we're going to add a property definition, which will allow the developer to set the label text above the placeholder. An added benefit of using the literal control is that it will allow the developer to add HTML tags in the label to control items, such as bold. In the following code, you can see the Text property within the control.

```
private string text = "";

public string Text
{
    get
    {
        return text;
    }
    set
    {
        text = value;
    }
}
```

So up to this point, this is a pretty basic user control. There's nothing inherently "CMS-like" except the namespace we added. However, as we mentioned earlier, we only want the label appear under certain conditions. Specifically, you want the label to appear when the Web Author is in either of two modes: AuthoringNew and AuthoringReedit. Based on the mode, we'll programmatically manipulate the visibility property of the literal control. In the following code, you'll see how we use the Web Author Context object and the mode enumeration provided in the PAPI to determine when the label should appear.

```
// Set a variable equal to the current Web Author Context
WebAuthorContext myContext = WebAuthorContext.Current;
// Check to see what mode we're in and set the visibility
accordingly
if(myContext.Mode == WebAuthorContextMode.AuthoringNew ||
    myContext.Mode == WebAuthorContextMode.AuthoringReedit)
    {this.OutputText.Visible=true;}
else
{this.OutputText.Visible=false;}
```

If we examine the code line-by-line, we find the following:

- We set a variable equal to the current WebAuthorContext (as much for space as for convenience, but not necessary).
- We determine whether we're in the AuthoringReedit or AuthoringNew mode of the Web Author. These two modes correspond to authoring within CMS. AuthoringReedit mode occurs when you're editing an exiting posting, while AuthoringNew is the mode during the creation of a new posting. In both cases, we set the visibility of the literal control to "true". Notice that we're using the WebAuthorContextMode enumeration to get a list of potential modes. If you've been watching the query string through the various exercises, you'll notice that it's possible to use the query string values to accomplish what we've done here—watch for particular values and conditionally set the visibility of the literal control. However, that methodology isn't as clean, and it tends to be difficult to nail down the combination of parameters.
- If both conditions are false (meaning we're not in either mode), we set the visibility of the literal to "false" so that it's not seen on the "live" site or even in Edit mode if the placeholders aren't visible.

Again, what we've done here isn't revolutionary. It is, however, very useful and utilizes the PAPI to create a "CMS aware" user control. This control can be used from project to project. Practically speaking, the control can be dragged from your project directly to the design surface. When the control is implemented, the developer simply sets the "text" property in the tag to the desired label for a placeholder as follows:

```
<uc1:cmsplaceholderlabel id="PressReleaseDateLabel" runat="server"
text="<b>Press Release Date:</b><br>">
</uc1:cmsplaceholderlabel>
```

Once you've done everything we've discussed so far, you should have a fully functional placeholder label. In addition, you could use this label control beyond basic labeling by adding some additional code. In Listing 29–1 you'll see the code for the BOTS Consulting placeholder label user control.

**Listing 29–1** Complete code for the BOTS Consulting PlaceholderLabel user control

```
namespace botsconsulting.usercontrols
{
    using System;
    using System.Data;
    using System.Drawing;
    using System.Web.UI;
    using System.Web.UI.WebControls;
    using System.Web.UI.HtmlControls;
    using Microsoft.ContentManagement.WebControls;

    /// <summary>
    ///        The placeholderlabel user control is used to place a
    ///        descriptive label above a placeholder.
    /// </summary>

    public abstract class CMSPlaceholderLabel : System.Web.UI.UserControl
    {

        private bool displayinauthormode = true;
        private bool displayineditmode = false;
        protected System.Web.UI.WebControls.Literal OutputText;

        public bool DisplayinAuthorMode
        {
            get
            {
                return displayinauthormode;
            }
            set
            {
                displayinauthormode = value;
            }
        }

        public bool DisplayinEditMode
        {
            get
            {
                return displayineditmode;
            }
            set
```

```
                {
                        displayinauthormode = value;
                }
        }

        private string text = "";

        public string Text
        {
                get
                {
                        return text;
                }

                set
                {
                        text = value;
                }
        }

        private void Page_Load(object sender, System.EventArgs e)
        {
                // Set default values for the control if no values are
given
                displayinauthormode = true;
                displayineditmode = false;

                // Set the literal control TEXT property based on the TEXT
property
                OutputText.Text = this.text;

                // Set a variable equal to the current Web Author Context
                WebAuthorContext myContext = WebAuthorContext.Current;
                // Check to see what mode we're in and set the visibility
accordingly
                if((myContext.Mode == WebAuthorContextMode.AuthoringNew ||
                        myContext.Mode ==
WebAuthorContextMode.AuthoringReedit)
                        && displayinauthormode)
                {this.OutputText.Visible=true;}
                else if ((myContext.Mode ==
WebAuthorContextMode.PresentationUnpublished)
                        && displayineditmode)
                {this.OutputText.Visible=true;}
```

```
         else
         {this.OutputText.Visible=false;}
    }


    #region Web Form Designer generated code
    override protected void OnInit(EventArgs e)
    {
         //
         // CODEGEN: This call is required by the ASP.NET Web Form
Designer.
         //
         InitializeComponent();
         base.OnInit(e);
    }


    ///             Required method for Designer support - do not
modify
    ///             the contents of this method with the code editor.
    /// </summary>
    private void InitializeComponent()
    {
         this.Load += new System.EventHandler(this.Page_Load);


    }
    #endregion
    }
}
```

In Listing 29–1 you'll notice that BOTS added a few elements to the basic placeholder label control we've talked about. Specifically, they added the ability to control in which mode the label is displayed. In other words, it may be useful for the control to display in Edit mode, even if the placeholders aren't visible. To handle this situation, BOTS added two new properties: DisplayinAuthorMode and DisplayinEdit Mode. The main difference is the addition of the extra condition to determine if the Web Author is in PresentationUnpublished, which corresponds to the mode the Web Author is in when the edit console is visible, but the content contributor can't author. Further, they integrated the two properties that allow the developer to set the modes in which the label should show itself. To help clarify the various states of the Web Author context, BOTS chose to distinguish the various modes of the Web Author as follows:

- **Live**: The site renders all approved content as if a subscriber were viewing the content.
- **Edit**: The site displays the edit console, but the pages look largely as they do when the site is in Live mode. No content contribution is possible.
- **Authoring**: The placeholders are visible, and an author can contribute content.

It's likely that you won't see these modes talked about in the Microsoft documentation, but we've found that this is a good way to classify the various states so that it's clear not only to the developers, but to the content contributors as well.

## Composite Controls

With CMS there are two opportunities to create custom composite controls. One opportunity is to create a custom server control. That is a control, very much akin to a user control, that uses existing server controls and creates a CMS-aware composite control. The other opportunity is to create a custom placeholder control. Both types of composite controls offer significant opportunities to extend the functionality of CMS. In the following sections, we'll examine both types of composite controls.

### Creating Custom Server Controls

Very similarly to creating user controls, creating custom CMS-aware server controls is simply a matter of creating a composite control that is aware of CMS. In our user control example, we made the control "aware" of the Web Author context by examining the mode of the WebAuthor Context. Once we knew the mode, we conditionally set the visibility of the literal control. By creating this kind of CMS awareness, we removed the need to add any code to the template, but provided a way to allow a label to appear over the placeholder only when the Web Author was in an authoring state.

Now, we could do something very similar with a server control. The server control would operate in the same way that our user control did, but we would be able to add a design-time interface to the control, and you would be able to add to the global assembly cache (GAC). The advantage would be that not only would the design interface allow either a developer or visual designer potentially to have more control over the server control during design, but since the control is in the GAC, there's no need to add it to each project separately.

Ultimately the decision is up to you. There's a good article on Microsoft's MSDN site that discusses how to decide between a server or user control, listing the advantages and disadvantages of each; see http://msdn.microsoft.com/library/en-us/cpguide/html/cpconcompositecontrolvsusercontrol.asp.

For examples of custom server controls, install the WoodgroveNet Bank sample site that ships with CMS. There are several custom server controls provided with the sample site. To download the sample site, you can follow the link to the download section for CMS at http://microsoft.com/downloads/results.aspx?productID=9A0DB489-0B68-4075-8D93-5540FB21E5DC&freetext=&DisplayLang=en.

## Creating Custom CMS Placeholders

Up to this point, we've been dealing with a fixed set of CMS placeholders that your content contributors use to add content. However, CMS provides a base placeholder class that can be inherited, which allows you to create your own placeholders. This very powerful feature of CMS provides an almost unlimited set of possibilities when it comes to extending CMS, especially as it relates to content contribution.

---

**NOTE:** The term "placeholder" is used often in this book, particularly in this chapter. For clarity, we are referring to the placeholder control in this section. The control is the element that you can drag from the Toolbox in VS.NET to the design surface. Also, please be aware that there is a standard .NET Web control called a PlaceHolder (with a capital H). The two controls are not related in any way.

---

Essentially, the base placeholder class provides the core services with regard to content. In the broadest sense, content is anything that you want to store in the repository. Content could be text or images, as we've dealt with previously in this book. Content could also be settings or other, noneditorial data that your application may need to store. The base placeholder class allows you to inherit this basic storage and retrieval functionality while adding your own application-specific functionality. In addition, it relieves you (the developer) from having to handle the switch between Live, Edit, and authoring modes; you simply implement the appropriate overrides, and CMS takes care of the rest.

Now, you may be asking yourself why you might create a custom placeholder at all. One driving reason is to allow you to store data in the repository. Further, it provides content contributors with direct access to that content while they're authoring. You wouldn't need a custom place- holder, for example, to allow an administrator to change a property of a channel, since administrators can use Site Manager. This distinction is key when you're planning your CMS site.

To begin, let's examine the BasePlaceholderControl class. In Fig- ure 29–3, we've looked up the class in the Object Browser.

BasePlaceholderControl is an inheritable class for building place- holders. In fact, all placeholders standard to CMS are based on this class. Within the class there are five primary methods that must be imple- mented when you are creating your custom placeholder.

- CreateAuthoringChildControls: This method is used to create the controls that will represent the authoring view of your custom placeholder. This method and CreatePresentationChild Controls replace CreateChildControls, typical of other .NET

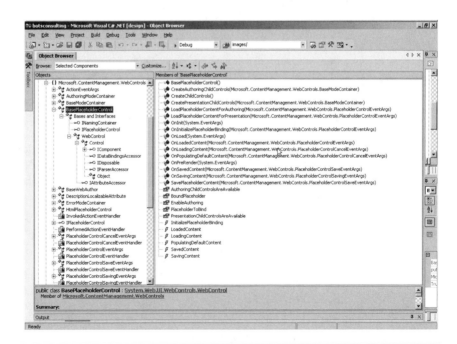

**Figure 29–3** The BasePlaceholderControl class in the Object Browser

controls. The CreateChildControls method (taken care of by the BasePlaceholderControl class) calls this method and Create PresentationChildControls at the appropriate time, based on the mode of the Web Author.

- CreatePresentationChildControls: This method, like the Create AuthoringChildControls method, is responsible for one half of the traditional CreateChildControls method you've probably worked with in the past. CreatePresentationChildControls is called when the Web Author is in some sort of presentation mode—those modes other than AuthoringNew and AuthoringReedit.

- LoadPlaceholderContentForAuthoring: LoadPlaceholderContent ForAuthoring is called when the placeholder renders in authoring mode. This method makes the content stored in the repository available to your authoring controls.

- LoadPlaceholderContentForPresentation: Like the LoadPlace holderContentForAuthoring method, LoadPlaceholderContent ForPresentation allows you to retrieve content from the repository. Unlike the authoring method, this method is used to retrieve the content for presentation—content displayed in modes other than AuthoringNew and AuthoringReedit.

- SavePlaceholderContent: This method is responsible for saving content to the repository. In SavePlaceholderContent you can connect the bound placeholder definition to the controls in your custom placeholder.

---

**NOTE:** Make sure that you call EnsureChildControls before you try to set the values of either the authoring or presentation controls. This will ensure that the authoring and presentation controls exist before you try to assign a value to them. If you don't, an exception will be raised. Also, the BasePlaceholderControl class does not call either LoadPlaceholderContentForPresentation or LoadPlaceholderContentForAuthoring on a postback.

---

Now that you have a good understanding of the five mandatory methods to implement, let's look at how you might implement each in an example within the BOTS Consulting site.

In the BOTS site, the developers wanted to provide a way for the content contributors to indicate the industry that a specific case study addressed. Although it's possible to accomplish this with a standard placeholder, the regular HTML placeholder allowed a little too much contribution flexibility (translation: It allowed the content contributors to enter any value). So, in an effort to provide a little more guided contribution, the BOTS Consulting developers created a drop-down list box placeholder. This placeholder allowed content contributors to choose the target industry for a case study from a set list of choices defined by the developers.

In order to create this control in your project, we'll first need to create a control library project within our current solution. This new project will hold all our new composite controls for the BOTS Consulting site. In our solution, we've chosen to call the new project botsconsultingwebcontrols. To create your own Web control library, use the following instructions:

1. Make sure you have an open solution. In our case, we have our BOTS Consulting solution open.
2. Right-click your solution and pick Add from the context menu.
3. Now, choose Add New Project from the second context menu that appears.
4. From the dialog that appears, pick Visual C# Projects from the left column (if you're using VB.NET, you should choose Visual Basic Projects).
5. Then, pick Web Control Library from the right column. *Do not* choose the Windows Control Library; that type of project is for Windows form projects.
6. Once you've chosen the correct project type, you should enter the name you wish to give your new project. In our case, we've called our new control library botsconsultingwebcontrols. In Figure 29–4 you'll see a screen shot of what you should be seeing at this point.
7. Click OK to create the new project.

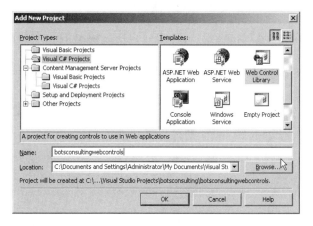

**Figure 29–4** Creating a new Web control library in VS.NET

Now that we have our new project, you'll need to add references to the appropriate CMS assemblies. To add the references, right-click the References folder in your new project and choose Add Reference from the context menu. When the Add Reference dialog appears, click the Browse button and browse to the CMS assembly directory *<Install Drive>*:\Program Files\Microsoft Content Management Server\Server\bin. At minimum, you'll need to add references to the following assemblies:

- Microsoft.ContentManagement.Common.dll
- Microsoft.ContentManagement.Publishing.dll
- Microsoft.ContentManagement.Publishing.Extensions. Placeholders.dll
- Microsoft.ContentManagement.Web.dll
- Microsoft.ContentManagement.WebControls.dll

After you've added the appropriate assembly references, we need to add the new control. Right-click the new project and pick Add from the context menu. Choose Add New Item. In the left column of the Add New Item dialog, choose Local Project Items, and in the right column, choose Web Custom Control. Once you've done that, enter the name of the new control in the name property. Our control will be aptly named DropDownPlaceholderControl. Now, simply click Open. What should appear next is the basic code that VS.NET supplies.

We now have to set up this new control to be a custom placeholder control. The first thing is to add the following namespaces to our control:

- Microsoft.ContentManagement.WebControls
- Microsoft.ContentManagement.Publishingnamespace

Next, change the "class" statement to inherit from the BasePlaceholderControl class instead of the more generic WebControl class. In Listing 29–2, you can see the C# code we've added to our control up to this point.

**Listing 29–2**  The initial code for our DropDownPlaceholderControl

```
using System;
using System.Web.UI;
using System.Web.UI.WebControls;
using System.ComponentModel;
using Microsoft.ContentManagement.Publishing.Extensions.Placeholders;
using Microsoft.ContentManagement.WebControls;
```

```
namespace botsconsultingwebcontrols
{
      /// <summary>
      /// Summary description for DropDownPlaceholderControl.
      /// </summary>
      [DefaultProperty("Text"),
           ToolboxData("<{0}:DropDownPlaceholderControl
runat=server></{0}:DropDownPlaceholderControl>")]
      public class DropDownPlaceholderControl :
Microsoft.ContentManagement.WebControls.BasePlaceholderControl
```

Once we have this basic structure in place, we'll need to add code to and remove code from our control to finalize our custom placeholder control. The first step is to remove the standard Text property VS.NET places in new controls. This property may be appropriate in some cases. However, in our control, we don't need the property, so we're going to remove it. Next, we need to add our mandatory functions. These were the functions we listed earlier in the chapter. In Listing 29–3, you can see the functions we've placed in our control.

**Listing 29–3** The mandatory functions that need to be included in custom placeholders

```
protected override void CreateAuthoringChildControls(BaseModeContainer
authoringContainer)
{
}

protected override void CreatePresentationChildControls(BaseModeContainer
presentationContainer)
{
}

protected override void
LoadPlaceholderContentForAuthoring(PlaceholderControlEventArgs e)
{
}

protected override void
LoadPlaceholderContentForPresentation(PlaceholderControlEventArgs e)
{
}
```

```
protected override void
SavePlaceholderContent(PlaceholderControlSaveEventArgs e)
{
}
```

After you've removed the Text property and added the functions in Listing 29–3, you should be able to successfully build your solution without errors.

To begin the actual coding of our custom placeholder control, let's start by creating the authoring environment. As we mentioned, we want our authors to be able to pick the appropriate industry focus for a given case study from a drop-down list. This list will have the following items in it by default: Pharmaceutical, Construction, Manufacturing, and Technology. First, we define a new private member variable in our class to hold a reference to our drop-down list (we'll need this later). In our example, we're going to call that new variable IndustryList. Once we've created our member variable, we'll need to add code to our Create AuthoringChildControls function to physically create the drop-down list control and add the list items. To see what this looks like, refer to Listing 29–4.

**Listing 29–4** The new member variable and an implemented CreateAuthoringChildControls function

```
protected System.Web.UI.WebControls.DropDownList IndustryList;

protected override void CreateAuthoringChildControls(BaseModeContainer
authoringContainer)
{
this.IndustryList = new DropDownList();
this.IndustryList.Items.Add(new
ListItem("Construction","<value>Construction</value>"));
this.IndustryList.Items.Add(new
ListItem("Manufacturing","<value>Manufacturing</value>"));
this.IndustryList.Items.Add(new
ListItem("Pharmaceutical","<value>Pharmaceutical</value>"));
this.IndustryList.Items.Add(new
ListItem("Technology","<value>Technology</value>"));
this.IndustryList.EnableViewState = false;
authoringContainer.Controls.Add(IndustryList);
}
```

In Listing 29–4 we're creating the authoring view of the placeholder. The first few lines of the function simply create the drop-down list. In this example, BOTS only had four industry options, so there are only four "manual" add statements. We're turning off the view state for the drop-down list control, because when switching between Edit and authoring modes, controls sometimes become "confused" and throw an exception. In the last statement, we're adding our drop-down list control to the authoring environment container. Without this statement, your control(s) won't render (as we found out the first time we created a custom placeholder).

Now that we have this much of the control, we should be able to test the basic control by adding it to a template. To add this new placeholder control to your template, you first should add it to your Toolbox in VS.NET. Adding this new placeholder to your Toolbox is pretty easy; just use the following instructions:

1. Open a template and make sure you're in Design view.
2. Once the template appears, click the Content Management Server tab in the VS.NET Toolbox. You should see the existing placeholder objects that are standard to CMS.
3. Right-click the Toolbox and pick Customize Toolbox from the context menu.
4. When the Customize Toolbox dialog appears, click the .NET Framework Components tab.
5. Click the Browse button in the lower right corner of the dialog box; the button will be above the OK/Cancel/Reset/Help buttons.
6. You'll have to navigate through your file system to find your Web control library project. Once you've located the project, select the "bin" directory and then the assembly that corresponds to your new control library. Depending on how you've set up your VS.NET environment, you may have "debug" and "release" folders within your "bin" folder.
7. Click the assembly and click OK.
8. Now, just select the specific controls you want to appear in the Toolbox. At this point, it's likely you only have one control, but you may have been very productive and gotten a few more done while you've been reading this. In Figure 29–5 you can see what our dialog looks like after we have selected our assembly and checked our DropDownListPlaceholder class.
9. Once you've selected your new placeholder, click OK.

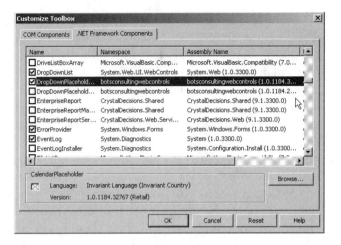

**Figure 29–5** The Customize Toolbox dialog with our new placeholder class selected

Your new placeholder will be shown in the Toolbox. In Figure 29–6, you can see our new placeholder in the Toolbox.

Now that you have the new placeholder in your Toolbox, just drag it onto your template. In the BOTS Consulting example, we've positioned the new placeholder just above the body copy. In this way, we can allow the content contributor to choose the industry focus before they begin to write the copy. Further, when the page is fully rendered, the industry focus will be the first element displayed on the page (after the title), so the reader instantly knows to what industry this case study applies.

Before we can truly "test drive" our new control, we need to add a placeholder definition to our TGI. Since this is a new placeholder type, there won't be a corresponding placeholder definition. However, we can use one of the existing placeholder definitions for our placeholder. In this example, we're going to use an XML placeholder definition, since the XML placeholder type makes it fairly easy to store data versus editorial text (which is probably better with an HTML placeholder).

As we learned in our earlier chapters, you'll want to open the Template Explorer window and find the TGI associated with your template. In our case, we're using the Case Study Detail TGI. You'll need to check out your template and click the ellipsis to call up the Placeholder Definition Collection Editor. Go ahead and create a new XML placeholder definition for the new placeholder you just added to your template. In our case, we've called this new placeholder definition CaseStudyIndustry. In Figure 29–7 you can see the new definition we've added.

**Figure 29–6** The new DropDownPlaceholderControl in our VS.NET Toolbox

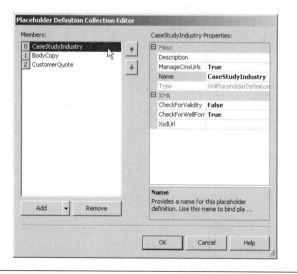

**Figure 29–7** The Placeholder Definition Collection Editor with the new XML placeholder definition

After you've added your definition, you'll need to bind the new definition to your placeholder. Go back to your template and click the placeholder control you added earlier. In the properties list, select the new placeholder definition in the PlaceholderToBind property. Notice that this placeholder doesn't discriminate among the various definitions that exist in the definition collection for this TGI. All the definitions that are in the TGI are listed in the drop-down list. We'll address this issue later, but be careful to pick the definition you just created; the placeholder will allow you to bind it to any of the definitions in the TGI, whether or not they're XML definitions.

With the new placeholder control added to the template and bound to our new placeholder definition, we're ready to test the new control. In Figure 29–8, you can see what our new placeholder control looks like in a case study. Keep in mind that the control will only render in authoring mode, and it doesn't "understand" how to save content as of yet. However, this is a good way to making sure you've achieved the right results so far.

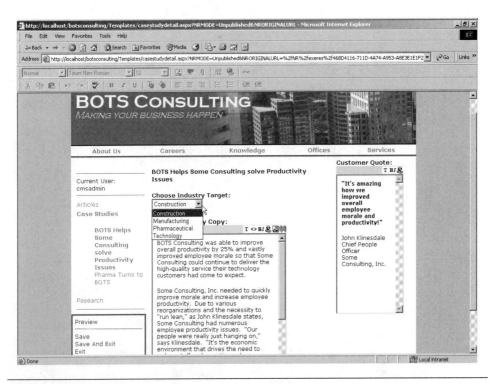

**Figure 29–8** A case study with the new drop-down list placeholder control

If all has gone well, your test drive should have been successful. We still need to wire up the rest of the functions so that our new placeholder is fully functional. Let's continue our construction by adding the code to SavePlaceholderContent. Again, this function is where we take the values that have been assigned to our child controls, in this case a drop-down list, and assign them to the bound placeholder in our TGI. You must make sure you call EnsureChildControls so that an exception isn't thrown at runtime. In Listing 29–5, you can see the code we've added to our SavePlaceholderContent function (the line breaks are not intentional).

**Listing 29–5** SavePlaceholderContent code in our drop-down list placeholder control

```
protected override void
SavePlaceholderContent(PlaceholderControlSaveEventArgs e)
{
      EnsureChildControls();
      try
      {
            ((XmlPlaceholder)this.BoundPlaceholder).XmlAsString  =
this.IndustryList.SelectedItem.Text;
      }
      catch (Exception ex)
      {
            string saveExceptionMessage = "Error saving placeholder contents:
" + this.GetType().Name + " :: " + this.ID + " :: " + ex.Message;
            Exception saveException = new Exception(saveExceptionMessage,
ex);
            throw saveException;
      }

}
```

As you can see in Listing 29–5, the code isn't terribly complex. We first ensure that our child controls are created; we then read the value from our drop-down list control and set the XmlasString property of the bound placeholder (again, in this case we're using an XML placeholder definition). CMS takes care of the rest. You'll notice that we're performing some light exception handling. Although we're using the standard exception message, you could create your own custom exception.

Next, we need to fill the LoadContentForAuthoring function. In this function, we're going to retrieve the content we saved previously. This function is the opposite of the prior function we talked about. Instead of assigning a value to the bound placeholder, based on the drop-down list, we're retrieving the value from the bound placeholder and finding the corresponding value in our drop-down list. In Listing 29–6 you can see how this function is constructed.

**Listing 29–6** The LoadContentForAuthoring function in our custom placeholder control

```
protected override void
LoadPlaceholderContentForAuthoring(PlaceholderControlEventArgs e)
        {
                EnsureChildControls();
                try
                {
                        ListItem savedSelectedIndustry =
this.IndustryList.Items.FindByValue(((XmlPlaceholder)this.BoundPlaceholder).
XmlAsString);
                        this.IndustryList.SelectedIndex =
this.IndustryList.Items.IndexOf(savedSelectedIndustry);
                }

                catch (Exception ex)
                {
                        string saveExceptionMessage = "Error loading
placeholder contents: " +
                                this.GetType().Name + " :: " + this.ID + " :: "
+ ex.Message;
                        Exception saveException = new
Exception(saveExceptionMessage, ex);
                        throw saveException;
                }
        }
```

Again, as with SavePlaceholderContent, we start by ensuring that our child controls are created with the EnsureChildControls call. After we've done that, we can retrieve the value from the placeholder. Because we're dealing with an XML placeholder and we're presenting the values in a drop-down list, setting up the control for the author takes a couple of extra steps. Namely, once we get the value back from the repository, we need to search the drop-down list control to find the value that matches what we've gotten back from the repository. Once we find the right index, we set the SelectedIndex property of the drop-down list to match. In this way, the content contributor is presented with the same value they entered earlier.

So now what? We've created an authoring environment, and we've saved the content to the repository and retrieved it again. What's next? Well, now we have to create the presentation controls. As you're probably aware by now, CMS always "lives" in two worlds: the authoring world and the presentation world. Although we've created the authoring world, we haven't addressed the presentation world. To create the presentation view of our placeholder, we have to implement two functions, which correspond closely to the authoring functions we've already covered. The two functions are CreatePresentationChildControls and LoadPlaceholderContentForPresentation.

We'll begin with CreatePresentationChildControls. This function is where you'll place the code to create the controls you want to appear when the Web Author is in modes other than AuthoringNew and AuthoringReedit. In our custom placeholder control, we're going to use the literal control to display the value chosen. In Listing 29–7 you can see how we've constructed our function.

**Listing 29–7** The CreatePresentationChildControls function in our DropDownListPlaceholder

```
private System.Web.UI.WebControls.Literal SelectedIndustry;

protected override void CreatePresentationChildControls(BaseModeContainer
presentationContainer)
{
        SelectedIndustry = new Literal();
        presentationContainer.Controls.Add(SelectedIndustry);
}
```

Kind of unexciting, huh? Since we're simply creating the presentation control environment, there isn't much to do. Again, we created a private member variable for our literal control, and in the function we physically created it. Once it existed, we added it to our presentation container. That's it.

Now that we have our presentation environment, we can fill it with content through the LoadPlaceholderContentForPresentation function (see Listing 29–8). In this function, we need to retrieve the content from the repository and assign the value to our literal control's Text property.

**Listing 29–8**  The code in the LoadPlaceholderContentForPresentation function

```
protected override void
LoadPlaceholderContentForPresentation(PlaceholderControlEventArgs e)
{

      EnsureChildControls();
      try
      {
            this.SelectedIndustry.Text =
((XmlPlaceholder)this.BoundPlaceholder).XmlAsString;

      }
      catch (Exception ex)
      {
            string saveExceptionMessage = "Error loading placeholder
contents: " +
                  this.GetType().Name + " :: " + this.ID + " :: " + ex.Message;
            Exception saveException = new Exception(saveExceptionMessage, ex);
            throw saveException;
      }

}
```

Notice in this function that you simply have to retrieve the value from the repository and assign the value to the literal control. That's it.

If you've followed along so far, you should have a functional drop-down list custom placeholder.

### Authoring-Only Custom Placeholders

Up to this point, we've focused on a fairly basic placeholder control. However, there are almost limitless variations. One specific variation is creating an authoring-only placeholder. There may be some business requirements that require content contributors to contribute content when authoring but not have the content show up in the live site. A good example of this is a placeholder that allows a content contributor to manipulate posting settings. In the BOTS site, there's an authoring-only placeholder that allows a contributor to change the start date of the posting while they're authoring.

A common challenge that some template designers have is providing a contribution environment that makes "sense" to a broad audience. For example, CMS provides some basic page properties that content contributors and developers can use. Unfortunately, depending on the skill level of the content contributor, the Page Properties dialog may be forgotten ("Oh, I didn't know that was there") or prove difficult to use ("I don't understand what all this means"). As a result, some of the productivity that could be gained by CMS is lost. There is a way, however, to get that back through using custom placeholders.

One of the elements of the BOTS Consulting Web site in the press release section is the date of the release. This date is taken from the Start Date property of a posting. By using the start date, contributors have the ability to create the release well in advance of the actual public release and have CMS publish the content when it's appropriate. Further, the release will always reflect the date it was released to the public. Unfortunately, the Start Date property is in the Page Properties dialog. As a result, it requires content contributors to go back and reset that property once they've saved the page. Often, contributors will forget to set this property, and it may even be missed during the workflow process. To combat this problem, the BOTS Consulting site has a custom placeholder control that's used only during authoring to allow the content contributor to set the date of the posting while they're authoring. In Figure 29–9 you can see what this placeholder looks like.

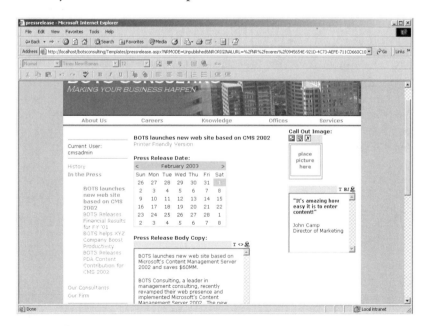

**Figure 29–9** The press release template with the calendar custom placeholder

Now, this is not revolutionary, but it does go a long way toward making contribution easier for a broader audience. Not only is the control available during authoring, but it should be relatively intuitive—you use a calendar to set the release date of the posting.

In the press release template, we are already using the StartDate property of the posting to display the release date, so we don't need the placeholder to display during any mode other than AuthoringNew or AuthoringReedit. In essence, we need an authoring-only placeholder. In order to create an authoring-only placeholder, we simply don't fully implement the two presentation-focused functions in the control, Load-ContentForPresentation and CreatePresentationChildControls. We still have to have them listed, but we won't add any code to them.

The next element of our control is the need to change the posting start date. For this we're just going to use a standard call to the PAPI to affect the posting's StartDate property. We want the StartDate property to be affected when the content contributor chooses a date on the calendar and saves the posting. Keep in mind, however, that the role of the person who changes the date may affect the workflow. Since page properties are the domain of the moderator, an author who changes the release date will force the need for moderator approval, *and* that posting will disappear from the site if it's already been published.

The complete code for the CalendarPlaceholder is shown in Listing 29–9.

**Listing 29–9**  The CalendarPlaceholder control code

```
using System;
using System.Web.UI;
using System.Web.UI.WebControls;
using System.ComponentModel;
using Microsoft.ContentManagement.Publishing;
using Microsoft.ContentManagement.Publishing.Extensions.Placeholders;
using Microsoft.ContentManagement.WebControls.Design;
using Microsoft.ContentManagement.WebControls;


namespace botsconsultingwebcontrols
{
    /// <summary>
    /// Summary description for CalendarPlaceholder control.
    /// </summary>
```

```
     [ SupportedPlaceholderDefinitionType(
typeof(HtmlPlaceholderDefinition)),DefaultProperty("CurrentDate"),
     ToolboxData("<{0}:CalendarPlaceholder
runat=server></{0}:CalendarPlaceholder>"),
     Description("Allows authors to change the start date of a posting while
adding content")]
     public class CalendarPlaceholder :
Microsoft.ContentManagement.WebControls.BasePlaceholderControl
     {
          private System.DateTime currentDate = System.DateTime.Now;
          private bool canSetPostingStartDate = false;
          private Literal alternateAuthoringControl;

          [Bindable(false),
          Category("Settings")]
          public System.DateTime CurrentDate
          {
               get
               {
                    return currentDate;
               }

          }


          protected System.Web.UI.WebControls.Calendar newCalendar;

          protected override void
CreateAuthoringChildControls(BaseModeContainer authoringContainer)
          {
               if (CmsHttpContext.Current.Posting.State.ToString() ==
"New")
               {

                    // If this is a new posting and it hasn't been saved
                    at least once
                    // just display a message to the author indicating
                    that they
                    // can't set the startpublishdate until the posting
                    has been
                    // saved at least once.
                    this.alternateAuthoringControl = new Literal();
                    this.alternateAuthoringControl.EnableViewState =
                    true;
```

```
                     // Set this boolean to false to ensure none of the
                     other operations
                     // will try and affect the startpublishdate or
                     placeholder value
                     canSetPostingStartDate = false;
                     authoringContainer.Controls.Add
                     (this.alternateAuthoringControl);
             }
             else
             {
                     // Assign the basic properties of the child control
                     this.newCalendar = new Calendar();
                     this.newCalendar.ID = "StartPublishCalendar";

                     // Explicitly set the EnableViewState property to
                     true
                     // If this isn't done, you'll occasionally receive an
                     // exception about improper casting
                     this.newCalendar.EnableViewState = true;

                     // Set the canSetPostingDate property to true so the
                     rest
                     // of the operations can occur
                     canSetPostingStartDate = true;

                     // Add the calendar control to the authoring
                     container
                     authoringContainer.Controls.Add(this.newCalendar);
             }
     }


     protected override void
CreatePresentationChildControls(BaseModeContainer presentationContainer)
     {
             // This function isn't implemented since this is an
             authoring
             // only placeholder
     }


     protected override void
LoadPlaceholderContentForAuthoring(PlaceholderControlEventArgs e)
     {

             EnsureChildControls();
```

```
                    try
                    {

                          // Only load content if this isn't a new posting,
                          since we can't set the start
                          // date unless the posting has already been saved
                          once.
                          if (canSetPostingStartDate)
                          {
                                // If this isn't a postback and the current
                                placeholder doesn't
                                // have any value
                                if((!Page.IsPostBack) &&
((HtmlPlaceholder)this.BoundPlaceholder).Text == "")
                                {
                                      this.newCalendar.SelectedDate =
currentDate;

                                      this.newCalendar.TodaysDate =
currentDate;

                                      this.newCalendar.VisibleDate =
currentDate;

                                }

                                // Assign the appropriate values to the
                                calendar control
                                // based on the placeholder value
                                else
                                {
                                      System.DateTime placeholderDate =
System.DateTime.Parse(((HtmlPlaceholder)this.BoundPlaceholder).Text);
                                      this.newCalendar.SelectedDate =
placeholderDate;

                                      this.newCalendar.TodaysDate =
currentDate;

                                      this.newCalendar.VisibleDate =
placeholderDate;
                                }
                          }
                    }
                    catch (Exception exp)
                    {
                          // Show error conditions in the console
                          string myExceptionMessage = "Error loading
placeholder contents: " +
```

```
                                 this.GetType().Name + " :: " + this.ID + " :: "
+ exp.Message;
                         Exception myException = new
Exception(myExceptionMessage, exp);
                         throw myException;
                   }
            }


         protected override void LoadPlaceholderContentForPresentation
(PlaceholderControlEventArgs e)
         {
               // This function isn't implemented since this is an
               authoring
               // only placeholder
         }

         protected override void SavePlaceholderContent
(PlaceholderControlSaveEventArgs e)
         {

               EnsureChildControls();
               try
               {
                     // Make sure we can set the startpublishdate of the
                     posting
                     if (canSetPostingStartDate)
                     {

                             // Make sure that the date selected on the
                             calendar is after
                             // the startpublish date of the channel.  Child
                             object start dates
                             // can't parent startpublish dates.
                             if
(this.newCalendar.SelectedDate.ToUniversalTime() < CmsHttpContext.Current.
Channel.StartDate)
                             {
                                   // Throw an exception to alert the
                                   content contributor
                                   // that they've broken the rules
                                   Exception myException = new
Exception("Posting start date prior to channel start date");
                                   throw myException;
```

```
                              }
                              else
                              {
                                      // Set the bound placeholder value equal
                                      to the calendar selected date

((HtmlPlaceholder)this.BoundPlaceholder).Html  = this.newCalendar.
SelectedDate.ToString();
                                              CmsHttpContext.Current.Posting.StartDate
= this.newCalendar.SelectedDate.ToUniversalTime();
                              }
                      }
                      else
                      {
                              // Store an empty string in the placeholder if
                              we can't affect
                              // the startpublishdate property of the posting
                              ((HtmlPlaceholder)this.BoundPlaceholder).Html
                              = "";
                      }
              }
              catch (Exception exp)
              {
                      // Show error conditions in the console
                      string myExceptionMessage = "Error loading
placeholder contents: " +
                              this.GetType().Name + " :: " + this.ID + " :: "
+ exp.Message;
                      Exception myException = new
Exception(myExceptionMessage, exp);
                      throw myException;
              }
      }


      protected override void OnPopulatingDefaultContent
(PlaceholderControlCancelEventArgs e)
      {

              // This function allows us to fill the placeholder with a
              default
              // value when the posting is new; since this control will
              not allow
```

```
    // authors to change the value until after the posting has
    been saved
    // once, we simply fill in a default value for the literal
    control.
        try
        {
                this.alternateAuthoringControl.Text = "You
                cannot set the release date until the release
                has been saved once.";
        }
        catch (Exception exp)
        {
                string myExceptionMessage = "Error loading
                placeholder contents: " +
                    this.GetType().Name + " :: " + this.ID +
                    " :: " + exp.Message;
                Exception myException = new
                Exception(myExceptionMessage, exp);
                throw myException;
        }


    }
  }
}
```

As you walk through the code, you'll probably notice a few differences between this placeholder control and the earlier example we used. There are some unique characteristics of this particular control that need to be noted.

- It's not possible to change the start date of a new posting. A posting doesn't truly exist until after it's saved once. As a result, we had to create a special condition that handled new postings (Authoring New) differently from postings that are being reedited (Authoring Reedit). In the case of a new posting that has never been saved, we simply show a literal control with a basic text message. Further, we don't change the placeholder value of the posting. In all other cases, the control displays a calendar that allows the content contributor to change the date.
- In connection with our earlier point, the BasePlaceholderClass has an event that's automatically registered and called OnPopulated

DefaultContent. This event allows you to control the initial content that a placeholder might be assigned in the case of a new posting. Because we're explicitly preventing any authoring when the posting is brand new, we use this event to change the Text property of the literal control. It's in this event where we specify the message to the author about not being able to change the release date.

■ The calendar control depends on a postback behavior as the user changes the selected date. This is normally fine. However, since we're authoring, the console will normally warn a content contributor if they try to navigate away from a posting while in authoring mode. Again, this is normally a good thing. However, when we select a different date in the calendar control, it looks to the console as if we're trying to navigate away. So, we made a small change to the default console. In the DefaultConsole user control, we check for the existence of the calendar placeholder. If this kind of placeholder exists on a page, we set EnableLeave AuthoringWarning to "false". In this way, the message about navigating away from the authoring environment will not appear as we change the selected value. The code we added to the console is provided in Listing 29–10.

**Listing 29–10** The code in the DefaultConsole to turn off the leave-authoring warning

```
System.Web.UI.Control myControl =
this.Page.FindControl("CalendarPlaceholder1");
if (myControl != null)
{
      this.Console1.EnableLeaveAuthoringWarning = false;
}
else
{
      this.Console1.EnableLeaveAuthoringWarning = true;
}
```

## Summary

In this chapter we discussed building CMS-aware controls and custom placeholder controls. Building a CMS-aware control is very similar to building other .NET controls, except a CMS-aware control "knows" how to react in the CMS environment (between authoring and live). This could be as simple as recognizing the various modes of the author or implementing features specific to a CMS object, like a posting. For our example, we demonstrated how to create a PlaceholderLabel user control and talked about how you could create a similar control as a composite server control.

We also built two custom CMS placeholders. In our examples, we demonstrated creating a custom placeholder that appeared to the author as a drop-down list. This control allowed the author to select the industry with which a specific case study was associated. In addition, we demonstrated how to create an authoring-only placeholder. The calendar placeholder we showed provided a mechanism for the content contributors to change the start-publish date of a posting while they were authoring.

Obviously our examples were presented within the context of the BOTS Consulting solution. However, the concepts and techniques shown here can be used across a wide variety of projects. What you should have seen here are the possibilities for custom controls to enhance and extend CMS. For additional examples of CMS-aware controls and custom placeholders, visit http://www.gotdotnet.com.

# CHAPTER 30

# Customizing the Web Author Console

The Web Author application is a fundamental component within the CMS architecture. It is this interface that empowers business users by allowing them to modify their Web pages. CMS was originally designed to remove the "Webmaster bottleneck," and it is ultimately the Web Author that accomplishes this goal. Of course, without the rest of CMS, the Web Author would not be very useful, but it is the Web Author that is at the "top of the stack." This is what most CMS users see when they interact with the server.

The Web Author is actually two entirely separate applications: the original ASP-based Web Author and the new Web Author .NET. This chapter will primarily discuss the .NET application, but the term "Web Author" will be used to describe both versions.

## Overview

Why would you want to customize the Web Author? Well, by customizing the Web Author, you can effectively change the workflow within CMS, change the rights of CMS user roles, or even change the functionality of CMS.

For example, if you remove the Submit option when a CMS author logs in, you have changed the way that the CMS workflow works. Now, instead of authors submitting changes, editors would have to do so. Along the same lines, if you remove the Move option when an author logs in, then you have effectively changed the rights of the CMS author role. If you add a link that allows an author to e-mail an editor, then you have changed the functionality of CMS. In many cases, altering the Web Author is the only way to make such customizations. Having a strong understanding of the Web Author architecture is vital if you want to take advantage of its potential.

There are innumerable reasons why you might choose to alter the Web Author console. Because of this, it is not possible for Microsoft to build all your desired features into the product. Instead, they must provide a flexible platform that allows you to make the required changes. The Web Author offers this flexibility. As you will see in this chapter, it is possible to make many types of customizations to both the appearance and the functionality of the Web Author.

# Anatomy of the Web Author .NET Console

The Web Author .NET application is constructed from many ingredients. The architecture is based on ASP.NET principles, so if you are familiar with ASP.NET, then you will be comfortable with the Web Author.

The console itself is contained within a .NET user control, the controls within the console are .NET server controls, and the underlying code is contained within .NET classes (e.g., the WebAuthorContext).

## Web Author Controls

There are a few different types of .NET server controls within the Web Author architecture (Figure 30–1): console controls, site mode container controls, action controls, and status controls. The fact that these controls are all .NET server controls offers great advantages in terms of class inheritance and development experience.

### Console Controls

CMS ships with two console controls. These two server controls are the authoring console and the error console. The controls are used to encapsulate the .NET server controls used by the Web Author. When you open the WoodgroveNet DefaultConsole.ascx file in design mode, you can see these two controls.

The authoring console appears when a CMS user clicks the Switch to Edit Mode link. The error console is displayed when the WebAuthor Context class encounters an error. To make things easy, the two controls

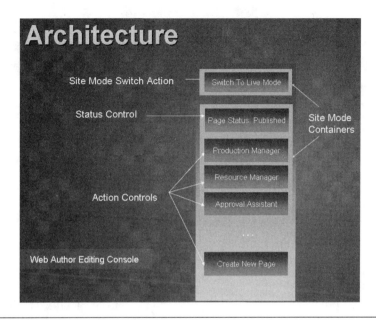

**Figure 30–1** Web Author .NET architecture

are displayed within the same .NET user control. For example, when you add the WoodgroveNet default console or the BOTS Consulting console to a template, you are also adding the error control.

### Site Mode Container Controls

Site mode containers enable Web Author controls to act differently under different Web Author modes. There are three types of container controls: presentation mode containers, authoring mode containers, and error mode containers. For example, looking at the source for the Default Console.ascx file, you can see container controls such as Presentation ModeContainer and AuthoringModeContainer. These containers give the CMS developer an easy way to organize the Web Author action and status controls. If you created a new custom control, you could add your control to one of these containers and you would not have to worry about the control appearing in the wrong CMS mode. In other words, you do not have to write any code to determine whether your control appears in the WebAuthorContext Published mode or authoring mode.

The mode containers support a number of different submodes, shown in Table 30–1.

**Table 30–1** Mode Container Submodes

| Mode Container | Submode | Description |
|---|---|---|
| Presentation | Published | This is the Live site mode. If a CMS user is logged in, the Switch to Edit Site link appears. |
| | Unpublished | Various action and status controls appear in this mode. The specific controls that appear are determined by the rights of the CMS user. For example, the Approve link will only appear if the current posting is in the "waiting for approval" state and the current user has rights to perform the approval. |
| | Both | Controls added to this section will appear in both Published mode and Unpublished mode. |
| Authoring | AuthoringNew | This mode is used when a page is first created. |
| | AuthoringReedit | This mode is available when an existing page is edited. |
| | Both | Controls added to this section will appear in both AuthoringNew mode and AuthoringReedit mode. |
| Error | FailedSaveNewPage | The Save action failed. |
| | OverlappedSave | More than one Save action was detected. |
| | FailedSavePlaceholder | A Save action failed when placeholder changes were being saved. |
| | FailedSubmit | The Submit action failed. |
| | FailedApprove | The Approve action failed. |
| | FailedDecline | The Decline action failed. |
| | FailedDelete | The Delete action failed. |

### Example: Displaying the Web Author Mode

You may be curious about these modes and when they come into play. Add this code to your DefaultConsole.ascx file to output the current Web Author mode.

```
using Microsoft.ContentManagement.WebControls;
<%
    WebAuthorContext webAuthor = new WebAuthorContext();
    string mode = webAuthor.Mode.ToString();
    Response.Write(mode);
%>
```

### Action Controls and Status Controls

These .NET server controls are the most obvious components within the Web Author console. Status controls are used to display information about CMS objects (such as the publication status of the current posting), and action controls allow CMS users to do things like create or edit the content on the Web site.

Action controls and status controls render HTML inside server control tags. Rather than restricting the rendering of the controls, they provide an object model to retrieve rendering details. For example, the Text property is used to show the text within the anchor tags, and the Action Javascript property determines the JavaScript that runs when the link is clicked.

The following are examples of Web Author action controls:

- Create New Page: Allows the user to create a new page.
- Move: Moves the page to another CMS channel.
- Save: Saves edits to the current page.
- Submit: Submits the page into the CMS workflow.
- Approve: Approves the saved changes and changes the live version to the saved version.

The following are examples of Web Author status controls:

- Posting State: Indicates the current stage in the CMS workflow.
- Lock Status: Shows which CMS author has locked the page.
- Version: Indicates whether another version of the page exists. For example, if the page has been edited but the changes have not

been approved, this control shows that the live version of the page is different from the version displayed in Unpublished mode.

Most of the Web Author action controls are contained within the container control for authoring. The only one that is visible in presentation mode is the link that allows a CMS author to switch to Unpublished mode. This is the Switch to Edit Site link that you see as a CMS user with authoring rights. The control has added logic that hides the link if the current user is the CMS guest account.

### WebAuthorContext Class

The WebAuthorContext class is the heart of the Web Author application. CMS offers different rendering of pages based on different modes. It is the WebAuthorContext class that allows the Web Author to manage these different modes. For example, in Published mode, CMS placeholders render content, but in Unpublished mode it is usual that they allow authors to edit the content. It is the WebAuthorContext.Current method that allows the Web Author to detect the current mode. Take a look at the CMS help files for a complete breakdown of the WebAuthor Context class.

This is the same class that handles the new PAPI event model. CMS developers can use the event model to perform custom actions based on changes to the CMS site—for example, when new pages are created. But this is a topic for another chapter.

## Working with the Default Console Control

The ASP.NET version of the CMS 2002 Web Author is conveniently packaged within a user control. Many Web Author changes can be made by simply modifying this one control. The following sections explore a few examples of changes that you might want to make to your CMS implementation.

### Changing Display Properties of the Default Console

In a CMS site, the Web Author console is exposed within a .NET user control. By implementing the console in this manner, the CMS development team has given users a great deal of flexibility over the presentation of the console. Simply by altering the user control, you can present the

Web Author console in a different manner. The following example demonstrates how to make such an alteration.

### Example: Altering the Border Color of the Web Author Console

If you have looked at the WoodgroveNet sample site, you have seen that the default Web Author console (Figure 30–2) is surrounded by a green border. Since it is likely that you are using a different color scheme, this is one of the most obvious changes that you might want to make. You can use this example as a basis for making a number of aesthetic changes to the Web Author console.

---

**NOTE:** You can try any of these examples using the BOTS Consulting site.

---

To alter this border color, open a browser window and navigate to your CMS site (e.g., http://localhost/WoodgroveNet/). If you are using Forms authentication, log in as a CMS user who has rights to edit the page. Next you need to click the Switch to Edit Mode link. This will show the Web Author console. Notice the border color of the Web Author console. For example, the WoodgroveNet console has a green border.

**Figure 30–2**  Web Author default console

If the CMS project is not already open, open it in Visual Studio .NET. For more information on this topic, refer to the CMS documentation ("Opening the WoodgroveNet Project in Visual Studio .NET"). In the Solution Explorer, expand the folder containing the DefaultConsole. ascx file. In the WoodgroveNet sample, this folder is called Console and contains the files used by the WoodgroveNet authoring console. Double-click the DefaultConsole.ascx file (e.g., C:\Program Files\Microsoft Content Management Server\Sample Data\WoodgroveNet\console\ DefaultConsole.ascx). This will open the file for editing. Click the HTML tab at the bottom of the window to switch to the HTML view. Before you alter this file, make sure you create a backup copy. Once you have created a backup copy, you can change the code that renders the Web Author console. For example, to change the border color of the control, you would alter the following code. Note that in the WoodgroveNet sample, this code starts at line 5.

Before:

```
<table width='100%' border='2' bordercolor='green' cellpadding='5'>
```

After:

```
<table width='100%' border='2' bordercolor='black' cellpadding='5'>
```

Once you are done, save the file DefaultConsole.ascx. Note that it is not necessary to build the project, since you have not altered the code-behind page. Go back to the browser window and refresh the page. You will see that the border around the console has changed color.

This is a simple example, but the example is a good one. By making this change, you can see that you have complete control over the presentation of the Web Author console.

## Adding and Removing Options from the Console

Imagine the following scenario. The Web manager of the BOTS Consulting site decides that it is not acceptable for an author to move a Web page from one part of the site to another. This decision is relayed to the CMS developers who must implement this business decision. Changing the Web Author console makes it easy to implement this policy. The following example shows how to remove a link from the Web Author console.

### *Example: Removing a Link from the Web Author Console*

This example shows a more substantial change to the Web Author console. Altering the functionality of the Web Author is tantamount to altering the CMS rights model or workflow. For example, you will now see how you can remove options from being displayed within the authoring console. By making a change like this, you are actually altering the rights of the CMS authors.

To make such a change, open a browser window and navigate to your CMS site. If you are using Forms authentication, log in as a CMS user who has rights to edit the page. Next you need to click the Switch to Edit Mode link. This will show the Web Author console. If the CMS project is not already open, open it in Visual Studio .NET. In the Solution Explorer, expand the folder containing the DefaultConsole.ascx file. In the WoodgroveNet sample, this folder is called Console and contains the files used by the WoodgroveNet authoring console. Double-click the DefaultConsole.ascx file to open it for editing. Click the HTML tab at the bottom of the window to switch to the HTML view. Before you alter this file, make sure you create a backup copy.

Once you have created a backup copy, you can delete the code that renders the link that you wish to remove. For example, to remove the Move link, you would delete (or comment out) this code. Note that in the WoodgroveNet sample, this code starts at line 105.

```
<CmsConsole:MoveAction id="MoveAction" runat="server">
    <A id="MoveAnchor" href="#" onclick="<%#
Container.ActionJavascript %>;return false" target=_self>
        <%# Container.Text %>
    </A><BR>
</CmsConsole:MoveAction>
```

Save the file DefaultConsole.ascx. Note that it is not necessary to build the project, since you have not altered the code-behind page. Go back to the browser window and refresh the page. You will see that the link no longer appears in the Web Author console. Based on this change, authors will not be able to move pages from one channel to another.

If you wanted to make a more selective change, you could simply check the current user's rights and then make a decision about whether to show or hide various options. The CMS API may not directly give you every check that you would like to make, but there are ways to get around this.

For example, if you want to check whether a user is an author, check whether the user has rights to create a page but not approve it. If you want a more specific check, you could create an object and only give your special user rights to that object. A good example is a hidden channel. Then you can check whether the current user has rights to that object. If the user does, then you have found the specific user that you are looking for. This method can be used to distinguish between CMS administrators and channel managers.

## Changing the "Real Estate" of the Console

Altering the presentation of the console might suit some scenarios, but quite often it is not enough. Fortunately, this does not present a problem for the Web Author's flexible design. When a more in-depth change is necessary, you can make more drastic alterations to the presentation of the console. For example, if you do not want the console to take up a lot of space on the page, you could change the controls so that they use less real estate. Here are a couple of examples of custom consoles.

### Example: A Dynamic "Drop-down" Web Author Console

This example shows how you can change your Web Author console so that it is presented as a drop-down list (Figures 30–3 and 30–4). This customization could use far less real estate on your page. Consequently,

**Figure 30–3** The drop-down Web Author console collapsed

**Figure 30–4** The drop-down Web Author console expanded

the CMS author will see little difference between the Published mode design and the authoring mode design.

The following code shows the important elements of the drop-down version of the Web Author console. Dynamic HTML is used to catch change events within the Select tags. Each Web Author control is enclosed between one of these Select tags. The complete code for this example is available for download at www.awprofessional.com/titles/0321194446.

```
<CmsConsole:Console runat="server" id="Console1">
      <script language="JavaScript">
function changeConsoleSelection(selection)
{
      var option = selection.options[selection.selectedIndex];
      if (option.actionJavascript != null )
      {
      var actionJavascript = option.actionJavascript;
      eval(actionJavascript);
      }
}
      </script>
. . .
<select onchange="changeConsoleSelection(this)"
ID="dropDownConsole" NAME="dropDownConsole">
  <option>Web Author Console</option>
. . .
<CmsConsole:PostingStatus id="PostingStatus1" runat="server">
   <B>Page Status:</B> <FONT color="red">
     <%# Container.Text %> </FONT> <BR /> </CmsConsole:PostingStatus>
. . .
<CmsConsole:CopyAction id="CopyAction1" runat="server">
   <option id=CopyAnchor actionJavascript="<%#
     Container.ActionJavascript %>">
   <%# Container.Text %> </option>
. . .
</CmsConsole:Console>
```

### Example: Floating Web Author Console

This example shows another useful console modification. Instead of having the console tied to a particular location on the page, you may want to allow your CMS users to move the console around as they see fit. This example renders the Web Author console as a floating DHTML window (Figure 30–5). Authors can easily drag the control anywhere they wish.

This is a popular console because it does not require any real estate on your page. If you already have a great template, you can add the console without having to make any changes.

The following code shows a small portion of the floating console implementation. This is the code that displays or hides particular elements within the console. This code is used to expand and collapse the control. The complete code for this example is available for download at www.awprofessional.com/titles/0321194446.

```
<script language="JavaScript">
function OpenCloseDiv(divName){
      if (divName.style.display == "none") {
            divName.style.display="block";
      }
      else {
            divName.style.display="none";
      }
}
```

**Figure 30–5** A floating Web Author console

```
</script>
<CmsConsole:Console id="Console1" runat="server">
      <DIV class="floatingConsole" id="editConsole"
ondblclick="OpenCloseDiv(editConsoleOptions)">
</CmsConsole:Console>
```

# Subclassing to Create a New Action Control

Altering the appearance of existing Web Author dialogs is not supported by Microsoft. However, in some cases, there are no real technical hurdles to doing so. For example, the Save New Page dialog is an ASPX file (installed by default to C:\Program Files\Microsoft Content Management Server\Server\IIS_CMS\WebAuthor\Dialogs\PageOperation\ AuthoringMode\PageSave\NewPageSaveDlg\NewPageSaveDlg.aspx). If you wanted to, you could go into the ASPX file and alter the dialog.

However, the real flexibility in the Web Author design is the fact that you can create your own .NET server controls by inheriting from the Web Author control classes. For example, if you wanted to create your own Create New Page action, you could inherit from the Microsoft. ContentManagement.WebControls.WebAuthorContext.BasePostback Action class and then add your own user interface. An added bonus to this model is that your customized control will still trigger CMS PAPI events. The same principle can be applied to the Web Author status controls.

## Classes for Creating an Action Control

There are three classes for creating an action control: BaseAction, Base-NewWindowAction, and BasePostbackAction.

To create an action control that triggers client-side JavaScript, you should inherit from the BaseAction class. You can then override the ActionJavascript property to define the code that runs when the user clicks the control. This type of control can be used to render custom dialog boxes.

The BaseNewWindowAction class allows a CMS developer to create a custom Web Author control that opens a dialog box. This class includes a property called UrlNewWindow, which determines the URL that should be opened when the control is clicked.

Another option is to create a custom Web Author action control that raises an ASP.NET postback event. If you want to create an action that does this, you should subclass your action from the BasePostbackAction class. The PerformAction method is used to specify the code that runs when the postback is raised.

## Example: The "createChannel" Action Control

To demonstrate the flexibility of the Web Author controls, this example shows how you might create a custom action control. One of the most commonly requested Web Author enhancements is the ability to create CMS channels directly from within the Web Author console. This is a perfect candidate for demonstrating custom action controls.

We will create a function called "createChannel" and then add it as an action control within the Web Author. The function will use the CMS PAPI to create a new channel under the root channel of the CMS Web site. The complete code for this example is available for download at www.awprofessional.com/titles/0321194446.

Once you have created your own subclass, you will want to override the functionality of the default control. You have a number of choices. The first option shown is overriding the Text property. This property determines the link text displayed on the console for the control. Other options are discussed later in this chapter.

### Creating Your Subclass

This first snippet shows the base code that we will use to subclass from a Web Author class. You can see that it adds references to a number of assemblies, and it inherits from the BasePostbackAction class. This piece of code also introduces the parentChannel member variable, which we will use to determine the parent channel of the new channel.

```
using System;
using System.ComponentModel;
using System.Collections;
using System.Web;
// Add references for MCMS namespaces
using Microsoft.ContentManagement.Publishing;
using Microsoft.ContentManagement.WebControls;
using Microsoft.ContentManagement.WebControls.ConsoleControls;
namespace CmsWebAuthorApplication
{
    public class CreateChannelAction : BasePostbackAction
    {
        // Instantiate MCMS HTTP Context
```

```
            CmsHttpContext cmsPapiHttpContext =
CmsHttpContext.Current;
            // Set the root channel as the default parent channel
            protected Channel parentChannel = null;
    }
}
```

### Creating Your Custom Action Function

This next section of code shows how you can create your own custom
properties to use in the action control. CMS developers can then change
these properties in the console file. Properties like this are powerful
tools in the .NET developer's toolbox. They encourage code reuse and
help avoid coding errors.

```
/// <summary>
/// Channel sets or returns the path for the parent channel.
/// </summary>
[
   Browsable(true),
   Description("Parent Channel"),
    Category("Behavior")
]
public string ParentChannel
{
    get { return parentChannel.Path; }
    // Get a channel object using its path.
    set { parentChannel =
CmsHttpContext.Current.Searches.GetByPath(value) as Channel;}
}
```

Next is the code that actually creates the channel. Looking through
this code you will see that it uses the CMS PAPI to create a channel
under a certain parent channel. The parent channel is determined by the
ParentChannel property. As one of the code comments notes, it is not
necessary to switch to Web Author Update mode to run this code. The
reason for this is that the base class already runs the code in Update
mode. Since this code is inherited from that base class, we get this functionality for free.

This code creates the channel, names it, and then commits the
change to the CMS database. If an error is encountered, the changes to
the CMS database are canceled.

```
// This function programmatically creates an MCMS channel
private void createChannel()
{
// Instantiate MCMS HTTP Context
CmsHttpContext cmsPapiHttpContext = CmsHttpContext.Current;
HttpContext httpContext = HttpContext.Current;
// Attempt to create a new channel
// Note that the BasePostbackAction performs in update mode so we
don't
// need to switch
try
{
// Identify the channel to create new channels within
Channel targetChannel = cmsPapiHttpContext.RootChannel;
    // Check if channels can be created within the target channel.
    // Note CreateChannel can still fail even if CanCreateChannels
returns true
    if (targetChannel.CanCreateChannels)
    {
    // If channels can be created, create a channel and name it
    //'ChannelFoo'
        Channel newChannel = targetChannel.CreateChannel();
        newChannel.Name = "ChannelFoo";
        // Commit changes to the MCMS database
        cmsPapiHttpContext.CommitAll();
    }
}
catch (Exception eCreateChannel)
{
    // Roll back changes if an exception occurs
    cmsPapiHttpContext.RollbackAll();
    throw eCreateChannel;
}
} //End createChannel
```

### Overriding the Text Property

If you override the Text property of the base class, you are able to specify the text that appears in the console.

It is possible to add code within the Text property. However, this code will run every time the control is rendered within the Web Author console. Below your function, add the following code. This will override the Text property of the base class.

```
public override string Text
   {
   get
   {
      //Show the text of the Create Channel link
      return "Create Channel";
      //Note that you could run other code within this property
   }
}
```

### Adding Your Custom Control to the Web Author Editing Console

Next you will add the class you have created as an action within the Web Author console. In the Solution Explorer window, expand the Console folder in the WoodgroveNet project. Open the DefaultConsole.ascx file. The console opens in Design view. To see the code, you will need to switch to HTML view. In this example, assume that you have added your control to the WoodgroveNet namespace. To register a prefix for the CmsWebAuthorApplication, position the cursor at the top of the DefaultConsole.ascx page and add the following code:

```
<%@ Register TagPrefix="CreateChannelActionConsole"
Namespace="CmsWebAuthorApplication"
Assembly="WoodgroveNet" %>
```

To add the CreateChannel class as an action to the default console, add the following code:

```
<!- The "parentChannel" property determines the parent channel for
the new channel ->
<CreateChannelActionConsole:CreateChannelAction
id="CreateChannelAction" runat="server" parentChannel="/Channels">
<a id="CreateChannelActionAnchor" onclick="<%#
Container.ActionJavascript %>;return false;" href="#"”><%#
Container.Text%>
</a></CreateChannelActionConsole:CreateChannelAction>
```

## Example: Some Other Properties That You Can Override

Refer to the CMS documentation for a complete list of Web Author class properties that you can use in your custom controls. Here are a few quick examples.

### Overriding the ActionJavascript Property

The ActionJavascript property is within the BasePostbackAction base class. This property returns a string that contains client-side JavaScript for displaying a custom dialog box that retrieves the name of the channel to be created.

The simple code that follows is an example meant to demonstrate the functionality of the ActionJavascript property. Adding this code will result in an alert message popping up when the control is clicked.

```
public override string ActionJavascript
{
    get
    {
    string javascriptOutput;
    javascriptOutput = "alert('ActionJavascript Override')";
    return javascriptOutput;
    }
}
```

### Overriding the Available Property

The Available property is another useful aspect of Web Author controls. This property allows you to add logic for determining when an action control should appear on the console. As you can imagine, this property is used by almost all Web Author controls.

Typically, it is the Web Author mode that determines when a control should be displayed. However, you could use any logic, based on your business needs. In this example, the Available property is used to check the current user's rights to the current parent channel. If the current user does not have rights to create channels, then the option is simply not displayed.

```
/// <summary>
/// Available overrides BaseAction.Available and returns a boolean
value
/// indicating whether the current user can create channels in the
/// parent channel.
/// </summary>
public override bool Available
{
    get
```

```
    {
    return parentChannel.CanCreateChannels;
    }
}
```

# Customizing the Web Author Toolbar

Note that the modifications described in this section are not supported by Microsoft Professional Support Services (PSS).

Another customization option for the Web Author is to insert custom commands into the Web Author toolbar. These commands allow for client-side manipulation of the code in the standard HTML placeholder control. Common examples are to insert commands so that users can insert or delete rows from a table or set the background color on a table cell.

In order to trigger custom client-side actions and manipulate content from the Web Author, you can add custom toolbars and buttons to the ActiveX toolbar. The Web Author toolbar docks to the browser window during authoring. You can modify this toolbar by including custom client-side VBScript in CMS templates.

## Example: Altering the Web Author Toolbar

Add the starter file (ActiveXToolbarHooks.vbs) found in C:\Program Files\Microsoft Content Management Server\Server\IIS_CMS\Web Author\Client\PlaceholderControlSupport.

In order to see what the standard toolbar does with these calls, you can look in the toolbar code file: *installation drive*\Server\IIS_CMS\ WebAuthor\Client\PlaceholderControlSupport \ActiveXEditing.vbs. This file shows you when these hooks are called and what you need to do to add buttons. Do not modify the ActiveXEditing file directly.

You will need to add a client-side reference to the ActiveXToolbar Hooks.vbs file in all authoring templates that require the custom functionality. The reference is only needed in authoring mode. For example, add the following to the template code (this code must be within the Web form):

```
<asp:PlaceHolder id="phActiveXScript" runat="server"
EnableViewState="False" />
```

Add the following code to the Page_Load method in the code-behind. This addition requires a "using" reference to the Microsoft. ContentManagement.WebControls namespace.

```
WebAuthorContext webContext = WebAuthorContext.Current;
if ((webContext.Mode == WebAuthorContextMode.AuthoringNew) ||
(webContext.Mode == WebAuthorContextMode.AuthoringReedit))
{
     HtmlGenericControl scriptControl = new
HtmlGenericControl("script");
     scriptControl.Attributes.Add("language", "vbscript");
     scriptControl.Attributes.Add("type", "text/vbscript");
     scriptControl.Attributes.Add("src",
"../Script/ActiveXToolbarHooks.vbs");
     phActiveXScript.Controls.Add(scriptControl);
}
```

You will need to do the same for any custom JavaScript files where you implement the behavior (i.e., CustomToolbar.js). You may need to change the path that references the VBScript. The path is set to "../Script" in the sample code.

Custom toolbar button images should be copied to &lt;installation drive&gt;\Server\IIS_CMS\WebAuthor\ Client\PlaceholderControlSupport\ ToolbarImages.

Refer to the following section for examples on how to add and hook up actions to buttons.

## Example: Adding Custom Editing Behavior to the Web Author

To demonstrate this concept, you will add a new button to the Web Author allowing users to add <acronym> tags to text. First, you need to add a button to the toolbar by inserting the following code into the OnToolbarInitialize subroutine in the ActiveXToolbarHooks.vbs file:

```
Dim CustomToolbar
Set CustomToolbar =
     document.ToolbarInterface.Toolbars.CreateToolbar
("CustomToolbar")
Call CustomToolbar.AddButton("AcronymButton", "", "acronym.gif",
"Insert Acronym")
```

This assumes there is a custom toolbar button named acronym.gif available. In the example, AcronymButton is the ID used to identify the button and "Insert Acronym" is the tooltip that will be shown when the user hovers over the button.

You can decide whether your button should be enabled by checking a standard button that has similar properties. For example, we can choose to allow acronyms if the Bold command is allowed by inserting the following code into OnToolbarStateInitialize:

```
If (pState.Item("Bold").Allowed = True) Then
     pState.Item("AcronymButton").Allowed = True
Else
     pState.Item("AcronymButton").Allowed = False
End If
```

You can choose to attach the enabling of the custom button to that of the Bold button because the placeholder must be set to allow TextMarkup. If this setting is not correct, CMS will strip out the <acronym> tag when the page is saved.

The following code should be used in OnToolbarUpdate to ensure that the button cannot be used in HTML source editing mode:

```
If bEditingSource Then
     pActiveHtmlEditor.ToolbarState.Item("AcronymButton").Enabled
= False
Else
        pActiveHtmlEditor.ToolbarState.Item("AcronymButton").
Enabled = True
End If
```

Then, using the OnToolbarEvent subroutine, you can hook up the button to a client-side JavaScript function. If you wanted, you could just code the client-side manipulation in VBScript, but it is often easier to code in JavaScript.

```
Select Case bstrId
     Case "AcronymButton"
     Call CreateAcronym(pActiveHtmlEditor.DOM)
End Select
```

In this case, the CreateAcronym function is defined in Custom Toolbar.js. This file is referenced from your template. You can model the code used to insert the acronym after the code used to create hyperlinks.

Refer to the WBC_CreateLink function found in <*installation drive*>\ Server\IIS_CMS\WebAuthor\Client\AuthFormClientIE.js.

The CreateAcronym function is passed a reference to the Document Object Model (DOM) for the placeholder. A list of the functionality available from the DOM is available from http://msdn.microsoft. com/library/default.asp?url=/workshop/author/dhtml/reference/dhtml_ reference_entry.asp. The function inserts the <acronym> tag into the HTML or changes the title if the <acronym> tag already exists.

The user input for the "title" attribute is received using a custom pop-up window that is opened as a modal dialog from the CreateAcronym function. It returns the title input by the user to the CreateAcronym function, using only client-side code. The supporting JavaScript file takes care of initializing the title if an existing acronym is being edited. It also handles passing the value back to the calling window when the user selects OK. The functionality of this pop-up is patterned after the hyperlink dialog found at <*installation drive*>\Server\IIS_CMS\ WebAuthor\Dialogs\ HLink\hlink.aspx. Refer to this file for guidance on how to implement custom client-side pop-up windows.

# Customizing the ASP Web Author

As mentioned at the beginning of this chapter, CMS 2002 ships with two versions of the Web Author. This section quickly discusses how you can make changes to the ASP version. Based on this example, you should get an idea of where to start if you want to make changes to the ASP Web Author.

## Adding an Option to the Web Author

This example shows how you can create a new action for the ASP version of the Web Author. Just like the .NET Web Author, the ASP version was designed to allow users to modify the console. The example adds a new link to the Web Author console. This new link opens a window that represents the new action page. The example shows that this new window could also be a CMS posting.

The first thing you will need to do is add a call to the new function in ConsoleUI.inc (the default location is C:\Program Files\Microsoft Content Management Server\Server\IIS_NR\System\WBC\Customizable\ SiteEmbeddedWBCLinks\ConsoleUI.inc). Keep in mind that there are different versions of the console. Choose which console you are using. The default console is the one located at C:\Program Files\Microsoft Content Management Server\Server\IIS_NR\System\WBC\Customizable\ SiteEmbeddedWBCLinks\WBCConsole\FlatHTMLConsole.

Add this code to the console file (line 210):

```
' -- 8) ASP Example link
If AutoSession.ThisChannel.CanSetProperties Then
  Response.Write("<br>" & vbCr & vbCr )
Dim urlASPExample, strChannelModeUpdate
urlASPExample =
Autosession.Searches.GetByPath("/Channels/Samples/ASPExample
").URLModeUnpublished
strChannelModeUpdate =
Autosession.ThisChannel.QuerystringModeUpdate
  %>
    <script language="Javascript">
    <!-
     function openWindow()
     {
       //Open the window for the ASP Example (in update mode)

window.open("<%=urlASPExample%>?<%=strChannelModeUpdate%>&PostingGU
ID=<%=Autosession.ThisPosting.GUID%>", "WorkflowProperties",
"height=610,width=650");
     }
    -->
    </script>
  <%
  Call WriteHrTagAndReset(bWriteHrTag)
  Call ShowASPExampleLink()
  End If
```

This code opens a new window and displays another CMS posting. You do not have to do it this way. In fact, the Web Author uses stand-alone ASP pages to open the action windows. But you can see from this example that either method is possible.

The next choice is which Web Author mode you would like to use to show the new action. For example, if you want to add the action during the regular Edit site mode, you should add your new call to EditSite Ops.inc (the default install location is C:\Program Files\Microsoft Content Management Server\Server\IIS_NR\System\WBC\Customizable\ SiteEmbeddedWBCLinks\WBCConsole\EditSiteOps.inc).

This code adds the link to the Web Author application (line 32):

```
' ---- [Public] This subroutine generates the html to show the "ASP
Example" link
Sub ShowASPExampleLink()
%><a href="#" onclick="JavaScript:openWindow();return false">ASP
Example</a><%
End Sub
'--/ASPExample---'
```

You can see that you get the posting object by its path. This method is easier to maintain than a GUID. However, a GUID search would be faster. The posting returned is the object that represents the UI for the command. For better encapsulation, you could put this code into an include file.

This example should help you add or remove options from the ASP version of the Web Author console. Unlike the .NET version of the Web Author, the ASP code is not compiled, so keep in mind that the complete code for the ASP Web Author is there for your viewing pleasure. Just be sure to check the legal statements about what changes are supported by Microsoft PSS.

# Summary

The Web Author provides the business user with an intuitive and accessible interface for content authoring and editing. In addition, the flexible design and ease of extensibility also offer CMS developers a great deal of customization potential.

The combination of the .NET control architecture and the CMS WebAuthorContext class also grant the CMS developer a powerful development experience. It is possible for CMS developers to not only alter the appearance of the Web Author console but also make significant changes to its functionality. As a CMS developer, you should not let yourself be confined by the traditional functionality of the Web Author application. Rather, you should explore your options and take time to experiment. You may discover a way to address many business problems and possibly impress your boss along the way.

However, it is important to remember that behind the seemingly straightforward architecture of the Web Author, there has been an awful lot of server coding. The Web Author is really the tip of the iceberg when it comes to the architecture of CMS.

# Extending the Publishing Workflow

## Overview

CMS provides a fairly straightforward and useful workflow process "out of the box." However, if you want to enhance the native capabilities, you'll need to add some custom workflow code. In this chapter we'll discuss how you can extend the standard workflow by developing business-specific logic within the workflow event model. We'll begin by examining each of the events in the workflow model. Then, we'll look at building a simple logging routine that will illustrate how the events fire in "real life" by placing event handlers in Global.ASAX. Finally, we'll show you how to build custom HTTP modules, and we'll provide some best practices for implementing workflow extensions.

## What Is Extending the Workflow?

To begin, let's do a quick review of the workflow native to CMS for new content; since we covered workflow earlier, we won't do that here in depth—we just want to refresh your memory.

CMS provides a basic three-step workflow process for new content. The process starts when an author creates a new posting in CMS, either through the Authoring Connector or through the Web Author. Once the author is finished creating the new posting, they save and submit it for approval. When they submit the posting, it is sent to the editor. Taking the "happy path" approach (ideal case), the editor has two options: accept the posting as is, or make changes and then accept it. Once the editor accepts the new content, the posting is sent to a moderator. Since this is the happy path, we'll also assume the moderator accepts the posting. Once that happens, the posting is "approved." The posting will move to the Published state once the current date and the posting's startpublish date are equal. This basic workflow path is what all postings follow (assuming you have each of these roles defined for your channels).

Now, there are two cases when a posting will not follow the happy path. The first case is when either an editor or a moderator declines the posting. In that case, the posting is "returned" to the author. The second case is when the posting already exists. If the posting isn't new and posting page properties such as startdate name or description don't change, a moderator is not involved in the workflow process; approving a content change to an existing posting only requires editor approval.

So, what does "extending" the workflow mean? Essentially, almost every step we described earlier affects the state of the posting (refer to Table 31–1 for a review of posting states). Every time an action is taken—save, submit, approve, decline—a posting's state changes; there's a begin state and an end state. For example, when the author creates a new posting and saves it, the state of that posting changes from New to Saved. If they submit a posting for editor approval, the state changes from Saved to WaitingForEditorApproval. Each step in the process only requires one individual in a role (one author to submit, for example) to

**Table 31–1** Posting States for New Postings

| Action (Role) | Begin State | End State |
| --- | --- | --- |
| Save (author) | New | Saved |
| Save (editor) | Waiting for Editor Approval | Saved |
| Submit (author) | Saved | Waiting for Editor Approval |
| Approve (editor) | Waiting for Editor Approval | Waiting for Moderator Approval |
| Approve (moderator) | Waiting for Moderator Approval | Approved |
| Decline (editor) | Waiting for Editor Approval | Editor Declined |
| Decline (moderator) | Waiting for Moderator Approval | Moderator Declined |

change the state. Besides the state change, nothing else really happens within CMS. So when we talk about extending the workflow, what we're really doing is governing how the state change occurs and what other operations might need to happen when a posting changes state.

---

**NOTE:** In Table 31–1 we qualified the action with a role, since both authors and editors can save, and editors and moderators can accept or decline. Also, there are two posting states that aren't represented here because there is no corresponding workflow event: Published and Expired. If you'd like more detailed information on basic CMS workflow, please refer to Chapter 6.

---

## A Review of the Publishing Events

As we mentioned in the previous section, extending the CMS workflow is all about state management. However, it's impossible to manage state if you can't "see" events as they fire. To solve this problem, CMS has several workflow events that are fired at various times in the workflow process. You extend the CMS workflow by adding business-specific logic to the appropriate event or events.

CMS workflow events are "fired" at various times in the workflow process. Each event is really an event pair—one event in the pair fires before a state change occurs, and one fires after. All events that fire before the state change end with "ing." All events that fire after a state change end in "ed." To make things a little more interesting, any given state change may involve one or more event pairs. In fact, there are always at least two event pairs firing for every posting state change, but there may be more.

In Table 31–2, we've provided a list of the standard workflow events and a brief description of when they fire.

To help you better understand how events fire, let's look at one example. In Figure 31–1, we show the flow of an event firing sequence for an approval action on an existing posting. As we described earlier, you can see how the "ing" event fires first and then the "ed" event fires. Also, you can see that there are actually two pairs of events in the sequence. CMS will always fire the Changing and Changed events regardless of what action is taken; in reality, the Changing and Changed events may fire more than once for certain workflow actions.

**Table 31-2**  Standard Workflow Events in CMS

| Workflow Event | Description |
| --- | --- |
| Approved | Fires after a posting has been approved |
| Approving | Fires just before a posting is approved |
| Changed | Fires after any change has occurred |
| Changing | Fires just before a change is made |
| Created | Fires after a posting has been created |
| Creating | Fires just before a posting is created |
| CustomPropertyChanged | Fires after a custom property value has been changed |
| CustomPropertyChanging | Fires just before a custom property value is changed |
| Declined | Fires when a posting has been declined |
| Declining | Fires just before a posting state is changed to declined |
| Deleted | Fires after a posting has been deleted |
| Deleting | Fires just before a posting is to be deleted |
| Moved | Fires after a posting has been moved |
| Moving | Fires just before a posting is moved |
| PlaceholderPropertyChanged | Fires after the value of a placeholder is changed |
| PlaceholderPropertyChanging | Fires just before the value of a placeholder is changed |
| PropertyChanged | Fires after a posting property has changed |
| PropertyChanging | Fires just before a posting property is changed |
| Submitted | Fires after a posting has been submitted |
| Submitting | Fires just before a posting is submitted |

When you're extending the CMS workflow, it's likely that you don't need to catch all events, just the specific ones that are germane to your process. Further, adding code to multiple events may have unexpected results if you're not careful.

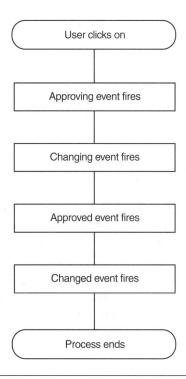

**Figure 31–1** The event firing order for an approval action

## Creating Event Handlers

There are two ways to handle events in CMS: through the Global.ASAX file or through custom HTTP modules. The decision of where to put your event handlers is a question of reusability. Putting your event handlers in the Global.ASAX file makes them a little less portable from project to project than writing a custom HTTP module. However, it's much easier to put event handlers in Global.ASAX. Ultimately, the choice is yours.

### Event Handlers in Global.ASAX

In order for the workflow events to fire, you first need to register the events. To register the CMS events, you need to add some code to the HTTPModules section of Web.Config. If you've used the CMS project templates and you've chosen MCMS Web Application, the code should already be added. However, if you started with a blank solution or the MCMS Empty Web Project, you'll have to add the following code manually:

```
<add name="CmsPosting" type="Microsoft.ContentManagement.
Publishing.Events.PostingEventsModule, Microsoft.ContentManagement.
Publishing"/>
```

Notice the name attribute of the "add" tag. This name will be used when you create the event handlers. The name is part of the "signature" for each of the event handlers. If you either don't add this module or your event handler signature and the registered module name don't match, your events will not fire.

Next, you'll need to add your event handler functions in Global.ASAX. Each event handler will correspond to a specific CMS event. As we mentioned earlier, you only need to create event handlers for those events that are germane to your project. Once you've added your signatures to Global.ASAX, you can begin to add code to them. In Listing 31–1 you'll find a list of all the event handlers available to you.

---

**NOTE:** The complete list of event handlers is also in the MCMS2002.CHM file provided with the product.

---

**Listing 31–1** The event handler signatures

```
public void CmsPosting_Approved( Object sender, ChangedEventArgs e ) {}
public void CmsPosting_Approving( Object sender, ChangingEventArgs e ) {}
public void CmsPosting_Changed( Object sender, ChangedEventArgs e ) {}
public void CmsPosting_Changing( Object sender, ChangingEventArgs e ) {}
public void CmsPosting_Created( Object sender, CreatedEventArgs e ) {}
public void CmsPosting_Creating( Object sender, CreatingEventArgs e ) {}
public void CmsPosting_CustomPropertyChanged( Object sender,
Microsoft.ContentManagement.Publishing.Events.PropertyChangedEventArgs e ) {}
public void CmsPosting_CustomPropertyChanging( Object sender,
PropertyChangingEventArgs e ) {}
public void CmsPosting_Declined( Object sender, ChangedEventArgs e ) {}
public void CmsPosting_Declining( Object sender, ChangingEventArgs e ) {}
public void CmsPosting_Deleted( Object sender,  ChangedEventArgs e ) {}
public void CmsPosting_Deleting( Object sender, ChangingEventArgs e ) {}
public void CmsPosting_Moved( Object sender, MovedEventArgs e ) {}
```

```
public void CmsPosting_Moving( Object sender, MovingEventArgs e ) {}
public void CmsPosting_PlaceholderPropertyChanged( Object sender,
Microsoft.ContentManagement.Publishing.Events.PropertyChangedEventArgs e ) {}
public void CmsPosting_PlaceholderPropertyChanging( Object sender,
PropertyChangingEventArgs e ) {}
public void CmsPosting_PropertyChanged( Object sender,
Microsoft.ContentManagement.Publishing.Events.PropertyChangedEventArgs e ) {}
public void CmsPosting_PropertyChanging( Object sender,
PropertyChangingEventArgs e ) {}
public void CmsPosting_Submitted( Object sender, ChangedEventArgs e ) {}
public void CmsPosting_Submitting( Object sender, ChangingEventArgs e ) {}
```

---

**NOTE:** In Listing 31–1, you'll notice that we occasionally specify the fully qualified namespace, and in some cases we don't. This is to avoid class ambiguity.

---

### Writing a Generic Handler

There are a few ways to approach writing handlers. One approach is to code to a generic event like Changing or Changed. Both of these events will fire, regardless of what you're doing with a posting. Coding to a generic event has the advantage of providing you with "access" to all events and all objects. For example, you'll be able to see when a posting is created as well as when a placeholder value changes. Of course, this could also be a downside, since you'll have to add some conditional logic to filter out what you don't want.

In the BOTS Consulting site, we've created a generic handler to log events to a text file. This is not a terribly realistic example, but we wanted to demonstrate how CMS workflow events fire; the best way to do that is to write a simple log program, which writes out all the events along with the particular object information. In our example, we're using a function we wrote to write a string to a file called BOTSLog.TXT.

In Listing 31–2, we've provided the generic event handler that logs the events to the event log. We've not provided the code to write to the text file, since that's a little out of scope for this example.

**Listing 31–2** Generic event handler

```
public void CmsPosting_Changing( Object sender, ChangingEventArgs e )
{
WriteLogEntry("A CHANGING event fired because a (an) "
        + e.Target.ToString() + " fired a " + e.Action.ToString().ToUpper()
        + " event.");
}
```

Although the example in Listing 31–2 isn't terribly complex, it does yield some interesting results. The log entries it produces give us insight into how CMS fires events. To test this code, we're going to create a new press release in the Press channel of BOTS. The Press Release Detail template has four HTML placeholders and one image placeholder. Based on this information, we should expect a number of events to fire. Remember, we're actually only catching this information in the Changing event, which means that everything we have in the log is only half of the transaction; this code will fire before any state changes occur, but doesn't log anything for the after event. The log output is provided in Listing 31–3 (we've numbered this list to make it more readable).

**Listing 31–3** The log output from the Changing event handler

```
1. A CHANGING event fired because a (an)
Microsoft.ContentManagement.Publishing.Channel fired a CREATE event.
2. A CHANGING event fired because a (an)
Microsoft.ContentManagement.Publishing.Posting fired a PROPERTYCHANGE event.
3. A CHANGING event fired because a (an)
Microsoft.ContentManagement.Publishing.Posting fired a PROPERTYCHANGE event.
4. A CHANGING event fired because a (an)
Microsoft.ContentManagement.Publishing.Extensions.Placeholders.
HtmlPlaceholder fired a PLACEHOLDERPROPERTYCHANGE event.
5. A CHANGING event fired because a (an)
Microsoft.ContentManagement.Publishing.Extensions.Placeholders.
HtmlPlaceholder fired a PLACEHOLDERPROPERTYCHANGE event.
6. A CHANGING event fired because a (an)
Microsoft.ContentManagement.Publishing.Extensions.Placeholders.
HtmlPlaceholder fired a PLACEHOLDERPROPERTYCHANGE event.
7. A CHANGING event fired because a (an)
Microsoft.ContentManagement.Publishing.Extensions.Placeholders.
ImagePlaceholder fired a PLACEHOLDERPROPERTYCHANGE event.
```

```
8. A CHANGING event fired because a (an)
Microsoft.ContentManagement.Publishing.Extensions.Placeholders.
ImagePlaceholder fired a PLACEHOLDERPROPERTYCHANGE event.
9. A CHANGING event fired because a (an)
Microsoft.ContentManagement.Publishing.Extensions.Placeholders.
ImagePlaceholder fired a PLACEHOLDERPROPERTYCHANGE event.
10. A CHANGING event fired because a (an)
Microsoft.ContentManagement.Publishing.Extensions.Placeholders.
HtmlPlaceholder fired a PLACEHOLDERPROPERTYCHANGE event.
```

What you should notice immediately is that there were more PlaceholderPropertyChange events than placeholders in our template (remember, we only have four in the press release template). What's going on here? Well, keep in mind that the Changing event fires anytime something changes in CMS. In this case, it appears that the image placeholder has more properties that change during the Save. To find out which properties are changing, we've added a specific handler to our Global.ASAX file.

### Writing a Specific Handler

Writing a generic handler is pretty easy, and, as you saw in our earlier example, you can get at a lot of information. However, you end up seeing literally everything that happens. Sometimes this is desirable, but in most cases you'll want to simply concentrate on specific events. In this case, you need to add a signature for the specific event.

Continuing our work with the press release template and the generic handler we already wrote, we've added a specific handler to get a closer look at the PlaceholderPropertyChanging events we saw. In our Global. ASAX, we've added the CmsPosting_PlaceholderPropertyChanging function and a reference to our WriteLogEntry function. This will allow us to gather more specific information about the events we were seeing in the Changing handler. In Listing 31–4 you can see exactly what we did.

**Listing 31–4** The new code in our PlaceholderPropertyChanging event

```
public void CmsPosting_PlaceholderPropertyChanging( Object sender,
PropertyChangingEventArgs e )
{
    WriteLogEntry("The PLACEHOLDERPROPERTYCHANGING event fired because "
        + ((Placeholder)e.Target).Name
        + "'s " + e.PropertyName + " property changed.");
}
```

After we added the code and looked in the log, we ended up with the output shown in Listing 31–5.

**Listing 31–5** Additional log data

```
1. A CHANGING event fired because a (an)
Microsoft.ContentManagement.Publishing.Channel fired a CREATE event.
2. A CHANGING event fired because a (an)
Microsoft.ContentManagement.Publishing.Posting fired a PROPERTYCHANGE event.
3. A CHANGING event fired because a (an)
Microsoft.ContentManagement.Publishing.Posting fired a PROPERTYCHANGE event.
4. The PLACEHOLDERPROPERTYCHANGING event fired because Calendar's Html
property changed.
5. A CHANGING event fired because a (an)
Microsoft.ContentManagement.Publishing.Extensions.Placeholders.
HtmlPlaceholder fired a PLACEHOLDERPROPERTYCHANGE event.
6. The PLACEHOLDERPROPERTYCHANGING event fired because BodyCopy's Html
property changed.
7. A CHANGING event fired because a (an)
Microsoft.ContentManagement.Publishing.Extensions.Placeholders.
HtmlPlaceholder fired a PLACEHOLDERPROPERTYCHANGE event.
8. The PLACEHOLDERPROPERTYCHANGING event fired because Disclaimer's Html
property changed.
9. A CHANGING event fired because a (an)
Microsoft.ContentManagement.Publishing.Extensions.Placeholders.
HtmlPlaceholder fired a PLACEHOLDERPROPERTYCHANGE event.
10. The PLACEHOLDERPROPERTYCHANGING event fired because CallOutImage's Src
property changed.
11. A CHANGING event fired because a (an)
Microsoft.ContentManagement.Publishing.Extensions.Placeholders.
ImagePlaceholder fired a PLACEHOLDERPROPERTYCHANGE event.
12. The PLACEHOLDERPROPERTYCHANGING event fired because CallOutImage's Alt
property changed.
```

```
13. A CHANGING event fired because a (an)
Microsoft.ContentManagement.Publishing.Extensions.Placeholders.
ImagePlaceholder fired a PLACEHOLDERPROPERTYCHANGE event.
14. The PLACEHOLDERPROPERTYCHANGING event fired because CallOutImage's Href
property changed.
15. A CHANGING event fired because a (an)
Microsoft.ContentManagement.Publishing.Extensions.Placeholders.
ImagePlaceholder fired a PLACEHOLDERPROPERTYCHANGE event.
16. The PLACEHOLDERPROPERTYCHANGING event fired because CallOutImageCaption's
Html property changed.
17. A CHANGING event fired because a (an)
Microsoft.ContentManagement.Publishing.Extensions.Placeholders.
HtmlPlaceholder fired a PLACEHOLDERPROPERTYCHANGE event.
```

So, as you can see, we were right about the properties. It appears that the image placeholder has three properties that change when a posting saves: ALT, HREF, and SRC. As a result, the changing event would fire three separate times, once for each property change. When you put all this together, the log shows the PlaceholderPropertyChanging event, followed by the more generic Changing event just as we predicted.

Now, it's possible to accomplish everything we've done here in the more generic handler. However, as we mentioned earlier, accomplishing everything we did here in the Changing event, for example, would require us to better qualify the event arguments—determining the object's type and then casting it. By using the PlaceholderPropertyChanging event, we already know we're getting a placeholder back, and the base placeholder type provides us with a way to get to most of the properties we need to make other decisions, such as the name or even the posting. Of course, if you need a specific property, you'll have to cast it to a more specific placeholder type, like HtmlPlaceholder, ImagePlaceholder, or AttachmentPlaceholder.

## Creating Custom HTTP Modules

Although using the HTTP module that CMS provides is generally the easiest to implement, you can also write a custom HTTP module. A custom HTTP module is implemented as a new class and can be used across CMS solutions. Building on the example we provided in the previous section, we're going to write a custom module for the PlaceholderProperty Changing event. We'll use the same code, but it will be contained in our new HTTP module class.

The first step is to add a new project to our BOTS Consulting solution. Once we have our new project, we need to add a new class. In our example, we've called our new class CMSPlaceholderPropertyChanging. The new class will inherit from IHttpModule. Because we're creating a custom module, we'll have to write an Init and a Dispose function to wire up the right event to our class. Again, we're going to wire up our class to the PlaceholderPropertyChanging event. In Listing 31–6 we've provided the code for our new class, and in Listing 31–7 you can see the modified log output, showing the influence of the new HTTP module.

**Listing 31–6** The new HTTP module class

```
using System;
using System.IO;
using System.Web;
using Microsoft.ContentManagement.Publishing;
using Microsoft.ContentManagement.Publishing.Events;
using Microsoft.ContentManagement.Publishing.Extensions;

namespace botsconsulting.Classes
{
    /// <summary>
    /// CMSPlaceholderPropertyChanging is a custom HTTP module for handling
    /// a placeholder property change.  It writes a line in a text file
    /// for every PlaceholderPropertyChangingEvent that occurs.
    /// </summary>
    public class CMSPlaceholderPropertyChanging : IHttpModule
    {

        // Implement the mandatory Init and Dispose functions
        public void Init(HttpApplication myEventContext)
        {
            PostingEvents myEvent = PostingEvents.Current;
            myEvent.PlaceholderPropertyChanging += new
PropertyChangingEventHandler(this.OnPlaceholderPropertyChanging);
        }
        public void Dispose()
        {
            PostingEvents myEvent = PostingEvents.Current;
            myEvent.PlaceholderPropertyChanging -= new
PropertyChangingEventHandler(this.OnPlaceholderPropertyChanging);
        }
```

```
            // Create a delegate for the event and a private
            // member variable to hold a reference to the event
            public delegate void CUSTOMPlaceholderPropertyChanging(Object
sender, PropertyChangingEventArgs e);
            private CUSTOMPlaceholderPropertyChanging myCMSHandler = null;

            // Wire up the event
            public event CUSTOMPlaceholderPropertyChanging
MyNewPlaceholderPropertyChangingEvent
            {
                add{myCMSHandler += value;}
                remove{myCMSHandler -=value;}
            }

            // Create the actual custom event logic.  In this case, we're
writing
            // to our BOTSLog as we did in the Global.ASAX example.
            public void OnPlaceholderPropertyChanging(Object sender,
PropertyChangingEventArgs e)
            {
                WriteLogEntry("CUSTOM HTTP MODULE - The
PLACEHOLDERPROPERTYCHANGING event fired because "
                    + ((Placeholder)e.Target).Name
                    + "'s " + e.PropertyName + " property changed.");
            }

            // The WriteLogEntry function for actually writing to the
            // text file
            private void WriteLogEntry(string eventLogEntry)
            {
                StreamWriter myLogfile = new
StreamWriter("c:\\BOTSLog.txt",true);
                myLogFile.WriteLine(System.DateTime.Now.ToString() + " :: "
+ eventLogEntry);
                myLogFile.Close();
            }

    }

}
```

Before your new HTTP module will operate properly within your solution, you must register it in the Web.Config file. This is something we covered in the Global.ASAX section. For the new module we just created, this is what we needed to add to our Web.Config file in the <httpModules> section:

```
<add type="botsconsulting.Classes.CMSPlaceholderPropertyChanging,
botsconsulting" name="myCustomEvent"/>
```

Once you've added the registration to Web.Config, you can run your solution. In our example, we ended up with the log entries shown in Listing 31–7 (we've only included a sampling of the output for brevity).

**Listing 31–7** The modified log output

```
1. A CHANGING event fired because a (an)
Microsoft.ContentManagement.Publishing.Extensions.Placeholders.
ImagePlaceholder fired a PLACEHOLDERPROPERTYCHANGE event.
2. CUSTOM HTTP MODULE--The PLACEHOLDERPROPERTYCHANGING event fired because
CallOutImage's Href property changed.
3. The PLACEHOLDERPROPERTYCHANGING event fired because CallOutImage's Href
property changed.
4. A CHANGING event fired because a (an)
Microsoft.ContentManagement.Publishing.Extensions.Placeholders.
ImagePlaceholder fired a PLACEHOLDERPROPERTYCHANGE event.
5. CUSTOM HTTP MODULE--The PLACEHOLDERPROPERTYCHANGING event fired because
CallOutImageCaption's Html property changed.
6. The PLACEHOLDERPROPERTYCHANGING event fired because CallOutImageCaption's
Html property changed.
7. A CHANGING event fired because a (an)
Microsoft.ContentManagement.Publishing.Extensions.Placeholders.
HtmlPlaceholder fired a PLACEHOLDERPROPERTYCHANGE event.
```

As you can see from Listing 31–7, our code in Listing 31–6 produced the same result as the code we added to Global.ASAX. We modified the log-writing statement slightly to highlight which lines were produced by our custom module verses the code that still remains in Global.ASAX.

# Best Practices for Extending Workflow

As with any development activity, there are some guiding principles for extending the CMS workflow. We have provided a few that we had to learn the hard way.

## Know What You're Doing

If you change posting properties during a workflow process, make sure you know what you're doing. This sounds like a simple piece of advice, but experience has shown that even if you *think* you know what you're doing, you still may be surprised by the result. Here are two examples.

- Making changes to objects in the workflow events may initiate the firing of an event. For example, if you change the name of a Posting object, it will fire the PostingPropertyChanging and Posting PropertyChanged event. Improperly implementing property changes causes a PublishingEventRecursiveHandlerException. Refer to the CMS 2002 documentation for the best practice when you are implementing property changes inside a workflow event.
- Certain properties are tied to certain roles, which may adversely impact the flow of a posting. For example, all content is the responsibility of the editor. If, during the workflow process, you change the value of a placeholder, for example, you could inadvertently change the state of a posting. If you change the value during the Submit event, you could revert the posting to a Saved state. Although this is inconvenient for the author and the editor, it's easily solved by resubmitting the posting programmatically; the site will remain unaffected. However, if you change a page property like the startdate, you've now effectively removed the posting from the production site, if it's an existing posting. The reason is that the page properties are not versioned, and page property changes require moderator approval before the posting can be published.

## Limit Notifications

Don't overdo notification. E-mail notifications are a nice feature to have. In fact, it's probably the most commonly implemented extension to the workflow (a code sample is provided in the Microsoft documentation). However, as you saw, a workflow event may fire more than once for a single operation. As a result, if you're not paying attention, you could inadvertently send multiple e-mail messages for the same action. Taking this a step further, consider a situation where you have tens or hundreds of authors and somewhat fewer editors. If you have an e-mail sent out for every submission, an e-mail could potentially be sent to every editor responsible for that channel (remember, roles are assigned per channel, and therefore events that fire notifications would only affect the groups assigned to that channel). The amount of e-mail generated from one author's activities is manageable. E-mail from the activities of even 20 authors may be overwhelming. Try creating some very specific business rules that govern how e-mail is sent, or provide a feature to allow editors to turn off e-mail notifications if they so desire. Alternatively, consider providing notifications through some other mechanism, such as tasks in Outlook. You'll still have to manage the volume, but tasks aren't as intrusive as e-mails.

### Wait for a While

Consider making no changes to the standard workflow process until you've had CMS in production for a while. It may sound counterintuitive, but you may find that "requirements" for workflow that business users initially communicated during the requirements phase aren't entirely accurate. Given the work involved in coding extensions to workflow, you should allow the system to run without extensions for some period of time. This will allow your business users to become accustomed to the tool and help you better understand how the users really work.

## Summary

In this chapter we examined how to extend the standard workflow in CMS. We started with a basic review of the various posting states. In essence, extending CMS workflow is about controlling the native states of a posting. Then, we discussed the various workflow events where you can code your business-specific logic. These events allow you to catch specific events and actions, binding them to your particular business process. Once the groundwork was laid, we demonstrated two different approaches to writing custom workflow extensions—one using the Global.ASAX file and standard event handlers, the other using custom HTTP modules. Finally, we discussed a few best practices for implementing your business logic within the workflow events of CMS.

# Publishing Dynamic Data in CMS

## Overview

A very common question from CMS users is, "How do I include dynamic data in my CMS application?" This data could come from other systems or straight from an external database. Often, there's a need to include this content as part of a template or a posting. However, this question is often posed in the context of how someone would integrate an application with CMS—existing ASP or ASP.NET pages that contain some unique functionality. Fundamentally, there isn't a straight answer. The decision of whether to integrate an existing application or dynamically display context inside of a CMS template needs further investigation.

In this chapter, we'll provide a framework for helping you decide how and what to include in a CMS-based application. We'll demonstrate a few examples of how to update placeholders with an external data source and how to simply display that content on a template.

## Why Would You Want to Integrate?

In a lot of cases, companies that are going to implement CMS for one Web application have several others that may or may not be migrated in the future. Often, these "legacy" Web sites have a great deal of functionality or are meant for one purpose, as opposed to an intranet that may be a collection of a number of different sites. Given how CMS operates, it's difficult to decide why and how you might consider re-writing these legacy sites using CMS. In some cases, it won't make sense to rewrite these applications; in other cases, it will. How do you decide?

CMS provides a rich environment for creating and maintaining Web sites. Conceptually, it's based on the idea that a developer will create a template, which will then be used by multiple authors to create some number of pages. Ideally, these templates will be used more than once across the site. A press release template, for example, could potentially be used for hundreds of postings. A summary template similarly could be used multiple times across the site. However, what if you had a phone directory application, for example? A very common interface for a phone directory is one ASP or ASP.NET page that allows a user to look up the phone number of a fellow employee. Do you write a template to replace the stand-alone ASP or ASP.NET page?

One of the basic questions of whether to convert an existing application involves reuse. Since CMS uses templates to create pages, the question really becomes, Does it make sense to develop a template for one posting? Further, if that template doesn't use any CMS functionality, is it worth the effort? Both questions are very relevant to the decision process; CMS is good for a lot of functions, but it doesn't fit in every circumstance. Here are some basic guidelines that you can use to help you decide whether to rewrite your existing applications or keep them outside of CMS.

*How many times could you reuse the template(s)?* Integration of an existing application really means that you'll create templates in CMS that contain the rewritten application's functionality. In other words, if you have a phone directory application that allows users to look up employees, you'll have to write CMS templates that perform the same function. Once you've built the templates, postings will have to be created within your site. Can you use those templates elsewhere? In this example, probably not. If you find that it's not possible or practical to reuse the templates you would create for the application, you might consider leaving it alone. However, if you could create one template that could be used across your site, it might be worth the effort. For example, instead of having one phone directory page for the entire company, perhaps you could create a template that allows a content contributor to specify a scope for the search. Maybe the template you create will be deployed for a divisional microsite instead of the whole company. This way each department could have its own employee directory page that searches just that department's employees. The same template could also be used at a higher level in the intranet for a more global search. Although this is essentially adding more functionality to the page, the additional functionality enables that template to be reused across the site, potentially providing needed flexibility as you turn over site management to content contributors. Also, instead of having a dedicated page for the phone directory, you could create a reduced interface that consists of just a first and last name field, which would be implemented as a user or server control. This new control could then be added to all templates in your CMS application.

*How much could you leverage from CMS?* Frankly, if you're going to rewrite your application in CMS, you should get benefit from it. At a very basic level, you can inherit the design of the site as well as the navigation. Your application can look just like all the other pages in your site. Plus if it moves or other pages in the site move, CMS will handle updating the navigation without your having to rewrite any code. Is there anything else? If we use the phone directory example, there could be some introductory text or field labels that could be turned into placeholders, allowing contributors to customize the form. We're not suggesting that you should "force" some change to the application to leverage CMS, but you do have some opportunities with CMS that may not have existed before.

*Are content contributors going to create instances of the application?* Sometimes, an application can exist in more than one place, or perhaps the application always produces one result, based on parameters. Our phone directory application is one example of potential reuse of the code across the site. However, suppose that you have code that creates a pie chart based on sales data from an ERP system or a database. If you have a number of groups wanting to include that kind of functionality in your site, it may be a good candidate for a template. You can build a template that allows content contributors to specify the parameters they want to use during the authoring process. At runtime, the code produces the appropriate pie chart. A variation on this would be to create a custom placeholder, which can be used across a number of templates.

*Would it be useful for content contributors to browse to the application?* If your application is a posting inside of CMS, users not only have the ability to create a hyperlink to the posting using the browse feature, but the application will automatically be included in the navigation. In this way, if the application moves, content contributors don't have to worry about modifying their content; CMS will automatically update all the links. This is true of "manually" created links or links that may have been programmatically rendered. This feature is especially useful when multiple links to an application may exist within your Web site.

*How much processing does the existing application do?* CMS necessarily adds overhead to a site. No matter how efficient any tool is, there is always additional processing that's required. That said, will the overhead of CMS be outweighed by the benefits it brings? If your existing application is processor intensive, you may not want to add an additional load. This is especially true if you're not able to leverage CMS in the application itself.

*If you're integrating data with CMS, how often does the data change?* CMS is indeed a dynamic solution. It dynamically generates a posting, based on the content in placeholders and the template. However, placeholder content doesn't usually change from view to view of the posting, unless an author changes the content. The data from this other system or database, conversely, may change frequently. Integrating data from an external system could mean programmatically filling placeholder values with the content from that external system or simply displaying the data as you would in any other Web application. If the data doesn't change that frequently or your business users want to have some workflow process to approve new content being published on the Web site, it may be appropriate to programmatically fill placeholder values. If your business users don't want to approve data changes or the data changes frequently, you may want to create a template without placeholders and simply place a data grid on the design surface, which will be filled at runtime. Again, you should consider template reuse. If the template you create for this data is only going to be used once, you may just simply want to leave it alone.

# Sample Integrations

As we suggested earlier in the chapter, there are a few ways to integrate CMS with your existing applications. To demonstrate what we mean, we've provided a couple of code samples to illustrate our point. The examples we've provided here are not an exhaustive list. In fact, our examples will probably be "best case" scenarios that probably don't exist in reality. However, the basics of each example should help you with your real integrations.

## Displaying Data from an External Data Source

Displaying dynamic data from an external source is a very common operation to perform within a Web application. Performing the same operation isn't fundamentally different in CMS. If anything, displaying data from a database is exactly the same in a CMS template as it is in an ASP. NET page, since CMS templates are in fact ASP.NET pages. However, to prove this point to you, we've provided a small example in Listing 32–1. In this listing, we demonstrate how to retrieve a record set from a database and display the result in a data grid control.

**Listing 32–1** Displaying external data in a data grid

```
using System;
using System.Collections;
using System.ComponentModel;
using System.Data;
using System.Data.OleDb;
using System.Drawing;
using System.Web;
using System.Web.SessionState;
using System.Web.UI;
using System.Web.UI.WebControls;
using System.Web.UI.HtmlControls;
using Microsoft.ContentManagement.Publishing;
namespace botsconsulting.Templates
{
    /// <summary>
    /// Summary description for generic.
    /// </summary>
    public class dataintegration : System.Web.UI.Page
    {
        protected Microsoft.ContentManagement.WebControls.RobotMetaTag
RobotMetaTag1;
        protected System.Web.UI.WebControls.Literal PageTitle;
        protected Microsoft.ContentManagement.WebControls.
SingleImagePlaceholderControl CallOut;
        protected Microsoft.ContentManagement.WebControls.
SingleImagePlaceholderControl CallOutImage;
        protected Microsoft.ContentManagement.WebControls.
HtmlPlaceholderControl CallOutImageCaption;
        protected System.Web.UI.WebControls.Literal BodyTitle;
        protected Microsoft.ContentManagement.WebControls.
HtmlPlaceholderControl BodyCopy;
        protected System.Web.UI.WebControls.DataGrid myDataGrid;
        protected botsconsulting.UserControls.header Header;
        private OleDbConnection myConnection;
        private void Page_Load(object sender, System.EventArgs e)
```

```
        {
                this.BodyTitle.Text = "<b>" +
CmsHttpContext.Current.Posting.DisplayName + "</b>";
                CreateOleDbConnection();
                BindDBtoDataGrid();
        }
        public void CreateOleDbConnection()
        {
                string myConnString = "Provider=SQLOLEDB.1;Integrated
Security=SSPI;Persist Security Info=False;Initial Catalog=Northwind;Data
Source=localhost;";
                myConnection = new OleDbConnection(myConnString);
        }
        public void BindDBtoDataGrid()
        {
                string myQuery = "Select LastName,FirstName,Title from
employees";
                OleDbCommand myCommand = new OleDbCommand(myQuery);
                myCommand.Connection = myConnection;
                myConnection.Open();
                myDataGrid.DataSource = myCommand.ExecuteReader();
                myDataGrid.DataBind();
                myCommand.Connection.Close();
        }
}
```

In this example, we connected to the Northwind database provided
with SQL Server. We selected all the records in the Employee table, displaying three columns in a data grid. Figure 32–1 shows what this template looks like with a posting in the BOTS Consulting site.

## Allowing Content Contributors to Select What Data Is Displayed

The earlier example is probably not a realistic example of what you
would do in an application. However, it does demonstrate that displaying
dynamic data in CMS isn't difficult. The real power, though, comes from
taking the previous example and building on it. Again, one of the reasons
you might integrate application code with a template is to provide content contributors with more flexibility in the deployment of that application. In this next example (Listing 32–2), we've created a custom

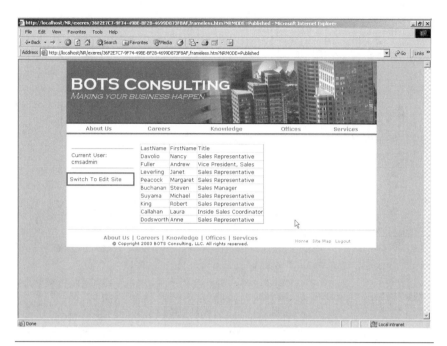

**Figure 32–1** Dynamic data template in the BOTS site

placeholder that allows a content contributor to determine which record to display on the live page.

**Listing 32–2** Using a custom placeholder to determine which record to display

```
using System;
using System.Data.OleDb;
using System.Web.UI;
using System.Web.UI.WebControls;
using System.ComponentModel;
using Microsoft.ContentManagement.Publishing.Extensions.Placeholders;
using Microsoft.ContentManagement.WebControls;
namespace botsconsultingwebcontrols
{
    /// <summary>
    /// Summary description for DropDownPlaceholderControl.
    /// </summary>
    [ToolboxData("<{0}:DataDrivenDropDownListPlaceholder
runat=server></{0}:DataDrivenDropDownListPlaceholder>")]
```

```
    public class DataDrivenDropDownListPlaceholder :
Microsoft.ContentManagement.WebControls.BasePlaceholderControl
    {

        protected System.Web.UI.WebControls.DropDownList IndustryList;
        protected System.Web.UI.WebControls.DataGrid SelectedEmployees;
        protected override void CreateAuthoringChildControls
(BaseModeContainer authoringContainer)
        {
            this.IndustryList = new DropDownList();
            this.IndustryList.Items.Add(new ListItem("Sales
Representative","Sales Representative"));
            this.IndustryList.Items.Add(new ListItem("Sales
Manager","Sales Manager"));
            this.IndustryList.Items.Add(new ListItem("Inside Sales
Coordinator","Inside Sales Coordinator"));
            this.IndustryList.Items.Add(new ListItem("Vice President,
Sales","Vice President, Sales"));
            this.IndustryList.EnableViewState = false;
            authoringContainer.Controls.Add(this.IndustryList);
        }
        protected override void SavePlaceholderContent
(PlaceholderControlSaveEventArgs e)
        {
            EnsureChildControls();
            try
            {
                ((HtmlPlaceholder)this.BoundPlaceholder).Html =
this.IndustryList.SelectedItem.Value.ToString();
            }
            catch (Exception ex)
            {
                string saveExceptionMessage = "Error saving
placeholder contents: " +
                    this.GetType().Name + " :: " + this.ID + " :: "
+ ex.Message;
                Exception saveException = new Exception
(saveExceptionMessage, ex);
                throw saveException;
            }
        }
        protected override void
LoadPlaceholderContentForAuthoring(PlaceholderControlEventArgs e)
        {
```

```
                    EnsureChildControls();
                    try
                    {
                            ListItem savedSelectedIndustry =
this.IndustryList.Items.FindByValue(((HtmlPlaceholder)this.BoundPlaceholder).
Text);
                            this.IndustryList.SelectedIndex =
this.IndustryList.Items.IndexOf(savedSelectedIndustry);
                    }
                    catch (Exception ex)
                    {
                            string saveExceptionMessage = "Error loading
placeholder contents: " +
                                    this.GetType().Name + " :: " + this.ID + " :: "
+ ex.Message;
                            Exception saveException = new Exception
(saveExceptionMessage, ex);
                            throw saveException;
                    }

            }
            protected override void CreatePresentationChildControls
(BaseModeContainer presentationContainer)
            {

                    SelectedEmployees = new DataGrid();
                    presentationContainer.Controls.Add(SelectedEmployees);

            }
            protected override void LoadPlaceholderContentForPresentation
(PlaceholderControlEventArgs e)
            {

                    EnsureChildControls();
                    try
                    {
                            // Grab the value from the placeholder
                            string mySelectedEmployees = ((HtmlPlaceholder)
this.BoundPlaceholder).Text;

                            // Open a new connect and perform a search for values
that match
                            // the save placeholder value
                            OleDbConnection myConnection;
```

```
                    string myConnString = "Provider=SQLOLEDB.1;Integrated
Security=SSPI;Persist Security Info=False;Initial Catalog=Northwind;Data
Source=localhost;";
                    myConnection = new OleDbConnection(myConnString);
                    string myQuery = "Select LastName,FirstName from
Employees where Title = '" + mySelectedEmployees + "';";
                    OleDbCommand myCommand = new OleDbCommand(myQuery);
                    myCommand.Connection = myConnection;
                    myConnection.Open();
                    // Fill the datagrid with the returned records
                    this.SelectedEmployees.DataSource =
myCommand.ExecuteReader();
                }
                catch (Exception ex)
                {
                    string saveExceptionMessage = "Error loading
placeholder contents: " +
                        this.GetType().Name + " :: " + this.ID + " :: "
+ ex.Message;
                    Exception saveException = new
Exception(saveExceptionMessage, ex);
                    throw saveException;
                }


        }
    }
}
```

In Listing 32–2 you can see how we fill the drop-down list box with
the four titles that exist in the Employee table. Then, during presentation, we perform a SQL query against the table to find all records that
have the selected value in the title field. In this way, the content contributor can select what employees they want to display based on the
employee title. We could have taken this a step further by filling the
drop-down list control with the actual values from the database as well.
The implementation you choose is up to you.

In Figures 32–2 and 32–3 you can see what each mode of the new
custom placeholder looks like.

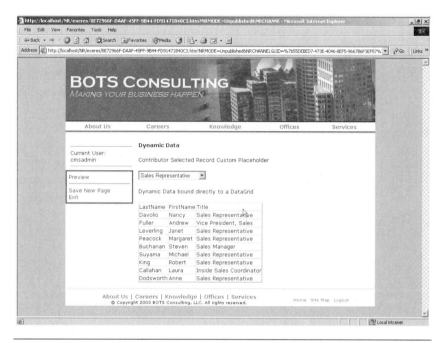

**Figure 32–2**  The new custom placeholder in authoring mode

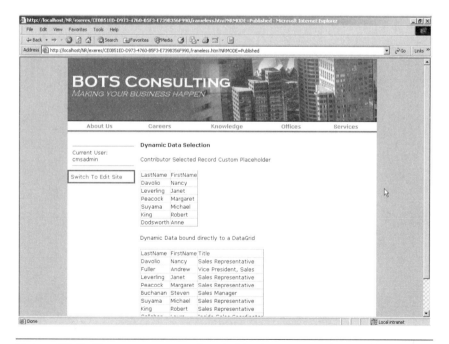

**Figure 32–3**  The new custom placeholder in presentation mode

## Summary

In this chapter we discussed how developers can integrate dynamic data or existing applications into a CMS-based solution. We discussed how you can go about determining whether it makes sense to integrate data or applications, posing a series of questions that you can ask as you consider the integration project. Next, we demonstrated two examples where we integrated dynamic data in a CMS template. The first example placed a data grid on a template and bound it to a data source. The next example extended the prior solution by allowing content contributors to select what data is displayed through the use of a custom placeholder.

# Web Services

For some time now, Web Services have been the buzzword technology that everyone is scrambling to support. For good reason—Web Services expose the inner workings of any application so they can work with external forces. Think of Web Services as a self-contained set of methods that can reside anywhere on the Internet and can be invoked remotely.

Web Services also bridge the technology gap. They offer a way for distributed applications to communicate from any platform or geographical location with any other platform or geographical location. Web Services are built on open protocols and standards. This makes it possible for any vendor to provide their version of a Web Service, and because they must follow the standards for their product to be classified as a Web Service, everyone can interact with it. For instance, communication is done over HTTP, a well-known, open protocol for communication. The method call and its parameters are done using SOAP, a well-known, open protocol for remote procedure calls based on XML, a well-known, open language for exchanging structured data. Since XML is just plain ASCII text, it can be generated and consumed by any platform regardless of programming language, Web server choice, or operating system. Web Services do require an HTTP (port 80) or HTTPS (port 443) exposure to the World Wide Web, also commonly, albeit inaccurately, referred to as the Internet (the Internet includes a much broader set of technologies, like FTP and SMTP). That global network is what makes Web Services compelling and is quite commonplace today in nearly every workplace and even most homes.

The World Wide Web also allows a Web Property's content to frequently be part of a much larger ecosystem with local, regional, and even global reach. Each partner uses different hardware and software enabled by disparate technologies and programming languages using diverse data stores. Trying to get tab A to squarely fit into slot B is a time-tested challenge. But the Internet introduced the world to connectivity unlike anything that preceded it. However, rampant use of that connectivity was hampered because of the unprecedented threat that same connectedness provides. Through it all, HTTP (port 80) remains the most ubiquitous stronghold for information exchange between parties anywhere, anytime. Out of that, Web Services emerged as a compelling means to allow the quasi-secure exchange of data throughout the global ecosystem.

This chapter explores how Web Services can be used by MCMS sites to exchange information. An entire alphabet soup of acronyms associated with Web Services is listed in Table 33–1, but we are not going to discuss them in depth.

Fortunately, we don't have to become experts in all these technologies to create a Web Service, because VS.NET and IIS handle much of

**Table 33–1** Web Services Acronym Soup Defined

| Acronym | Explanation | Use |
| --- | --- | --- |
| HTTP | HyperText Transport Protocol | This protocol allows us to send a SOAP message to a Web Service requesting information or processing, and allows the Web Service to send us a response. |
| SOAP | Simple Object Access Protocol | This includes the name of the method we want the Web Service to execute and any parameters we are passing to that method. |
| UDDI | Universal Data Description Interface | This centralized repository catalogs Web Services, allowing others to discover a Web Service we have written or for us to discover a Web Service that others have written. This works somewhat like the Yellow Pages. |
| WSDL | Web Service Definition Language | This describes the methods available from a Web Service, what protocols can be used to call them, what the methods do, what parameters are allowed or required, and what data type those parameters need to be so that our SOAP message can correctly call a specific Web Service method. |

**Table 37–5** *(Continued)*

| Acronym | Explanation | Use |
|---------|-------------|-----|
| WSIL | Web Service Inspection Language | This relative newcomer is similar to UDDI in that it allows for the discovery of Web Services, but it uses a decentralized model. This works more like a business card. In many ways, WSIL is like an RSS Weblog for Web Services. |
| XML | eXtensible Markup Language | This language follows a standard that can be validated, and although typically used to describe data, it is also used to format our SOAP message. |
| XSL | eXtensible Stylesheet Language | This language is used for creating a style sheet that describes how data sent over the Web using XML is to be presented to the user. |

the dirty work for us. For instance, although we will be using WSDL, SOAP, and XML in our code sample, we will hardly even know that they were needed. Anyway, much has been written about these standards and can be easily found on the Internet, should additional information about them be required.

## Common Uses

Web Services associated with a CMS Web Property are typically used for one of two purposes: syndication (conduction) to any platform or aggregation (consumption) from any platform.

However, the sky is the limit. Anything that can be done via the CMS Publishing API (PAPI) in a stand-alone application could theoretically be made available via a Web Service. So, for instance, if we wanted to create a Web Service that would provide the name and GUID of all postings that expire in the next week, we could do that from any application that could call our Web Service. Further, if we wanted to create a Web

Service that allowed our customer to change the ExpiryDate of one of those postings, we could do that. So, common use may lie in the eye of the beholder.

That said, we are going to focus on the two purposes mentioned at the beginning of this segment. From a technical perspective, these two scenarios are distinguished by whether the CMS system will be the publisher or the consumer of Web Services. If it is syndicating its data, it will be the publisher, and if it is aggregating, it will be the consumer.

## Content Syndication

Syndication can be defined as a distribution of information to various destinations for repurposing or republishing in another context. Noncomputer examples of syndication include the sale of a comic strip, column, television series, or movie for simultaneous republication in newspapers, periodicals, independent television stations, or theaters. The content typically remains the same, but the advertising surrounding the content, the placement or presentation of the content, or even the purpose of the content may be altered.

Syndication is accomplished by replicating data across systems, commonly done as a batch process running at a fixed time interval. This causes duplication of data across systems and creates a potential disconnect between the data being used by the destination applications and the up-to-date data held by the source system. This solution can be complex to manage but is often required to meet the business need.

Syndication can also be accomplished by creating a real-time interaction between applications. This can lead to fresh reuse of content without resorting to "screen scraping" or manual cutting and pasting. Usage of the syndicated content may create potential subscription fee revenue.

Far more scenarios exist (see the Decisions That Must Be Made section), but whatever method is employed, CMS syndicated content is typically only available when it has been approved for publishing.

## Content Aggregation

Aggregation is the flip side of syndication. It can be defined as a collection of related information from various sources for repurposing or republishing in another context. Today aggregators typically gather syndicated content into an indexed, searchable, and potentially categorized collection of links to that content. That content can be displayed in a homogeneous user interface with all relevant data presented simultaneously. This allows a user to visit a single site and interact with content from many sites. Since large volumes of data can be automatically collected, the user can filter and search for just the content that they want to view. The information can be summarized or repurposed, as previously described. Also, since the aggregator collects new content continuously, the site can stay as fresh as its freshest syndicate. For large, effective aggregators, that can mean a Web site that changes very rapidly.

## Decisions That Must Be Made

When content is to be syndicated, there are several decisions that must be made in order to determine the best means of sharing that content. These decisions can have a significant impact on the success of the syndication. These are not necessarily presented in any order, since the importance of each decision is dependent on the situation. What is a good choice in one situation may be a poor choice in another situation.

### Redundant versus Centralized

It will be important to decide whether the content that is syndicated will be copied to the aggregator or kept in a central store. Making a redundant copy of the data requires a repository and space at the aggregator. If the content changes or is removed, the change may need to be reflected in the copy. This can become quite complex if there are multiple aggregators. That could certainly lead to synchronization issues and potentially lead to stale or even inaccurate content. If the content doesn't change (such as a comic strip), this is less of an issue.

There is also the potential for alternative utility of the aggregated data. Once data is gathered together from various sources, it can become quite compelling. For instance, there is a certain utility for our credit card holder to know when we've never made a late payment. But when all our creditors aggregate their individual payment experiences into a credit bureau, that collective information has a utility that wasn't available to the credit card company before it was centralized.

However, there is a compelling argument for having a single source of truth that all aggregators simply point to. Practically every Web site has links to other content. If every Web site were required to keep a copy of the information that they currently only point to, practically every Web site would become unmanageable within one day. Also, if the content needs a high level of security, spreading copies of it around will certainly increase the risk that it may be exposed. Using a single source will typically provide a more consistent set of information, especially if there are complex or proprietary algorithms that must be performed.

### Scheduled versus Real Time

Almost all Web Properties have peak times when their hardware is pushed to its limit and other times when it is nearly idle. God willing, we spend more time at peak than at idle. However, it may be necessary to have information scheduled to be copied locally at times when the servers are not busy so that the content is available locally when the servers are busy. Sometimes, performance is key, especially if the data needed is voluminous. Imagine if we wrote a Web Service to retrieve all products sold at the local grocery in the last quarter so that we could show the top ten–selling products to our customer. If someone is waiting at the other end of that query, they may want to go get a cup of coffee or have lunch. Getting that content the night before and interacting with local, potentially even summarized data would significantly improve the experience. Trend analysis or other complex calculations that require the context of other content are good candidates for scheduled syndication.

However, sometimes, regardless of the performance hit, real-time, up-to-date information is key. Imagine if our stockbroker used last night's price for the stock we wanted to buy today, or if our bookie used yesterday's odds for the race we want to bet on today. Not good. These situations require the freshest information possible. However, they need good designs to prevent latency or, worse, unavailability. How many bets do you think the bookie will take if ten minutes before race time he loses access to the odds? We also might want to use real-time access if we only care about a small unanticipatable portion of a large data set. If our customer only looks at their balance once every six months, it would probably be overkill to schedule the move of every customer balance every 20 minutes so that it would be current when they asked. A real-time lookup on a central repository would likely be the best solution in that case.

### Push versus Pull

Whether the content will be sent to the syndicate or retrieved by the aggregator can potentially be one of the most difficult decisions that must be made. Politics, turf, security, clout, relationship, profit, trust, the number of potential consumers, who holds the biggest stick, who had the idea, technical savvy, how often the content could change, and a whole host of other factors (including all the other factors discussed in this section) can influence this decision. If the content owner wants to control precisely what content is going to be syndicated, to whom, and when that content should be available, they will probably opt to push their content. The more complex those rules get, the more likely it will be pushed. The push will typically be synchronous with an event at the syndicate, and the aggregator will have little control over the timing of the receipt of that content. However, the aggregator will probably store that information redundantly for instant availability when it is requested by their customer, and the information will probably be as fresh as it can be.

On the other hand, if the interaction needs to be at the behest of the consumer, a pull model will need to be created. It wouldn't make any sense for a company to push their stock price out to every partner every time it changed. That content would most likely be pulled by the partner when it was needed. It also wouldn't make sense for a bank to push every transactional change out to all their branches in anticipation that one of their customers may walk into that branch. The branch would selectively pull that content when they needed it.

### Private versus Open Access

The decision about who will be allowed access to this content will typically be far more cut and dried. If we need to control who gains access to the content, it will need to be private. It may even be fee based (that is the compelling promise of Web Services for some industries). If Gartner (example of private content) started giving away its analysis to the public, their current revenue model would have to change. Likewise, if Google (example of open access content) started charging for each search, their current revenue model would have to change. In fact, neither would likely survive the change.

### RSS versus Web Service

RSS (Really Simple Syndication, created by Netscape and championed by UserLand, or RDF Site Summary, based upon a Web standard for metadata called RDF) is an XML-based standard format that allows the syndication of lists of hyperlinks along with other information, or metadata, that helps viewers decide whether they want to follow the link. Any list-oriented content—such as news headlines, press releases, job listings, conference calendars, and rankings (like top ten lists), to list a few—is a good candidate for an RSS feed. Powerful tools exist for consuming aggregated RSS feeds, but most require an existing aggregator. Although there are thousands of RSS feeds on a wide variety of topics, there must be a groundswell of public interest in syndicating the same type of content before aggregating it makes sense. So, there is wide adoption in some sectors, while there is no adoption in others. We'd be more likely to find a deep and fresh channel about a rock star than we would about airline ticket prices.

With Web Service syndication, anything is possible. That can actually make it more difficult to get a groundswell of people sharing content about the same thing. Although Web Services are based upon standards, their implementation is typically very proprietary. There are growing means by which aggregators can consolidate content from Web Services, but public adoption is more difficult because there isn't the same kind of strict standards with regard to content organization as there is with RSS. However, partner (B2B) adoption is high for proprietary solutions.

### Partial versus Complete

This decision will likely be determined based upon the size of the content universe and the need for the aggregator to have the complete set of content available. As with push versus pull, a large number of external influencers could make this decision difficult. However, typically it will make sense to provide access either to a single item or segment of the content or to all of it. Certainly, our bank isn't going to allow us to access all the accounts when we pull transactional content into our accounting software. It may be all of our content, but it isn't all of the bank's content. If the data is relatively volatile, syndicating only the altered content would be impractical. It would probably make more sense to send the entire universe of data to a redundant store each evening. However, direct, real-time access to specific content could be the best way to handle content that tends to be highly volatile. If we take a cue from RSS, it may be good to syndicate pointers, URLs, or IDs to the actual content. The aggregator would then funnel the user through to the source if their interest was piqued with the teaser.

### Add versus Add/Change/Delete

Like the examples given at the beginning of this discussion, some content never changes. Consider a comic strip—once it is syndicated, changes do not occur. The same is true of a newspaper column, press release, transcript, school report card, lab test results, and lots of other content. Content that doesn't change is obviously easier to syndicate. Once it is out, it needs no maintenance. It can live in as many repositories as it finds its way into because the source system never needs to alter it. This is by far the most prevalent kind of syndication in place today.

However, for other content, change or removal is likely or other maintenance may be necessary. If the syndicate must be privy to the whereabouts of its syndicated content at all times so that they can keep it current, they will likely need an add/change/delete strategy. In essence, transactional syndication will probably require an approach that allows the syndicate to maintain any redundant copies with methods that allow alteration and deletion of previously syndicated content.

## Horizontal or Vertical (Who Cares?)

Much ado is frequently made about whether a Web Service is horizontal or vertical to CMS. The evaluation is somewhat subjective and there isn't a significant benefit to knowing whether a Web Service is horizontal or vertical. Nevertheless, two questions need to be answered.

- Is the Web Service interface generic enough to be used for any CMS application or not?
- Does the consumer need intimate knowledge of the underlying CMS application or not?

Basically, if the interface is so specific that the consumer doesn't need to know much about your application, it is considered a vertical Web Service (exaggerated example of a vertical WebMethod: GetYahoo PressReleasesForYear(string yearToRetrieve)). But if the interface is very generic, requiring the consumer to have an intimate knowledge of your CMS application information architecture, it is considered a horizontal Web Service because it is similar to PAPI in its style (exaggerated example of a horizontal WebMethod: GetPostings(string postingChannel Path, string postingClient, string postingType, string postingYear, string optionalPostingID)). Figure 33–1 attempts to illustrate these classifications pictorially.

## Web Service Security

Can I secure my Web Service? This is controversial at best, and many people do not think enough attention has been given to this topic. Web Services give anyone with access to the Internet the potentially published (UDDI, WSIL) and certainly discoverable (WSDL) detailed

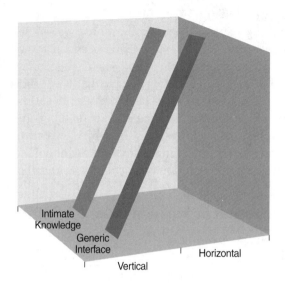

Intimate
Knowledge

Generic
Interface

Horizontal

Vertical

**Figure 33–1** Horizontal or vertical Web Service

information necessary to invoke code on our publicly accessible servers. It stands to reason that we may want to restrict that access to specific people. We may even want to charge for it. We certainly want to minimize the likelihood that malicious attacker(s) could wreak havoc or worse on those servers.

Almost everything about this topic is well beyond the scope of this chapter. Suffice it to say that in the Microsoft environment that CMS runs in, all the customary means available to secure a traditional Web site are available to secure a Web Service. These include, but are not limited to, the following:

- IIS virtual directory–based security using Windows: Basic, Digest, or Integrated Windows authentication (NTLM or Kerberos) or restricting by IP address.
- .NET Framework–based security using Windows: Basic, Digest, or Integrated Windows authentication (NTLM or Kerberos) in conjunction with IIS, Microsoft Passport authentication, Forms, or Client Certificates.
- Third-party digital certificate–based security.
- Windows file system–based security using role- or user-based Access Control Lists (ACLs), which implies the use of Windows authentication.

- SQL Server role- and user-based security. (Note that CMS uses a specific database user to access the CMS database, and the CMS database structure is internal to Microsoft and not documented for public consumption or alteration. Direct access to the CMS data structures is not supported by Microsoft.) However, it is possible to keep highly restricted data in a separate database and control access using built-in SQL Server security on that data store.

Of course, we could (and many do) build our own proprietary security methods, storing the credentials of valid users in LDAP, a database, or the file system and managing access to Web Services using code written specifically for this purpose.

Other means of protecting access to your assets could include the following:

- Encryption: .NET provides strong encryption algorithms, or you can simply encrypt the entire communication via SSL.
- Obfuscation: Don't publish, describe, or name your Web Service anything that would help a user know what to expect from it. Remove the WSDL, and require a private object structure that only your partners know. Use an IP address with no domain attached to it.
- Restrict physical access: Configure hardware appliances such as a firewall, router, or NIC card to only allow access under certain conditions. Keep the servers under lock and key and out of public areas.
- Monitor: Implement an Intrusion Detection System (IDS) that can write rules to keep out known-to-be-bad packet requests (remember NIMDA) and to watch for patterns of abuse and automatically block Denial Of Service (DOS)-like attacks on any element of a Web Property, including a Web Service.

These are but a few of the techniques in the arsenal of security mechanisms that could be deployed to protect our Web Service.

For the code sample in this chapter, we will use IIS Integrated Windows authentication, populating the SoapHttpClientProtocol.Credentials property with the value stored in CredentialCache.DefaultCredentials for the currently logged-in user. This way we can be sure that security is not a hindrance to learning about the topic at hand. Since we are running these examples on a single box, the credentials for one system can easily be shared by the other system. We will, however, follow the best practice of creating a Web Service in a separate Web application from CMS so that different security settings can be applied.

Of course, some Web Services will need to be offered to the anonymous public, and that is possible too. CMS will need guest access enabled, the guest user will need the authority to do whatever the Web Service requires, and IIS will need anonymous access enabled.

# Setup for Coding CMS Web Services

The code sample in this chapter assumes that managing CMS assets (Channels, Postings, Templates, and so on) in a Web Property is understood and a good portion of the CMS PAPI is instinctive. Therefore, screen shots will only be shown for results and directives specific to this chapter. Please refer to other chapters in this book for CMS non–Web Service details. Also, the simple error handling in the code throughout the code sample isn't meant to be the model for how to handle CMS exceptions; there is an application code block from Microsoft on how to do exception handling in .NET.

But before we can begin coding our Web Services, we need to do a little setup work. The BOTS Consulting Web site already has a channel structure and navigation that will accommodate what we will call Job Offerings. However, there are currently no general, summary, or detail templates or postings in that section of the BOTS Web site. So we will need to create them. Not to worry—we'll keep it very simple.

---

**NOTE:** You don't need to have BOTS to create the code in this chapter. Just create or use channels, templates, and postings in your own site and change the names accordingly.

---

The steps we will go through to set up the BOTS Web site follow, first in brief and then in detail. It should take no more than about ten minutes to set up this environment.

1. Set up the channel hierarchy (three easy channels).
2. Set up the templates (two easy templates).
3. Set up the template files and associate them with templates (two easy template files).
4. Code the template files (relatively simple code is provided).

5. Build the solution in VS.NET (three-finger salute but not Ctrl-Alt-Del).
6. Create the postings (two easy postings).
7. Install the Woodgrove sample data site (standard setup).

## Set Up Channel Hierarchy

Using the Site Manager, ensure that we have, at a minimum, the channel hierarchy characterized in Table 33–2.

The jobs channel was called "growth" for Growth Opportunities in other parts of the book. But "jobs" for Job Offerings seemed a better descriptor for this code sample.

When you are done, it should look something like Figure 33–2.

**Table 33–2**  Channel Hierarchy for BOTS Job Offerings

| Channel | Parent Channel | Display Name | Default Page | Script URL |
|---|---|---|---|---|
| botsconsulting | Channels | BOTS Consulting | default | empty |
| careers | botsconsulting | Careers | default | empty |
| jobs | careers | Job Offerings | default | empty |

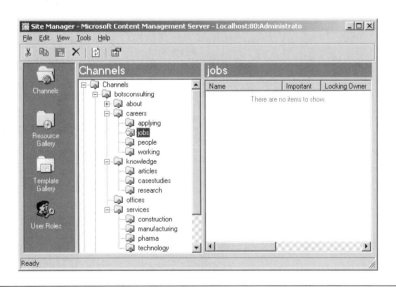

**Figure 33–2**  Channel hierarchy for BOTS Job Offerings

## Set Up Templates

Using the VS.NET MCMS Template Explorer, create the logical templates characterized in Table 33–3 (take the default values for all unspecified properties).

We added the two circled templates in Figure 33–3. Note that they are not yet associated with a template file, so the icon looks broken and there is a red check mark because they are still checked out.

## Set Up Template Files and Associate with Templates

Using the VS.NET Solution Explorer, create two physical template files in the Templates directory by copying the existing generic.aspx template file. Name them jobsummary.aspx and jobdetail.aspx, and save them to disk.

**Table 33–3** Templates for BOTS Job Offerings

| Template | Parent Template | Placeholder Definition Type | Placeholder Definition Name |
| --- | --- | --- | --- |
| JobSummary | BOTS Consulting | none | none |
| JobDetail | BOTS Consulting | HtmlPlaceholder Definition | JobDescription |

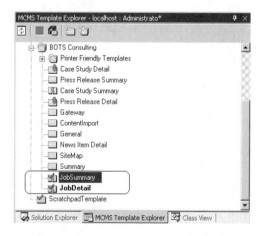

**Figure 33–3** Templates for BOTS Job Offerings

**NOTE:** If you aren't using the BOTS code, the generic.aspx template file is just a stub that includes the header, footer, and left navigation used on the Web site. It also has the default console and a Web Form literal called BodyTitle in the content portion of the file. You could easily use a standard MCMS template file and add your own custom interface.

Using the VS.NET MCMS Template Explorer, associate the Template File property of the JobSummary template with the jobsummary.aspx file, and the TemplateFile property of the JobDetail template with the jobdetail.aspx file. The icon for each template should become unbroken, and if you check them, the red check mark should go away.

Back in the VS.NET Solution Explorer, edit the jobsummary.aspx file. Add a Web Form placeholder control named SummaryOfPostings just below the existing literal control in the content portion of the file. It should look something like Figure 33–4.

Edit the jobdetail.aspx file. Add an HtmlPlaceholderControl named JobDescription just below the existing literal in the content portion of the file. Also, choose JobDescription from the drop-down list for the PlaceholderToBind property. The result should look something like Figure 33–5.

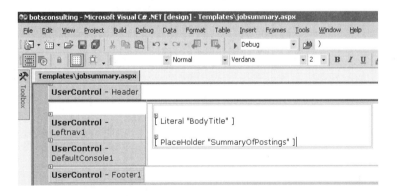

**Figure 33–4**  jobsummary.aspx

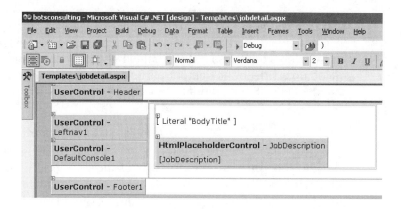

**Figure 33-5** jobdetail.aspx

## Code the Template Files

Replace the Page_Load function in the jobsummary.aspx template file with the following code:

```csharp
private void Page_Load(object sender, System.EventArgs e)
{
  HtmlAnchor cmsPostingLink;
  Literal cmsPostingDate;

  CmsHttpContext cmsContext = CmsHttpContext.Current;

  //Show the Posting DisplayName at the top of the content
  BodyTitle.Text = "<b>" +
    HttpUtility.HtmlEncode(
      CmsHttpContext.Current.Posting.DisplayName) +
    "</b>";
  //Go through all the Postings in this Channel and Add details to
  //the SummaryOfPostings Web Form Placeholder for each Posting
  //sorted by StartDate
  //Do not include the Posting named default
  PostingCollection cmsChannelPostings =
    cmsContext.Channel.Postings;
  if (cmsChannelPostings != null)
  {
    cmsChannelPostings.SortByStartDate(false);
    foreach (Posting cmsPosting in cmsChannelPostings)
    {
      if (cmsPosting.Name != "default")
```

```
    {
      //Format Hyperlink
      cmsPostingLink = new HtmlAnchor();
      cmsPostingLink.HRef = cmsPosting.Url;
      cmsPostingLink.InnerText = cmsPosting.DisplayName;
      cmsPostingLink.Attributes.Add("style","COLOR: gray");

      SummaryOfPostings.Controls.Add(new LiteralControl("<p>"));
      SummaryOfPostings.Controls.Add(cmsPostingLink);
      SummaryOfPostings.Controls.Add(new LiteralControl(
        "<br />Posted: " +
        cmsPosting.StartDate.ToLongDateString()));
      SummaryOfPostings.Controls.Add(new LiteralControl("</p>"));
    }
  }
 }
}
```

The code basically shows a URL and StartDate for each posting in the channel except the default posting.

Ensure that the namespace and public class (initially called "generic" if copied from generic.aspx) near the top of the file are unique in your project. You may want to provide a more detailed comment.

```
namespace botsconsulting.Templates
{
  /// <summary>
  /// Summary description for jobsummary.
  /// </summary>
  public class jobsummary : System.Web.UI.Page
```

This is the only custom code in this template file.

Replace the Page_Load function in the jobdetail.aspx template file with the following code:

```
private void Page_Load(object sender, System.EventArgs e)
{
  //Show the Posting DisplayName at the top of the content
  BodyTitle.Text = "<b>" +
    HttpUtility.HtmlEncode(
      CmsHttpContext.Current.Posting.DisplayName) +
    "</b>";
}
```

Ensure that the namespace and public class (initially called "generic" if copied from generic.aspx) near the top of the file are unique in your project. You may want to provide a more detailed comment.

```
namespace botsconsulting.Templates
{
  /// <summary>
  /// Summary description for jobdetail.
  /// </summary>
  public class jobdetail : System.Web.UI.Page
```

This is the only custom code in this template file.

## Build the Solution in VS.NET

This is an important step—don't miss it. You can use Ctrl-Shift-B or choose Build Solution from the Build menu. Clearly, but hopefully unnecessary, you must deal with any errors before continuing.

## Create Postings

Once the build is successful, browse to http://localhost/botsconsulting/careers/jobs in Internet Explorer.

**NOTE:** For the top navigation to work properly, you may want to create a posting named "default" in the careers channel. This posting can be based upon any template that allows navigation to the channel's children. However, it isn't required for this code sample to function. You could even create the default posting in the careers channel using the JobSummary template if you like. Give it a name of "default" and a display name something like "Check out our Job Offerings."

Follow these steps to create the default posting based upon the Job Summary template in the jobs channel:

1. Click the Switch to Edit Site link on the right side of the channel Welcome page.
2. Click the Create New Page link.
3. Locate and click the BOTS Consulting link in the template gallery.
4. Locate the JobSummary template and click its Select icon.

**5.** There are no placeholders on this template, so simply click the Save New Page link.

**6.** Type "default" into the Name text box.

**7.** Type "Job Offerings" into the Display Name text box.

**8.** Click OK to dismiss the dialog.

**9.** Click the Approve link.

**10.** Click the Switch to Live Site link.

Figure 33–6 shows what this default summary page will look like after the next steps are complete.

Follow these steps to create the default posting based upon the Job Summary template in the jobs channel:

**1.** Click the Switch to Edit Site link in the Web Author console of the default page in the jobs channel.

**2.** Click the Create New Page link.

**3.** Locate and click the BOTS Consulting link in the template gallery.

**4.** Locate the JobDetail template and click its Select icon.

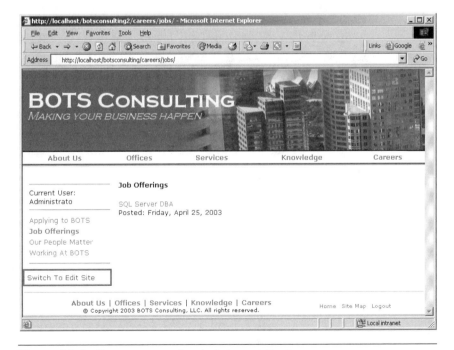

**Figure 33–6** Summary posting in Internet Explorer

5. Enter a job description like "SQL Server 2000 DBA must know DTS" into the placeholder.
6. Type "BOTS.12345" into the Name text box.
7. Type a job title like "SQL Server DBA" into the Display Name text box.
8. Click OK to dismiss the dialog.
9. Click the Approve link.
10. Click the Switch to Live Site link.

Clicking the Job Offerings link on the left navigation should take you to the posting in the jobs channel named default, which should look something like Figure 33–6.

Clicking the SQL Server DBA link should take you back to the detail page for that posting, and it should look something like Figure 33–7.

## Install Woodgrove Sample Data Site

The Woodgrove Bank sample that comes with CMS will be used to syndicate postings to the BOTS Consulting Web site. So if you don't already

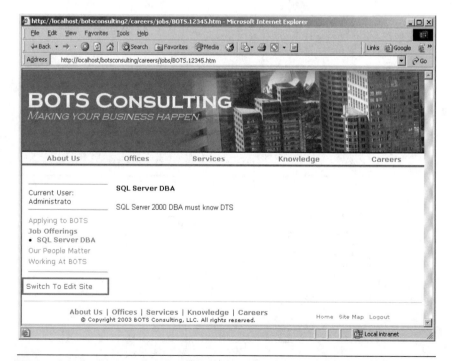

**Figure 33–7** Detail posting in Internet Explorer

have Woodgrove installed, you need to do that now. There are detailed instructions for installing the sample both in the CMS help file and on MSDN. As always, you have the option of using your own site and just changing the names as needed.

That is all the setup we need to do, so let's code up a Web Service!

# Building a Web Service

For our first example, let's suppose that BOTS Consulting has a pretty good relationship with some of its clients including, coincidentally, Woodgrove Bank (the Woodgrove sample that comes with CMS will be modified to complete this code sample). Whenever Woodgrove, or other BOTS partners, posts a job posting on their Web site, BOTS would like to have it show on their Web site as well. If Woodgrove changes their job posting, BOTS would like their site to reflect the modified posting on their Web site. If Woodgrove deletes their posting, BOTS would like their Web site to reflect this deletion.

So, in cooperation with Woodgrove and its other partners, BOTS Consulting wants to create a Web Service that their partners would call to accomplish these tasks. This horizontal, real-time, push Web Service hosted by BOTS will syndicate a redundant copy of each job opportunity sent from BOTS' partners. That makes BOTS the aggregator of job postings for their partners.

First a Woodgrove author will submit a new or changed posting for approval. Then a Woodgrove approver will approve the posting, which will be the catalyst for calling the BOTS Web Service to syndicate the content. Figure 33–8 shows this scenario pictorially.

Later a Woodgrove approver will delete the posting, which will be the catalyst for calling the BOTS Web Service to remove the content previously syndicated. Typically, we expect that the posting will simply expire rather than get deleted. The ExpiryDate is syndicated with the content, and the BOTS Web Service will set the syndicated posting to expire at the same time as the Woodgrove posting. If we presume the clocks on the separate servers are somewhat in sync, both postings will expire simultaneously. Figure 33–9 shows this scenario pictorially.

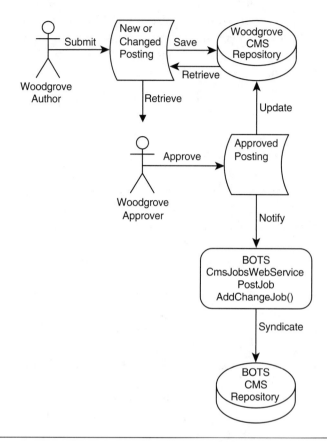

**Figure 33–8**   Add or change push syndication

## Create the BOTS Web Service VS.NET Project

We begin by building the BOTS Web Service that Woodgrove will call. It is wise and easier to isolate the Web Service code from the existing BOTS VS.NET project.

### Step 1

So, crack open VS.NET and open a new C# MCMS Web Service VS.NET project (Figure 33–10).

Be sure to choose MCMS Web Service from the Visual C# Projects folder under the Content Management Server Projects folder. If, instead, you choose ASP.NET Web Service from the root-level Visual C#

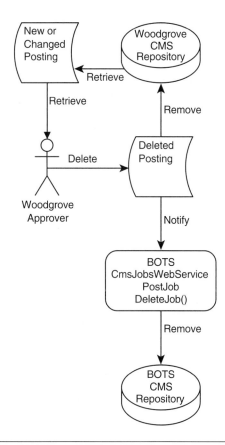

**Figure 33–9** Delete push syndication

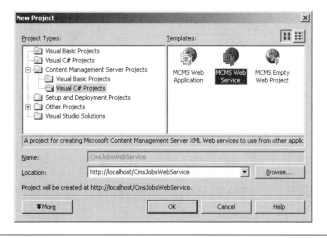

**Figure 33–10** New C# MCMS Web Service VS.NET project

Projects folder, a lot of configuration in the Web.config file will be missing, and although CMS will work for most things, when we try to do something other than retrieve data, we will end up with exceptions. The error message will indicate that we need to add the PostingEvents Module to the <httpmodules> section of Web.config with the name CmsPosting. Let's avoid all that by selecting the MCMS Web Service project template from the correct folder. That way, all the appropriate references, assemblies, and httpmodules will have already been added to the project for us.

### Step 2

Using the VS.NET Solution Explorer, right-click the project name, CmsJobsWebService, and select Add a Web Service from the Add menu of the resulting pop-up. In the resulting dialog, choose Web Service from the list of templates in the Web Project Items folder, and name the new Service PostJobToBOTS.asmx (Figure 33–11; this time we do not want to use the Content Management Server folder).

This will be our actual Web Service assembly. However, we want an easy way to communicate multiple parameters via XML to the Web Service. To do this, we are going to create a serializable public class in the next few steps.

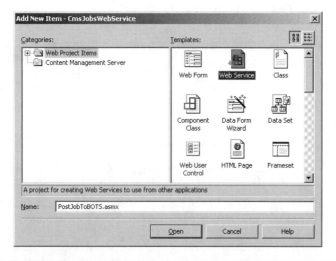

**Figure 33–11** New Web Service named PostJobToBOTS.asmx

**Figure 33–12** New class named JobPosting.cs

## Step 3

Again, right-click the project name, CmsJobsWebService, and select Add a Component from the Add menu of the resulting pop-up. This time, in the resulting dialog, choose Class from the list of templates in the Web Project Items folder, and name the new class JobPosting.cs (Figure 33–12; again, we do not want to use the Content Management Server folder).

## Step 4

Near the top of the code window for JobPosting.cs, change the namespace from CmsJobsWebService to BOTS.CmsJobsWebService. The namespace used here must be the same as the namespace used in the Web Service for the two classes to interact locally. Add a nice comment to the summary area and add the [Serializable] attribute to the class. More on the value of the [Serializable] attribute later. The code should look something like the following:

```
using System;

namespace BOTS.CmsJobsWebService
{
  /// <summary>
  /// This class provides an efficient way to share information
```

```
/// with our partners about an Approved Job Posting. The class
/// is marked as Serializable so we can easily dehydrate its
/// state into XML, pass it to our partner so they can hydrate
/// it back and use it.
/// </summary>
[Serializable]
public class JobPosting
{
  //1. Public Properties
  public String JobEmployer;
  public String JobPostingID;
  public String JobPostingName;
  public DateTime JobPostingStartDate;
  public DateTime JobPostingExpiryDate;
  public String JobTitle;
  public String JobDescription;

  //2. Constructor, required by .NET Framework
  public JobPosting()
  {
  }
 }
}
```

## Step 5

The first code in the class defines the public properties for this class. We can hold information in these properties in much the same way that we used structures in the past. If we wanted to, we could have used regular set and get blocks to access private variables, but since no additional processing is needed and to keep the example short, we just make the variable itself public. For jobs that are syndicated to BOTS, these properties represent the data that BOTS anticipates. The syndicate will need to adopt their data to these fields. The first property, JobEmployer, should identify the company that is calling the Web Service. The next four are characteristics about the posting, and the last two are about the job itself. The JobTitle property will be used to populate the DisplayName of each posting that is created/updated. The code after the second comment is the .NET required class constructor. Save your changes.

### Step 6

Return to the top of the code window for the PostJobToBOTS assembly (PostJobToBOTS.asmx.cs). We need to add two `using` statements. The first statement is included for interacting with Publishing objects and the second for working with Placeholders. We also need to change the namespace from CmsJobsWebService to BOTS.CmsJobsWebService (to match the namespace given in the JobPosting class), add a nice comment to the summary area, and add the `[WebService]` attribute to the class. The code near the top of the file should look something like the following (preceded by several `using` statements inserted by default):

```
using Microsoft.ContentManagement.Publishing;
using
  Microsoft.ContentManagement.Publishing.Extensions.Placeholders;

namespace BOTS.CmsJobsWebService
{
  /// <summary>
  /// Summary description for CmsJobsWebService.PostJobToBOTS.
  /// </summary>
  [WebService (Namespace="http://botsconsulting.com")]
  public class PostJobToBOTS : System.Web.Services.WebService
  {
    public PostJobToBOTS()
    {
```

The `[WebService]` attribute is the key to exposing this class as a Web Service. By adding `Namespace="http://botsconsulting.com"` to this attribute, we avoid the warning we would get later about using the http://tempuri.org namespace.

### Step 7

Uncomment the HelloWorld example provided near the bottom of the code window, build the solution (Ctrl-Shift-B), and then point the browser to our Web Service (should be http://localhost/CmsJobsWeb Service/PostJobToBOTS.asmx) to make sure that everything is working properly. Since debug is set to true by default in a new MCMS Web Service, right-clicking the PostJob.asmx file in the Solution Explorer, clicking Set As Start Page, and then pressing F5 launches a browser window (Figure 33–13) where we can not only debug but test as well.

**Figure 33–13** Testing the Web Service

If you see a message that reads "This Web service is using http://tempuri.org/ as its default namespace" followed by a verbose recommendation, the Namespace property we discussed in step 6 is missing from the [WebService] attribute. Clicking the Service Description will display XML that describes the class and its methods. This XML is called the WSDL, Web Service Description Language, discussed near the beginning of this chapter in Table 33–1. Clicking the HelloWorld link and subsequently on the Invoke button that follows will result in a new window that shows the XML string that would be returned to the caller of the HelloWorld Web Service. Getting this simple example to function properly is a must before continuing. If it is working for you, let's continue. If not, there are dozens of examples on MSDN, on GotDotNet.com, and even in the .NET Framework SDK that should help get you going.

### Step 8

Next, replace the entire HelloWorld example and its comment with the following four private functions. We will be using them when we are coding the public method of our Web Service.

The first private function simply logs errors to a file.

```
private void LogErrorToFile(string errorMessage)
//******************************************************************
//Write Error to File
//******************************************************************
```

```
{
  try
  {
    //1. Write Error to File
    System.IO.StreamWriter logFile =
      new System.IO.StreamWriter(<@>"C:<\\>ErrorLog.txt", true);
    logFile.WriteLine(errorMessage);
    logFile.Close();
  }
  catch{}
}
```

The second private function was introduced in Chapter 25 in Listing 25–1. It is used to create an authenticated CMSApplicationContext using the currently logged-on Windows user, typically in Update PublishingMode.

```
private CmsApplicationContext GetAuthenticatedCmsApplicationContext
  (PublishingMode cmsMode)
//******************************************************************
//Adapted from Listing 25-1 Function to Create an Application
//Context. Create a new CmsApplicationContext and authenticate it
//Pass the created Context back to the calling method.
//******************************************************************
{
  //1. Declare a Context variable
  CmsApplicationContext cmsContextApp = null;
  try
  {
    //2. Grab a new Application Context
    cmsContextApp = new CmsApplicationContext();

    //3. Assign current Windows User to a WindowsIdentity variable
    //    This will only work if IIS is set to Windows
    //    Authentication and Guest Access is enabled in the SCA
    System.Security.Principal.WindowsIdentity identCurrentUser =
      System.Security.Principal.WindowsIdentity.GetCurrent();

    //4. Log in to CMS
    //    Use the currently authenticated Windows User credentials
    //    Put Context into the PublishingMode passed to the function
    cmsContextApp.AuthenticateUsingUserHandle(
      identCurrentUser.Token,       cmsMode);
```

```
  //5. Return the Authenticated Context
  return cmsContextApp;
}
catch(Exception eError)
{
  //6. Write Error to File
  LogErrorToFile(eError.Message.ToString());

  //7. Return the null Context in the event of an error
  return cmsContextApp;
}
}
```

The third private function was also introduced in Chapter 25, in
Listing 25–3. Given a Channel, a Name, and a Template, the function is
used to create an uncommitted Posting.

```
private Posting CreateNewPosting(
  Channel parentChannel, string newPostingName,
  Template cmsTemplate)
//****************************************************************
//Adapted from Listing 25-3 Function to Create New Posting.
//Create a new Posting in the parentChannel using the
//newPostingName based upon the cmsTemplate all passed to the
//function. Pass the created Posting back to the calling method.
//****************************************************************
{
  //1. Declare a Posting variable
  Posting cmsPosting = null;

  try
  {
    //2. Determine if the user has sufficient rights to create
    //   a Posting from the would-be parent Channel
    if(parentChannel.CanCreatePostings)
    {
```

```
      //3. Create the Posting using the Template passed
      cmsPosting = parentChannel.CreatePosting(cmsTemplate);

      //4. Validate successful creation
      if(cmsPosting != null)
      {
        //5. Give it the Name passed to the function
        cmsPosting.Name = newPostingName;
      }
    }
    //6. Return the created Posting
    return cmsPosting;
  }
  catch(Exception eError)
  {
    //7. Write Error to File
    LogErrorToFile(eError.Message.ToString());

    //8. Return the null Posting in the event of an error
    return cmsPosting;
  }
}
```

And finally, the fourth private function simply isolates the process of systematically generating a name from data provided, so that it can consistently be done from several areas of our Web Service. We will concatenate the jobEmployer, a period, and the jobID (without the curly brackets) into a name that will help us relocate the created Posting if it is changed or deleted in the future. By including the jobEmployer value in the name, we ensure uniqueness across partner postings, providing a potentially beneficial sorting mechanism while maintaining the ability to find the created Posting later.

```
private string GenerateJobName(string jobEmployer, string jobID)
//****************************************************************
//Concatenate JobEmployer and ID to consistently form a name
//****************************************************************
{
```

```
//1. Declare temp variable to hold jobname
string jobName = "";
try
{
  //2. Strip out all spaces (could do any kind of tailoring here)
  jobName = jobEmployer.Replace(" ", "");

  //3. Concatenate the GUID without the curly brackets to the
  //   Employer name separated with a period
  //   This is done so that we can identify this Posting later
  jobName += "." + jobID.Substring(1,36);

  //4. Return concatenated name
  return jobName.ToString();
}
catch(Exception eError)
{
  //5. Write Error to File
  LogErrorToFile(eError.Message.ToString());

  //6. Return empty name
  return jobName.ToString();
}
}
```

Next we create our first WebMethod.

## Step 9

BOTS will need to provide its partners with a function that they can call (in a Web Service this is called a WebMethod) to add or change a job when it is approved on their Web Property. Making a function available to the outside world via a Web Service is relatively painless in VS.NET. We simply ensure that the function is public and is preceded with the [WebMethod] attribute. The AddChangeJob WebMethod code is explained with comments throughout but will also be discussed after the code is presented.

```
[WebMethod]
public string AddChangeJob(JobPosting job)
{
  try
  {
```

```
//1. Grab an Authenticated Context in Update PublishingMode
//   using the GetAuthenticatedCmsApplicationContext function
//   from Listing 25-1
CmsApplicationContext cmsContextApp =
  GetAuthenticatedCmsApplicationContext(PublishingMode.Update);


//2. Grab the jobs Channel in which the Posting will exist
//   Cast the result of the Searches object as a Channel
Channel cmsChannel =
  cmsContextApp.Searches.GetByPath(
  "/Channels/botsconsulting/careers/jobs/")
  as Channel;


//3. Generate a consistent name for the Posting from data
//   provided. The resulting name will look something like:
//   Woodgrove.12345
string jobName = GenerateJobName(job.JobEmployer,
  job.JobPostingID);


//4. Grab this Posting for update if it already exists
Posting cmsPosting =
  cmsContextApp.Searches.GetByPath(
  "/Channels/botsconsulting/careers/jobs/" + jobName)
  as Posting;


//5. If no Posting was found, create one
if (cmsPosting == null)
{
  //6. Grab the Template upon which to create the Posting
  //   Cast the result of the Searches object as a Template
  Template cmsTemplate =
    cmsContextApp.Searches.GetByPath(
    "/Templates/botsconsulting/JobDetail")
    as Template;


  //7. Create a new Posting
  cmsPosting = CreateNewPosting(cmsChannel, jobName,
    cmsTemplate);
}
```

```
//8. Verify we have a Posting
if (cmsPosting != null)
{
  //9. Set the Posting data, by synchronizing the Start/Expiry
  //   dates. The postings are automatically published and
  //   expired together.
  cmsPosting.DisplayName = job.JobTitle.ToString();
  cmsPosting.StartDate   = job.JobPostingStartDate;
  cmsPosting.ExpiryDate  = job.JobPostingExpiryDate;

  //10. Grab the description placeholder
  HtmlPlaceholder cmsPlaceholder =
    cmsPosting.Placeholders["JobDescription"]
  as HtmlPlaceholder;

  //11. Set the description placeholder's content
  //    The caller will include everything that they want to
  //    show in this single syndicated Posting in this field
  cmsPlaceholder.Html = job.JobDescription;

  //12. Submit the Posting
  //    This will kick off whatever workflow BOTS has decided
  //    to implement for the user we authenticated with
  cmsPosting.Submit();

  //13. Commit all changes. If not explicitly called, the
  //    disposition of changes is based upon
  //    RollbackOnSessionEnd
  cmsContextApp.CommitAll();
}

//14. Dispose of the stand-alone Application Context
cmsContextApp.Dispose();

//15. Let the caller of the Web Service know the job succeeded
return jobName + " successfully syndicated";
}
catch(Exception eError)
{
  //16. Write Error to File
  LogErrorToFile(eError.Message.ToString());
```

```
    //17. Let the caller of the Web Service know an error occurred
    return job + eError.Message.ToString();
  }
}
```

The parameter passed to this WebMethod function is of type Job Posting. That is the public class that we created earlier in this chapter. When the caller invokes this AddChangeJob method of our Web Service, they will need to pass it a JobPosting object. With .NET this is easy. They simply create an instance of our public JobPosting class that is exposed to them, populate it with the data that they would like to syndicate, and then pass the instance as if they were calling a local component's method. Because the class has the [Serializable] attribute, the .NET Framework will automatically serialize the object as XML and transfer it to the Web Service where it will automatically be deserialized, and BOTS can use it as if it were a local object. All of the state that was present when the object was serialized will be back when it is deserialized. Frequently, this is referred to as deflating and inflating, or dehydrating and hydrating an object. Very cool.

The jobName under comment 3 is of interest. Because CMS allows us to use a different DisplayName from the actual name of the Posting, we are using two pieces of information that the caller provides to create a name for the syndicated Posting that users won't see but has great utility for us. The naming convention should keep the jobs sent to BOTS in uniquely named Postings. Also, because CMS has a search that we can use to find specifically named assets, the naming convention provides us with a convenient way to determine if we have created this Posting before. By naming the Postings in this way, we can also sort the PostingCollection by Name, assuming that BOTS might set this up with more companies than just Woodgrove, yielding a list of Postings ordered by ID within Employer. That could prove to be very helpful. Woodgrove will be sending us a GUID as an ID, so it is highly unlikely that anyone else would ever send the same ID, but it is feasible that as BOTS expands this service, two companies could send Postings with the same ID. The naming convention protects us against that scenario by including the Employer in the name.

However, this solution is not at all bulletproof. We obviously should do a lot more exception handling. For instance, under comment 6 we search for a hard-coded Template but we never validate that it was successfully found before we create our new Posting. Or if the jobName returns empty, we proceed to create a Posting with no name. We also don't do any bounds or content checking, so a malicious or just careless partner could introduce potentially hazardous content (maybe voluminous garbage, maybe containing a script or some kind of hack, maybe spam, or worse).

The way it is set up right now, the JobDescription Placeholder will only contain plain text. So, no matter how elegant the content is that a client sends, our current Posting will present it with no frills. BOTS may want to consider changing the JobDescription Placeholder to allow for FullFormatting.

### *Step 10*

We need one final [WebMethod]. If BOTS partners decide to remove a job posting before or even after it has expired, BOTS needs to reflect that deletion. The DeleteJob WebMethod code is explained with comments throughout.

```
[WebMethod]
public string DeleteJob(JobPosting job)
{
  try
  {
    //1. Grab an Authenticated Context in Update PublishingMode
    //    using the GetAuthenticatedCmsApplicationContext function
    //    from Listing 25-1
    CmsApplicationContext cmsContextApp =
      GetAuthenticatedCmsApplicationContext(PublishingMode.Update);

    //2. Generate a consistent name for the Posting from data
    //    provided. The resulting name will look something like:
    //    Woodgrove.12345
    string jobName = GenerateJobName(job.JobEmployer,
      job.JobPostingID);

    //3. Grab this existing Posting for syndicated deletion
    Posting cmsPosting =
      cmsContextApp.Searches.GetByPath(
      "/Channels/botsconsulting/careers/jobs/" + jobName)
      as Posting;

    //4. Check to see if the Posting was found, if it was delete it
    if (cmsPosting != null)
    {
```

```
    //7. Delete the Posting
    cmsPosting.Delete();

    //8. Submit the Posting
    //   This will kick off whatever workflow BOTS has decided
    //   to implement for the user we authenticated with
    cmsPosting.Submit();

    //9. Commit all changes. If not explicitly called, the
    //   disposition of changes is based upon
    //   RollbackOnSessionEnd
    cmsContextApp.CommitAll();
}

    //10. Dispose of the stand-alone Application Context
    cmsContextApp.Dispose();

    //11. Let the caller of the Web Service know the job succeeded
    return jobName + " successfully deleted";
}
catch(Exception eError)
{
    //12. Write Error to File
    LogErrorToFile(eError.Message.ToString());

    //13. Let the caller of the Web Service know an error occurred
    return job + eError.Message.ToString();
}
}
```

Build the PostJobToBOTS Web Service solution in VS.NET. Our Web Service is now complete. Let's modify the Woodgrove Web site to consume it.

## Consuming a Web Service

If you haven't looked before, it may be helpful to see what a Woodgrove job posting looks like. Browse to the Careers section of the Woodgrove sample site. From anywhere on the Woodgrove site, we can choose Careers from the About Us menu option in the top navigation, or typing

the following URL should get there: http://localhost/WoodgroveNet/
About+Us/Careers/. A summary of existing job postings is shown. Clicking
one of the postings should show a screen something like Figure 33–14.

At the top of the posting is the display name for the posting (Account
Manager, in this example) followed by four fields: Job Title, Job Description, Qualifications, and Application Instructions (this section is not
labeled). Click the Switch to Edit Site link and then click the Edit link to
see the actual placeholders that are being populated. These placeholders
are named in the associated template in VS.NET.

The BOTS AddChangeJob WebMethod only accepts a JobTitle and
a JobDescription, so we will need to consolidate a few of these fields or
leave off the content. We don't want the Posting to be incomplete, so we are
going to concatenate the Woodgrove JobDescription, Qualifications, and

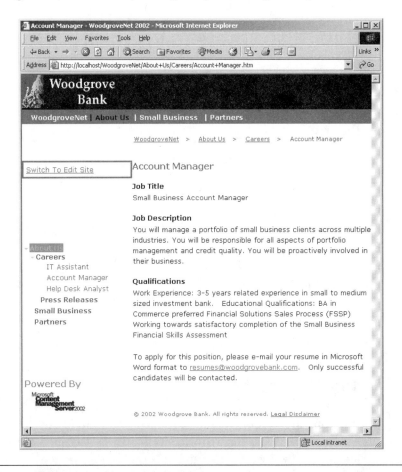

**Figure 33–14** Woodgrove job posting

ApplicationInstructions placeholder data into the single JobDescription field in the BOTS Web Service.

When a Web Service is consumed, a proxy class is typically created that contains all the properties and methods that the Web Service exposes publicly. When the properties and methods on the proxy class are called, they handle the marshalling of the parameters into SOAP, sending the SOAP request over HTTP, receiving the response from the Web Service, and then unmarshalling the return value. In short, the proxy class will make the BOTS Web Service behave as if it were a local component. VS.NET makes creating this proxy class a snap.

### Creating a Proxy Class to the Web Service

Open the Woodgrove sample in VS.NET and right-click the References folder. Select Add and then Add Web Reference from the resulting pop-up menu. In the Add Web Reference dialog (Figure 33–15), type the URL of the BOTS Web Service we built in the last section, http://localhost/CmsJobsWebService/PostJobToBOTS.asmx, into the Address text box and press Enter.

We can see the DeleteJob and AddChangeJob WebMethods, so this is the Web Service that we want. The JobPosting class is not a Web Method, so it is not listed, but it is also available for use from the Web

**Figure 33–15** Add Web Reference dialog

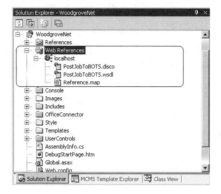

**Figure 33–16** Added Web Reference

Service. Click the Add Reference button at the bottom of the dialog, and VS.NET will create a new folder called Web References in which the PostJob Web Service is loaded (Figure 33–16).

Adding this Web Reference in VS.NET prepares the proxy class that we can use to refer to the Web Service public methods and objects locally, and the necessary code to interact with the actual Web Service will be created by VS.NET on our behalf. We simply need to refer to the proxy class methods and object. For instance, we will use localhost.Add ChangeJob(thisJob) to access the AddChangeJob Web Service.

## Consuming the AddChangeJob Web Service

Remember, the requirements as depicted in Figure 33–8 show that the AddChangeJob Web Service WebMethod is invoked when a Woodgrove job posting is approved. The stub for the CmsPosting_Approved event can be found in the Woodgrove Global.asax file.

---

**NOTE:** Using the events in the Global.asax file is covered in depth in Chapters 6 and 31.

---

Locate and populate the CmsPosting_Approved function in the Global.asax file with the following code:

```
protected void CmsPosting_Approved(Object sender,
  ChangedEventArgs e)
{
```

```
try
{
  //1. Grab the posting that is being Approved
  Posting cmsPosting = e.Target as Posting;

  //2. Check to see if it is in the Woodgrove Careers channel
  if (cmsPosting.Parent.Name == "Careers")
  {
    //3. Grab the object that will pass our data as XML to BOTS
    localhost.JobPosting jobToPost  = new localhost.JobPosting();

    //4. Populate the Employer and Posting characteristic fields
    jobToPost.JobEmployer         = "Woodgrove Bank";
    jobToPost.JobPostingID        = cmsPosting.Guid.ToString();
    jobToPost.JobPostingName      = cmsPosting.Name.ToString();
    jobToPost.JobPostingStartDate = cmsPosting.StartDate;
    jobToPost.JobPostingExpiryDate = cmsPosting.ExpiryDate;

    //5. Grab the approved Postings Title placeholder and
    //   populate the JobTitle to pass to BOTS using the Html
    //   placeholder property
    HtmlPlaceholder cmsPlaceholder =
      cmsPosting.Placeholders["Title"] as HtmlPlaceholder;
    jobToPost.JobTitle = cmsPlaceholder.Html;

    //6. Grab the approved Postings JobDescription placeholder
    //   and assign its Html to a temporary variable
    cmsPlaceholder = cmsPosting.Placeholders["JobDescription"]
      as HtmlPlaceholder;
    string jobDescription = cmsPlaceholder.Html + "<br><br>";

    //7. Grab the approved Postings Qualifications placeholder
    //   and append its Html to the temporary variable
    cmsPlaceholder = cmsPosting.Placeholders["Qualifications"]
      as HtmlPlaceholder;
    jobDescription += cmsPlaceholder.Html + "<br><br>";

    //8. Grab the approved Postings ApplicationInstructions
    //   placeholder and append its Html to the temporary
    //   variable
    cmsPlaceholder =
      cmsPosting.Placeholders["ApplicationInstructions"]
      as HtmlPlaceholder;
    jobDescription += cmsPlaceholder.Html + "<br><br>";
```

```
        //9. Assign the temporary variable to the BOTS JobDescription
        jobToPost.JobDescription = jobDescription.ToString();

        //10. Create the proxy object to PostJobToBOTS Web Service
        localhost.PostJobToBOTS postJobToBOTS =
          new localhost.PostJobToBOTS();

        //11. Use the same credentials on BOTS that we are using in
        //     Woodgrove. This is but one way to authenticate to the
        //     Web Service.
        postJobToBOTS.Credentials =
          System.Net.CredentialCache.DefaultCredentials;

        //12. Invoke the BOTS WebMethod to Add or Change a Job
        postJobToBOTS.AddChangeJob(jobToPost);
    }
  }
  catch(Exception eError)
  {
    //13. Write Error to File
    System.IO.StreamWriter logFile =
      new System.IO.StreamWriter(<@>"C:<\\>ErrorLog.txt", true);
    logFile.WriteLine(eError.Message.ToString());
    logFile.Close();
  }
}
```

We use the CmsPosting_Approved event rather than the CmsPosting_
Approving event because we want to call the Web Service after the local
posting has been successfully approved rather than before that processing begins.

## Consuming the DeleteJob Web Service

The requirements as depicted in Figure 33–9 show that the DeleteJob
Web Service WebMethod is invoked when a Woodgrove job posting is
deleted. The stub for the CmsPosting_Deleted event can be found in
the Woodgrove Global.asax file.

Locate and populate the CmsPosting_Deleted function in the Global.asax file with the following code:

```
protected void CmsPosting_Deleted(Object sender,
  ChangedEventArgs e)
{
  try
  {
    //1. Grab the posting that is being Approved
    Posting cmsPosting = e.Target as Posting;

    //2. Check to see if it is in the Woodgrove Careers channel
    if (cmsPosting.Parent.Name == "Careers")
    {
      //3. Grab the object that will pass our data as XML to BOTS
      localhost.JobPosting jobToPost = new localhost.JobPosting();

      //4. Populate the Employer and Posting characteristic fields
      jobToPost.JobEmployer  = "Woodgrove Bank";
      jobToPost.JobPostingID = cmsPosting.Guid.ToString();

      //5. Create the proxy object to the PostJobToBOTS Web Service
      localhost.PostJobToBOTS postJobToBOTS =
        new localhost.PostJobToBOTS();

      //6. Use the same credentials on BOTS that we are here
      postJobToBOTS.Credentials =
        System.Net.CredentialCache.DefaultCredentials;

      //7. Commit the pending delete. This is only necessary
      //   because both CMS solutions are hosted on localhost and
      //   there is a single transaction limit per CommitAll called
      e.Context.CommitAll();

      //8. Invoke the BOTS WebMethod to Delete a Job
      postJobToBOTS.DeleteJob(jobToPost);
    }
  }
  catch(Exception eError)
  {
    //9. Write Error to File
    System.IO.StreamWriter logFile =
```

```
        new System.IO.StreamWriter(<@>"C:<\\>ErrorLog.txt", true);
    logFile.WriteLine(eError.Message.ToString());
    logFile.Close();
  }
}
```

We use the CmsPosting_Deleted event rather than the CmsPosting_Deleting event because we want to call the Web Service after the local posting has been successfully deleted rather than before that processing begins.

It is important to note that the code under comment 7 is required only if the two CMS solutions are running on the same server. This is due to the fact that CMS only allows for a single posting to be deleted for each CommitAll. So, near the end of the CmsPosting_Deleted event, just before we call the Web Service, we simply explicitly commit the local posting's uncommitted deletion. This way when we call the Web Service and attempt to commit that posting's deletion we don't end up trying to commit both of them at the same time.

Build the modified Woodgrove solution in VS.NET.

# Testing the Web Service

This is the fun part. We get to see it all working in unison.

## Open the Two CMS Solutions

1. Open BOTS: Using IE, browse to the Job Offerings section of the BOTS Consulting Web site. From anywhere on the BOTS site, we can choose Careers from the top navigation and subsequently choose Job Offerings from the left navigation, or typing the following URL should get there: http://localhost/botsconsulting/careers/jobs. If no other postings have been added, this summary page will look like Figure 33–6, shown earlier in this chapter. If you created the solution in your own site, pull up the Job Offerings summary page.

2. Open Woodgrove: In a second IE window, browse to the Careers section of the Woodgrove sample site. From anywhere on the Woodgrove site, we can choose Careers from the About Us menu option in the top navigation, or typing the following URL should get there: http://localhost/WoodgroveNet/About+Us/Careers/.

There should be a summary of postings based upon the Job Posting ASPX template under the Careers heading.

## Create a New Woodgrove Job Posting

1. Click the Switch to Edit Site link in the Web Author console of the default page in the jobs channel, unless the posting is already in Unpublished mode.
2. Click the Create New Page link.
3. Locate and click the About Us Net link in the template gallery.
4. Locate the Job Posting ASPX template and click its Select icon.
5. Enter a job title like "Programmer Analyst" into the first placeholder.
6. Enter a job description like "Proven development skills in .NET XML Web Services." into the second placeholder.
7. Enter qualifications like "Must know C#" into the third placeholder.
8. Enter "how to apply" information like "Call us at 555-1212" into the fourth placeholder.
9. Click the Save New Page link.
10. Since Woodgrove shows the name of the posting on their summary, we must give it a displayable name. Type "Programmer Analyst Posting" into the Name text box.
11. Click OK to dismiss the dialog (the Name will automatically be used as the Display Name as well).
12. That will fire the code we wrote in the CmsPosting_Approved, unless the channel requires that the posting be explicitly approved. If the new posting is still in a Saved state rather than a Published state, click the Approve link.

Our new Programmer Analyst Posting should be visible in the Woodgrove browser (Figure 33–17), and if we refresh the BOTS site in the other browser, we will see it was syndicated here as well (Figure 33–18).

## View the Syndicated Content Aggregated in BOTS

1. Click the Programmer Analyst link in the BOTS Job Offerings summary, and we see that the detailed contents of the syndicated posting are even displayed (Figure 33–19).
2. Click the Switch to Edit Site link in the Web Author.

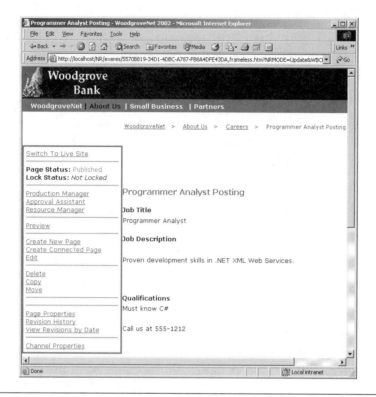

**Figure 33-17**   New Woodgrove posting

3. Scroll down and click the Page Properties link. The name of the posting will show that this posting was syndicated to BOTS from Woodgrove Bank. The Woodgrove GUID will be visible in the name too.

4. Click the Cancel button to dismiss the Page Properties dialog.

## Change the Woodgrove Posting and Syndicate the Change

1. Toggle back to the Woodgrove browser.

2. While still on the Programmer Analyst Posting, click the Edit link in the Web Author.

3. Change the Job Title placeholder from "Programmer Analyst" to "Programmer II."

4. Change the Qualifications placeholder from "Must know C#" to "Must know VB.NET."

5. Click the Save and Exit link in the Web Author.

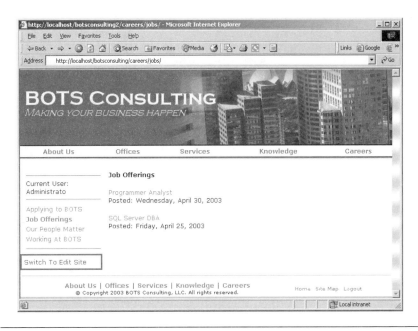

**Figure 33–18** Syndicated to BOTS summary

6. Click the Approve link in the Web Author if the page didn't automatically go through approval.
7. Once the posting is in the Published state, toggle back to the BOTS browser.
8. Refresh the BOTS browser (Figure 33–20).

## Delete the Woodgrove Posting and Syndicate the Deletion

1. Toggle back to the Woodgrove browser.
2. While still on the Programmer Analyst Posting, click the Delete link in the Web Author.
3. The system will prompt "Deleting this page will remove it permanently from the system. Continue?"
4. Click OK to continue.
5. The posting will be deleted, and the Woodgrove site will be returned to the Careers summary page.
6. Toggle back to the BOTS browser.
7. Click the Job Offerings link in the left navigation.
8. The posting delete will have been syndicated to BOTS, and the summary will again look like Figure 33–6.

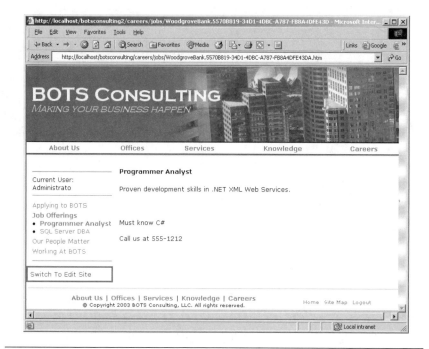

**Figure 33–19**  Syndicated to BOTS detail

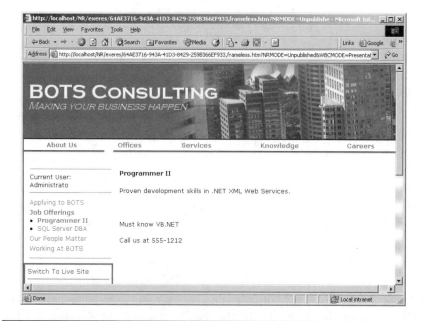

**Figure 33–20**  Changes Syndicated to BOTS

## Summary

After coming to a complete understanding about the concepts of syndication and aggregation, we successfully created an entire sample Web Service that interfaces two independent CMS Web Properties. We called that Web Service from two events within the exiting Woodgrove sample site, syndicating the creation, alteration, and deletion of a posting in the BOTS Consulting sample site.

The next part of the book focuses on performance from a monitoring and a capacity planning perspective. Because CMS dynamically generates all content returned to the user, this is a very important area of CMS development.

# CMS Performance

# Performance Planning

CMS has been designed to run large Web sites. In fact, it is large Web sites that benefit the most from the features of CMS. But this does not mean that CMS site designers can forgot about performance considerations. Most developers could easily write code that would bring any Web site to a crawl. The onus is on the site designers and developers to research performance questions so that they can produce the fastest pages possible.

Performance is not something that is added to a Web site after it is finished. It is an essential part of the site design, development, and deployment. Consider performance at each stage of your project, and you will save yourself an awful lot of effort.

## Designing High-Performance CMS Sites

Although you should consider performance in each phase of your CMS project, the design phase is certainly the most important. Designing a site with performance in mind will help you code and deploy a fast site.

### ASP versus ASP.NET

When you are planning your CMS site, one of the first decisions must be whether to use ASP or ASP.NET. Ultimately, the decision is based on many factors, but from a performance viewpoint, the advantages of ASP.NET are quite clear.

The most obvious benefit of ASP.NET is the new output caching mechanism. This new feature is provided within the ASP.NET framework. Output caching is discussed later in this chapter. Also, considering that ASP.NET performs so well, most of the topics in this chapter will discuss ASP.NET site considerations.

## Caching

The single greatest difference you can make in the performance of your code is your caching strategy. If you are serious about performance, then you need to get serious about your caching design. Early in your Web site design process, you should identify which parts of your site and which parts of each page could be cached. Generally speaking, you will want to cache the code that takes the longest to run. However, if you have a highly personalized site, you might not want to implement caching at all. As with most decisions, you need to find the technological solution that best addresses your business needs.

A number of different caching techniques are described in this chapter. You will need to balance these different caches (see Figure 34–1) according to the resources that you have available. For example, both ASP.NET output caching and CMS node caching use memory resources. In general, you will want to use output caching on as much of your site as possible. However, if you cannot fit all your most popular pages in the output cache, you will want to ensure that you allocate sufficient resources to the CMS node cache. There is no easy rule to follow. You will have to test your site to find the appropriate balance.

For more information about caching, refer to "Best Practices for Improving MCMS Web Site Performance" in the MCMS 2002 documentation.

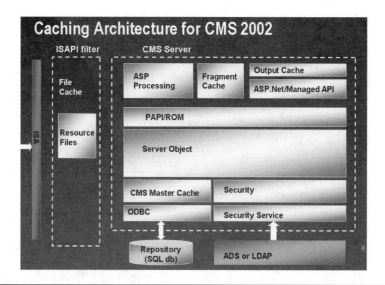

**Figure 34–1** CMS 2002 caching architecture

### The Working Set

The term "working set" is used to refer to the set of pages that are most frequently accessed. This group of pages usually accounts for roughly 80% of the site traffic. For this reason, caching the working set results in the greatest performance gain across the site.

The default configuration for ASP.NET output caching is to use up to 60% of total physical memory. Using this configuration, a CMS server with 1GB of physical RAM can store roughly 2,500 pages in the output cache. Of course, this number is significantly influenced by the size of the pages. If your working set is larger than 2,500, you may want to consider dedicating some testing to determine the size of these pages. Once you have done this, you can target the "heavy" pages and try to scale them down. Refer to the CMS partner page (http://www.microsoft.com/cmserver/partners) for information about companies that offer products that perform these types of tests.

If you find that you are still having trouble getting your working set into the cache, you should consider increasing the server's memory or partitioning your site across multiple CMS servers. This topic is discussed later in this chapter.

Another key point to mention is that the size of the output cache does not significantly affect performance. This means that you can safely increase the resources allocated to the output cache without worrying that this in itself will negatively affect performance. The ASP.NET output caching mechanism is intelligent enough that this is not a concern. As long as increasing this memory allocation is not starving other systems of memory, then it is a good use of your resources.

### ASP.NET Output Caching

As mentioned already, caching is your best way to increase performance. The next point to consider is that ASP.NET output caching is the most effective caching mechanism. Output caching is so effective that the output-cached WoodgroveNet site performance is over 400% better than the WoodgroveASP site.

Since ASP.NET output caching is implemented within the .NET Framework, this technique obviously applies only to ASP.NET pages. However, it is so effective that it's worth considering migrating to ASP.NET purely to use this feature. Figure 34–2 shows the impressive impact of output caching.

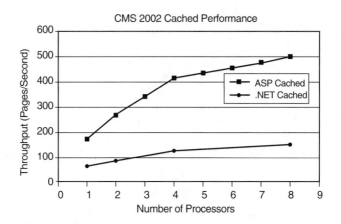

**Figure 34–2** WoodgroveNet with .NET output caching and WoodgroveASP with ASP fragment caching

This chart is dramatic, but it is also important to show the results when pages are served from outside the cache. This is referred to as a "cache miss." Figure 34–3 shows what happens when cache misses increase.

The tests show that performance is seriously affected by cache misses. When a cache miss occurs, quite often it results in a trip to the database and also a write to the CMS node cache. This work is considerably slower than simply serving the cached HTML.

The reason that output caching is so effective is that it is the first operation that the server attempts. If the HTML for the page is cached, it is not necessary to do any other calculations. The cached HTML is

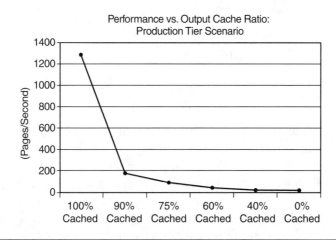

**Figure 34–3** .NET output cache ratio

simply sent to the browser client. It is possible to cache entire pages or fragments of pages. Performance is obviously optimized if the whole page is cached. However, the decision about how to implement this method of caching will be determined by your business requirements. For example, you may have some legal information displayed on your site. If your business requires that this data is always up to date, it may be that it can never be cached. In this case, you would not be able to output cache the entire page.

Partial-page caching is also an important means of using output caching. For example, you could choose to only cache your navigation controls. Whether you cache the whole page or just part of the page, a number of custom settings are available. For example, you can set the cache lifetime. You can also set some CMS-specific properties such as "vary by cms role". This allows you to cache the page content based on the role of the user who is accessing the site.

For more information about output caching, refer to the MCMS documentation, the WoodgroveNet sample site, and the ASP.NET documentation.

### ASP Fragment Caching

If you are not running an ASP.NET site, then your best bet is to implement ASP fragment caching. CMS provides a built-in mechanism for doing this, but there are other choices. For example, if you are running Microsoft Commerce Server (CS) 2002, you might decide to use the CS LRU cache instead of the CMS fragment caching mechanism.

Fragment caching works in a similar fashion to ASP.NET output caching. The idea is to compile pieces of HTML and then serve these from memory instead of compiling them each time they are needed. Of course, ASP fragment caching can be used on any site since it does not require the ASP.NET framework or ASPX pages.

Figure 34–4 shows the benefit of fragment caching on the Woodgrove ASP site.

The following brief example shows how fragment caching is implemented in ASP code. For a more thorough example of this, refer to the WoodgroveASP sample site available on MSDN.

```
<%
      'Display HTML for left navigation of this posting
      'First check LRU cache, if it is not found then compile and
   'populate the LRU cache.
```

```
Dim strHtml, strKey
strKey = Autosession.This.GUID & "left nav"
strHTML = cache.lookup(strKey)
If strHtml = "" then
        'Execute code to compile the required HTML
        strHtml = compiledHtml
        cache.add(strKey, strHtml)
End If
Response.Write(strHtml)
%>
```

### CMS Node Cache

If a page is not available via output caching or fragment caching, CMS will have to assemble the HTML. To maximize the performance of this assembly process, CMS has a number of its own caching strategies. Only a couple of these caches are discussed here since many of them are not meant to be configured by users. Refer to Chapter 3, CMS Architecture, for more details about these caches.

The performance of the CMS server is highly dependent upon its customized caching strategies. The most prominent of these is the CMS node cache. The node cache is used to store various types of data—for example, the channel structure, the template gallery items, and the placeholder content.

Since the node cache is so important, it can easily be adjusted by CMS administrators. To configure this cache, open the Server Configuration Application (SCA) and click the Cache tab (see Figure 34–5). This allows you to alter the number of nodes in the node cache.

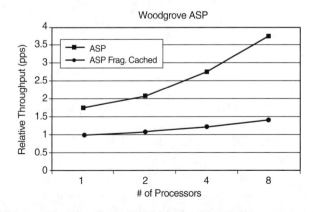

**Figure 34–4**  Fragment caching on the WoodgroveASP site

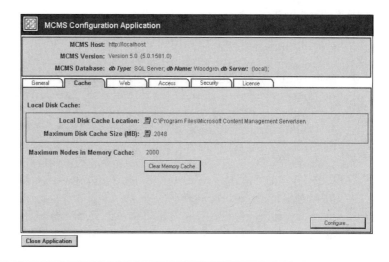

**Figure 34–5** Cache settings in the SCA

As mentioned previously, you do not want to blindly increase this number. The more nodes you have in the CMS cache, the less memory there is available for output caching. You will need to find the right balance. Refer to the next chapter for information about CMS performance counters. These counters can help you find the right balance for your available resources.

### Disk Cache

The other cache that can be configured in the SCA is the disk cache. The disk cache stores data that would otherwise have to be retrieved from the CMS database. To minimize the trips to SQL Server, these files are cached on the server's hard drive. The combination of this cache and the inherent performance of SQL Server is so effective that SQL Server is rarely the performance bottleneck for a CMS site. This is true even when a significant number of CMS servers are accessing a single SQL Server. More often, the CMS server CPU is simply not able to keep up with the writes to all the appropriate caches.

To make use of this cache, you must have sufficient disk space available on your CMS server. Do not set the disk cache size so high that the server could run out of empty space. One recommendation from Microsoft is to keep the Internet Information Services (IIS) logs on a different drive from the CMS disk cache. This is one example of how disk space can be freed up for use by CMS.

## Template Design Considerations

CMS template design almost equates to CMS performance design. If your templates are designed well, it is straightforward to deploy a high-performance CMS site. If your template performs poorly, then you may find that you have to spend substantial time tweaking your caches and adding more resources to your deployment.

When you are creating CMS templates, trade-offs have to be made between offering increased flexibility and increased performance. Just as in any other Web site, the fastest templates are the ones that run the least amount of code and serve the least amount of data. On a CMS site, placeholders are used to store content, but each added placeholder also requires more code to run. The fastest CMS templates are those that have few placeholders with small amounts of data.

## Placeholder Data

The amount of data in placeholders has a significant effect on the performance of CMS pages. But this is a very straightforward principle. Just as in any other Web site, the more data you send to the client, the slower the page will render. For CMS users, it is key to remember that placeholders do not nullify this principle. A well-administrated CMS site will include guidelines for authors about the size and type of content that can be included on a particular page. Since image placeholders usually contain more data than HTML placeholders, the type of placeholder can also have an affect on performance. Make sure that your template design decisions include this consideration.

Another issue with large amounts of placeholder data is that caching is no longer as effective. You may save time compiling HTML, but this savings can be negated if the cached HTML is so large that transferring it across the wire takes a long time. Figure 34–6 demonstrates how throughput is affected as the size of placeholder data increases. In this test, each line of content contained 36 characters.

## Number of Placeholders

Placeholder data is an important factor, but the number of placeholders is also important. All too often, site developers give in to pressure from their authors and try to build the ultimate template. The problem with trying to please everyone with one template is that you end up with so many placeholders that you significantly degrade performance. Each placeholder that you add requires the server to fetch and render more

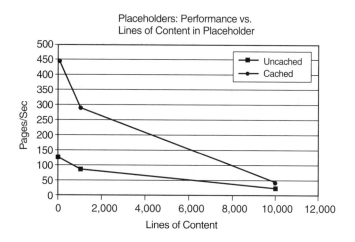

**Figure 34–6** Placeholder size performance

content. This clearly increases the amount of code that the server must execute.

Of course, there are other considerations. You do not want to create too many templates, because this leads to many different problems. Some sites find that after years of running their CMS system, they have produced so many templates that site management becomes awkward. The trick is to find a balance between performance and flexibility. CMS 2002 provides the ability to create your own placeholders. A custom placeholder may allow you to significantly decrease the number of place-holders on your template.

Microsoft has suggested that keeping the number of placeholders—on each template—under 100 is important. Although each site has its own performance goals, this is an awful lot of placeholders. If you find that you are using more than 20 placeholders on a page, then take a step back and consider if what you really need is another template.

Figure 34–7 shows how the number of placeholders affects perfor-mance of the site.

## Postings and Other CMS Containers

CMS containers are virtual structures. For example, you will not find anything resembling the CMS channel structure within your file system. Based on this architecture, CMS containers must be inflated from the database and cached on the server. These operations take time and are a significant factor in the performance of a CMS site. Fortunately, there

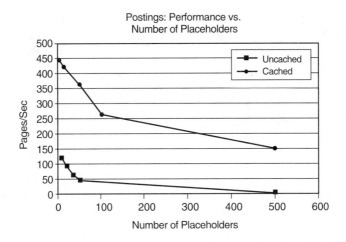

**Figure 34–7** Placeholder number performance

are ways to mitigate this performance hit. A well-designed CMS site will not suffer from this issue.

The solution is quite simple. Make sure that all your CMS containers are organized in a distributed hierarchy. When it comes to adding channels, template galleries, resource galleries, and user roles, divide your container content into well-proportioned trees. Microsoft has suggested that you should keep your container content to less than 300 items. The most important case of this rule is the root level of the container trees. Figure 34–8 illustrates this point.

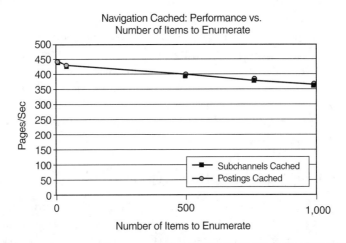

**Figure 34–8** Performance of navigation code based on postings in a single container

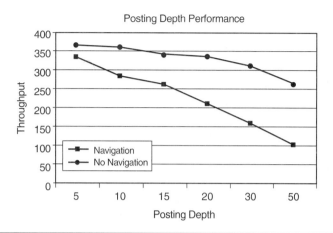

**Figure 34–9** Posting depth performance

In addition to the number of items in your containers, consider the depth of your trees. Rather than having few deep trees, divide your containers into trees that balance both depth and width. If you have to make a choice, depth is preferential to width. Figure 34–9 shows the results of deep channel structures.

## CMS Resources

CMS resources have many benefits. They allow a single file to be easily used in many places and by many authors. However, just as in any other Web site, resource files should be used carefully. These files generally comprise a significant portion of the data downloaded to the Web browser client. Resources can be any sort of file. However, for simplicity's sake, image files will be used as the default example.

CMS resources are the files stored within a CMS resource gallery. If you add a file directly to a template or add a file directly within a placeholder, then these files are not managed by CMS. Management has advantages but it also comes with a performance implication. This impact can be mitigated by caching your resources. If all your CMS resources are cached, they will behave just like resources on any other Web site. Refer to the earlier section about adjusting the size of your CMS disk cache.

# Developing High-Performance CMS Sites

This section discusses optimizing performance when you are coding CMS sites. In the previous main section, we already touched on the importance of writing efficient code for site navigation. Now we will cover other issues that CMS developers need to be mindful of when writing code for CMS templates.

## Navigation

Effective navigation is clearly essential to any Web site. However, making navigation effective and making it perform well may be conflicting goals. But this is the pessimist's view of the question; another way to think about it is that navigation is an excellent opportunity to improve the performance of your templates. A little time spent tweaking your navigation code can result in a large difference in your performance numbers.

Just like any other aspect of your site design, the major factor to consider when you think about navigation is how much work you are doing. For example, if you include many different types of navigation on every page, then you will be running more code than if you were to pick and choose between different navigation options. You may decide that the most popular pages in your working set should have less navigation code than other pages.

The WoodgroveNet sample site uses a number of different types of navigation. On most pages, there is a standard tree control on the left, a tab-style navigation across the top, and a breadcrumb control just below the tabs. But this is a small site. If some of the pages could not fit in the output cache, then it would be important to consider whether all these controls were necessary on all pages.

Once you have narrowed down which controls are required on each page, the next consideration is how much code is being run for each control. The most obvious example of this point is the tree control. If your channel structure is deep, it could take some time to render the control. This is true even if you are only displaying the current level of the tree. The key to using tree navigation is to use lazy enumeration. Lazy enumeration is the practice of only compiling the HTML that is necessary to display at any given time. When the WoodgroveNet left navigation control was originally built, it did not use lazy enumeration. This raised a flag during the CMS performance testing, and the control was quickly revised to only enumerate the channels that are expanded.

Once you have run the minimum amount of code required to render your navigation controls, make sure that you run this code as few times as possible. Unless your navigation changes based on factors such as personalization, you will probably find that caching your navigation results in a substantial performance benefit. Figures 34–10 and 34–11 show the importance of caching your navigation controls.

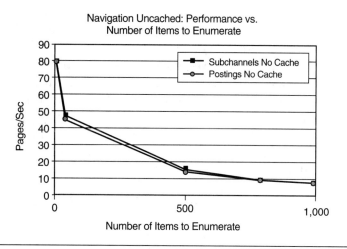

**Figure 34–10** Navigation performance without caching

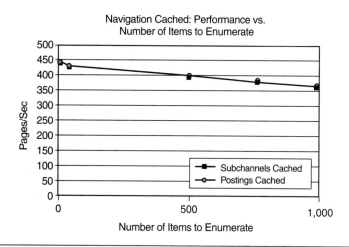

**Figure 34–11** Navigation performance cached

## CMS PAPI Searches

Not all CMS PAPI searches are created equal. For example, if you want to search your whole site for a particular posting, then a GUID search will be the fastest. The reason for this is quite simple: When searching for a GUID, CMS goes directly to the node table and retrieves the object. Other searches, such as searching by path, require processing before the object's GUID is found. Once the GUID is found, the GUID search is performed.

Not all searches require the same amount of processing; one search in particular must be handled with care. This is the custom property search. There are good and bad uses for this tool. Consider the case of meta information. Many sites use custom properties to store metadata. This information is then used for various purposes. Figure 34–12 illustrates what happens if you try to use this information to find postings across an entire site. This is a poor use of custom property searches.

Custom property searches are not inherently flawed. They can be used efficiently and very effectively. If you have already performed a different search, then you can use custom property searches on a smaller sample. For example, if you want to find all the postings that contain a certain custom property value, first narrow down the search by keeping all these postings within a certain channel. A GUID search can be used to retrieve the channel, and then a custom property search can be used to go through the postings in that channel. Based on the previous information, this would narrow down the postings searched to less than 300. This same principle should be applied to searching for channels.

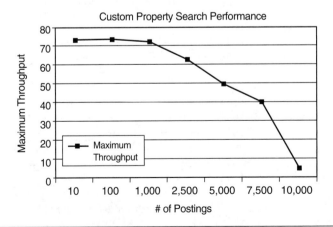

**Figure 34–12** Custom property search performance

# Deploying High-Performance CMS Sites

The architecture of your site can have a substantial impact on the performance of your pages. However, it is worth noting again that this is not the best place to start your performance planning. Only after you have optimized all the other areas of your design should you then consider how to improve the performance of your deployment. This game plan will result in the best-performing site with the least amount of hardware and the simplest deployment architecture.

## Dedicated Hardware

One of the most obvious ways to increase the performance of your CMS deployment is to use dedicated hardware. Although you could run other applications, such as SQL Server, on the same machine as the CMS server, this is clearly not the best strategy.

Another point to consider is that having other applications running on the CMS server will make your performance testing much more complicated. As the various applications compete for resources, there could be a number of permutations of resource usage that are difficult to diagnose. With a dedicated CMS server and a dedicated SQL server, it is much easier to get reliable performance numbers.

## Scaling Up

You may not feel that it is important for your site to scale, but will this be true in the future? Someday, you may need the added flexibility that performance scaling offers. "Scaling up" is the process of maintaining performance as you increase the number of CPUs within your CMS server. In the long run, scaling up could save you money on hardware. Rather than adding another machine, you could save time and money by adding another processor to your CMS server.

However, it is important to realize that adding processors will not result in a linear increase in performance. If you go from one processor to two, you might not see a 100% increase in performance. But you may not require that sort of increase. If you are just under your performance goals, adding an extra processor may be a good solution.

Figure 34–13 illustrates the scale-up results for WoodgroveNet. The numbers have been adjusted so that both cached and uncached results start with a value of one. The actual throughput for cached pages on one

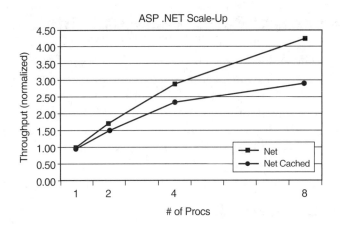

**Figure 34–13** CMS scale-up results

processor was over seven times greater than for uncached pages. The throughput for eight processors showed a difference of almost five times.

## Scaling Out

"Scaling out" is the process of maintaining performance across a server farm. CMS servers support this type of clustering; because of this, CMS is able to run extremely large Web sites. For example, Microsoft has recently deployed dynamic CMS sites on Microsoft.com. To see an example, you can navigate to http://www.microsoft.com/cmserver. This is the first of many scheduled CMS deployments across Microsoft.com. It would certainly not be possible to run a site that gets as much traffic as Microsoft.com without using a scale-out model. Even a static Web site would not be able to handle sites of this size if they had to run on a single server.

Clustering is achieved using load balancing. As client requests hit the sites, they first go to the load balancer and then are routed to the Web server that is best able to serve the request. There are two flavors of load balancing: software load balancing and hardware load balancing. Software load balancing, such as Windows Network Load Balancer, is often the cheaper of the two options. However, hardware load balancing is able to handle a much greater load. Make sure that you investigate your needs before you invest in either option. Figure 34–14 shows the benefits of scaling a CMS site across many machines.

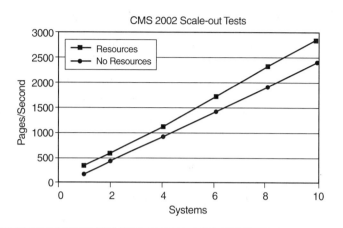

**Figure 34–14** CMS scale-out results

Note that deploying CMS servers in a cluster is also important in cases where failover and reliability are among the top priorities. If your Web site must be running all the time, then you will need to have at least two CMS clusters. Refer to the Microsoft deployment white paper for more information.

## Site Partitioning

It is unlikely that most sites will need to worry about partitioning. However, if your performance requirements cannot be met by scaling up and scaling out, you will need to partition your site over multiple CMS server clusters.

Partitioning a site can provide many performance benefits. Obviously, a smaller working set means that more pages in the set can be cached. Also, the principle of dedicated hardware applies because you are dedicating hardware not only to CMS but to specific parts of your site.

A candidate for site partitioning would be one with extremely high traffic and a very large working set. Microsoft points out that a server using the maximum of 4GB of memory might be able to cache a working set of 10,000 pages. If your site happens to have a working set of 20,000 pages, then you may need to divide your site into two clusters. Each cluster would contain half of the Web site pages. Keep in mind that this site would likely have hundreds of thousands of pages and would constitute one of the largest Web sites in the world.

## Authoring and Performance

CMS servers are most efficient when many read and few write operations are occurring. This is, of course, the most popular usage pattern for
any Web site. However, you may find that authoring on your CMS server
is affecting performance to an unacceptable degree. The best possible
deployment scenario is to separate your CMS servers into an authoring
environment, a test environment, and a production environment. For
added security, the production tier is generally the only one that is accessible across the Internet.

Having a dedicated authoring environment allows you to bundle
your content updates into regular deployment packages and minimizes
the impact to the production tier. The most obvious example of this is
the many caches that are affected by authoring. When CMS authors
change content, they are invalidating the many caches on the server.
This is particularly important for coarse caches such as the ASP.NET
output cache.

Keeping in mind the impact to caching, you can imagine how writing
to the CMS server can substantially impact your performance. Not only
are you performing writes to the database, but then this data must be
written into the many caches on the system.

Even so, it is quite possible that authoring against your production
tier will still leave you within acceptable performance limits. There are
administrators running large CMS sites who are comfortable with the
performance and security implications of authoring on their production
tier. One of the main factors in this decision is how important it is to have
updates go live immediately. News sites, for example, may find that their
business needs conflict with their desire to improve performance by
caching content. They may accept that their authors will be constantly
updating and creating pages. But this is their business and therefore is
their most important consideration.

## Authentication Module

Authentication is the action of identifying a user. This action, just like
any other, carries with it a performance implication. The test results in
Figure 34–15 demonstrate that CMS sites experience roughly a 10%
performance improvement when the CMS authentication module is
removed from the web.config file.

The obvious question is, when can this module be removed safely?
Only remove your authentication module if your entire site is available

to the CMS guest user. If you have portions of your site that are meant only for specific users, you will need the authentication module in order to identify these users.

If you require authentication for part of your site and still want to take advantage of this performance improvement, you can consider partitioning your site across different CMS servers. This would allow you to remove the module from the cluster that does not require authentication.

## Read-Only versus Read/Write CMS Sites

Using the CMS SCA, it is quite easy to change a CMS site from read/write to read-only. As mentioned in Chapter 3, when a CMS server is in read-only mode, roughly 90% of interaction with the database is through stored Structured Query Language (SQL) procedures. An example of this is a read-only CMS server caching CMS pages. When the server is writing—such as creating new CMS pages—approximately 50% of database queries are ad hoc server queries and the other 50% are stored procedures.

The fact that so much of the processing is happening through stored procedures adds up to roughly a 10% performance increase over read/write sites. Also, a performance increase comes from not having any cache flushes occurring.

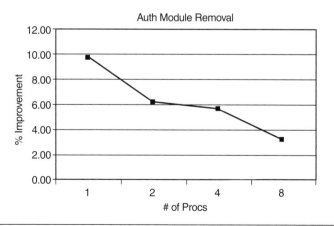

**Figure 34–15** Authentication module removal

### CMS Background Processing

CMS background processing is responsible for cleaning up CMS servers. For example, performance of a CMS server is increased by the fact that background processing will remove deleted items from the CMS SQL Server database. These items include CMS pages, channels, and resources. Removing these items during background processing allows better performance during authoring and keeps the database size as small as possible.

Background processing has been significantly improved in CMS 2002. Almost all the work has been moved to the SQL Server. This provides a significant performance gain for the CMS server. However, it does not mean that background processing has no performance impact.

If a browser client requests content that is cached, the CMS server will continue to serve this content as normal. If, on the other hand, the content needs to be retrieved from the CMS database, then there could be a performance hit. The reason for this is that the CMS server might be contending with background processing for the SQL Server resources. Based on this, your CMS server performance will be optimized if you run background processing during your lowest traffic period.

## Network Latency

Just like any other Web site, CMS sites are affected by the performance of their network. Network latency is the delay caused by data moving across your network architecture. This topic is outside the scope of this book, but it is important to realize that your network latency can impact your CMS server performance.

There are a few points that can easily be noted here. Microsoft advises that CMS performance will be best when the CMS server is on the same network switch as the database server. Keep in mind that security measures, such as firewalls, can also impact your network performance.

## IIS Performance

As you know, CMS is not a Web server. The pages sent to a browser client are all coming from IIS. Based on this fact alone, it is important to ensure that your IIS server is optimized for performance. Keeping this in mind, you can make some CMS-specific changes that will provide performance gains.

The best candidate for IIS performance gains applies only to read-only sites. As mentioned earlier, the best deployment scenario for CMS performance is to separate the authoring servers from the production servers. If your site is deployed in this architecture, you will also be able to set your production servers to be read-only. As mentioned earlier, simply setting the server to read-only will result in a performance gain. However, given this scenario, you have an additional option.

If your CMS server is running as read-only, it is possible for you to remove one of the CMS ISAPI filters. The Resolution HTML Packager filter is only used when CMS authors are comparing different historical versions of content. If your site is read-only, you can safely remove this filter and benefit from a small increase in performance.

The filter can be removed from within the Internet Information Services Manager. From this interface, go to your Web site properties. Once there, you can click on the ISAPI Filters tab and remove the filter.

# SQL Server Performance

Contrary to what many people think, SQL Server is seldom the bottleneck on a runtime CMS site. One SQL Server can easily handle a significant Web farm of CMS servers. Make sure that you have investigated other performance tuning options before you start to spend a great deal of effort trying to optimize your database. You may find that your time is better spent investigating your caching plan or the efficiency of your templates.

There is one scenario where SQL Server could be stressed by a CMS site. This is when a lot of authoring is occurring at the same time as a lot of traffic. With this in mind, you need to remember a few key points about optimizing your CMS SQL Server database. The most important point is that you will improve your performance if you dedicate a SQL Server machine to your CMS database. SQL Server is able to handle a tremendous load, so this may not be required, but it is certainly the first consideration when you are contemplating this topic.

If you are using your SQL Server for many databases, then you should consider how you will prevent resource contention issues. For best performance, the SQL Server databases should be separated from their transaction logs. This separation should occur across different physical drives.

SQL Server performance is a broad topic and will not be discussed in depth in this book. Refer to the SQL Server documentation for a more thorough discussion of this topic at http://go.microsoft.com/fwlink/ ?LinkId=9512.

## Security and Performance

As with most design topics, security and performance can often be conflicting goals. If you protect your entire CMS site with a protocol such as Secure Sockets Layer (SSL), you will certainly incur a performance penalty. To mitigate this impact, you should carefully consider which parts of your site require such security mechanisms. For example, most CMS sites will only use SSL for their login page.

If you do decide to use SSL with your CMS pages, keep in mind that any data on the page will be encrypted before it is sent across the wire. This includes both text and image data. To maximize your performance, make sure that the SSL-protected pages are light (i.e., few graphics and as little text as possible).

For more information about secure Web sites, refer to the security chapters in Part IV of this book and to article Q247658, "Building Secure ASP.NET Applications: Authentication, Authorization, and Secure Communication," in the Microsoft Knowledge Base (http://msdn.microsoft. com/library/default.asp?url=/library/en-us/dnnetsec/html/SecNetch04.asp).

## Summary

Learning about CMS-specific issues is important when considering the performance of your CMS Web site deployment. In this chapter, a number of vital considerations have been discussed. Performance testing, on the other hand, is very similar to testing any other Web site. There are many resources out there that can help you with testing the performance of your CMS site.

When you are designing any site, it is important to test and test often. The same holds true for performance testing a CMS site. The next chapter covers Transaction Cost Analysis (TCA). You can apply the techniques that you have learned in this chapter to the TCA for your site. Here is a summary of performance considerations.

- Ensure that your CMS servers have ample physical memory. Windows 2003 Advanced Servers can use up to 4GB of RAM. Making more memory available can be the fastest, cheapest, and easiest way to increase your performance.
- Clarify your working set and ensure that these pages are cached. The next chapter will provide information about how to define the working set on your site.
- Minimize the frequency of cache flushes caused by content updates.
- Make sure that your CMS template code is as efficient as possible.
- Use a container hierarchy that is neither too wide nor too deep.
- Limit the number of placeholders on a template. Each additional placeholder adds more code to the template.
- Limit the amount of data in your placeholders. Just as in any other Web site, you want to keep your pages as light as possible.
- Use PAPI searches wisely; GUID searches are the fastest.

# Performance Testing and Capacity Planning

Although it is important to have specific performance knowledge about CMS when you are designing a CMS site, it is not as important to have such knowledge when you are testing the site. Performance testing for CMS sites is much the same as testing any other ASP or ASP.NET Web site.

It is remarkable how often performance planning is neglected during the Web site planning phase. Quite often it is an afterthought. At the end of the process, when the site is completed, it is deployed to the production environment and only then tested for performance. This is a recipe for disaster. When planning your CMS site project, make sure to schedule performance tests at a stage when you will actually be able to resolve any issues that are found. Do not make the mistake of running your first tests when you are already rushing to meet impending deadlines.

The previous chapter discussed how to build high-performance CMS sites. This chapter discusses how to create your performance goals and how to test your results. The key message of this chapter is "test early and test often."

## Performance Goals

At the start of your CMS project, you should have the performance goals nailed down. This gives everyone in the Web design and coding process a realistic chance to succeed. If you do not provide specific goals, you are not giving your people a chance. The only thing worse than not having targets is increasing the expectations near the end of the project. Keep in mind that your Web site is designed and coded based on the original numbers. If someone changes those numbers, it could result in a substantial redesign.

Creating your performance goals should be a scientific process. If you are already running a Web site and you want to move that Web site to CMS, then you have the data that you require to create your goals. Simply check your Web site statistics and base your performance goals on these numbers. On the other hand, if you are creating a site from scratch or making major alterations, the task is far more involved.

Of course, there is a paradox when you try to estimate your initial performance goals. The closer the testing environment gets to your final site, the more complex the simulation becomes. At some point, you will compromise the efficiency of your test by spending too much time creating the setup. In other words, the closer the simulation gets to the actual site, the less time you save doing the prototype. At some point, you may as well wait for the site to be finished. Nonetheless, this initial testing should be done. Have your developers mock up the best prototype possible. This will give you some confidence that your initial numbers are well founded.

How you determine your performance goals for a new site is a business question. However, there are a number of things that you can do to help nail down realistic goals. Based on the requirements of your site, you can prototype features and then do some performance tests. These tests can be used to help calculate the performance necessary to meet your business needs and your budget.

The following are some of the factors that you should consider when creating your performance goals.

## Site Traffic

This is the most common interpretation of performance. Web developers often talk about how many "hits" the site can handle. Although the term is used to describe a number of different counting techniques, the principle idea is the same. The intent is to define the number of people who can simultaneously surf the site and still have a decent user experience.

Obviously, this is one of the most important considerations, but it certainly does not give you all the information that you require to draft your performance goals. Do not convince yourself that this one measurement will encompass all your performance needs.

## Authoring

Regardless of whether you separate your production and authoring environments, the number of authors you support will still be a consideration.

You may have different performance goals for each environment, but you will want both your site visitors and your authors to have a pleasant experience.

Quite often, the "design-time" performance of CMS sites is neglected. Make sure that your performance tests include some sort of realistic authoring cases.

## Usage Profile

How your site is used can be as important as how much your site is used. Later in this chapter we will discuss how usage profiles are used in performance testing. If you do not take this into consideration, you could find that most of your traffic is heading to your slowest pages. This will substantially skew your performance numbers.

## Applications

The type of code that you run on your site will dramatically affect how quickly you can serve pages. In fact, this is probably the single greatest consideration that you have the power to change (other than telling people not to visit your site).

Many sites offer some sort of personalization for their visitors. This is an example of an application that you may wish to run. The action of checking which user is viewing your site will cost you CPU cycles. Other examples include integration with back-end systems and code that makes your Web more visually interesting. One example of this is DHTML menus. They may look cool, but they are adding work to the client browsers.

The balance that you will search for is the amount of functionality that you can offer your users and still keep their interest. If you do not offer them anything, then they might get bored. But if you try to give them too much, your site could slow to a crawl. It is not always easy to find balance. You need to do performance testing and usability testing so that you can make an educated decision.

## Budget

Given an unlimited budget, virtually any site could meet any performance goals. But this is not the world that we live in. Your performance goals will most likely be constrained by your hardware budget.

Just as with any other bugs, fixing performance problems early in your project will save you a tremendous amount of time and money.

According to Steve McConnell's *Code Complete* (Microsoft Press, 1993), "Microsoft's application division has found that it takes 3 hours to find and fix a defect using code inspection . . . and 12 hours to find and fix a defect using testing." Test your site early and test it often.

### Time

Time is often the trump card in arguments about project plans. You may simply have to concede that your performance is partially dependent upon the amount of optimization that can be done within the time that you are allotted. The last chapter discussed how you could save time in your performance tuning by starting early in the project plan. Design your site with performance in mind. Do not try to add it all at the end.

# Performance Testing

This section discusses how you can hunt down any potential problems. Also, as previously discussed, performance testing will be necessary if you want to draft realistic performance goals.

Ideally, you will include performance testing in the development of each component within your site. Whether it is your personalization code or your navigation, you should test it to see if it performs well enough to be included in the final version of your site.

## Performance Counters

In the area of performance testing, the best new feature of CMS 2002 is the performance counters. Performance counters allow you to monitor various values as you run your performance tests. Although these performance counters are not the most useful ones for calculating your performance numbers, they are very useful when you are diagnosing problems.

Table 35–1 shows the complete list of performance counters provided in MCMS 2002.

For more information about how to set up and use performance counters, refer to MSDN (http://msdn.microsoft.com/library/default. asp?url=/library/en-us/cpguide/html/cpconmonitoringaspnetapplication performance.asp). You can also refer to the CMS help topic "Measuring and Testing Site Performance" for more information about CMS-specific considerations.

**Table 35–1** Performance Counters

| Counter | Counts | Description |
| --- | --- | --- |
| Active Enterprise (AE) Node objects | Number of active MCMS COM objects on the server | These are the COM nodes created as each request is processed. Each request will generate many COM objects in the AEServer object, which are then destroyed as the processing completes. This counter is a snapshot of the number of COM objects active at any one time and is a reflection of the amount of processing activity within the MCMS server. |
| | | In itself this does not provide a direct gauge of performance; however, high values would demonstrate a very active MCMS site. If the site is under-performing, this value can be decreased by using techniques such as caching the navigation controls, which in turn could improve performance. |
| AE Node objects created/sec | Number of AE Node objects created per second | As above, but this provides the average activity over time. |
| Guest sessions | Number of guest sessions on the server | This is the number of current connections to the MCMS server that are authenticated as a Guest user. |
| | | This is more for informational purposes than to adjust performance, although it could be used to identify peaks of activity. |
| Guest sessions opened/sec | Number of guest sessions opened per second | As above, but this provides the average activity over time. |

*(continued)*

**Table 35–1** *(Continued)*

| Counter | Counts | Description |
|---|---|---|
| Authenticated sessions | Number of authenticated sessions connected to server | This is the number of current authenticated connections to the MCMS server.<br><br>This is more for informational purposes than to adjust performance, although it could be used to identify peaks of activity. |
| Authenticated sessions opened/sec | Number of authenticated sessions opened per second | As above, but this provides the average activity over time. |
| Edit sessions | Authoring or development sessions connected to server | This is the number of current authenticated connections to the MCMS server that are in Edit mode.<br><br>This is more for informational purposes than to adjust performance, although it could be used to identify peaks of activity. Edit activity on an MCMS server can have a significant impact on performance. |
| Edit sessions opened/sec | Number of authoring or development sessions opened per second | As above, but this provides the average activity over time. |
| ISAPI sessions | Number of Internet Server API (ISAPI) sessions opened by server | Provides the number of connections currently in the MCMS ISAPI filter performing URL transformations. If you have a high number of these, it may mean that the URL transformation is taking a long time, which may be adjusted by increasing the node cache size. |
| ISAPI sessions opened/sec | Number of ISAPI sessions opened per second | Tells you how many connections are opened per second in the MCMS ISAPI filter. Provides the number of URL requests to MCMS per second. |

**Table 35–1** *(Continued)*

| Counter | Counts | Description |
| --- | --- | --- |
| Master cache nodes | Number of items in internal MCMS master cache | Number of nodes in master cache. This is limited by the node cache size set in the SCA. If this value is less than the setting in the SCA, then this is an indication that all requested MCMS nodes are currently cached. If this value is close to or above the value in the SCA, then this is an indication that the setting in the SCA is not high enough to allow all requested nodes to be cached. |
| Shared nodes | Number of items/nodes referenced by server, including master cache items | This value is related to the number of master cache nodes; however this value will reflect multiple versions (e.g., checked in and checked out) of the same master node. |
| Shared nodes created/sec | Shared nodes created per second | This is a reflection of the increase in size of the node cache as new nodes are cached. |
| | | If the master node cache value is close to or above the value in the SCA and this value is high, then this is a clear indication that objects are being moved into and out of cache, which will lower performance. |
| Cache hits/sec | Rate of cache hits on master cache | A high value here relative to the following value implies an effective use of cache. |
| Cache misses/sec | Rate of cache misses on master cache | A high value here relative to the preceding value implies an inefficient cache setting. |

*(continued)*

**Table 35–1** *(Continued)*

| Counter | Counts | Description |
|---|---|---|
| Data access operations/sec | Number of data access operations executed per second | This is the count of accesses to the SQL Server database. A high value could imply one of several things: The node cache value may be too small; the resource cache may be too small; or there is a need to cache search results. |
| Exceptions thrown | Number of exceptions thrown by server | This is informational and provides a count of exceptions thrown. If this is increasing rapidly over time, it could indicate problems on the server or in the code base. |
| Number of MCMS connections | Number of open MCMS application connections | This is informational and provides an indication of the load on the MCMS server. It includes all current connections to the MCMS server at a point in time. It includes the ISAPI connections plus all other connections. |

## Measuring Performance

How you determine your performance numbers determines how realistic those numbers will be when you deploy your site to the Web.

There are three steps to creating a performance test. First, you need to create a realistic usage profile. Next, you create test scripts, and finally, you run your test scripts. The following subsections discuss each of these steps.

### Step 1: Create a Usage Profile

Your usage profile will be used as the game plan for your stress testing. Without the profile, you cannot be sure that you are focusing on the right portions of your site. For example, you may have a section of your site that is used frequently but performs worse than the rest of the site. You will want to ensure that you address the performance issues for these pages. Usage profiles will be discussed in more detail later in this chapter.

For more information about a usage profile, refer to "Creating a Usage Profile for Site Capacity Planning" (http://go.microsoft.com/fwlink/ ?LinkId=9508).

### Step 2: Create a Test Script

There are different tools that you can use to stress your site. The most popular tool is Microsoft Application Center Test (ACT). This tool is designed to simulate load on your Web site.

Once you have created a usage profile, you will have a good idea of the URLs that will get hit in each visit. Hitting these URLs with a stress tool will give you performance numbers for each visit. You can either record a test script or programmatically create a test script.

For more information about ACT, refer to this URL: http://msdn. microsoft.com/library/default.asp?url=/library/en-us/act/htm/actml_ main.asp.

### Step 3: Use a Stress Tool to Run the Script against Your Site

Running the stress tool against your site will give you the opportunity to use performance counters. Which counters you record will depend upon your business needs, but typical Web site stress tests measure CPU usage and ASP.NET (or ASP) requests.

For more information about throughput, refer to "Understanding Performance Testing" (http://go.microsoft.com/fwlink/?LinkId=9511).

## Usage Profiles

Creating realistic usage profiles is fundamental to effective performance testing. A usage profile is a representation of your site visitors' behavior while they are surfing your site.

Generally, usage profiles consist of the following information:

- Average session length of the user
- List of pages visited
- Total number of pages visited in a session
- Frequency at which each page is visited

You will not need to model all these parameters, but you will need to accurately model pages that are hit and the frequency with which they are hit.

### Average Session Length

"Session" is a word that is far too overloaded. In the context of usage profiles, think of a session as a unique visit from a user. One user may have many unique visits to a site. As the user surfs around the site, their one session might involve hitting many pages. Within those pages are many elements that can access many files. For example, one site might contain pieces cached in memory or various images from your hard drive.

The average session length represents the average number of minutes from the start of a user's visit to the end of the visit. You will need to use your IIS logs to gather information about the length of each session.

### Pages Visited

Page views define the way that users surf a Web site. You can check your IIS logs to see the URLs for the pages that are being accessed the most.

### Number of Pages

Tracking the number of pages visited will allow you to create usage profiles that match your users. By looking at how many pages are surfed, you can create stress scripts that include the appropriate number of URLs.

If you have statistics for the average session length, you can use this number and the number of pages visited to calculate the frequency of page visits.

### Frequency of Page Visits

This statistic is important because it indicates how quickly your users navigate through your site. If you have a lot of content on your pages, you may find that users spend some time before moving on to the next page. However, if your users click rapidly through pages, then you would want to consider this when creating your usage profiles.

## Web Usage Statistics

There are numerous tools and services available for interpreting Web site usage. If you want to do this work yourself, you can use your IIS logs to compile the information that you require.

The goal of performance testing is to plan for peak periods on the Web site. Generally, site operators consider peak to be three times their normal load. With this in mind, you should try to gather usage statistics from a period long enough that it includes periods that are as close to your peak usage as possible. After having done this, you can identify a peak period and use those numbers for your testing. Typically, a sample of a day is used.

## Page Requests

To get pages per second, you might want to record a script using ACT. Then open the script and take out any redirects. In other words, leave in URLs like http://localhost/mysite/default.htm. But, on an ASP site, you would want to take out anything like http://localhost/mysite/. The reason for this is that this URL is simply a redirect and does not correspond to a page hit.

However, on an ASP.NET site, you would not want to have a URL like http://localhost/mysite/ right next to the URL http://localhost/mysite/default.htm. These two URLs are equivalent, and therefore one of them could be considered a redirect. Having done this, you can use your performance counters to calculate pages per second. Once you have warmed up the site by running the test for a few minutes before you start to record, ASP.NET (or ASP) requests per second will equal pages per second. This is a rough method, but it generally works well.

We have now completed our discussion of one of the main methods of performance testing a Web site: prototype modeling. This method involves running tests on hardware similar to the production environment and on applications that model your production code.

In summary, the way to use this method is to create a test environment as close to your production environment as possible. Then you would create your usage profile, simulate this profile using a stress tool, and determine the throughput of the profile in pages per second. Based on this, you can extrapolate the number of concurrent users that your site can support. You can use rules of thumb like 30 seconds per click per user, or you can use the statistics in your usage profile. Once you have all this information, you can take your throughput and divide it by the number of clicks for each user. For example, if your site renders 100 pages per second and your users click 1 page per second, then you could support 100 concurrent users.

We will now move on to the other popular strategy for performance testing: Transaction Cost Analysis (TCA).

# Transaction Cost Analysis

The Transaction Cost Analysis methodology is used to provide mathematical calculations for capacity planning. You can also use TCA principles to find performance bottlenecks on your site. Each operation is isolated and examined. Remember that creating accurate usage profiles is the first step to successful TCA analysis.

The benefit of this paradigm is that you do not have to model your environment the same way that you would using the prototype modeling approach. TCA is far more granular and therefore more flexible. For example, it may allow you to test on hardware that is not the same as your performance environment. Furthermore, you will be able to modify things like your usage profiles without having to run any new tests.

Once you have initial values for your TCA analysis, you will be able to use them for future changes to your site. Rather than analyzing the entire site, you can focus purely on the sections that have changed.

For the purposes of this chapter, we are using the example of CPU utilization. However, the TCA principles can be applied to other costs. For example, you might want to analyze the performance of your SQL Server machine or the memory usage of your Web server.

For more information about the TCA methodology, refer to the following articles:

- "Using Transaction Cost Analysis for Site Capacity Planning," http://go.microsoft.com/fwlink/?LinkId=9509. This article provides a hands-on guide to using TCA. We highly recommend that you read this paper before you read the rest of this chapter.
- "Capacity Model for Internet Transactions," http://go.microsoft.com/fwlink/?LinkId=9507. This article provides an overview of the TCA methodology.
- CMS 2002 white paper "Transaction Cost Analysis and Capacity Planning for MCMS 2002."

## Page Cost Strategy

This is the strategy that we will be exploring in this chapter. The reason that we will use this method is that it is the most reliable way to test the performance of a CMS site. Depending on your business and your site, you may decide to use one of the other strategies. But even if you do, page cost will be a useful test for you. Page cost is the easiest because the tests are straightforward. You use a stress tool and record the results of one page. There isn't much that can go wrong with this strategy.

Since you have already read the TCA paper listed earlier (you did read it, right?), you have seen the example of a site performing various "operations." In our discussion, you can equate these operations with page cost.

## Using Page Cost to Test Your CMS Site

Based on the page types identified for the site, the following tables can be produced. These numbers are based on the fictitious BOTS Consulting site.

Each of these tables represents a page from the usage profile. After using the performance counters to gather the cost of each page, you then average out the cost and calculate the total cost of the site.

What we will now do is create three scripts that hit each page individually. The scripts will be executed such that the processor will be at or near 85% utilization. Keep in mind that most sites try to run their production machines at about 35% utilization. This allows them to scale to a peak load of three times the normal traffic. We are using 85% for these tests to check the performance near the peak load. Having run these scripts, we will record the CPU utilization and the pages-per-second throughput.

Tables 35–2 through 35–4 illustrate the CPU cost for each of the three pages that we are testing. We gather this information by running an ACT script against the URL for the page and then recording the Windows performance counter for CPU utilization.

**Table 35–2** Page 1: Home Page

| Measurement | Value |
|-------------|-------|
| CPU usage | 0.80 (MHz) |
| Throughput | 100 (pages per second) |

**Table 35–3** Page 2: Case Study

| Measurement | Value |
|-------------|-------|
| CPU usage | 0.85 (MHz) |
| Throughput | 150 (pages per second) |

**Table 35–4** Page 3: Article

| Measurement | Value |
|---|---|
| CPU usage | 0.90 (MHz) |
| Throughput | 200 (pages per second) |

## Calculating Users Based on CPU Capacity

Calculating the number of users that your site can support is one of the key aims of performance testing. In fact, this one measurement is often the catalyst for all performance testing. The formula for calculating CPU capacity is the number of processors multiplied by the megahertz rating of the CPU.

$$\text{CPU capacity} = (\text{number of processors}) \times \text{speed}$$

The next number to calculate is the target CPU capacity. This will determine your goal for CPU capacity. You will need to determine what you think your target should be. A value of 80% is often used because it allows some room in case your usage spikes for some period of time. For example, if your site happened to be mentioned by some large news site, you might find that you need that extra 20% of capacity.

$$\text{Target CPU capacity} = \text{CPU capacity} \times .80$$

It is then a simple matter to determine how many simultaneous users you are able to support on one machine.

$$\text{User capacity} = \text{target CPU capacity} / \text{Web CPU cost per user}$$

## Cost Table for Pages

Once you have numbers for each page, you can create a table such as Table 35–5. For this example, we are using fictitious numbers for the BOTS Consulting site, with one 1,000MHz processor.

The total CPU cost for each page is calculated with this formula:

Total CPU cost =
(CPU usage $\times$ number of processors $\times$ CPU speed)/requests per second

For example:

$$\text{Page 1 total CPU cost} =$$
$$(0.01 \times 1 \times 1,000)/110 = 0.09$$

## Using Usage Profiles for TCA

Now we know the cost of individual pages. Based on our usage profile, we can add in the page distribution numbers, shown in Table 35–6. This determines how much of the traffic we expect each page to carry.

For this example, we will continue to use fictitious numbers from performance testing on the BOTS Consulting site. We will use these numbers to demonstrate how to calculate the user capacity for a CMS site. We will also assume that the Web server has one 1,000MHz processor.

**Table 35–5**  Total CPU Cost for Each Page in the Profile

| Pages | Requests per Second | CPU Usage (MHz) | Total CPU Cost (MHz/Request) |
|---|---|---|---|
| Page 1: Home Page | 110 | 0.80 | 7.27 |
| Page 2: Case Study | 120 | 0.85 | 7.08 |
| Page 3: Article | 130 | 0.95 | 7.31 |

**Table 35–6**  Distribution of Traffic

| Posting Operation | Distribution |
|---|---|
| Page 1 | 50% |
| Page 2 | 30% |
| Page 3 | 20% |
| Total | 100% |

Next we can take our numbers from the CPU cost table (Table 35–5) and add in the data about the distribution of the load (Table 35–6). This gives us the cost of the particular usage profile, shown in Table 35–7. Table 35–8 shows the result of calculating the pages-per-second cost of the distribution profile.

As we learned earlier in this chapter, once you have all this information, you can take your throughput and divide it by the number of clicks for each user. In this example, our site renders roughly 111 pages per second. If our users click 1 page per second, then we could support 111 concurrent users.

Remember that your usage profile could include the rate that your users are clicking through your site. If we found that our IIS logs indicated that the average session length was ten minutes and the average pages per session was 20, then the click rate would be 0.017 pages per second per user. Based on this rate, we could support 6,517 concurrent users (110.79 pages per second / 0.017 pages per second per user).

Now that you have these numbers for a 1,000MHz processor, you could change the processor power to 2,000MHz. Without running any new tests, you would know that you would be able to support 13,034 concurrent users. You could also alter your user profile distributions and calculate the resulting effect on your performance numbers. And finally, you could change the code on one page and then just test the new page. You would not have to run all the other page tests again.

**Table 35–7** CPU Cost for Distribution Profile

| Pages | Distribution Profile | CPU Cost for Profile |
|---|---|---|
| Home Page | 50% | $7.27 \times 0.5 = 3.635$ |
| Case Study | 30% | $7.08 \times 0.3 = 2.124$ |
| Article | 20% | $7.31 \times 0.2 = 1.462$ |
| Total | 100% | 7.221 |

**Table 35–8** CPU Cost of Profile

| Server CPU | Target CPU | Web CPU Cost for Profile | Pages/Second for Profile |
|---|---|---|---|
| 1,000 | $1,000 \times .80 = 800$ | 7.221 | 110.79 |

## Troubleshooting Performance Issues

From the perspective of a CMS developer, the first step in any performance investigation is to verify whether or not the performance issue is actually a CMS problem. The Microsoft PSS support team for CMS actually spends a good portion of its time chasing down problems that are not the result of a CMS issue.

To determine whether an issue is directly related to CMS, take as much of the code from the problematic template as possible and run it outside of a CMS context. In other words, put the code into a stand-alone ASPX (or ASP) page and see what sort of performance difference exists. If the code runs considerably faster outside of CMS, then you can start to think about CMS-specific considerations.

Obviously, this is more difficult to do if the code is using the CMS PAPI. But the key message is to not just assume that the issue is a CMS problem. Try to narrow it down to a particular template and then a particular section of code. You can do this by practicing the all-important methodology of "one thing at a time." Try removing each component until you find the code that is dragging.

Table 35–9 lists a number of issues and their possible causes and solutions.

**Table 35–9** Troubleshooting Performance Issues

| Behavior | Solution |
|----------|----------|
| Rate of cache misses is high. | Examine size and balance of caches. Ensure that output cache directives are correct and the durations are appropriate. |
| Rate of cache misses is high plus data access operations are high. | Adjust your cache settings and usage. This could also be the result of large searches—try caching the most common searches. |
| Rate of cache misses is high plus number of master node cache items is high. | Increase the size of the master node cache—ideally your peak node cache requirements should be around 80% of allocated node cache size to allow for shared nodes. You can also use this in conjunction with the ASP.NET performance counters for the output cache to trace the caching of data before MCMS. |

*(continued)*

**Table 35–9** *(Continued)*

| Behavior | Solution |
|---|---|
| Number of exceptions thrown by server is high. | Check the event log. |
| The cost for your authenticated users is much higher than for guest users. | Check your authentication mechanism for potential issues. |
| Web server is starved for resources. | Check the performance counters to see what is using the most resources. |

# Summary

Performance testing is a vital component in your Web site development plan. Ensure that you have provided yourself with adequate time and resources for proper performance testing. Do not wait until your site is completely finished before you start your performance testing.

As each feature is built, you can use the prototype modeling or the TCA methodology to analyze the performance of the code. This will help you find performance issues early in the process. This will save you time and money since you will detect defects when they are easier to fix.

This chapter discussed various aspects of performance testing and the TCA methodology. For more information about these topics, refer to *Performance Testing Microsoft .NET Web Applications*, by the Microsoft Application Consulting and Engineering Team (Microsoft Press, 2003).

# Tips and Techniques

## Overview

Some of our most frustrating moments have been trying to figure out solutions to "problems." In some cases these problems are the result of what CMS can or cannot do. However, it's more often that we simply have a challenging requirement to meet and we're not sure what the solution is.

In this chapter, we provide you with a frequently asked questions (FAQ)-style summary of some of the challenges we've run across and how we solved them. This list is by no means complete. However, we hope that it will give you insight into some common challenges and, perhaps, lead you to your own answers as you develop on the platform.

## Building a Site Map with Recursive Navigation

In traditional Web site development, the developer controlled navigation. This model worked pretty well, since they also controlled content contribution. However, after you've implemented CMS, the business users really control the site. More to the point, even if the developers wanted to maintain navigation manually, it's almost impossible to keep up with even a modestly sized contributor group. As a result, developers must create a mechanism that can effectively react to a site without inherently knowing what the structure of that site is. This is especially apparent when we are talking about a site map. To this end, CMS provides two mechanisms for allowing developers to create code that can elegantly and effectively react to an ever changing site structure: the Publishing API (PAPI) and Site Manager.

To begin, Site Manager allows developers and content contributors to create a structure that defines the organization of their site in the form of channels. This channel structure is easily defined through Site Manager and through the constant contribution of postings within CMS. Then, the Publishing API provides the ability to access that structure, exposing properties like URL, Display Name, and Name in addition to an unlimited number of custom properties. Once you have a structure and a way to access it, programmatic recursion of that structure allows developers to be freed from the bonds of having to know the structure up front. To illustrate this point, let's examine the BOTS Consulting site map.

In Figure 36–1 you'll see a picture of Site Manager, exposing the channel structure of the BOTS Web site. Be careful to note the channels and the structure.

Now, let's look at the actual site map in the site. In Figure 36–2 you'll notice that all the channels defined in Site Manager are exposed in the site map page. In this case the BOTS IT department decided that they only wanted to expose the sections of the site (the channels) and not the actual pages. It's relatively trivial to include postings as well; just keep in mind that it may affect performance since you're exposing many more objects.

**Figure 36–1** In Site Manager you can see the channel structure for BOTS

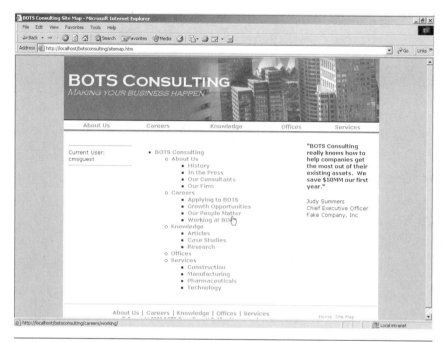

**Figure 36–2** The BOTS Consulting site map

In Listing 36–1 you can see our site map function. In this function, we're adding literal and HtmlAnchor controls to a .NET placeholder control we've embedded in our user control.

**Listing 36–1** A sample recursive site map control

```
public void BuildSiteMap(Channel startChannel)
{
    // Add an unordered list tag to our .NET placeholder control
    this.SiteMap.Controls.Add(new LiteralControl("<UL>"));

    // Create a new link and assign the appropriate values from the channel
    // startChannel object.
    HtmlAnchor navigationLink = new HtmlAnchor();
    navigationLink.InnerText = startChannel.DisplayName;
    navigationLink.HRef = startChannel.Url;
    navigationLink.Attributes.Add("style","FONT-WEIGHT: bold; COLOR: gray");

    // Add the new link to our .NET placeholder control
    this.SiteMap.Controls.Add(new LiteralControl("<LI>"));
```

```
    this.SiteMap.Controls.Add(navigationLink);
    this.SiteMap.Controls.Add(new LiteralControl("</LI>"));

    // Get a collection of channels in the current channel
    ChannelCollection subChannels = startChannel.Channels;
    // Make sure that we got a collection
    if (subChannels != null)
    {
        // Call our BuildSiteMap function for each of the subchannels
        foreach(Channel subChannel in subChannels)
        {
            this.BuildSiteMap(subChannel);
        }

    }
    // Close the unordered list tag and add it to our .NET placeholder
control
    this.SiteMap.Controls.Add(new LiteralControl("</UL>"));
}
```

In this example, we accept one parameter, which is the starting point for the site map. From there we recursively traverse our tree structure, "discovering" all the channels in our site. We've hardcoded how the site map displays (a large unordered list), but this can certainly be expanded to include formatting as a parameter.

## Impersonation

Impersonation is a way to programmatically log on as a user who is different from the actual physical user. In the context of CMS, there are a few reasons why you might want to implement this feature. For example, let's suppose that the current user is an author and you would like to give them the ability to create a channel. The only sure way to provide them with this functionality is to make them a channel manager or an administrator. Obviously, this route is not always the best one and it tends to be unilateral—yes, you've given them the ability to create channels, but you've also provided them with certain authority over security, channel properties, and content approval. This is not ideal. So, the real answer to the problem is impersonation.

Essentially, it is possible to programmatically and temporarily log on as a generic, impersonated user with certain rights—in this case as either an administrator or a channel manager—perform the operation you need to perform, and log that generic user out.

The first step is defining what functionality you would like to expose. Building off of the example we provided earlier, let's suppose that BOTS Consulting wants to give their editors the ability to create new channels in the Knowledge section so that it's possible for editors to create new classifications of "knowledge" as the firm changes over time. Since editors don't inherently have this ability, you'll first need to create a user ID under which this operation can be performed. In this example, we've created a generic user called IMPCHANNELADMIN. This user is defined as a channel manager in the Knowledge section.

---

**NOTE:** You could also create an administrator-level account, but since the requirement was specific to the Knowledge section, we didn't want to give the impersonated user too much power. The choice is up to you.

---

The next step is to create an interface that allows the editor to provide the channel properties for the new channel (see Figure 36–3). In

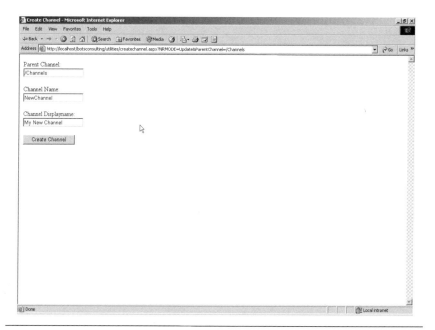

**Figure 36–3** Sample interface for a channel creation tool

this example, you need to create a form that allows the editor to enter the name and display name for the new channel.

Once the interface is defined, you need to add the code to support the operation. In this case, the form will allow the user to enter the properties and, on postback, log on as the generic administrator, create the channel, and return a success or failure message. In Listing 36–2 you will see a rough sample of how to create the impersonation logic.

**Listing 36–2**  Creating a Web-based channel creation solution using impersonation

```
private void Page_Load(object sender, System.EventArgs e)
{
      try
      {
            // Show the current user
            this.CurrentUser.Text = CmsHttpContext.Current.User.
ServerAccountName;

            // Set parent channel from the query string
            // We assume that you would create a link from a posting in the
            // site to this page, enabling the user to create a channel.
            // When you call the page, you provide the current channel's path
            // as a query string parameter.  You could equally pass the
            // parent's GUID.
            if (Request.Params["ParentChannel"] != null)
            {
                  this.txbParentChannel.Text = Request.Params
["ParentChannel"];

                  // Create a reference to the channel
                  Channel objParentChannel = (Channel)CmsHttpContext.Current.
Searches.GetByPath(this.txbParentChannel.Text);

                  // Make sure the channel exists
                  if (objParentChannel == null)
                  {
                        this.DisplayNonExceptionMessage("The specified
channel does not exist.");
                  }
            }
            else
            {this.DisplayNonExceptionMessage("No parent channel specified");}
      }
```

```
        scatch(Exception eException)
        {
                this.DisplayExceptionMessage(eException);
        }


}


public CmsApplicationContext AuthenticateasAdminUser()
{
        CmsApplicationContext newContext = new CmsApplicationContext();
        newContext.AuthenticateAsUser("WinNT://cmsdemo1/cmsadmin","password",
PublishingMode.Update);
        return newContext;
}


private void CreateNewChannel (CmsApplicationContext myContext)
{

        try
        {
                // Create a channel object representing the parent channel
                Channel objParentChannel =
(Channel)myContext.Searches.GetByPath(this.txbParentChannel.Text);

                // Create the new channel, assign the name and displayname
                // properties as provided by the user and commit the transaction
                Channel objNewChannel =
(Channel)objParentChannel.CreateChannel();
                objNewChannel.Name = this.txbName.Text.ToString();
                objNewChannel.DisplayName = this.txbDisplayName.Text.ToString();
                myContext.CommitAll();
                this.DisplayNonExceptionMessage("New channel created
successfully.");
        }

        catch(Exception eException)
        {
                this.DisplayExceptionMessage(eException);
        }


}


private void DisplayExceptionMessage(Exception eException)
{
```

```
    this.lblMessage.Text = "An exception occurred:<br>Message: "
        +eException.Message.ToString()+"<br>Source: "+eException.Source;
}

private void DisplayNonExceptionMessage(string strMessage)
{
    this.lblMessage.Text = strMessage;
}

private void btnCreateChannel_Click(object sender, System.EventArgs e)
{
    CreateNewChannel(AuthenticateasAdminUser());
}
```

In our example, we clearly broke some basic rules of security by embedding the user ID and password in the code. Keep in mind that this is just a sample. The overall concept, however, could be useful in extending the Web Author to allow a moderated ability to expand the structure of your site. A variation on this code could be a check to see what role the user occupies and to limit the channel creation ability to editors instead of everyone. Also, we're using the CmsApplication Context object for a few reasons:

- It allows us to authenticate inline without having to set a cookie and redirect.
- We leave the existing user's credentials intact on their machine.
- We can use this method whether or not we're using Forms or Windows authentication.

If you are using Forms authentication and you want to log the current user out, log your impersonated user in, perform the operation, and then log the original user back in, it's possible to do that with CmsForms Authentication. We found our methodology easier, though, since you don't have to worry about persisting the current user's credentials somewhere.

## Anonymous Content Contribution

Building upon our impersonation example, there may be times when it's not a matter of granting additional abilities to an existing content contributor, but granting limited authoring capabilities to an anonymous user. For example, say you wanted to create a knowledge base (similar to Microsoft's) that allowed anyone in your company to contribute an article. However, you didn't want to grant a large population authoring rights to CMS. An alternative would be to build a basic Web form that collected all of the appropriate content, along with a display name, and programmatically created a posting. You would then programmatically submit the content for approval. In this way, you could allow anonymous content contribution and still maintain control of what content was published. Once the new article was approved, it would automatically show up on your site.

## Creating an Alternate Version of a Posting

Alternate versions of postings are useful in presenting existing content in different formats. For example, you may want to create a "print friendly" version, at the simplest level, or you may need to create a PDA version, which presents a little more of a challenge. In either case, it's easy enough to create a new template that formats the content appropriately and then create a connected posting. We don't think you should have to create a new posting every time you add content. Instead, there should be a way to simply "reformat" existing content on the fly. It's possible to do just that, by dynamically associating a posting's content with an alternate template. The idea was provided by the earlier version of CMS (2001), which had a direct API call to accomplish what we're doing here (there are good reasons why it was dropped, though). Since CMS 2002 no longer supports that API call, you'll have to write a little code to replicate that functionality. The following code was provided by Pat Miller (of Microsoft) on the Microsoft-hosted newsgroup microsoft.public. cmserver.general; we simply commented it a bit more and changed some variable names to protect the innocent (see Listing 36–3).

**Listing 36–3** Repurposing content programmatically—dynamic template switching

```
public string UrlUsingAlternateTemplate(string templateName)
{
    // Set a variable to the current CMS Context
    CmsHttpContext myContext = CmsHttpContext.Current;

    // Set a variable to point to the current posting; we'll use this
    // object to get to its template and to that template's
```

```
      // connected templates.
      Posting thisPosting = myContext.Posting;

      if ( thisPosting != null )
      {
            // Retrieve a reference to the current posting's
            // template
            Template thisTemplate = thisPosting.Template;
            if ( thisTemplate != null )
            {
                  // Use the requested template name to find it in the
                  // collection connected templates.
                  Template templateToSwitchTo =
thisTemplate.ConnectedTemplates[templateName];
                  if ( templateToSwitchTo != null )
                  {
                        // Determine whether the TGI we found is connected
                        // to a physical template file.
                        if ( templateToSwitchTo.SourceFile != "" )
                        {
                              // Return the source path and file of the
                              // alternate template, along with the query
                              // string of the current posting.  The query
                              // string will indicate the GUID of the posting
                              // (which contains the content) to display
                              // within the context of the alternate template.
                              return templateToSwitchTo.SourceFile + "?" +
                                    Request.QueryString.ToString();
                        }
                        else
                        {
                              return null;
                        }
                  }
                  else
                  {
                        return null;
                  }
            }
            else
            {
                  return null;
            }
      }
```

```
    else
    {
        return null;
    }
}
```

In Listing 36–3 we're using the connection between the current posting's template and its connected templates. In other words, this function will only work if you have templates with connected templates in your solution. One advantage to this approach is that all connected templates share the same placeholder definitions, so you're assured that content in the original posting shows up on the alternate version. Keep in mind, however, that you're passing in the name of the template as a string. This will only work if all the connected templates have unique names.

## How Do I Debug a CMS Project?

Generally, you can debug a CMS project as you would any other ASP.NET application, using the built-in debugging facility in VS.NET. However, because of the way CMS works—the ASPX files aren't run directly—you can't simply set the startup page in your VS.NET project to a template file. To debug a CMS project, you can use either of the following techniques:

- Manually attach to the ASPNET_WP.EXE process and then open Internet Explorer and browse to your site.
- Create a small ASPX page that redirects to a posting in your site. In your project, set the startup page to that redirect ASPX file. Now, simply press F5.

If you'd like more detail on debugging, refer to Chapter 12, Designing Templates.

# Why Am I Prompted for Logon Credentials When I Have Windows Authentication Enabled?

There are two sets of permissions that must be in sync for your CMS site to operate properly. One set of permissions are set in CMS, through Site Manager. The other set of permission are the specific Access Control Lists (ACLs) for the directory where your solution files are stored. If you change the ACLs on the project folders, it's possible to prevent users from accessing the site. For example, if we were to change the ACLs for our templates folder in the BOTS site to disallow the CMS guest account, our anonymous access would stop working; CMS would still allow access to the content, but since the template can't run, the site won't operate. However, if you create a special folder in your project to hold templates that are appropriate only for postings accessed by certain individuals, then it's possible to block access to the postings based on those templates by changing the ACLs on that folder. This could work for you or against you depending on your situation. Using this technique, you can create a more secure site, or a completely inaccessible site if you don't set the permissions correctly.

# Reducing the Number of Clicks to Attachments

As we've mentioned several times in this book, there are really two audiences for your CMS site: content contributors and content consumers. As a result, there are some cases where the site should operate differently depending on who's using the site. For example, let's suppose that you create a template that allows content contributors to upload attachments. Let's further suppose that the attachment is the only content on that page. In this case, all the attachment templates are summarized in some list on the site as well.

If we were subscribers, the only thing we would be interested in is the attachment. We don't want to have to click a link to get to a posting and then click the link to the attachment. Instead, we should be able to simply click the link to the posting and automatically be redirected to the attachment.

Conversely, if we were the author, we would be interested in getting to that posting if the site were in Edit mode (remember the rule: You must be able to navigate to where you want to affect content). So how do you resolve the needs of these two distinct audiences? Easy. Create an attachment redirect template.

OK, let's review the "rules" for this template:

- When a user clicks a link to a posting containing just an attachment, they should be automatically redirected to the posting.
- When the site is in Edit mode, authors should be able to click the link to the posting and actually get to the posting without being redirected.

Well, that seems simple enough. It is. In Listing 36–4 you can see the code that you'll need to put in the code-behind of the attachment template to make all this work.

**Listing 36–4** The code for the redirect attachment template

```
private void Page_Load(object sender, System.EventArgs e)
{
      this.BodyTitle.Text = "<b>" + CmsHttpContext.Current.Posting.
DisplayName + "</b>";

      // Call the redirect logic
      HandleRedirect();
}
private void HandleRedirect()
{
      // Set a reference to the current Web Author Context
      WebAuthorContext currentWebAuthor = WebAuthorContext.Current;

      // Check to see if the various conditions where we don't want to
      // redirect exist.  If so, just stay on the posting.  If not, redirect
      // to the attachment.
      if ((currentWebAuthor.Mode != WebAuthorContextMode.AuthoringNew) &&
            (currentWebAuthor.Mode != WebAuthorContextMode.AuthoringReedit) &&
            (currentWebAuthor.Mode !=
WebAuthorContextMode.PresentationUnpublished) &&
            (currentWebAuthor.Mode != WebAuthorContextMode.TemplatePreview))
      {
            string redirectUrl = ((AttachmentPlaceholder)CmsHttpContext.
Current.Posting.Placeholders["WhitepaperAttachment"]).Url;
      Response.Redirect(redirectUrl);
      }
}
```

As you can see, the code for this improvement is pretty simple. However, techniques like this can really mean the difference between a good implementation of CMS and one that just didn't quite make it.

# Creating Navigation with Existing .NET Server Controls

Almost every navigation example in this book used literals, tables, and a few HTML Anchors to create navigation. Although this is a perfectly acceptable, and sometimes preferable, method of creating navigation in your site, it's also possible to use other server controls, like a Tree control or a Datalist. To make it easier on us to describe, we'll call this methodology "creating navigation with alternative controls."

In Listings 36–5 and 36–6, we show you two ways of creating navigation using alternative controls. Keep in mind that, in the case of the Tree control specifically, there are performance considerations that aren't apparent in our samples and Microsoft doesn't support this control any longer (it's included in the IE Web Controls).

**Listing 36–5**  Creating a site map with a Tree control

```
protected Microsoft.Web.UI.WebControls.TreeView myTreeView;

private void Page_Load(object sender, System.EventArgs e)
{
    // Set the "root" of our site map to the home channel of
    // BOTS consulting
    Channel myStartChannel =
(Channel)CmsHttpContext.Current.Searches.GetByPath("/Channels/botsconsulting");

    // Turn off the lines and the plus/minus signs, making
    // the tree control look less like a "tree"
    myTreeView.ShowLines = false;
    myTreeView.ShowPlus = false;
    // Call the BUILDSITEMAP function, passing in the starting
    // channel and a null reference for the parentChannel (since
    // we're starting with the root)
    BuildSiteMap(myStartChannel,null);
}
/// <summary>
/// This function recursively builds a site map using a TreeControl.
```

```csharp
/// The function only displays the channels and not the postings to
/// improve performance. The function will generally work well on
/// smaller sites, but may be sluggish on larger, more complicated
/// sites.
/// </summary>
/// <param name="(Channel) startChannel"></param>
/// <param name="(TreeNode) parentTreeNode"></param>
public void BuildSiteMap(Channel startChannel, TreeNode parentTreeNode)
{
    // Create a new tree node
    TreeNode myNewNode = new TreeNode();

    // Add the styles we want to our node (yes, we could have used
    // CSS, but we were lazy)
    myNewNode.DefaultStyle.Add("FONT-FAMILY","verdana");
    myNewNode.DefaultStyle.Add("FONT-WEIGHT","bold");
    myNewNode.DefaultStyle.Add("COLOR","gray");

    // Set the NavigateUrl property to the URL of the current channel
    // Set the Text property to the displayname
    myNewNode.NavigateUrl = startChannel.Url;
    myNewNode.Text = startChannel.DisplayName;

    // Check to see if the parentTreeNode is null.  If it is
    // this is the first time this function has been called, so
    // we know we're at the root.
    if(parentTreeNode == null)
    {
        // Add the new node to the myTreeNode control on our user
        // control.
        myTreeView.Nodes.Add(myNewNode);
    }
    else
    {
        // If we were given a parent, add our new node to that
        // parent node and make sure it's expanded.
        parentTreeNode.Nodes.Add(myNewNode);
        parentTreeNode.Expanded = true;
    }
    // If the current channel has subchannels, recursively
    // call this function to finish out the rest of the tree.
    if (startChannel.Channels.Count > 0)
    {
        foreach(Channel subChannel in startChannel.Channels)
```

```
        {
                BuildSiteMap(subChannel,myNewNode);
        }
    }
}
```

The code in Listing 36–5 resides inside a user control. The user control had a Tree control added at design time, and we create the nodes within the tree at runtime. During the Page_Load event, we simply set up the Tree control and get a reference to the root channel. We then recursively traverse the tree to gather all the nodes. As we mentioned in the code comments, this particular implementation will work for relatively small sites. However, we've seen similar implementations on larger sites perform poorly, through a combination of sheer processing time and the size of the resulting property bag. If you implement this control on your site, be sure to properly load test the site to ensure optimal performance.

Next, in Listing 36–6, you'll see a sample of our left navigation using a Datalist. In this sample, we're creating a data source dynamically from the collection of postings and then binding that data source to our Datalist. A display template handles all of the formatting. Thanks to Drew Jones for this contribution.

**Listing 36–6** Creating navigation with a Datalist

```
protected System.Web.UI.WebControls.DataList myDataList;
private string startchannelpath;
public string startChannelPath

{
    get
    {
        return startchannelpath;
    }
    set
    {
        startchannelpath = value;
    }
}

private void Page_Load(object sender, System.EventArgs e)
```

```
{
    // Check to see if a path has been provided by the developer
    // If one hasn't been provided, get the path to the current channel.
    if(startChannelPath =="")
    {startchannelpath = CmsHttpContext.Current.Channel.Path;}

    // Set a reference to the channel indicated by the startChannelPath
    // property
    Channel startChannel = (Channel)CmsHttpContext.Current.Searches.
GetByPath(startchannelpath);

    // If an invalid path was provided, set the startChannel to the current
    // channel
    if (startChannel == null)
    {startChannel = CmsHttpContext.Current.Channel;}

    // Call the navigation function
    BuildNavigation(startChannel);
}

public void BuildNavigation(Channel startChannel)
{
    // Check to see if startChannel is null
    if (startChannel != null)
    {
        // Set the datasource of my list to the collection of channels
        myDataList.DataSource = startChannel.Channels;

        // Bind the DataList to the datasource
        myDataList.DataBind();
    }
}
```

The code in Listing 36–6 sets up the Datalist and binds the collection of postings. However, you also have to provide a "template" that defines how to display the data when it's rendered. In our case, we just want a simple list. In Listing 36–7 we've provided the item template that controls the display of the Datalist. In Figure 36–4, you can see the result of this new user control when it is added to the general template in the BOTS site. We've simply added it just below the existing navigation. It fundamentally looks the same as the original navigation; it just ultimately required fewer lines of code to create. It may not be appropriate for all situations, but we thought it was cool.

**Listing 36–7**  Item template for the Datalist

```
<table border=0>
    <tr>
        <td> </td>
        <td>
            <hr size=1>
            <asp:DataList id="myDataList" runat="server"
Font-Name="Verdana">

                <ItemTemplate>
                    <a style="COLOR: gray" href="<%#
DataBinder.Eval(Container.DataItem,"Url")%>">
                        <%# DataBinder.Eval(Container.DataItem,
"DisplayName") %>
                    </a>
                </ItemTemplate>

            </asp:DataList>
            <hr size=1>
        </td>
    </tr>
</table>
```

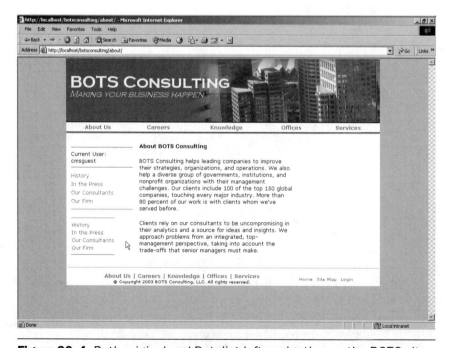

**Figure 36–4**  Both original and Datalist left navigation on the BOTS site

# Summary

In this chapter we've provided several tips and techniques. Again, there's lots of material that could be written about this topic, and we highlighted a few tips that we felt were interesting. However, we also encourage you to develop your own techniques. When you do, please share them with the rest of us through the various communities on the Web. A great resource to share code samples and white papers is at http://www.gotdotnet.com.

# PART IX

# Moving Forward with CMS

# Upgrading or Migrating Your Site to Content Management Server 2002

Whether you are new to Microsoft's Content Management Server (CMS) or you have deployed the earlier product, implementing CMS will involve getting your existing site into this new tool. In the following sections, we discuss the steps necessary to migrate your site and how to upgrade from CMS 2001. In the case of a migration, we assume that you do not have CMS 2001 installed; therefore, we will show you the additional steps that you will need to accomplish to successfully complete a migration from your current Web site to CMS 2001. If you are upgrading from CMS 2001, we assume that you've largely completed the non-CMS-related work before implementing the 2001 product. However, since CMS 2002 uses an entirely different framework for developing sites, we still recommend reviewing the migration section, even if you are already running CMS 2001.

## Migrating Your Existing Site to CMS 2002

As an organization's Web sites mature, many firms look to Web content management (WCM) systems like Microsoft's Content Management Server 2002 to help them manage their Web content. Not only does CMS offer a flexible platform with which to create and maintain sites, more fundamentally, it provides business users with the ability to directly control one of the most important customer touch points that businesses have today. Unfortunately, most firms misjudge the work involved in the migration effort. They often underestimate the work to move the functionality, the content conversion (e.g., moving content from static pages to CMS's repository), and the impact on day-to-day operations caused by a radical change in how Web site management is conducted. As a result, many implementations of CMS aren't as smooth as they should be—not because of the tool, but because of the process.

In this chapter, we'll introduce a framework for structuring the conversion of your site. This framework will allow you to appropriately plan for and manage the process of introducing CMS into your organization, as well as help you anticipate "gotchas" before they become a problem. Specifically, we'll review activities such as content inventory, functionality inventory, deployment strategy, information architecture (IA) review and template design, approval/review workflow, role definition, content conversion, and technical and content contributor training. Some of these activities may sound obvious, but they're often not given enough weight, which leads to problems throughout the project.

# Content Inventory

A content inventory is a complete list of all content that you want to manage within CMS 2002. Think of a content inventory as taking stock of everything that makes up your current Web site. This may sound a little tedious and perhaps unnecessary; however, consider that most Web sites are usually "owned" by a number of parties. With multiple people or groups contributing content, it's difficult to track and/or know what is actually out there. Performing a full content inventory will provide the following:

- *A complete list of all Web pages and/or content included in your Web site:* Again, Web sites tend to grow organically through interaction with multiple groups or people; most firms don't know what they have until they make a concerted effort to go through a discovery process.
- *A mechanism to account for all content that needs to be converted (or not):* It would be foolhardy to think it is possible to know whether a conversion was successful without knowing what the precondition was. In other words, this is a way to ensure that you have successfully converted all of your content by comparing it with a known list of what your site had. A thorough content inventory is a great quality assurance (QA) resource when you are performing the final testing.

- *A way of assigning content ownership:* As part of implementing CMS, you will define a workflow process. This workflow process will determine what people or groups are involved in producing and approving content. As the first step, you will have to identify the current owners of each piece of content. Often, firms will begin the process of converting their sites without the involvement of the key stakeholders—generally because they don't know who they are. This condition usually leads to user community dissatisfaction or errors in the conversion. Determining content ownership up front will greatly reduce these issues.

- *What content can be removed from the Web site:* Implementing CMS provides the unprecedented opportunity to review what content is published on your Web site. Most companies have probably gone through one or two revisions of their site by now; however, most have not concentrated on reviewing the content as a part of the redesign process. Usually, this means that a great deal of the content on the site has likely "evolved" over time. As a result, you may find that some content isn't relevant or is simply outdated. In either case, you may wish to remove this content when you convert your site. A side benefit is that this exercise may reduce the work necessary to migrate your site, since you're reducing the content you have to convert.

- *Content consistency review:* Through a combination of factors like content evolution, multiple group involvement, and ownership changes, content on a Web site could and does become inconsistent over time. For example, over time a product or service's positioning changes—because of product maturity, new product uses, product bundling, or simple product changes. As a result, a product's content changes to account for this metamorphosis. However, did all of the Web content change? Is it possible that out of the tens, hundreds, or thousands of references, descriptions, or links to your product, some of them are out of sync? Could the same product be positioned differently across your site (especially if the same product is cross-sold between different business units)? A content inventory will help highlight these inconsistencies and serve as a checklist for fixing them.

- *Missing content:* A thorough content inventory (in a conversion project) is a way of determining what content you currently have. However, if you are adding new sections to your site or you are reorganizing your site, you may be missing content in one or more areas. In this case, a content inventory will help point out missing content before it becomes necessary to create it.

■ *Guidance for information architecture, template design, and content conversion:* How is your current content structured? Do you have groupings of similar content? Are there patterns to your content? The answers to these questions are important to discover during the content inventory. Again, since you are converting your site, it is likely that you already have an information architecture and a solidified design. As with any site, yours will have changed over time, this will be your opportunity to ensure that your information architecture changed along with it.

# Functionality Inventory

A functionality inventory, like a content inventory, is a way of taking stock of what your Web site does. Too many times, developers are given an existing application and told, "Here, build this." Unfortunately, even the most gifted developer would not be able to discover every feature or function within the application. At best, they may be able to discover half the features in the existing application. Imagine being handed Microsoft Word, never having worked with the application before, and being asked to re-create it from scratch. This situation is often where developers find themselves, and it often leads to failed implementations.

A functionality inventory is a collaborative effort between the business folks and the IT/development staff. The inventory serves two functions: review of the existing functionality and a road map for the new site. The review is helpful in knowing what the site does today. In the same way that a content inventory can help point out content that everyone may not have known about, the functionality inventory provides the baseline functionality that your converted Web site must have when the project is finished. Does the site have a "contact us" page? How many contact pages? How can customers order products and services? Is there one way or many ways to download white papers? Over time, Web sites tend to collect functionality as they collect content. Different developers, different managers, changes in technology, and changes in technique all lead to situations where a Web site grows functionally—sometimes inconsistently and often sprawling.

Once you've identified what your site does, what is your new site going to do? This is the other important benefit of the functionality

## The "Already Built" Syndrome

We have, on more than one occasion, been presented with an existing application and told to simply "convert" it to some new platform. In this context, the word "convert" seems to indicate that there is some process by which an existing application can be morphed, upgraded, and/or magically transformed into a new version of itself running on the latest technology with little or no effort, since "it already exists." The truth, however, is that most applications can't simply be "converted"—they have to be rewritten. This means that no matter how much of the application already exists, the existing application will have to be rewritten, from scratch, to yield the "converted" application.

Consider this: If the government wanted to convert all asphalt-based roads to cement-based roads, they would literally have to rebuild, from scratch, every road. It's true that some of the work necessary for a brand-new road has been done (cutting down trees, clearing land, and so on), but it doesn't diminish the fact that the old asphalt road must be torn up and the new cement road laid in its place.

In the same way, it's true that users will expect the application to operate in a particular way, and the application's functionality should be well known (although that's not as true as we'd like). However, it still doesn't mean that it's any easier to convert to a new technology. Keep this in mind, since many of you will be "converting" from ASP-based applications to ASP.NET.

inventory. After you have identified what your site does, you can effectively plan for what you need to develop. This is not necessarily a straightforward exercise. Do not think that once you've finished your functionality inventory, you're done. The inventory will tell you what features your site has and, in some cases, what you can potentially eliminate.

Beyond what we've identified here, there are other benefits to the functionality map:

- *Traceability for QA:* Once you've built the new Web site, what do you test and how should it operate? The functionality inventory will provide you with a way of tracing functionality in your new Web site back to what you had in the older version.
- *Resource and effort planning:* Many companies engage in a development effort without fully understanding what the work effort will be. We're not suggesting that the functionality inventory will provide you with a complete picture, but it will give you a start. By understanding what features the current site has, you can better plan what resources will be necessary to help build or rebuild that

functionality in the new site. In addition, very few companies are likely to have the original developers available to them; the functionality inventory will help the new developers understand the site better.

- *Removing duplication:* Are there multiple "contact us" forms? How about ordering processes? Is functionality implemented consistently? A functionality inventory will expose all these issues. Since you're re-creating your site, this is the opportunity to do some housecleaning.

- *Guidance for template design:* In CMS, the templates will house the functionality in your site. If you know what functionality exists and how it operates, you can more effectively design the templates that support your site. In general, a goal of CMS is to try to leverage one template for as many pages as practical. If you understand the functionality within your site, you may be able to create more robust templates to support multiple sections of your site. Without this information, you will probably create more templates than are necessary, thereby increasing the development effort necessary to rebuild your site.

## Information Architecture Review and Template Design

Without a doubt, the most important aspect of a Web site is the information architecture. The IA defines how information is organized on your site—from the relationship between pages to the organization of information within a page. Whether or not you've consciously developed an IA, every site has one. Although some sites have a more logical and clear IA, moving to CMS will solidify the IA of your site, removing ambiguity caused by content contribution. As a result, it's a good idea to fully review and document an IA before moving your site to CMS.

The first step in creating a formal IA is to develop an information architecture diagram. This diagram, sometimes loosely referred to as a site map, is the equivalent of an organizational chart for your site. It shows all the content categories and all the pages, determines the nomenclature for these items, and illustrates where each page or category will be housed (under what parent category). Truly, the IA becomes a map of how end users get from point A to point B.

Now, the IA isn't just the site diagram. In addition, the IA includes page layout. Sometimes called schematics or wire frames, these documents illustrate the layout of content and functionality within a particular page (a posting, in CMS terms). Where is the search field? Where and how does the global navigation appear? These questions and many others are answered by the page schematics.

More than a few companies have viewed IA development as trivial, but it is generally more complicated than most firms expect. Within the context of a CMS implementation, these exercises have a tremendous impact on the project's success. The mere nature of CMS removes some of the arbitrary nature of site development. For example, when developers are in complete control, they can make decisions about nomenclature, site structure, and page layout as they code; when you have many developers working on the project, you may end up with different interpretations of nomenclature and layout. However, CMS reduces these inconsistencies by providing one place to retrieve the site organization (channel structure) and by implementing a template structure. The templates, in turn, are used by the content contributors to create pages within the site. The channel structure is what the developed code reads to display the navigation on the site. This is not to say that CMS reduces site flexibility. In fact, CMS sites can be extremely flexible. CMS simply creates a constant environment for end users, content contributors, and developers, and consistently reinforces this structure no matter how much content is added.

Earlier in this chapter, we discussed the content and functionality inventory. Those two documents will serve as the foundation for all of the work you'll perform in this phase. In fact, in conjunction with the content inventory, the IA may point out what content needs to be removed, "fixed," or added.

At BOTS Consulting, the business users developed the information architecture shown in Figure 37–1.

Once the information architecture is developed, you can directly translate that into a channel structure in CMS. Whereas the IA is the logical organization of your content, the channel structure represents the physical storage. In addition, as you have seen in prior chapters, the channel structure forms the foundation of your site's navigation. If we were to translate the information architecture for BOTS Consulting into a channel structure, it might look something like Figure 37–2.

In the figure, you can see how the IA was translated into the channel structure. The IA descriptions become the channel Display Name property, and the channel name is a shortened version of the description. Also notice that although there may be items listed on the IA (links to pages or channels) more than once, they will not be listed in the channel

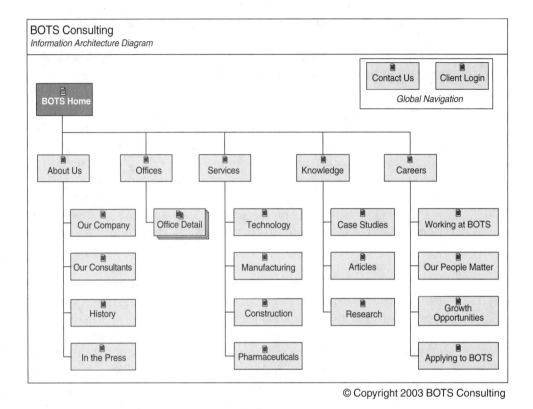

© Copyright 2003 BOTS Consulting

**Figure 37-1**  Sample information architecture for BOTS Consulting

structure in the same way; remember, the channel structure is the physical representation of a logical architecture—a navigation element may appear logically in more than one place, but it will be physically represented only once.

# Workflow

In Chapter 6, we discussed developing code to support your workflow processes. However, how do you know what you need to develop? Workflow must necessarily include all activities from creation through destruction of your content. Since you already have an existing Web site, you already have a workflow process. Is that process documented? Does it include everything from creation through destruction? Does everyone in the organization understand the process? Is it enforceable? With

---

**BOTS Consulting Channel Structure Document**

This document represents the actual channel structure of CMS, based on the Information Architecture Diagram.

| Channels | Channel Description (title on IA) |
|---|---|
| **\about** | About Us |
| \company | Our Company |
| \consultants | Our Consultants |
| \history | History |
| \press | In the Press |
| **\offices** | Offices |
| **\services** | Services |
| \technology | Technology |
| \manufacturing | Manufacturing |
| \construction | Construction |
| \pharma | Pharmaceuticals |
| **\knowledge** | Knowledge |
| \casestudies | Case Studies |
| \articles | Articles |
| \research | Research |
| **\careers** | Careers |
| \working | Working at BOTS |
| \people | Our People Matter |
| \growth | Growth Opportunities |
| \applying | Applying to BOTS |

---

**Figure 37–2** BOTS Consulting channel structure

CMS, you can apply a consistent and enforceable workflow process for all content. Depending on your organization, this may or may not be a good thing, but you must understand what your company does and how it operates to effectively implement the right technology with CMS.

To make sure you are ready to move to CMS, perform the following exercises to discover if you have enough information about your workflow process.

- *Talk to the business stakeholders.* Does everyone who "owns" a portion of the Web site understand how content makes its way to the site? Ask them to describe the process as they understand it. Keep in mind that if you are part of the group that initially created the process, the answer the stakeholder gives you may be what you want to hear, not what actually happens.
- *Review company policies on document/content retention.* It is paramount that you understand how your company retains and destroys

documents or content. Although most firms have long-standing document retention policies, they do not necessarily have a Web site retention policy. Sometimes Web sites, although they represent a public source of information about your company, are not considered a "document" as defined in document retention policies. It is one thing to keep paper in a box for seven years; it is an entirely different matter to preserve Web content for that long—technology changes, products are expired, and computer media radically changes (e.g., do you have a 5¼-inch floppy drive?). You should determine if your legal or compliance department has issued guidelines specifically targeting Web content. If so, these guidelines will be helpful in designing a system that appropriately preserves and/or destroys content, when the time comes (hint: It's not likely to include Content Management Server 2002). In addition to basic guidelines, it is important to understand the parameters of those guidelines. For example, has your company provided standards for Web content preservation—format, expectations for recovery, whether it has to be noneditable? Ask questions, get good answers, and your company will thank you.

- *Consider automated and people-based workflow processes.* There are typically a number of steps to publishing content on the Web. Some of those steps require human interaction and some do not. When you develop your formalized workflow, make sure to include both. For example, when an author finishes creating content and submits that content for approval, you can automatically send an e-mail to the editor(s) involved in reviewing the page. However, a human must review and potentially edit submitted content. Both processes—sending e-mail and reviewing the content—must be completed in order for the page to be published, and therefore must be included in any documented workflow.

- *Consider how you implement automated workflow features.* A very common workflow process is to send an e-mail after an event (e.g., on submit, on decline, on approve). An e-mail can be a very effective way of notifying that some action has been taken or that someone must take an action (e.g., reviewing content). However, since the e-mail is an automated feature, someone involved in the workflow process may quickly become overwhelmed by the volume. You should consider very carefully how you implement any notification process, or consider alternatives. For example, if you use Outlook as your mail client, consider using the Task List and adding a task to an editor's Task List when they need to review content, instead of sending the editor an e-mail. Although e-mail is the example we used here, there are a number of automated workflow features that will often confound the most well-prepared developer. Thorough testing is the only sure way of catching these oversights before your users do.

In the workflow process diagram shown in Figure 37–3, the subject matter expert (SME) is responsible for beginning the workflow by creating a case study. Once the SME is finished, they submit the posting to the technical director for the practice area. The technical director reviews the case study to ensure that the SME has accurately described the work and that the outcome reflects BOTS Consulting's process for solving this customer's specific problem. If the technical director approves the content, the posting is then reviewed by the practice manager, who also has the ability to make changes to the content; primarily, the practice manager is looking to ensure that the case study fits an "ideal" customer. If either of these individuals declines the case study, it is returned to the original author for corrections.

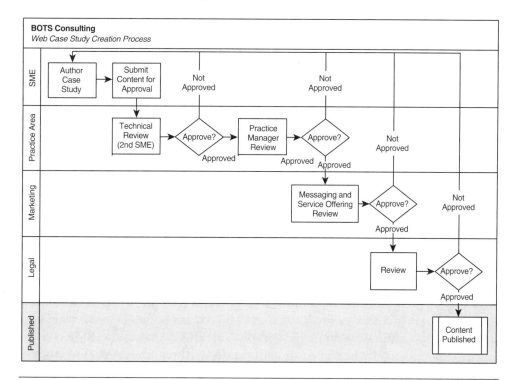

**Figure 37–3** Example workflow process for BOTS Consulting

After the practice area finishes reviewing the content, the posting moves on to the marketing department. Like the practice area, marketing is responsible for reviewing the content. However, in this case, instead of reviewing the content for technical accuracy, marketing wants to ensure that the case study accurately represents the firm. Further, they wish to ensure that the case study is written in the right tone of voice and that any offerings mentioned in the case study are consistently described.

Now, without continuing the description of the BOTS workflow, you should be seeing a pattern here. Not only are we providing a visual representation of the workflow, but we're also providing a narrative. In this way, you are providing everyone with a clear understanding of what happens to content as well as who is involved. The workflow diagram and written description will help your business users and the developers create the appropriate workflow actions within CMS.

# Role Definition

In the preceding workflow process, we illustrated how BOTS Consulting handles the production of its content. However, this workflow diagram only shows the BOTS business definitions. It does not map the business definitions to actual roles within CMS. In Chapter 6, we showed how CMS defines various roles. In order to make this process work, you need to map each business user to a specific CMS role.

In BOTS Consulting, there are several groups represented. The SME creates the case study, the technical director and practice manager edit and review the content, and the marketing department also edits and reviews. Finally, the legal department approves the copy produced, and the case study publishes to the Web site. Now, to map each of these groups to a role, we need to quickly review the CMS roles involved in content creation:

- *Author:* The author role allows individuals to create and edit their own content; this role does not allow an individual to modify other authors' content (while in the workflow process), but they can submit content for approval. In BOTS's case, the SME should rightly be put in an author role for the purposes of case studies; the SME simply creates the case studies and submits that content for review and approval.

- *Editor:* The editor role allows individuals to create their own content as well as edit and review other authors' content. This role also has the responsibility of approving content within the site. Where BOTS is concerned, there are three likely candidates for the role of editor: the technical director, the practice manager, and marketing. Each of these people requires the ability to edit someone else's work and needs the ability to approve content.
- *Moderator:* A moderator approves placement of content and all page properties. Within the context of CMS, moderators are only involved in the initial approval of the posting properties created during the content creation process. Unless the attributes of a posting are changed (i.e., start date, display name, important flag, and so on), the moderator isn't involved in subsequent content changes. BOTS's legal department will be a likely candidate for the moderator role. This assumes, however, that they don't want to be involved in the future changes in the content. If this assumption is not accurate, then BOTS may wish to put the legal department in an editor role.

It is important that you understand how your firm creates and approves content. Ensuring that the right individuals are put in the right roles in CMS will minimize the amount of custom workflow code required to power your Web site.

## Content Import

Once you have finished all the other steps in this process, you have to import your content into CMS. Importing your content (or content conversion, as it is sometimes called) is the process of creating postings within CMS and filling the placeholders within those postings with the content in your existing site.

Since most sites are rather unique, it would be difficult to describe what you specifically must do to convert your content. However, there are two general approaches to migrating your content: an automated import and a manual import.

## Automated Import

If your current site is already in a structured format (e.g., in a database or using templates), then it may be possible to directly import your content. The following code sample demonstrates, in C#, how to programmatically create a posting, populate the placeholders, and submit it for approval.

```
using System;
using System.Collections;
using System.ComponentModel;
using System.Data;
using System.Drawing;
using System.Web;
using System.Web.SessionState;
using System.Web.UI;
using System.Web.UI.WebControls;
using System.Web.UI.HtmlControls;
using Microsoft.ContentManagement.Publishing;
using Microsoft.ContentManagement.Publishing.Extensions.
Placeholders;
using Microsoft.ContentManagement.Web.Security;

namespace botsconsulting.ContentImport
{
    /// <summary>
    /*
    This page allows for an automated import of structured
content
    The file assumes that you have two server controls on your
ASPX file:
            - A list box called lstImportList
            - A button called btnGo

    This is meant to be a template file, associated with a TGI.
Once you've created
    your template, you must create a posting to run the code.
    */
    /// </summary>

    public class ContentImport : System.Web.UI.Page
    {
            protected Microsoft.ContentManagement.WebControls.
RobotMetaTag RobotMetaTag1;
```

```
            protected System.Web.UI.WebControls.ListBox
lstImportList;
            protected System.Web.UI.WebControls.Button btnGO;

            private void Page_Load(object sender, System.EventArgs e)
            {
                if (CmsHttpContext.Current.Mode !=
Microsoft.ContentManagement.Publishing.PublishingMode.Update)
                {
                    Response.Redirect(CmsHttpContext.Current.
Posting.UrlModeUpdate);
                }
                if (!this.IsPostBack)
                {this.AddLogEntry("Current CMS Publishing Mode: "
+ CmsHttpContext.Current.Mode);}
            }
            private bool CreatePosting(string strPostingName,
string strTitle, string strByLine, string strTeaser, string
strBodyCopy)
            {
                // CreatePosting handles the work of creating the
new posting.  It takes the necessary parameters to create
                // the new posting, but assumes the channel and
template.  This code could be expanded to include those
                // items as well.

                // Create a reference to the channel where the
posting will be created
                Channel objRootChannel = CmsHttpContext.Current.
RootChannel;
                try
                {
                    // Make sure that the current user can add
postings to the channel
                    if (objRootChannel.CanCreatePostings)
                    {
                        // Create a reference to the template
you're going to use with the new posting
                        Template objArticleTemplate =
(Template)CmsHttpContext.Current.Searches.GetByPath("/Templates/
Insight/HTMLArticle");

                        // Create the new posting in the
channel
```

```
                                Posting objNewPosting =
objRootChannel.CreatePosting(objArticleTemplate);

                                // Give the posting a name, display
name and fill in the placeholders
                                objNewPosting.Name = strPostingName;
                                objNewPosting.DisplayName = strTitle;
                                HtmlPlaceholder objPlaceholder =
(HtmlPlaceholder)objNewPosting.Placeholders["strArticleAuthor"];
                                objPlaceholder.Html = strByLine;
                                objPlaceholder =
(HtmlPlaceholder)objNewPosting.Placeholders["strArticleTeaser"];
                                objPlaceholder.Html = strTeaser;
                                objPlaceholder =
(HtmlPlaceholder)objNewPosting.Placeholders["strArticleBodyCopy"];
                                objPlaceholder.Html = strBodyCopy;

                                // Put an entry in the list box
indicating you've successfully added the posting
                                this.AddLogEntry (objNewPosting.Name
+ " added successfully.");

                                // Commit the change to the CMS
repository
                                CmsHttpContext.Current.CommitAll();

                                // Submit the new posting for
approval
                                objNewPosting.Submit();

                                // Return a successful import
                                return true;
                        }
                        else
                        {
                                // If the user does not have
sufficient rights, add an entry to the list box
                                this.AddLogEntry("User did not have
sufficient rights to add a posting.");
                                return false;
                        }
                }
                catch
                {
```

```
                        // If an exception is thrown, simply add an
entry to the list box
                        this.AddLogEntry("An exception was thrown
when trying to create the posting.");
                        return false;
                }


        }
        private void ImportContent()
        {
                // Add two entries to the list box, indicating
the process has begun and who is logged on
                this.AddLogEntry("Starting import.");
                this.AddLogEntry("User logged on: " +
CmsHttpContext.Current.User.ClientAccountName.ToString());


                // Try to create the posting, passing in the
appropriate values.  While this call
                // only passes a single argument, you can pass in
multiple argues by looping through
                // a recordset or other data source.
                if (!CreatePosting("MyPageName","My Title","First
placeholder value","Second placeholder value","Third placeholder
value"))
                {
                        this.AddLogEntry("Import failed.");
                }
                else
                {
                        this.AddLogEntry("Import succesful.");
                }
        }
        public void AddLogEntry(string strLogEntry)
        {


                // This is a simple progress log that adds items
to the list box
                ListItem lstItem = new ListItem();
                lstItem.Text = System.DateTime.Now + " :: " +
strLogEntry;
                lstImportList.Items.Add(lstItem);
        }
        #region Web Form Designer generated code
        override protected void OnInit(EventArgs e)
```

```
              {
                      //
                      // CODEGEN: This call is required by the ASP.NET
Web Form Designer.
                      //
                      InitializeComponent();
                      base.OnInit(e);
              }

              /// <summary>
              /// Required method for Designer support - do not
modify
              /// the contents of this method with the code editor.
              /// </summary>
              private void InitializeComponent()
              {
                      this.btnGO.Click += new
System.EventHandler(this.btnGO_Click);
                      this.Load += new
System.EventHandler(this.Page_Load);

              }
              #endregion

              private void btnGO_Click(object sender,
System.EventArgs e)
              {
                      ImportContent();
              }
         }
}
```

In Figure 37–4 you can see how this automated import process works. The interface is rudimentary but serves its purpose.

## Manual Import (Copy-and-Paste Method)

Frankly, most Web sites are not very structured. If your Web site is like most, it would be difficult or impossible to extract content from HTML files (primarily because it would be difficult to distinguish between HTML for formatting and HTML that is necessary for the content). As a result, manually copying and pasting content from your old site to the new one is what a lot of firms end up doing.

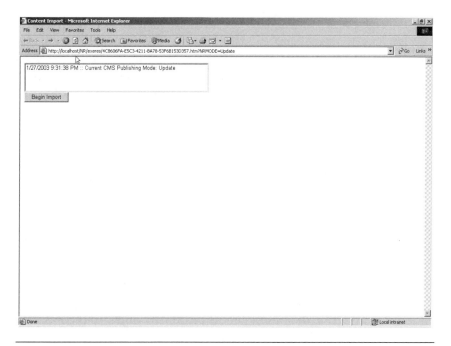

**Figure 37–4** View of the template as a posting

Ultimately, you will probably end up using a combination of the automated and manual methods. There will probably be a number of pages that have some regular structure to them. These pages may be imported through some scripted import, since they follow some regular pattern (developers like consistency). However, the vast majority will likely follow an inconsistent format. As a result, it will be impossible to extract the content in an automated way. On the upside, these inconsistent pages do make for a great training exercise for your content contributors (see the next section).

## Technical and Content Contributor Training

There are two types of training curricula that need to be developed: technical and content contributor. The technical track will target your technical staff, largely made up of your development staff responsible for implementing CMS. However, keep in mind that running a Web site is more than a development effort—your network security and data center folks will also want to understand how CMS integrates with the current technical infrastructure. When looking for training programs, you should certainly consider the Microsoft certified training courses. In addition, there are a number of commercial firms that offer short fix-priced engagements targeted at providing practical experience by allowing your staff to work with professionals who have implemented the tool.

Now, training your content contributors is a little trickier. Unlike training your technical staff, teaching your business users the tool is not useful. Most courses are structured to use a sample site, which will bear no resemblance to your new Web site. As a result, the training program will not be very effective in teaching your content contributors how to use this tool in conjunction with your Web site. Remember, what the content contributors see is not CMS but your Web site using CMS functionality; there will be many features that are not "native" CMS. For example, you may implement a feature that allows a business user to simply click a link that reads "Click Here to Add Another News Story." In the background, you programmatically pick the appropriate template and create the posting in the current channel. In this case, you are technically using standard CMS functionality, but it is not something a commercial course would teach. Consider developing your own custom course for your site. In addition to being able to teach the specific steps that a content contributor must take to add new content to your site, you will be able to dramatically reduce the training time required; most commercial courses are at least five days, with a heavy emphasis on technical training.

## Upgrading from CMS 2001 to 2002

The basic installation of CMS 2002 is straightforward, and the documentation from Microsoft is pretty clear. There are, however, some major changes (as you have seen) between the products that must be taken into account. Specifically, we will discuss the following: backing up your existing site, uninstalling CMS 2001, finding and reviewing your old templates, and running in mixed mode. As with any upgrade, you should refer to the product documentation for specifics.

## Backing Up Your Existing Site

For obvious reasons, the most important task to do when upgrading your site is to back up your existing implementation. There are three parts to your site: file-based assets, customizations, and the repository. Each part needs to be handled separately as you upgrade.

- *File assets:* The file assets are files that aren't included in the repository. These file assets include everything from your include files to the images that make up your site design. If you have created a special directory for all these assets, the process of backing them up is probably trivial.
- *Customizations:* Customizations are a little harder to track down, especially if you did not implement the site you are upgrading. When we talk about customizations, we are talking about any additional code added to CMS-supplied files. For example, a common customization is to send e-mail when someone submits content for approval. This code can usually be found in the Workflowhooks.inc file. When you upgrade, you should capture all of these kinds of files, because when you uninstall CMS 2001 in the next step, you'll lose those files. Since there are other "hook" files in CMS 2001, you should perform a thorough review of your current CMS implementation to ensure that nothing is missed.
- *Your repository:* Your repository is the SQL database to which your CMS server(s) connects. If you are not sure what database or database server you are using, you can look at the Server Configuration Application (SCA); it is located under Programs > Content Management Server > Server Configuration Application. The SCA lists the database server and database at the top of its main interface. Since the upgrade process makes changes to the database structure and contents, it is a good idea (no, it is a *great* idea) to have a backup before you run the installation process.

## Uninstalling CMS 2001

CMS 2001 and CMS 2002 cannot exist on the same server. As a result, you must uninstall CMS 2001 before running the CMS 2002 installation process. Uninstalling CMS 2001 is as simple as going to the Control Panel, picking Add/Remove Software, finding CMS 2001 on the list, and uninstalling the application. Depending on your implementation, you will have one or all of the following: the server, Site Builder, and Site Stager. In a standard implementation, CMS installs in *X*:\Program Files\ Microsoft Content Management Server, where X is the drive on which you installed the server. Be sure to uninstall all components of CMS 2001 before running the CMS 2002 installation process.

## Finding and Reviewing Your Templates

One of the changes in CMS 2002 is that your templates are now stored on the file system. When the upgrade process runs, it removes the templates from the database and places them on the file system. For each template in your old 2001 site, a template gallery item (TGI) will be created and a physical ASP file will be created in a subdirectory of NR (depending on your implementation).

Once the upgrade is complete, you can begin reviewing and converting your templates. One advantage of the new TGI/physical file model of CMS 2002 is that you can replace the underlying template file without affecting the TGI or its relationship to your postings. In CMS 2002, postings are technically associated with the TGI, not the template file. When you rewrite your ASP templates in ASP.NET, you can simply point the TGI to a new template file. The same is true with placeholders. Each placeholder control is bound to a placeholder definition, just as a template file is tried to a TGI. As you add placeholder controls to your new template, bind those placeholder controls to the placeholder definitions created during the upgrade process.

## Running in Mixed Mode

CMS 2002 supports both ASP and ASP.NET templates. If you install a clean copy of CMS 2002, you'll be asked whether you want CMS to support mixed mode; essentially, you'll need to instruct setup whether you want to support both ASP- and ASP.NET-based templates, or just the ASP.NET-based templates. In the case of an upgrade, CMS does not give you a choice; once you have finished your upgrade process, you'll be running in mixed mode.

Running in mixed mode is very much like running mixed verses "native" mode in Windows 2000, in the sense that you are supporting two different architectures. In the case of Windows 2000, you were (or are) supporting both Domain security and pure Active Directory. In the case of CMS 2002, you are supporting both ASP 3.0 and ASP.NET (all the files to support both are installed as part of running in mixed mode). In your converted templates, you will still see the old Autosession object, along with other elements such as Channels and Postings. There are some differences between the 2002 COM API and the 2001 version (most notably the way placeholders and the edit console are handled), but there is little material difference.

---

**NOTE:** There is really no way to take your server out of mixed mode. During the installation process, all the files necessary to support both ASP.NET and ASP templates were installed. If you want a "clean" CMS 2002 installation, you will have to create an export package, copy off your project, reinstall the server on a clean database, copy your project back, and import the CMS package you made earlier.

---

## Summary

In this chapter, we have reviewed how to migrate your non-CMS site to Content Management Server as well as reviewing some key points when you are upgrading from CMS 2001. If you are migrating your site from an unstructured to a structured environment, you must spend more time up front examining your site. We pointed out several tools that you could use to document your site, such as an information architecture, a functionality inventory, and a content inventory. In addition, we discussed two approaches for importing your content, understanding content workflow, defining the workflow roles, and training both your content contributors and your technical staff.

If you are upgrading your site from CMS 2001 to 2002, there are some additional tasks that you must be aware of. First and foremost, backing up your existing implementation is key to a successful upgrade. We also discussed where to find your old templates and how to convert them to .NET templates.

# PART X

# Appendixes

# HTTP Reference

## Overview

The Hypertext Transfer Protocol (HTTP) is an application-level protocol that defines the information interchange between HTTP clients, commonly known as Web browsers, and HTTP servers, commonly referred to as Web servers. HTTP uses the request-response message mechanism for communication between a client and a server. An HTTP client opens a connection and sends a request message to an HTTP server; the server then returns a response message, usually containing the resource that was requested. After delivering the response, the server closes the connection. HTTP is a stateless protocol—that is, it does not maintain any connection information across requests.

Three versions of HTTP have been used on the Internet since 1990: 0.9, 1.0, and 1.1. The HTTP version number consists of a major and a minor part. A minor number change implies the addition of some field values that do not change the general message-parsing algorithm. Major numbers are changed when the format of the message is altered.

The first version of HTTP was HTTP/0.9. It was a simple protocol for ASCII data transfer across a TCP/IP-based network. The next version, HTTP/1.0, was defined by RFC 1945. It brought significant changes to the original protocol by allowing both requests and responses to contain metadata describing the data being transferred, as well as additional modifiers. The requests and responses are based on the message format defined by the Multipurpose Internet Mail Extensions (MIME) in RFC 1521 and later in RFC 2045. For example, the introduction of a content-type header allowed multimedia data transfer from the server to the client, so that client software can display not only ASCII text but other media types, such as images, sound, and video. That's what made possible GUI desktop browsers as we know them today.

Both request and response messages consist of an initial line, zero or more header lines, a blank line (i.e., a CRLF—carriage return, line feed—by itself), and an optional message-body. Initial lines for requests and responses are different. Header lines are usually different as well; however, some headers may be used in both requests and responses. The general format for request and response messages is as follows:

```
<initial line>
Header1: value1
Header2: value2
...
HeaderN: valueN

<optional message-body>
```

Initial lines and headers should end in CRLF; CR and LF here mean ASCII values 13 and 10.

A typical example of HTTP/1.0 request-response interchange is shown in Figure A–1. In this example, a browser sends a request to a server asking for a file called page.html located in the root folder of the Web server. The HTTP initial request line has three parts, separated by spaces: a method name, the local path of the requested resource, and the version of HTTP being used, as follows:

```
GET /page.html HTTP/1.0
```

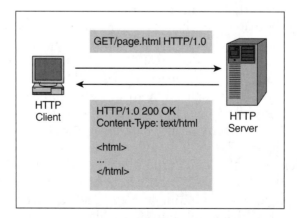

**Figure A–1** HTTP/1.0 client-server interaction

When the server gets the request, it retrieves the file, forms a response, and sends the response back to the requesting client as follows:

```
HTTP/1.0 200 OK
Content-Type: text/html

<html>
...
</html>
```

The initial response line is called the status line. It has three parts separated by spaces: the HTTP version, a status code, and a reason phrase describing the status code. The Content-Type header specifies the media type of the data being sent to the client in the response's message body in the format of the MIME type. Because the server is sending back an HTML file, the MIME type is text/html. The body of the message contains the requested resource; the header lines and the body are separated by a blank line (CRLF).

HTTP/1.1 is defined by RFC 2616. It extends the functionality of HTTP/1.0 by adding support for virtual server hosting, persistent connections between the client and the server, caching, hierarchical proxies, and gateways. For example, an HTTP/1.1 request must include the Host header that identifies a Web server, as shown in Figure A–2.

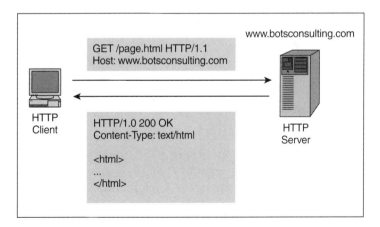

**Figure A–2**  HTTP/1.1 client-server interaction

> **NOTE:** Modern browsers, as well as HTTP proxy servers, include
> support for both HTTP/1.0 and 1.1. However, users can easily disable
> HTTP/1.1 on their client software if they want. Also, it is possible to
> configure a proxy server to use only HTTP/1.0. These factors mean
> that Web servers need to support both HTTP/1.1 and HTTP/1.0
> so that they are able to communicate with the widest possible
> variety of requesting clients.

The rest of this appendix looks into the formats, methods, header
fields, and status codes for HTTP requests and responses. It includes
partial quotes from RFC 2616. For the detailed specification, refer to
the full version of RFC 2616.

# HTTP Request

An HTTP request from a client to a server defines the HTTP method to
be applied to a requested resource, the identifier of the resource, and
the HTTP protocol version in use on the client. The request may include
the MIME-like header fields that indicate the purpose of a request and
provide additional information.

The initial request line begins with a method token, followed by the
Request-URI and the protocol version, and ending with CRLF. The elements are separated by the space (SP) character, as follows:

```
Request-Line = Method SP Request-URI SP HTTP-Version CRLF
```

The resource upon which to apply the request is identified by a
Request-URI (Uniform Resource Identifier).

> **NOTE:** As far as HTTP is concerned, Uniform Resource Identifiers are
> simply formatted strings that identify—via name, location, or any other
> characteristic—a resource. A Uniform Resource Locator (URL) is a form
> of URI.

The most common form of Request-URI is that used to identify a
resource on a Web server. In this case, the path of the URI is transmitted
as the Request-URI in the initial line, and the network location of the

URI is transmitted in a Host header field. For example, when a user types or clicks http://www.botsconsulting.com/about/default.htm in a browser, an HTTP/1.1 client will create a TCP connection to port 80 of the host www.botsconsulting.com and send the following at the beginning of the request:

```
GET /about/default.htm HTTP/1.1
Host: www.botsconsulting.com
```

**NOTE:** A Request-URI cannot be empty. If the path is not present in the original URL, it *must* be given as "/" (the server root).

## HTTP Methods

HTTP method names are case-sensitive. The methods defined in RFC 2616 are as follows:

- The **OPTIONS** method represents a request for information about the communication options available on the request-response chain identified by the Request-URI. This method allows the client to determine the options and/or requirements associated with a resource, or the capabilities of a server, without implying a resource action or initiating resource retrieval.
- The **GET** method means retrieve whatever information (in the form of an entity) is identified by the Request-URI. If the Request-URI refers to a data-producing process, it is the produced data that will be returned as the entity in the response and not the source text of the process, unless that text happens to be the output of the process.
- The **HEAD** method is identical to GET except that the server *must not* return a message-body in the response. The meta information contained in the HTTP headers in response to a HEAD request *should* be identical to the information sent in response to a GET request.
- The **POST** method is used to request that the server accept the entity enclosed in the request as a new subordinate of the resource

identified by the Request-URI in the Request-Line. POST is designed to allow a uniform method to cover the following functions:

- Annotation of existing resources
- Posting a message to a bulletin board, newsgroup, mailing list, or similar group of articles
- Providing a block of data, such as the result of submitting a form, to a data-handling process
- Extending a database through an append operation.

The actual function performed by the POST method is determined by the server and is usually dependent on the Request-URI. The posted entity is subordinate to that URI in the same way that a file is subordinate to a directory containing it, a news article is subordinate to a newsgroup to which it is posted, or a record is subordinate to a database.

- The **PUT** method requests that the enclosed entity be stored under the supplied Request-URI. If the Request-URI refers to an already existing resource, the enclosed entity *should* be considered as a modified version of the one residing on the server. If the Request-URI does not point to an existing resource, and that URI is capable of being defined as a new resource by the requesting user agent, the server can create the resource with that URI.
- The **DELETE** method requests that the server delete the resource identified by the Request-URI. This method *may* be overridden by human intervention (or other means) on the server. The client cannot be guaranteed that the operation has been carried out, even if the status code returned from the origin server indicates that the action has been completed successfully.
- The **TRACE** method is used to invoke a remote, application-layer loopback of the request message. The final recipient of the request *should* reflect the message received back to the client as the entity-body of a 200 (OK) response.
- The **CONNECT** method name is reserved for use with a proxy that can dynamically switch to being a tunnel (e.g., SSL tunneling).

**NOTE:** The list of methods allowed by a resource can be specified in an Allow header field (see the General Header Fields section in this appendix). The return code of the response always notifies the client whether a method is currently allowed on a resource, since the set of allowed methods can change dynamically. An origin server *should* return the status code 405 (Method Not Allowed) if the method is known by the origin server but not allowed for the requested resource, and 501 (Not Implemented) if the method is unrecognized or not implemented by the origin server.

## Request Header Fields

The request header fields allow the client to pass additional information about the request, and about the client itself, to the server. These fields act as request modifiers, with semantics equivalent to the parameters on a programming language method invocation.

The request header fields defined in RFC 2616 are as follows:

- The **Accept** header field can be used to specify certain media types that are acceptable for the response. Accept headers can be used to indicate that the request is specifically limited to a small set of desired types, as in the case of a request for an inline image.
- The **Accept-Charset** header field can be used to indicate what character sets are acceptable for the response. This field allows clients capable of understanding more comprehensive or special-purpose character sets to signal that capability to a server that is capable of representing documents in those character sets.
- The **Accept-Encoding** header field is similar to Accept, but restricts the content-codings that are acceptable in the response.
- The **Accept-Language** header field is similar to Accept, but restricts the set of natural languages that are preferred as a response to the request.
- The **Authorization** header field value consists of credentials containing the authentication information of the user agent for the realm of the resource being requested.
- The **Expect** header field is used to indicate that particular server behaviors are required by the client.
- The **From** header field contains an Internet e-mail address for the human user who controls the requesting user agent, if given. This is not supported by most browsers.
- The **Host** header field specifies the Internet host and port number of the resource being requested, as obtained from the original URI given by the user or referring resource (generally, an HTTP URL). The Host field value *must* represent the naming authority of the server or gateway given by the original URL. This allows the server or gateway to differentiate between internally ambiguous URLs, such as the root "/" URL of a server for multiple host names on a single IP address.

- The **If-Match** header field is used with a method to make it conditional. A client that has one or more entities previously obtained from the resource can verify that one of those entities is current by including a list of their associated entity tags in the If-Match header field.
- The **If-Modified-Since** header field is used with a method to make it conditional: If the requested variant has not been modified since the time specified in this field, an entity will not be returned from the server; instead, a 304 (Not Modified) response will be returned without any message-body.
- The **If-None-Match** header field is used with a method to make it conditional. A client that has one or more entities previously obtained from the resource can verify that none of those entities is current by including a list of their associated entity tags in the If-None-Match header field. The purpose of this feature is to allow efficient updates of cached information with a minimum amount of transaction overhead.
- The **If-Range** header field allows a client to "short-circuit" the second request. Informally, its meaning is "If the entity is unchanged, send me the part(s) that I am missing; otherwise, send me the entire new entity." If a client has a partial copy of an entity in its cache and wants to have an up-to-date copy of the entire entity in its cache, it could use the Range request header with a conditional GET (using either If-Unmodified-Since or If-Match, or both.) However, if the condition fails because the entity has been modified, the client would then have to make a second request to obtain the entire current entity-body.
- The **If-Unmodified-Since** header field is used with a method to make it conditional. If the requested resource has not been modified since the time specified in this field, the server *should* perform the requested operation as if the If-Unmodified-Since header were not present.
- The **Max-Forwards** header field provides a mechanism with the TRACE and OPTIONS methods to limit the number of proxies or gateways that can forward the request to the next inbound server. This can be useful when the client is attempting to trace a request chain that appears to be failing or looping in midchain.
- The **Proxy-Authorization** header field allows the client to identify itself (or its user) to a proxy that requires authentication. The Proxy-Authorization field value consists of credentials containing

the authentication information of the user agent for the proxy and/or realm of the resource being requested.

- The **Range** header field allows the client to define the byte range specifications that apply to the sequence of bytes in the entity-body (not necessarily the same as the message-body). A byte range operation *may* specify a single range of bytes or a set of ranges within a single entity. HTTP retrieval requests using conditional or unconditional GET methods *may* request one or more subranges of the entity instead of the entire entity, using the Range request header, which applies to the entity returned as the result of the request

- The **Referer** header field allows the client to specify, for the server's benefit, the address (URI) of the resource from which the Request-URI was obtained (the "referrer," although the header field is misspelled). The Referer request header allows a server to generate lists of back-links to resources for interest, logging, optimized caching, and so on.

- The **TE** header field indicates what extension transfer-codings the client is willing to accept in the response and whether it is willing to accept trailer fields in a chunked transfer-coding. Its value may consist of the keyword "trailers" and/or a comma-separated list of extension transfer-coding names with optional accept parameters.

- The **User-Agent** header field contains information about the user agent originating the request. This is for statistical purposes, the tracing of protocol violations, and automated recognition of user agents for the sake of tailoring responses to avoid particular user agent limitations. User agents *should* include this field with requests. The field can contain multiple product tokens and comments identifying the agent and any subproducts that form a significant part of the user agent.

# HTTP Response

The HTTP response message consists of an initial status line, one or more header fields, a blank line (CRLF) and an optional message body. The status line consists of the protocol version followed by a numeric status code and its associated textual phrase, with each element separated by space (SP) characters, as follows:

```
Status-Line = HTTP-Version SP Status-Code SP Reason-Phrase CRLF
```

The Status-Code element is a three-digit integer result code of the attempt to understand and satisfy the request. The first digit of the Status-Code defines the class of response. The last two digits do not have any categorization role. The Reason-Phrase is intended to give a short textual description of the Status-Code; the Reason-Phrase is intended for the human user. The client is not required to examine or display the Reason-Phrase.

## HTTP Status Codes

The HTTP status codes and their corresponding Reason-Phrases as defined in RFC 2616 are as follows:

- 1xx: Informational—The request was received; continuing process.
  - 100—Continue
  - 101—Switching Protocols
- 2xx: Success—The action was successfully received, understood, and accepted.
  - 200—OK
  - 201—Created
  - 202—Accepted
  - 203—Non-Authoritative Information
  - 204—No Content
  - 205—Reset Content
  - 206—Partial Content
- 3xx: Redirection—Further action must be taken in order to complete the request.
  - 300—Multiple Choices
  - 301—Moved Permanently
  - 302—Found
  - 303—See Other
  - 304—Not Modified
  - 305—Use Proxy
  - 307—Temporary Redirect
- 4xx: Client Error—The request contains bad syntax or cannot be fulfilled.
  - 400—Bad Request
  - 401—Unauthorized
  - 402—Payment Required
  - 403—Forbidden
  - 404—Not Found

- 405—Method Not Allowed
- 406—Not Acceptable
- 407—Proxy Authentication Required
- 408—Request Time-out
- 409—Conflict
- 410—Gone
- 411—Length Required
- 412—Precondition Failed
- 413—Request Entity Too Large
- 414—Request-URI Too Large
- 415—Unsupported Media Type
- 416—Requested Range Not Satisfiable
- 417—Expectation Failed
- 5xx: Server Error—The server failed to fulfill an apparently valid request.
  - 500—Internal Server Error
  - 501—Not Implemented
  - 502—Bad Gateway
  - 503—Service Unavailable
  - 504—Gateway Time-out
- 505—HTTP Version Not Supported

HTTP status codes are extensible. HTTP applications are not required to understand the meaning of all registered status codes, though such understanding is obviously desirable. However, applications *must* understand the class of any status code, as indicated by the first digit, and treat any unrecognized response as being equivalent to the *x*00 status code of that class, with the exception that an unrecognized response *must not* be cached.

## Response Header Fields

The response header fields allow the server to pass additional information about the response that cannot be placed in the status line. The header fields give information about the server and about further access to the resource identified by the Request-URI.

The response header fields defined in RFC 2616 are as follows:

- The **Accept-Ranges** header field allows the server to indicate its acceptance of range requests for a resource.

- The **Age** header field conveys the sender's estimate of the amount of time since the response (or its revalidation) was generated at the origin server. A cached response is "fresh" if its age does not exceed its freshness lifetime.
- The **ETag** header field provides the current value of the entity tag for the requested variant.
- The **Location** header field is used to redirect the recipient to a location other than the Request-URI for completion of the request or identification of a new resource. For 201 (Created) responses, the Location is that of the new resource that was created by the request. For 3xx responses, the Location *should* indicate the server's preferred URI for automatic redirection to the resource. The field value consists of a single absolute URI.
- The **Proxy-Authenticate** header field *must* be included as part of a 407 (Proxy Authentication Required) response. The field value consists of a challenge that indicates the authentication scheme and parameters applicable to the proxy for this Request-URI.
- The **Retry-After** header field can be used with a 503 (Service Unavailable) response to indicate how long the service is expected to be unavailable to the requesting client.
- The **Server** header field contains information about the software used by the origin server to handle the request.
- The **Vary** header field value indicates the set of request header fields that fully determines, while the response is fresh, whether a cache is permitted to use the response to reply to a subsequent request without revalidation. For uncacheable or stale responses, the Vary field value advises the user agent about the criteria that were used to select the representation. A Vary field value of "*" implies that a cache cannot determine from the request headers of a subsequent request whether this response is the appropriate representation.
- The **WWW-Authenticate** header field *must* be included in 401 (Unauthorized) response messages. The field value consists of at least one challenge that indicates the authentication scheme(s) and parameters applicable to the Request-URI.

# General Header Fields

There are several headers that are applicable for both request and response messages. These header fields apply only to the overall message being transmitted; they do not apply to the entity being transferred. The general header fields defined in RFC 2616 are as follows:

- The **Cache-Control** header field is used to specify directives that *must* be obeyed by all caching mechanisms along the request-response chain. The directives specify behavior intended to prevent caches from adversely interfering with the request or response. These directives typically override the default caching algorithms. Cache directives are unidirectional in that the presence of a directive in a request does not imply that the same directive is to be given in the response.
- The **Connection** header field allows the sender to specify options that are desired for that particular connection and *must not* be communicated by proxies over further connections.
- The **Date** header field represents the date and time at which the message was originated. The field value is an HTTP-date, it *must* be sent in RFC 1123 date format. For example,

```
Date: Sun, 9 Mar 2003 08:09:10 GMT
```

- The **Pragma** header field is used to include implementation-specific directives that might apply to any recipient along the request-response chain. All pragma directives specify optional behavior from the viewpoint of the protocol; however, some systems *may* require that behavior be consistent with the directives. For example,

```
Pragma: no-cache
```

- The **Trailer** header field value indicates that the given set of header fields is present in the trailer of a message encoded with chunked transfer-coding. An HTTP/1.1 message *should* include a Trailer header field in a message using chunked transfer-coding with a nonempty trailer. Doing so allows the recipient to know which header fields to expect in the trailer.
- The **Transfer-Encoding** header field indicates what (if any) type of transformation has been applied to the message-body in order

to safely transfer it between the sender and the recipient. This differs from the content-coding in that the transfer-coding is a property of the message, not of the entity. For example,

```
Transfer-Encoding: chunked
```

- The **Upgrade** header field allows the client to specify what additional communication protocols it supports and would like to use if the server finds it appropriate to switch protocols. The Upgrade header field is intended to provide a simple mechanism for transition from HTTP/1.1 to some other, incompatible protocol.
- The **Via** header field *must* be used by gateways and proxies to indicate the intermediate protocols and recipients between the user agent and the server on requests, and between the origin server and the client on responses. It is intended to be used for tracking message forwards, avoiding request loops, and identifying the protocol capabilities of all senders along the request-response chain.
- The **Warning** header field is used to carry additional information about the status or transformation of a message that might not be reflected in the message. This information is typically used to warn about a possible lack of semantic transparency from caching operations or transformations applied to the entity body of the message.

## Entity Header Fields

Entity header fields define meta information about the entity body or, if no body is present, about the resource identified by the request. Some of this meta information is optional; some might be required.

The entity header fields defined in RFC 2616 are as follows:

- The **Allow** header field lists the set of methods supported by the resource identified by the Request-URI. The purpose of this field is strictly to inform the recipient of valid methods associated with the resource.
- The **Content-Encoding** header field is used as a modifier to the media type. When present, its value indicates what additional content codings have been applied to the entity body, and thus what decoding mechanisms must be applied in order to obtain the media

type referenced by the Content-Type header field. Content-Encoding is primarily used to allow a document to be compressed without losing the identity of its underlying media type.

- The **Content-Language** header field describes the natural language(s) of the intended audience for the enclosed entity. Note that this might not be equivalent to all the languages used within the entity-body.

- The **Content-Length** header field indicates the size of the entity-body, in decimal number of octets, sent to the recipient or, in the case of the HEAD method, the size of the entity-body that would have been sent had the request been a GET.

- The **Content-Location** header field *may* be used to supply the resource location for the entity enclosed in the message when that entity is accessible from a location separate from the requested resource's URI.

- The **Content-MD5** header field contains an MD5 digest of the entity-body for the purpose of providing an end-to-end message integrity check (MIC) of the entity-body. (Note: An MIC is good for detecting accidental modification of the entity-body in transit but is not proof against malicious attacks.)

- The **Content-Type** header field indicates the media type of the entity body sent to the recipient or, in the case of the HEAD method, the media type that would have been sent had the request been a GET.

- The **Content-Range** header field is sent with a partial entity body to specify where in the full entity body the partial body should be applied.

- The **Date** header field contains the date and time at which the message was originated.

- The **Expires** header field contains the date and time after which the response is considered stale.

- The **Last-Modified** header field indicates the date and time at which the server believes the document being sent to the browser was last modified.

## Summary

This appendix provided a brief reference to HTTP requests and responses, including format, methods, headers, and status codes.

# Publishing API Reference

## CmsHttpContext Parentage

Table B–1 shows the complete parentage of the CmsHttpContext class. The properties and methods listed in italics in the table are defined by the class in the column header and then inherited by the derived class(es) to the left. So, for instance, only Current, UserCacheKey, and ChannelItemIsVisible are coded in the CmsHttpContext class, whereas Equals, GetHashCode, GetType, and ToString are coded in the System. Object class and then inherited by the CmsContext class, the CmsAsp Context class, and finally the CmsHttpContext class.

**Table B–1** CmsHttpContext Parentage

| CmsHttpContext | CmsAspContext | CmsContext | System.Object |
|---|---|---|---|
| **Public Properties** | | | |
| Channel | *Channel* | | |
| ChannelItem | *ChannelItem* | | |
| CmsQueryString | *CmsQueryString* | | |
| *Current* | | | |
| IsDefaultGuest Enabled | IsDefaultGuest Enabled | *IsDefaultGuest Enabled* | |
| IsLoggedIn AsGuest | IsLoggedIn AsGuest | *IsLoggedIn AsGuest* | |
| IsUsingTemplate | *IsUsingTemplate* | | |

*(continued)*

**Table B–1** *(Continued)*

| CmsHttpContext | CmsAspContext | CmsContext | System.Object |
|---|---|---|---|
| Mode | Mode | *Mode* | |
| Placeholder DefinitionTypes | Placeholder DefinitionTypes | *Placeholder DefinitionTypes* | |
| Posting | *Posting* | | |
| RollbackOn SessionEnd | RollbackOn SessionEnd | *RollbackOn SessionEnd* | |
| RootChannel | RootChannel | *RootChannel* | |
| RootResource Gallery | RootResource Gallery | *RootResource Gallery* | |
| RootTemplate Gallery | RootTemplate Gallery | *RootTemplate Gallery* | |
| Searches | Searches | *Searches* | |
| ServerTime | ServerTime | *ServerTime* | |
| SessionSettings | SessionSettings | *SessionSettings* | |
| Temporary UploadFolder | Temporary UploadFolder | *Temporary UploadFolder* | |
| User | User | *User* | |
| *UserCacheKey* | | | |
| UserCanApprove | UserCanApprove | *UserCanApprove* | |
| UserCanAuthor | UserCanAuthor | *UserCanAuthor* | |
| UserCanEdit Resources | UserCanEdit Resources | *UserCanEdit Resources* | |
| UserCanEdit Templates | UserCanEdit Templates | *UserCanEdit Templates* | |
| UserCan ModifySite | UserCan ModifySite | *UserCan ModifySite* | |

**Public Methods**

| CmsHttpContext | CmsAspContext | CmsContext | System.Object |
|---|---|---|---|
| AcceptBinary File | AcceptBinary File | *AcceptBinary File* | |
| ChannelItemIs Visible | *ChannelItem IsVisible* | | |
| CommitAll | CommitAll | *CommitAll* | |

**Table B–1** *(Continued)*

| CmsHttpContext | CmsAspContext | CmsContext | System.Object |
|---|---|---|---|
| Dispose | Dispose | *Dispose* | |
| Equals | Equals | Equals | *Equals* |
| GetHashCode | GetHashCode | GetHashCode | *GetHashCode* |
| GetType | GetType | GetType | *GetType* |
| Propagate Parameter | Propagate Parameter | *Propagate Parameter* | |
| ResolveUrl | *ResolveUrl* | | |
| RollbackAll | RollbackAll | *RollbackAll* | |
| ToString | ToString | ToString | *ToString* |
| UserHasRight ToBrowse | UserHasRight ToBrowse | *UserHasRight ToBrowse* | |

A handful of methods are inherited directly from System.Object. But the CmsContext class is the base class in which most of the CMS functionality is found.

---

**NOTE:** If a Web page is not a CMS Posting, even though it is running within IIS, it cannot access CmsHttpContext.

---

Table B–2 defines all the members listed for CmsHttpContext in Table B–1.

**Table B–2** CmsHttpContext Member Descriptions

| CmsHttpContext | Description |
|---|---|
| **Public Properties** | |
| Channel | Gets the Channel object representing the current channel. |
| ChannelItem | Gets the ChannelItem for the current Web page. |
| CmsQueryString | Gets a formatted QueryString string containing only the CMS-specific name/value pairs from the current QueryString. |

*(continued)*

**Table B–2** *(Continued)*

| CmsHttpContext | Description |
|---|---|
| *Current* | Gets the CmsHttpContext for the current HttpRequest. |
| IsDefaultGuestEnabled | Gets a value indicating whether guest user access is enabled for CMS. |
| IsLoggedInAsGuest | Gets a value indicating whether the user is logged in as a guest. |
| IsUsingTemplate | Gets a value indicating whether the current Web page is a Template. |
| Mode | Gets the current PublishingMode for the current session. |
| Placeholder DefinitionTypes | Gets the collection of allowed PlaceholderDefinition types for a CMS site. |
| Posting | Gets the Posting for the current Web page. |
| RollbackOnSessionEnd | Gets or sets a value that indicates whether uncommitted changes are rolled back when the session ends. |
| RootChannel | Gets the Channel at the root of the channel hierarchy. |
| RootResourceGallery | Gets the ResourceGallery at the root of the resource hierarchy. |
| RootTemplateGallery | Gets the TemplateGallery at the root of the template gallery hierarchy. |
| Searches | Get the Searches object that is used to search the CMS site. |
| ServerTime | Gets the current Coordinated Universal Time (UTC) of the CMS database server. |
| SessionSettings | Gets the SessionSettings for the current session. |
| TemporaryUpload | Gets the path of the temporary upload folder for Folder the CMS folder. |
| User | Gets the User, which represents the currently logged in user. |
| *UserCacheKey* | Gets a unique string for all users that have the same run-time browsing rights in the system. |
| UserCanApprove | Gets a value indicating if the user has rights to approve postings in the CMS site. |
| UserCanAuthor | Gets a value indicating if the user has rights to create and author postings. |
| UserCanEditResources | Gets a value indicating if the user has rights to edit Resource objects in the CMS site. |

**Table B–2** *(Continued)*

| CmsHttpContext | Description |
|---|---|
| UserCanEditTemplates | Gets a value indicating if the user has rights to create and edit templates in the CMS site. |
| UserCanModifySite | Gets a value indicating if the user has rights to make changes in the CMS site. |
| **Public Methods** | |
| AcceptBinaryFile | Loads a file from the file system and loads it into the database as an internal resource and returns a new URL for the resource. |
| ChannelItemIsVisible | Indicates whether the ChannelItem item is visible to the current user. |
| CommitAll | Commits changes to all CMS Publishing API objects that have been modified during the most recent session transaction. |
| Dispose | Releases all file handles and all unmanaged memory resources held by the CmsContext and objects retrieved directly or indirectly from CmsContext. |
| Equals | Determines whether two Object instances are equal. |
| GetHashCode | Serves as a hash function for a particular type, suitable for use in hashing algorithms and data structures like a hash table. |
| GetType | Gets the Type of the current instance. |
| PropagateParameter | Adds a name/value pair to CMS-generated URLs for the remainder of the session. |
| ResolveUrl | Makes URLs that are not generated by CMS compatible with the CMS Site Stager. |
| RollbackAll | Rolls back changes made to any CMS Publishing API objects that have been modified in the current session transaction. |
| ToString | Returns a String that represents the current object type. |
| UserHasRight ToBrowse | Indicates if the user has permissions to browse the current ChannelItem. |

## CmsApplicationContext Parentage

Table B–3 shows the complete parentage of the CmsApplicationContext class. As in the CmsHttpContext table, the properties and methods listed in italics are defined by the class in the column header and then inherited by the derived class(es) to the left.

**Table B–3** CmsApplicationContext Parentage

| CmsApplicationContext | CmsContext | System.Object |
|---|---|---|
| **Public Constructors** | | |
| *CmsApplicationContext* | | |
| **Public Properties** | | |
| IsLoggedInAsGuest | *IsLoggedInAsGuest* | |
| Mode | *Mode* | |
| PlaceholderDefinitionTypes | *PlaceholderDefinitionTypes* | |
| RollbackOnSessionEnd | *RollbackOnSessionEnd* | |
| RootChannel | *RootChannel* | |
| RootResourceGallery | *RootResourceGallery* | |
| RootTemplateGallery | *RootTemplateGallery* | |
| Searches | *Searches* | |
| ServerTime | *ServerTime* | |
| SessionSettings | *SessionSettings* | |
| TemporaryUploadFolder | *TemporaryUploadFolder* | |
| User | *User* | |
| UserCanApprove | *UserCanApprove* | |
| UserCanAuthor | *UserCanAuthor* | |
| UserCanEditResources | *UserCanEditResources* | |
| UserCanEditTemplates | *UserCanEditTemplates* | |
| UserCanModifySite | *UserCanModifySite* | |

**Table B–3** *(Continued)*

| CmsApplicationContext | CmsContext | System.Object |
|---|---|---|
| **Public Methods** | | |
| AcceptBinaryFile | *AcceptBinaryFile* | |
| *AuthenticateAsCurrentUser* | | |
| *AuthenticateAsGuest* | | |
| *AuthenticateAsUser* | | |
| *AuthenticateUsingUserHandle* | | |
| CommitAll | *CommitAll* | |
| Dispose | *Dispose* | |
| Equals | Equals | *Equals* |
| GetHashCode | GetHashCode | *GetHashCode* |
| GetType | GetType | *GetType* |
| PropagateParameter | *PropagateParameter* | |
| RollbackAll | *RollbackAll* | |
| ToString | ToString | *ToString* |
| UserHasRightToBrowse | *UserHasRightToBrowse* | |

The CmsApplicationContext class inherits all its properties directly from the CmsContext class without alteration and without the CmsAsp Context class that CmsHttpContext uses. The following properties are not available as they were in the CmsHttpContext class: Channel, ChannelItem, CmsQueryString, Current, IsUsingTemplate, Posting, and UserCacheKey. The following methods are also not available: Channel ItemIsVisible and ResolveUrl. This makes sense because this Context is used in the absence of a Posting URL, so there isn't a current Posting, Channel, or QueryString to reference.

Table B–4 defines all the unique members listed for the Cms ApplicationContext class in Table B–3.

**Table B–4** CmsApplicationContext Unique Member Descriptions

| CmsApplicationContext | Description |
|---|---|
| **Public Constructor** | |
| CmsApplicationContext | Creates a new instance of the CmsApplication-Context class. |
| **Public Methods** | |
| AuthenticateAsCurrentUser | Attempts to log in to CMS as the current user. |
| AuthenticateAsGuest | Attempts to log in as the default guest user for CMS. |
| AuthenticateAsUser | Attempts to log in as the specified user. |
| AuthenticateUsingUserHandle | Authenticates the user using the Windows user handle. |

# Channel Parentage

Table B–5 shows the complete parentage of a CMS Channel class. The properties and methods listed in italics in the table are defined by the class in the column header and then inherited by the derived class(es) to the left. So, for instance, only GetHashCode is coded in the CmsObject class, whereas Equals, GetType, and ToString are coded in the System.Object class and then inherited by the CmsObject class. All these members are inherited by the HierarchyItem class, the ChannelItem class, and finally the Channel class. AllChildren, for example, is coded in the Channel class and is not inherited by any other class.

**Table B–5** Channel Parentage

| Channel | Channel Item | Hierarchy Item | Cms Object | System. Object |
|---|---|---|---|---|
| **Public Properties** | | | | |
| AllChildren | | | | |
| *ApplyOuter ScriptToPostings* | | | | |

**Table B–5**  *(Continued)*

| Channel | Channel Item | Hierarchy Item | Cms Object | System. Object |
|---|---|---|---|---|
| *CanCreateChannels* | | | | |
| *CanCreatePostings* | | | | |
| CanDelete | CanDelete | *CanDelete* | | |
| CanSet Properties | CanSet Properties | *CanSet Properties* | | |
| ChangeDate | *ChangeDate* | | | |
| *Channels* | | | | |
| CreatedBy | CreatedBy | *CreatedBy* | | |
| CreatedDate | CreatedDate | *CreatedDate* | | |
| Custom Properties | *Custom Properties* | | | |
| *DefaultPostingName* | | | | |
| *DefaultResource Gallery* | | | | |
| *DefaultTemplate Gallery* | | | | |
| Description | Description | *Description* | | |
| DisplayName | *DisplayName* | | | |
| DisplayPath | *DisplayPath* | | | |
| ExpiryDate | *ExpiryDate* | | | |
| Guid | Guid | *Guid* | | |
| IsDeleted | IsDeleted | *IsDeleted* | | |
| IsHidden Mode Published | *IsHidden Mode Published* | | | |
| IsImportant | *IsImportant* | | | |
| IsRobot Followable | *IsRobot Followable* | | | |
| IsRobot Indexable | *IsRobot Indexable* | | | |
| *IsRoot* | | | | |

*(continued)*

**Table B–5** *(Continued)*

| Channel | Channel Item | Hierarchy Item | Cms Object | System. Object |
|---------|--------------|----------------|------------|----------------|
| IsWorkingRevision | IsWorking Revision | *IsWorking Revision* | | |
| LastModifiedBy | Last ModifiedBy | *Last ModifiedBy* | | |
| LastModifiedDate | LastModified Date | *LastModified Date* | | |
| Name | Name | *Name* | | |
| *OuterScriptFile* | | | | |
| OwnedBy | OwnedBy | *OwnedBy* | | |
| Parent | *Parent* | | | |
| Path | Path | *Path* | | |
| *Postings* | | | | |
| QueryString | *QueryString* | | | |
| QueryString Mode Unpublished | *QueryString Mode Unpublished* | | | |
| QueryString ModeUpdate | *QueryString ModeUpdate* | | | |
| RevisionDate | RevisionDate | *RevisionDate* | | |
| SortOrdinal | *SortOrdinal* | | | |
| StartDate | *StartDate* | | | |
| Url | *Url* | | | |
| UrlInner | *UrlInner* | | | |
| UrlInnerPlain | *UrlInnerPlain* | | | |
| UrlModePublished | *UrlModePublished* | | | |
| UrlModeUnpublished | *UrlModeUnpublished* | | | |
| UrlModeUpdate | *UrlModeUpdate* | | | |

**Public Methods**

*CreateChannel*

*CreateConnected Posting*

**Table B–5** *(Continued)*

| Channel | Channel Item | Hierarchy Item | Cms Object | System. Object |
|---|---|---|---|---|
| *CreatePosting* | | | | |
| Delete | Delete | *Delete* | | |
| Equals | Equals | Equals | Equals | *Equals* |
| GetByRelativePath | *GetBy RelativePath* | | | |
| GetHashCode | GetHash Code | GetHash Code | *GetHash Code* | |
| GetType | GetType | GetType | GetType | *GetType* |
| IsDescendantOf | IsDescendant Of | *IsDescendant Of* | | |
| ToString | ToString | ToString | ToString | *ToString* |

Channels inherit much of their functionality from ChannelItem and HierarchyItem.

Table B–6 defines all the members listed for the Channel class in Table B–5.

**Table B–6**  Channel Member Descriptions

| Channel | Classification | Description |
|---|---|---|
| **Public Properties** | | |
| AllChildren | Child object | Gets all the Channels and Postings within this Channel. |
| ApplyOuter ScriptTo Postings | Read/write | Gets or sets a value indicating whether the outer script should be executed for Posting objects. |
| CanCreate Channels | User right | Gets a value indicating whether the user has the necessary rights to create new Channel objects within this Channel. |

*(continued)*

**Table B–6** *(Continued)*

| Channel | Classification | Description |
|---|---|---|
| CanCreate Postings | User right | Gets a value indicating whether the user has the necessary rights to create new Postings within this Channel. |
| CanDelete | User right | Gets a value indicating whether the current user has sufficient rights to delete this class instance. |
| CanSet Properties | User right | Gets a value indicating whether the current user has sufficient rights to modify the properties of this class instance. |
| ChangeDate | Read-only | Gets the Coordinated Universal Time (UTC) when ChannelItem was last changed. |
| Channels | Child object | Gets the Channel objects within this Channel. |
| CreatedBy | Read-only | Gets the User that created this class instance. |
| CreatedDate | Read-only | Gets the UTC when the HierarchyItem was created. |
| Custom Properties | Child object | Gets the CustomPropertyCollection for this ChannelItem object. |
| Default PostingName | Read/write | Gets or sets the name of the default Posting for this Channel. |
| Default Resource Gallery | Read/write | Gets or sets the default ResourceGallery for this Channel. |
| Default Template Gallery | Read/write | Gets or sets the default Template Gallery for this Channel. |
| Description | Read/write | Gets or sets descriptive text for this class instance. |
| DisplayName | Read-only | Gets and sets the display name for this Channel Item object. |
| DisplayPath | Read-only | Gets the fully qualified path of a ChannelItem. |
| ExpiryDate | Read/write | Gets and sets the UTC at which this Channel Item expires and ceases to be a visible part of the published Web site. |
| Guid | Read-only | Gets a string representation of the globally unique identifier (GUID) for this object. |

**Table B–6**  *(Continued)*

| Channel | Classification | Description |
|---|---|---|
| IsDeleted | Read-only | Gets a value indicating whether this class instance has been deleted, regardless of whether the deletion has been committed. |
| IsHidden Mode Published | Read/write | Gets and sets a flag indicating whether this ChannelItem is hidden in the navigation hierarchy of the live (published) CMS Web site. |
| IsImportant | Read/write | Gets or sets a value indicating whether a ChannelItem is important. |
| IsRobot Followable | Read/write | Gets and sets a value indicating whether Web robots should follow any hyperlinks found in the Web page corresponding to this ChannelItem object. |
| IsRobot Indexable | Read/write | Gets and sets a value indicating whether Web robots should index the Web page corresponding to this ChannelItem object. |
| IsRoot | Read-only | Gets a value indicating whether this Channel is the root Channel in the channel hierarchy. |
| IsWorking Revision | Read-only | Gets a value indicating whether the Hierarchy Item is a working revision. |
| Last ModifiedBy | Read-only | Gets the User that last modified the Hierarchy Item. |
| Last ModifiedDate | Read-only | Gets the UTC when this HierarchyItem was last modified. |
| Name | Read/write | Gets or sets the name of this HierarchyItem. |
| OuterScript | Read/write | Gets or sets the outer script file for this Channel. |
| FileOwnedBy | Read-only | Gets the User who currently owns the class instance. |
| Parent | Child object | Gets the Channel that contains this Channel Item object. |
| Path | Read-only | Gets the fully qualified path of the Hierarchy Item. |
| Postings | Child object | Gets the Postings within this Channel. |
| QueryString | Read-only | Gets the URL QueryString parameters for this ChannelItem. |

*(continued)*

**Table B–6** *(Continued)*

| Channel | Classification | Description |
| --- | --- | --- |
| QueryString Mode Unpublished | Read-only | Gets the URL QueryString parameters used to view this ChannelItem when in Unpublished mode. |
| QueryString ModeUpdate | Read-only | Gets the URL QueryString parameters used by this ChannelItem when in Update mode. |
| RevisionDate | Read-only | Gets a System.DateTime that gets the UTC when this historical revision of this Hierarchy Item was created. |
| SortOrdinal | Read/write | Gets and sets the relative position of this ChannelItem with respect to its sibling Channel Item objects. |
| StartDate | Read/write | Gets and sets the UTC at which this Channel Item becomes visible in the published Web site. |
| Url | Read-only | Gets the URL for this ChannelItem object. |
| UrlInner | Read-only | Gets a URL that references the ChannelItem, bypassing the outer script file. |
| UrlInnerPlain | Read-only | Gets a URL that references the ChannelItem, bypassing the outer script file and not propagating any QueryString parameters from the current request. |
| UrlMode Published | Read-only | Gets the URL for this ChannelItem in Published mode. |
| UrlMode Unpublished | Read-only | Gets the URL for this ChannelItem in Unpublished mode. |
| UrlMode Update | Read-only | Gets the URL for this ChannelItem in Update mode. |

**Public Methods**

| | | |
| --- | --- | --- |
| Create Channel | Creating and deleting | Creates a new Channel within the current Channel. |
| Create Connected Posting | Creating and deleting | Creates a new Posting in this Channel that is connected to the specified Posting. |
| Create Posting | Creating and deleting | Creates a new Posting in this Channel. |

**Table B–6**  *(Continued)*

| Channel | Classification | Description |
| --- | --- | --- |
| Delete | Creating and deleting | Deletes the HierarchyItem. |
| Equals | System | Determines whether two Object instances are equal. |
| GetBy RelativePath | Child object | Locates a ChannelItem in the channel hierarchy according to its position relative to this Channel Item. |
| GetHash Code | Read-only | Gets the hash code for the object. |
| GetType | Read-only | Gets the Type of the current instance. |
| IsDescendant Of | Read-only | Determines whether this object is a descendant of the specified object. |
| ToString | System | Returns a String that represents the current object type. |

We have included a classification column in Table B-6. This is not a CMS classification. It was included to make it easier to locate the discussion about each member in Chapter 25.

## Posting Parentage

Table B–7 shows the complete parentage of a CMS Posting class. The properties and methods listed in italics in the table are defined by the class in the column header and then inherited by the derived class(es) to the left. So, for instance, only GetHashCode is coded in the CmsObject class, whereas Equals, GetType, and ToString are coded in the System. Object class and then inherited by the CmsObject class. All these members are inherited by the HierarchyItem class, the ChannelItem class, and finally the Posting class. CanApprove, for example, is coded in the Posting class and is not inherited by any other class.

**Table B–7** Posting Parentage

| Posting | Channel Item | Hierarchy Item | Cms Object | System. Object |
|---|---|---|---|---|
| **Public Properties** | | | | |
| *CanApprove* | | | | |
| CanDelete | CanDelete | *CanDelete* | | |
| *CanMove* | | | | |
| CanSet Properties | CanSet Properties | *CanSet Properties* | | |
| *CanSubmit* | | | | |
| ChangeDate | *ChangeDate* | | | |
| *ChangeToken* | | | | |
| *ConnectedPostings* | | | | |
| *ConnectedTemplates* | | | | |
| CreatedBy | CreatedBy | *CreatedBy* | | |
| CreatedDate | CreatedDate | *CreatedDate* | | |
| Custom Properties | *Custom Properties* | | | |
| Description | Description | *Description* | | |
| DisplayName | *DisplayName* | | | |
| DisplayPath | *DisplayPath* | | | |
| ExpiryDate | *ExpiryDate* | | | |
| Guid | Guid | *Guid* | | |
| *HasInaccessible ConnectedPostings* | | | | |
| *IsConnected* | | | | |
| IsDeleted | IsDeleted | *IsDeleted* | | |
| IsHiddenMode Published | *IsHiddenMode Published* | | | |
| IsImportant | *IsImportant* | | | |
| IsRobot Followable | *IsRobot Followable* | | | |
| IsRobot Indexable | *IsRobot Indexable* | | | |

**Table B–7**  *(Continued)*

| Posting | Channel Item | Hierarchy Item | Cms Object | System. Object |
|---------|--------------|----------------|------------|----------------|
| IsWorking Revision | IsWorking Revision | *IsWorking Revision* | | |
| *LastApproved DeclinedBy* | | | | |
| LastModified By | LastModified By | *LastModified By* | | |
| LastModified Date | LastModified Date | *LastModified Date* | | |
| Name | Name | *Name* | | |
| OwnedBy | OwnedBy | *OwnedBy* | | |
| Parent | *Parent* | | | |
| Path | Path | *Path* | | |
| *Placeholders* | | | | |
| QueryString | *QueryString* | | | |
| QueryString Mode Unpublished | *QueryString Mode Unpublished* | | | |
| QueryString ModeUpdate | *QueryString ModeUpdate* | | | |
| *RevisionCause* | | | | |
| RevisionDate | RevisionDate | *RevisionDate* | | |
| SortOrdinal | *SortOrdinal* | | | |
| StartDate | *StartDate* | | | |
| *State* | | | | |
| *StateApprovedVersion* | | | | |
| *StateUnapproved Version* | | | | |
| *Template* | | | | |
| Url | *Url* | | | |
| UrlInner | *UrlInner* | | | |

*(continued)*

**Table B–7** *(Continued)*

| Posting | Channel Item | Hierarchy Item | Cms Object | System. Object |
|---|---|---|---|---|
| UrlInnerPlain | *UrlInnerPlain* | | | |
| UrlMode Published | *UrlMode Published* | | | |
| UrlMode Unpublished | *UrlMode Unpublished* | | | |
| UrlMode Update | *UrlMode Update* | | | |
| *WorkingRevision* | | | | |

**Public Methods**

| Posting | Channel Item | Hierarchy Item | Cms Object | System. Object |
|---|---|---|---|---|
| *AcquireOwnership* | | | | |
| *Approve* | | | | |
| *Approvers* | | | | |
| *CopyTo* | | | | |
| *Decline* | | | | |
| Delete | Delete | *Delete* | | |
| Equals | Equals | Equals | Equals | *Equals* |
| GetBy RelativePath | *GetBy RelativePath* | | | |
| GetHash Code | GetHash Code | GetHash Code | *GetHash Code* | |
| GetType | GetType | GetType | GetType | *GetType* |
| IsDescendant Of | IsDescendant Of | *IsDescendant Of* | | |
| *MoveTo* | | | | |
| *ReleaseOwnership* | | | | |
| *RevisionForDate* | | | | |
| *Revisions* | | | | |
| *Submit* | | | | |
| ToString | ToString | ToString | ToString | *ToString* |
| ValidateChangeToken | | | | |

Like Channels, Postings inherit much of their functionality from ChannelItem and HierarchyItem.

Table B–8 defines all the members listed for the Channel class in Table B–7.

**Table B–8** Posting Member Descriptions

| Posting | Classification | Description |
|---|---|---|
| **Public Properties** | | |
| CanApprove | User right | Gets a value indicating whether the Posting requires approval and whether the current user has sufficient rights to either approve or decline it. |
| CanDelete | User right | Gets a value indicating whether the current user has sufficient rights to delete this class instance. |
| CanMove | User right | Gets a value indicating whether the current user has sufficient rights to move the Posting to another Channel. |
| CanSetProperties | User right | Gets a value indicating whether the current user has sufficient rights to modify the properties of this class instance. |
| CanSubmit | User right | Gets a value indicating whether the Posting requires submitting and whether the current user has rights to do so. |
| ChangeDate | Read-only | Gets the Coordinated Universal Time (UTC) when ChannelItem was last changed. |
| ChangeToken | Read-only | Gets a value used to determine whether a modification has occurred in a Posting. |
| ConnectedPostings | Child object | Gets the collection of Postings that are connected to the current Posting. |
| ConnectedTemplates | Child object | Gets the collection of templates connected to the template associated with this Posting. |
| CreatedBy | Read-only | Gets the User that created this class instance. |

*(continued)*

**Table B–8**  *(Continued)*

| Posting | Classification | Description |
| --- | --- | --- |
| CreatedDate | Read-only | Gets the UTC when the HierarchyItem was created. |
| CustomProperties | Child object | Gets the CustomPropertyCollection for this ChannelItem object. |
| Description | Read/write | Gets or sets descriptive text for this class instance. |
| DisplayName | Read-only | Gets and sets the display name for this ChannelItem object. |
| DisplayPath | Read-only | Gets the fully qualified path of a Channel Item. |
| ExpiryDate | Read/write | Gets and sets the UTC at which this ChannelItem expires and ceases to be a visible part of the published Web site. |
| Guid | Read-only | Gets a string representation of the globally unique identifier (GUID) for this object. |
| HasInaccessible ConnectedPostings | Read-only | Gets a value indicating whether the Posting is connected to other Postings that the user does not have rights to access. |
| IsConnected | Read-only | Gets a value indicating whether this Posting is connected to other Postings. |
| IsDeleted | Read-only | Gets a value indicating whether this class instance has been deleted, regardless of whether the deletion has been committed. |
| IsHiddenMode Published | Read/write | Gets and sets a flag indicating whether this ChannelItem is hidden in the navigation hierarchy of the live (published) CMS Web site. |
| IsImportant | Read/write | Gets or sets a value indicating whether a ChannelItem is important. |
| IsRobotFollowable | Read/write | Gets and sets a value indicating whether Web robots should follow any hyperlinks found in the Web page corresponding to this ChannelItem object. |

**Table B–8** *(Continued)*

| Posting | Classification | Description |
|---|---|---|
| IsRobotIndexable | Read/write | Gets and sets a value indicating whether Web robots should index the Web page corresponding to this ChannelItem object. |
| IsWorkingRevision | Read-only | Gets a value indicating whether the HierarchyItem is a working revision. |
| LastApproved DeclinedBy | Read/write | Gets a value that identifies the CMS user that last approved or declined the Posting. |
| LastModifiedBy | Read-only | Gets the User that last modified the HierarchyItem. |
| LastModifiedDate | Read-only | Gets the UTC when this HierarchyItem was last modified. |
| Name | Read/write | Gets or sets the name of this Hierarchy Item. |
| OwnedBy | Read-only | Gets the User who currently owns the class instance. |
| Parent | Child object | Gets the Channel that contains this ChannelItem object. |
| Path | Read-only | Gets the fully qualified path of the HierarchyItem. |
| Placeholders | Child object | Gets a collection of named Placeholder objects associated with this Posting. |
| QueryString | Read-only | Gets the URL QueryString parameters for this ChannelItem. |
| QueryStringMode Unpublished | Read-only | Gets the URL QueryString parameters used to view this ChannelItem when in Unpublished mode. |
| QueryStringMode Update | Read-only | Gets the URL QueryString parameters used by this ChannelItem when in Update mode. |
| RevisionCause | Child object | Gets the cause of a revision for historical revisions of this Posting. |
| RevisionDate | Child object | Gets a System.DateTime that gets the UTC when this historical revision of this HierarchyItem was created. |

*(continued)*

**Table B–8** *(Continued)*

| Posting | Classification | Description |
|---|---|---|
| SortOrdinal | Read/write | Gets and sets the relative position of this ChannelItem with respect to its sibling ChannelItem objects. |
| StartDate | Read/write | Gets and sets the UTC at which this ChannelItem becomes visible in the published Web site. |
| State | Read-only | Gets the state of the current version of this Posting. |
| StateApproved Version | Read-only | Gets the state of the Approved version of this Posting, regardless of whether it is the current version. |
| StateUnapproved Version | Read-only | Gets the state of the Unapproved version of this Posting, regardless of whether it is the current version. |
| Template | Child object | Gets the template used to create this Posting. |
| Url | Read-only | Gets the URL for this ChannelItem object. |
| UrlInner | Read-only | Gets a URL that references the Channel Item, bypassing the outer script file. |
| UrlInnerPlain | Read-only | Gets a URL that references the ChannelItem, bypassing the outer script file and not propagating any QueryString parameters from the current request. |
| UrlModePublished | Read-only | Gets the URL for this ChannelItem in Published mode. |
| UrlMode Unpublished | Read-only | Gets the URL for this ChannelItem in Unpublished mode. |
| UrlModeUpdate | Read-only | Gets the URL for this ChannelItem in Update mode. |
| WorkingRevision | Child object | Gets the working revision of this Posting. |
| **Public Methods** | | |
| AcquireOwnership | Managing | Takes ownership of the Posting, thereby restricting editing by others. |

**Table B–8** *(Continued)*

| Posting | Classification | Description |
| --- | --- | --- |
| Approve | Managing | Marks a Posting for approval. |
| Approvers | Child object | Checks which CMS users have rights to approve the Posting in its current state. |
| CopyTo | Managing | Copies the current Posting to the specified Channel. |
| Decline | Managing | Marks a Posting as declined. |
| Delete | Managing | Deletes the HierarchyItem. |
| Equals | System | Determines whether two Object instances are equal. |
| GetByRelativePath | Child object | Locates a ChannelItem in the channel hierarchy according to its position relative to this ChannelItem. |
| GetHashCode | Read-only | Gets the hash code for the object. |
| GetType | Read-only | Gets the Type of the current instance. |
| IsDescendantOf | Read-only | Determines whether this object is a descendant of the specified object. |
| MoveTo | Managing | Moves this Posting to the specified Channel. |
| ReleaseOwnership | Managing | Releases the ownership of a Posting previously acquired using AcquireOwnership. |
| RevisionForDate | Child object | Returns the historical revision of a Posting for a specified date and time (GMT). |
| Revisions | Child object | Returns a collection of historical revisions of a Posting. |
| Submit | Managing | Marks a Posting as submitted. |
| ToString | System | Returns a String that represents the current object type. |
| ValidateChangeToken | Managing | Confirms that the Posting has not been altered since the last time it was read and that it is in the expected state for the next edit operation. |

We have included a classification column in the Table B-8. This is not a CMS classification. It was included to make it easier to locate the discussion about each member in Chapter 26.

## Placeholder Parentage

Table B–9 shows the complete parentage of the CMS Placeholder class. The properties and methods listed in italics in the table are defined by the class in the column header and then inherited by the derived class(es) to the left. So, for instance, only GetHashCode is coded in the

**Table B–9** Placeholder Parentage

| Placeholder | CmsObject | System.Object |
|---|---|---|
| **Public Properties** | | |
| *Datasource* | | |
| *Datasource.RawContent* | | |
| *Definition* | | |
| *Name* | | |
| *Posting* | | |
| **Public Methods** | | |
| Equals | Equals | *Equals* |
| GetHashCode | *GetHashCode* | |
| GetType | GetType | *GetType* |
| ToString | ToString | *ToString* |
| **Protected Constructors** | | |
| *Placeholder Constructor* | | |
| **Protected Methods** | | |
| *BeginWrite* | | |
| *EndWrite* | | |
| *RetrieveContent* | | |
| SaveContent | | |

CmsObject class, whereas Equals, GetType, and ToString are coded in the System.Object class and then inherited by the CmsObject class. All these members are inherited by the Placeholder class. Datasource, for example, is coded in the Placeholder class and is not inherited by any other class.

Table B–10 defines all the members listed for the Placeholder class in Table B–9.

We have included a classification column in Table B–10. This is not a CMS classification. It was included to make it easier to locate the discussion about each member in Chapter 27.

**Table B–10** Placeholder Member Descriptions

| Placeholder | Classification | Description |
|---|---|---|
| **Public Properties** | | |
| Datasource | Read/write | Gets and sets a data source for this Placeholder, allowing it to detour where it saves and loads its data from. |
| Datasource.RawContent | Read/write | Gets or sets the raw data to be saved and returned. |
| Definition | Child object | Gets the PlaceholderDefinition that governs this Placeholder. |
| Name | Read-only | Gets the name of this Placeholder. |
| Posting | Child object | Gets the Posting to which this Placeholder belongs. |
| **Public Methods** | | |
| Equals | System | Determines whether two Object instances are equal. |
| GetHashCode | Read-only | Gets the hash code for the object. |
| GetType | Read-only | Gets the Type of the current instance. |
| ToString | System | Returns a String that represents the current object type. |
| **Protected Constructors** | | |
| Placeholder Constructor | Other | Creates a new instance of the Placeholder class. |

*(continued)*

**Table B–10** *(Continued)*

| Placeholder | Classification | Description |
|---|---|---|
| **Protected Methods** | | |
| BeginWrite | Other | Raises the PlaceholderPropertyChanging event to prepare for updating a Placeholder property. |
| EndWrite | Other | Raises the PlaceholderPropertyChanged event to end the Placeholder property update process. |
| RetrieveContent | Other | Retrieves the raw content from the CMS Content Repository. |
| SaveContent | Other | Saves Placeholder content as it is ready to be stored in the CMS Content Repository. |

# PlaceholderDefinition Parentage

One of the key properties in the Placeholder structure is the Definition object. So important and unique is this object that we provide the parentage of the PlaceholderDefinition in the following tables. The CanCache, InjectTypeProperty, and ReflectAsReadOnly properties inherited from CustomReflectableObject are protected and must be overridden to use them, so we left them out of the tables. Likewise, the protected properties GetEditor and GetPropertyOwner are not intended to be used directly from code and are also left out of the tables.

Table B–11 shows the complete parentage of the CMS Placeholder Definition class, using the same rules as the Placeholder table.

**Table B–11** PlaceholderDefinition Parentage

| Placeholder | CustomReflectableObject | System.Object |
|---|---|---|
| **Public Properties** | | |
| *Description* | | |
| *IsReadOnly* | | |
| *Name* | | |

**Table B–11**  *(Continued)*

| Placeholder | CustomReflectableObject | System.Object |
|---|---|---|
| **Public Methods** | | |
| *Clone* | | |
| *CreatePlaceholder* | | |
| *Delete* | | |
| *DeserializeObject* | | |
| Equals | Equals | *Equals* |
| GetAttributes | *GetAttributes* | |
| GetClassName | *GetClassName* | |
| GetComponentName | *GetComponentName* | |
| GetConverter | *GetConverter* | |
| GetDefaultEvent | *GetDefaultEvent* | |
| GetDefaultProperty | *GetDefaultProperty* | |
| GetEvents | *GetEvents* | |
| GetHashCode | GetHashCode | *GetHashCode* |
| GetProperties | *GetProperties* | |
| GetType | GetType | *GetType* |
| *Serialize* | | |
| ToString | ToString | *ToString* |
| **Public Events** | | |
| *PropertyChanged* | | |
| **Public Constructors** | | |
| *PlaceholderDefinition Constructor* | | |
| **Protected Methods** | | |
| *BeginRead* | | |
| *BeginWrite* | | |
| *EndWrite* | | |
| *OnCloned* | | |

Table B–12 defines all the members listed for the Placeholder Definition class in Table B–11.

Again, the classification column in Table B–12 is not a CMS classification. It was included to make it easier to locate the discussion about each member in Chapter 27.

**Table B–12** PlaceholderDefinition Member Descriptions

| Placeholder | Classification | Description |
| --- | --- | --- |
| **Public Properties** | | |
| Description | Read/write | Gets or sets a description for the PlaceholderDefinition. |
| IsReadOnly | Read-only | Indicates whether the PlaceholderDefinition is read-only. |
| Name | Read/write | Gets or sets the name of a PlaceholderDefinition. |
| **Public Methods** | | |
| Clone | Creating and deleting | Creates a new PlaceholderDefinition object that is a copy of the current PlaceholderDefinition. |
| CreatePlaceholder | Creating and deleting | Creates a new Placeholder based on this PlaceholderDefinition. |
| Delete | Creating and deleting | Marks a PlaceholderDefinition as deleted and removes it from the Template to which it belongs. |
| DeserializeObject | Creating and deleting | Deserializes the PlaceholderDefinition contained in a System.Xml.XmlNode. |
| Equals | System | Determines whether two Object instances are equal. |
| GetAttributes | Read-only | Gets the collection of attributes for the PlaceholderDefinition. |
| GetClassName | Read-only | Gets the name of the class for the PlaceholderDefinition. |
| GetComponentName | Read-only | Gets the name of the component for the PlaceholderDefinition. |

**Table B–12** *(Continued)*

| Placeholder | Classification | Description |
|---|---|---|
| GetConverter | Read-only | Gets a .NET converter for use with the PlaceholderDefinition. Converters are primarily used for string-to-value conversions, and they themselves have a multitude of members. |
| GetDefaultEvent | Read-only | Gets the default event for a PlaceholderDefinition, if any. |
| GetDefaultProperty | Read-only | Gets the default property for a PlaceholderDefinition, if any. |
| GetEvents | Read-only | Gets the events that are declared or inherited by the Placeholder Definition. |
| GetHashCode | Read-only | Gets the hash code for the object. |
| GetProperties | Read-only | Gets the collection of properties for the PlaceholderDefinition. |
| GetType | Read-only | Gets the Type of the current instance. |
| Serialize | Creating and deleting | Serializes the Placeholder Definition to an XML string using an optional System.Xml.XmlWriter. |
| ToString | System | Returns a String that represents the current object type. |
| **Public Events** | | |
| PropertyChanged | Creating and deleting | Occurs after any property of a PlaceholderDefinition has changed. |
| **Public Constructors** | | |
| Placeholder Definition Constructor | Creating and deleting | Is the constructor for the PlaceholderDefinition class. |

*(continued)*

**Table B–12** *(Continued)*

| Placeholder | Classification | Description |
|---|---|---|
| **Protected Methods** | | |
| BeginRead | Other | Checks that neither the current PlaceholderDefinition nor the Template to which the Placeholder Definition belongs has been deleted and committed. |
| BeginWrite | Other | Checks that the current user has sufficient rights to edit the PlaceholderDefinition. |
| EndWrite | Other | Saves the most recent change made to a PlaceholderDefinition to the CMS server. |
| OnCloned | Other | Allows a custom placeholder definition (derived from Placeholder Definition) to perform custom actions when an instance is cloned. |

# Index

Note: Italicized page locators indicate figures/tables.

# Also from Addison-Wesley

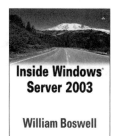

0-7357-1158-5

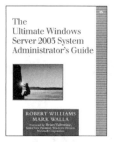

0-201-79106-4

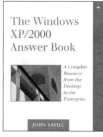

0-321-11357-8

0-321-13345-5

0-201-61621-1

0-672-32125-4

0-201-77574-3

0-321-12698-X

0-201-61613-0

0-7357-1192-5

0-201-61576-2

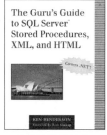

0-201-70046-8

0-201-74203-9

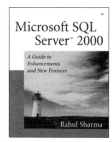

0-201-75283-2